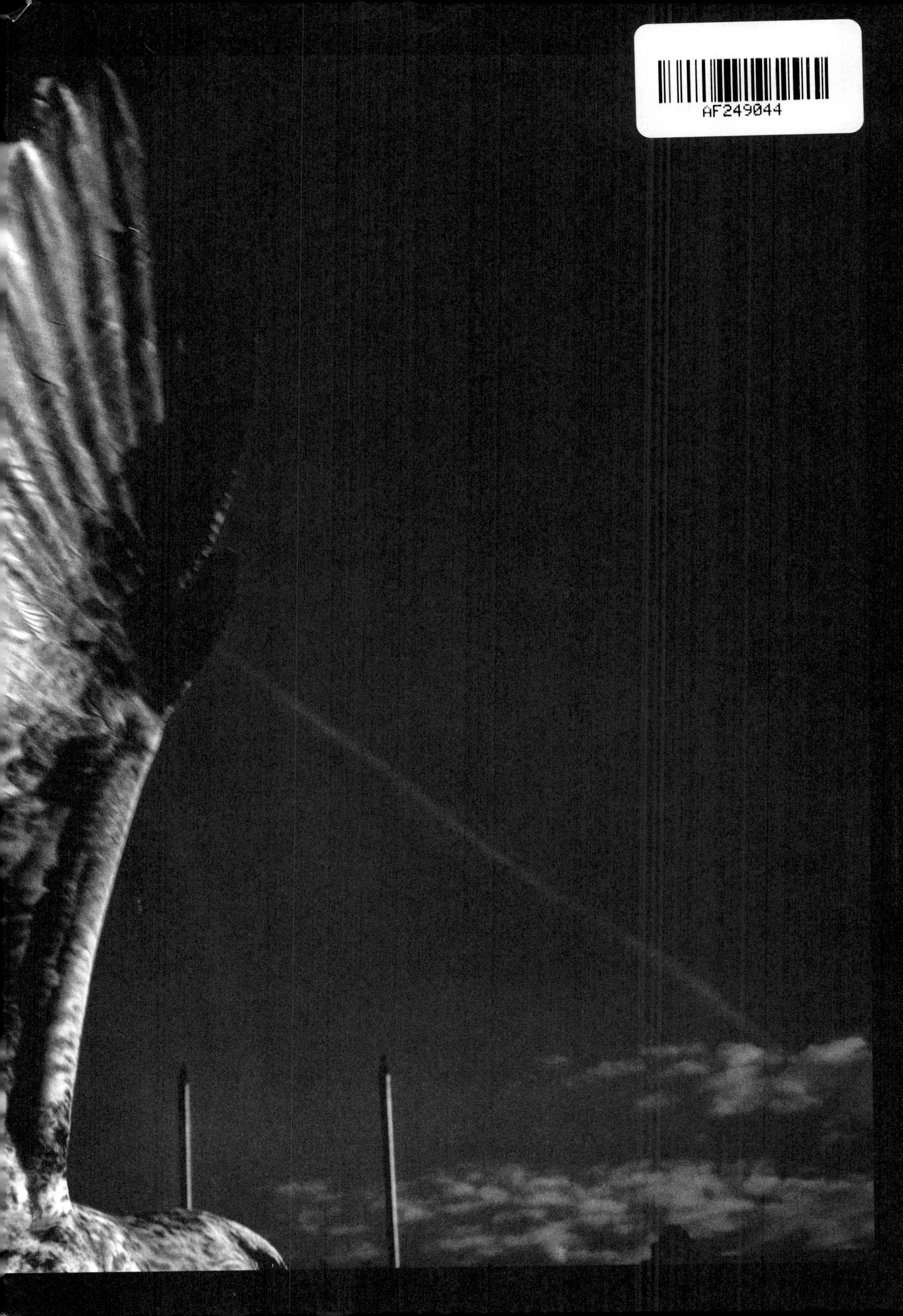

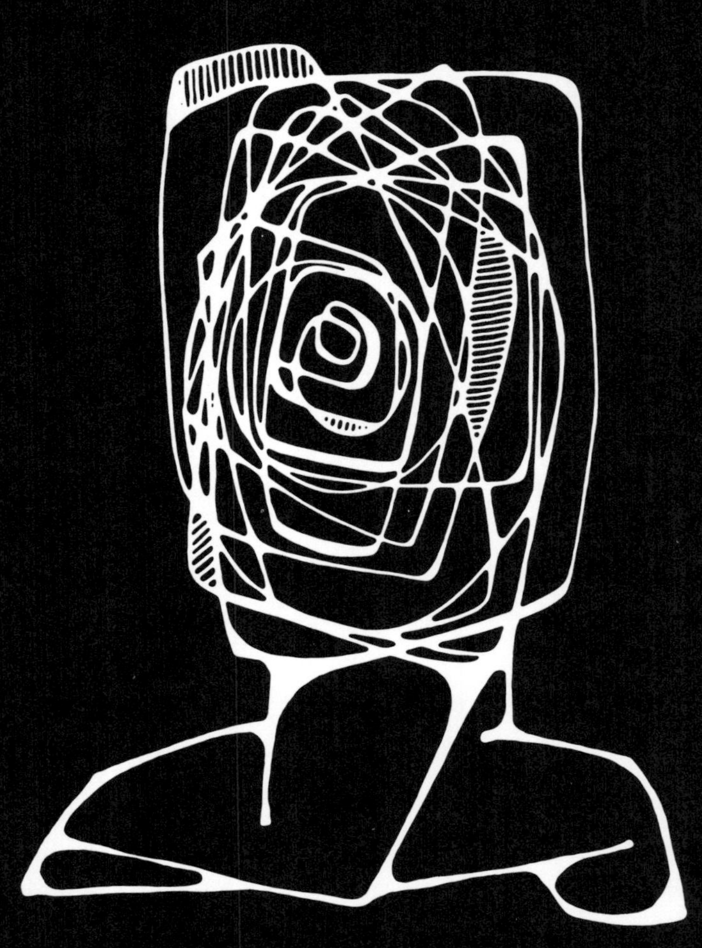

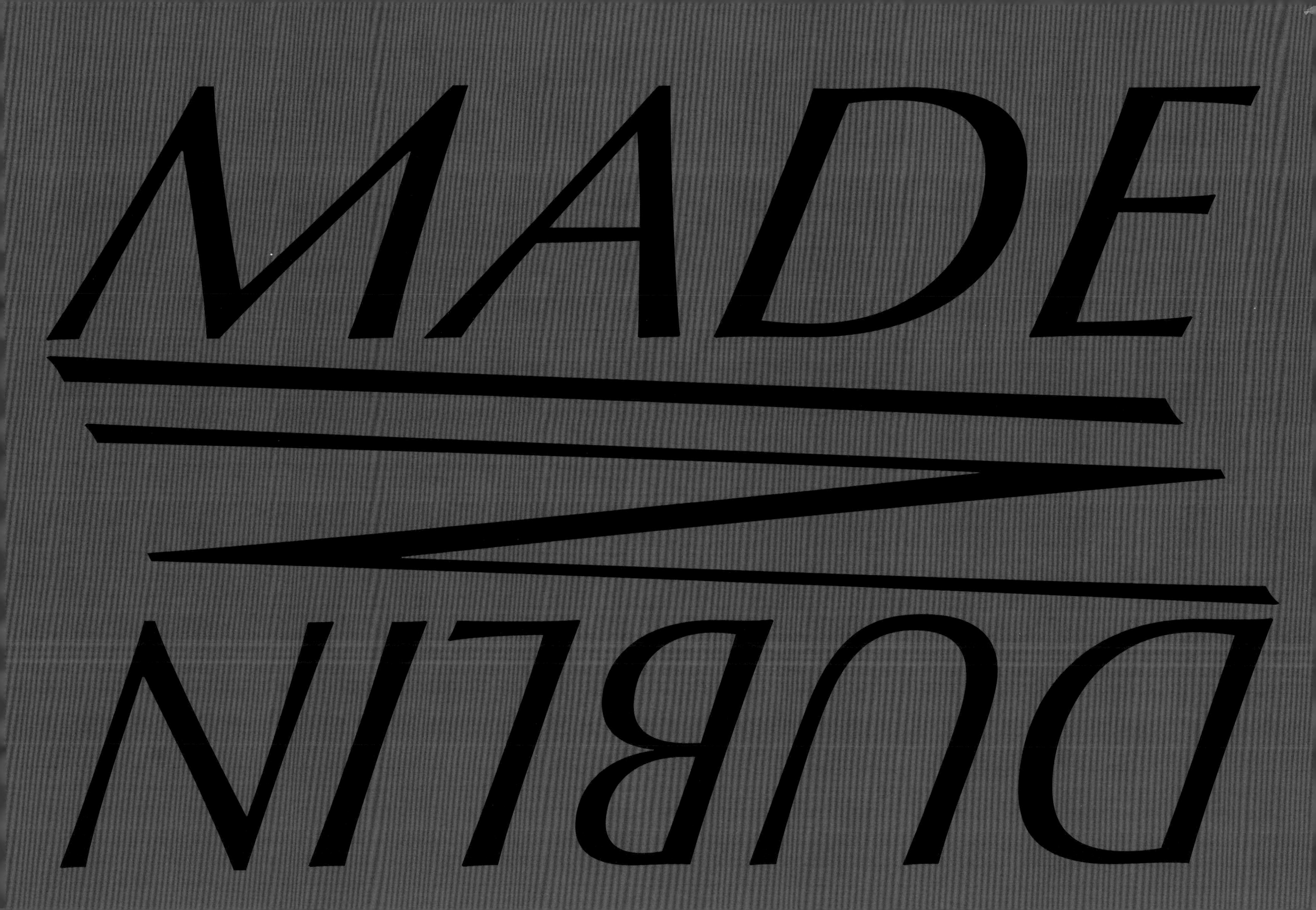
MADE IN DUBLIN

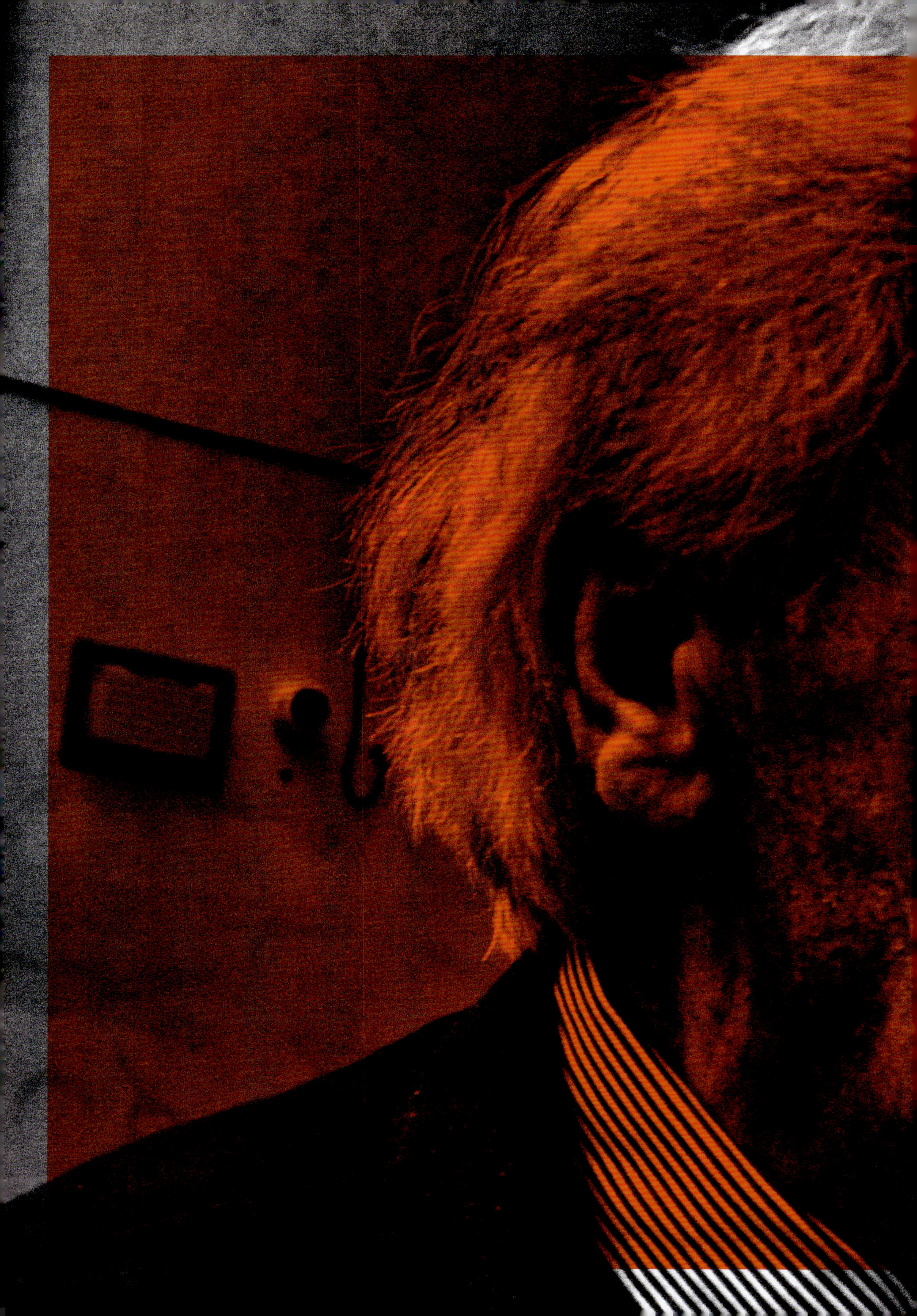

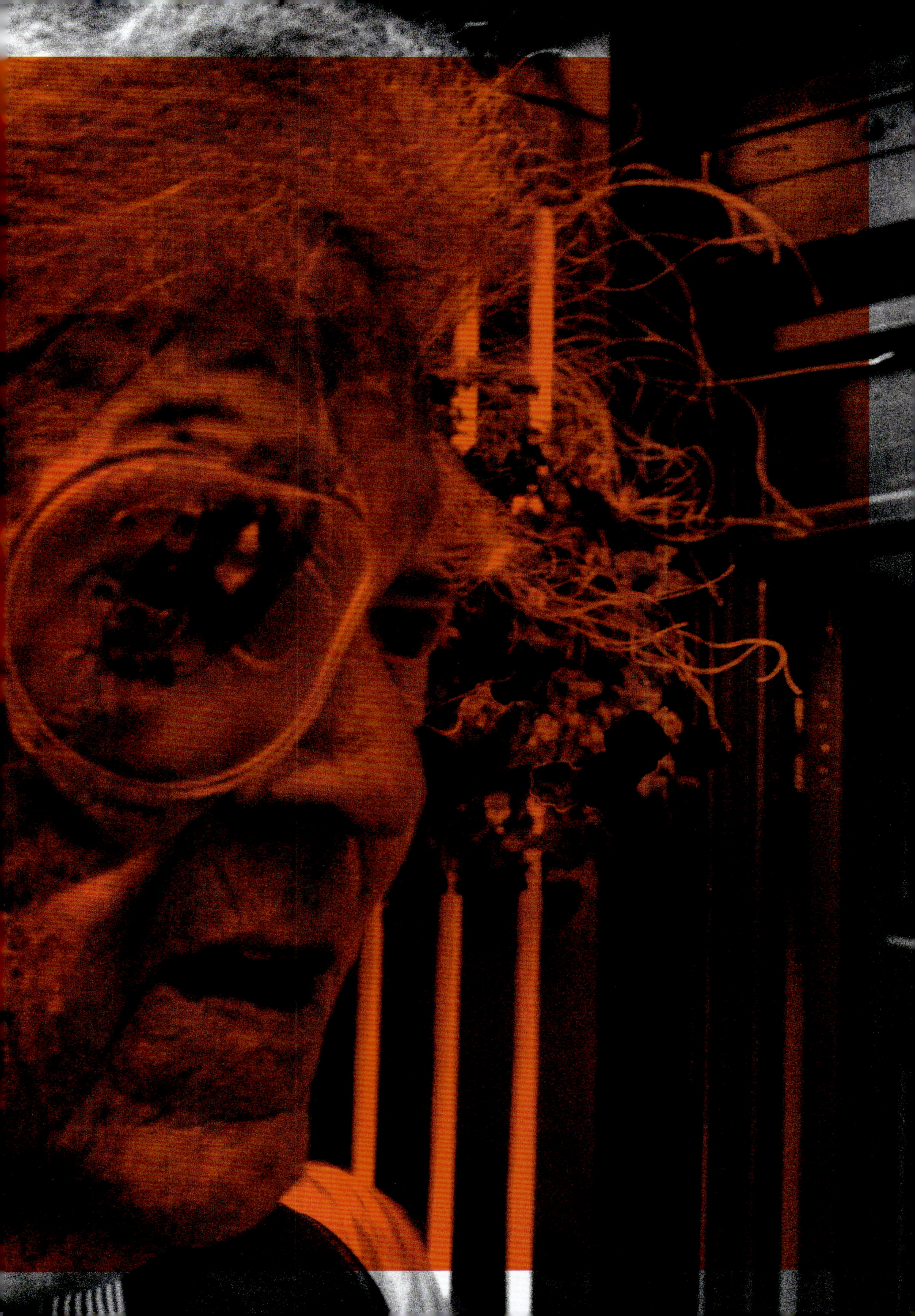

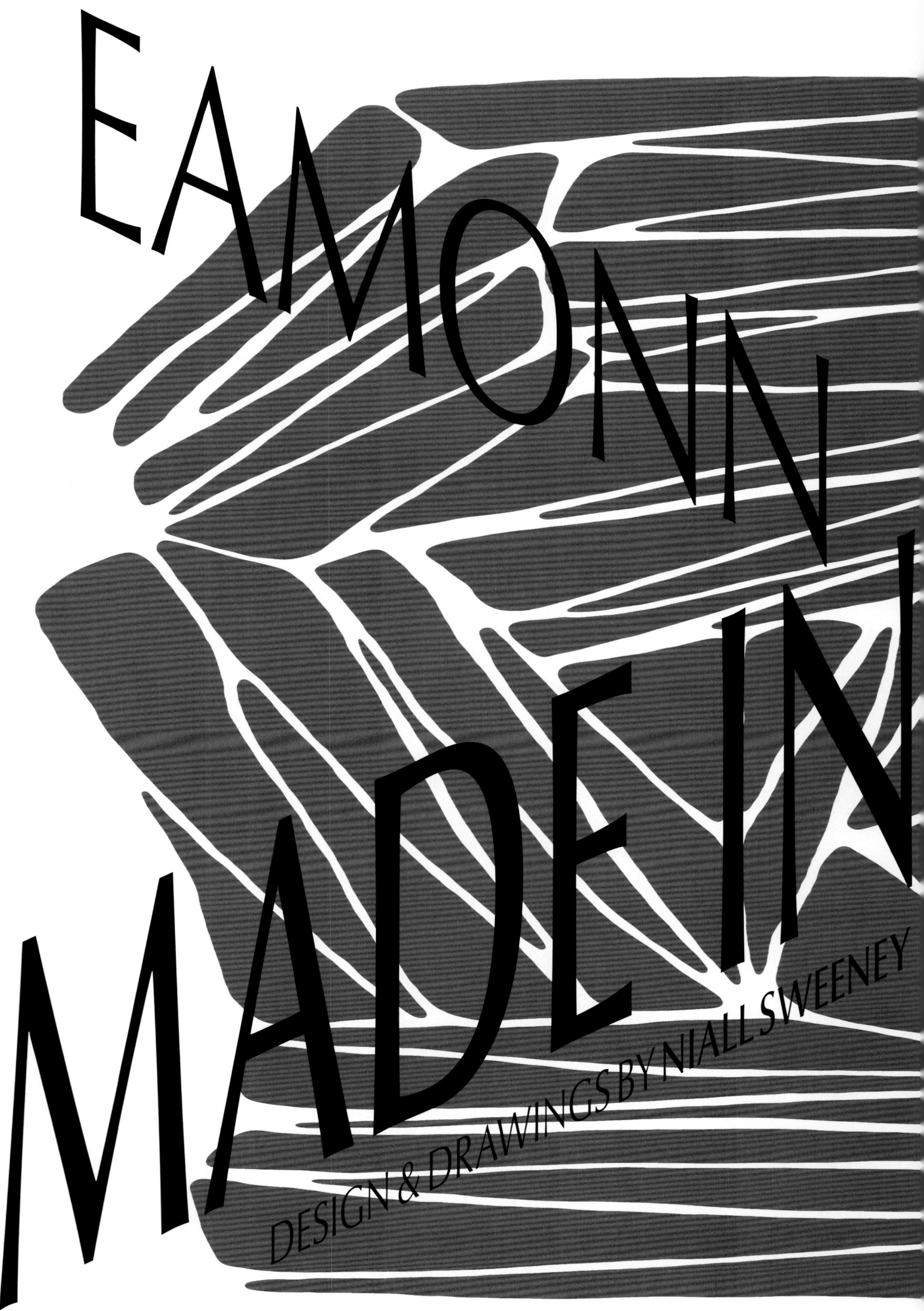

EAMONN
MADE IN
DESIGN & DRAWINGS BY NIALL SWEENEY

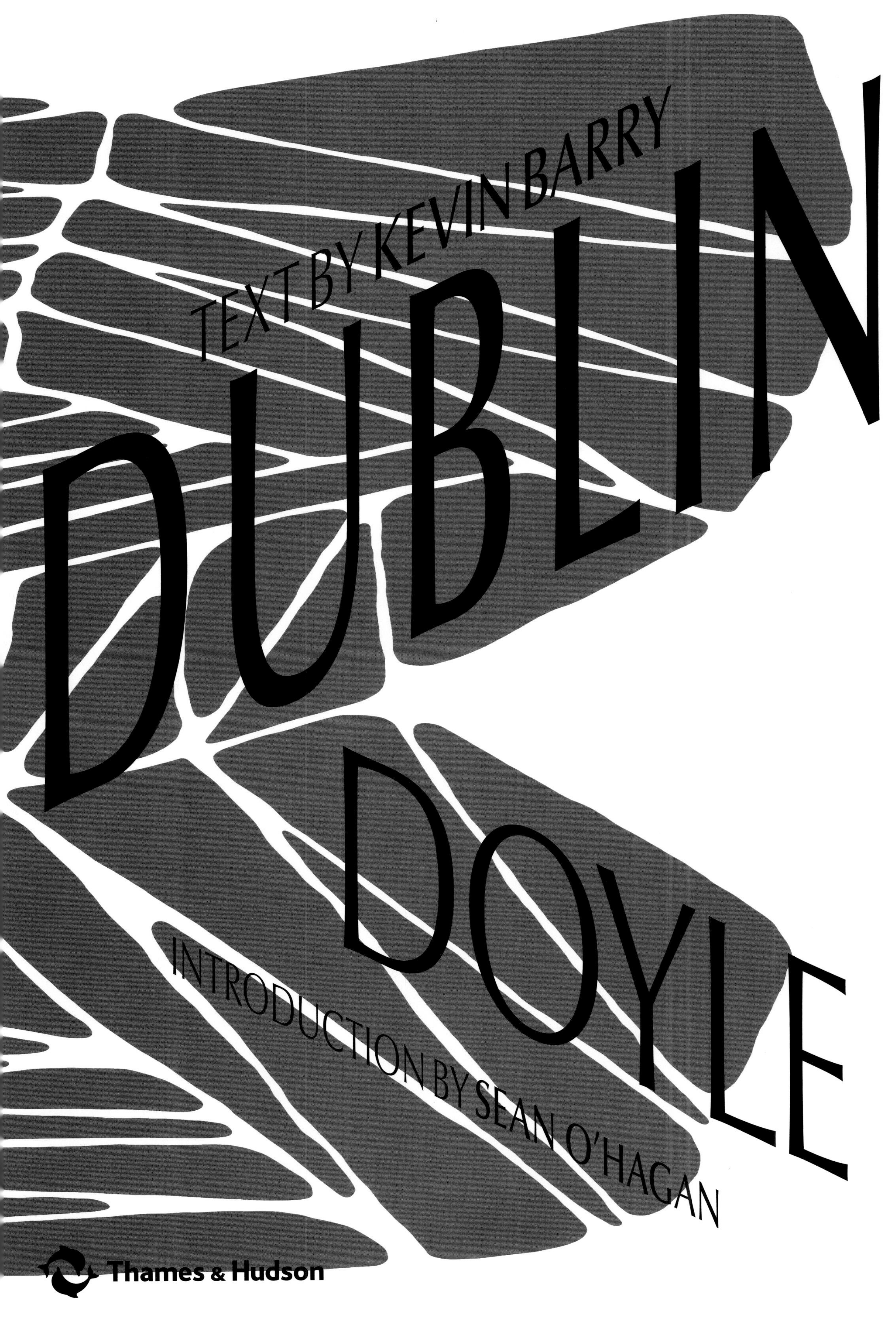

TEXT BY KEVIN BARRY
DUBLIN
DOYLE
INTRODUCTION BY SEAN O'HAGAN
Thames & Hudson

EAMONN DOYLE: MADE IN DUBLIN
© 2019 Thames & Hudson Ltd, London

Photographs © 2019 Eamonn Doyle
Text © 2019 Kevin Barry
Introduction © 2019 Sean O'Hagan
Drawings © 2019 Niall Sweeney
Design by Pony Ltd, London

First published in 2019 in the United States
of America by Thames & Hudson Inc.,
500 Fifth Avenue, New York, New York 10110

www.thamesandhudsonusa.com

Library of Congress Control Number 2018945041

ISBN 978-0-500-54508-9

Printed and bound in China by C&C Offset
Printing Co. Ltd

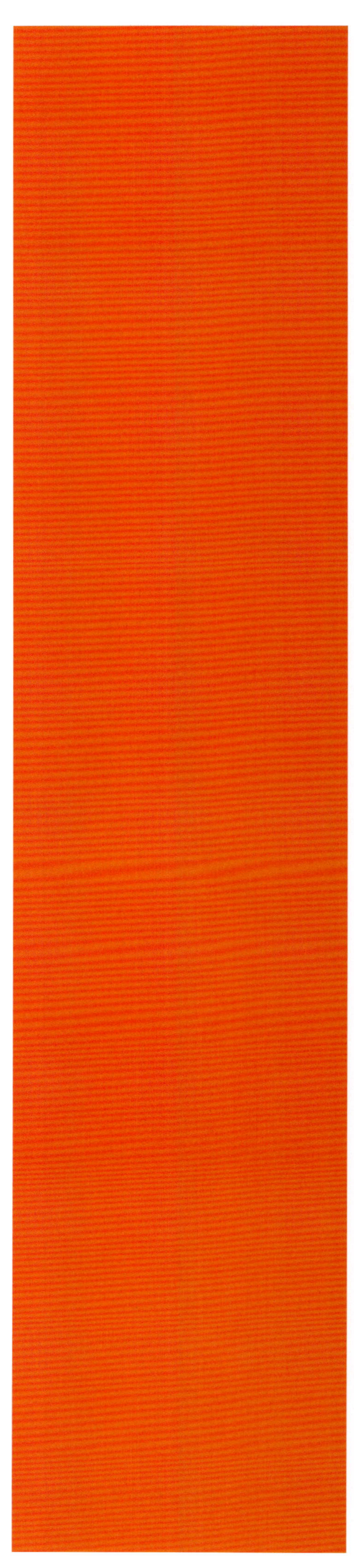

CONTENTS

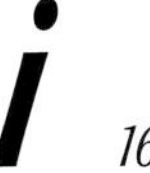

ON

End.

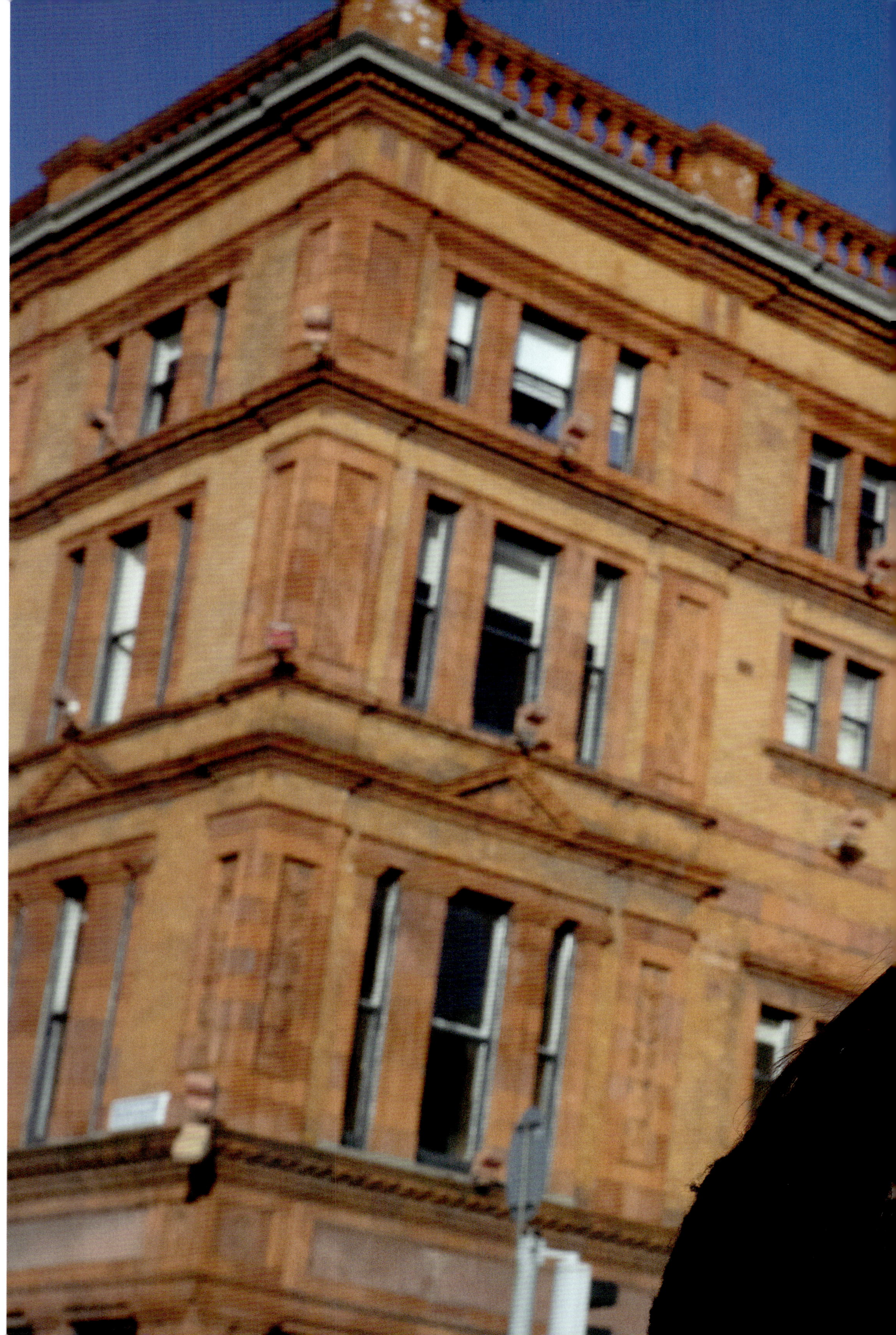

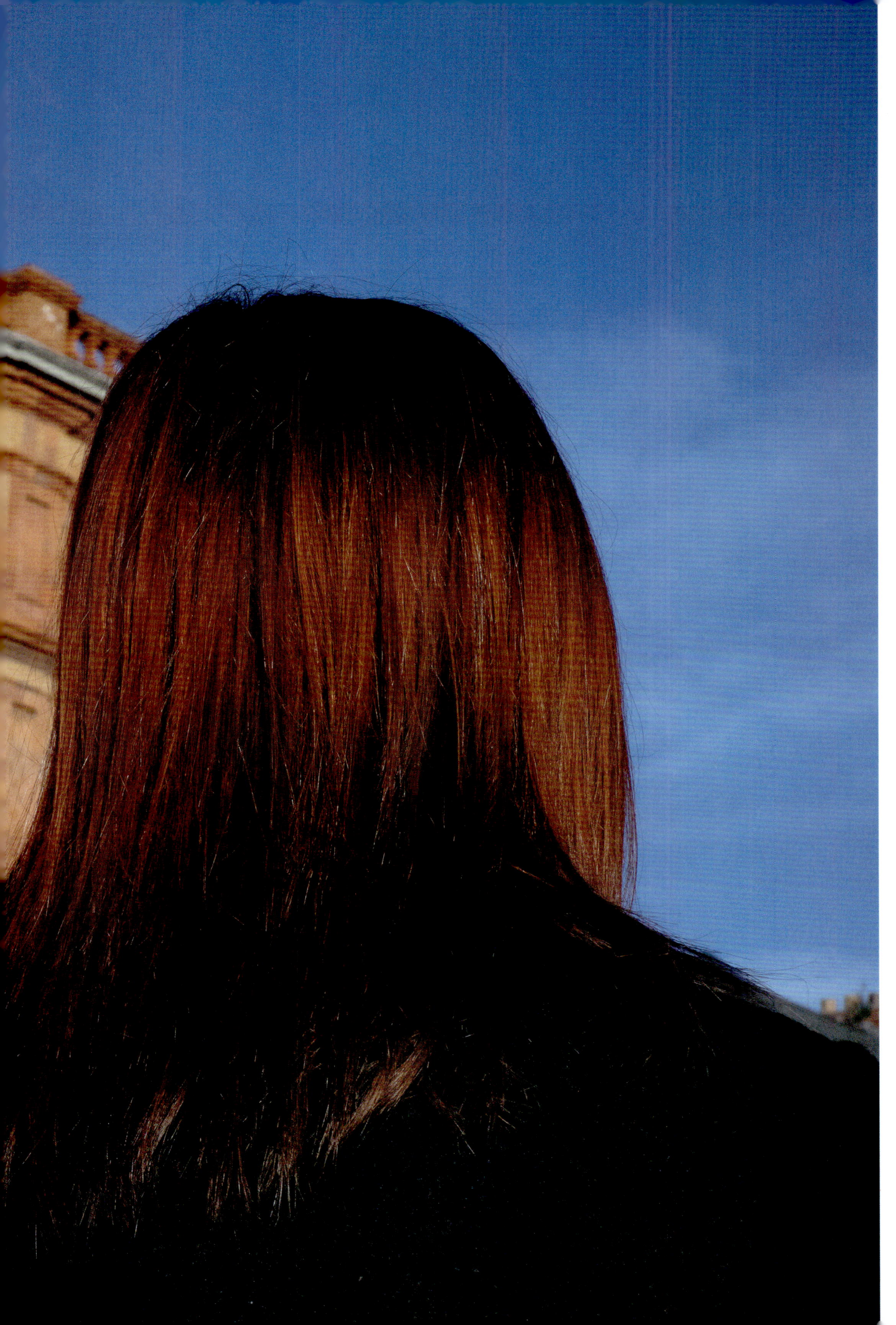

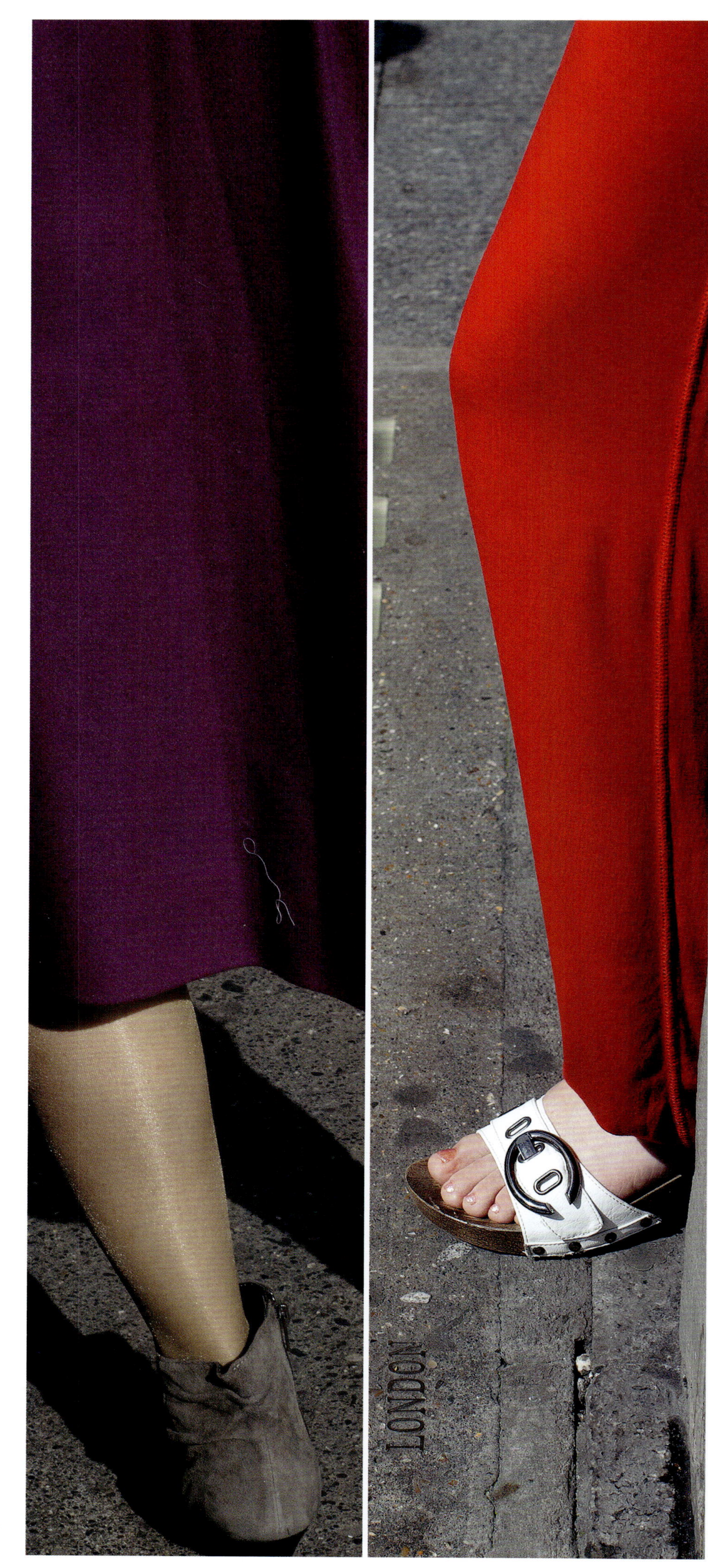
LONDON

Made In Dublin is the city as cinema, just as it revealed itself in real time through the lens of Eamonn Doyle, re-staging the intertwined looping dramas of the physical city, its light and texture, its psyche, and the movements of its people, as they unfold and pass through. It is about the shapes and beats that they, that *we*, unconsciously throw together as one. The images of Eamonn's Dublin trilogy have all been made over a short period of years, in the same place and in no particular order, with their thematic patterns and subjects emerging as the work grows exponentially. Though Eamonn has self-published episodic extracts from the trilogy as three acclaimed books, *i*, *ON* and *End.* (which also provide the structure of this book), *Made In Dublin* is the first time that the whole work has been brought together in print as the collaborative, greater entity that it continues to be.

Niall Sweeney

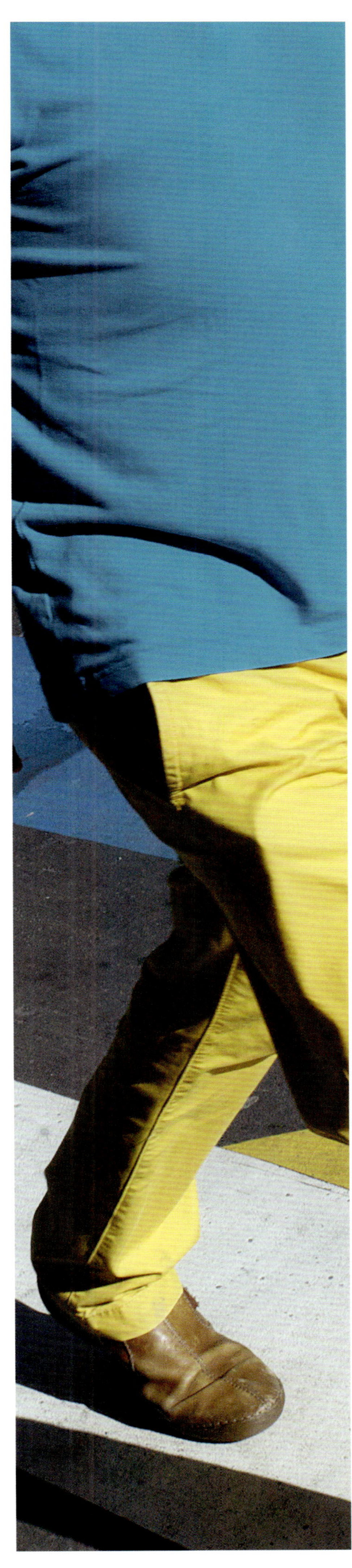

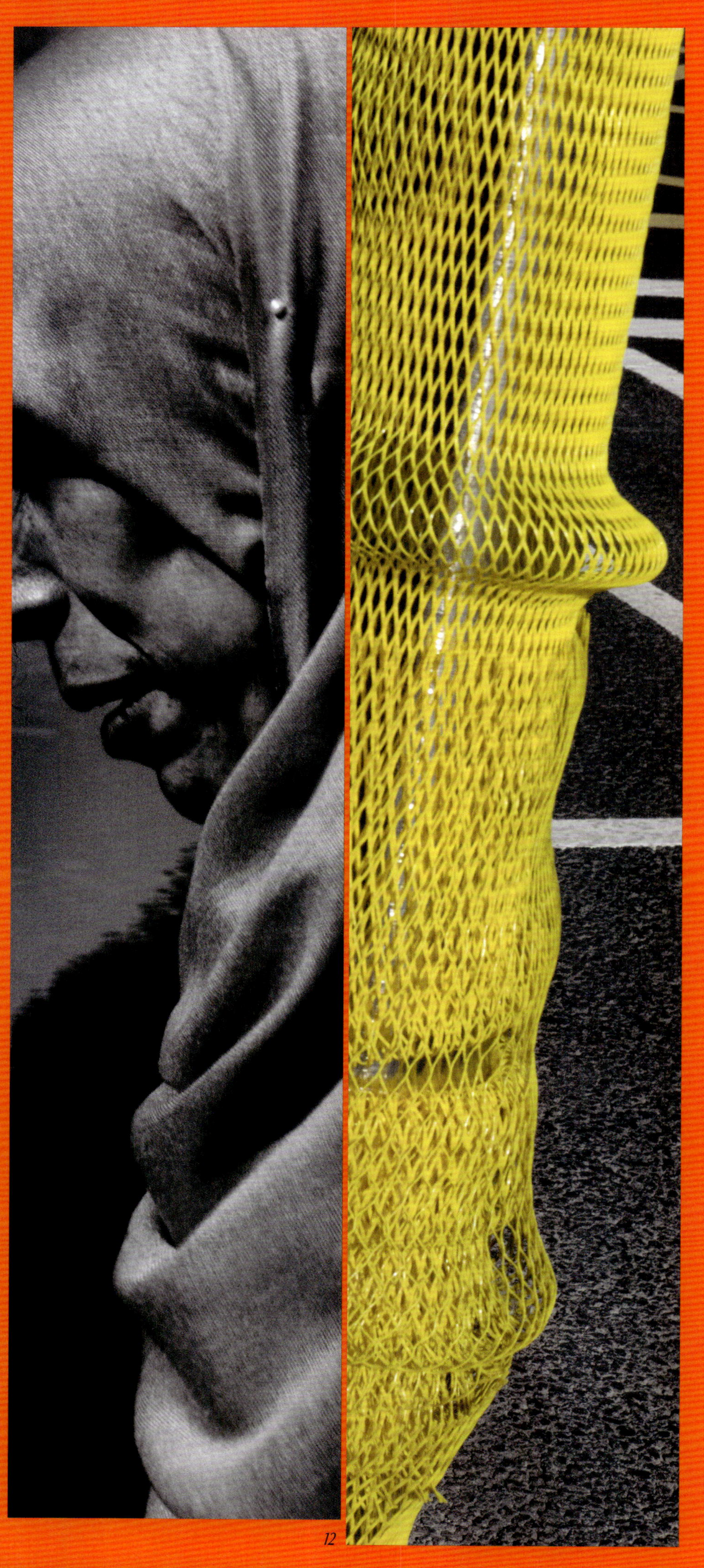

The Irish poet Patrick Kavanagh believed that the parochial was universal, that all human life was contained in the small, rural Irish parish he grew up in. James Joyce adhered in his own way to the same principle. Having fled Ireland for a long exile in Europe, he evoked the atmosphere, people and places of his native city, Dublin, with an almost forensic eye for minute geographical detail.

Photography, too, is well-suited to the evocation of the particular, the local. Pioneering colour photographer Saul Leiter made his impressionistic images of New York within a two-block radius of his East Village apartment. Joan Colom, a master of monochrome atmosphere, was drawn again and again to the notorious neighbourhood of El Raval in Barcelona, where prostitutes worked by night on the tough, working-class streets. On the streets of Dublin, Eamonn Doyle works in this tradition, staying close to home in order to create a portrait of a contemporary city that is now less compact and more diverse than Joyce's richly complex but essentially monocultural city.

The striking street portraits that comprise *i*, Doyle's first photobook, were taken within a half-mile radius of his house in north Dublin. Many of them, he told me, were shot 'within ten metres of my front door.' Some of his subjects were the elderly residents of north Dublin, who he photographed as they went about their daily business, often alone and unnoticed on streets not that far from the city centre. They are unsettlingly quiet images — the book's title is a nod to the great Irish poet of silence, Samuel Beckett, echoing his play *Not I*. In *i*, Doyle's subjects seem to exist in a world of their own, shot from above and often from behind as they move slowly through what appears to be a deserted Dublin. Their solitude is accentuated by the absence of the usual tired tropes of street photography — signage, crowds, traffic and the frantic kinetic movement of people.

Although he had graduated with a diploma in photography in 1991, Doyle had not pursued the medium since leaving college, working instead in the music business, running a studio and independent record label (DI Recordings, specializing in electronic music) and curating Dublin's Electronic Arts Festival (DEAF). In his mid-forties, he began taking photographs again, for no particular reason except a growing fascination with the city and the people passing his door.

Back in 1991, Doyle had bought a recording studio through a pre-social-media crowd-funding campaign. Contacting hundreds of people asking them to 'lend me a tenner' to invest in the studio, he managed to raise thousands. His relationship with long-time collaborators David Donohoe, an electronic musician and producer, and Niall Sweeney, an artist who has worked on the design of almost all of Doyle's projects to date, stems from this time. He has approached photobook publishing in much the same way he released records, which as Doyle elaborates, 'was basically to go ahead and make the thing, package it and hope it sells somehow.'

Like many emerging artists, Doyle sent a copy of his first book to the acclaimed British photographer and photobook collector Martin Parr, hardly expecting a response. It was only when he found that Parr had described *i* as 'the best street photobook I have seen in a decade' that Doyle began to realize just how groundbreaking his images were. As orders for the book mounted, another early champion of the work, well-known London photography gallerist Michael Hoppen, started to represent Doyle and show his work in his Chelsea gallery.

Since then, Doyle has self-published two further acclaimed photobooks set in Dublin: *ON* and *End*. In both, the subjects are more varied, and the city looms larger, often in stark monochrome. The dramatic angles sometimes make his Dubliners seem almost threatening, their stern faces set, their strides purposeful. Even amid the cut and thrust of the contemporary city, though, many of his subjects seem alone. A close-up of a woman in a headscarf makes her seem oddly holy. In another strangely mythic image, a man in a hat and overcoat walks down a deserted street like a lone hero in an existential western movie — except the landscape is 1930s social housing. The term 'street photographer' damns Doyle with faint praise. He is a chronicler of the city, of all its myriad small dramas, and its inhabitants — who are as oblivious to each other as they are to the man with the camera at their heels.

One of Doyle's most dramatic photographs from *ON* is a stark monochrome print that shows a group of people striding purposefully up O'Connell Street, the Gate Theatre outlined in the background beneath a sky streaked by vapour trails. In the foreground, a muscular young man in a tight t-shirt is shot as if from ground level. His demeanour suggests aggression, but his aura is all to do with framing, composition and proximity. For someone with, by his own confession, a shy nature, Doyle seems fearless when it comes to photographing people up close on the often edgy streets of Dublin's north side.

The portrait of the striding man takes on a dramatic monumentalism in Doyle's acclaimed exhibitions of the Dublin trilogy of work. In installations that sometimes include multi-screen configurations as well as prints, images loom over the viewers, taking up an entire wall, while others, smaller or in grids, are glimpsed through windows. In a contained space, the immersive sensory drama is total. Always accentuated by an electronic soundscape in exhibition (or here in this book by Kevin Barry's atmospheric prose), Doyle's images merge the macro and the micro to evoke the energy and edginess of the street wherever and however presented, while simultaneously showing how an artist with a strong commitment to the book as an art form itself can also energize a space in the most dynamic way.

Made In Dublin holds fast to these ideas, and the radical design of the original books. It is, in essence, an evocation of the contemporary Dublin cityscape in all its vibrant energy and infinite human variety. It emphasizes the creative cohesiveness of Doyle's Dublin trilogy — how the three volumes, viewed together and augmented by a selection of previously unseen photographs and sequences, comprise a vivid and sustained portrait of a city and a culture in flux. In his images, Eamonn Doyle shows us how much Dublin — and, by extension, Ireland — has changed of late, as it has moved, sometimes uneasily, from a pre-modern to a post-modern society. And how much it has, against all the odds, stayed the same.

Sean O'Hagan

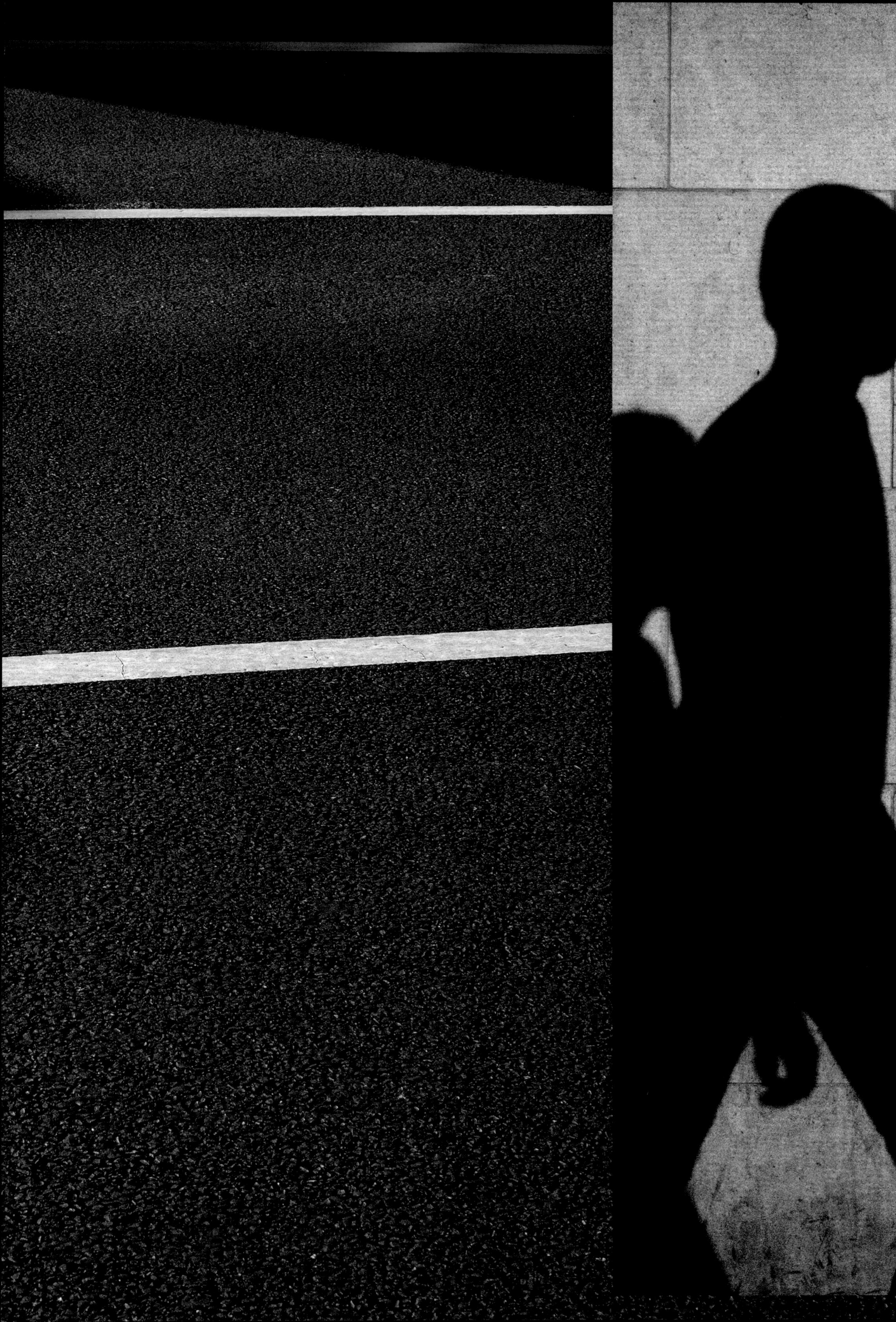

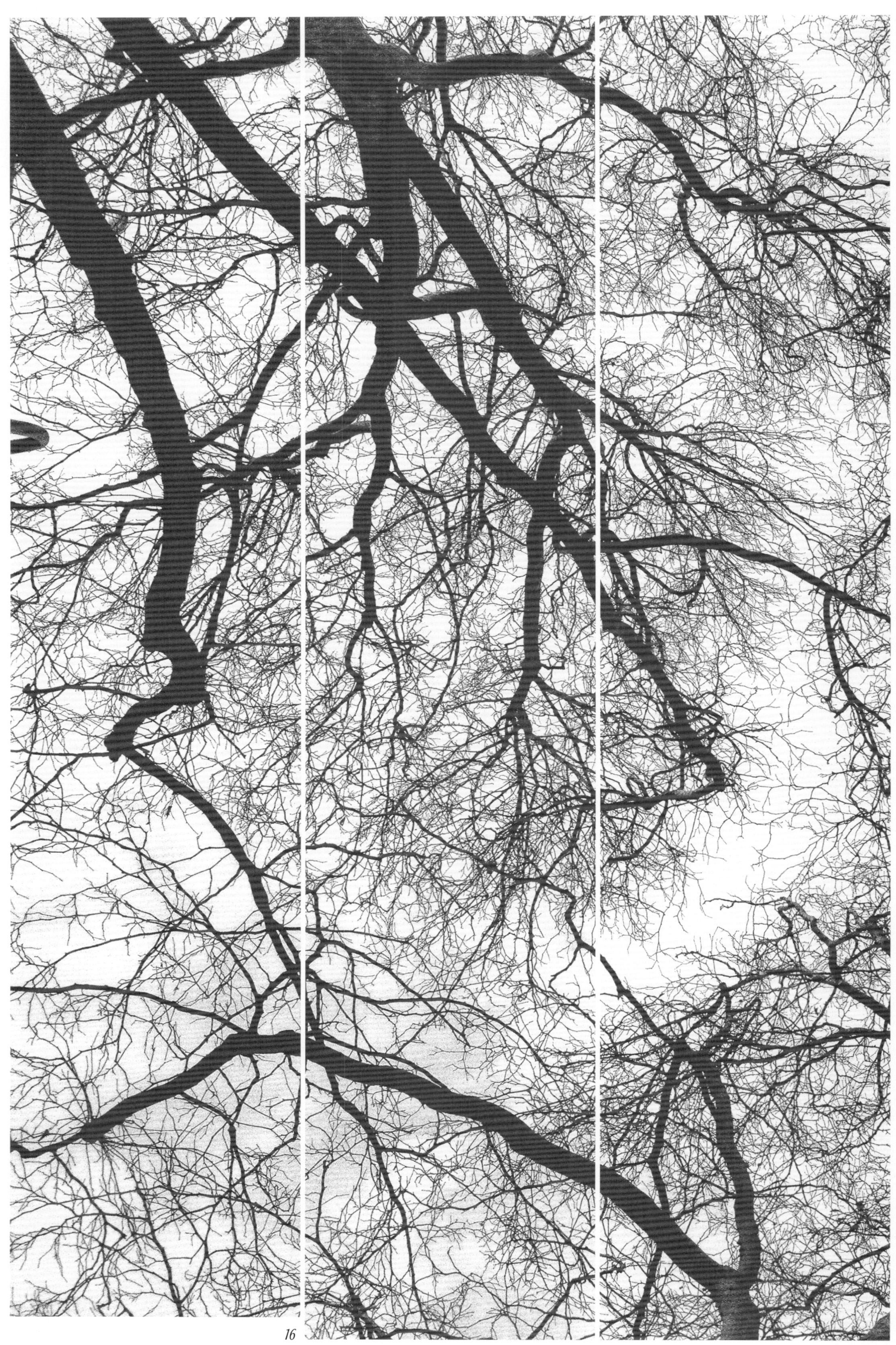

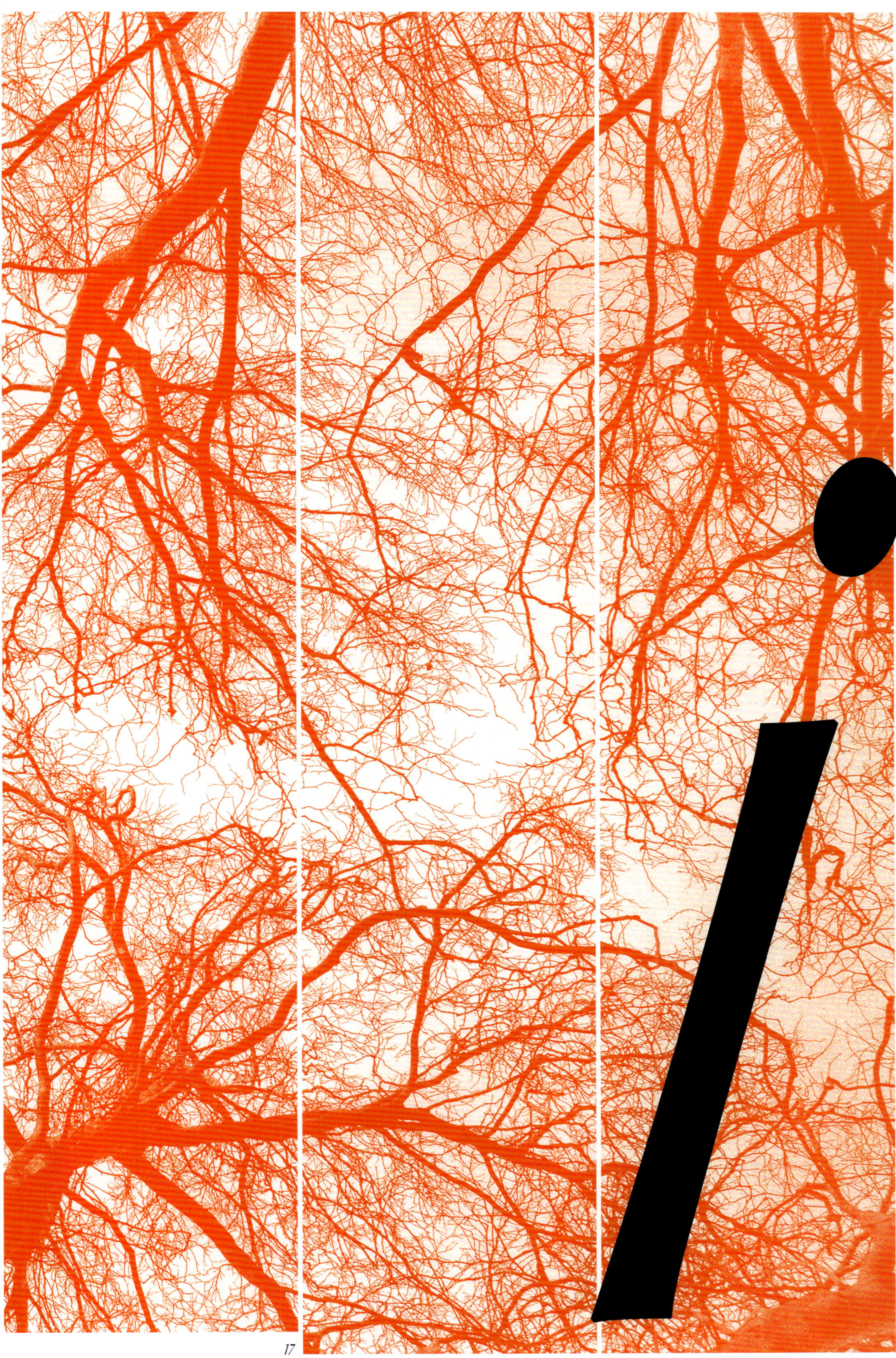

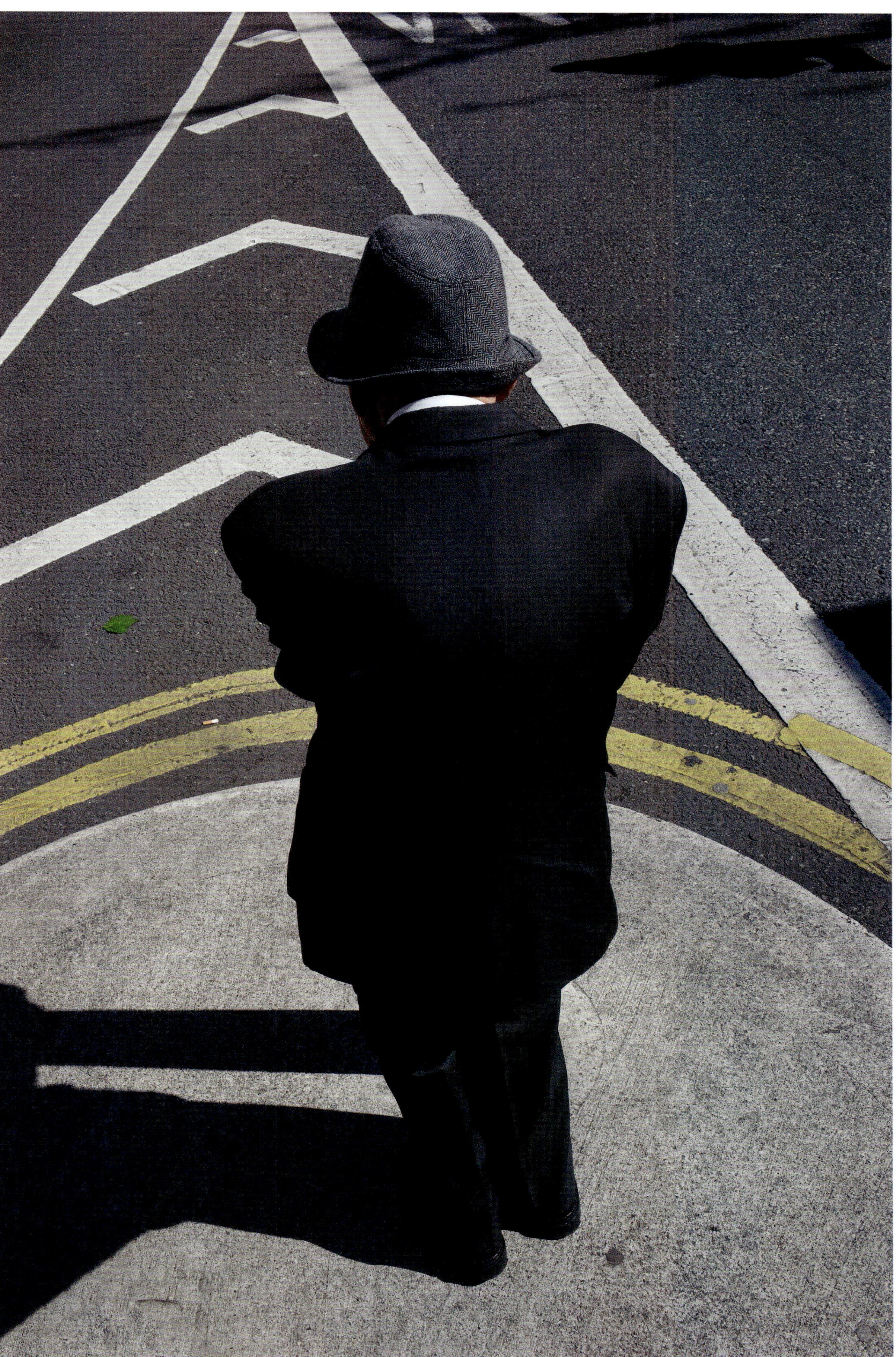

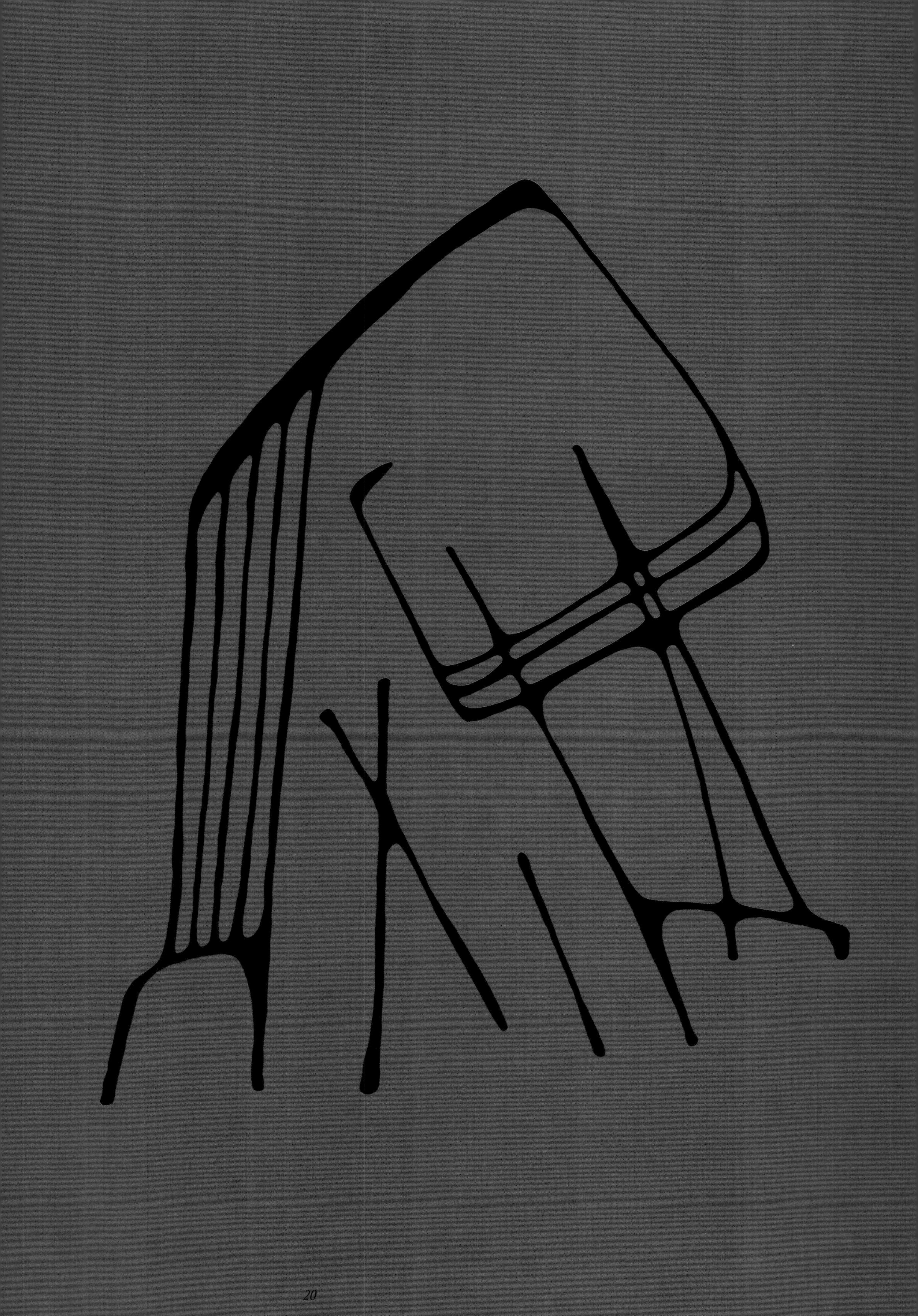

THERE IS A THREADED PULSE that runs
beneath the surface of this street. Sometimes, in one of those
quiet, eerie moments of the night when the city briefly stills itself,
as if to open out its sighs, you can almost hear it — you can hear
it as a kind of low, insistent throbbing, almost a rhythmic
sequence, and at once you'll know that it contains dark
information. It tells us that we are all being drawn in the same
general direction. It tells us that we are all being led along
the thread of the pulse. It tells us that we are all on the way out.

The city is disappearing all around us. Day by day, and night
by night, we are drawn down beneath the surface of its streets
to its underworld, and here we will for a short while linger and
learn to leave our time behind.

Here, too, each of us (every guttersnipe Orpheus and every
bargain-shop Eurydice) will suffer the cuts of memory's knives —
First love.
The last time we knew bliss.
The music that we heard.
The pain that was suffered;
the white screech of our anxieties.
The faces of our enemies and worse,
much worse, our friends.
Diminuendo, in musical notation, marks the fade out or
the dying fall. Age, too, is measured out in a slow diminuendo.
Slowly we make the distance from ourselves. The movement
of the street becomes slower, the street becomes longer,
and the city becomes the body. It speaks to us in a dying fall.

And we can hear, just now, as a pocket of silence opens
and allows it, the threaded pulse that tells us again our time
is passing.

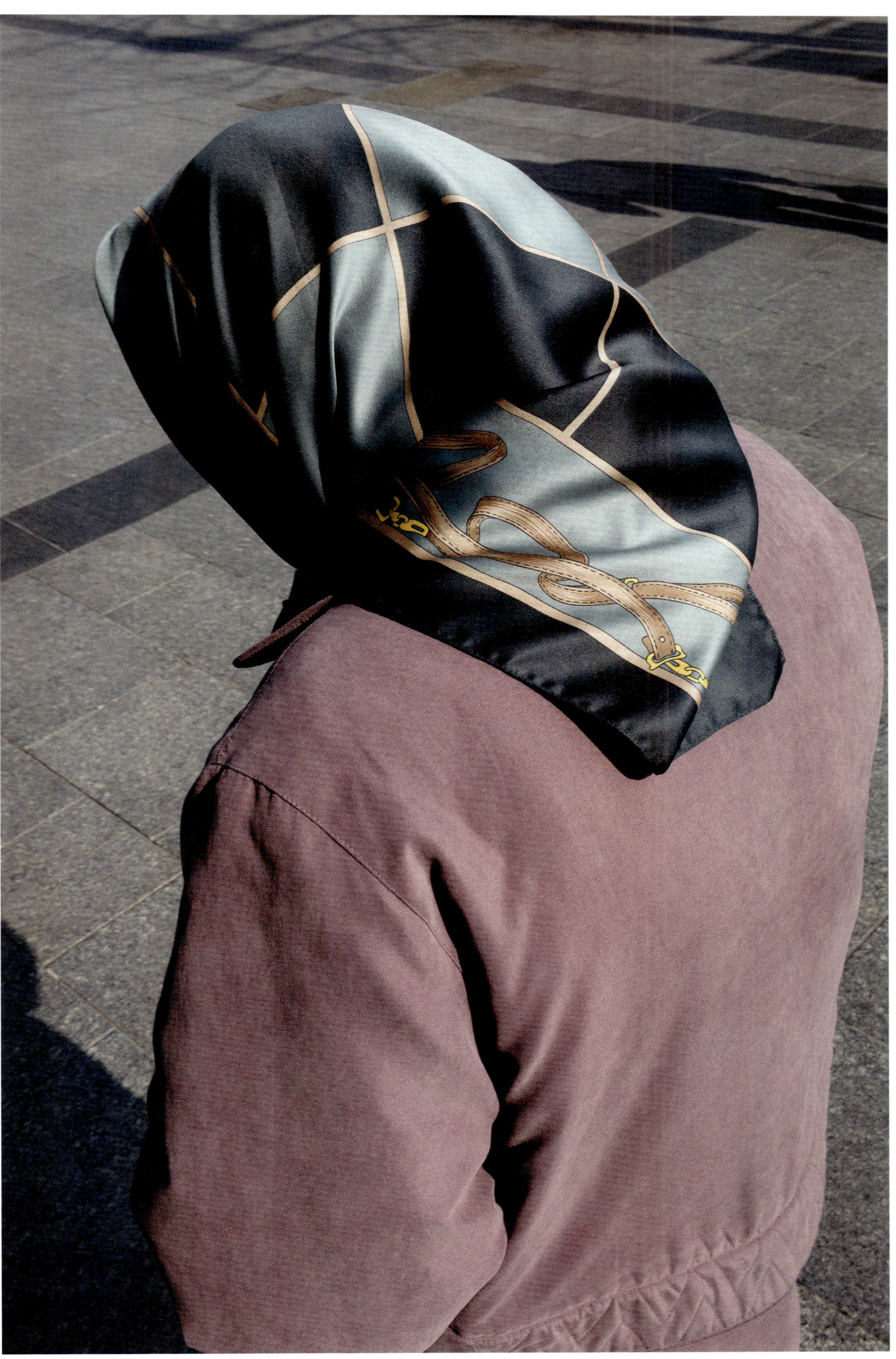

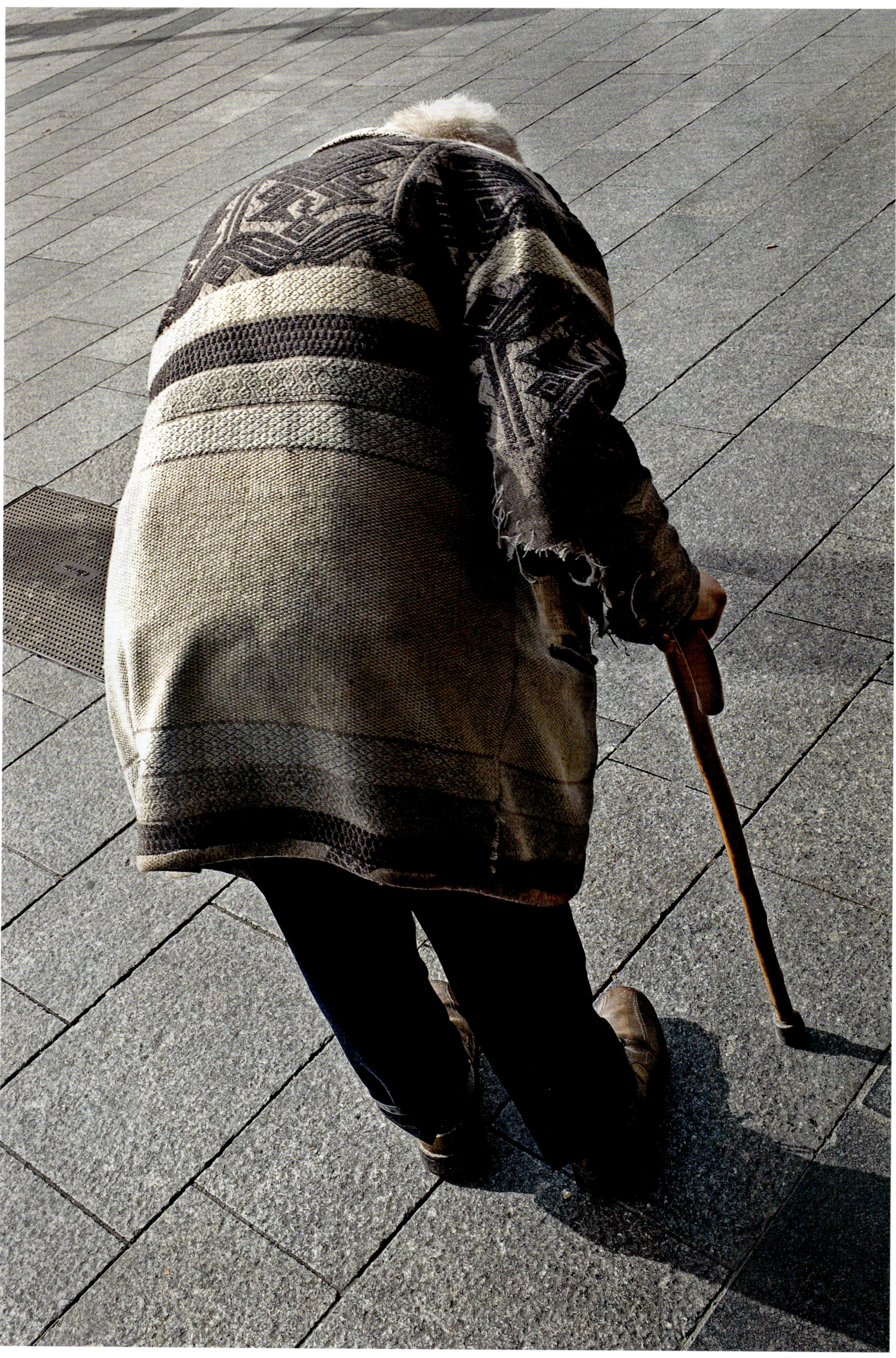

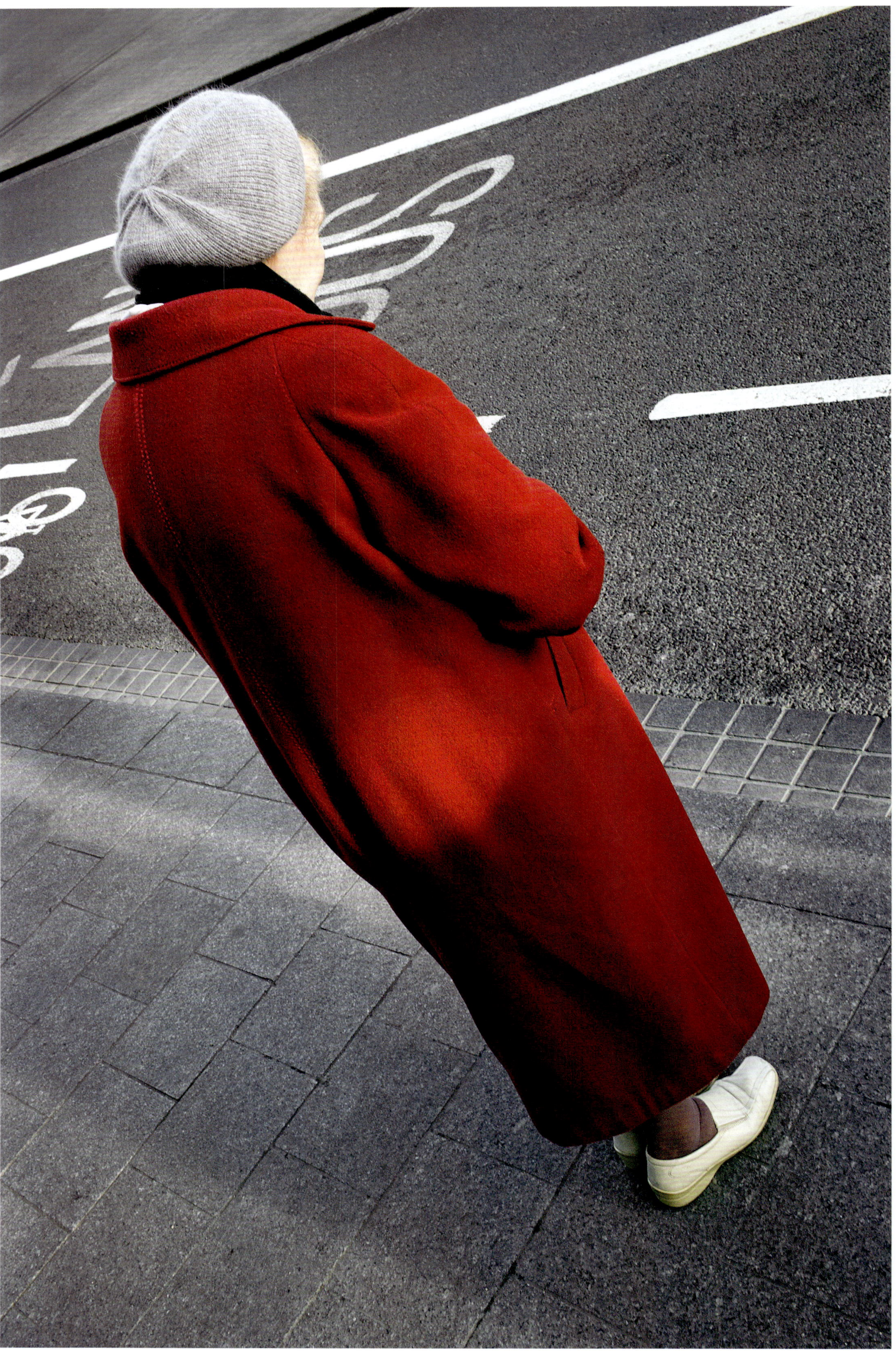

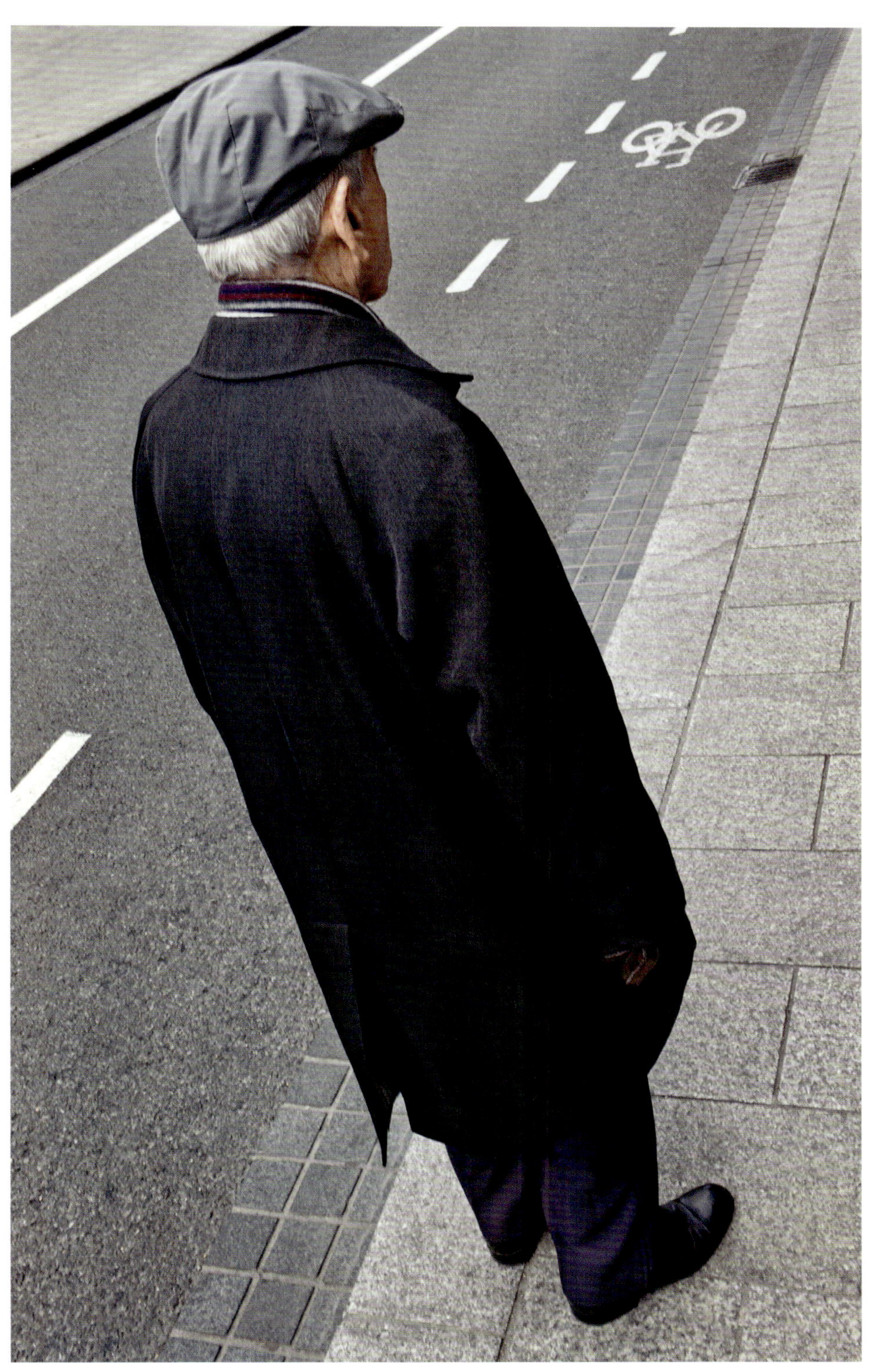

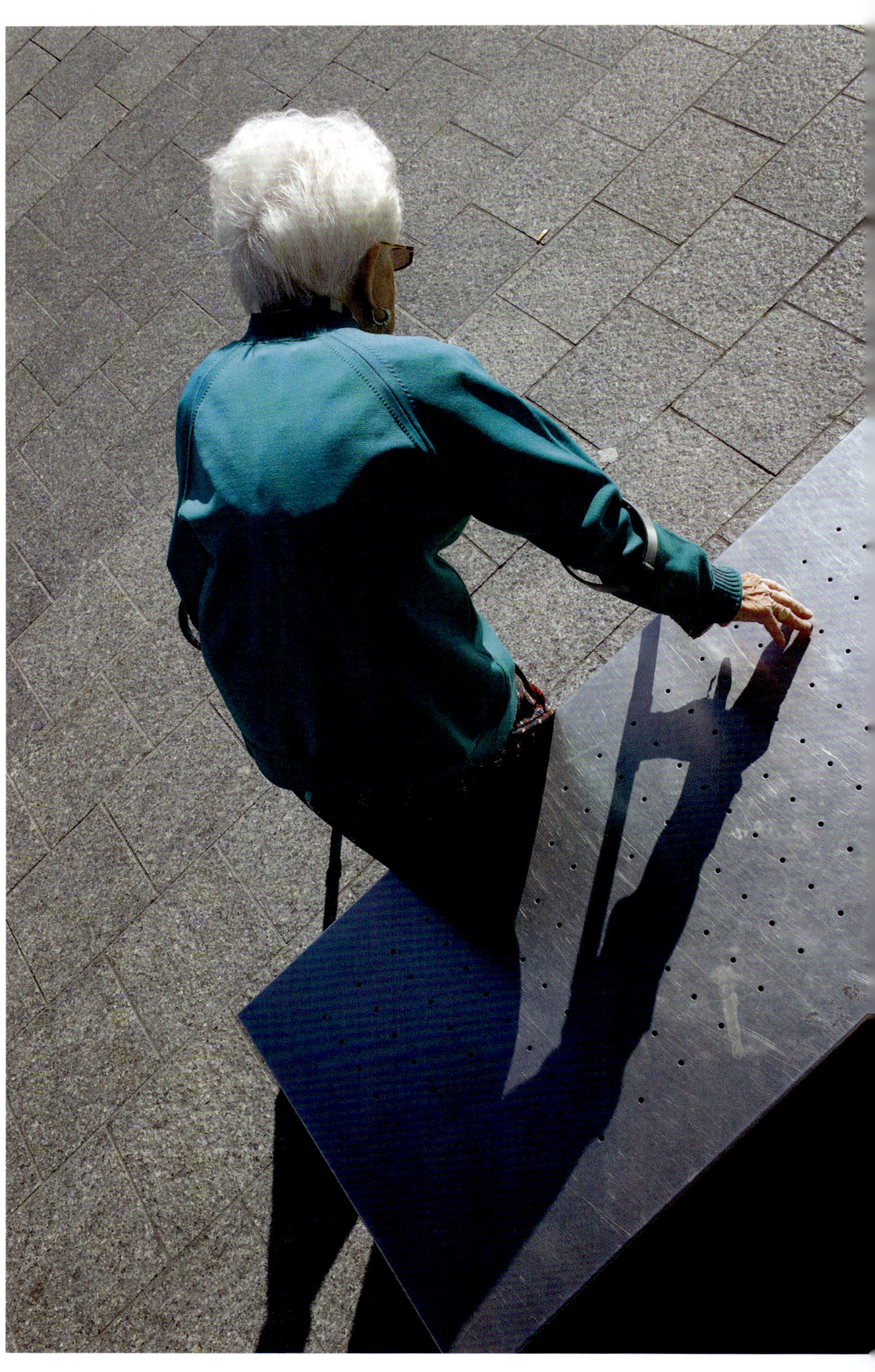

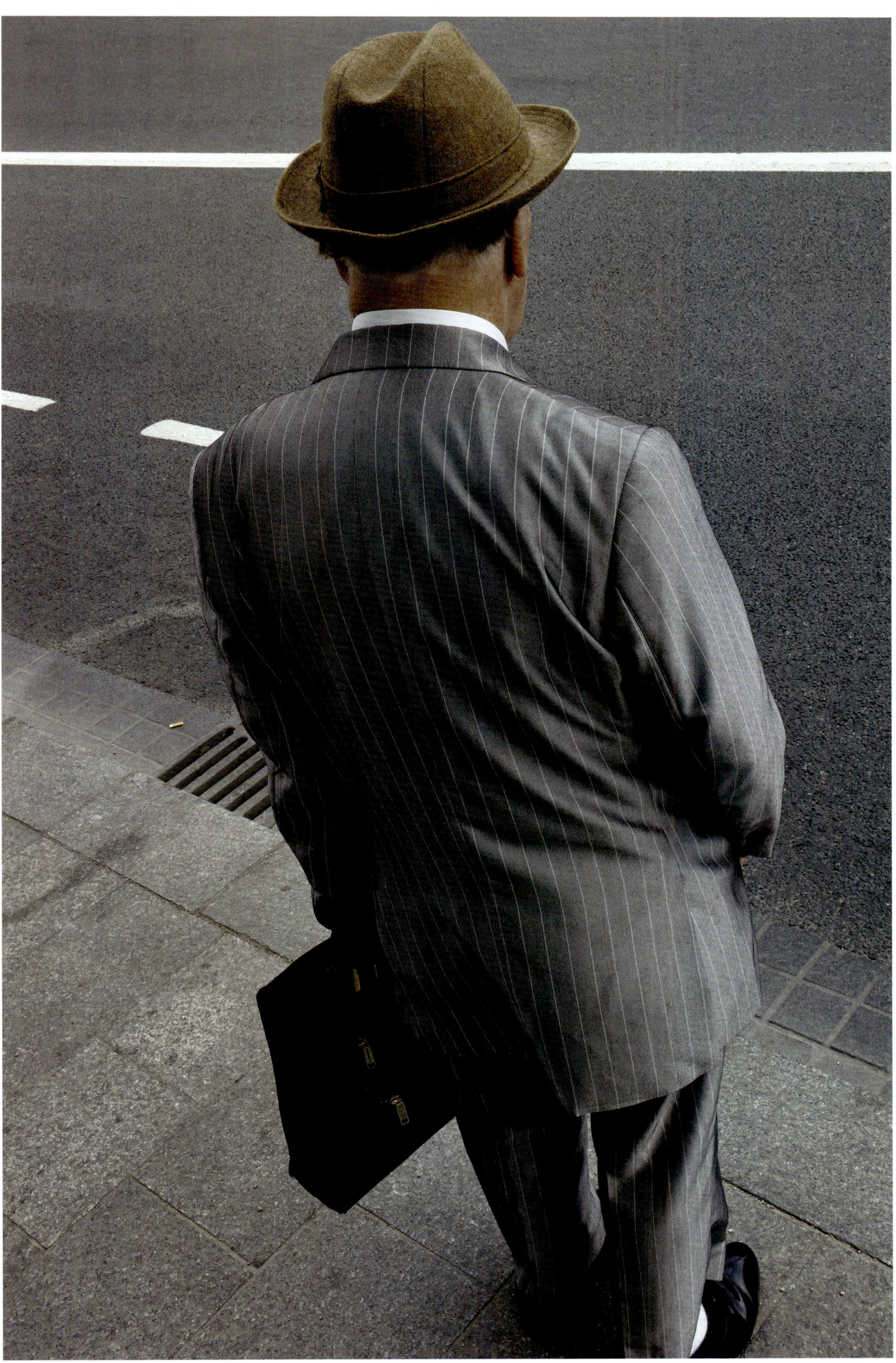

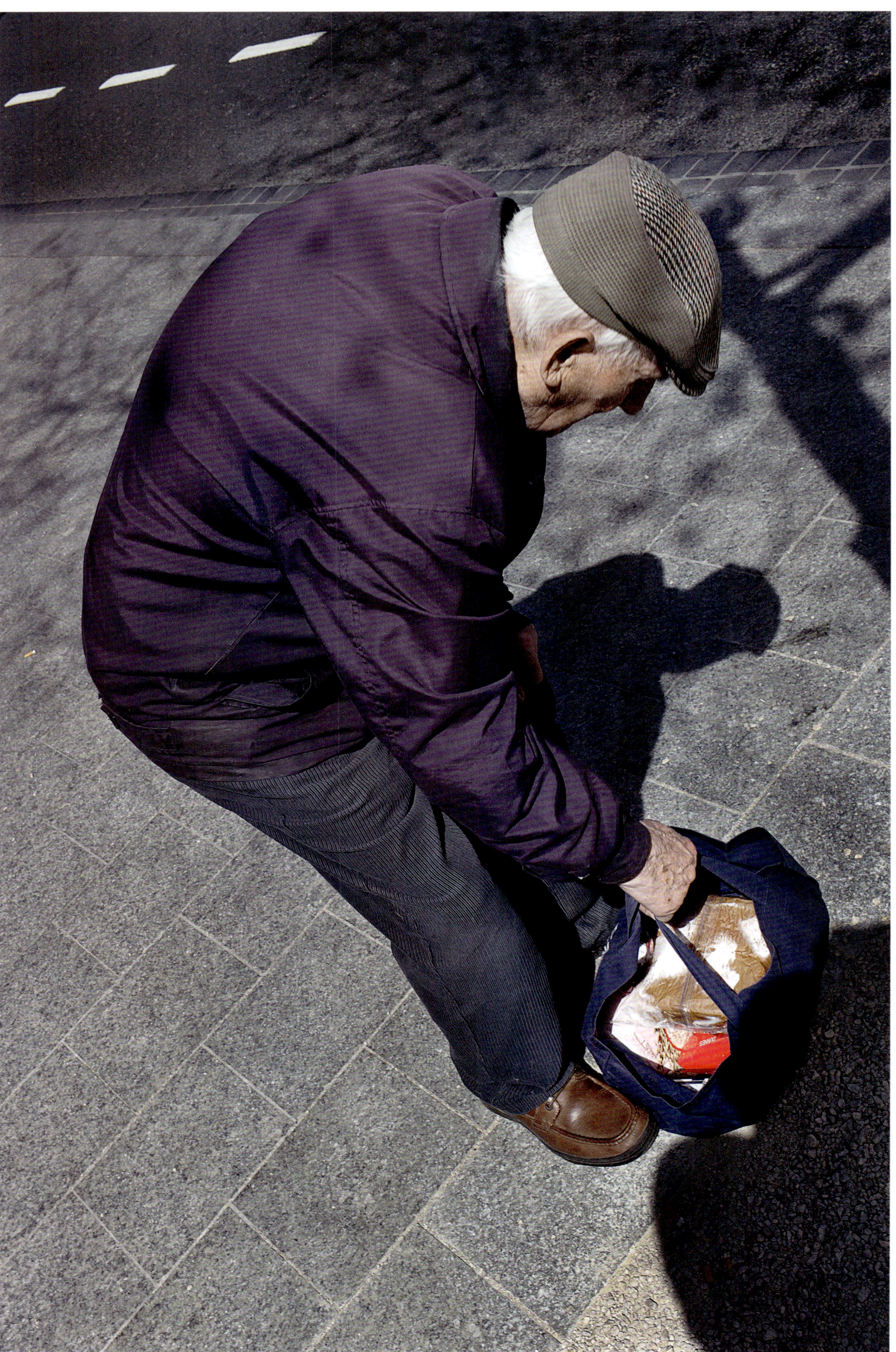

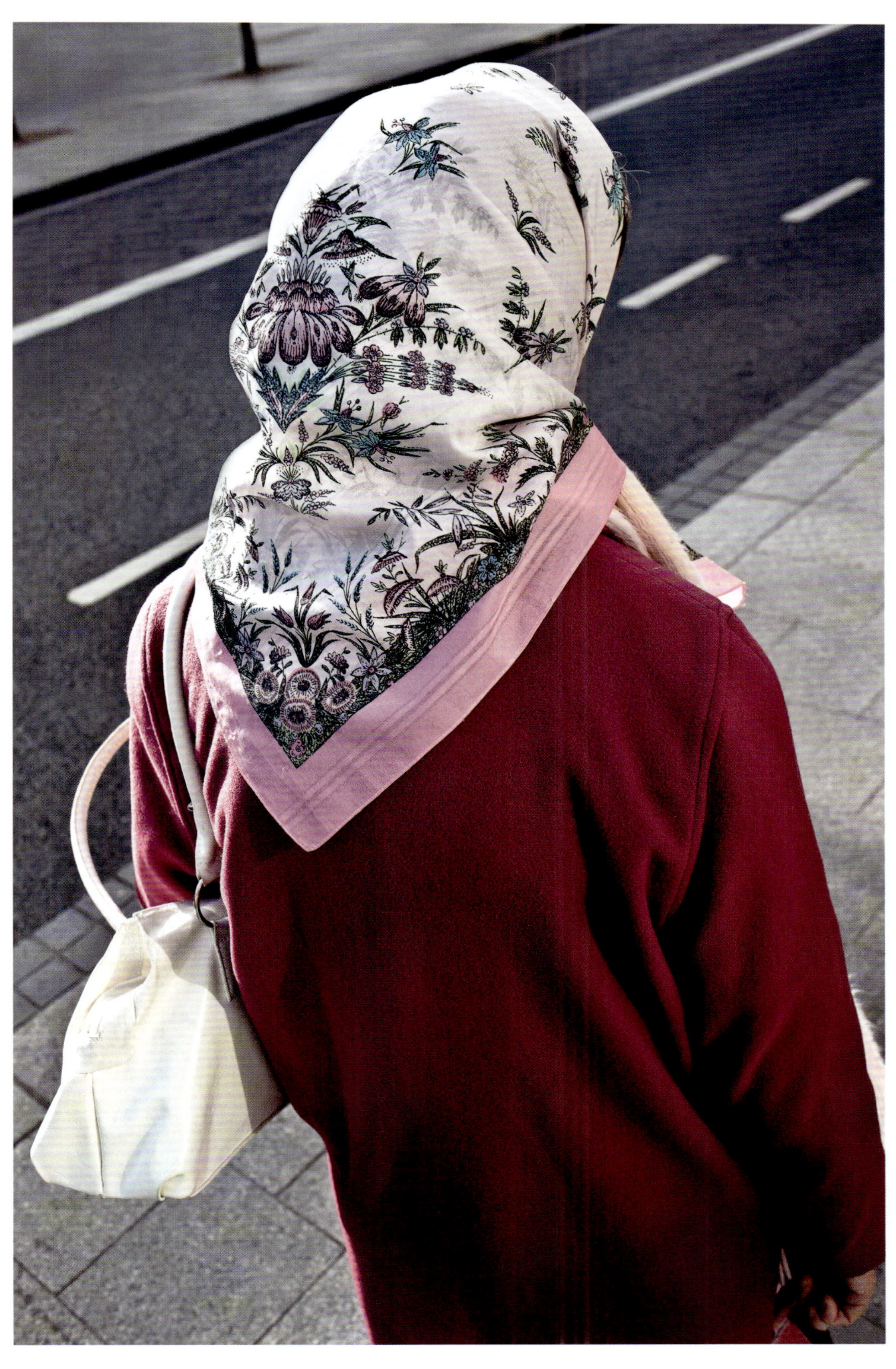

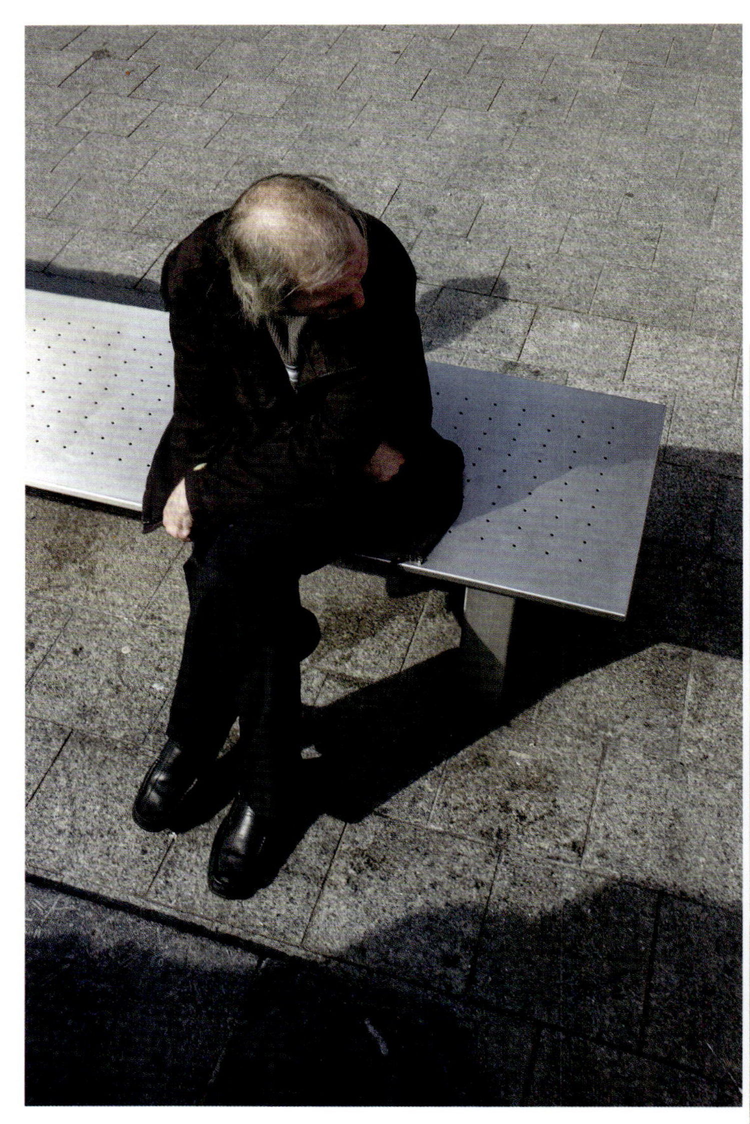

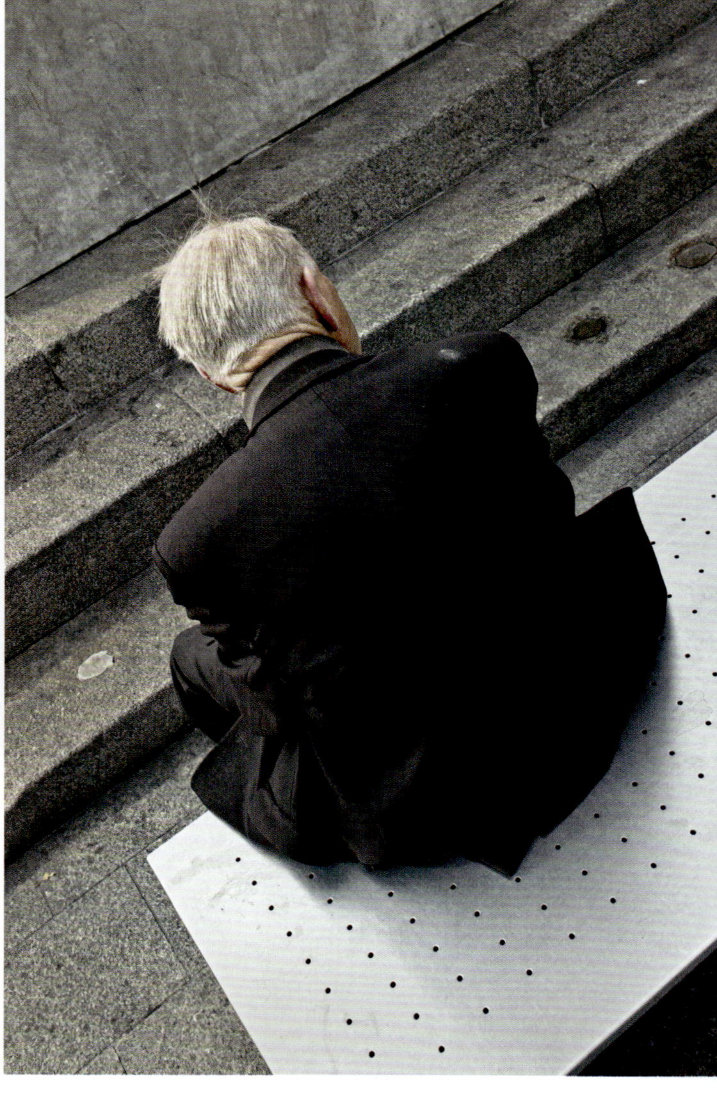

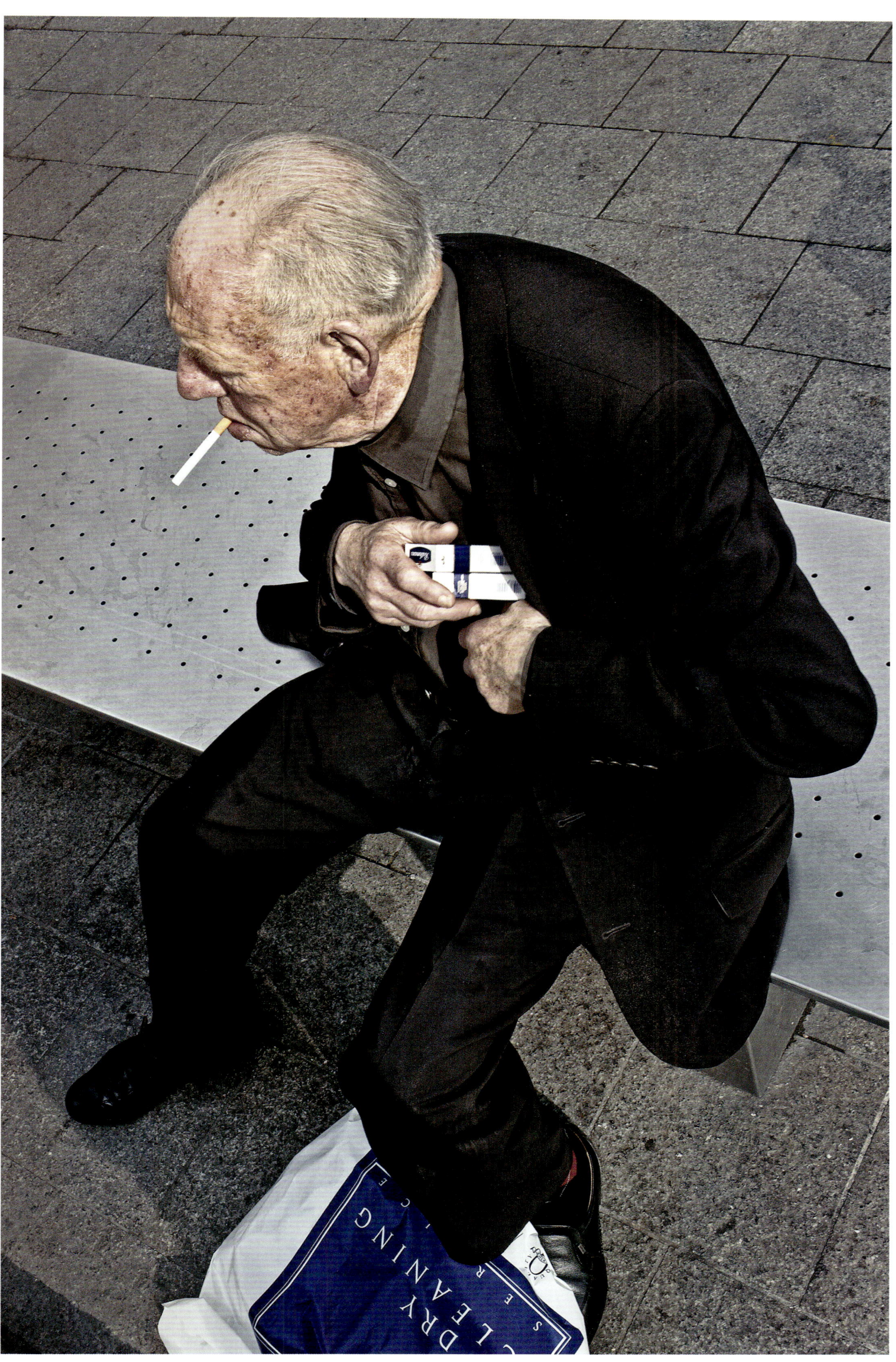

DRY
CLEANING
SERVICE

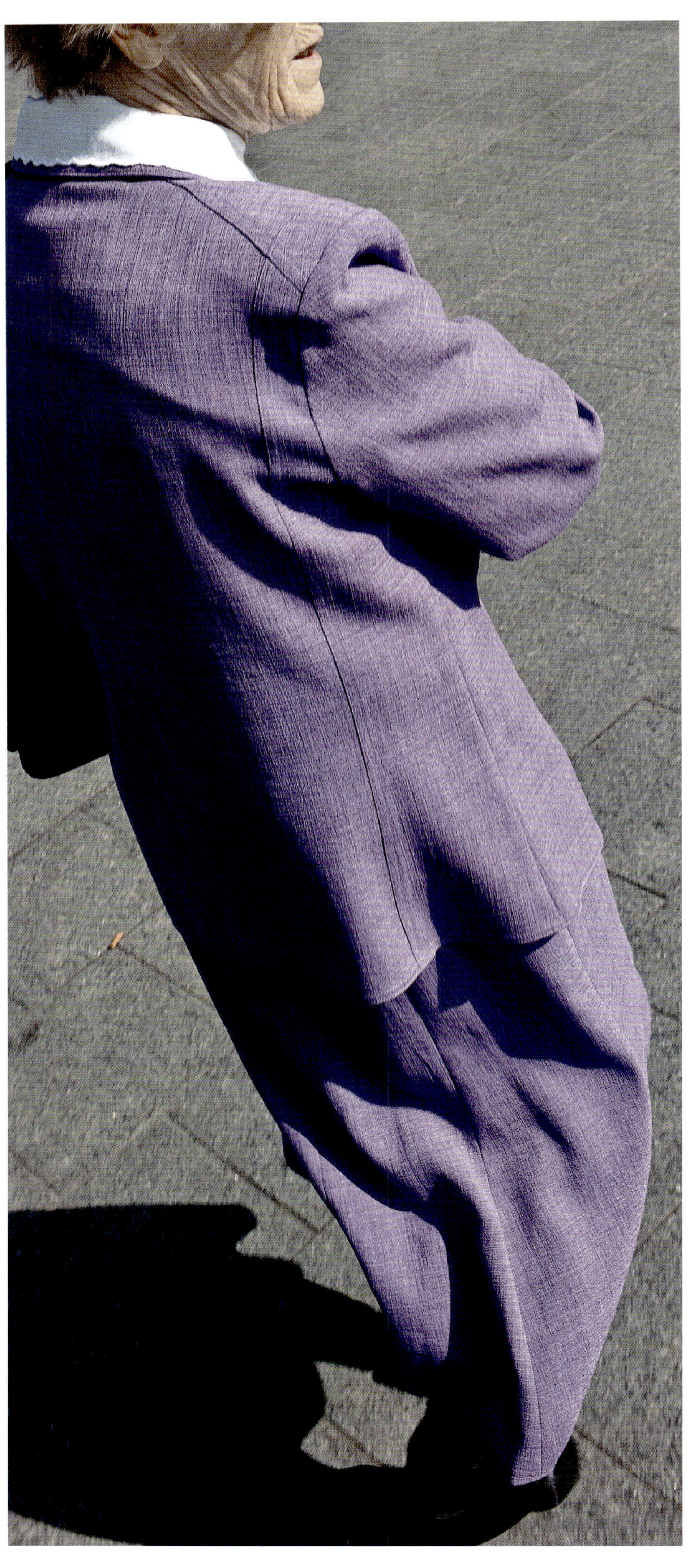

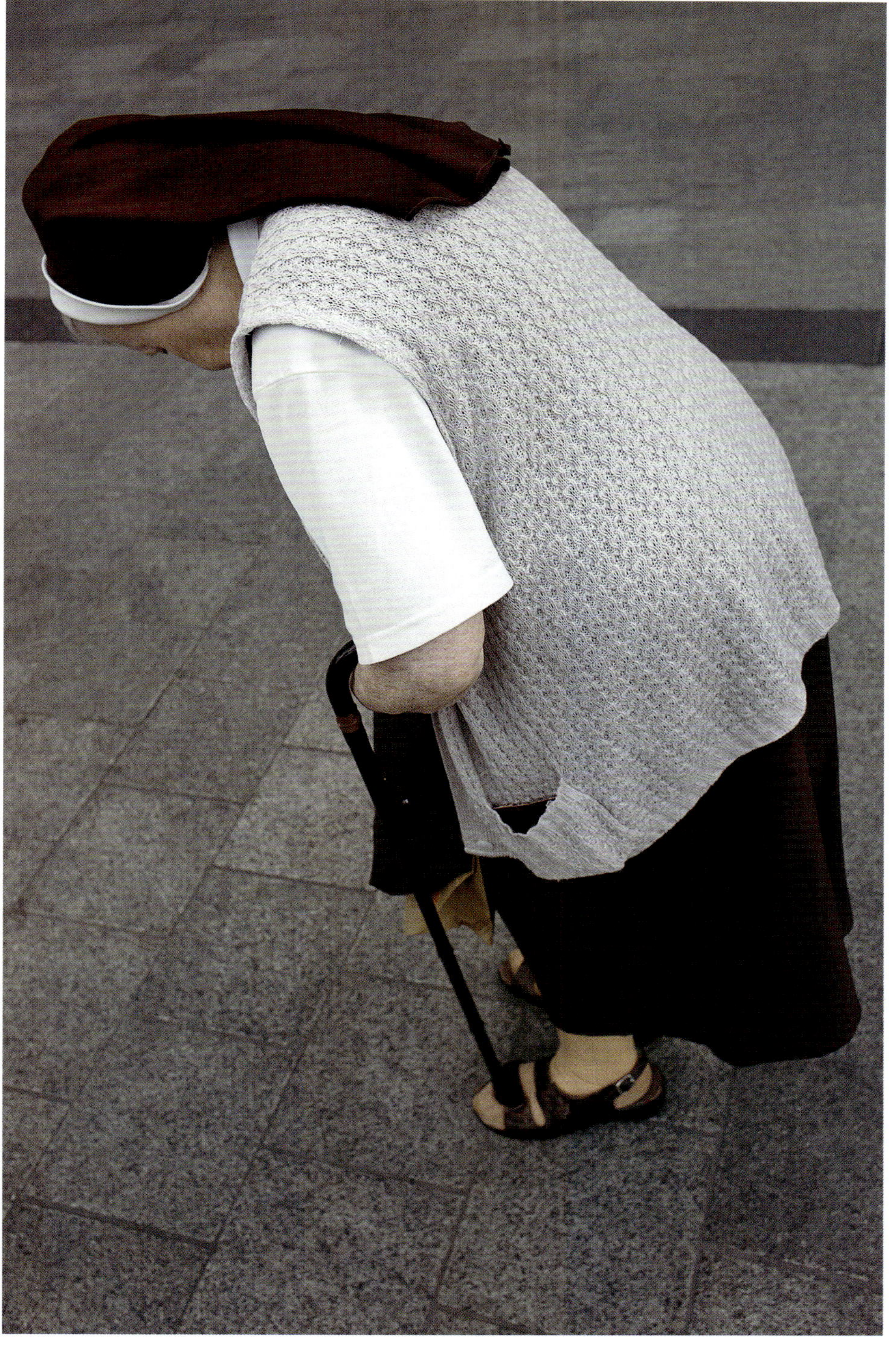

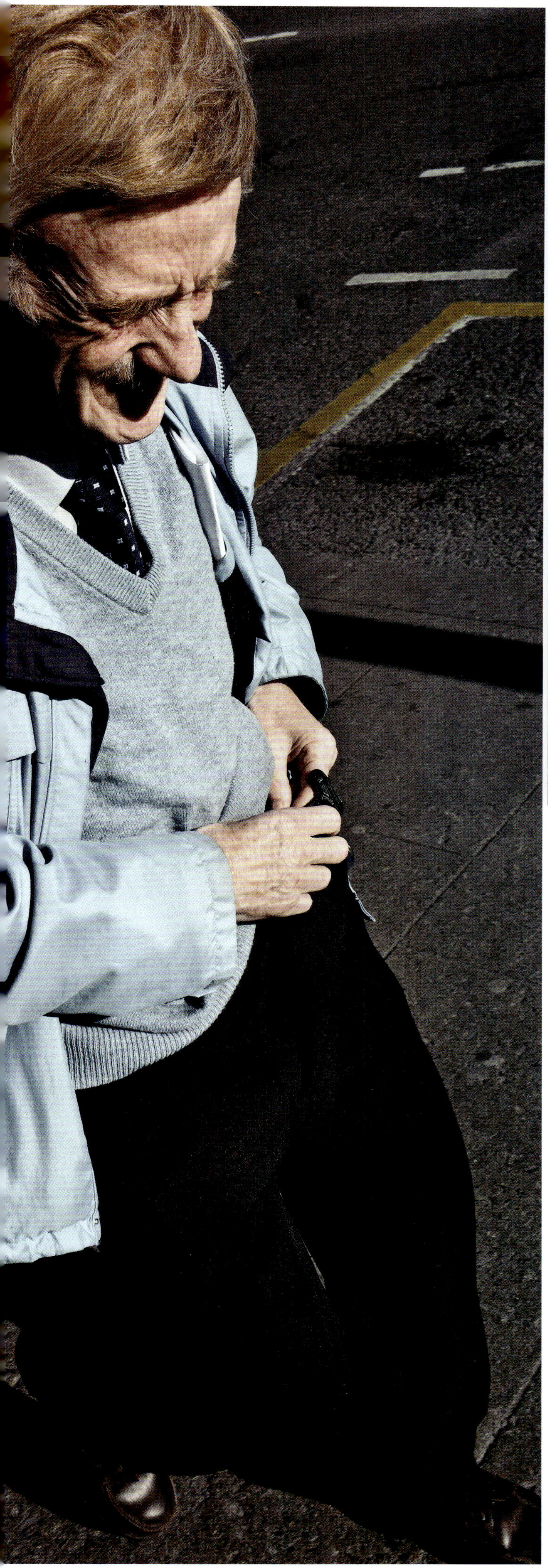

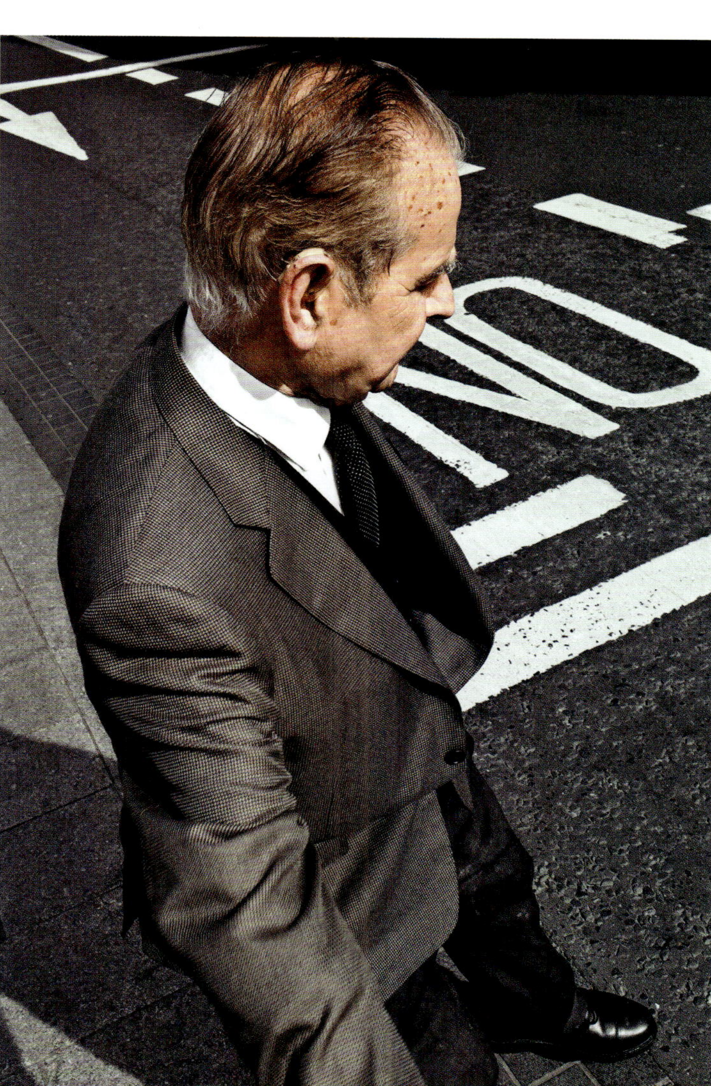

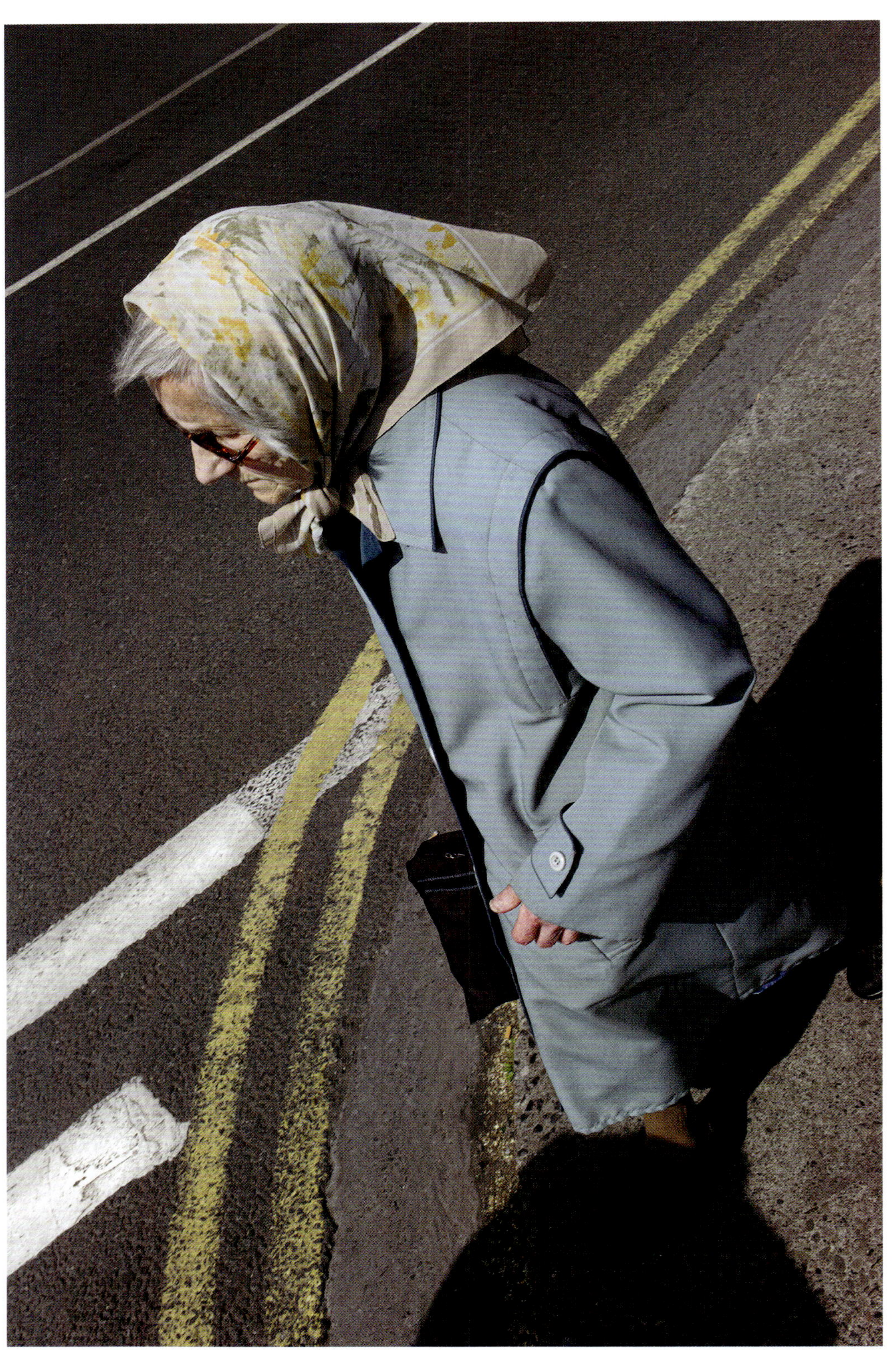

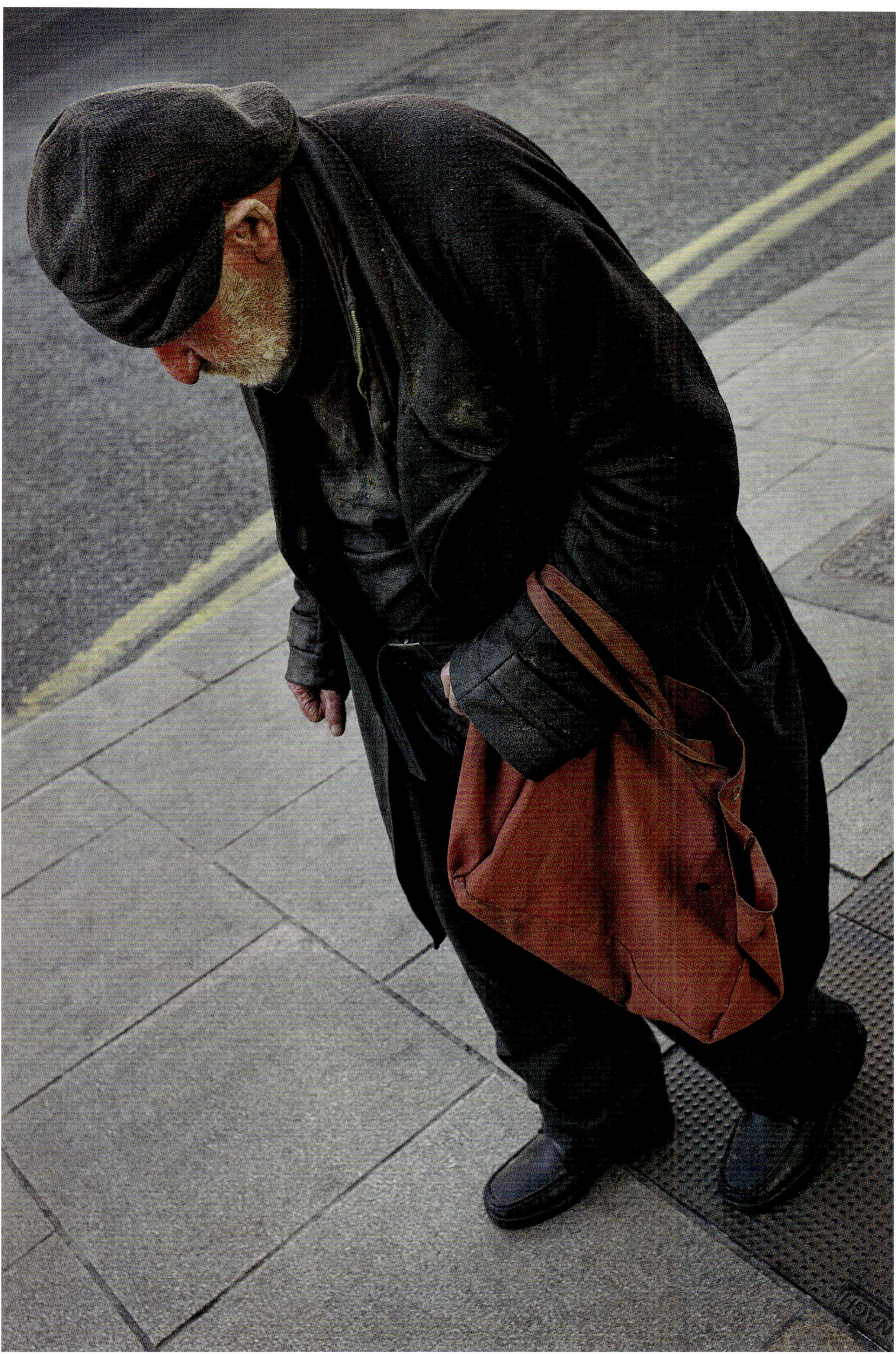

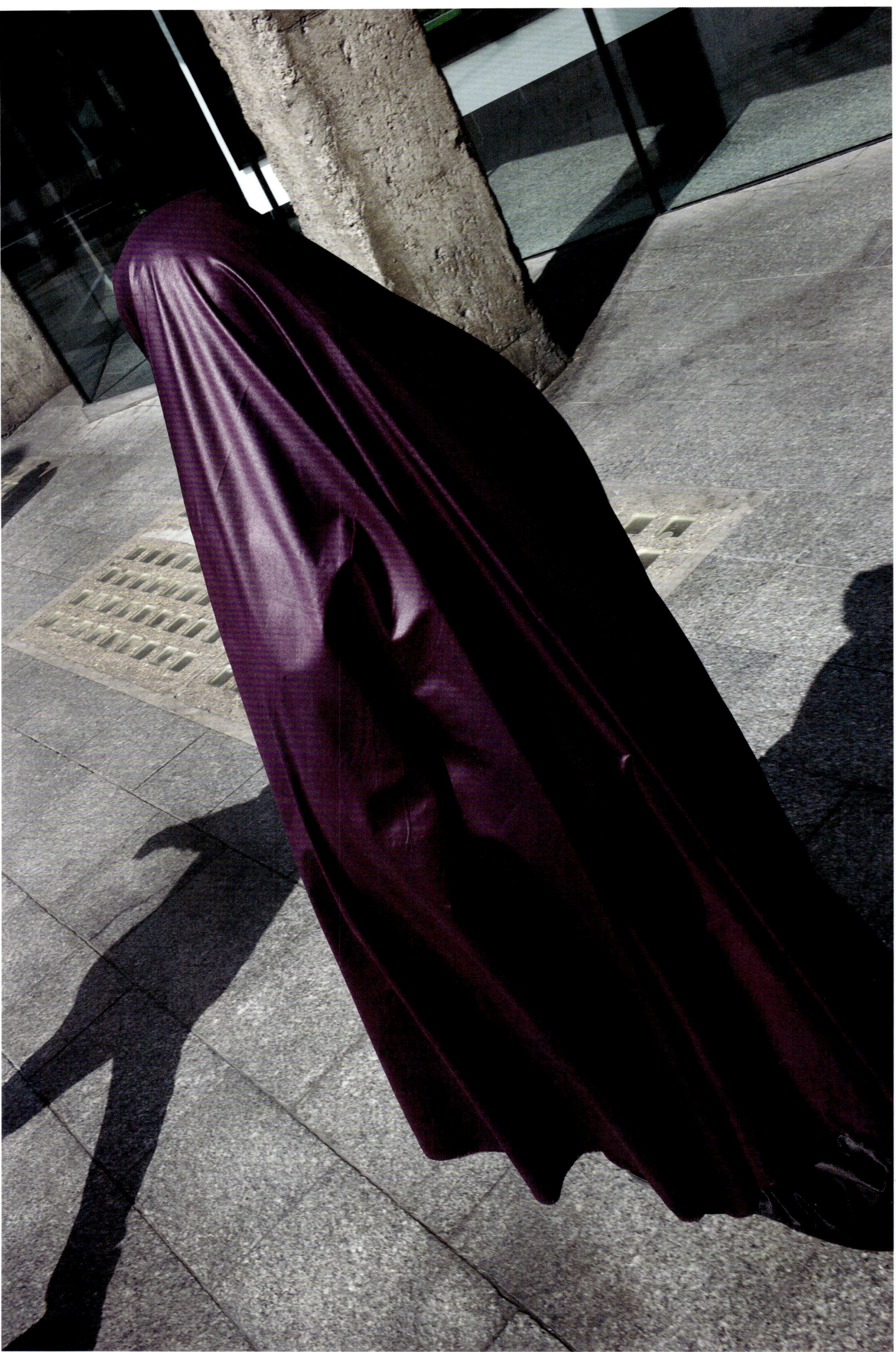

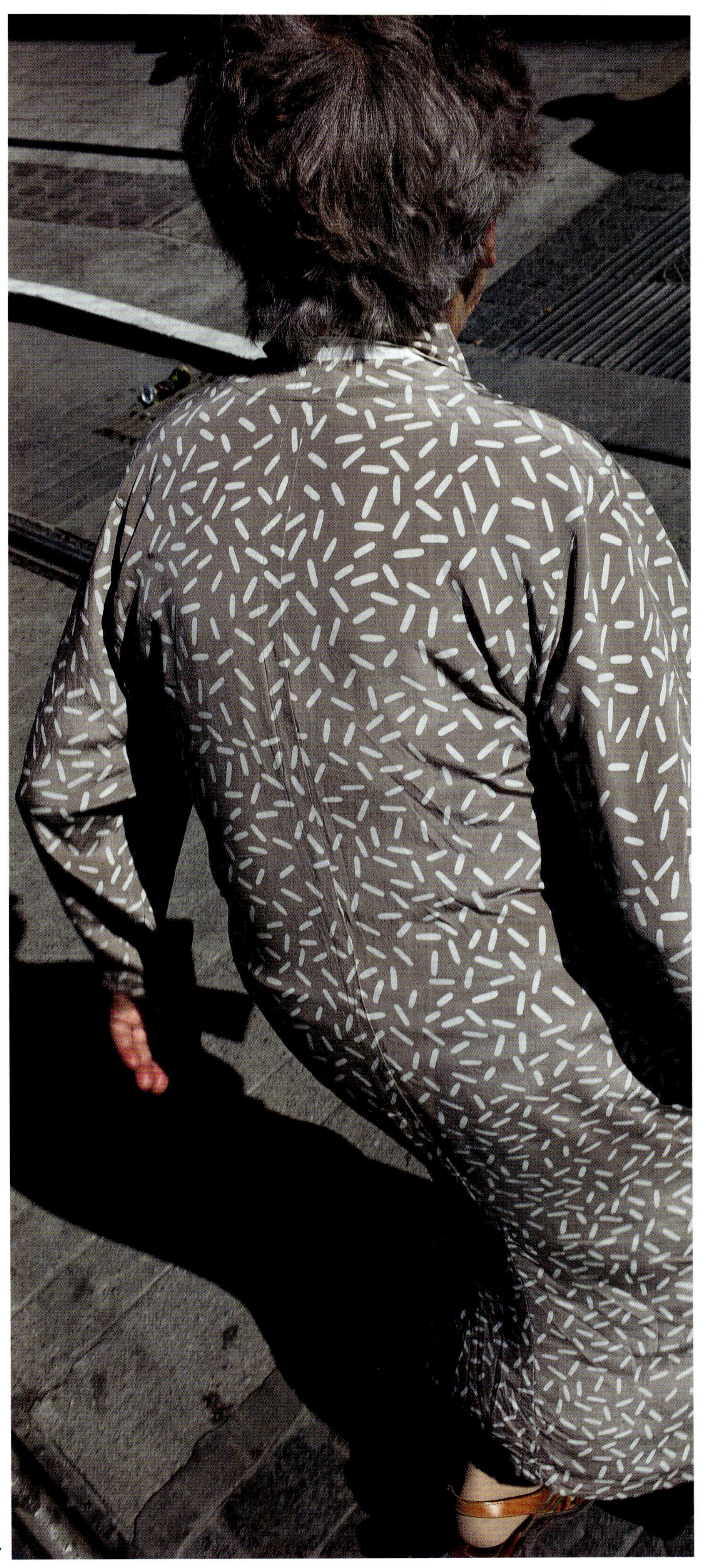

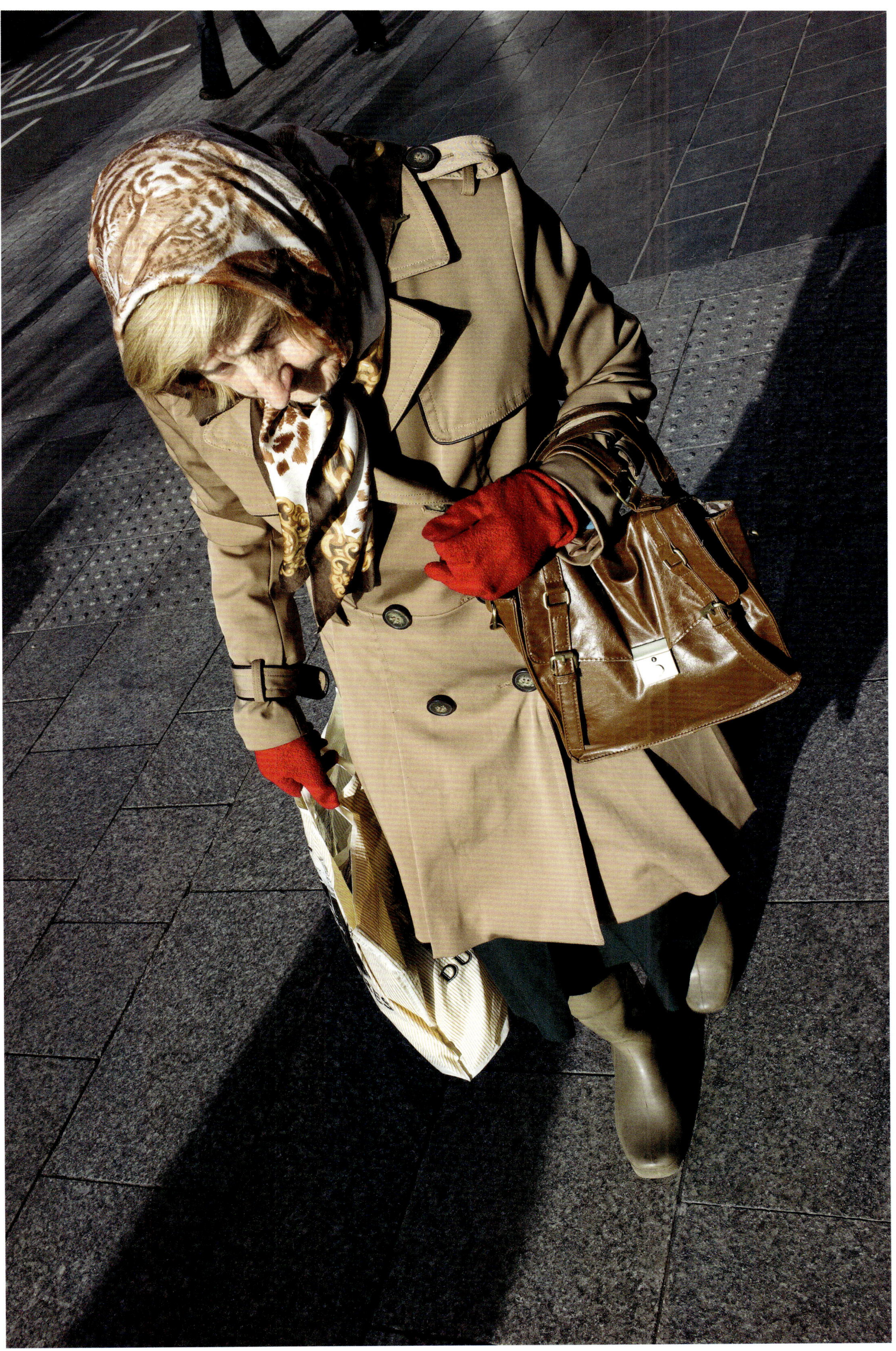

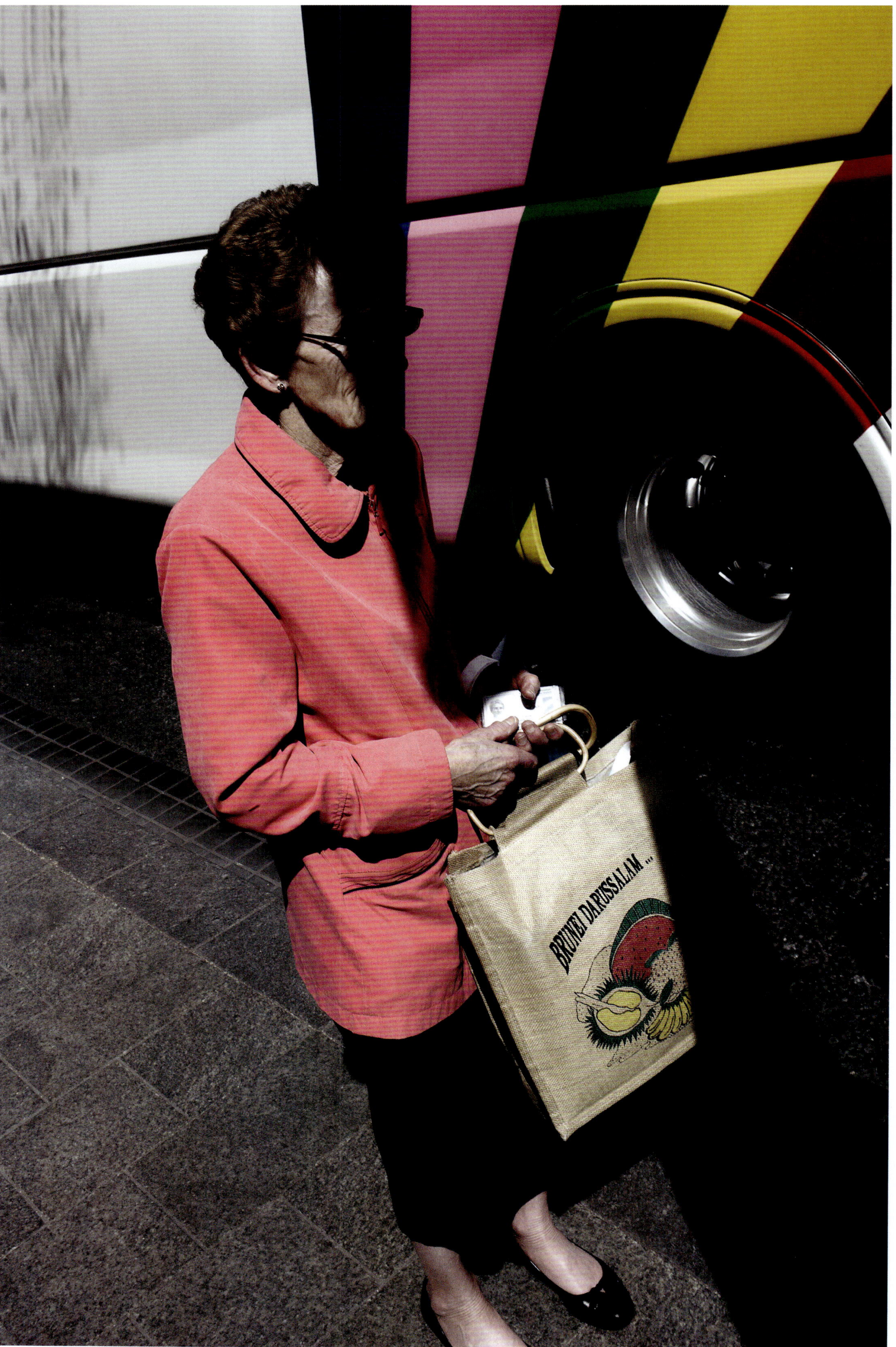
BRUNEI DARUSSALAM ...

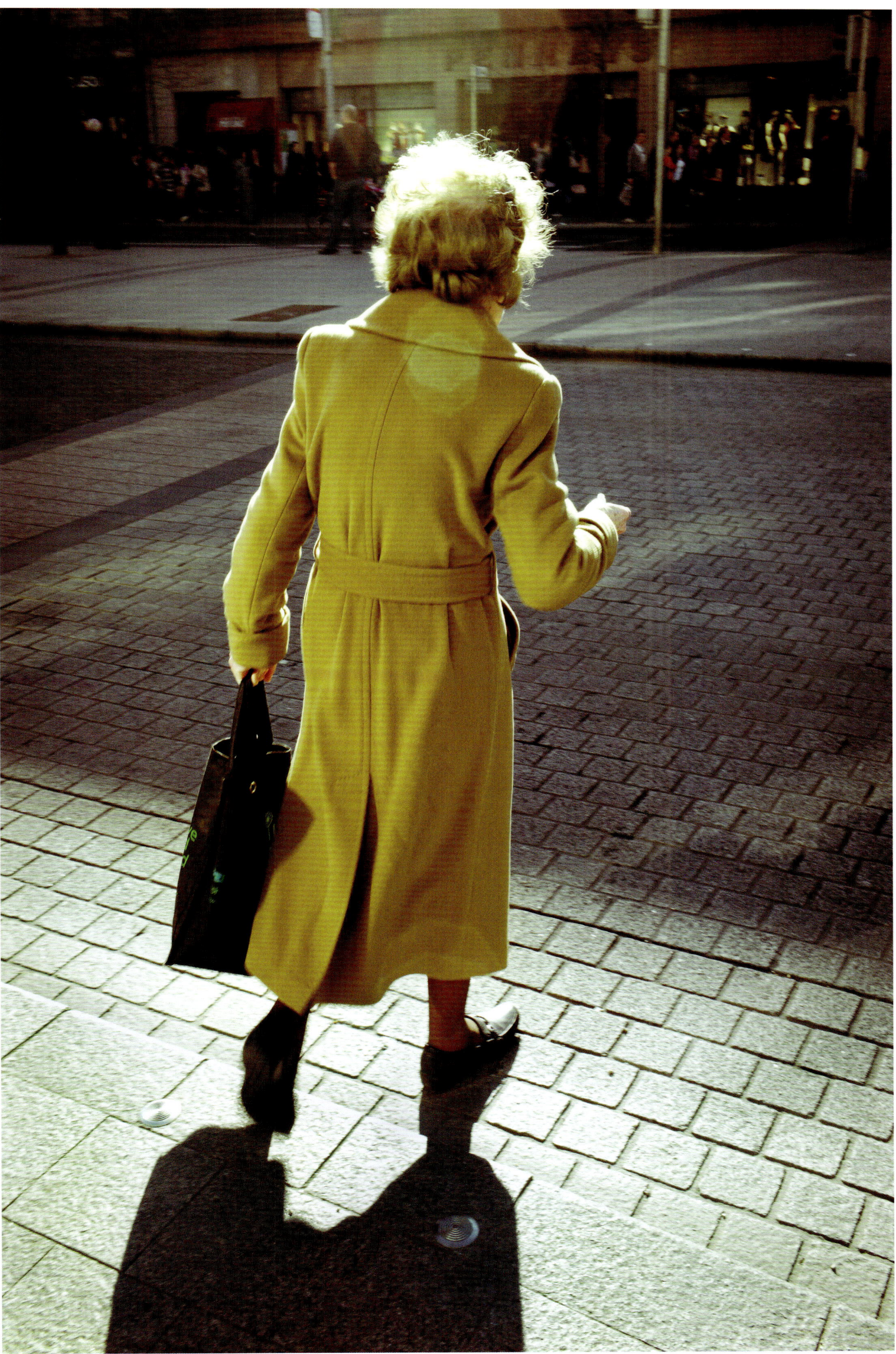

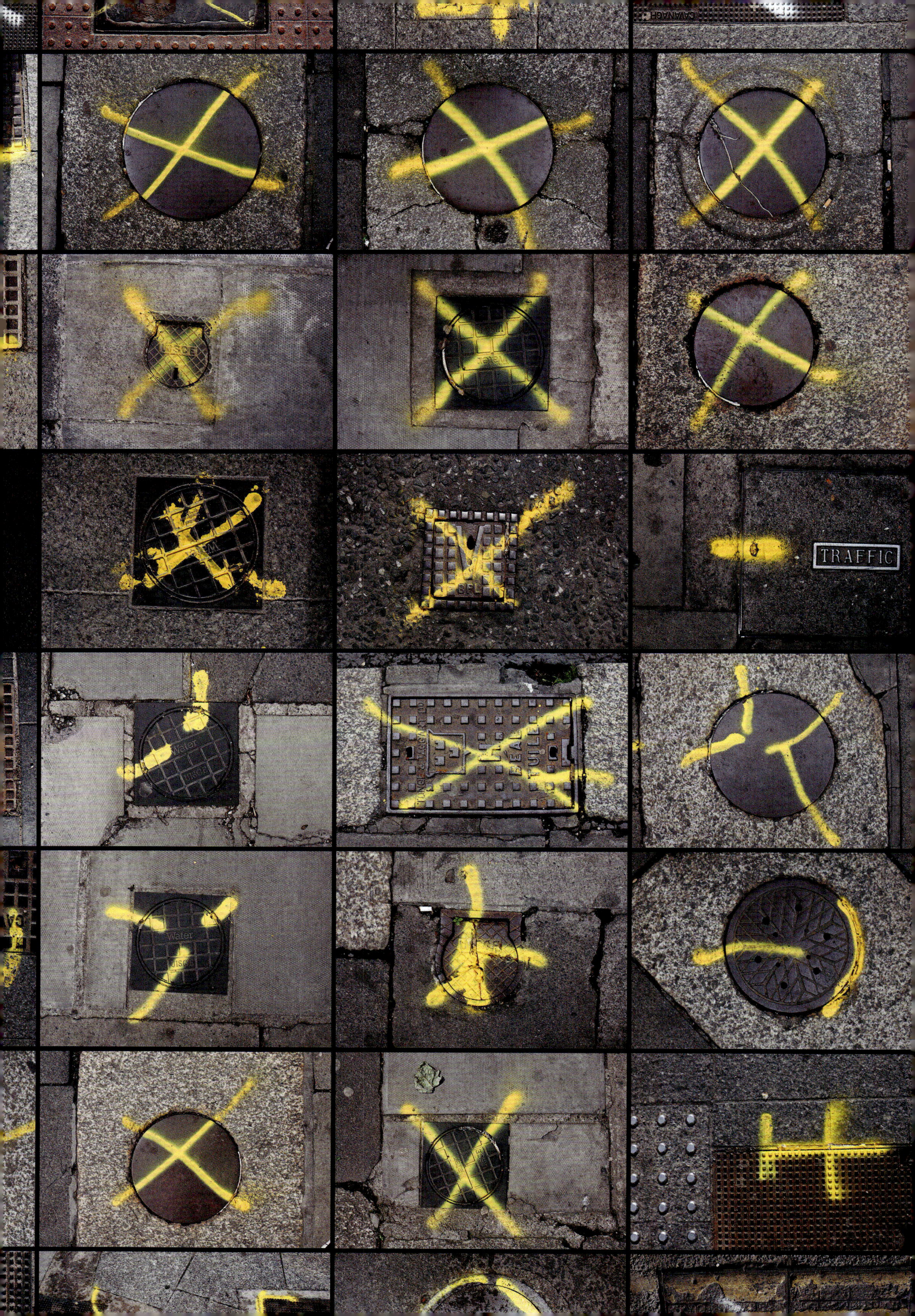

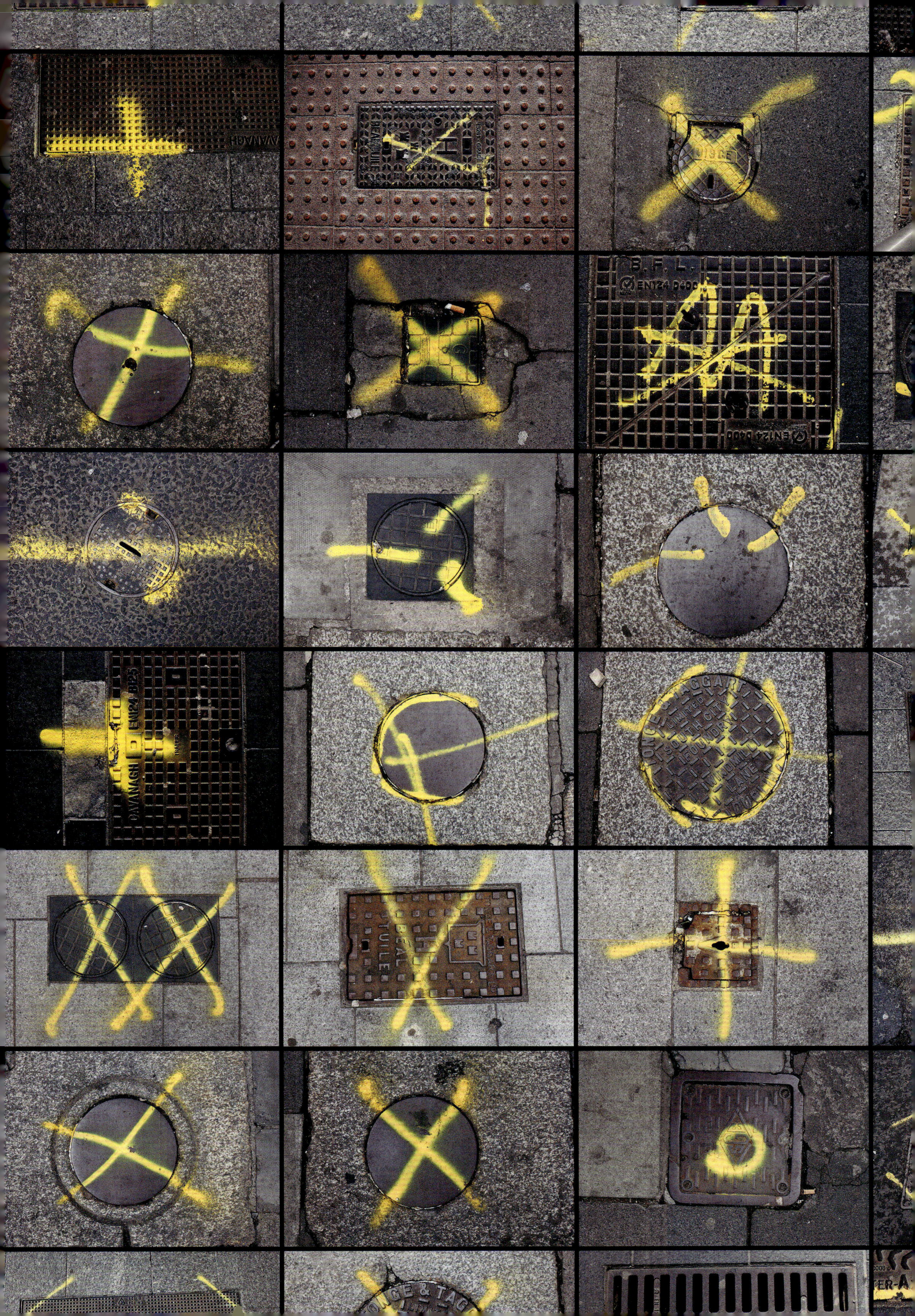

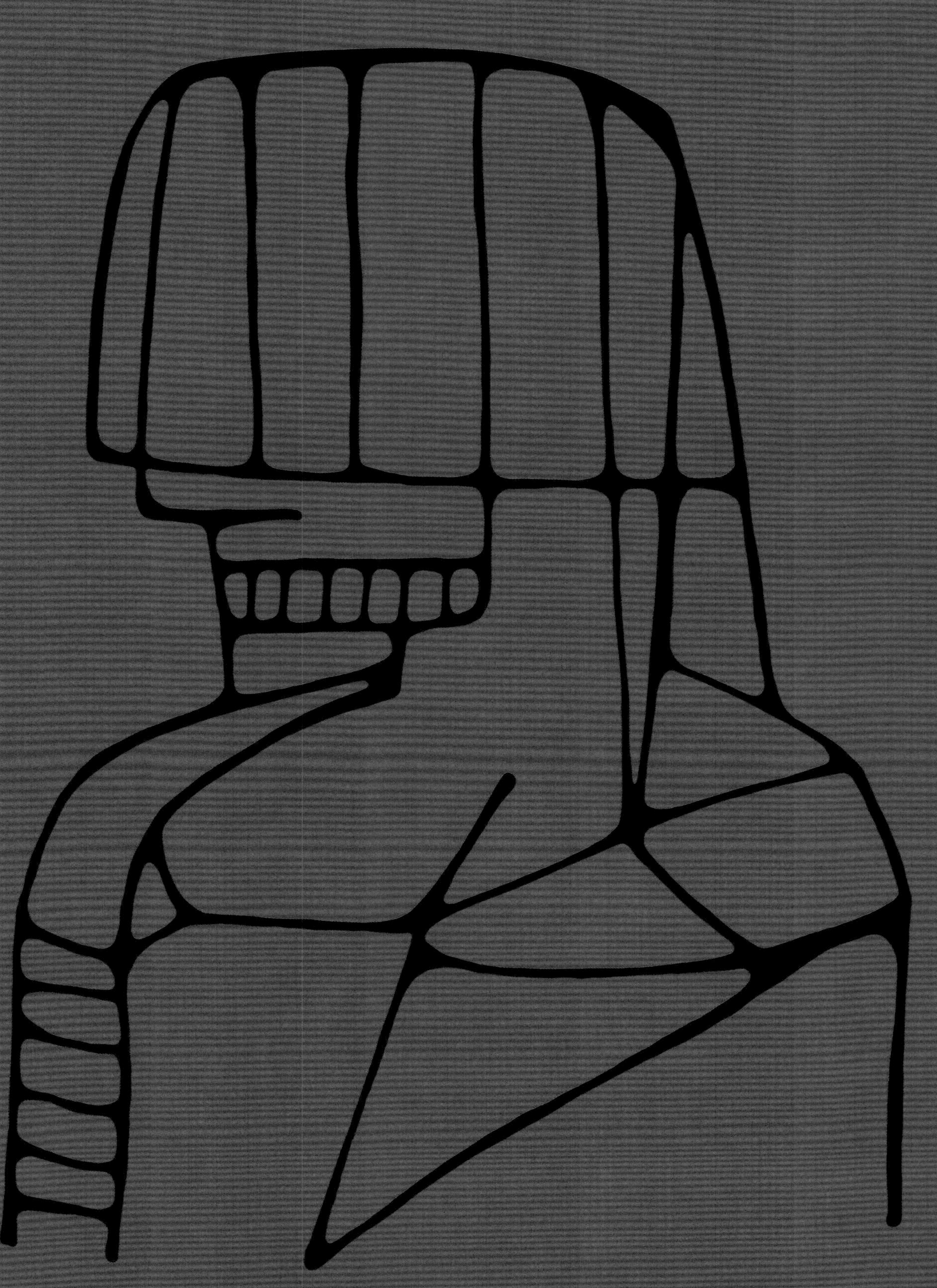

ONE NIGHT IN EARLY JUNE I was crossing O'Connell Bridge heading north with no notion on my mind more complicated than a bowl of noodles on Parnell Street when I was stopped up by a young addict.

You were supposed to meet me here last week, he said.

I had never seen the boy before, but I was not surprised by his delusion — as we spoke, he was dreamily popping little blue pills from a plastic card and swallowing them. These are the opioids that are bought over the internet to break down reality and wipe the identity clean.

I don't think you know me at all, I said, and I gave him a couple of euro and I made to move on, but gently he stopped me up again with a palm pressed lightly to my shoulder.

Come here and I tell you, he said. I think I seen the angel.

When was this? I said.

Just now, he said.

Where? I said.

Along the quays, he said. Just here.

And yes, he told me, in an awed but certain tone, yes he had seen the angel above the river, and she had spoken to him even, but he could not recall exactly what it was that she had said.

I walked on, drawn on the threaded pulse that runs beneath the streets, past the taxi rank and the Garden of Remembrance, and I wondered what it was that the angel above the river had said.

She said —

This place will endure and you will not. The flesh will fall from your arrogant bones. But these streets exist through each of their every moment still, because on the surface of the city all of time is unfixed, and the river will move as it always does through these gaudy lives and carnal songs, and the buildings and the bridges will creak and sway and collapse; and there will be nights again when better men and women come by here for a while, and there will be nights again when worse.

The Poles were drinking in their Parnell Street bars; the Chinese ate busily at late suppers; the rainbow flags flew all along North Great George's Street.

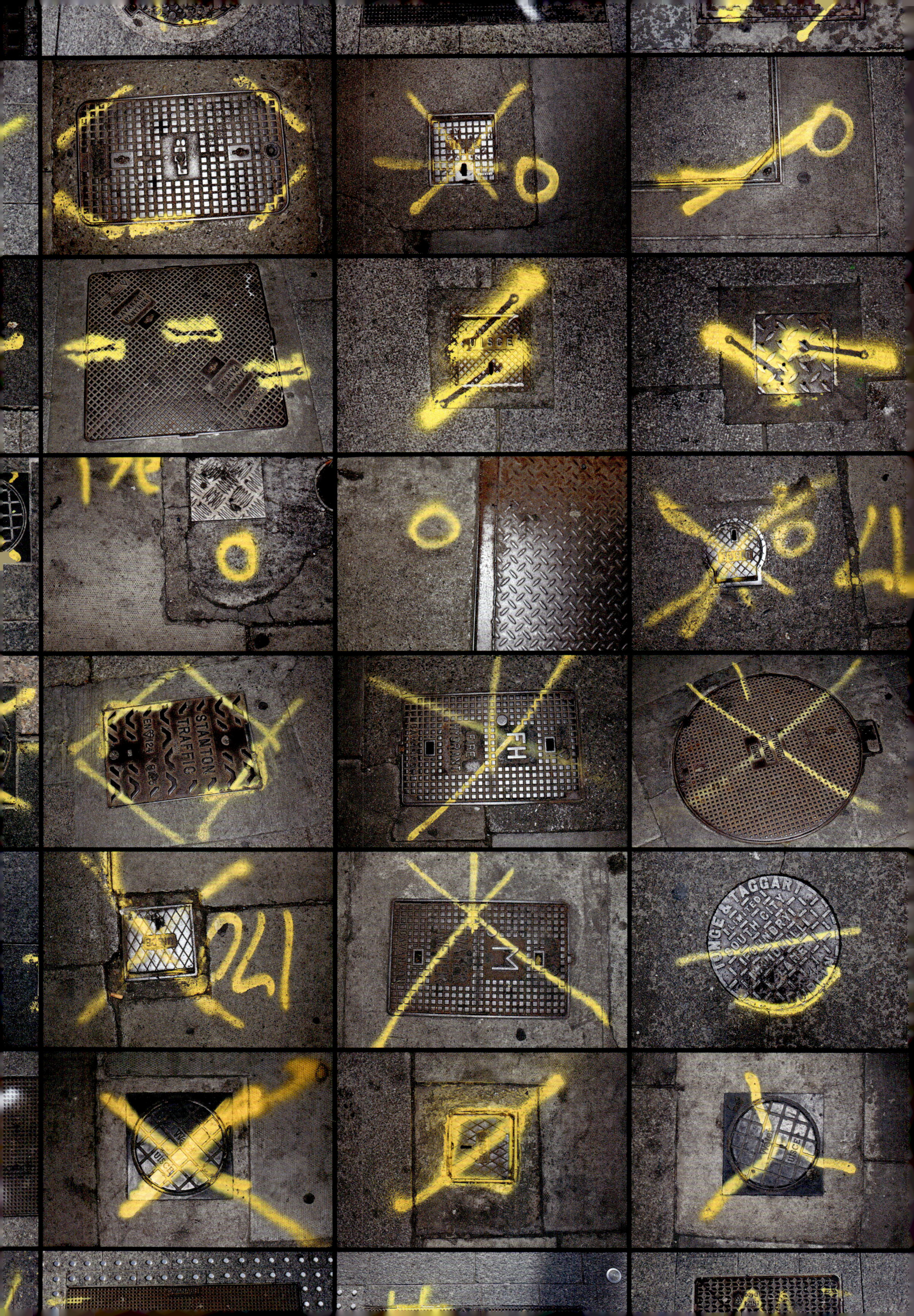

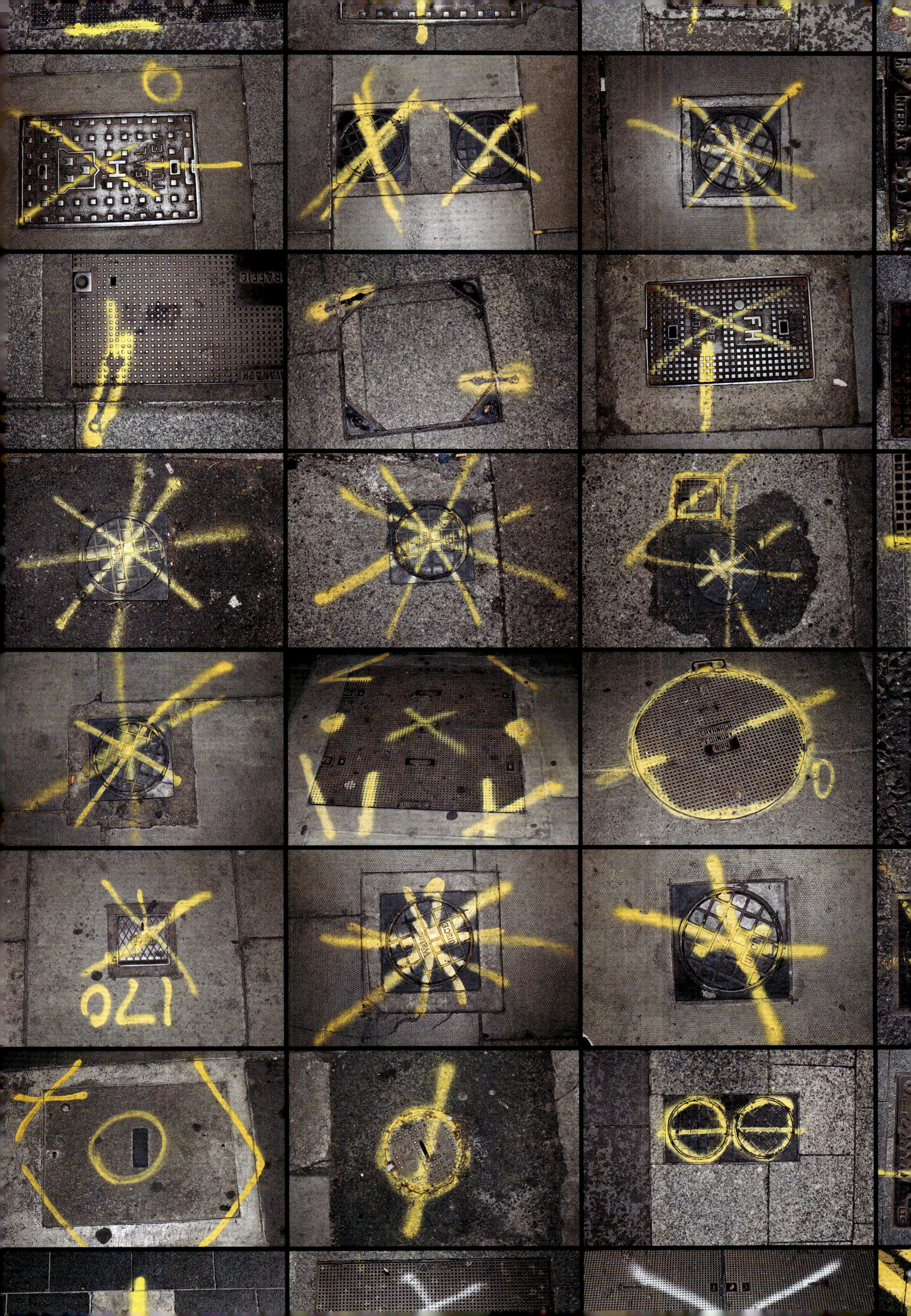

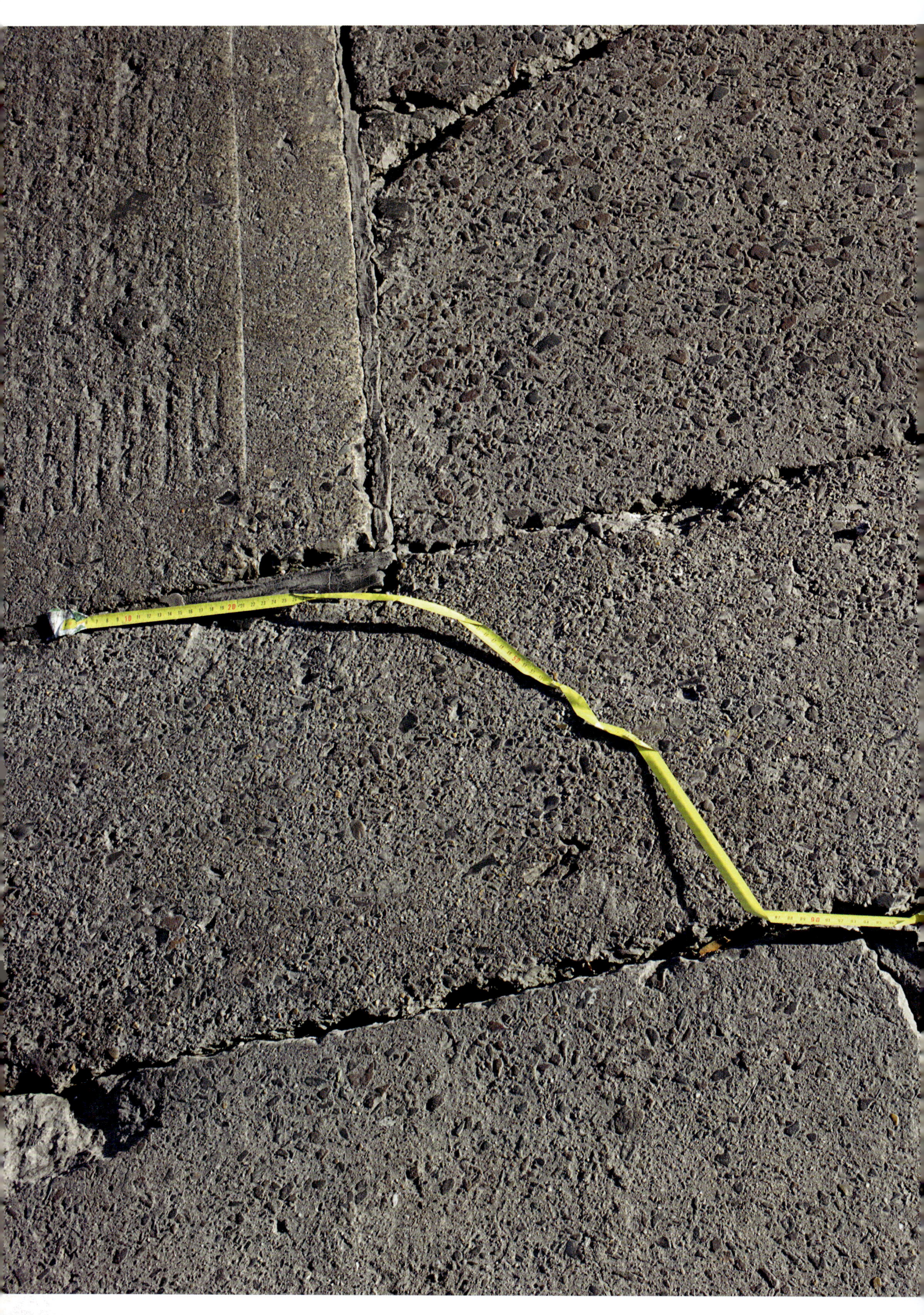

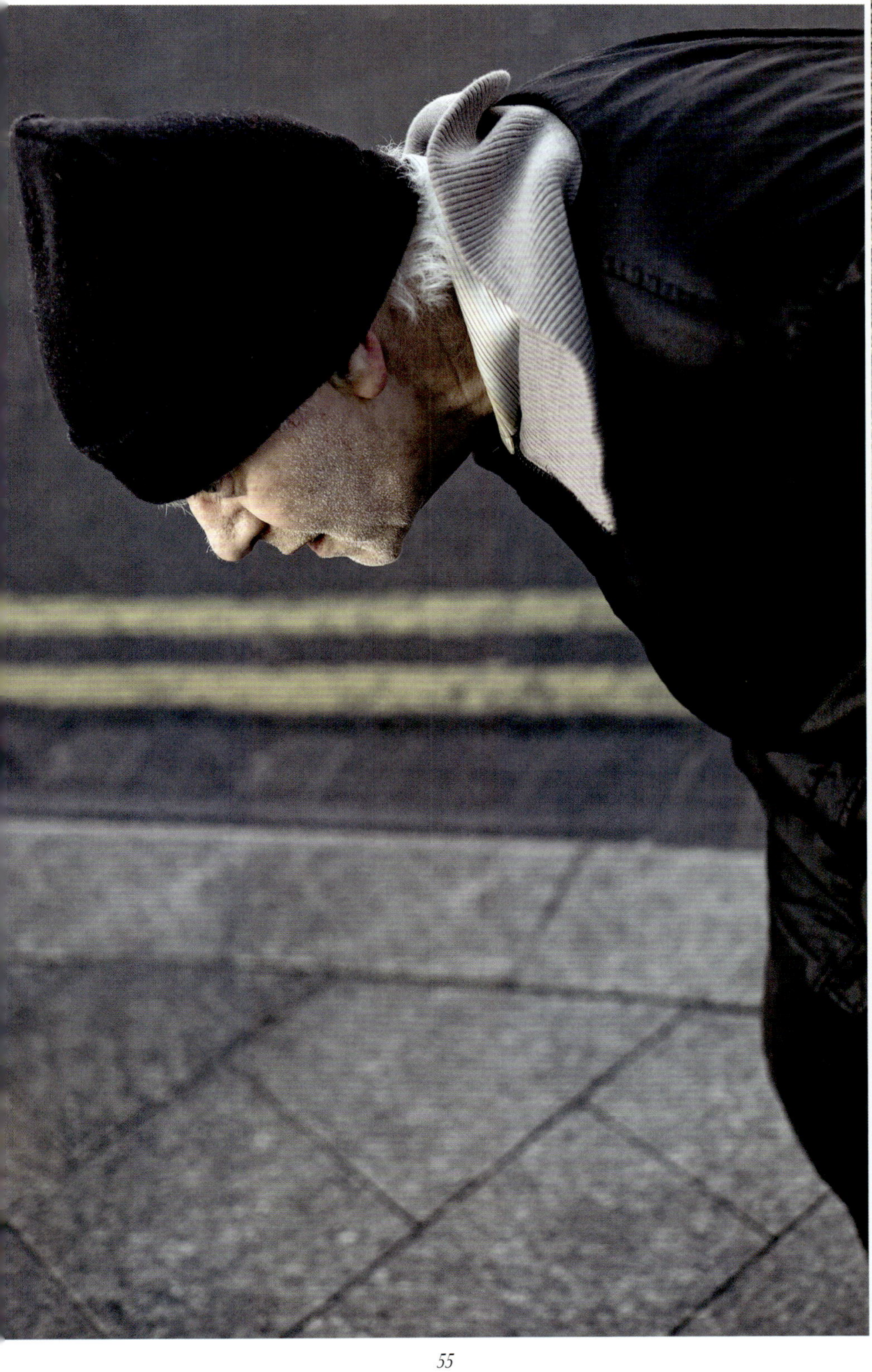

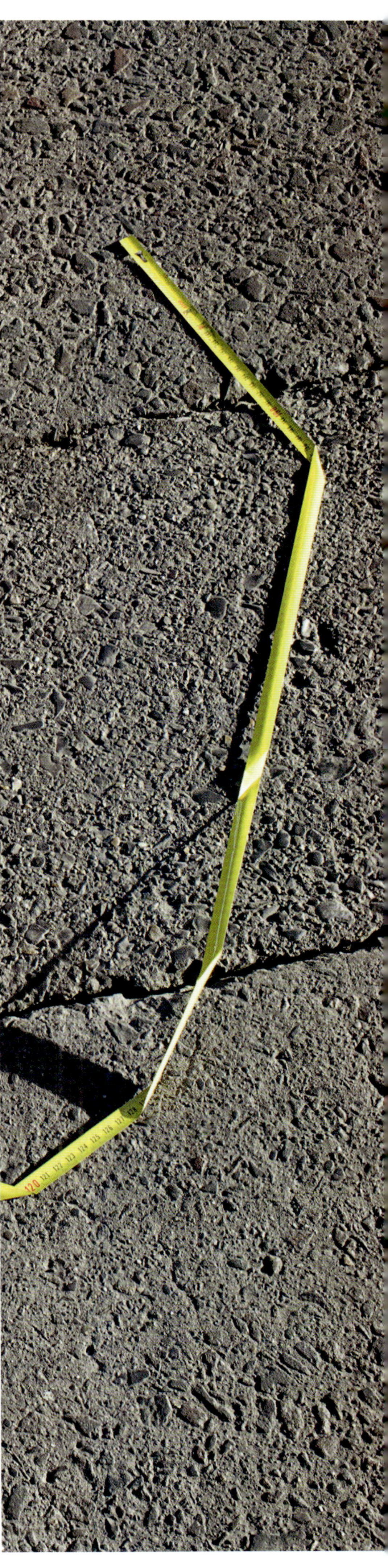

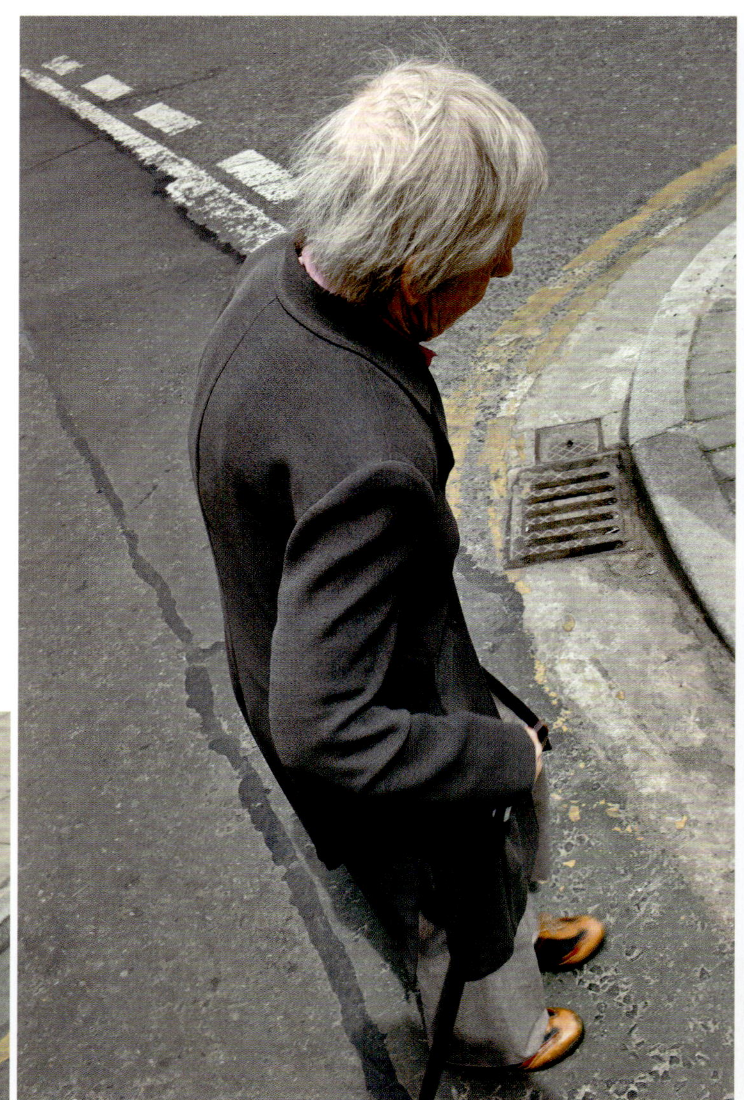

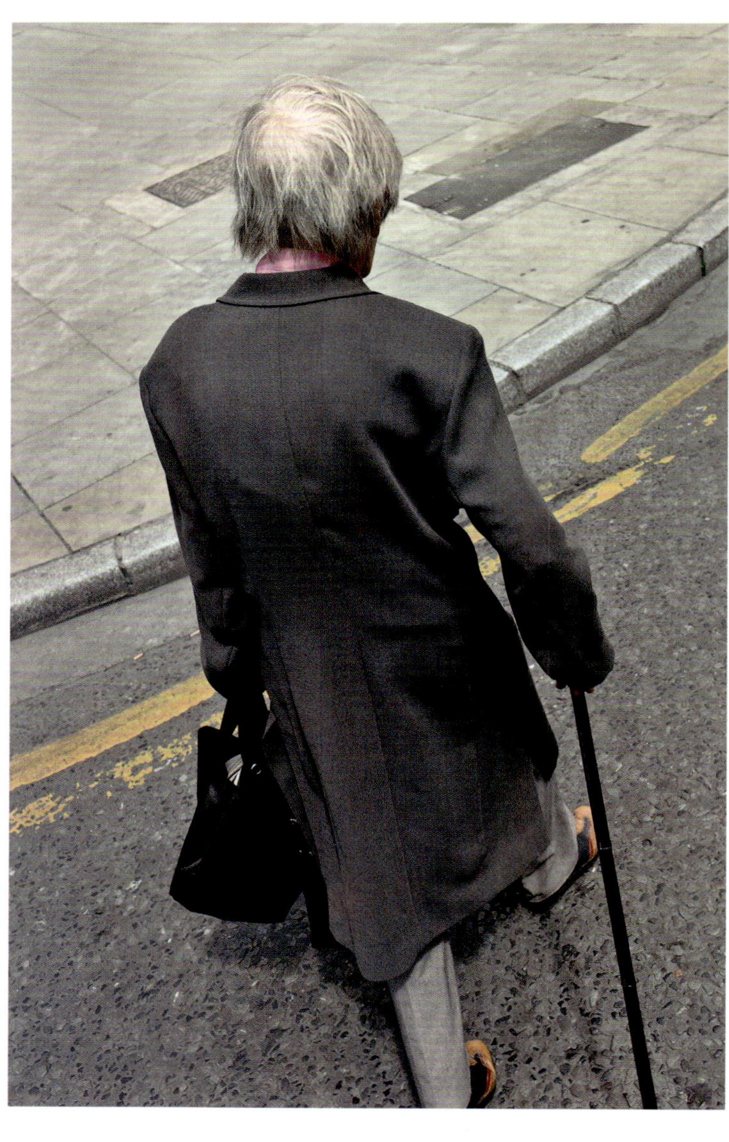

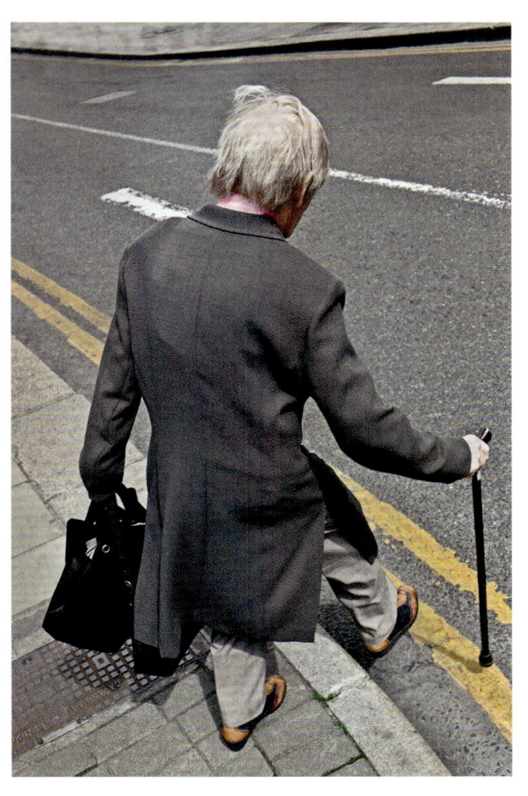
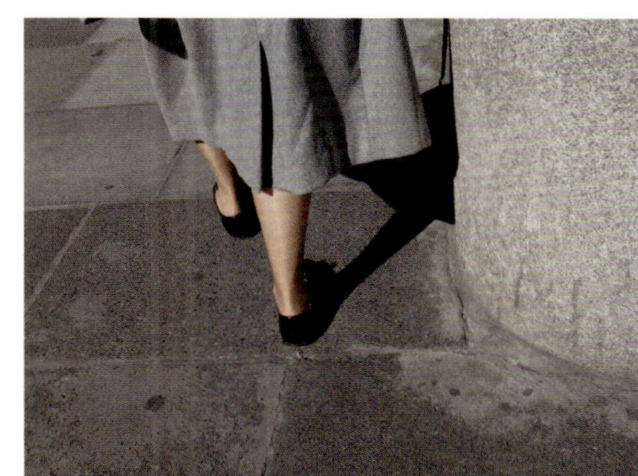
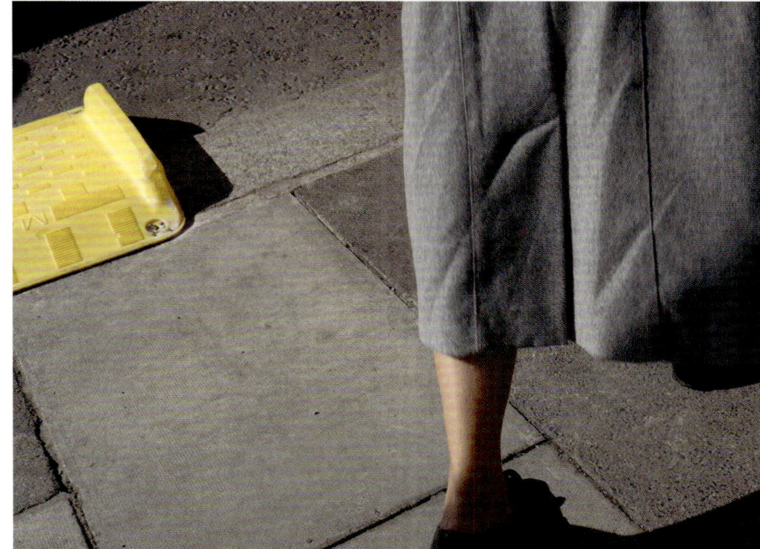

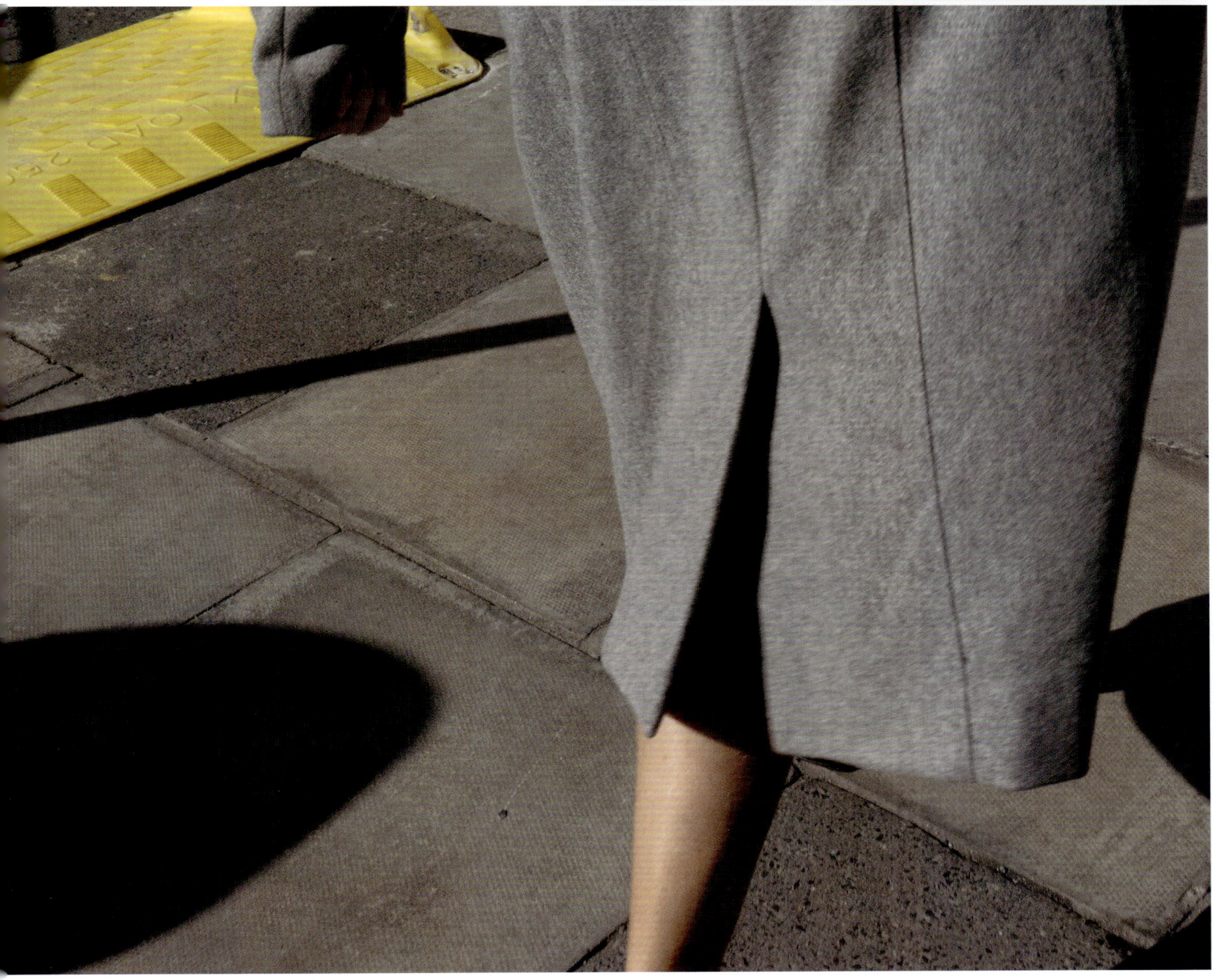

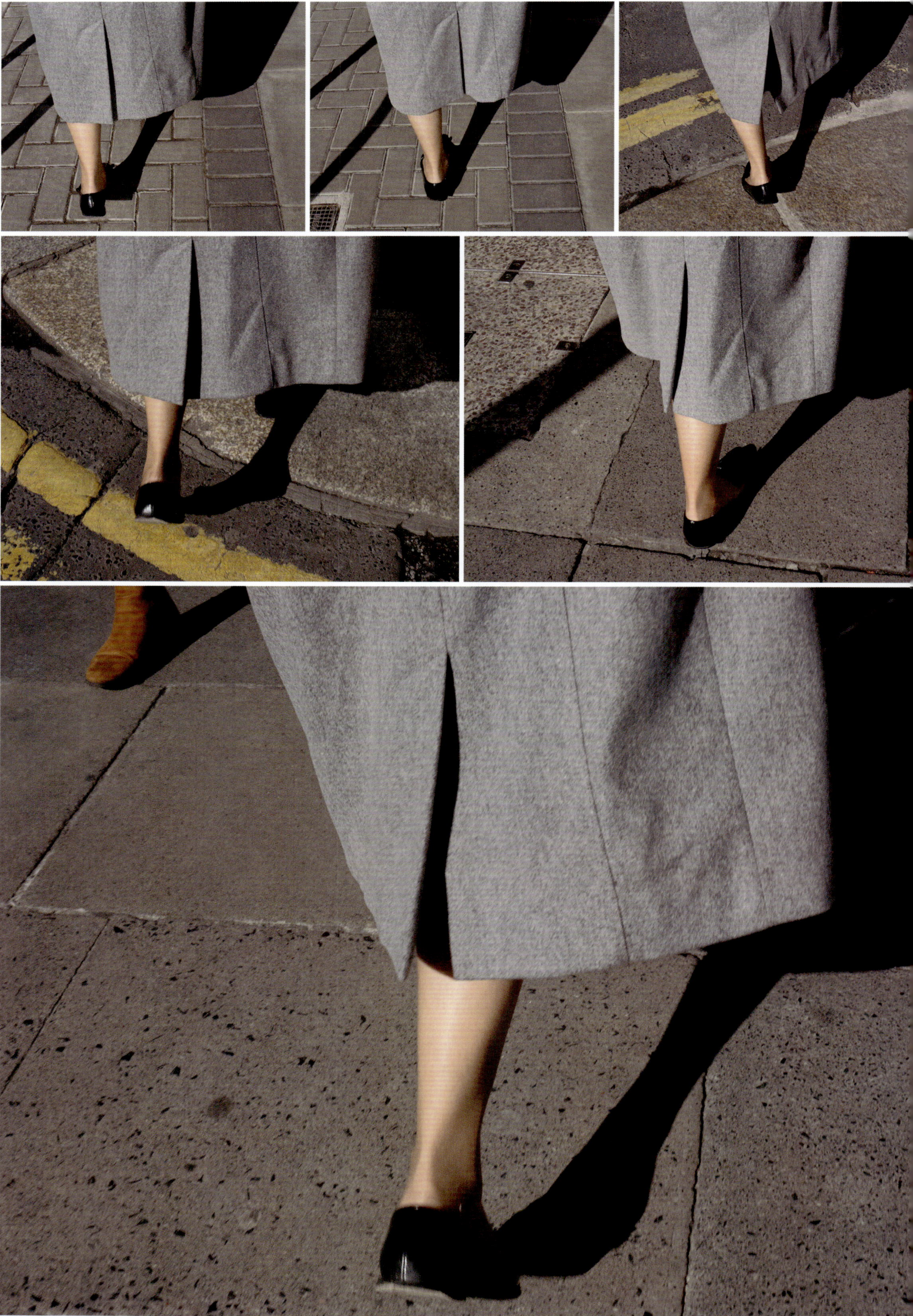

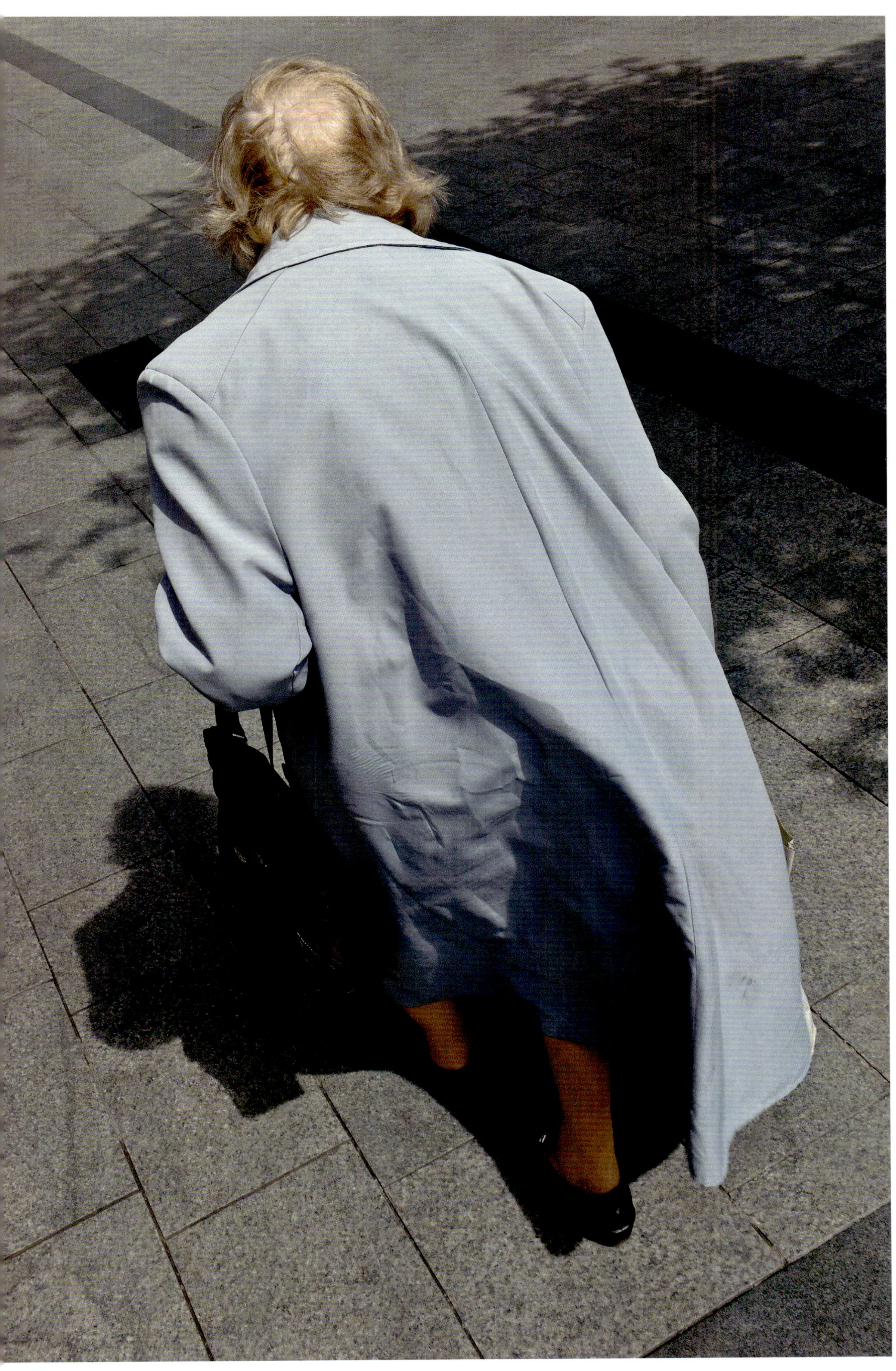

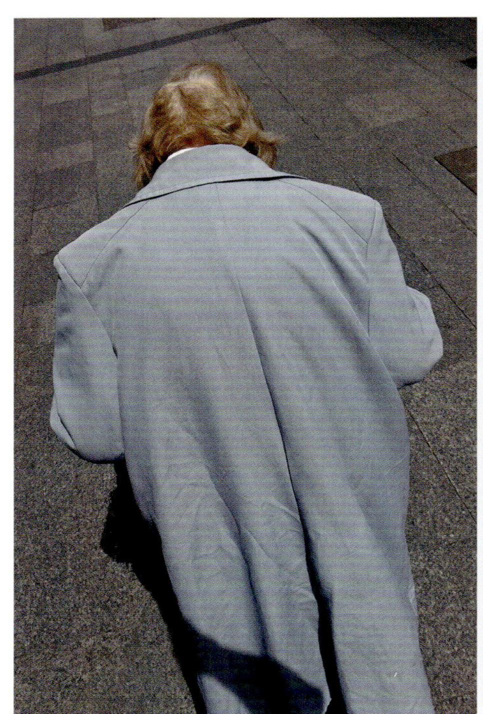

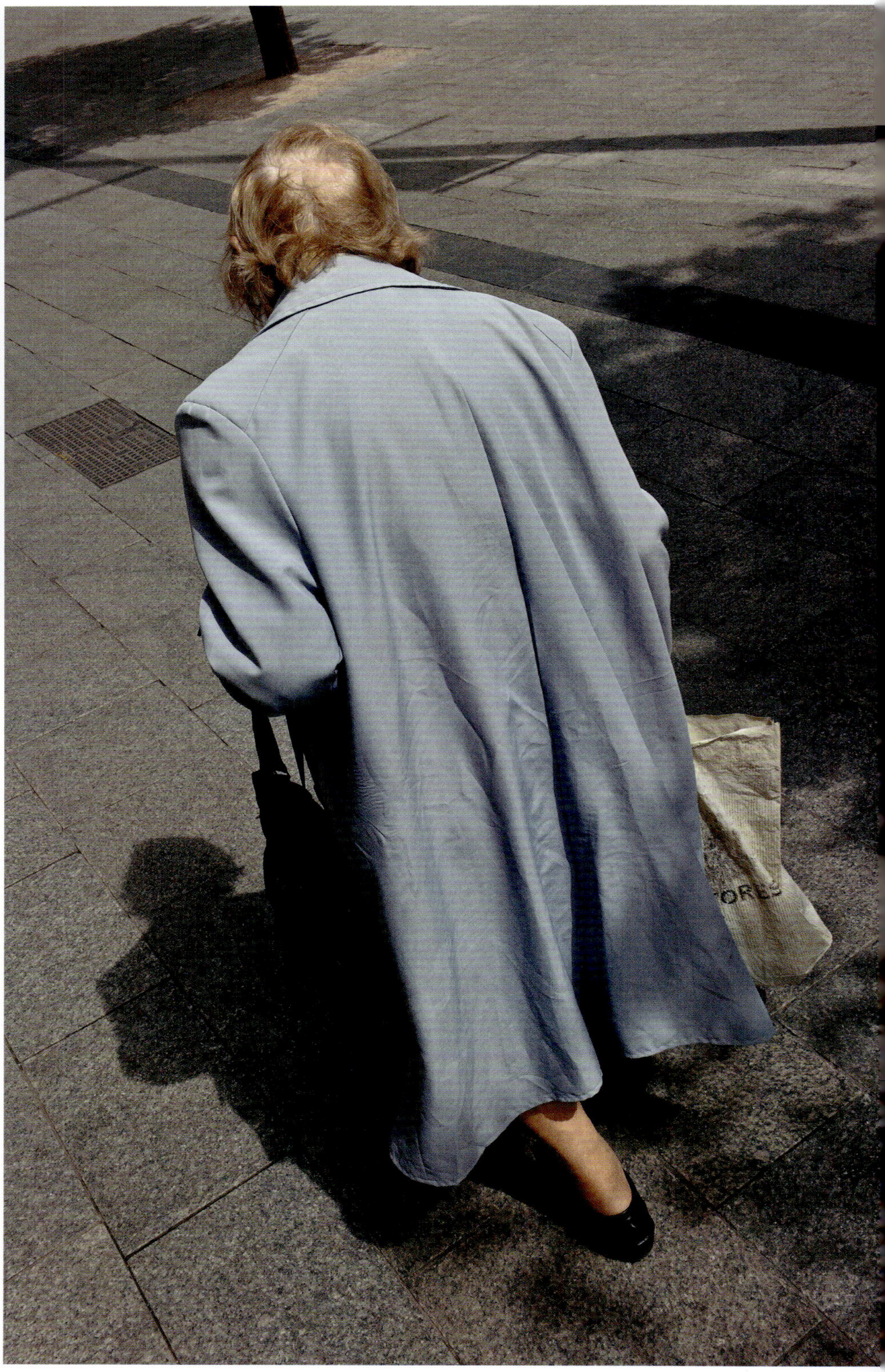

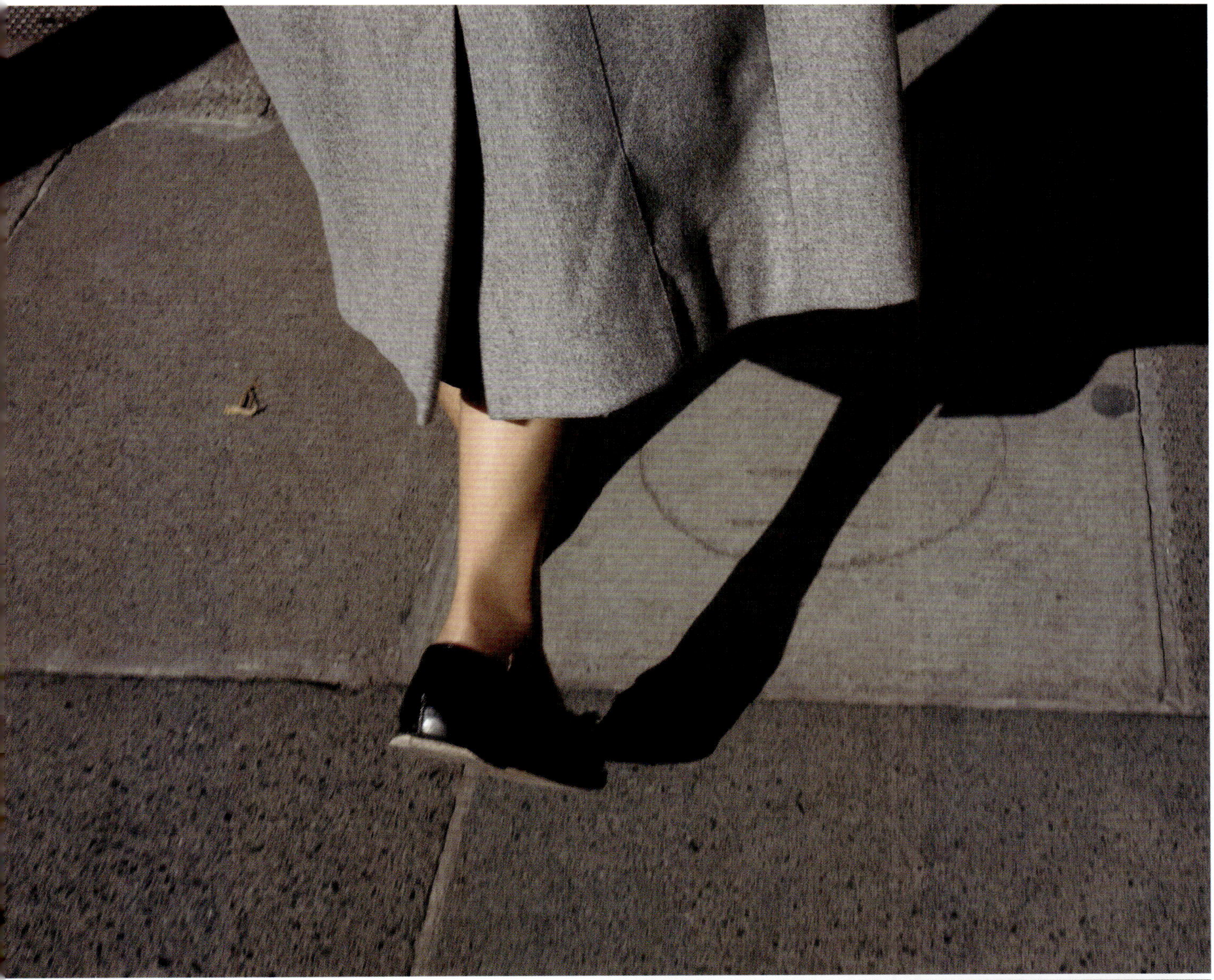

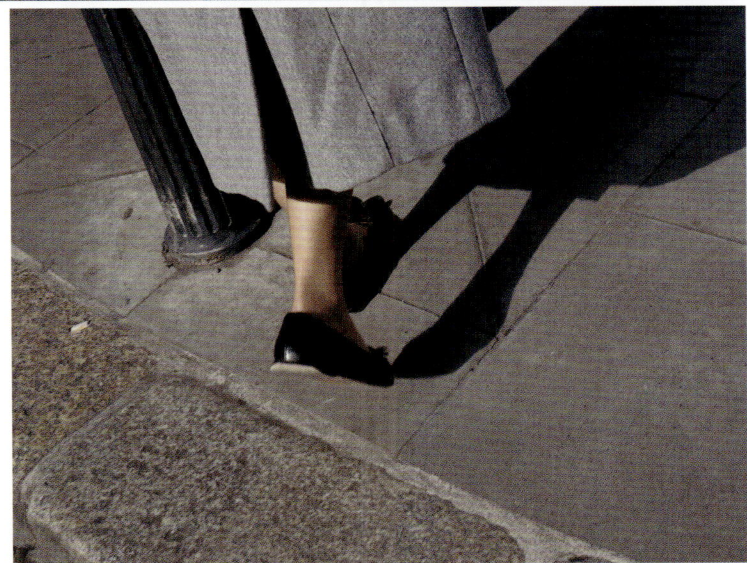

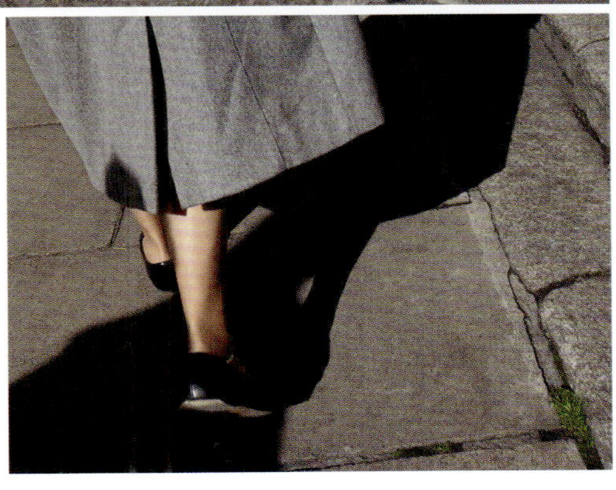

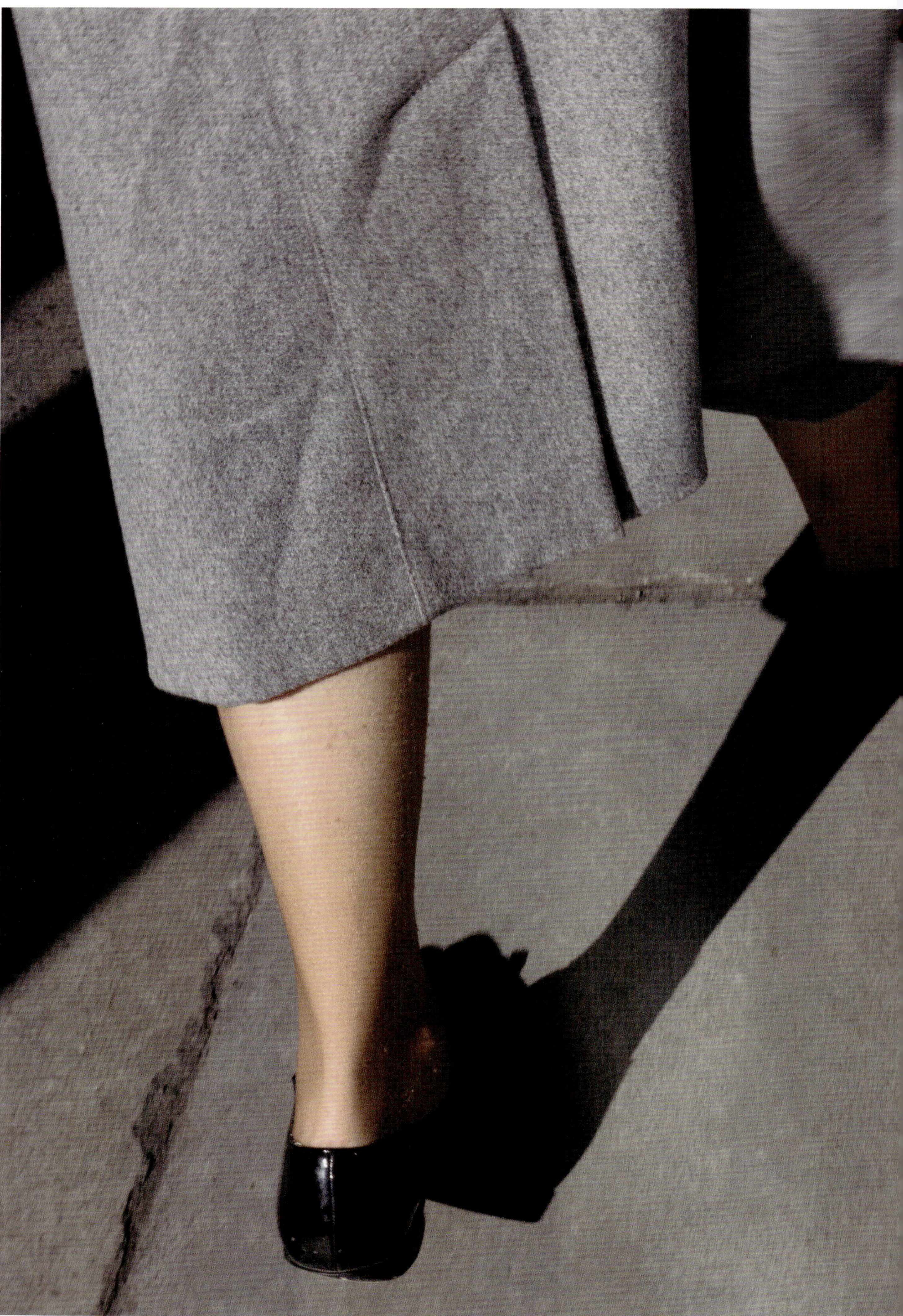

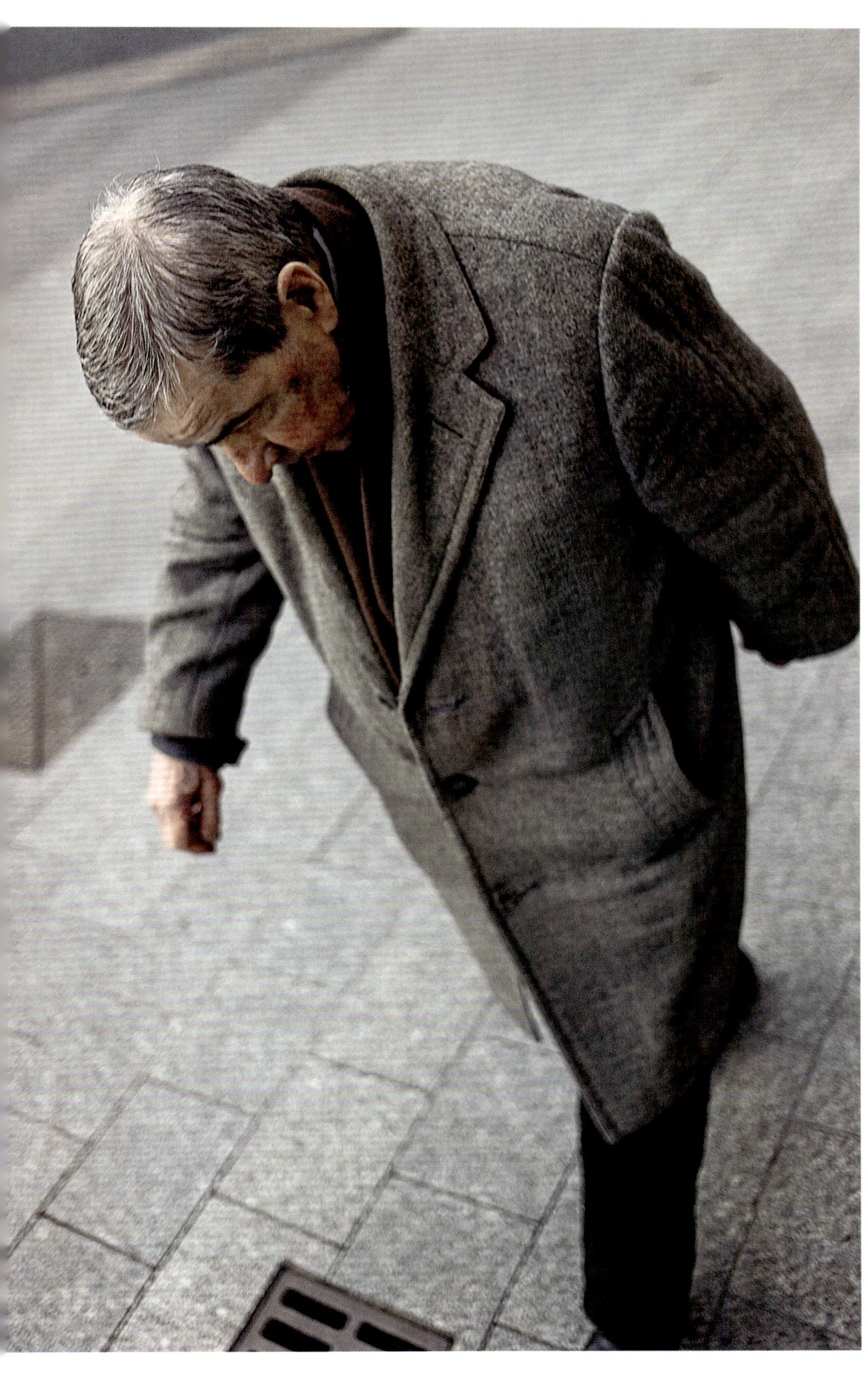

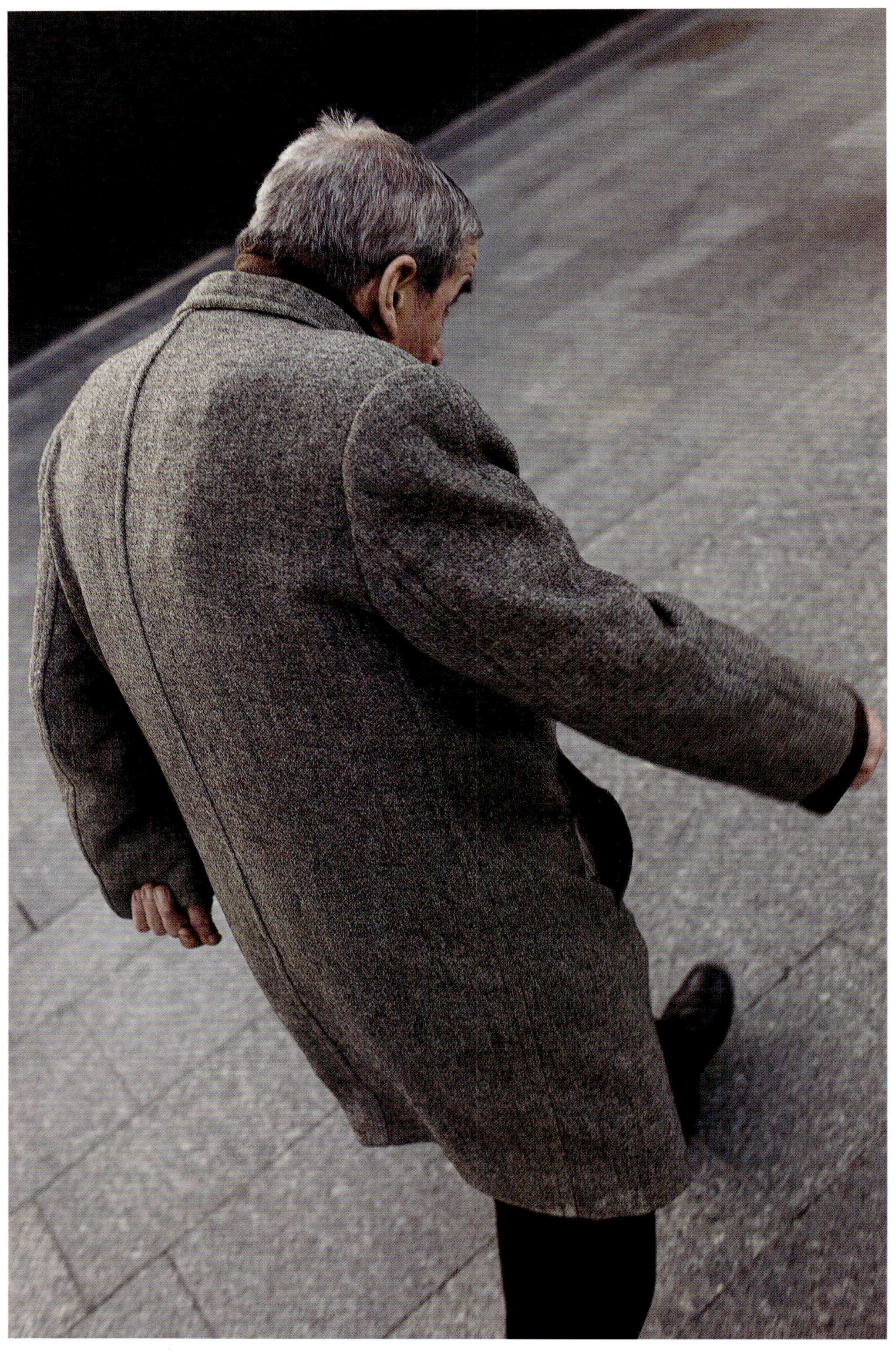

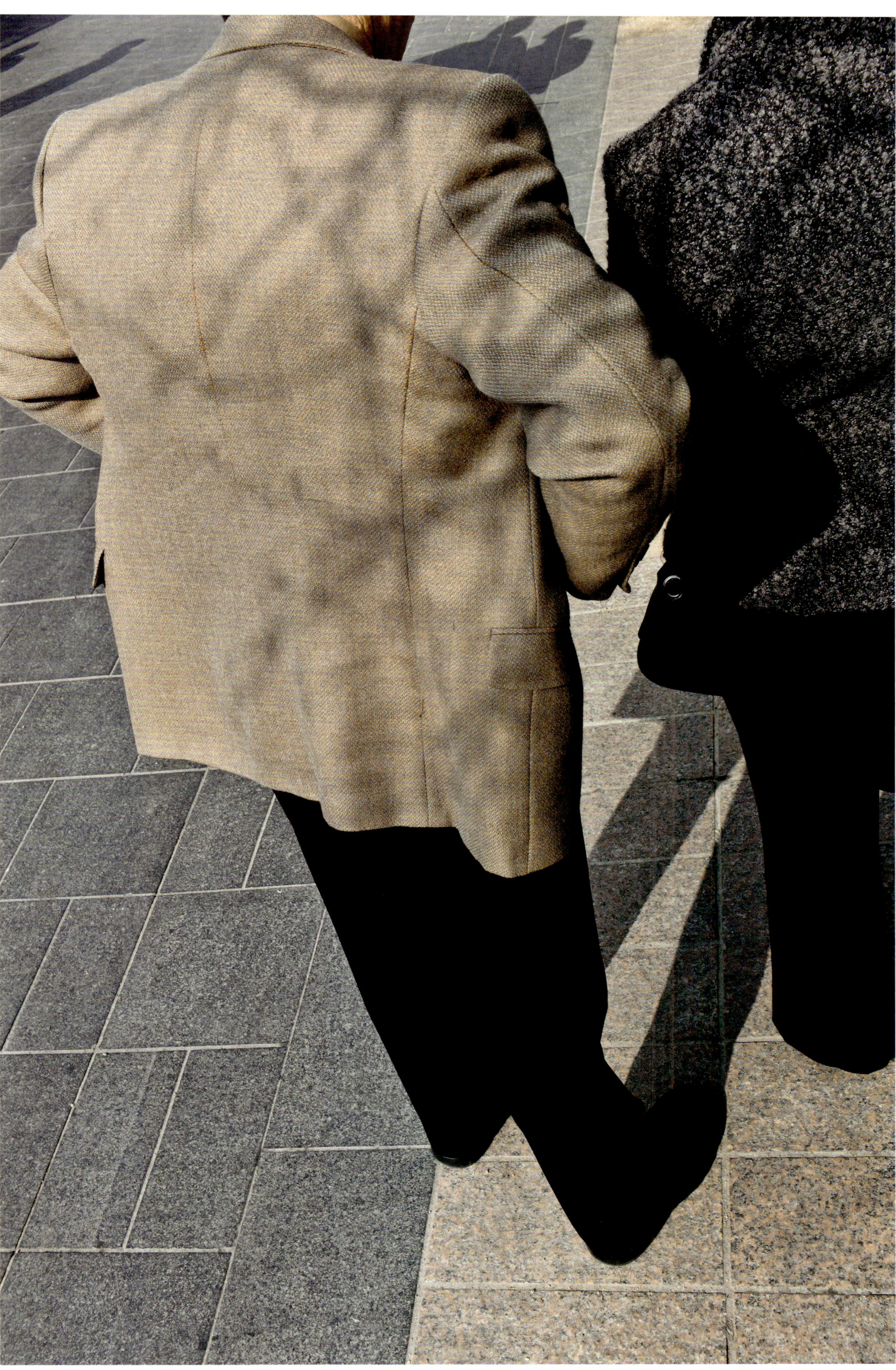

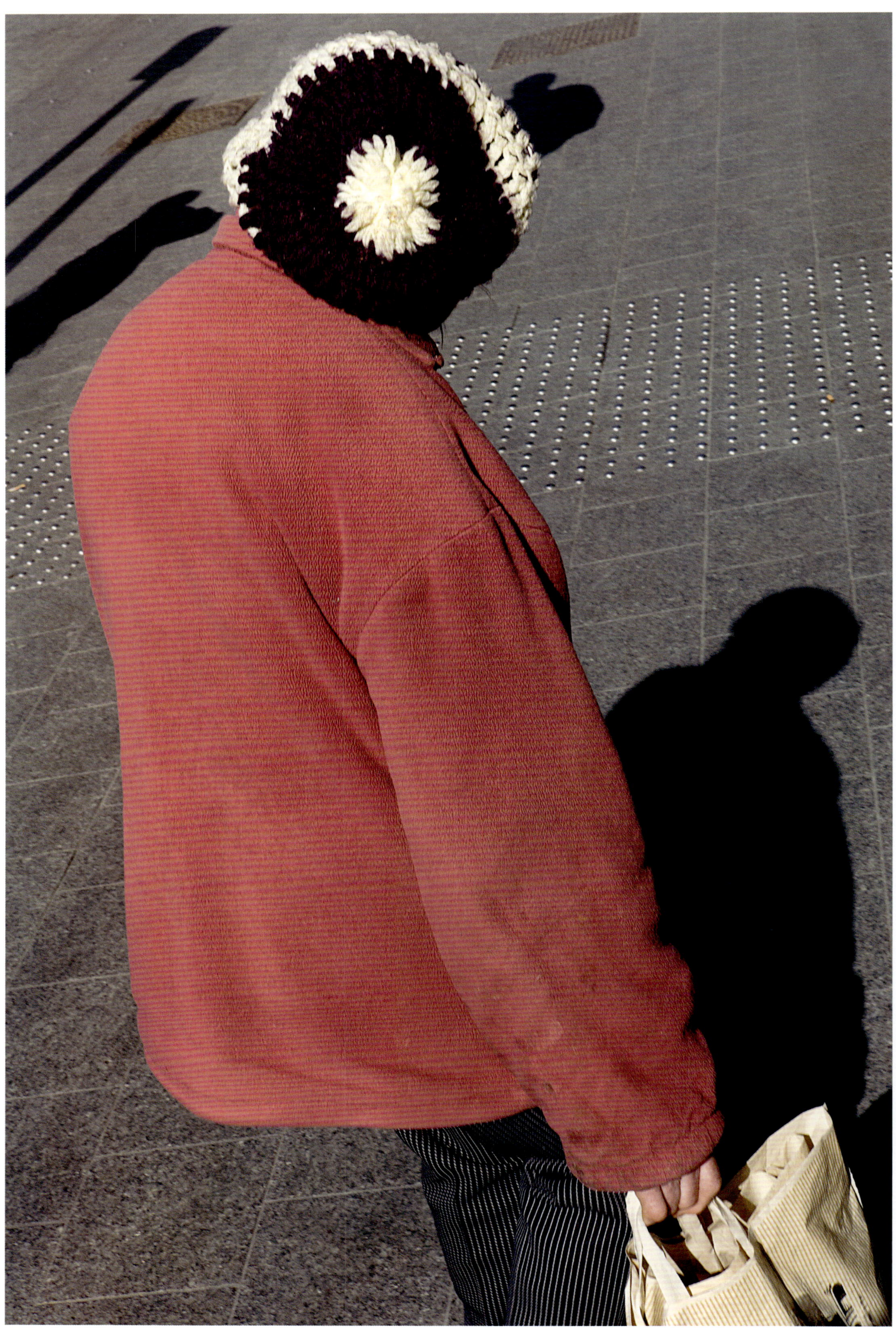

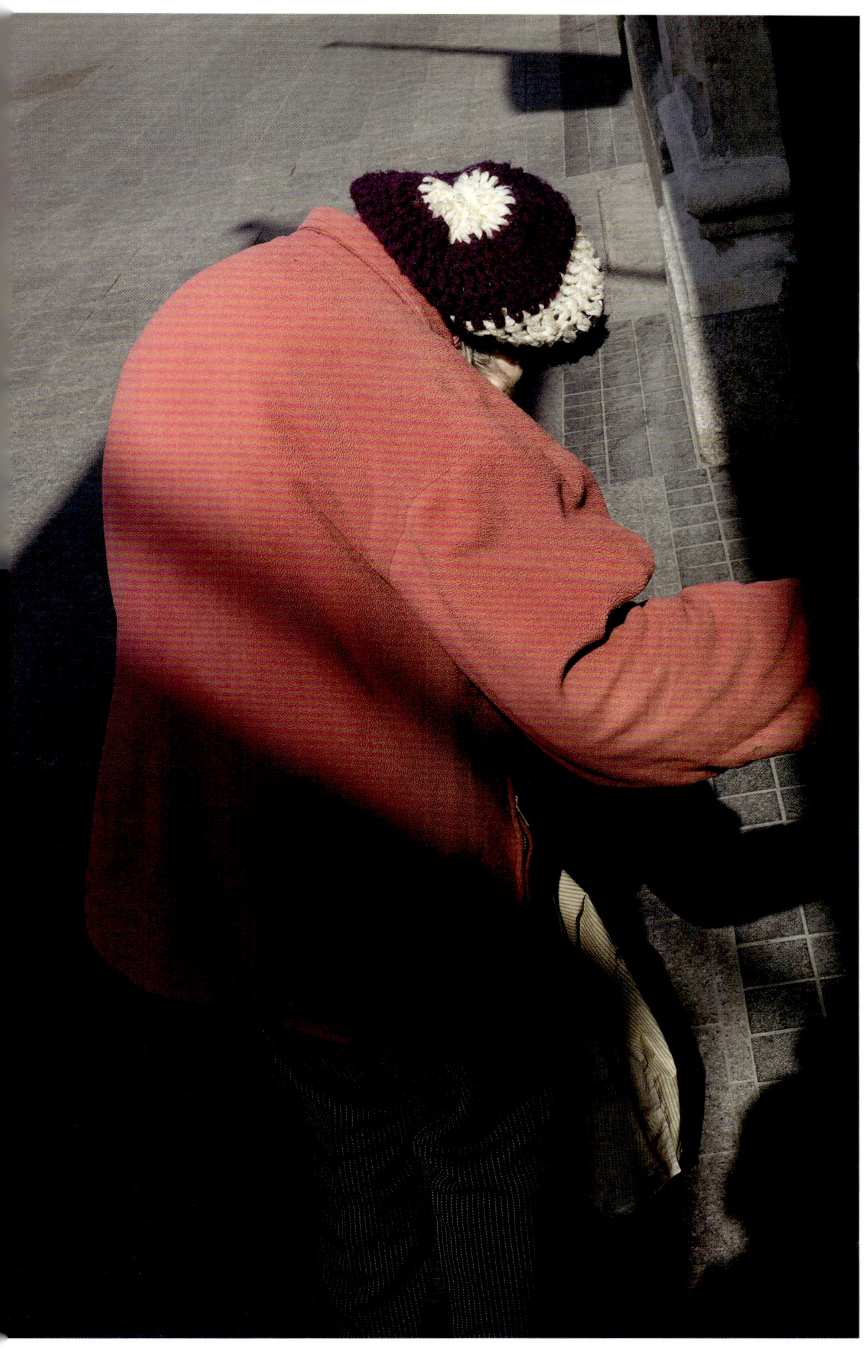

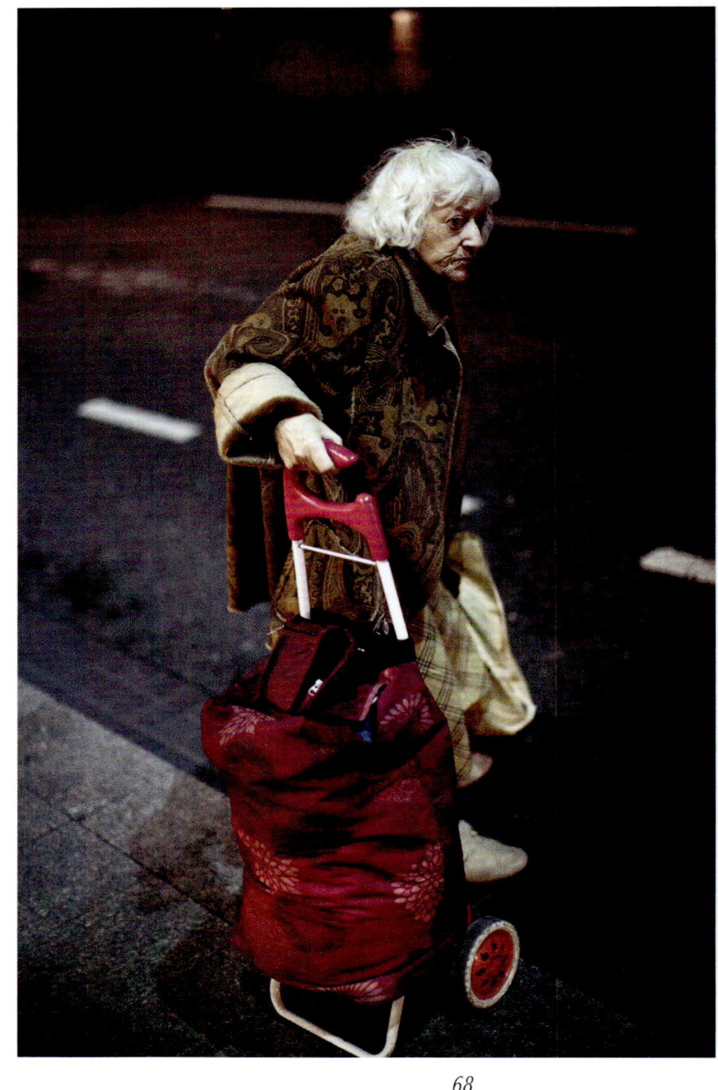

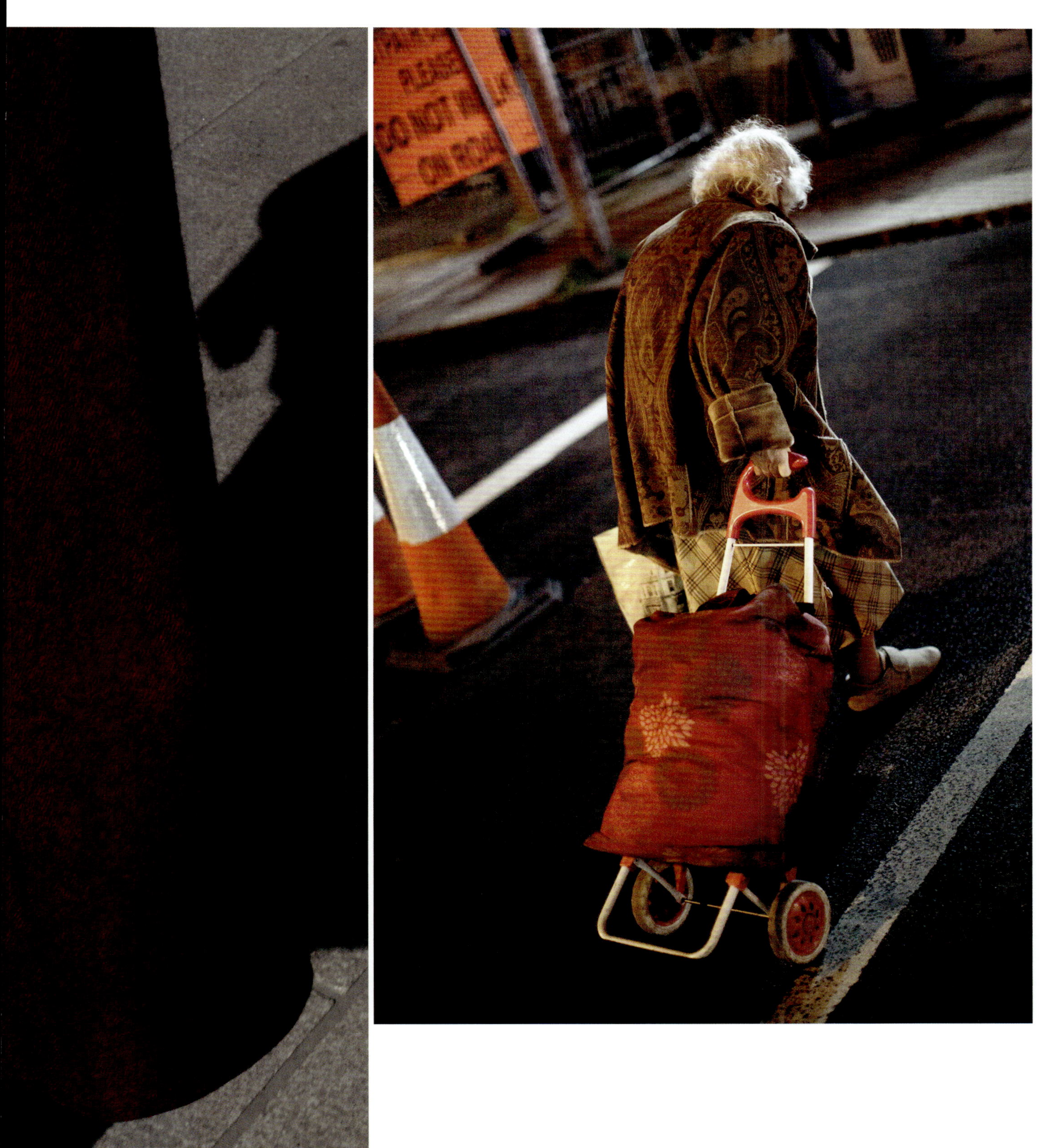
PLEASE
DO NOT
ON ROAD

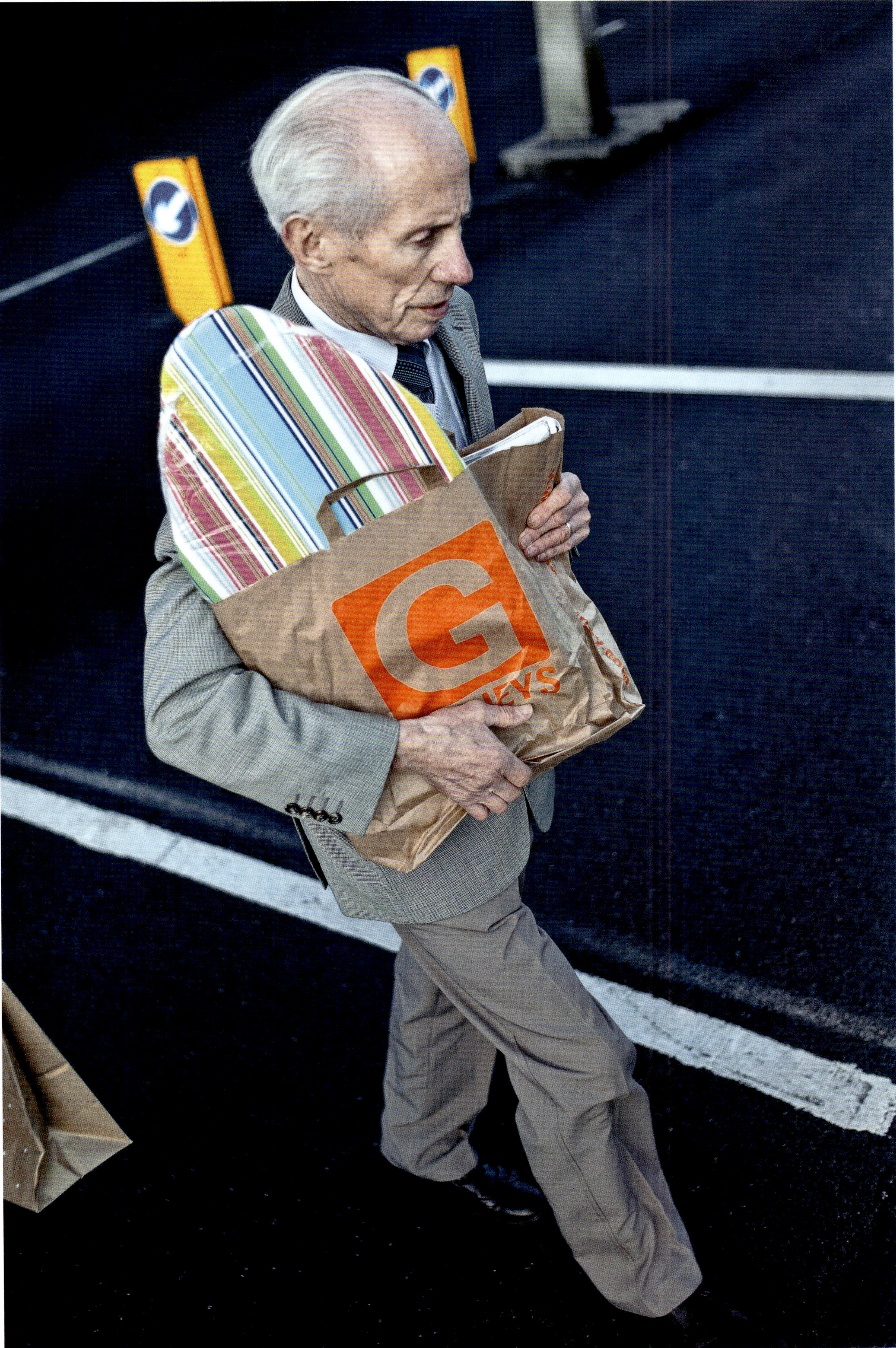

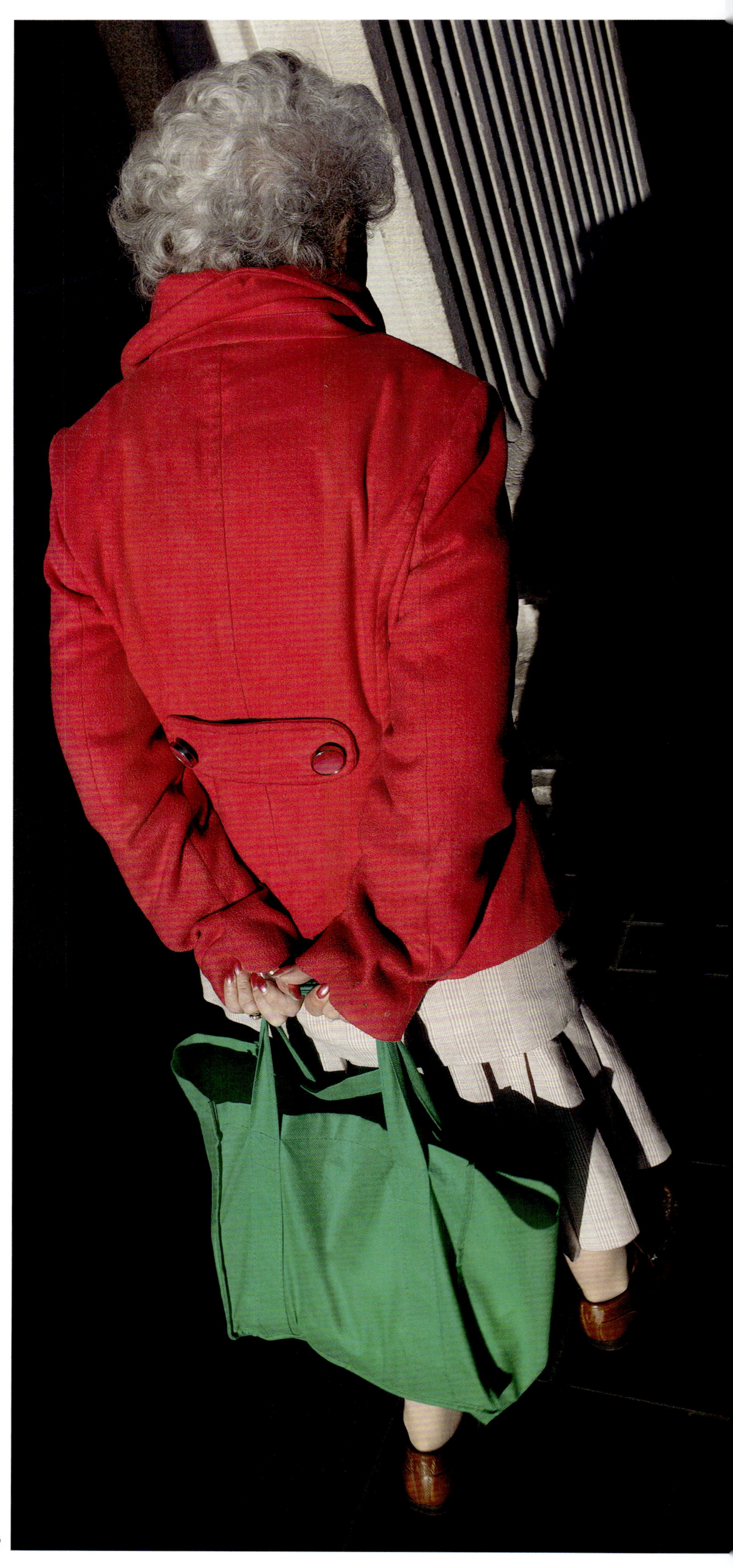

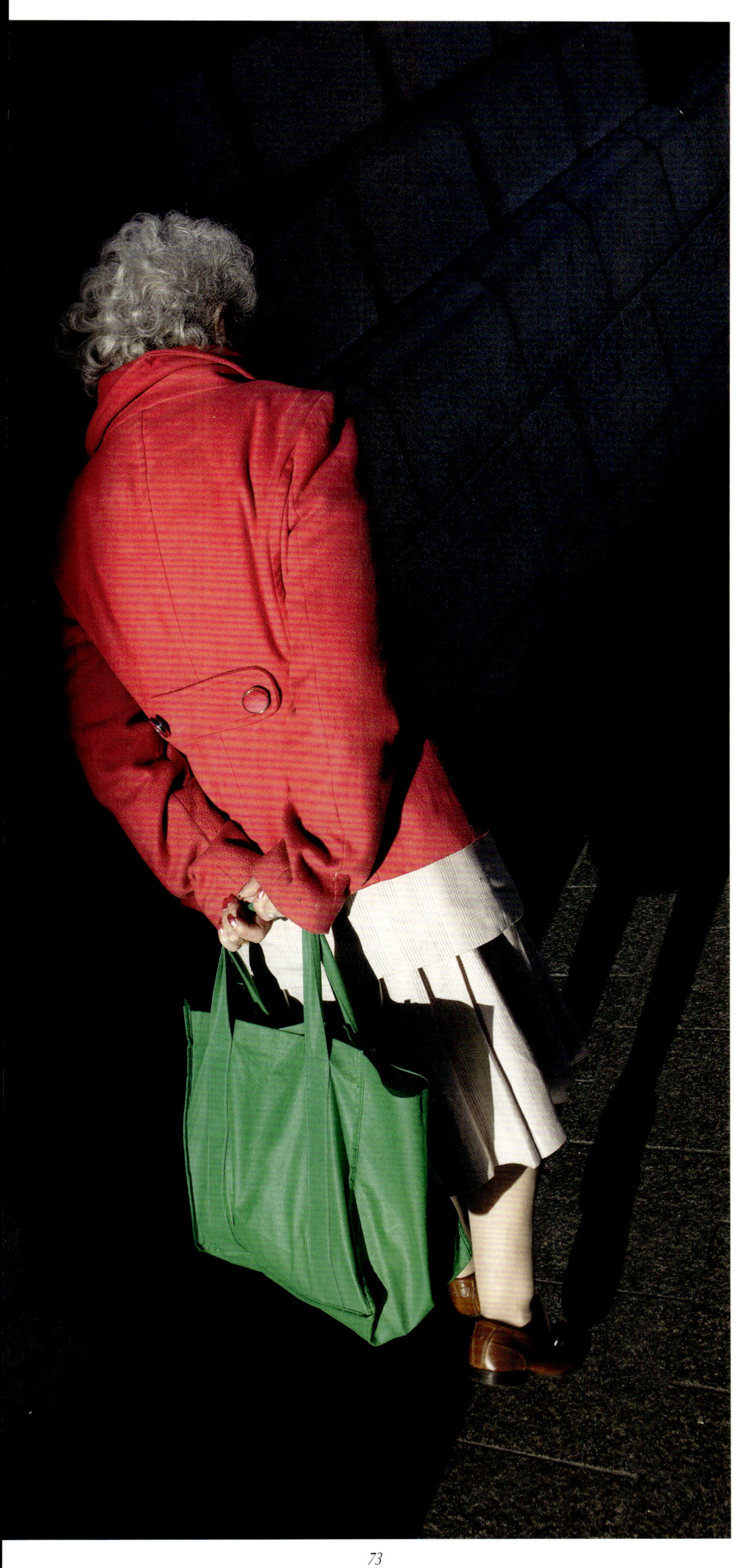

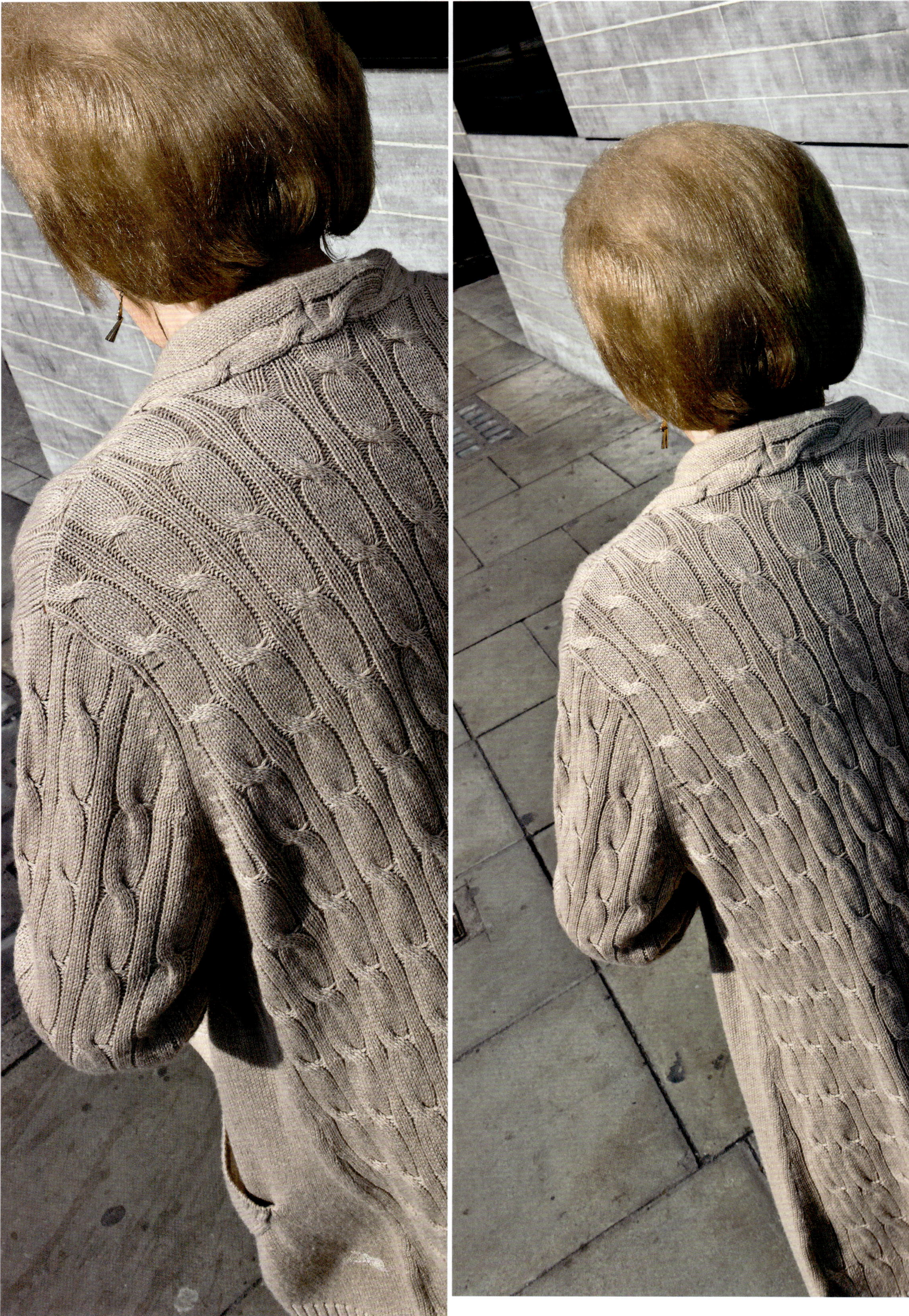

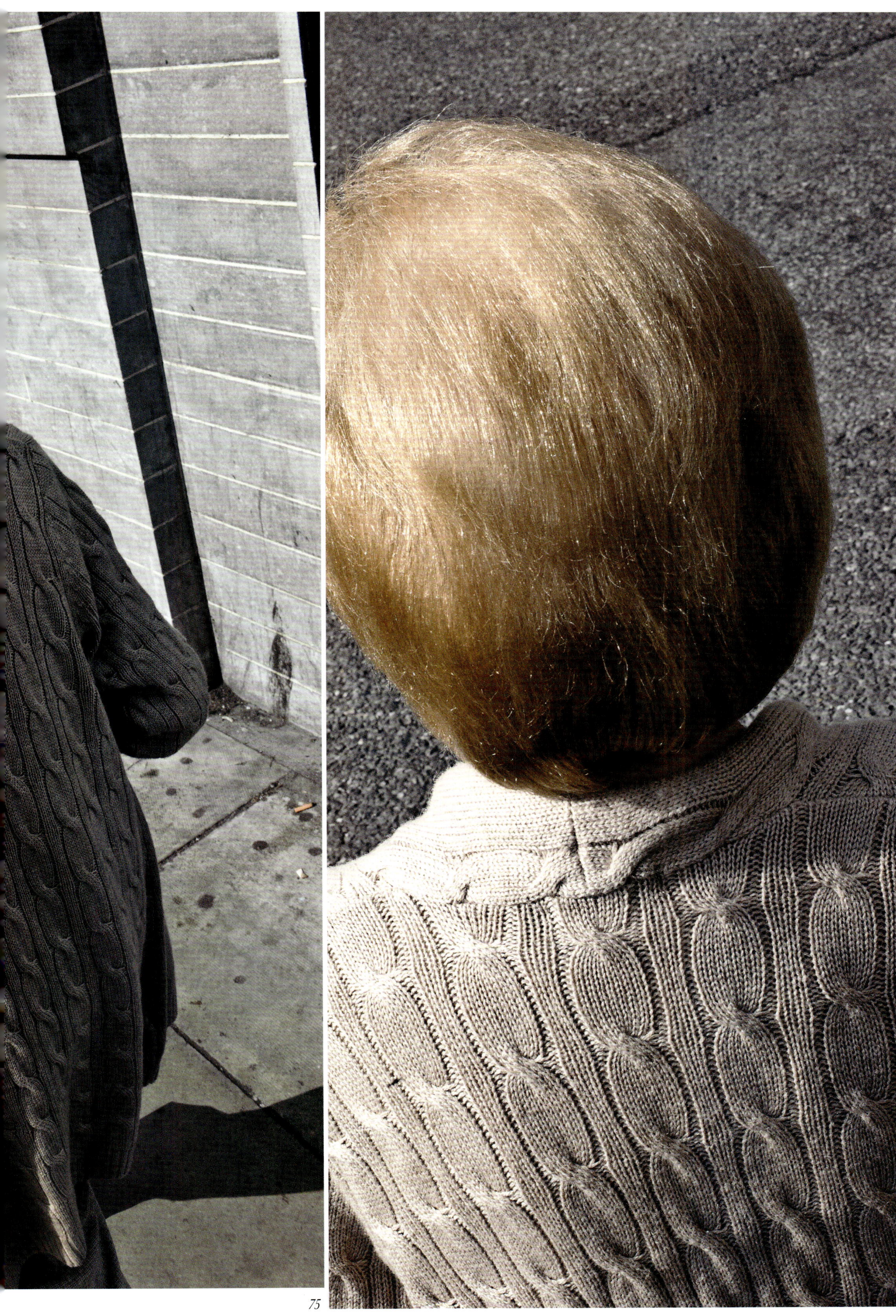

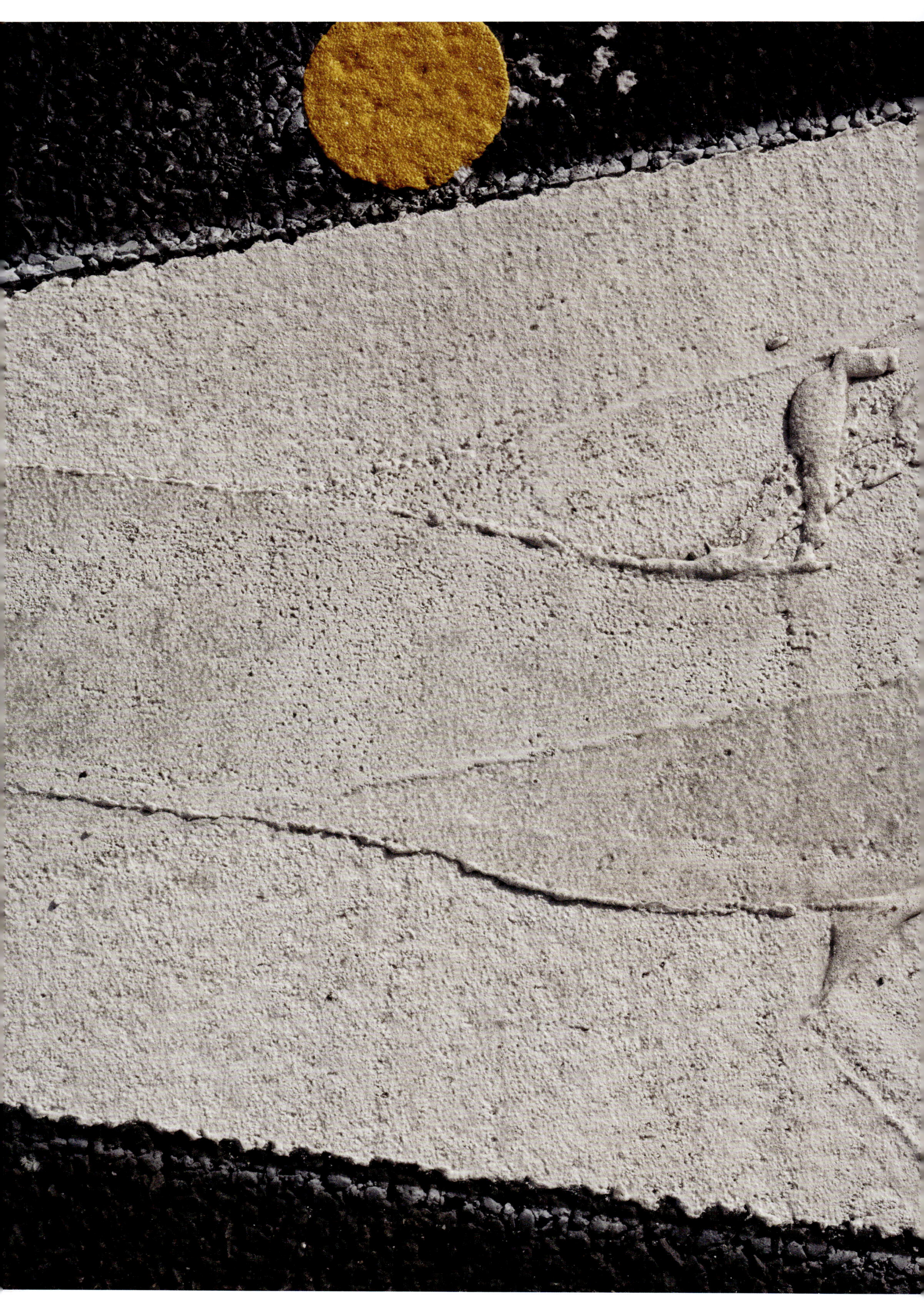

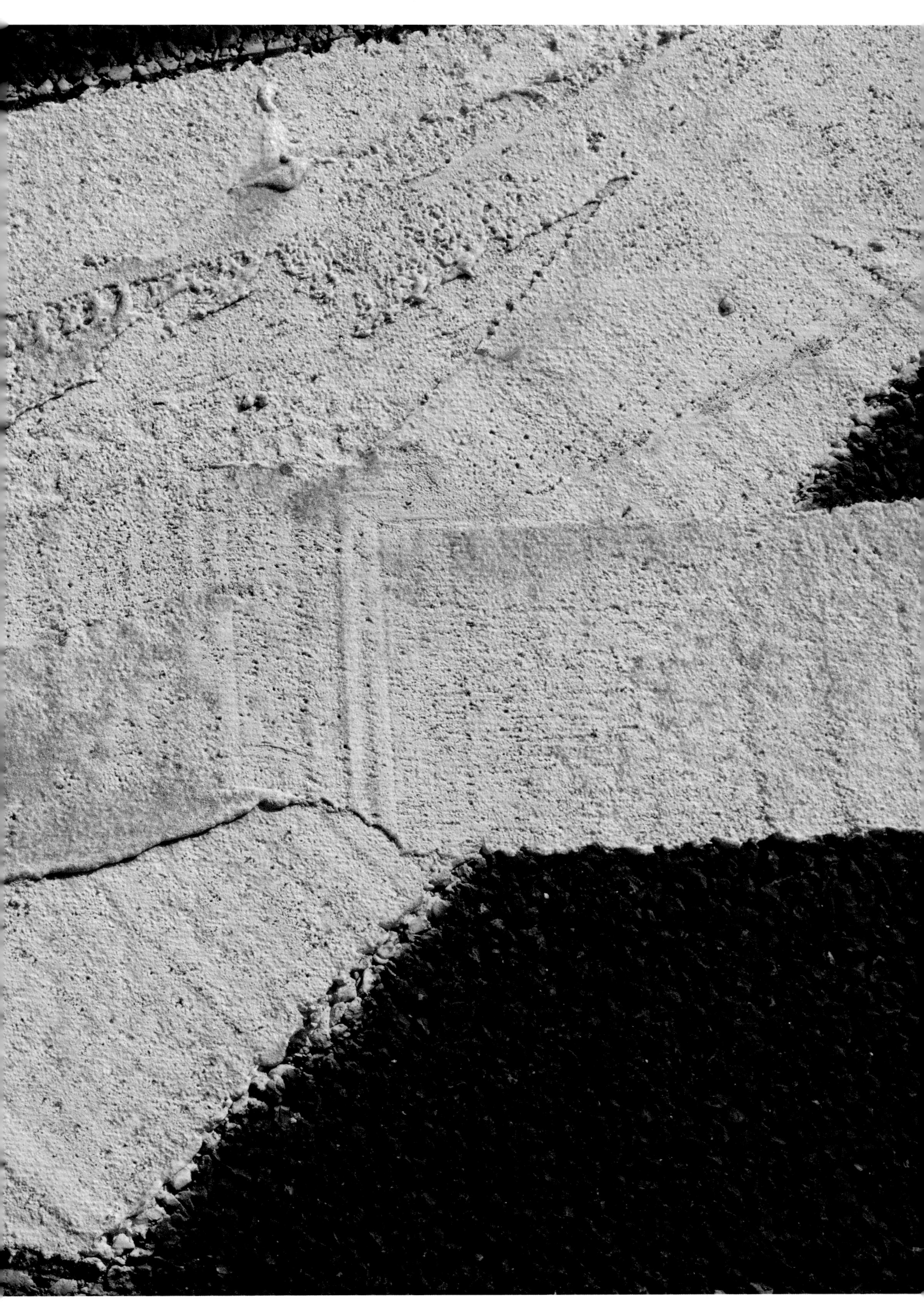

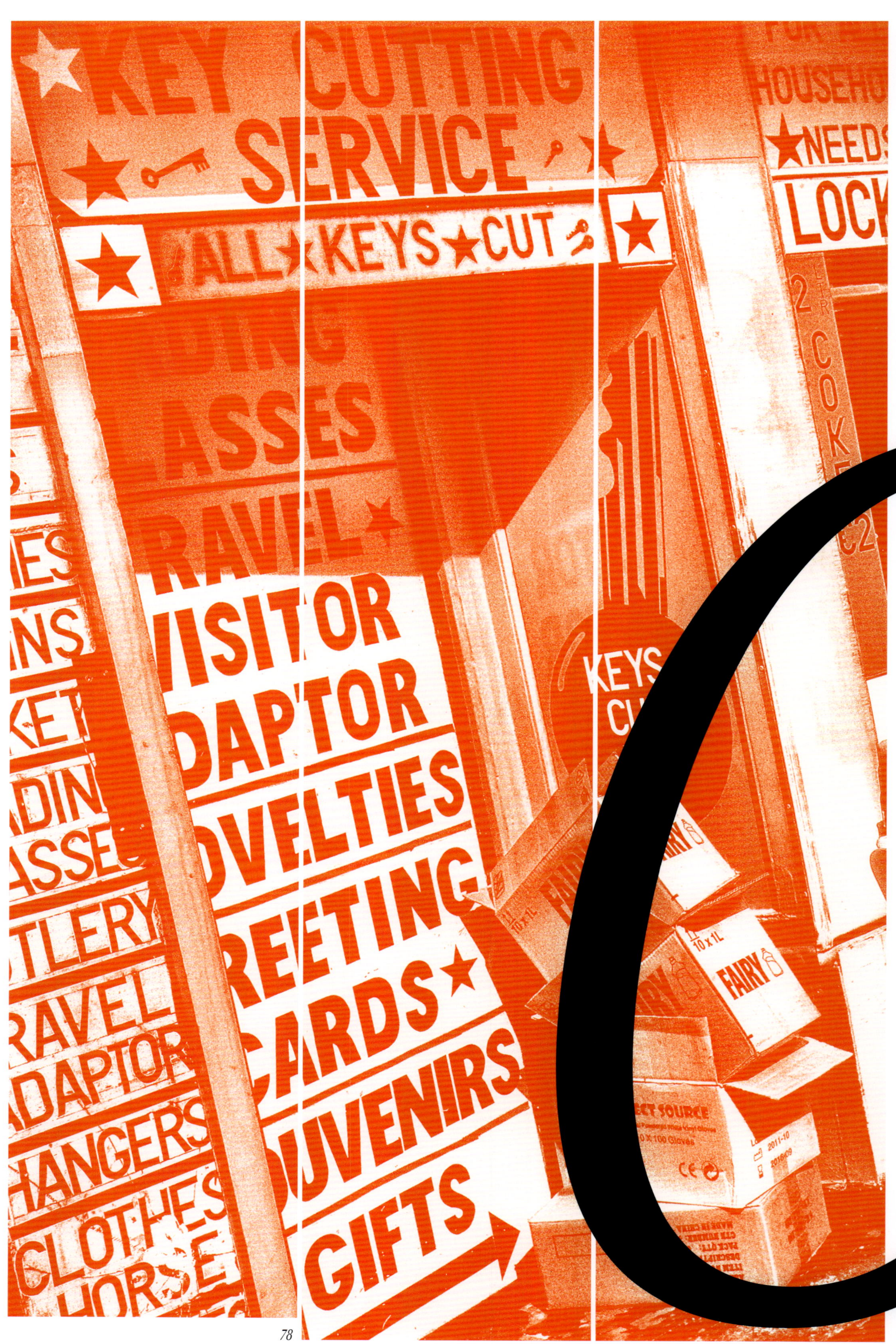
KEY CUTTING
SERVICE
ALL ★ KEYS ★ CUT
HOUSEHO
★ NEEDS
LOCK
VISITOR
ADAPTOR
NOVELTIES
GREETING
CARDS ★
SOUVENIRS
GIFTS
KEYS
CUT
FAIRY
FAIRY
COKE
£2
VISITOR
ADAPTOR
LADIN
GLASSES
CUTLERY
TRAVEL
ADAPTOR
HANGERS
CLOTHES
HORSE

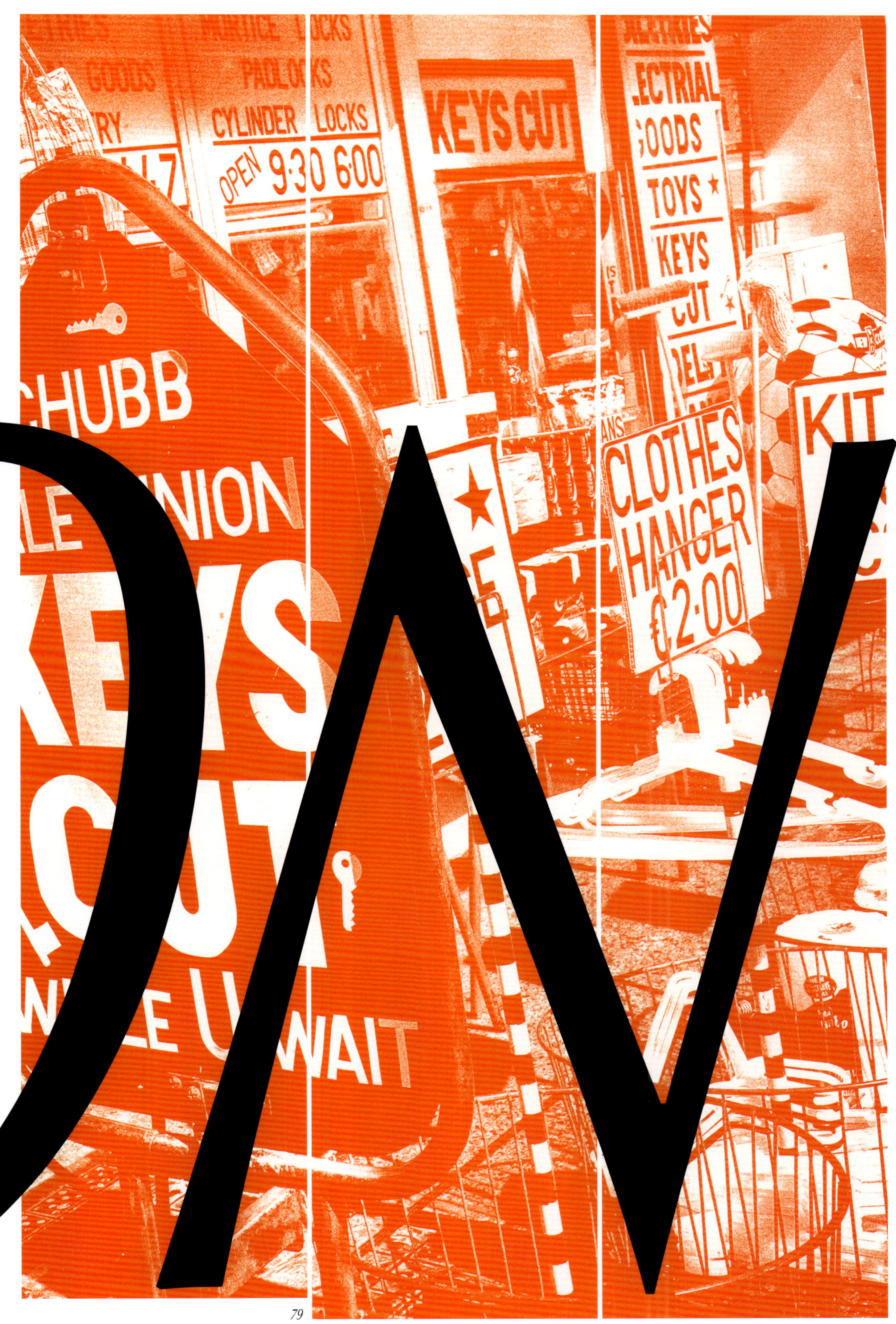
PATTERNS LOCKS
GOODS
PADLOCKS
CYLINDER LOCKS
OPEN 9·30 600
KEYS CUT
ELECTRIAL
GOODS
TOYS ★
KEYS
CUT ★
CHUBB
UNION
KEYS
CUT
WAIT
CLOTHES
HANGER
₤2·00
KIT

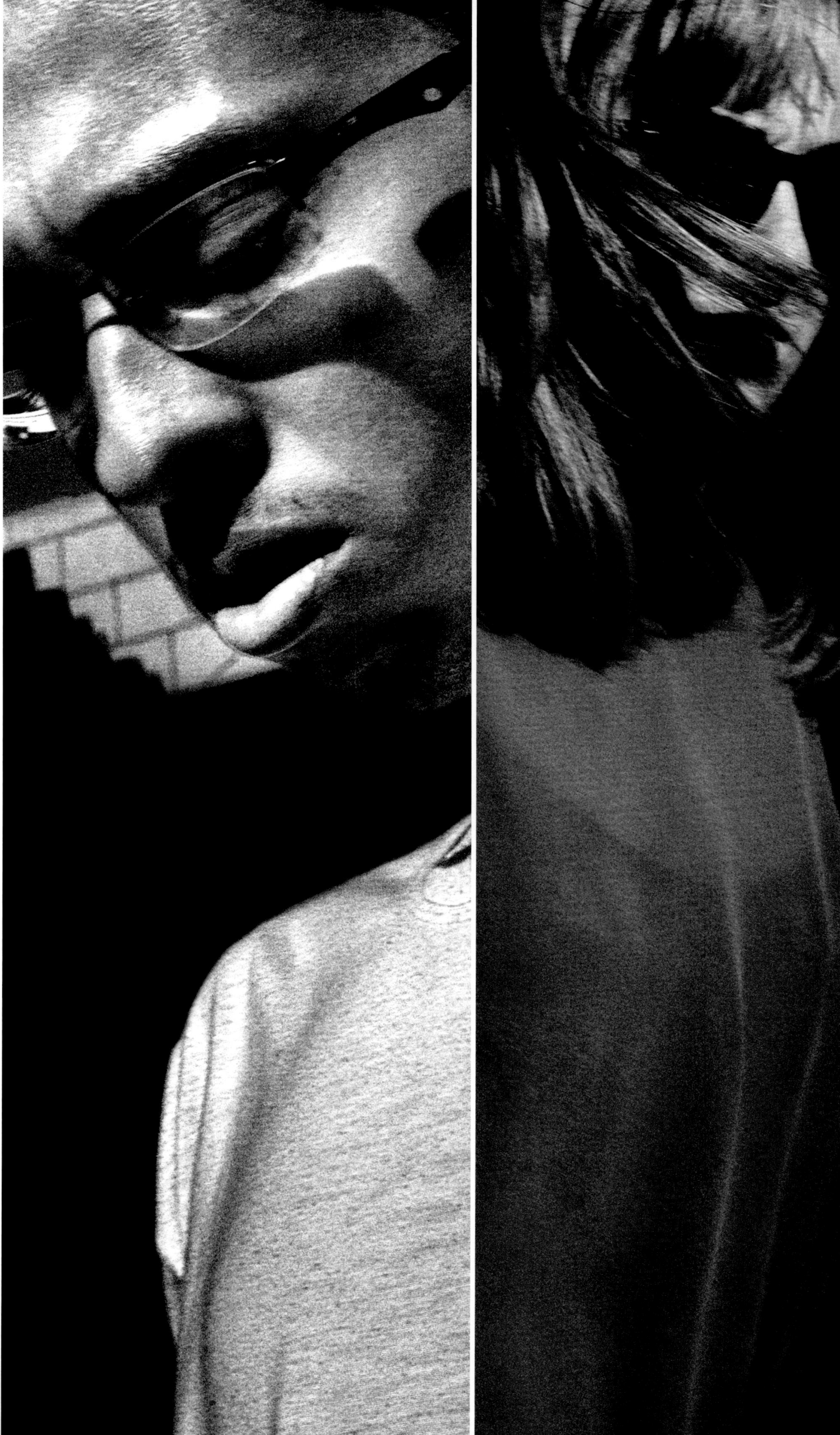

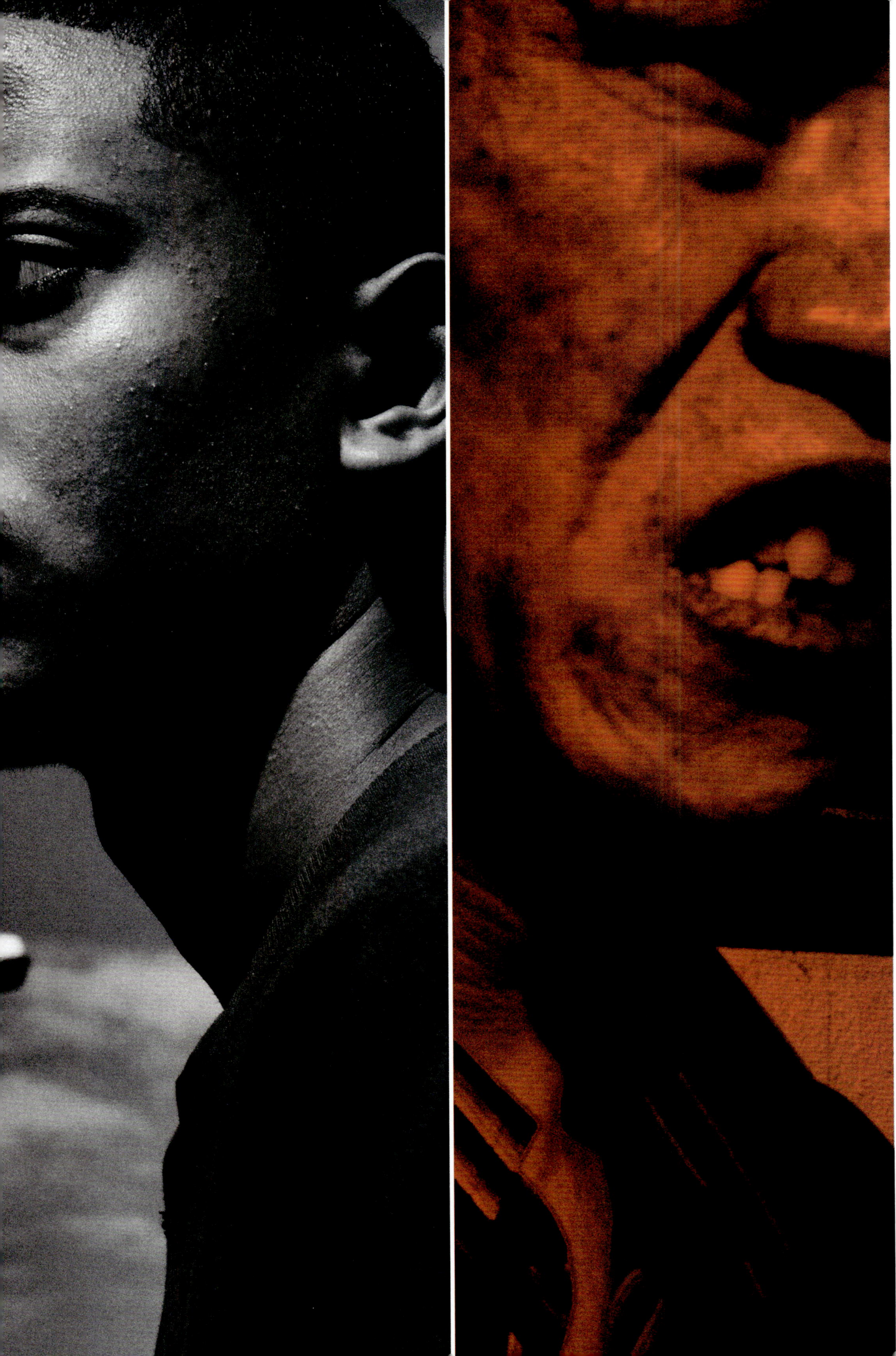

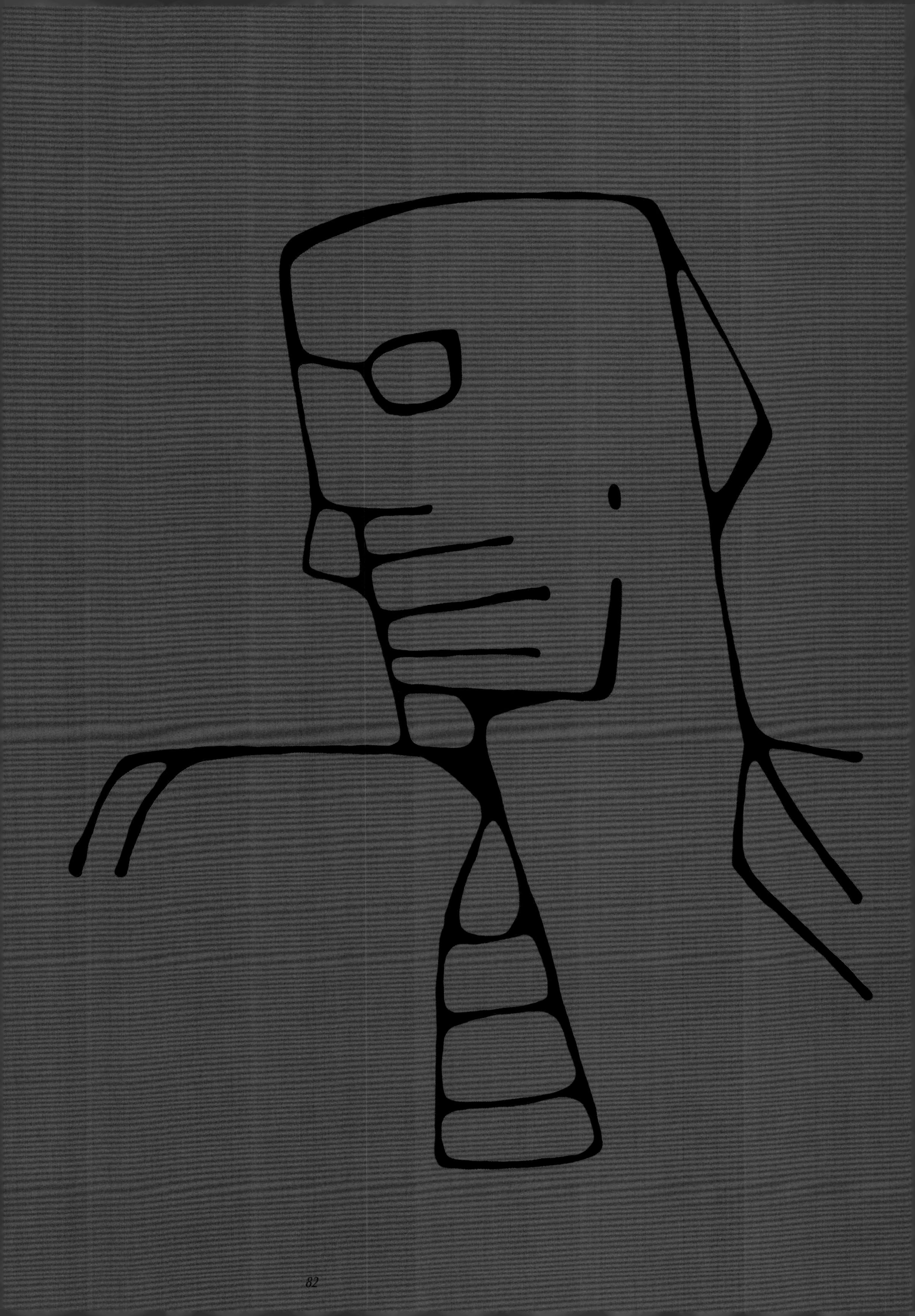

THE AGONIES OF LOVE —

She was supposed to meet me on Tuesday night — and I'm stood there, I'm like a bloody sap, I'm jawing on the air — but she did not show up. I waited for an hour. Now I don't think she's that into me anymore.

He was supposed to take me to meet his mother but he did not turn up. I think what it is? Is that he's ashamed of me.

I can't stand not to be around her anymore. I don't want to see her happy with him. I don't want to see her happy with anybody else.

His family? They all hate me. I know this. They all go quiet when I come in. They just look at their phones. They don't talk to me. I can see what they're thinking. They're thinking … her?

I believe she's sleeping with somebody else.

I can't get him out of my mind.

I'm obsessed by her. I can't sleep or eat or live right because of her. All I want to do is think about her and think about what it would be like to get to kiss and hold her.

I never believed in this old talk you hear about thunderbolts and the sky opening up and instant love shooting down and all the fireworks and the earth moving and all of that stuff but then what happened? She opened her sweet mouth and said like five kind words to me and I thought I was going to have to be hospitalized. I thought I was going to have to be put on a drip.

So I turned, acting all casual, or as casual as I could make it, and I dropped the hard word on her — I said, are we on?

We love each other. That's all that matters. And I would kill for him, actually.

I want her to know one thing and one thing only. She will regret this. I was the one for her. Until her dying breath. She will regret this.

He think he Daddy Cool. He think he Mister Somebody. But he an Ass Wipe is what he is.

Love? Don't be talking to me about love.

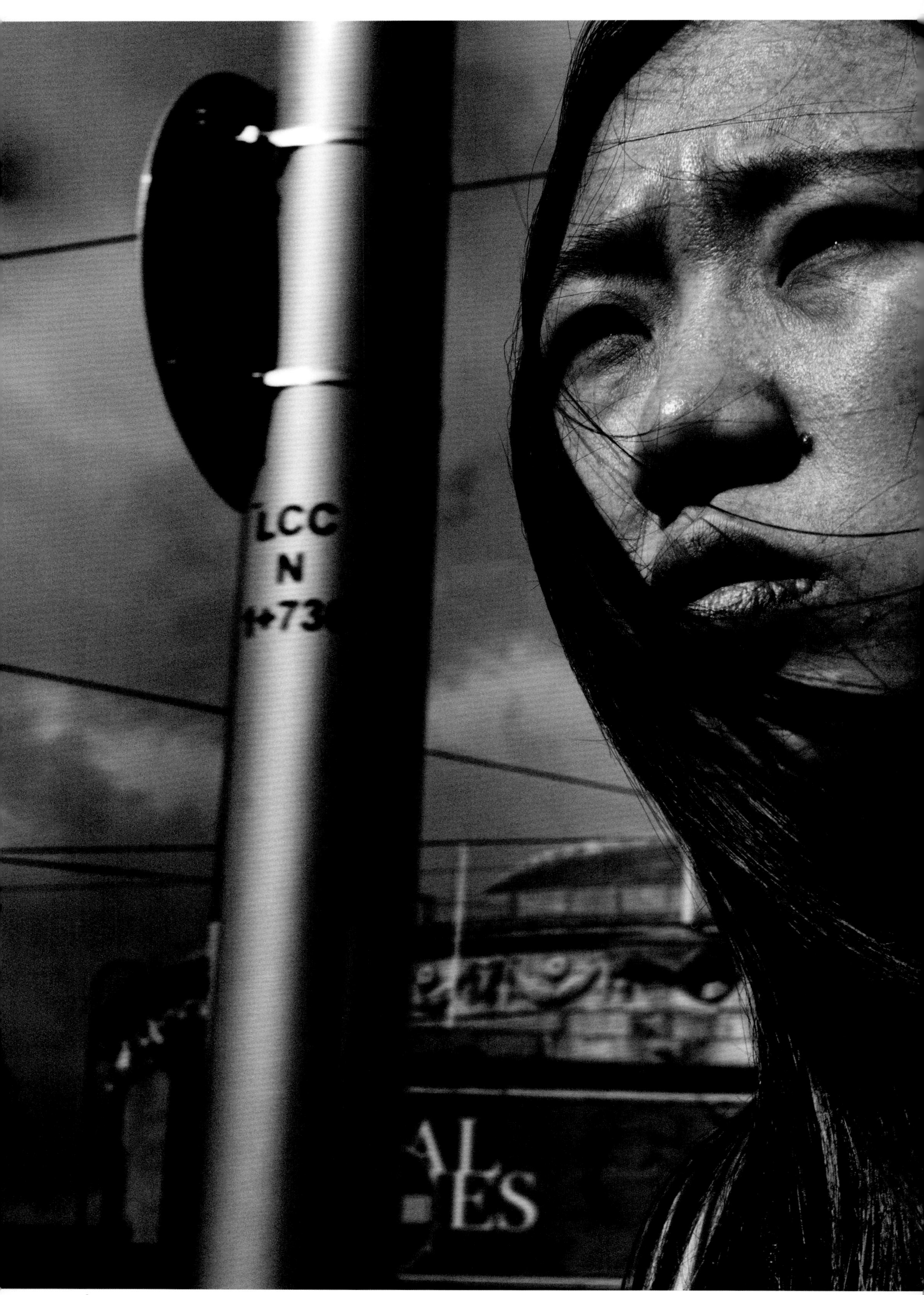

LCC
N
1+73

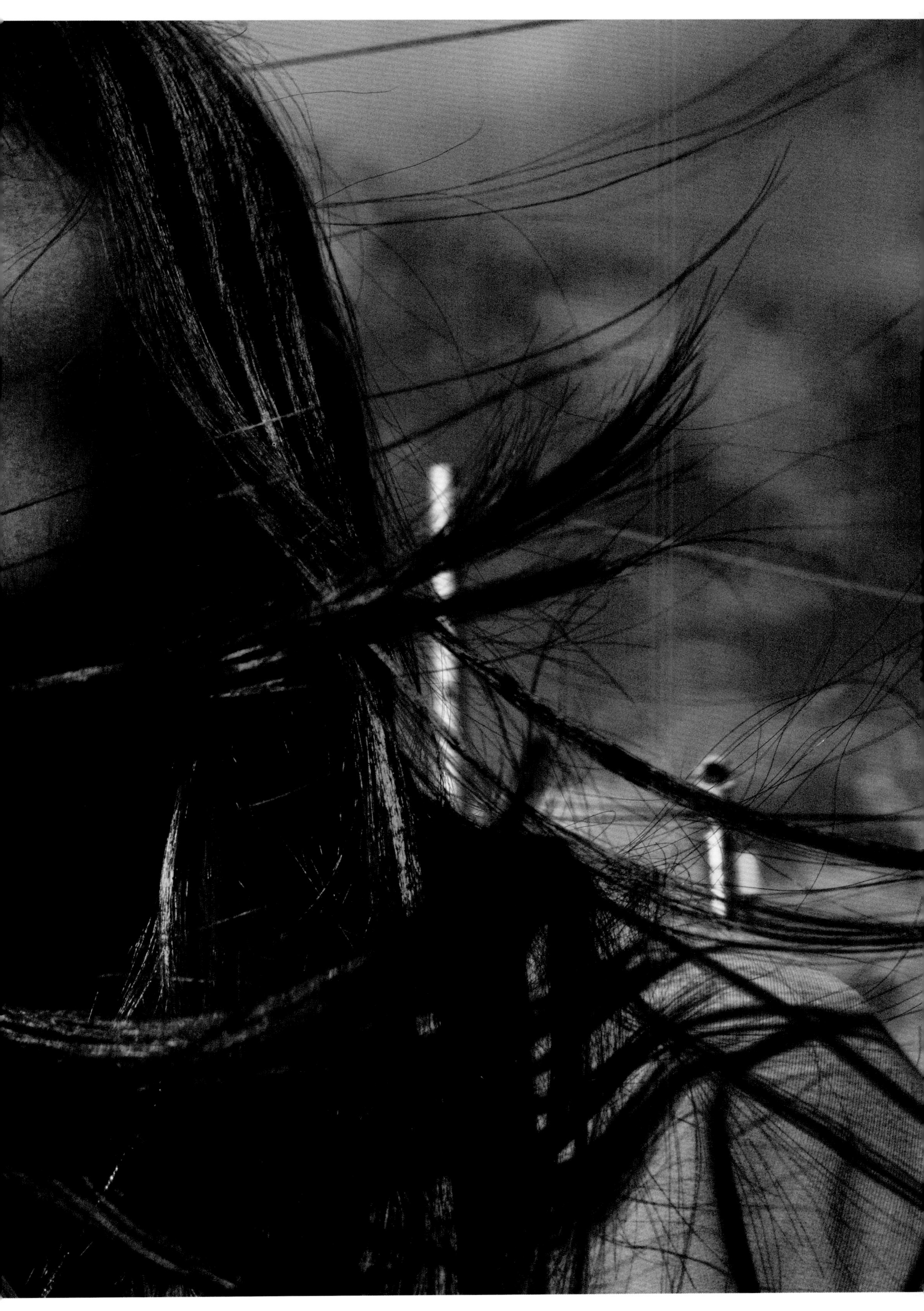

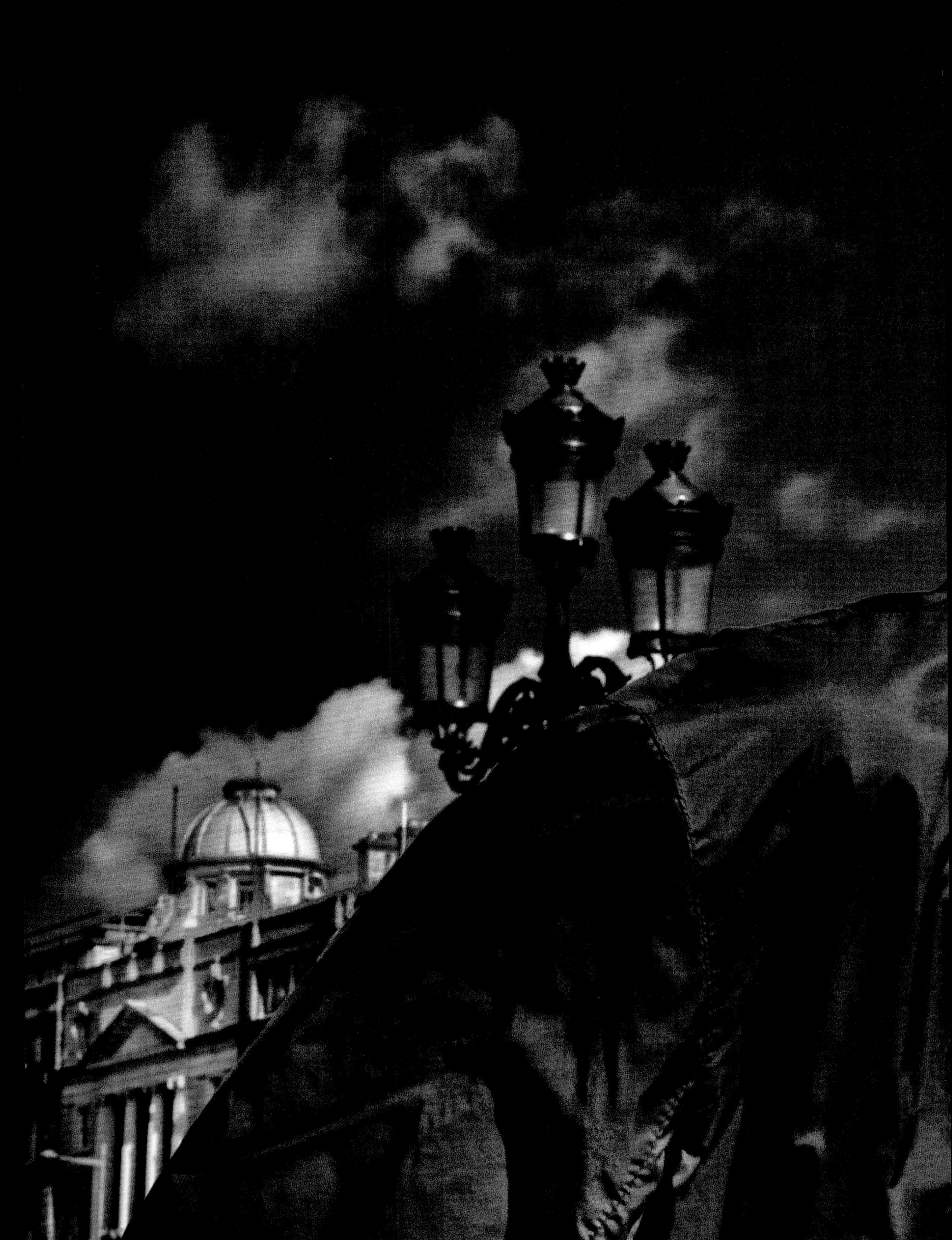

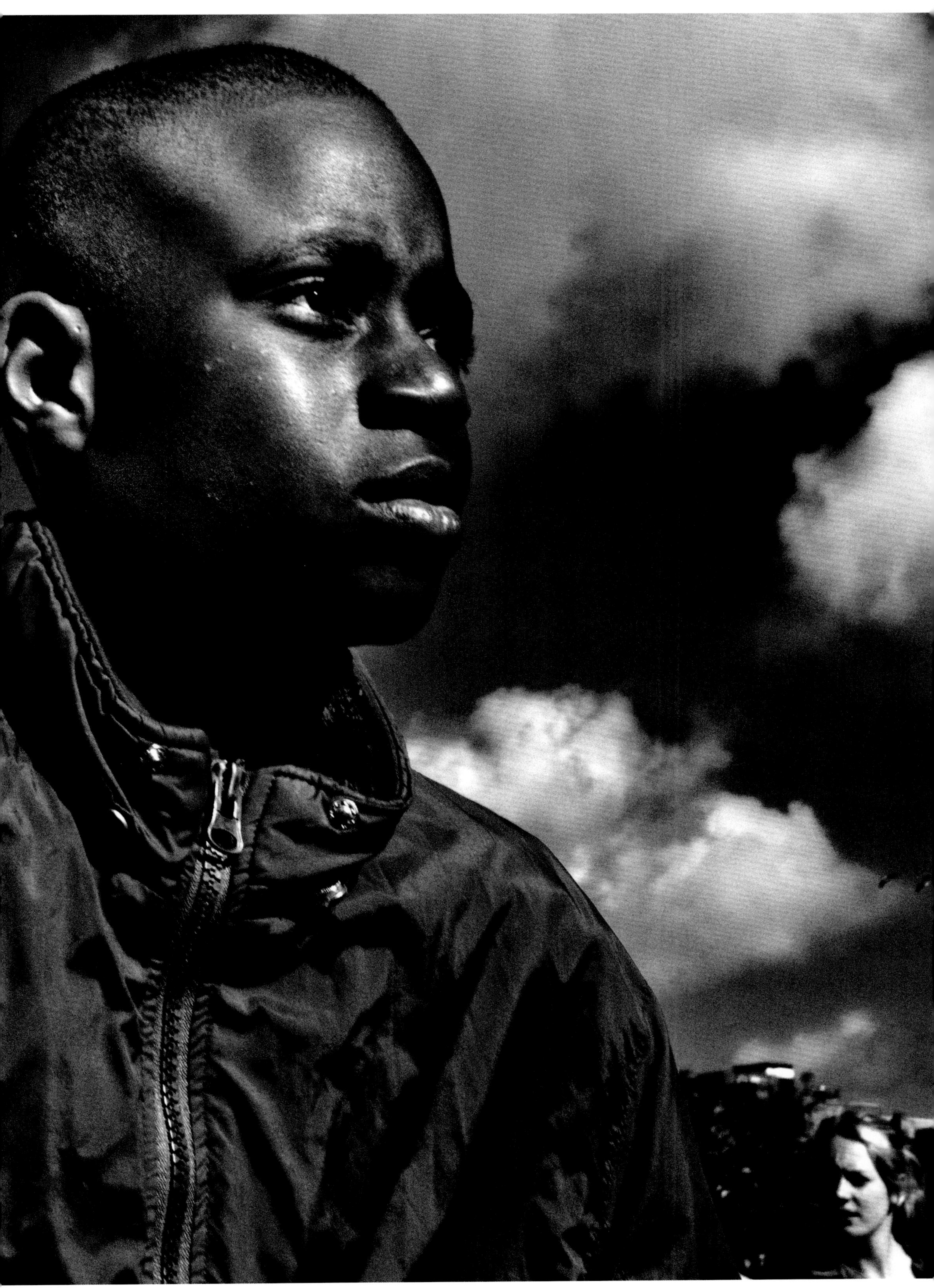

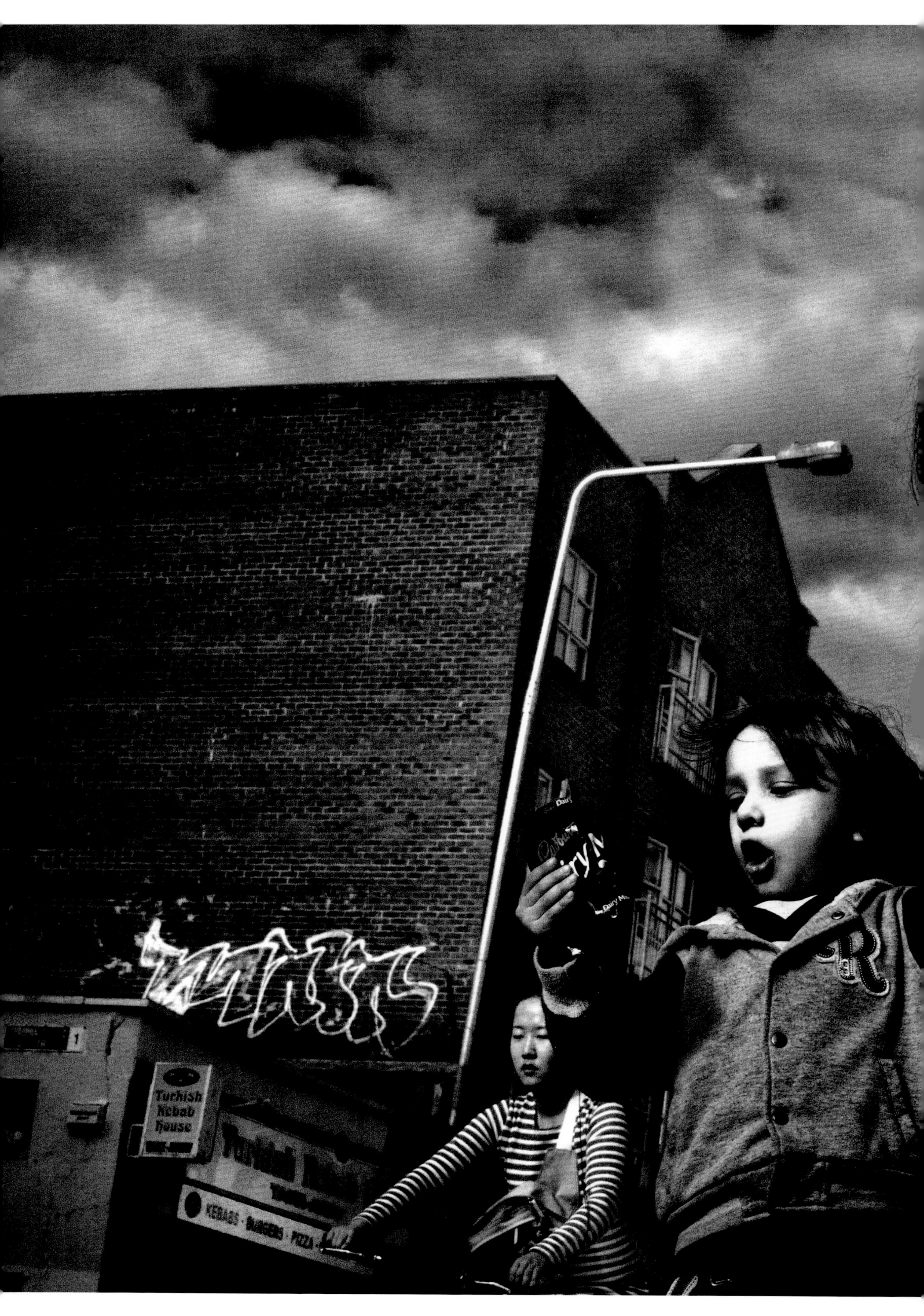
Turkish
Kebab
House
KEBABS · BURGERS · PIZZA
Dairy M
Dairy M
R

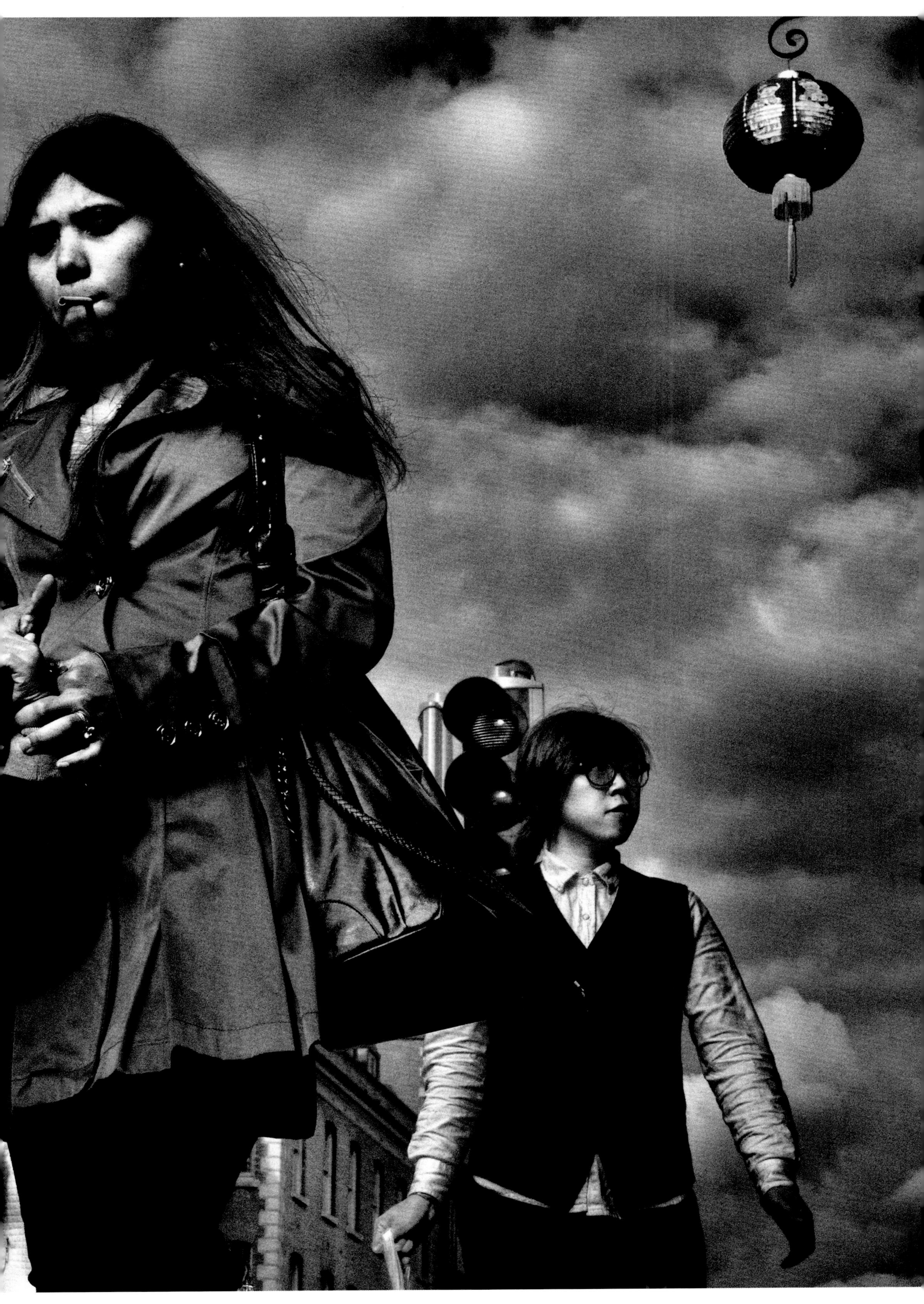

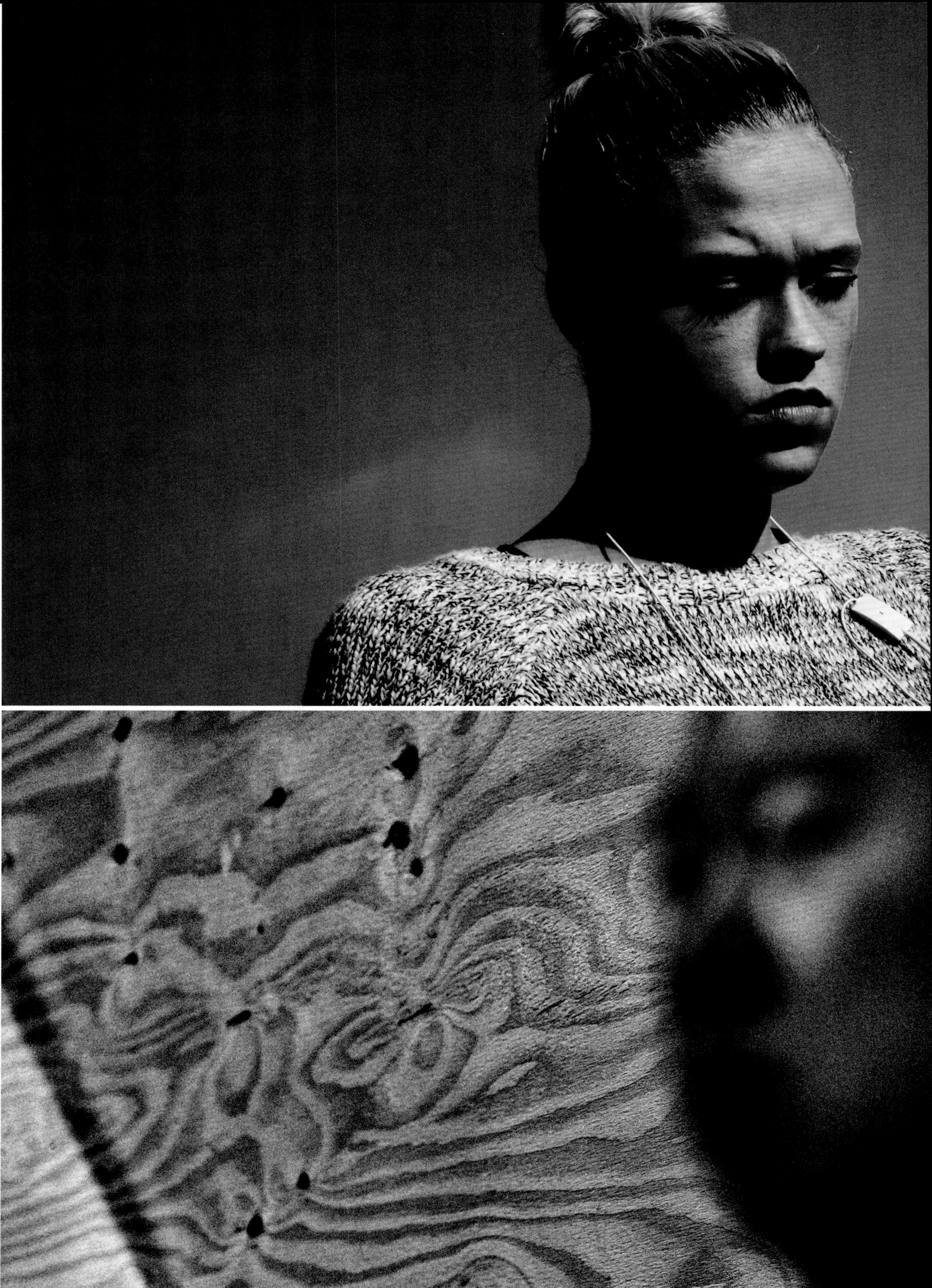

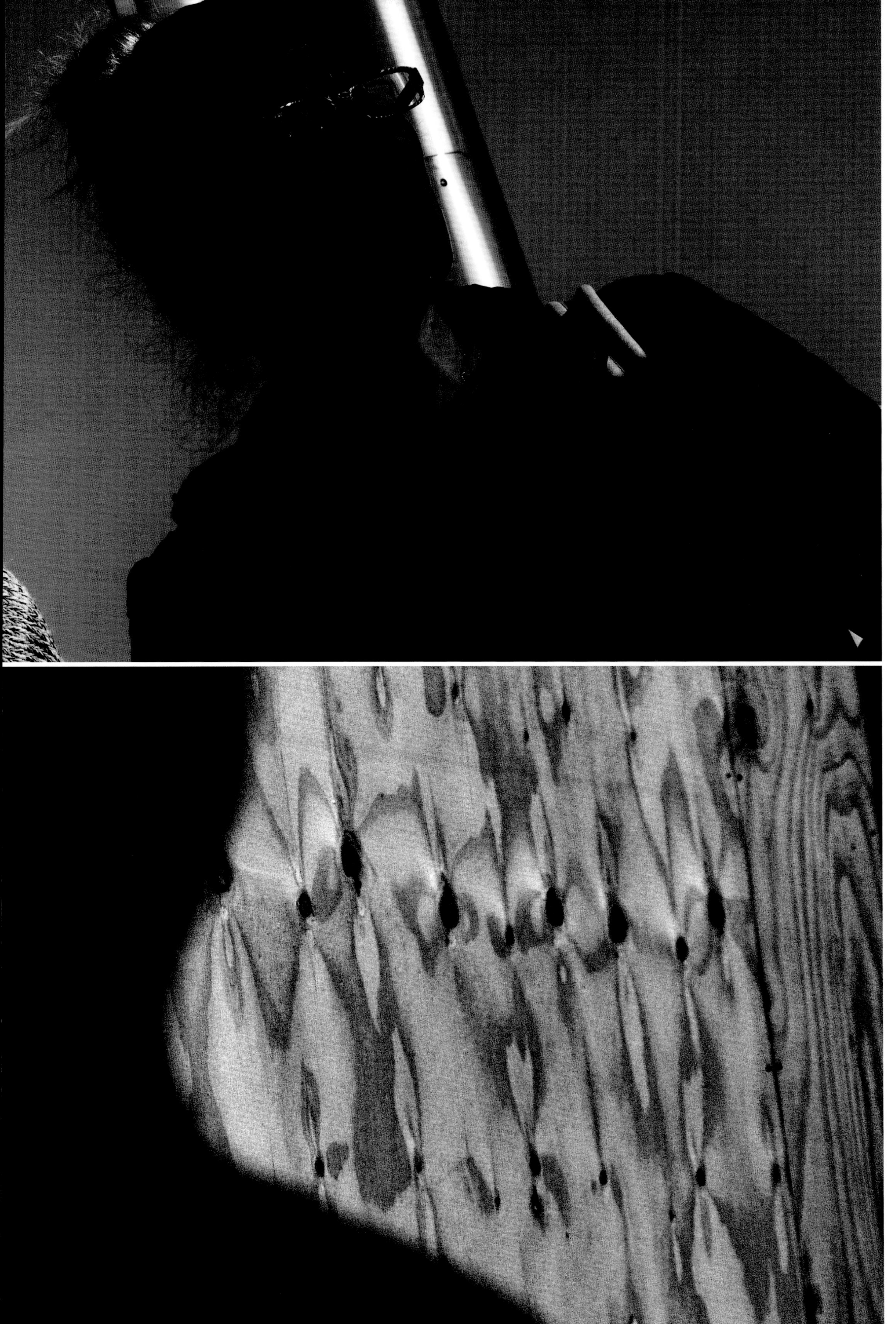

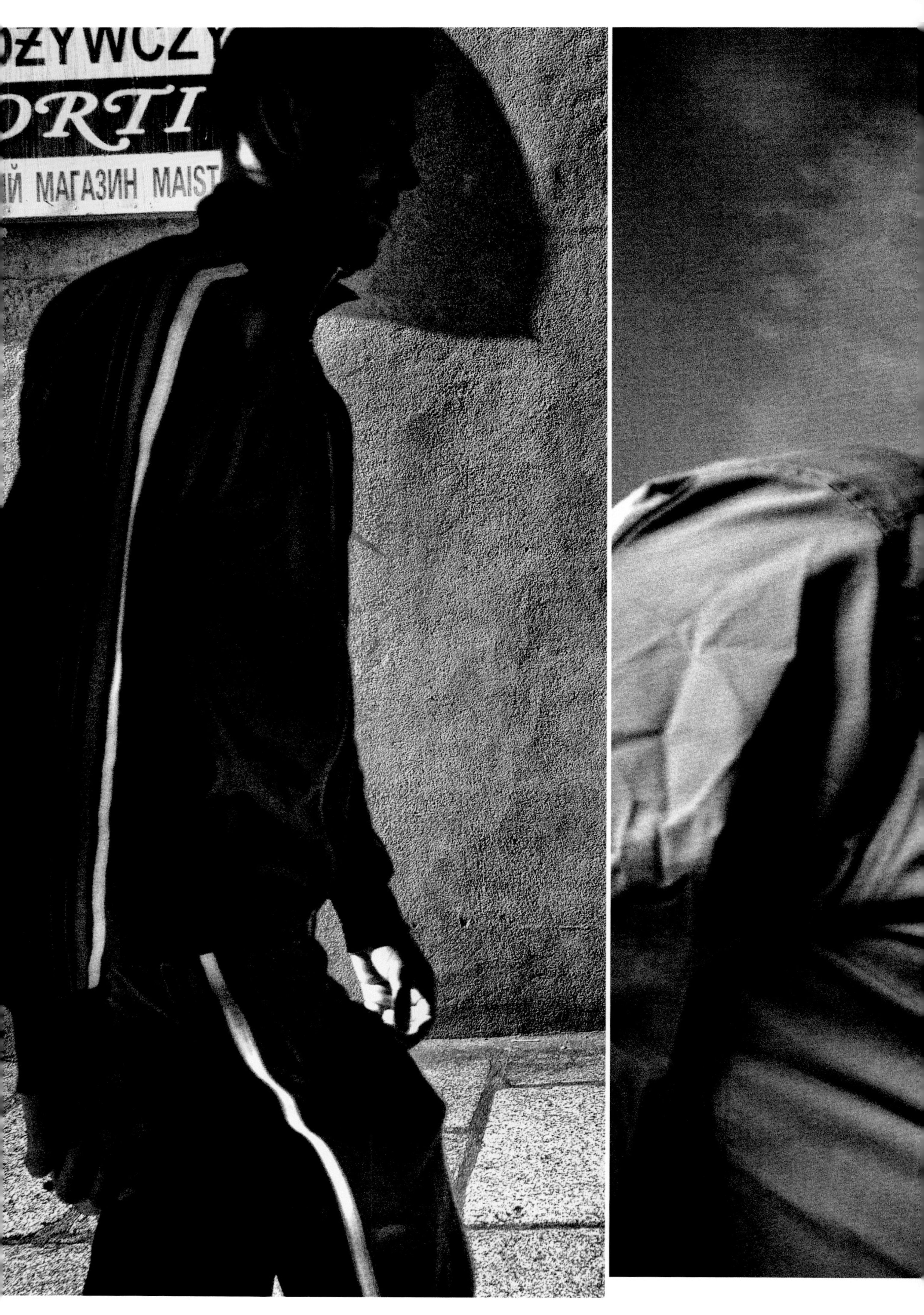
OŻYWCZY
ORTI
Й МАГАЗИН MAIST

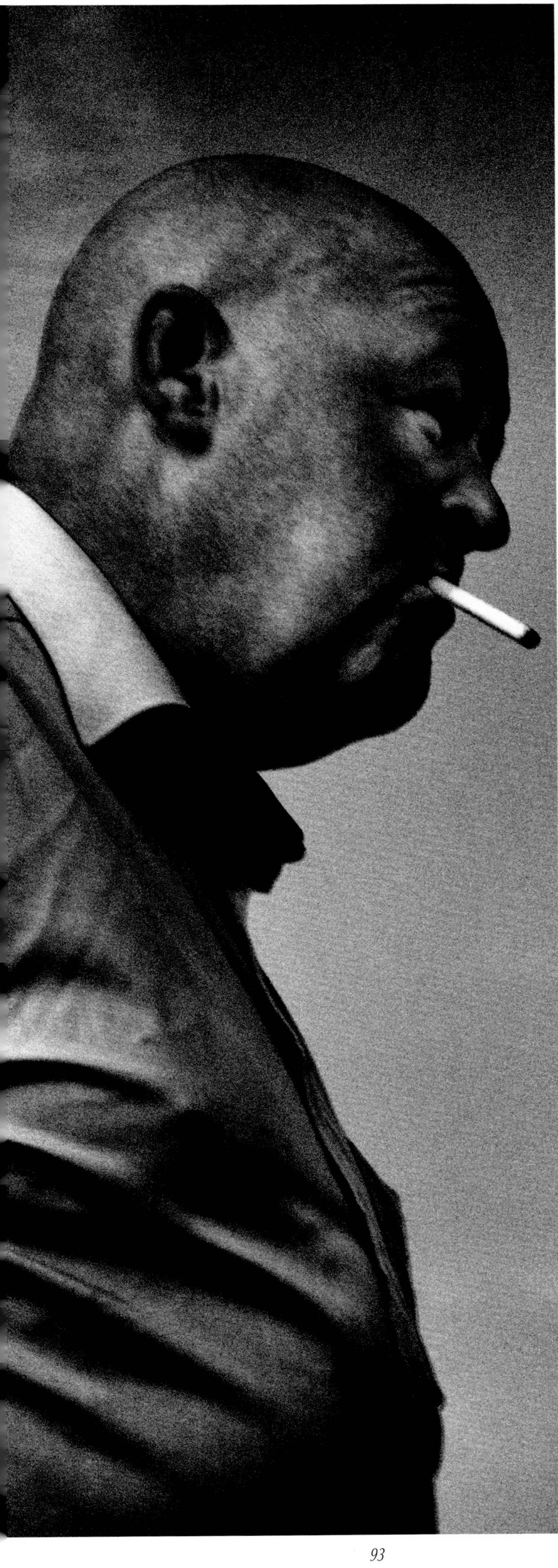

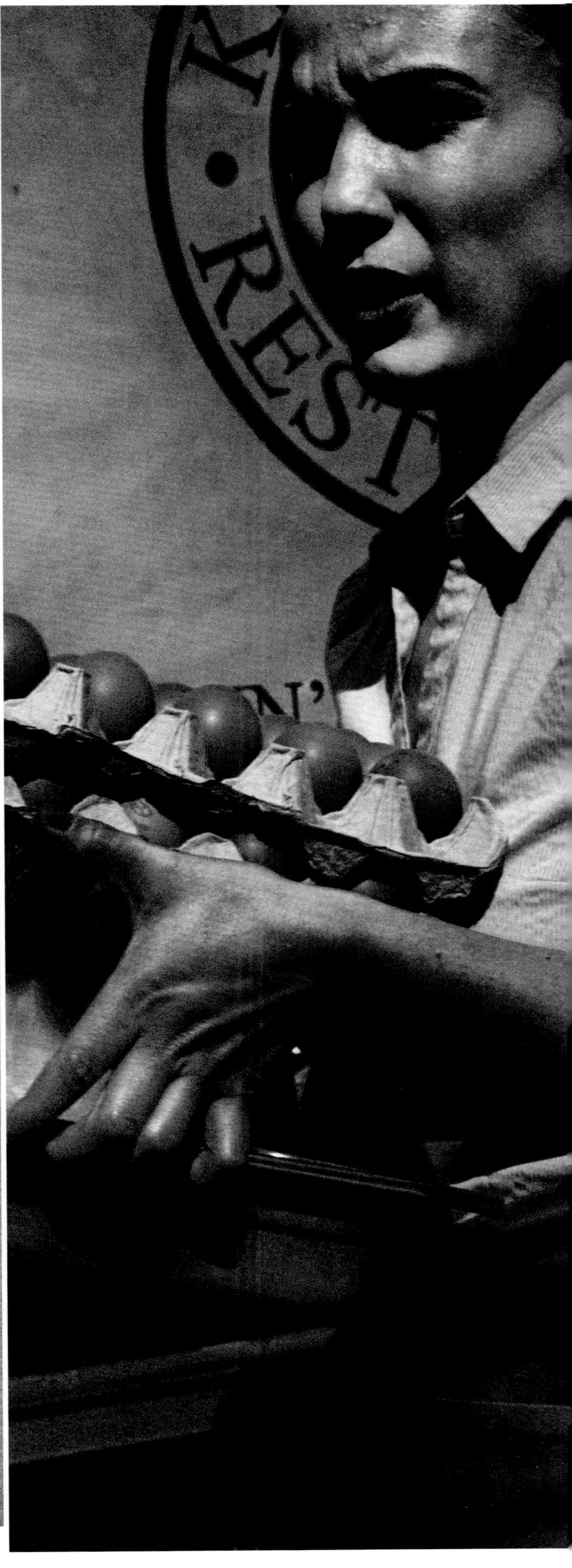

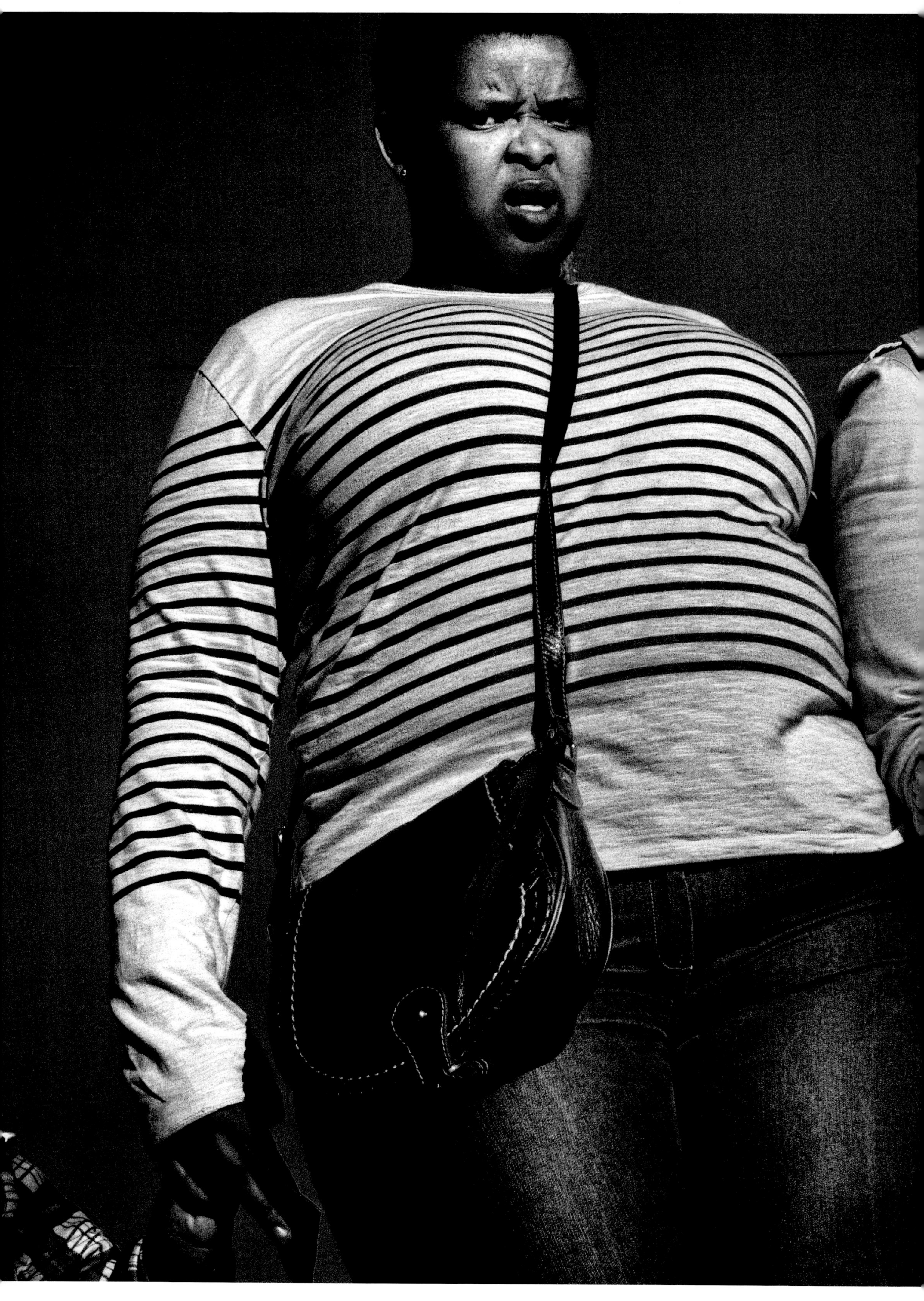

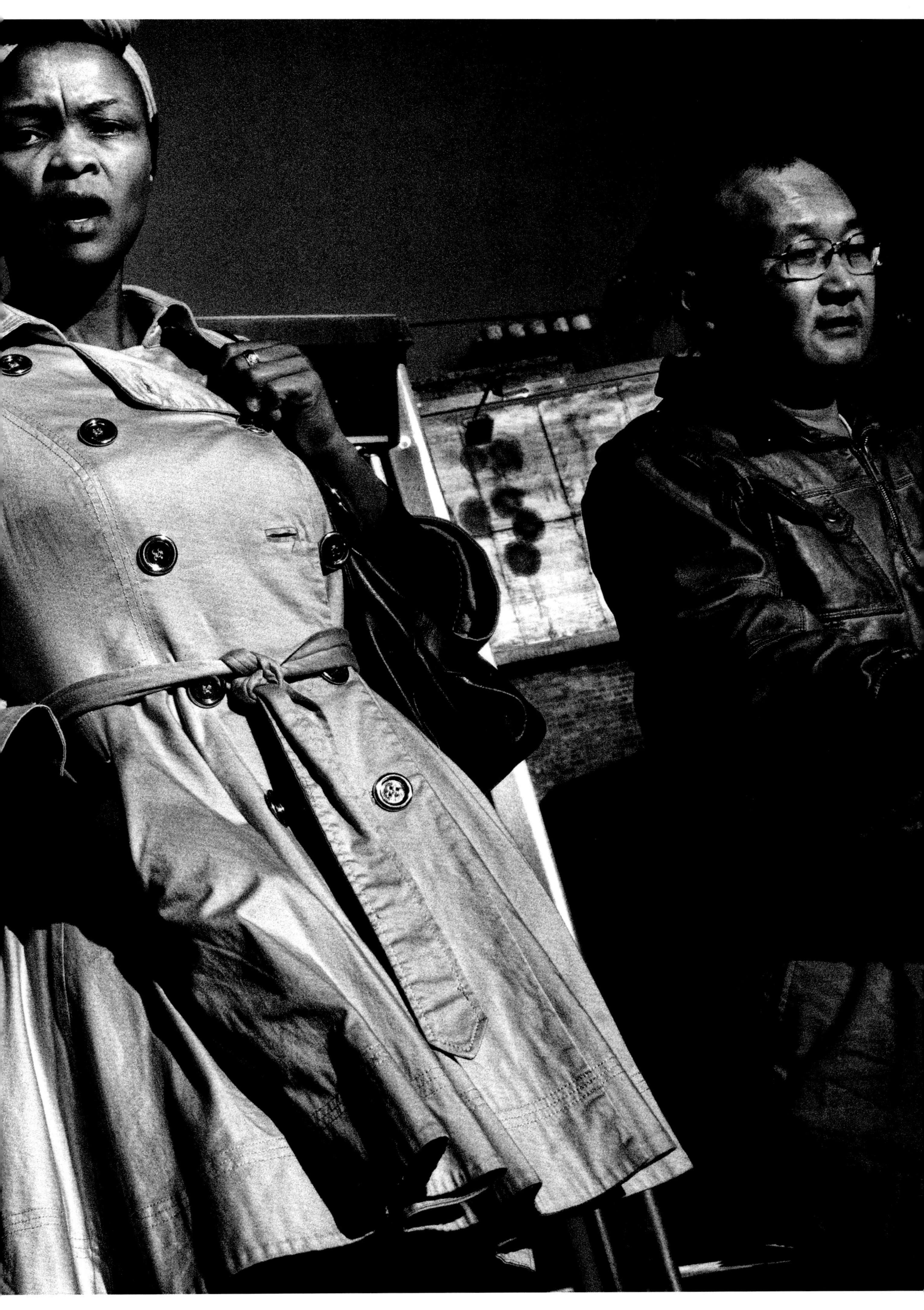

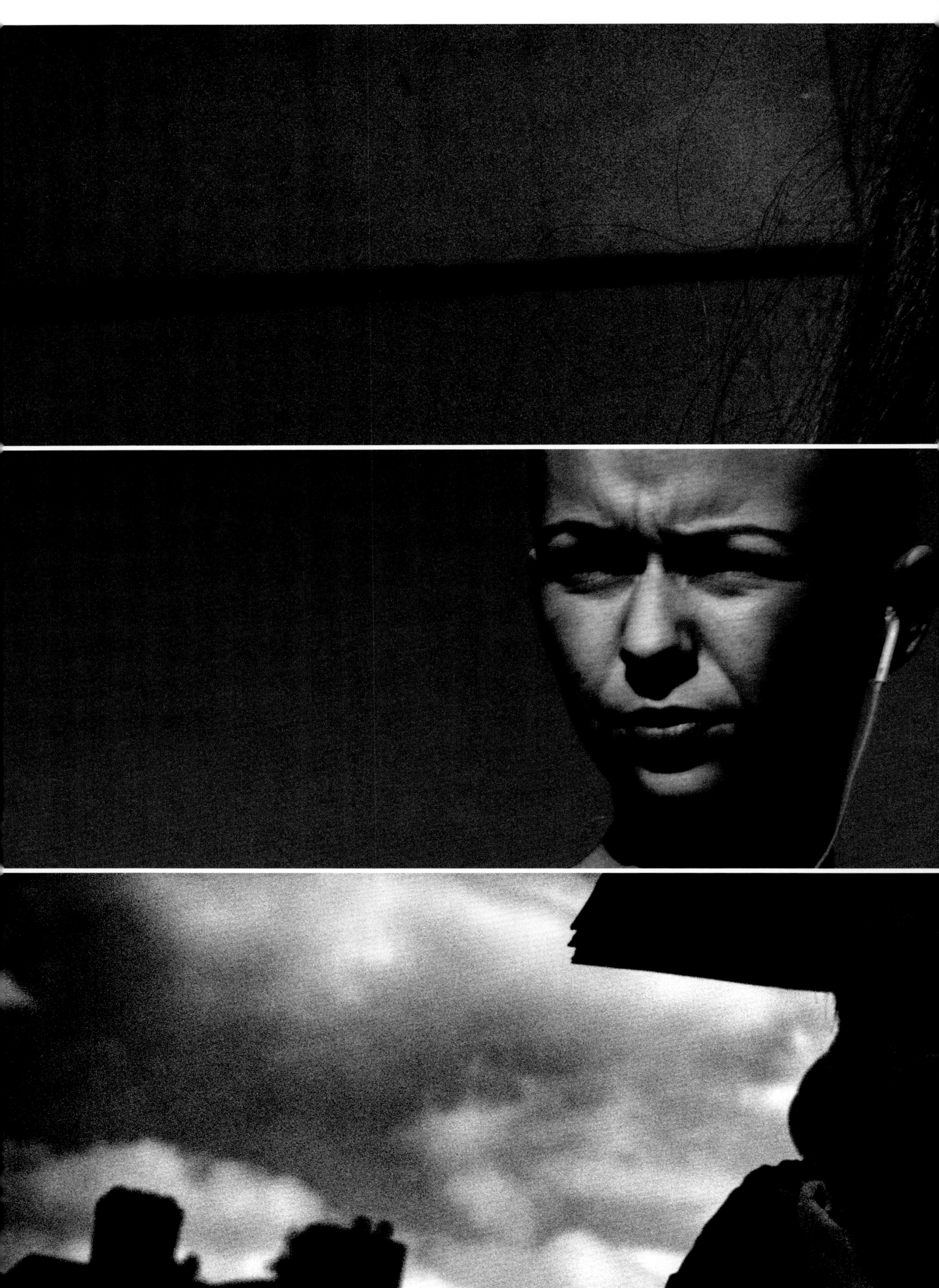

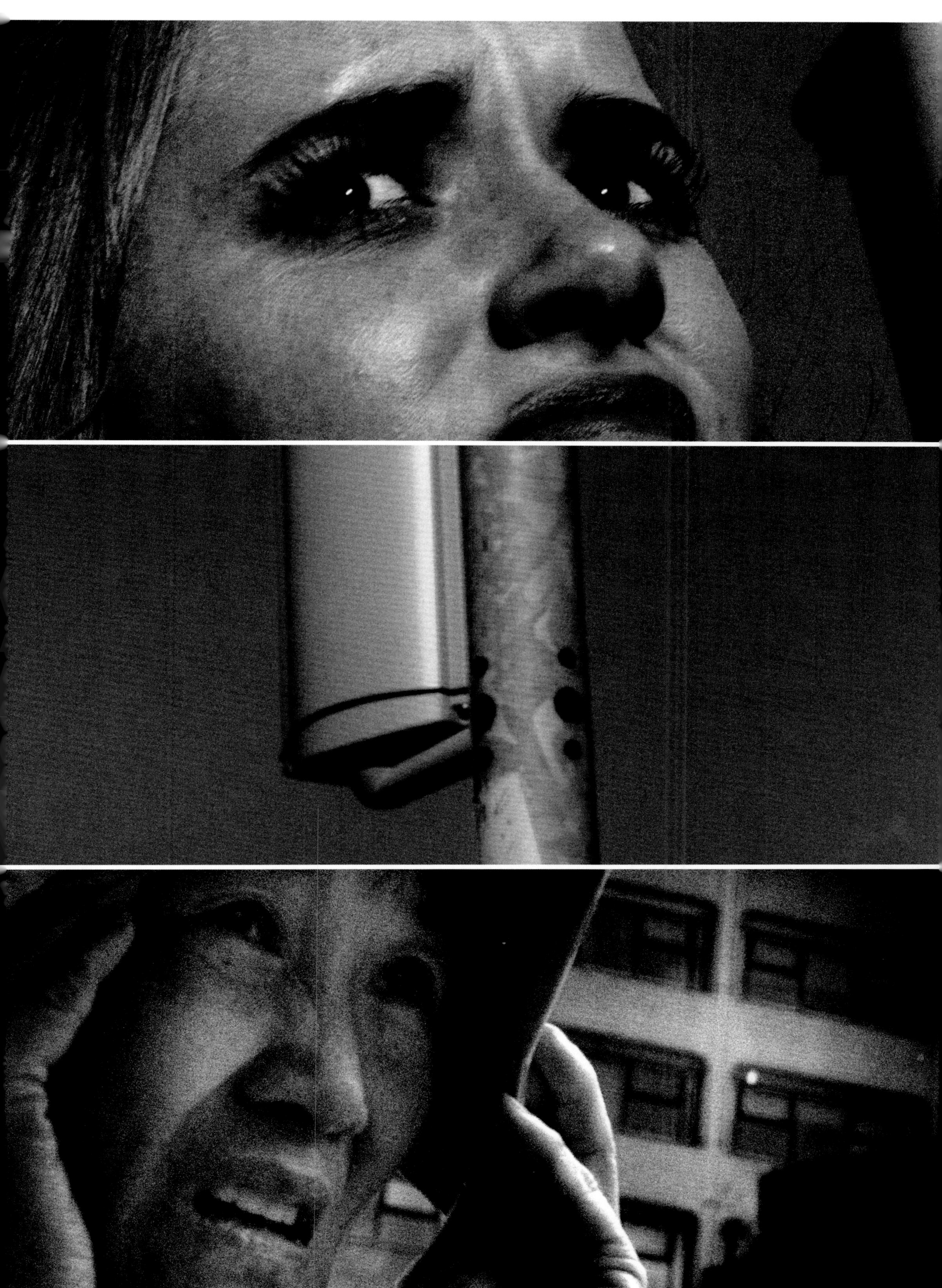

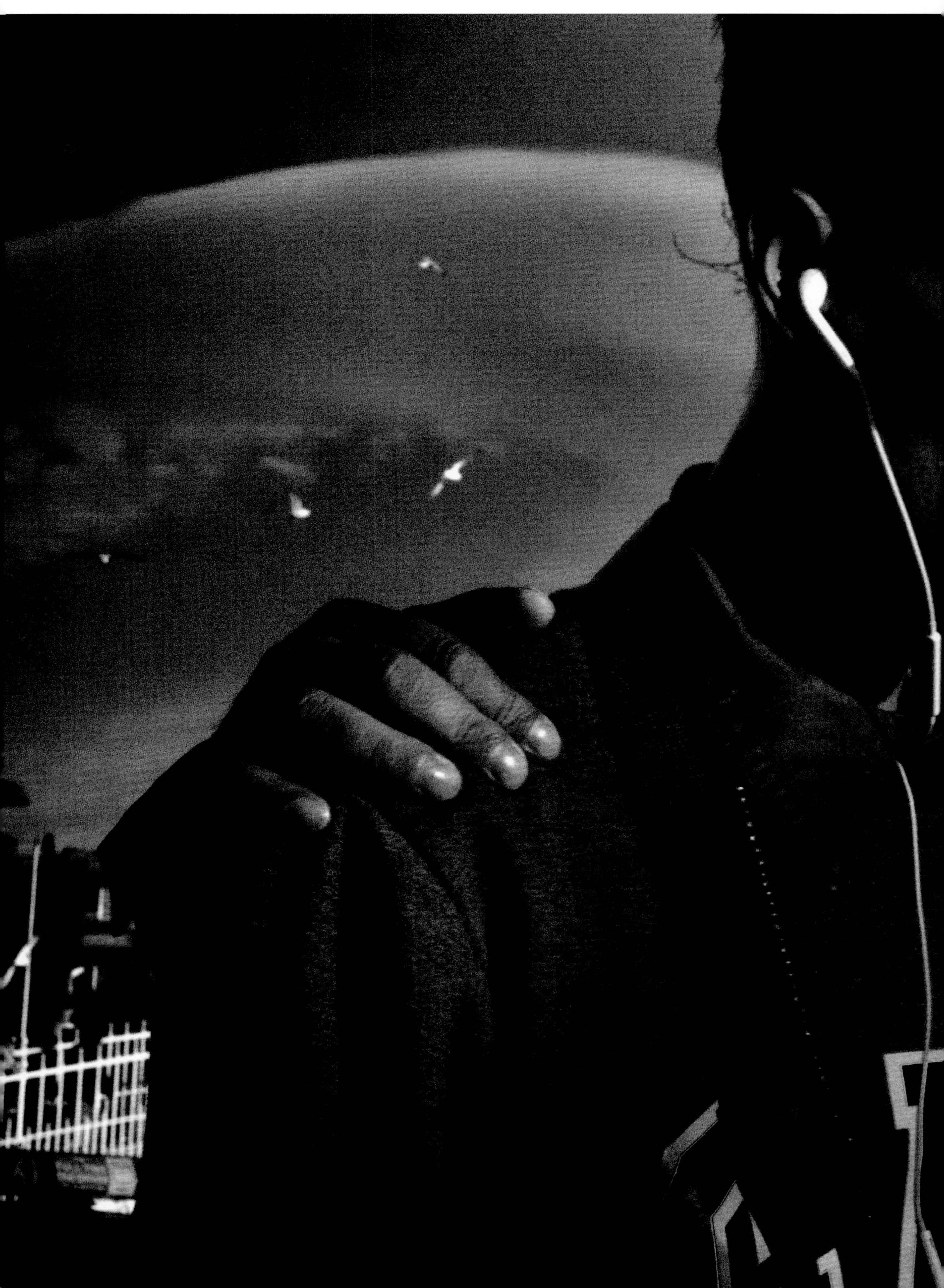

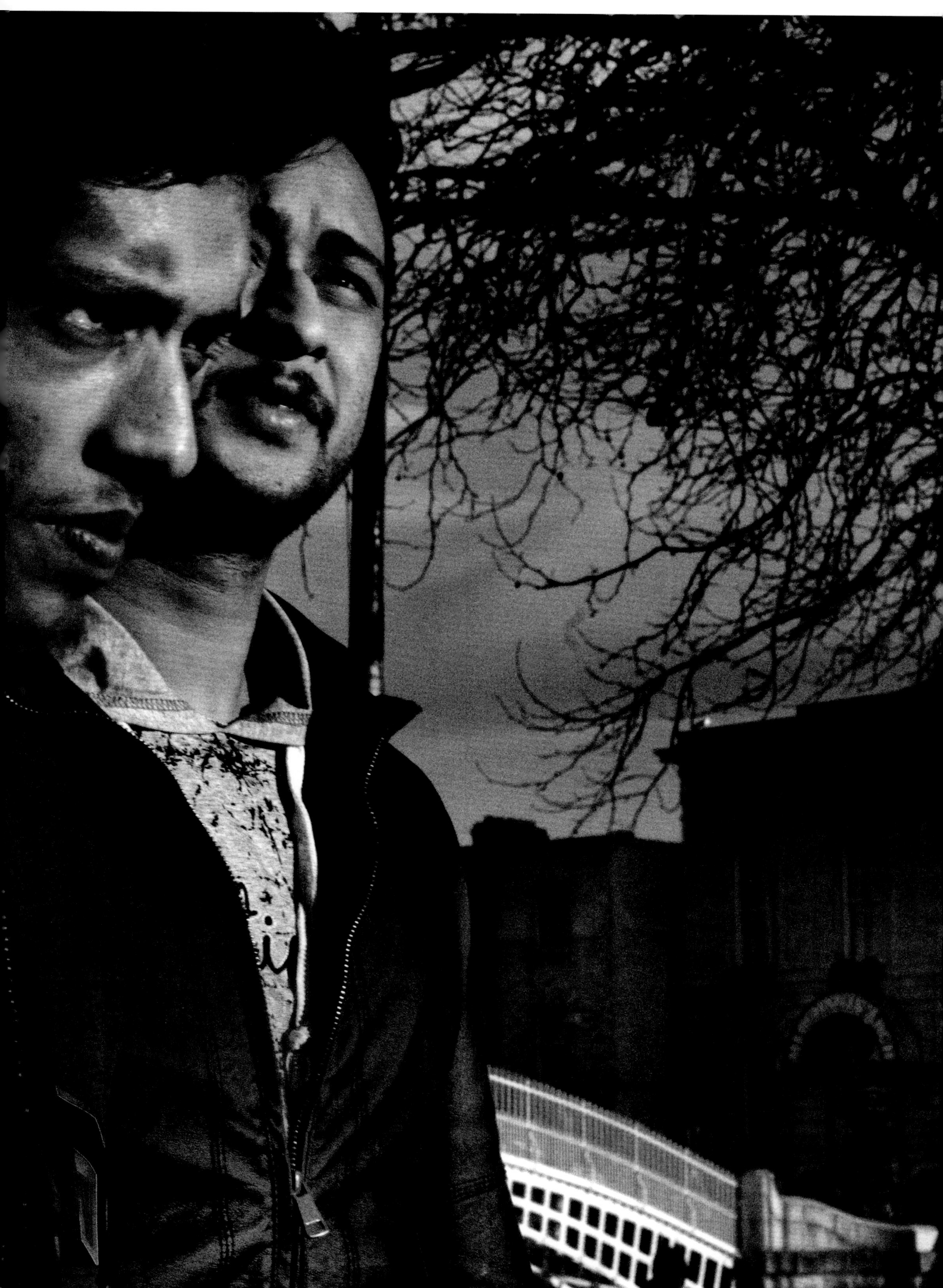

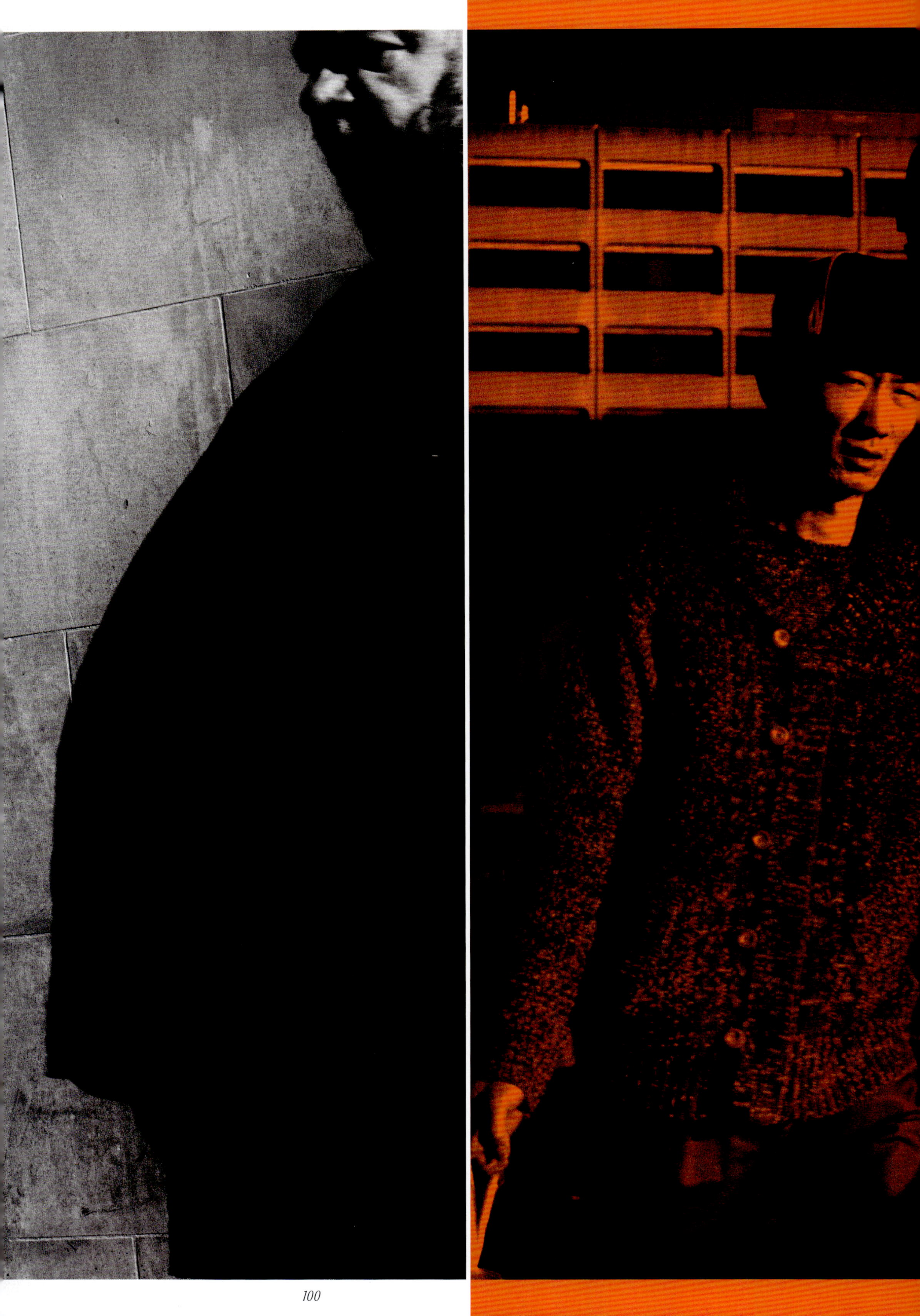

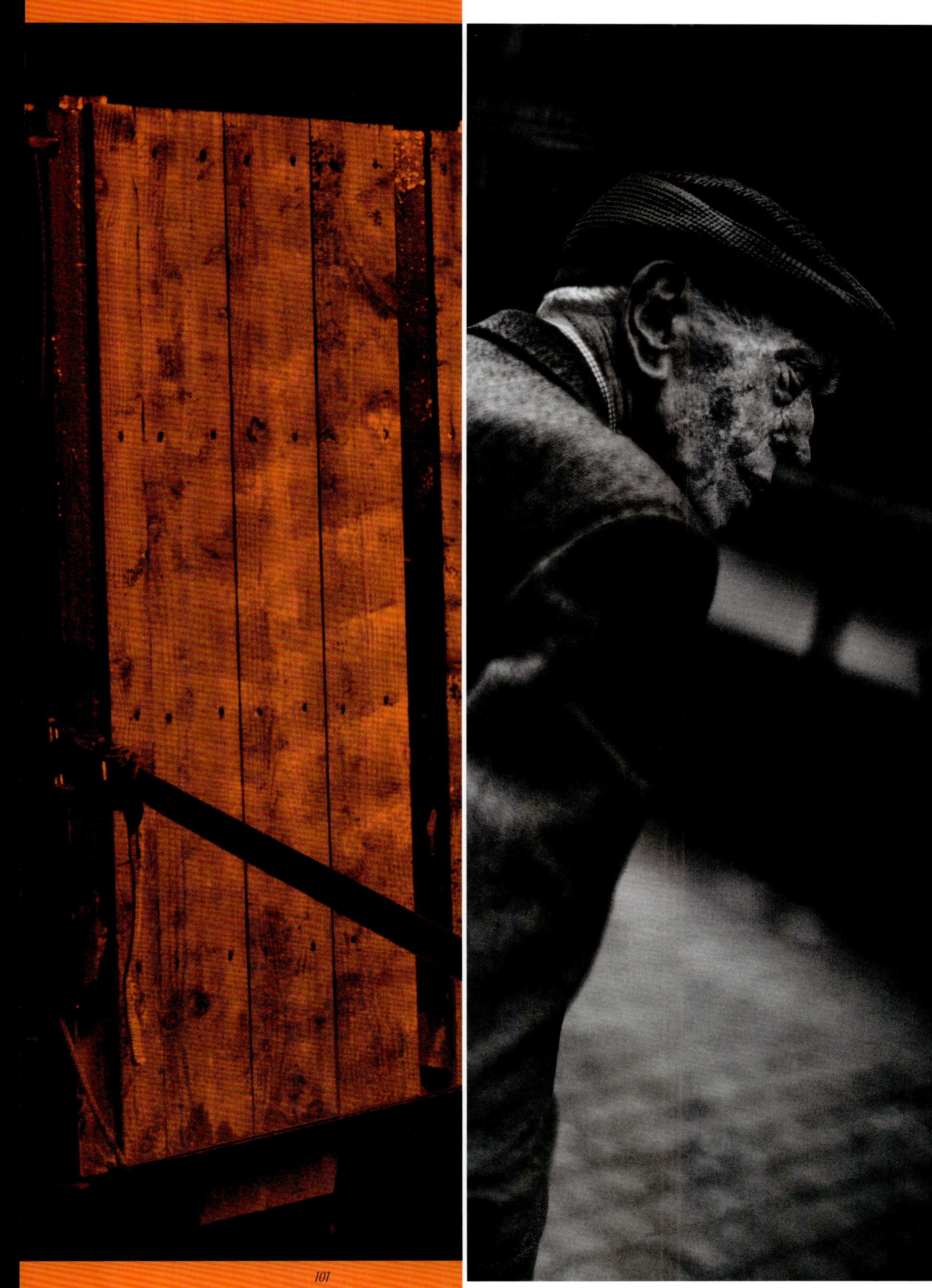

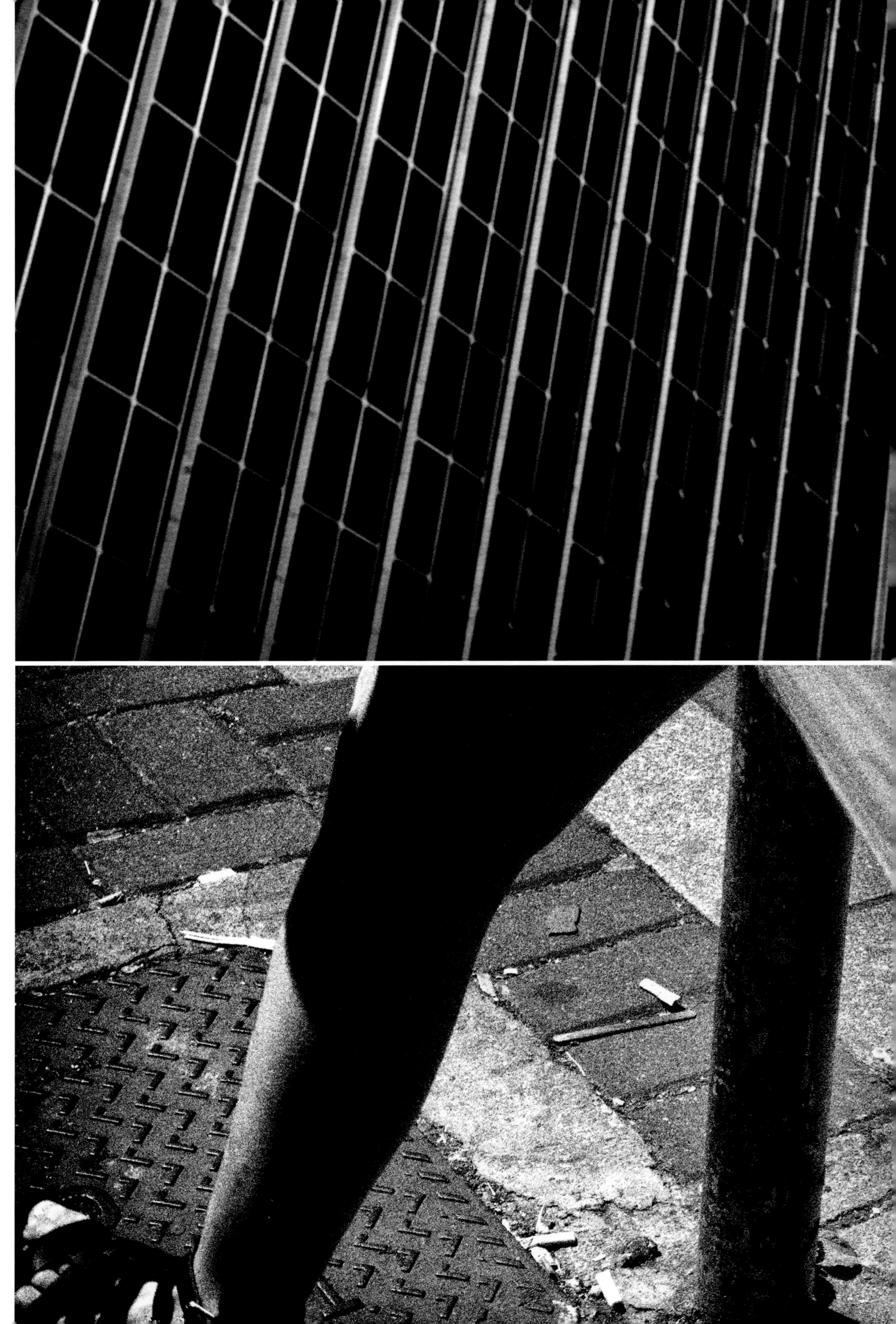

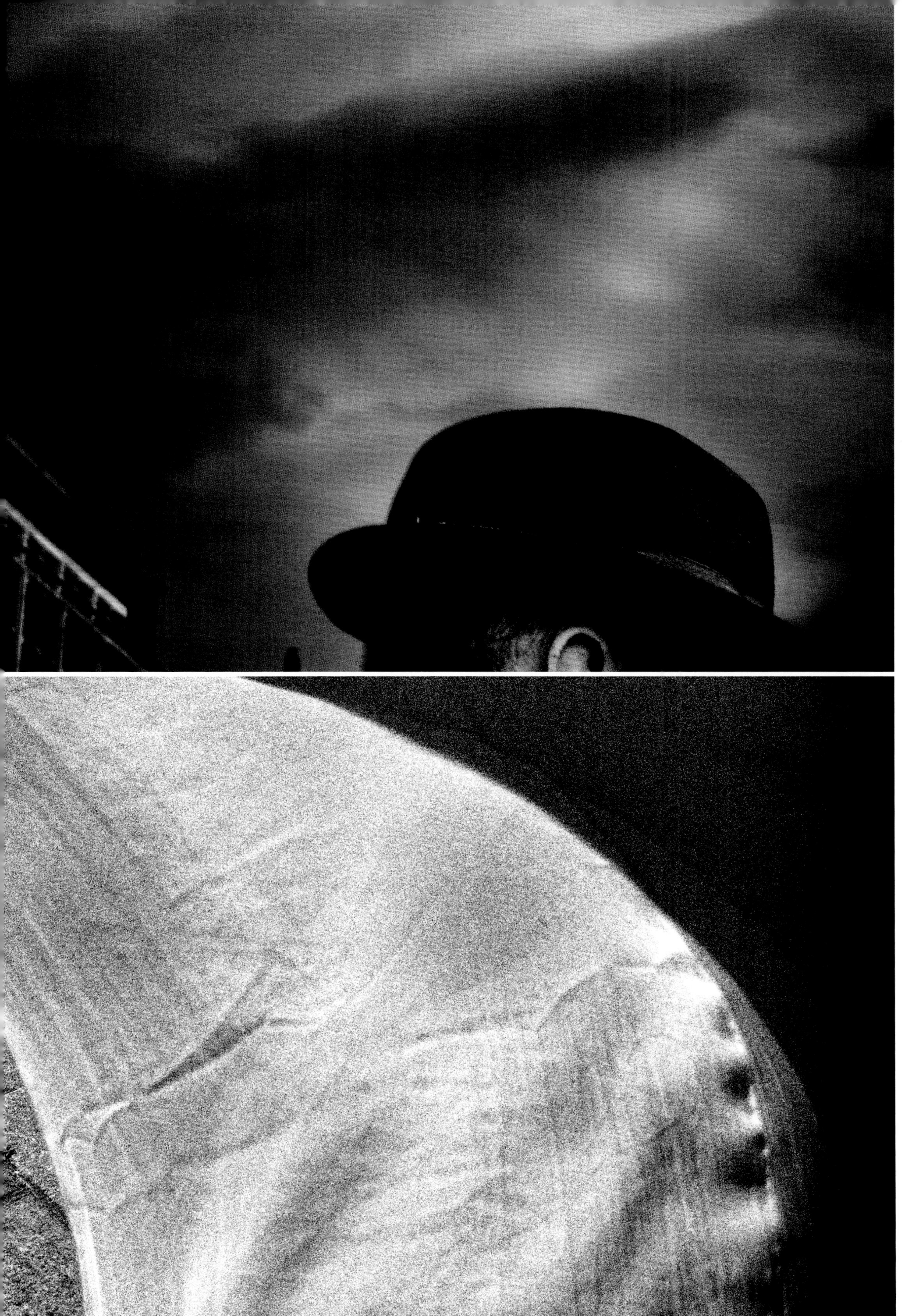

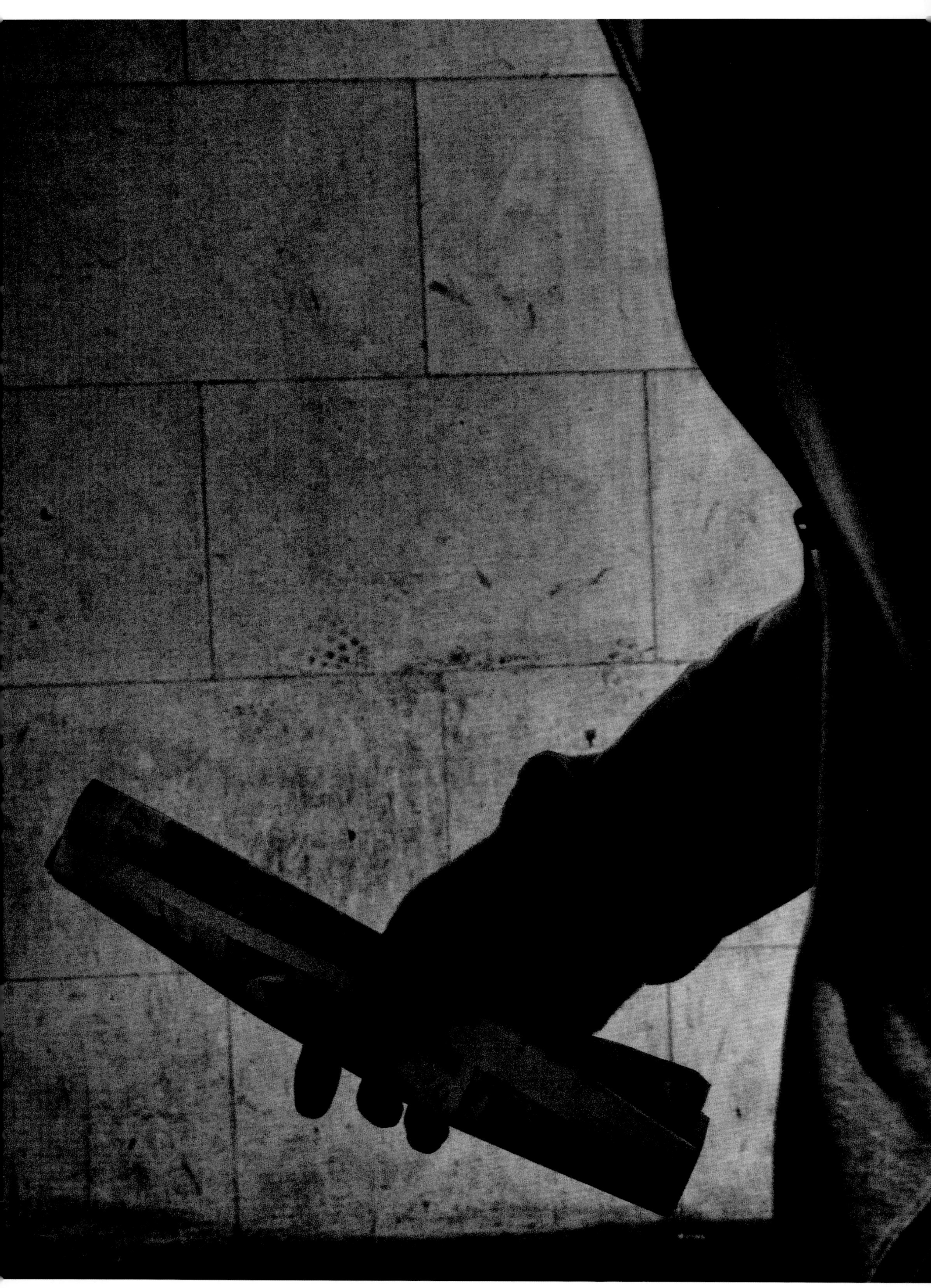

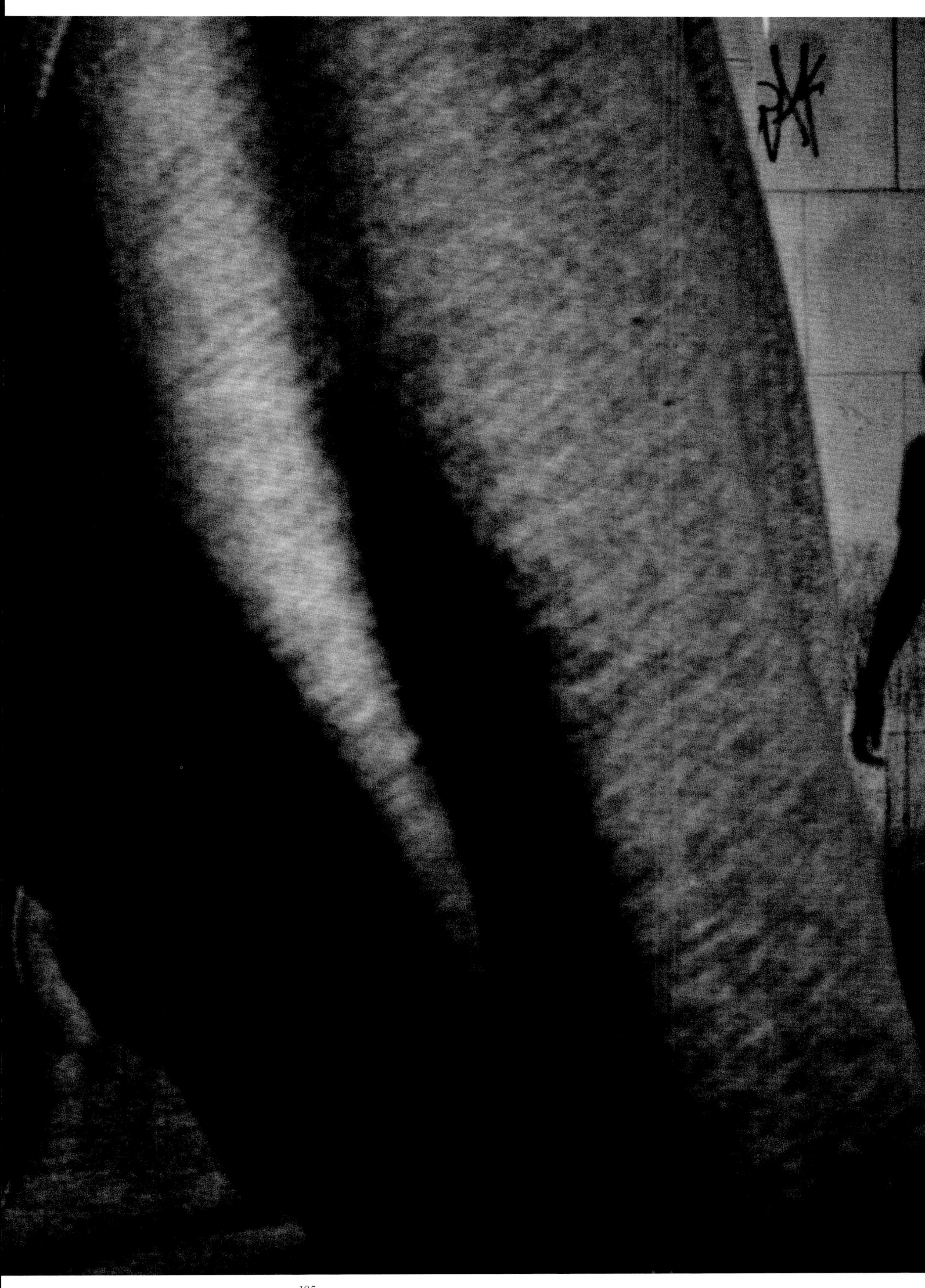

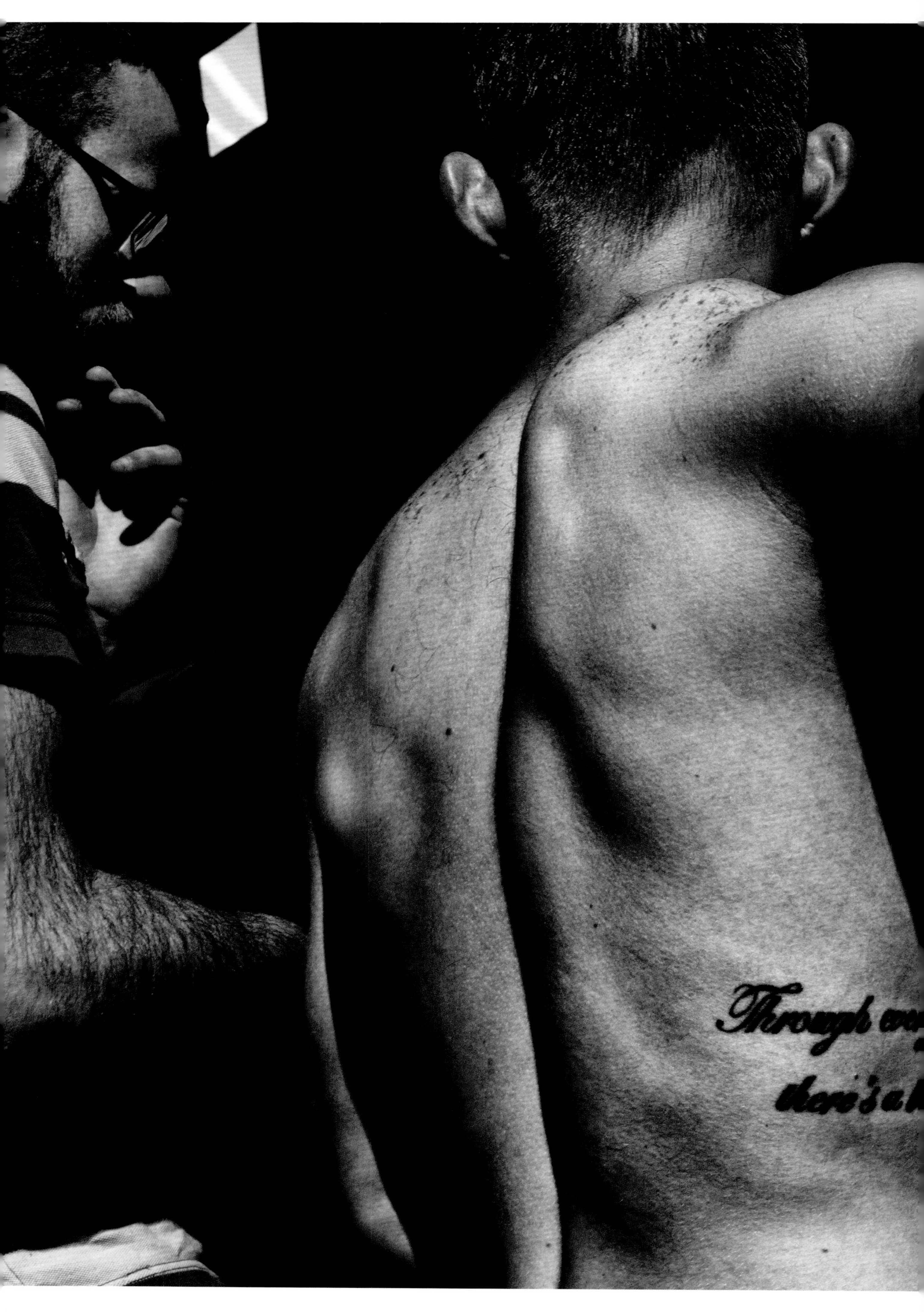
Through eve
there's a l

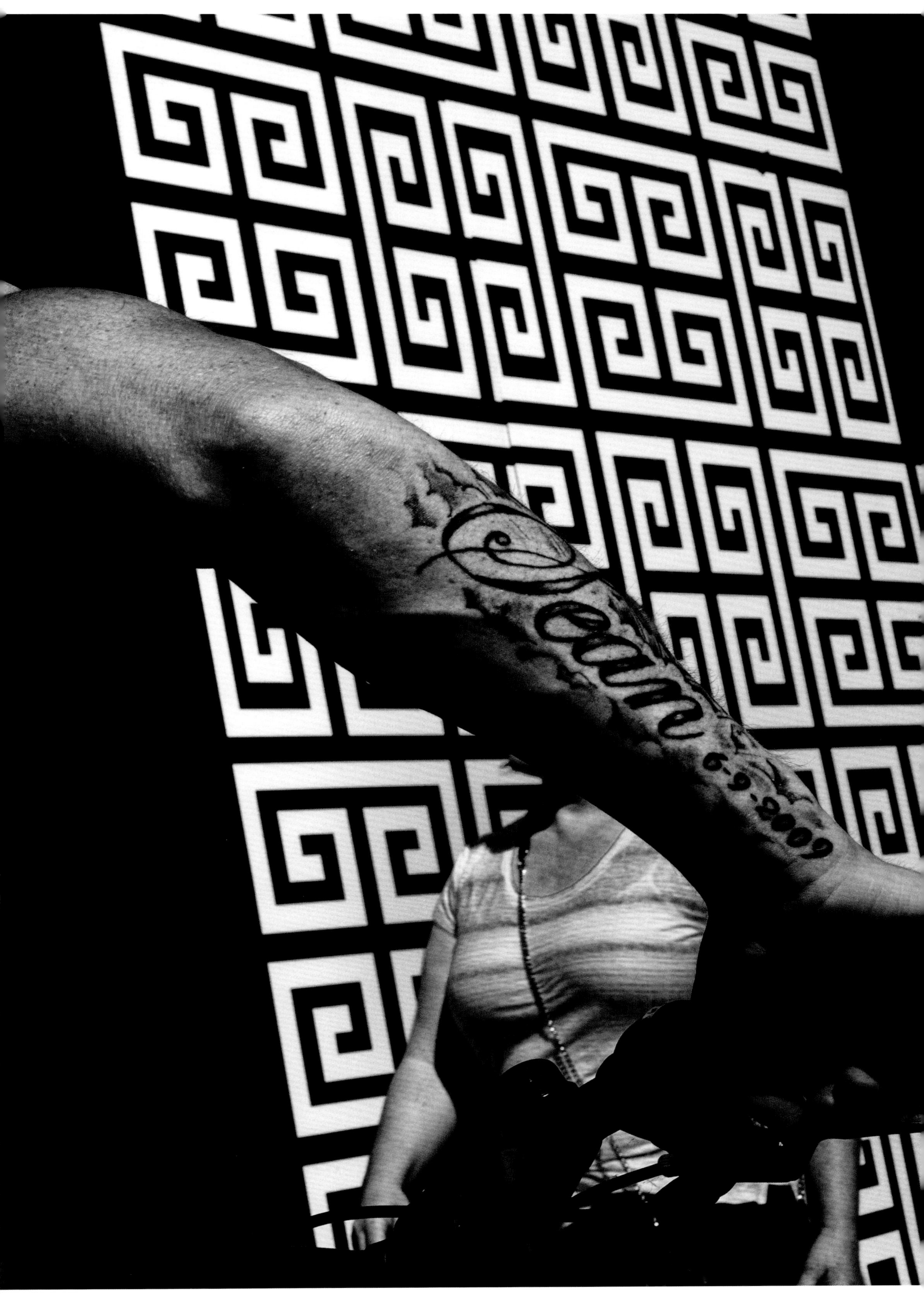
Jean
6-9-2009

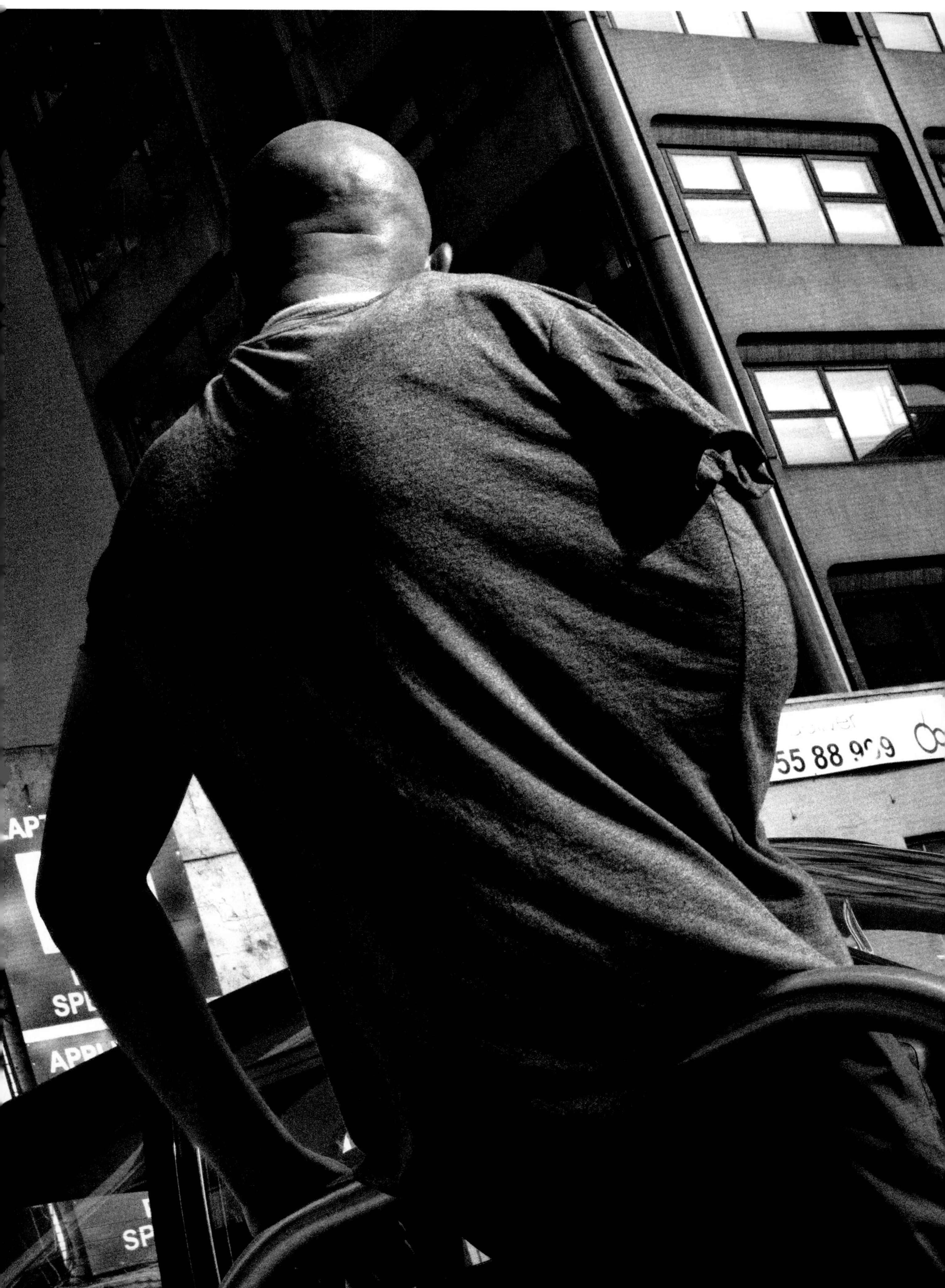

55 88 99 9
APT
SP
APP
SP

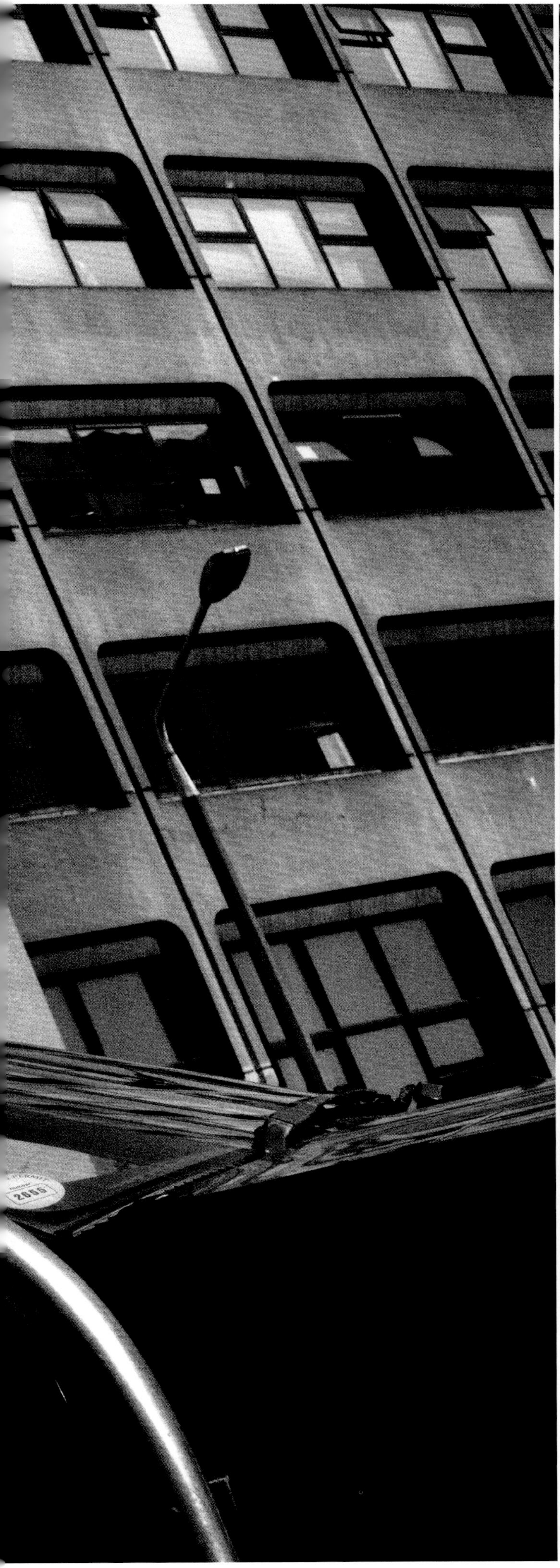

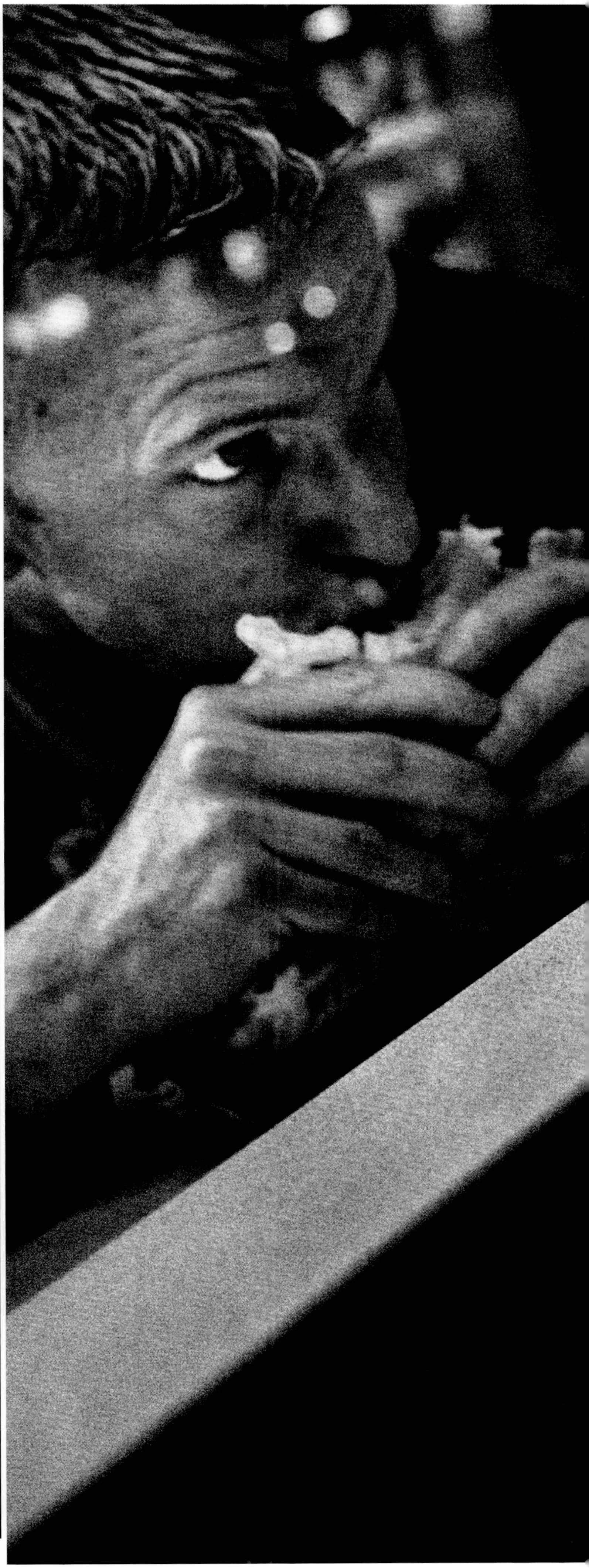

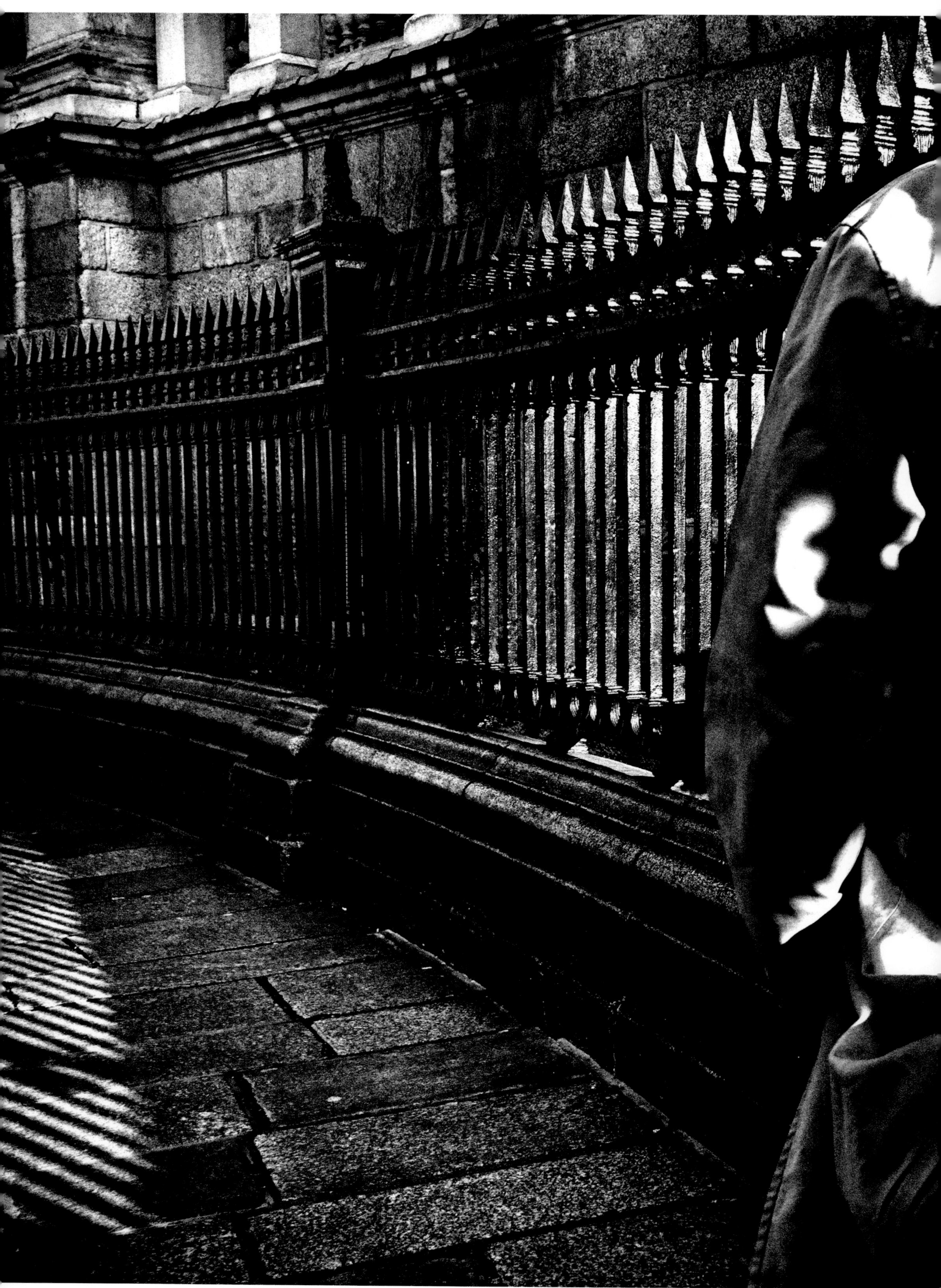

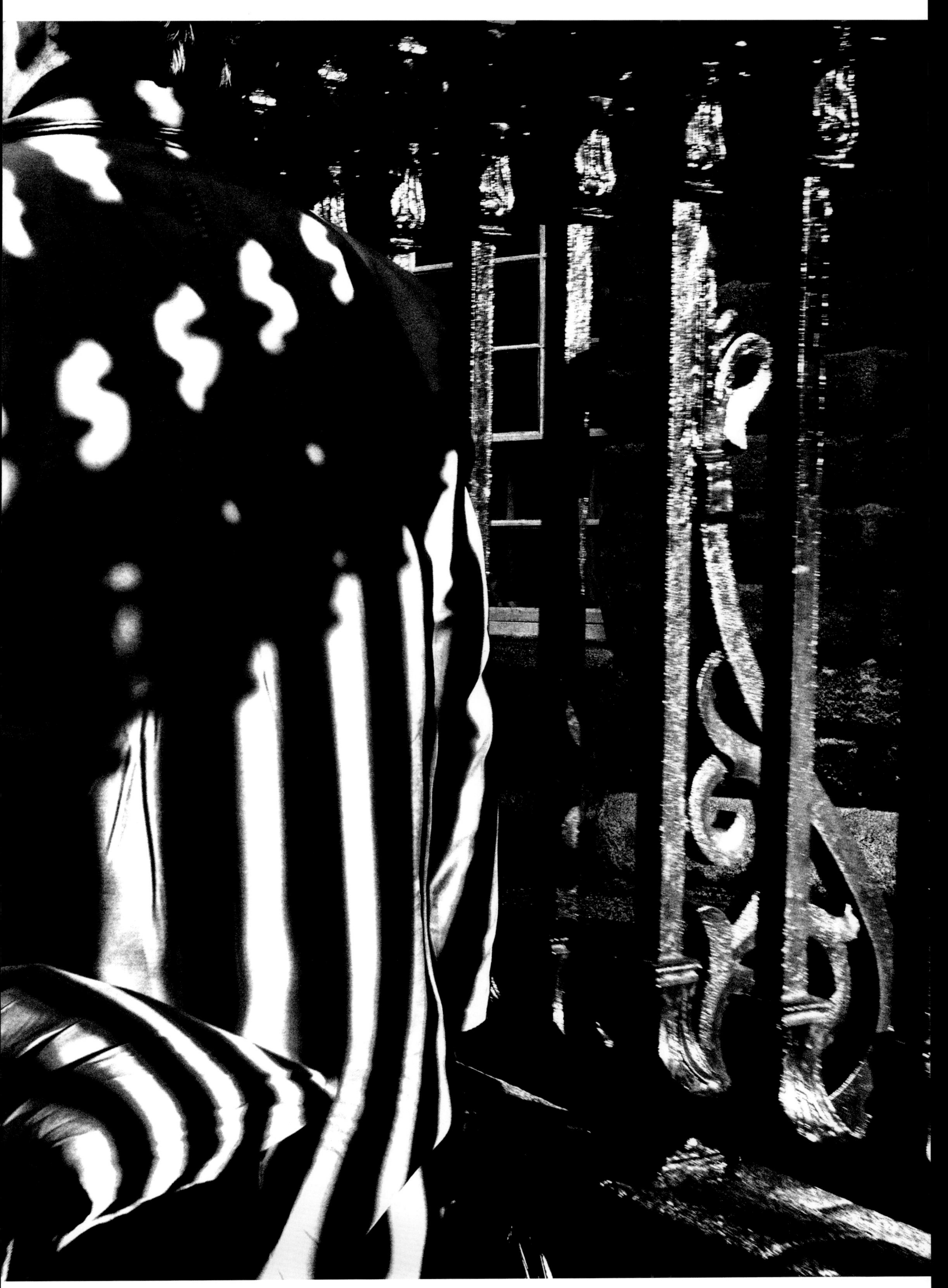

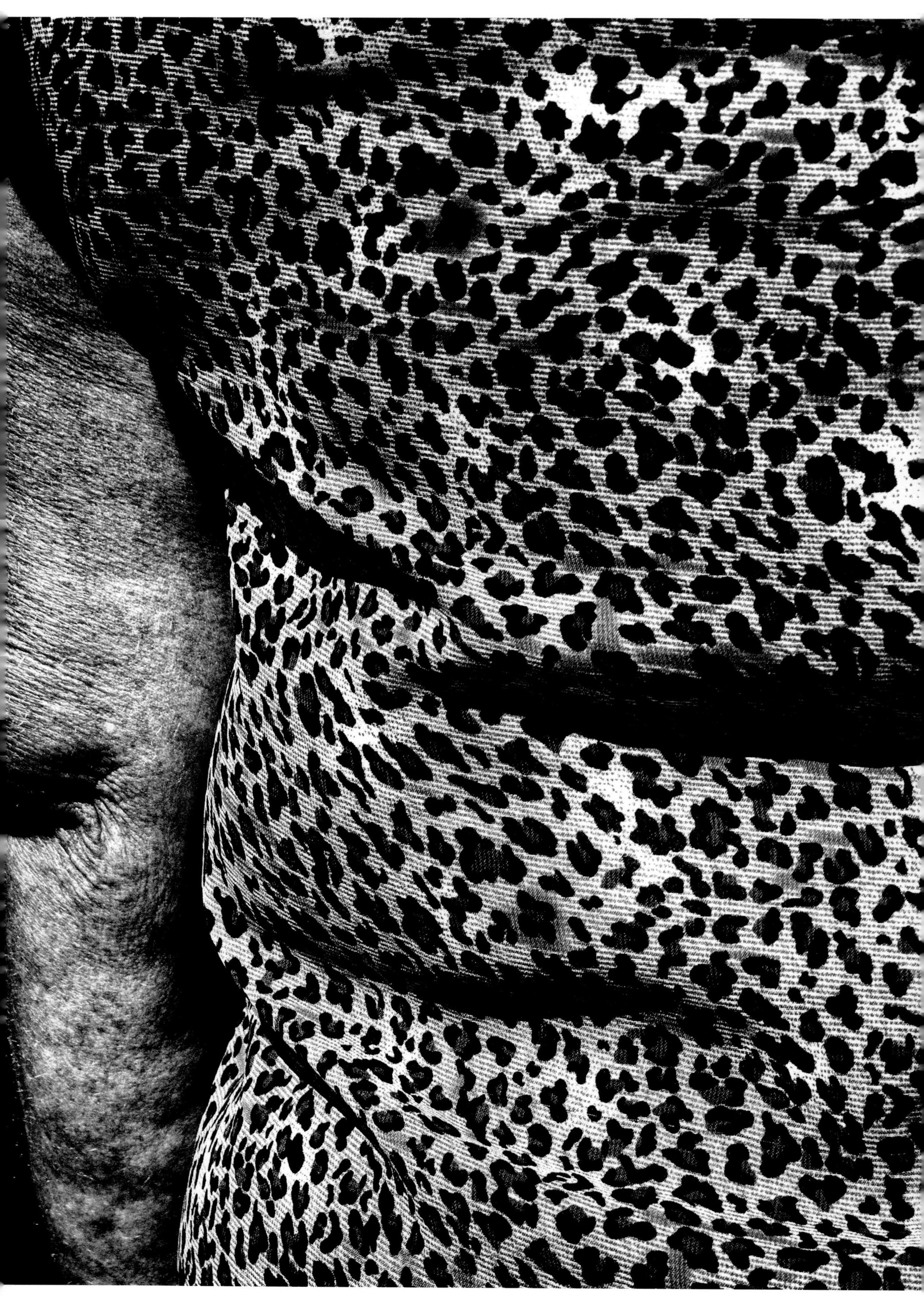

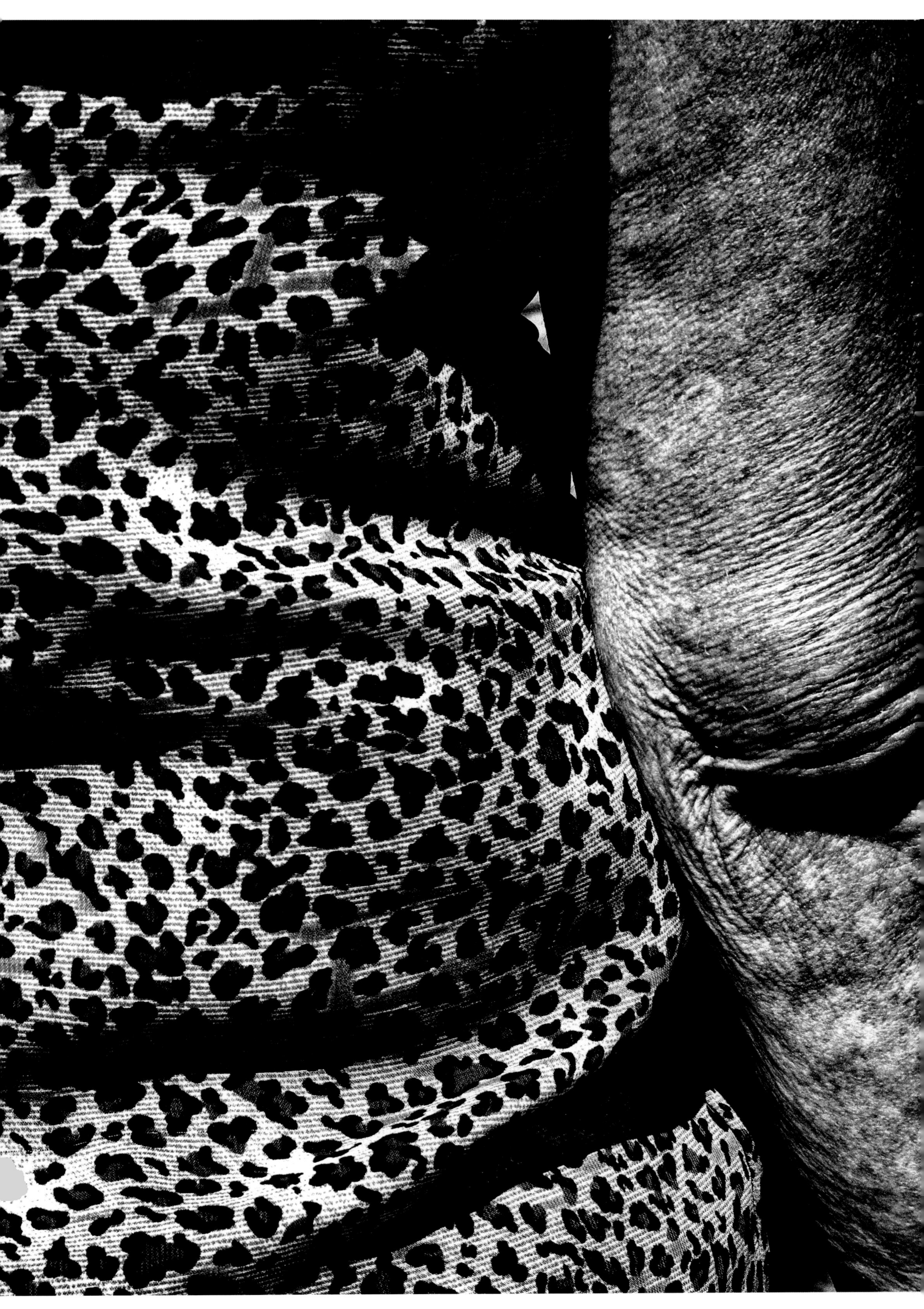

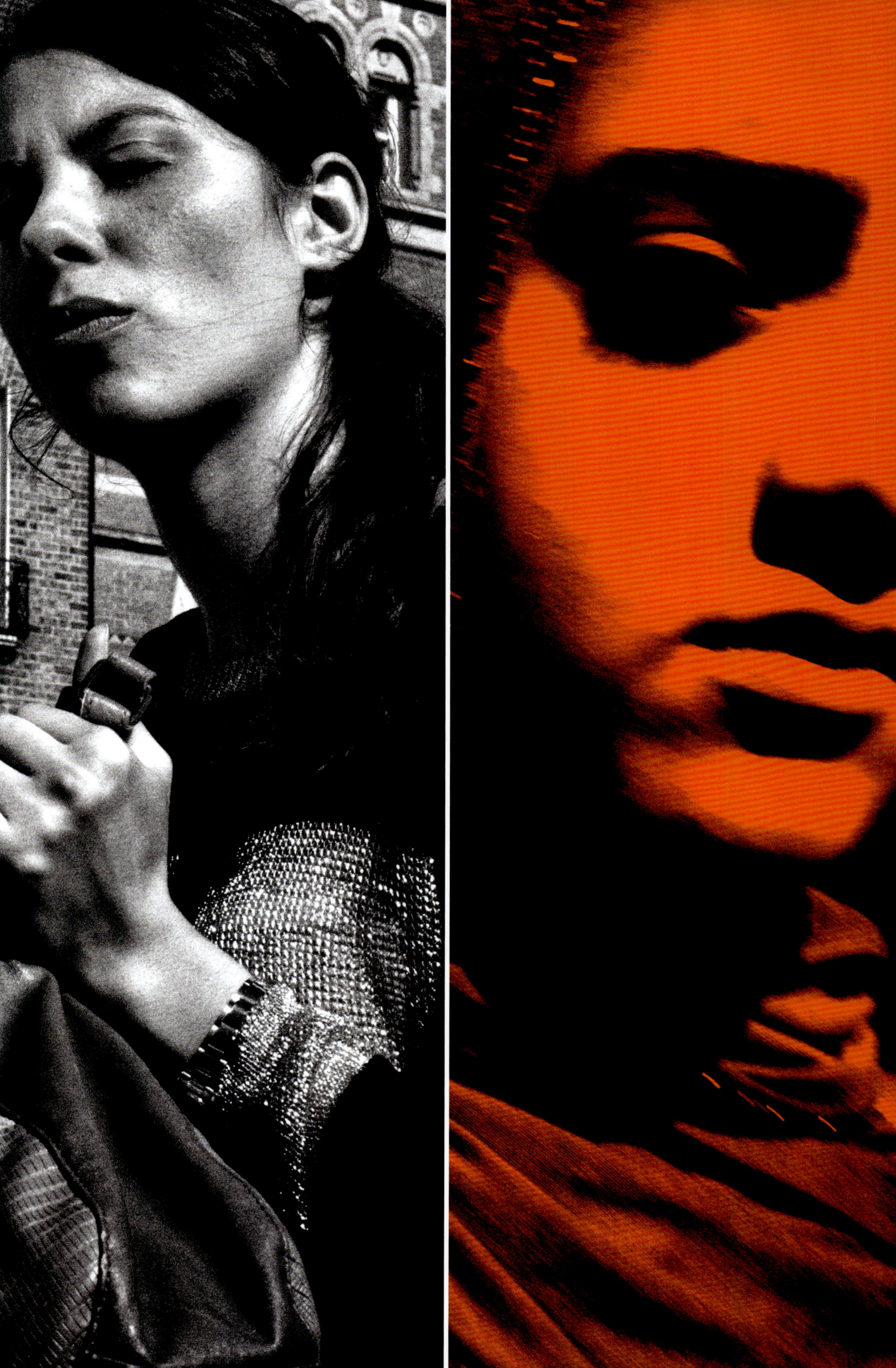

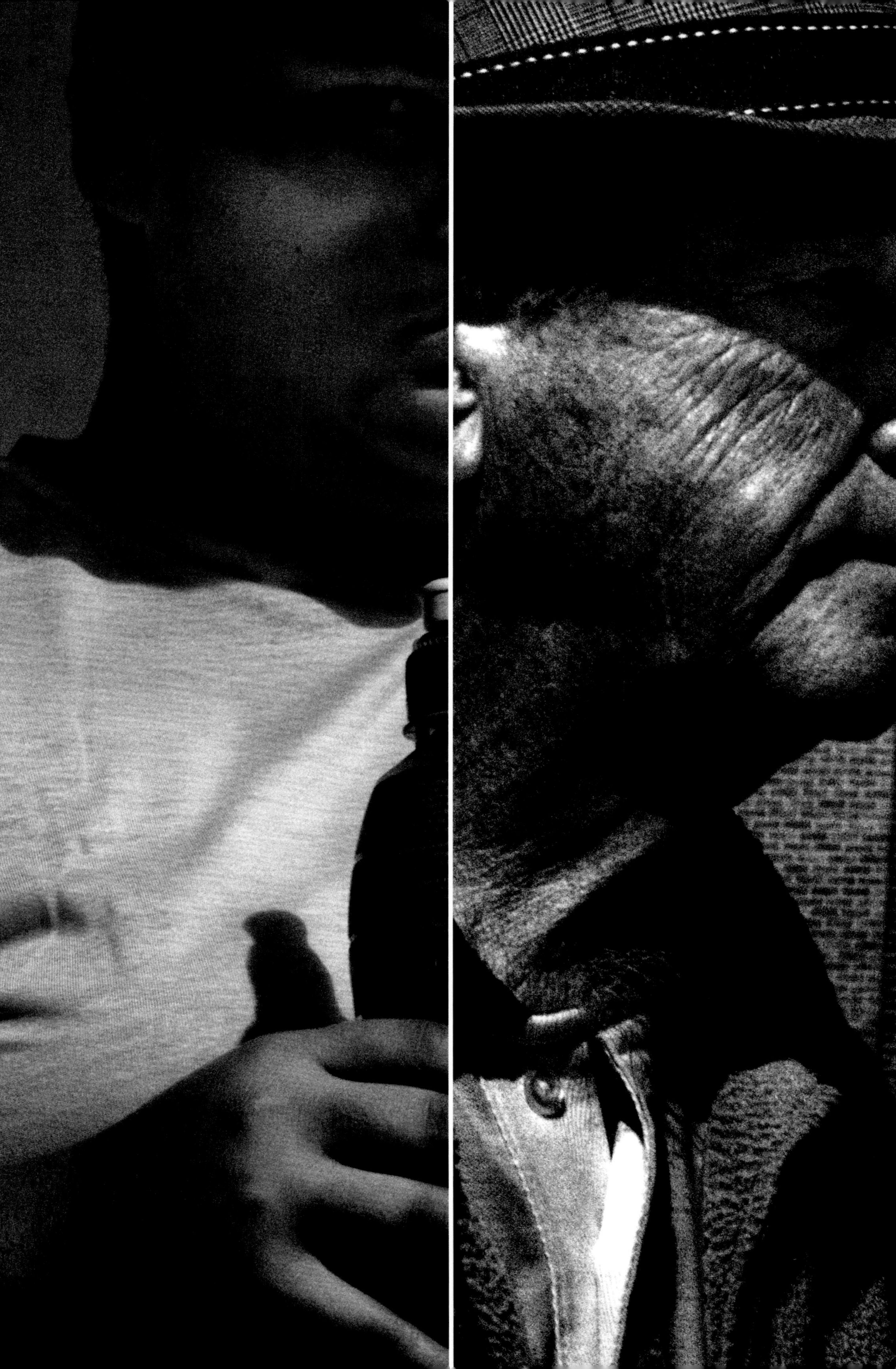

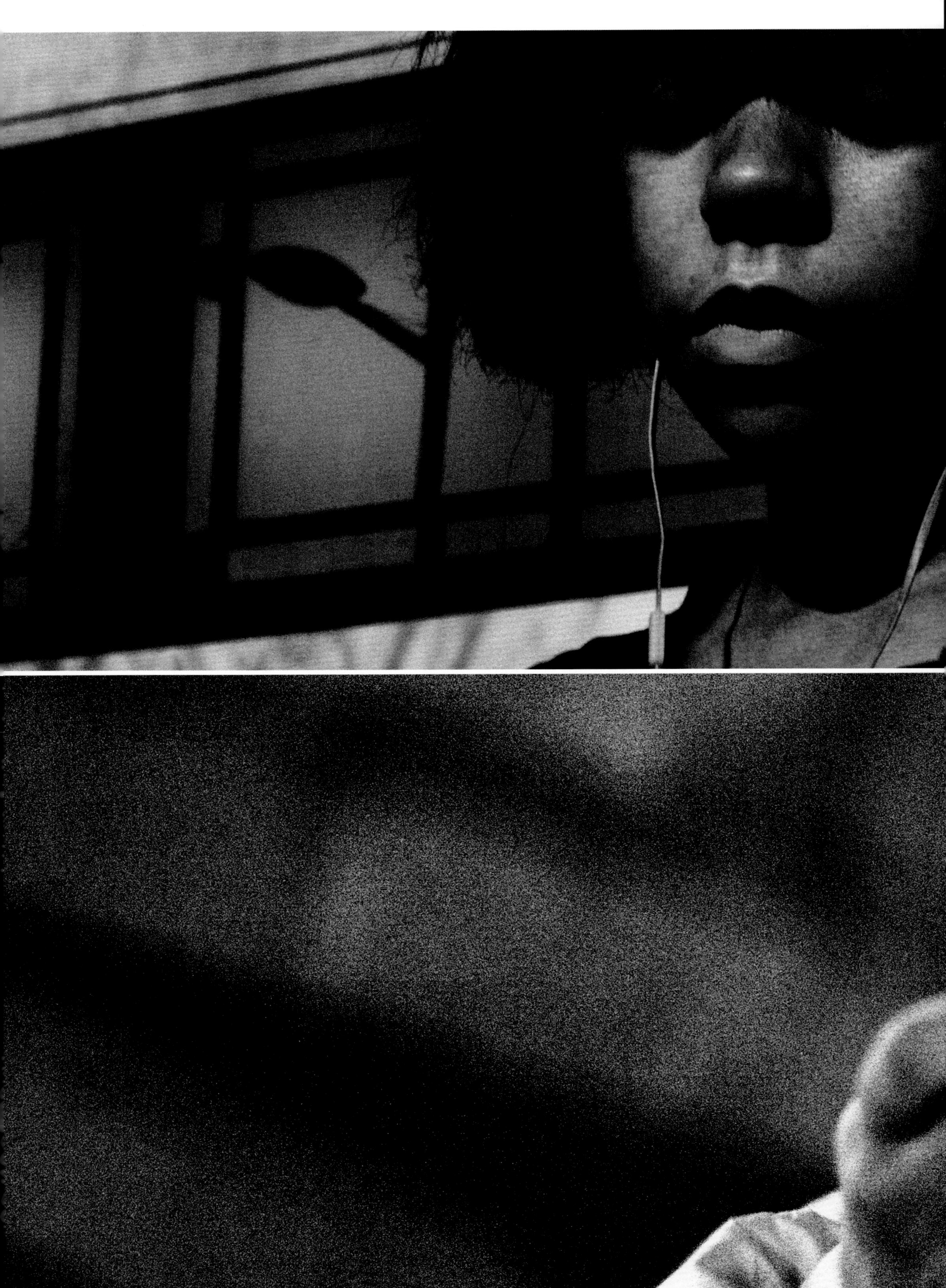

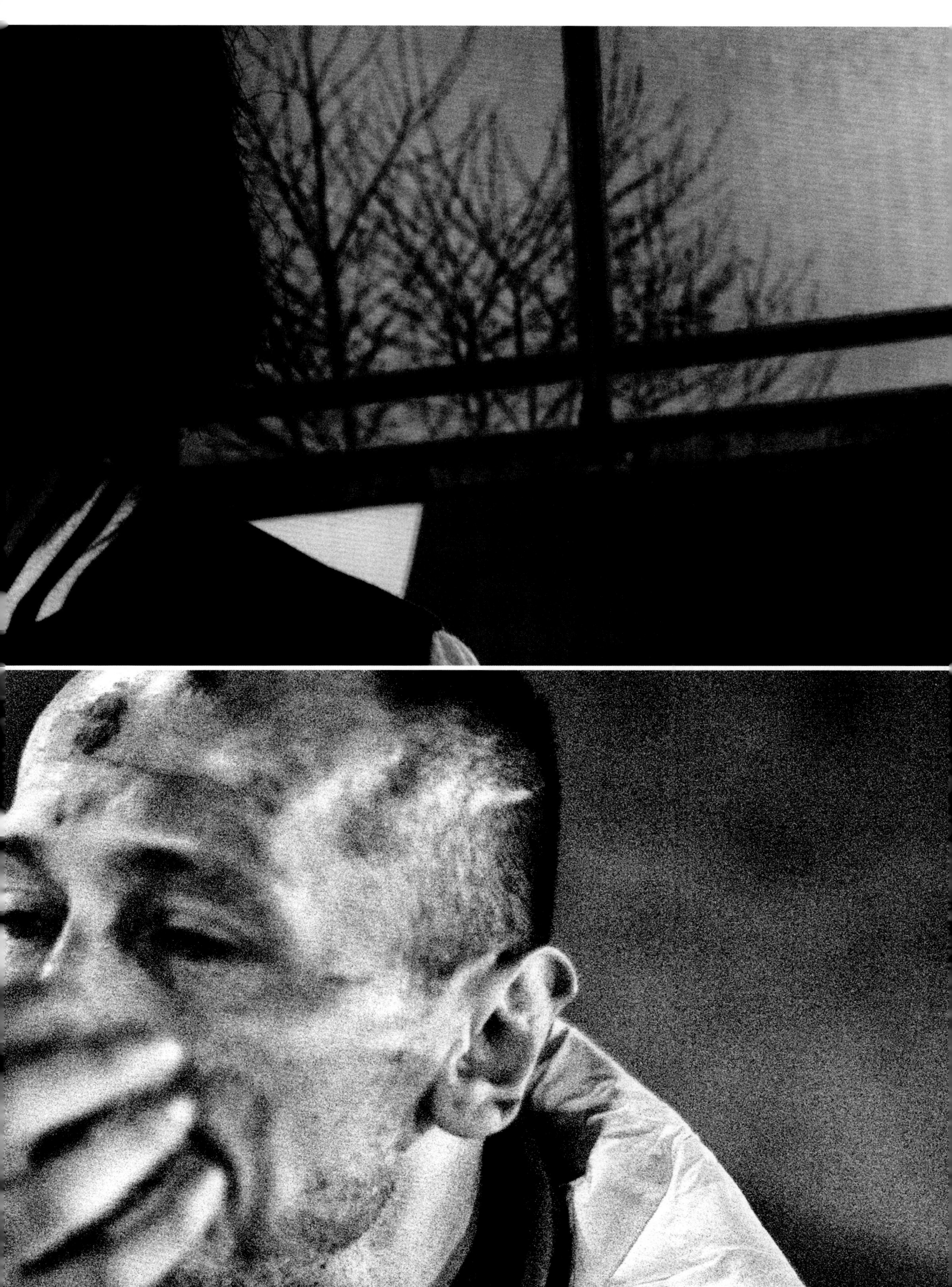

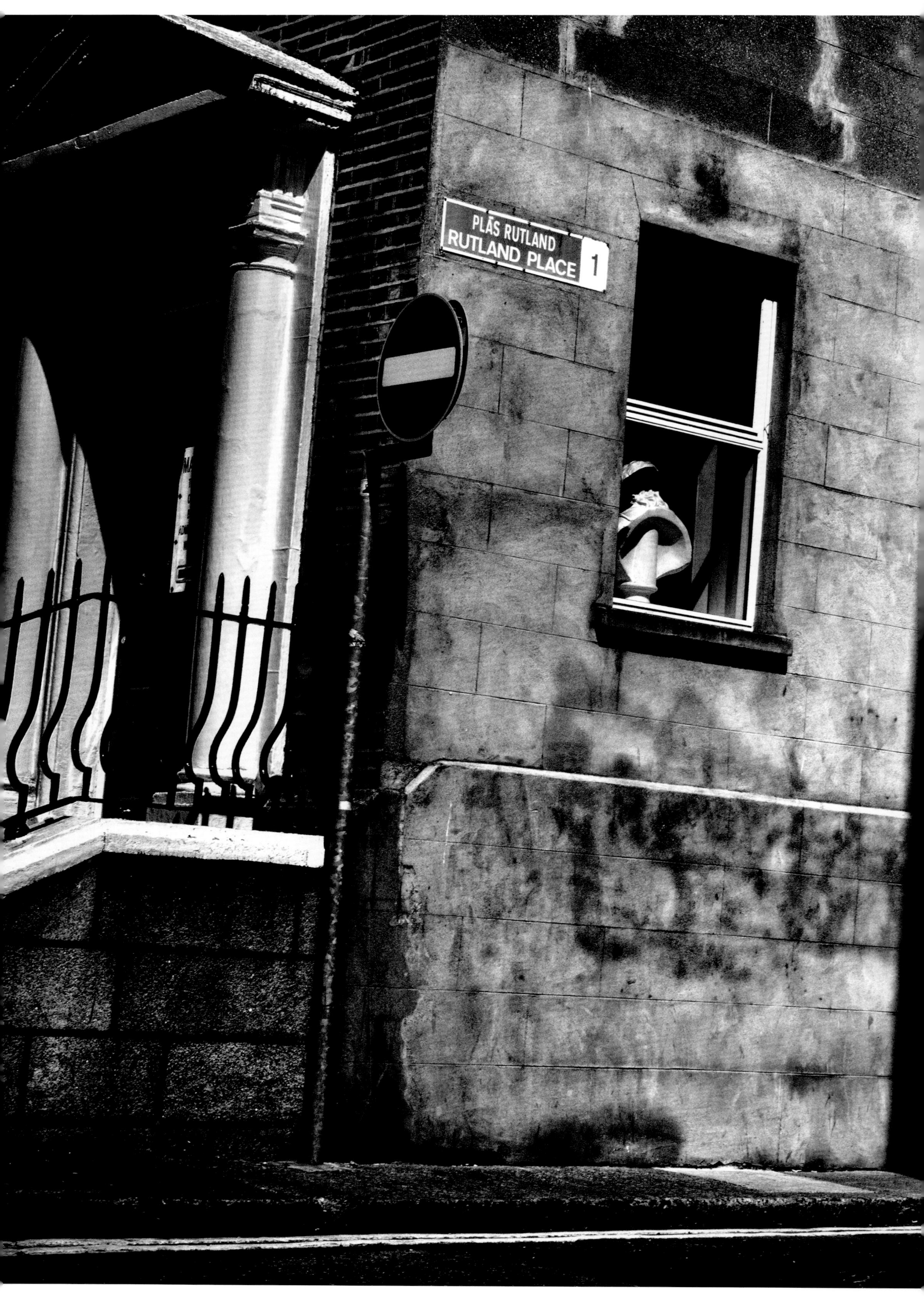

PLÂS RUTLAND
RUTLAND PLACE 1

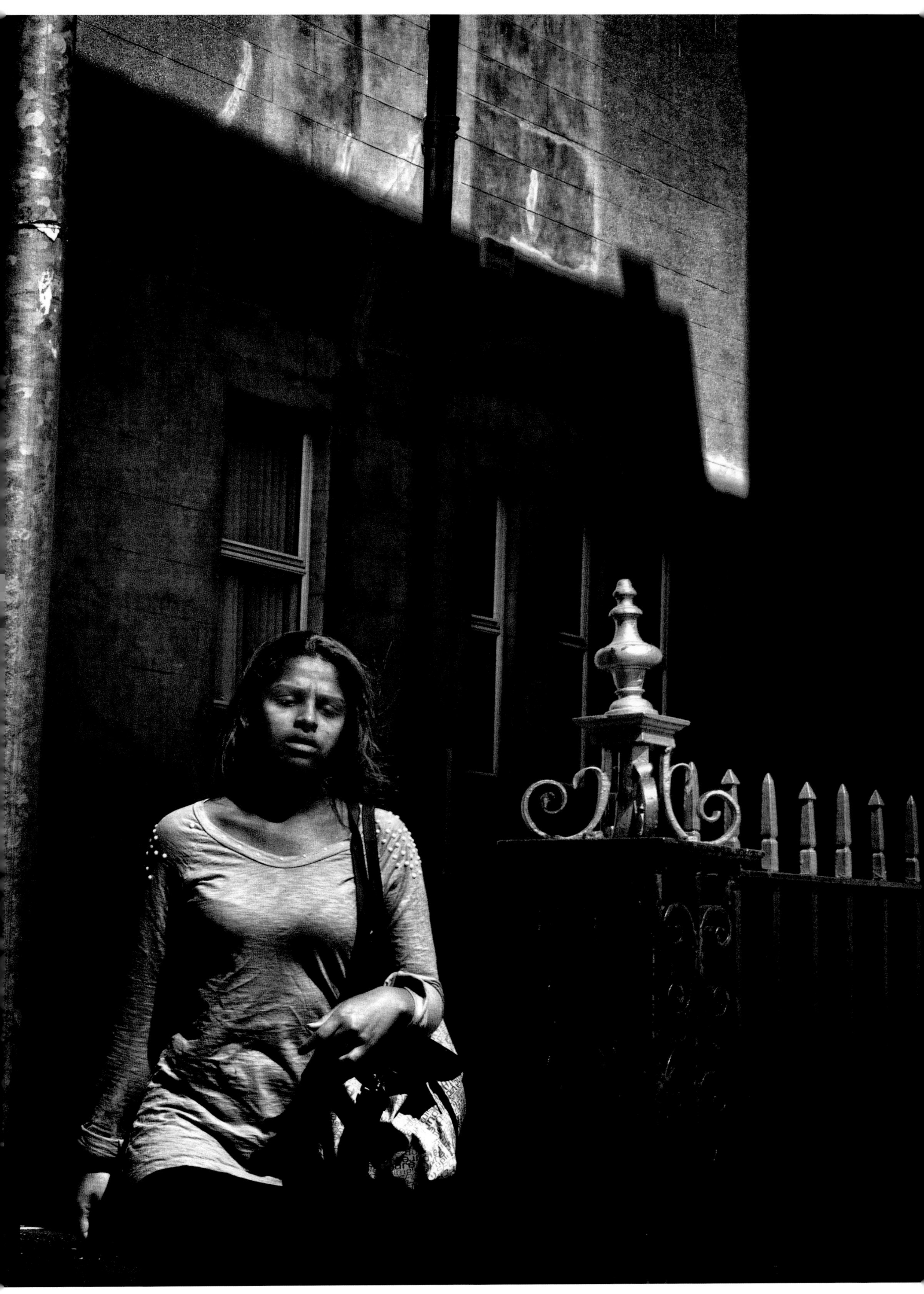

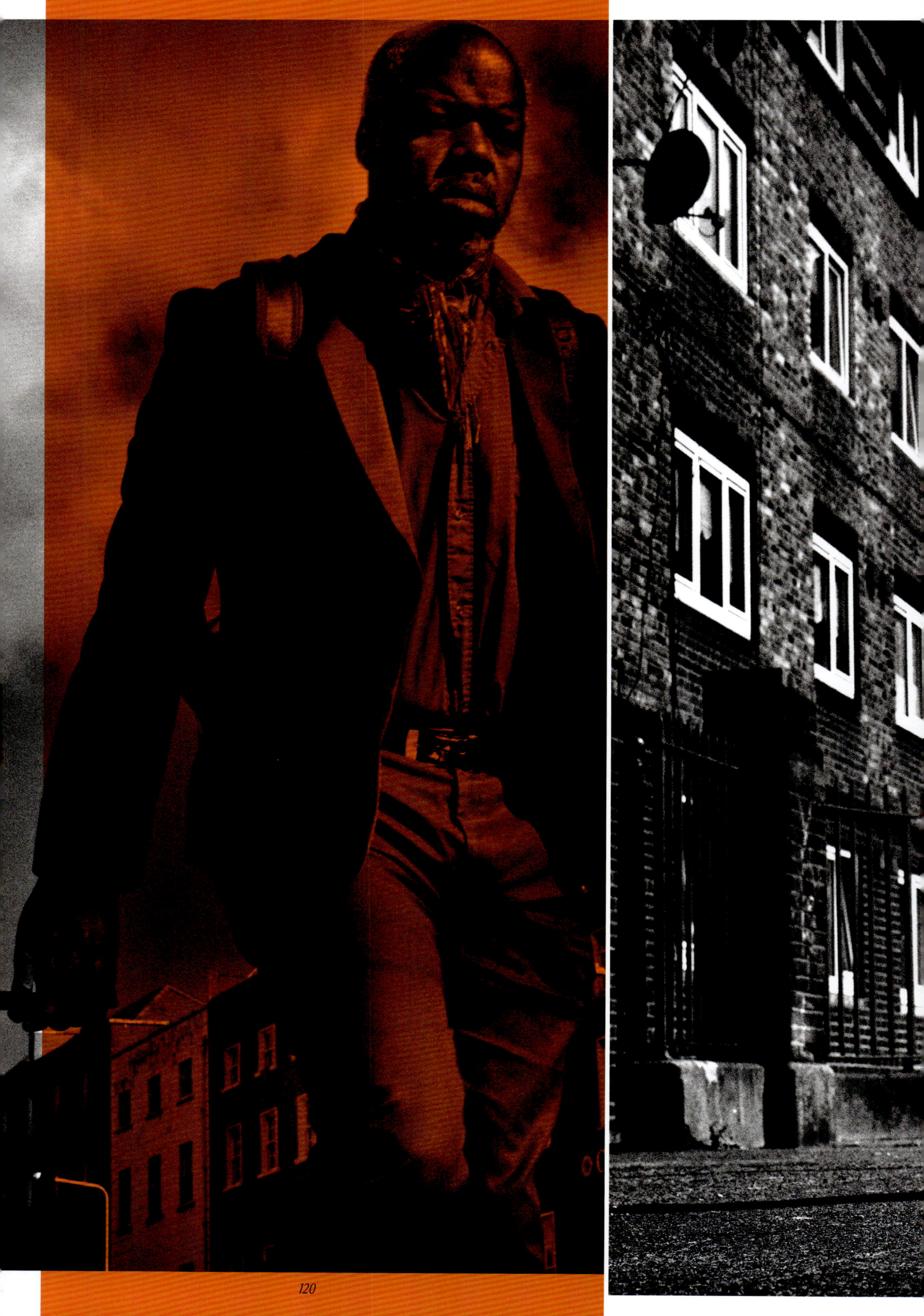

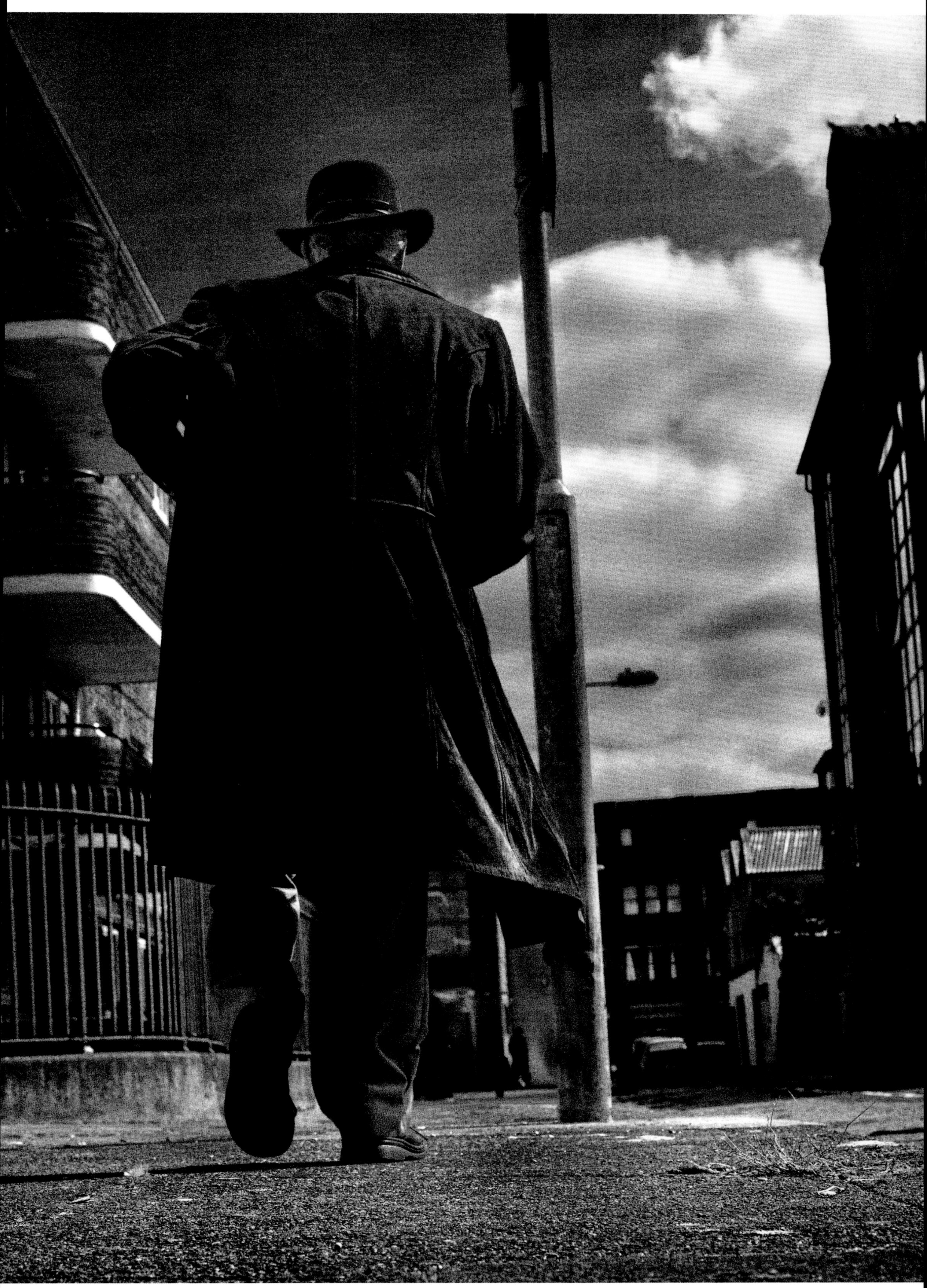

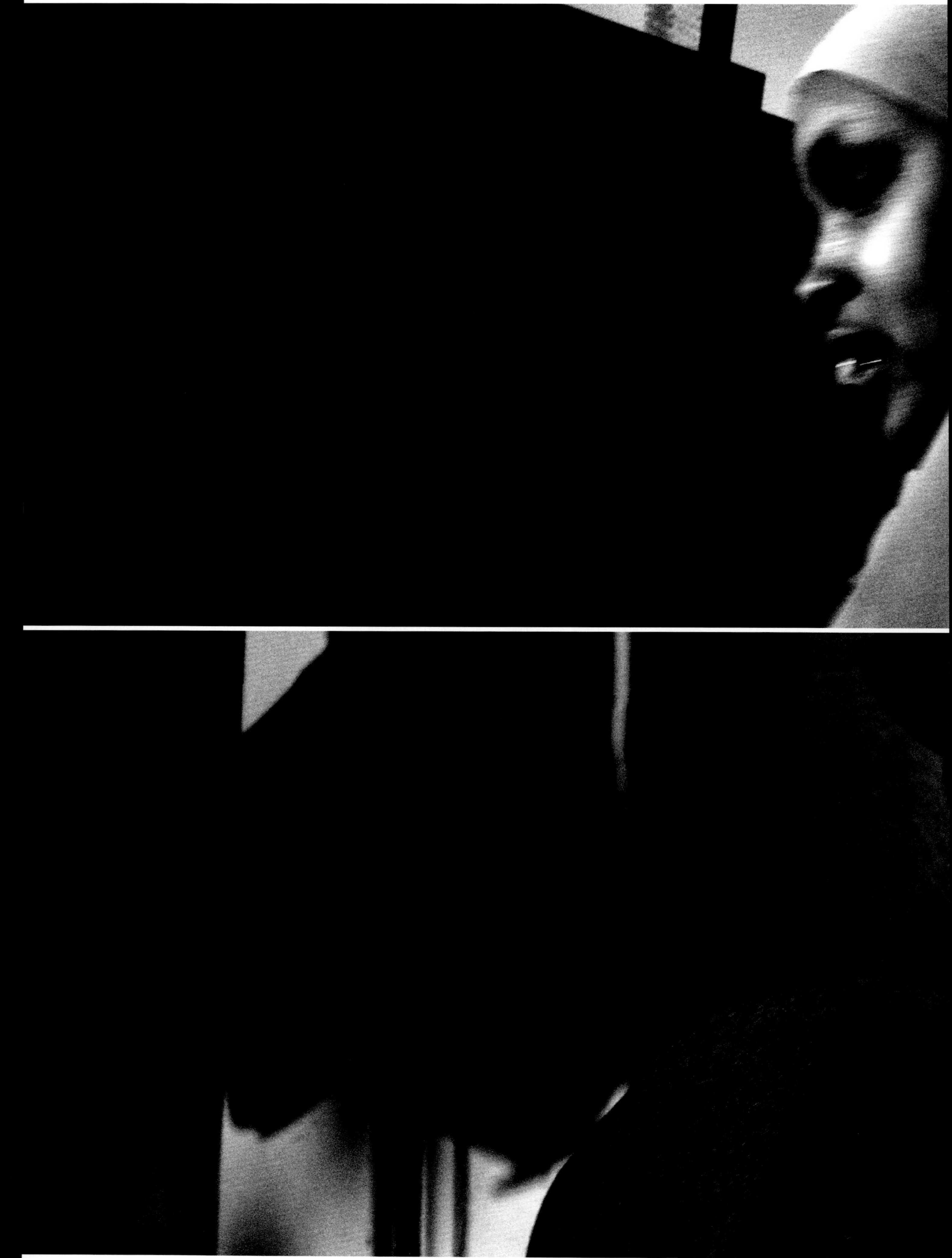

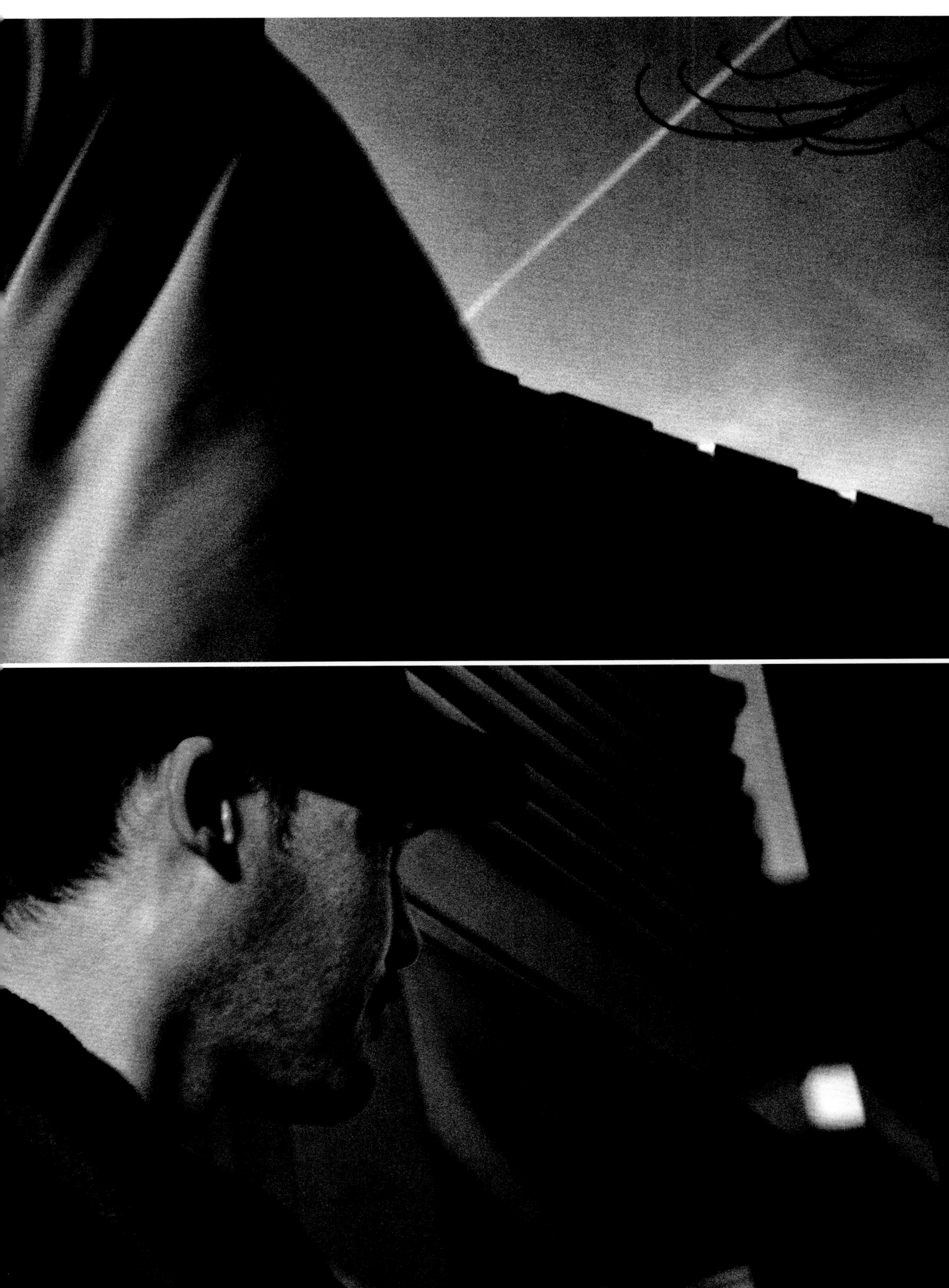

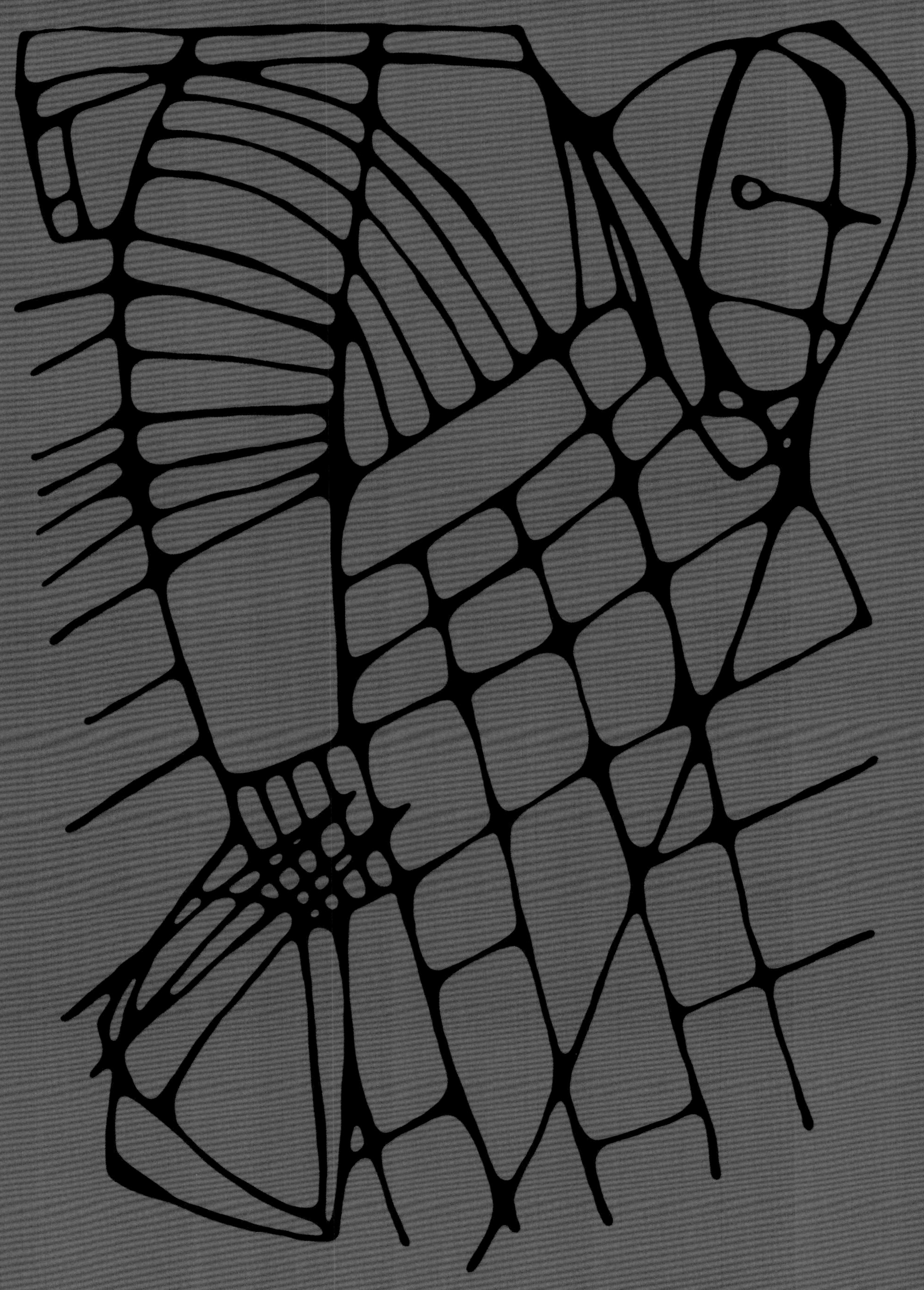

I LISTEN TO MONEY SINGING every day of my life. It is the mad song that sends me helter skelter around these streets. It calls to me from the high windows. It belts a brassy chorus from the rooftops. I try not to let it get into my head but it gets into my head and turns it into a sack of snakes.

Money makes my lips move as I walk down the street. I do my sums on my lips as I wait for the lights to change. Is it money that will tell me when my light turns green?

I am down on my knees for it.

I am racing through the night for it.

I am hurting people for it.

I want it so very badly.

I need it right now.

But then at the edges of my life — and always this is towards the end of the day; it's a feeling of the dusklight — I can see the limits appear and I know that I will never have enough. I feel like I'm constantly battling through my life about, I don't know, about five grand short? Five grand would sort out absolutely fuckloads. But where is it going to come from?

I can hear money singing to me in the night. It is like the taunting of an old love song. It says that I am all you'll ever need of sweetness and light — this is what money sings to me.

Money could turn my life into cinema.

I can taste it on my lips.

I need its protein and its salt.

I need its sugar-love.

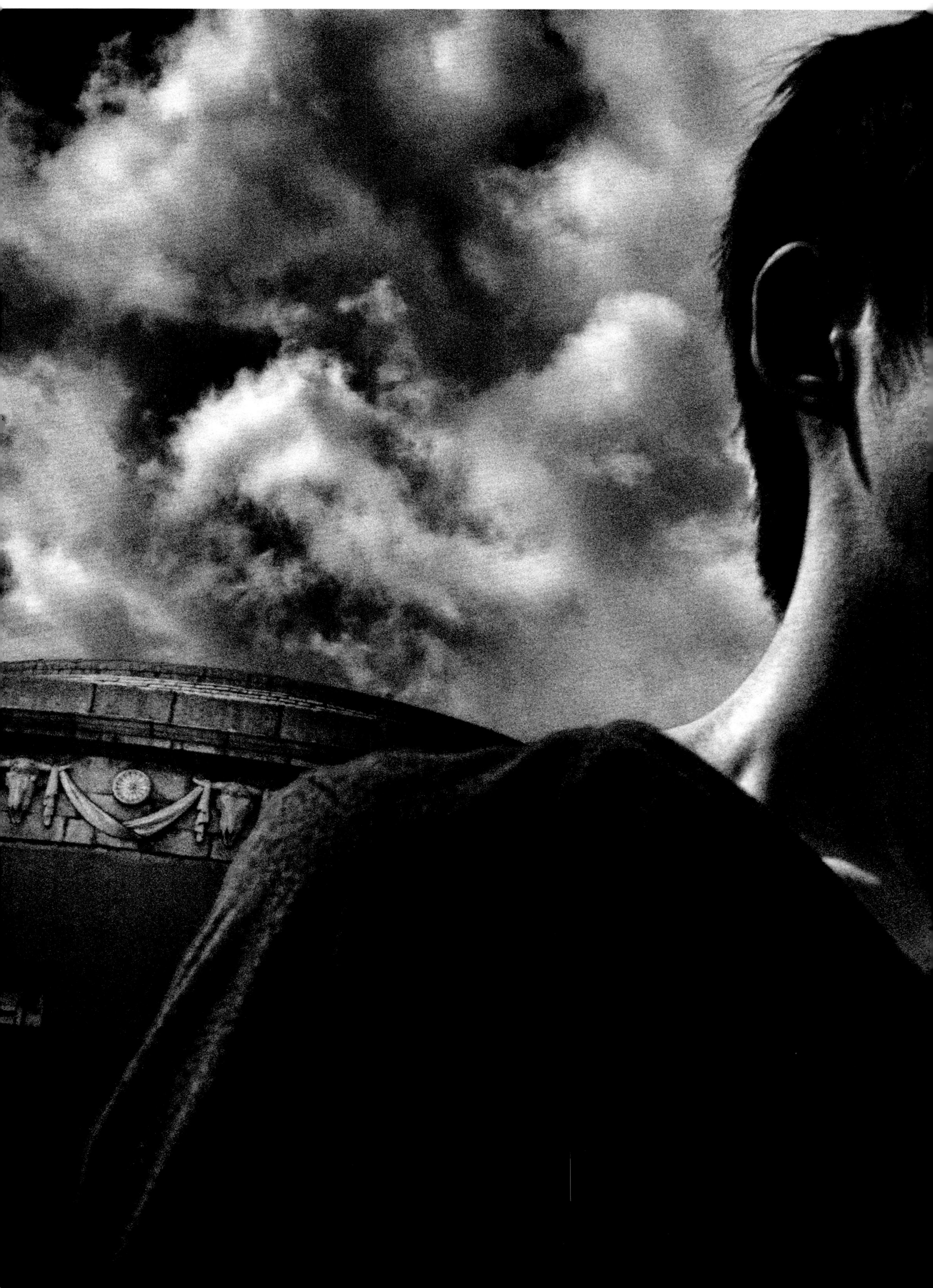

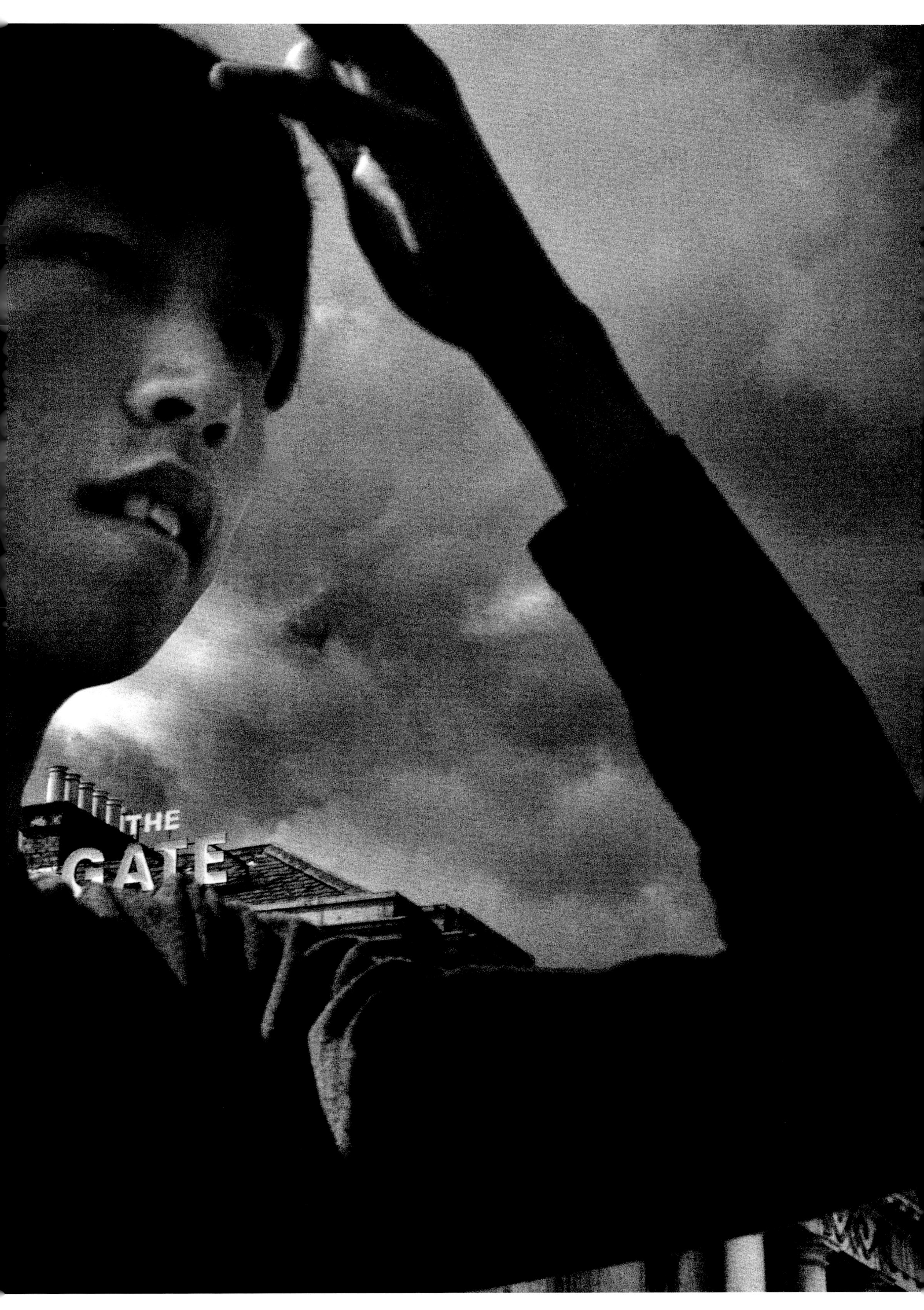
THE
GATE

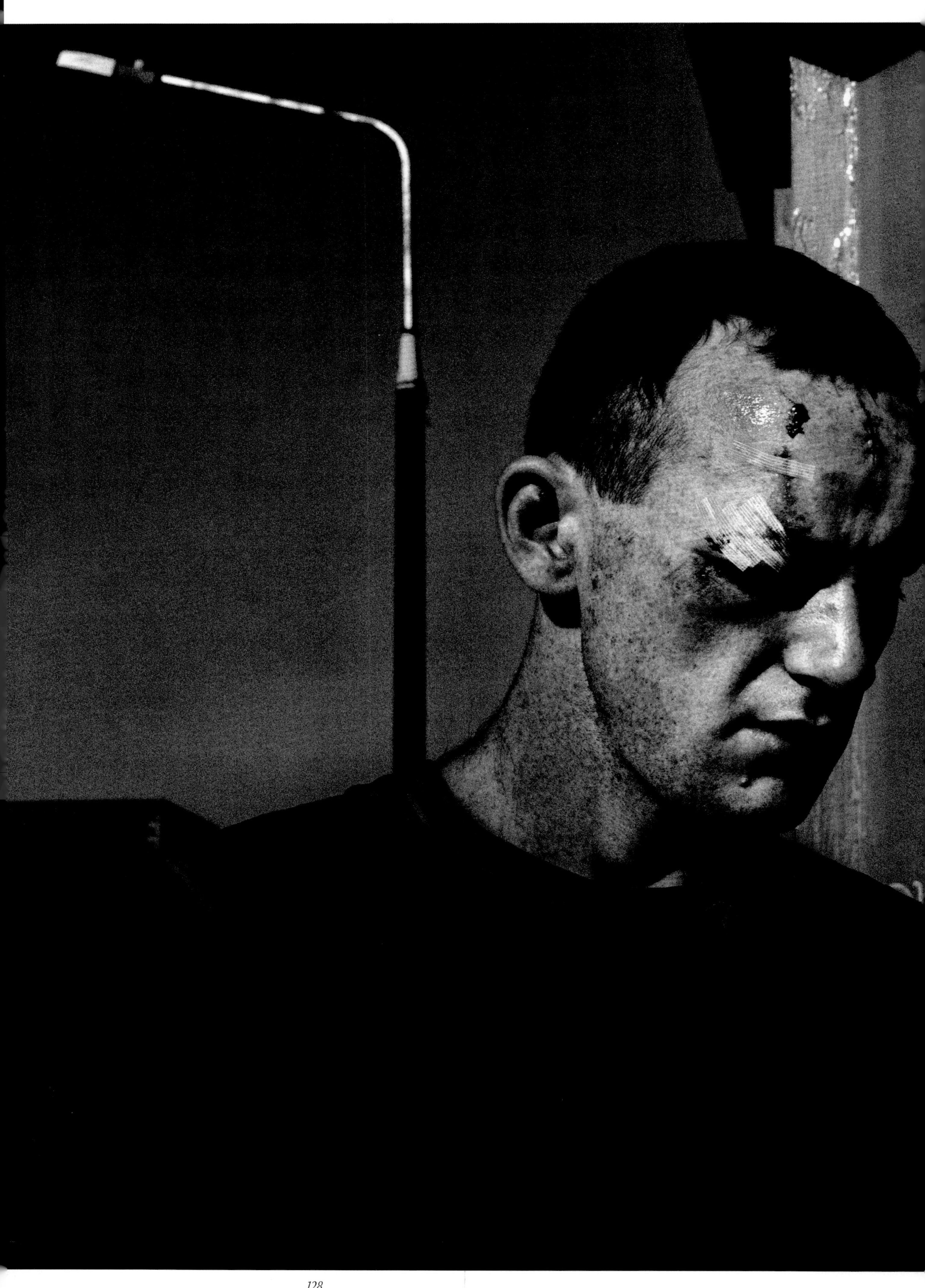

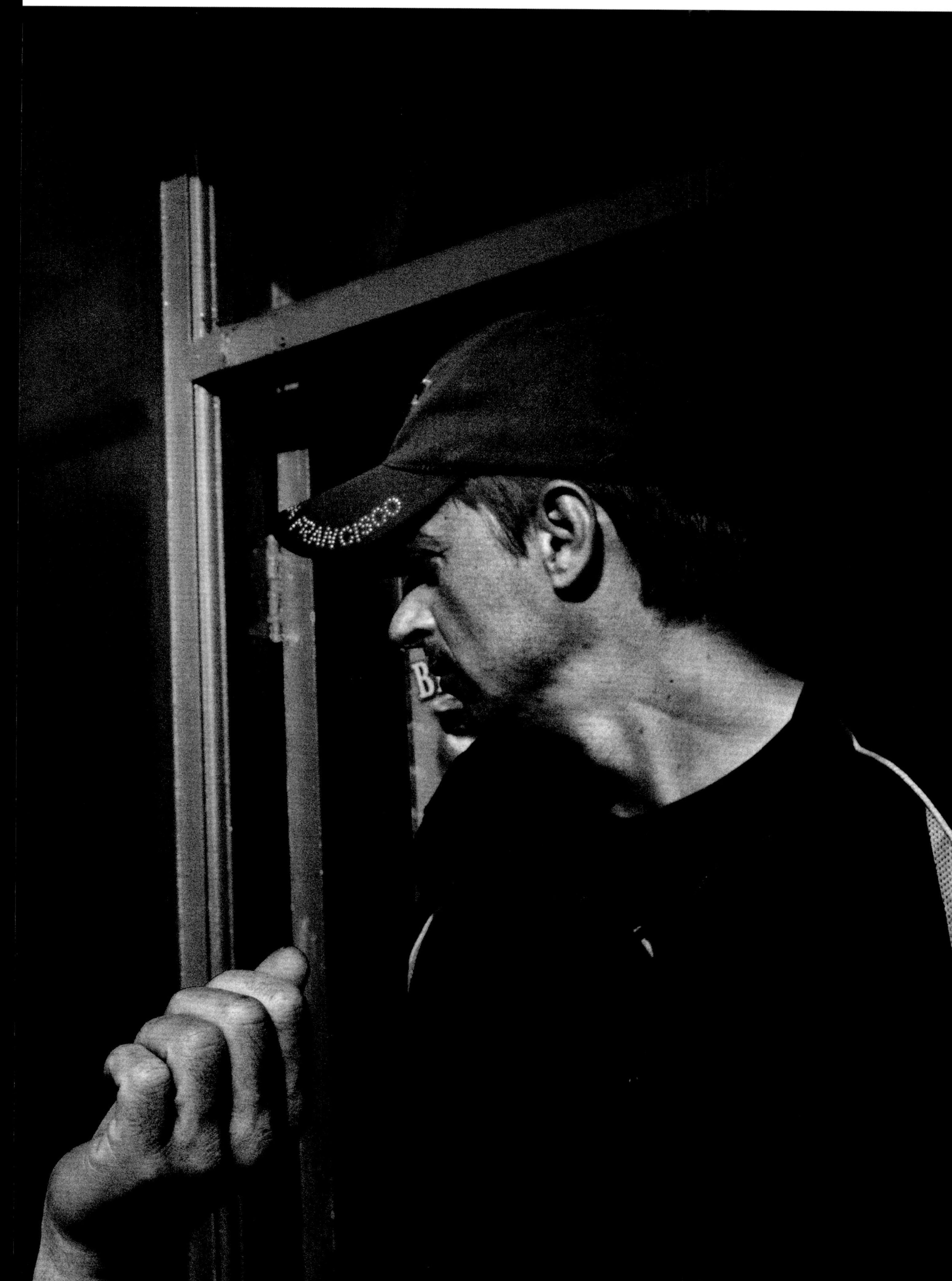

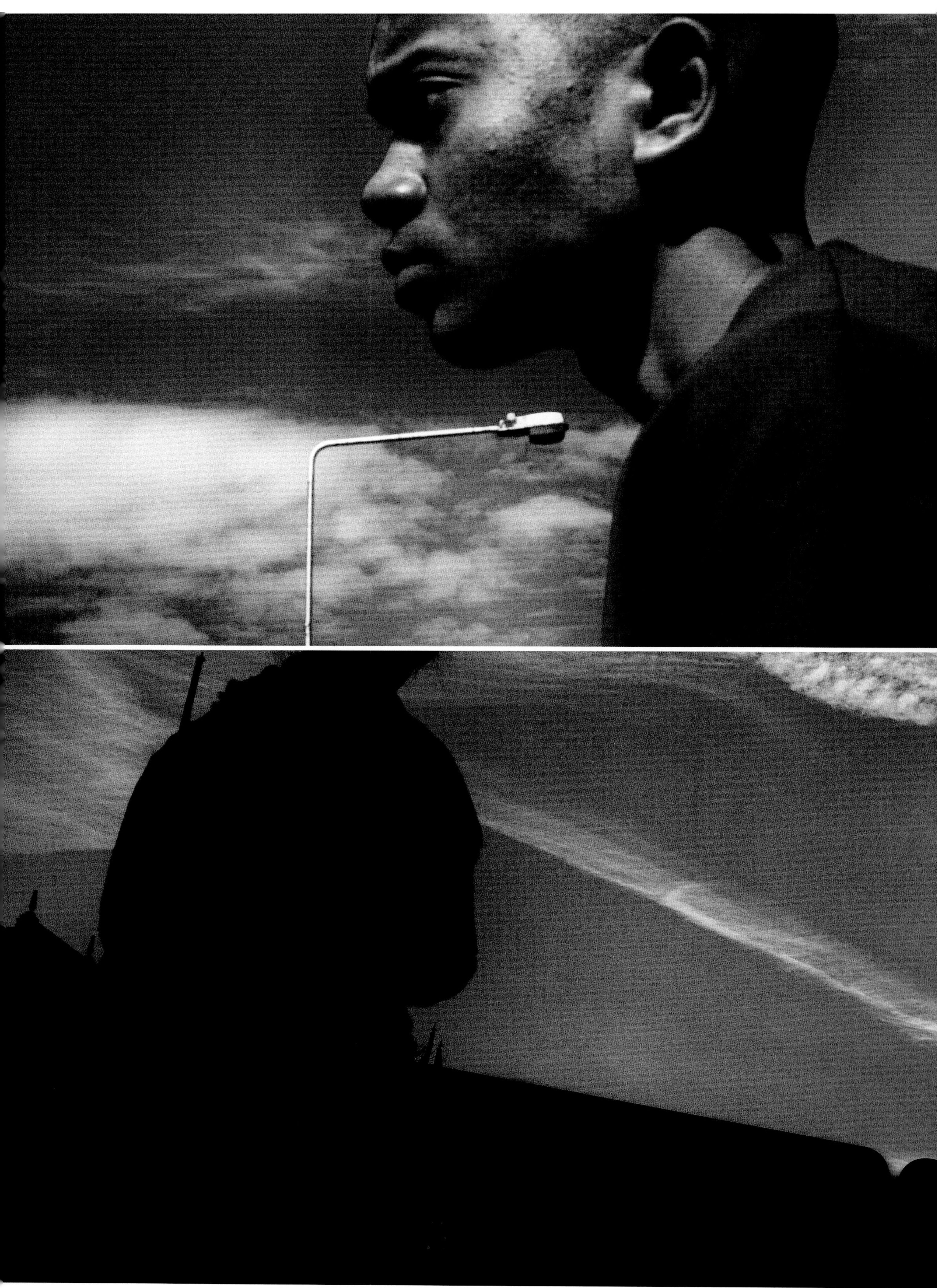

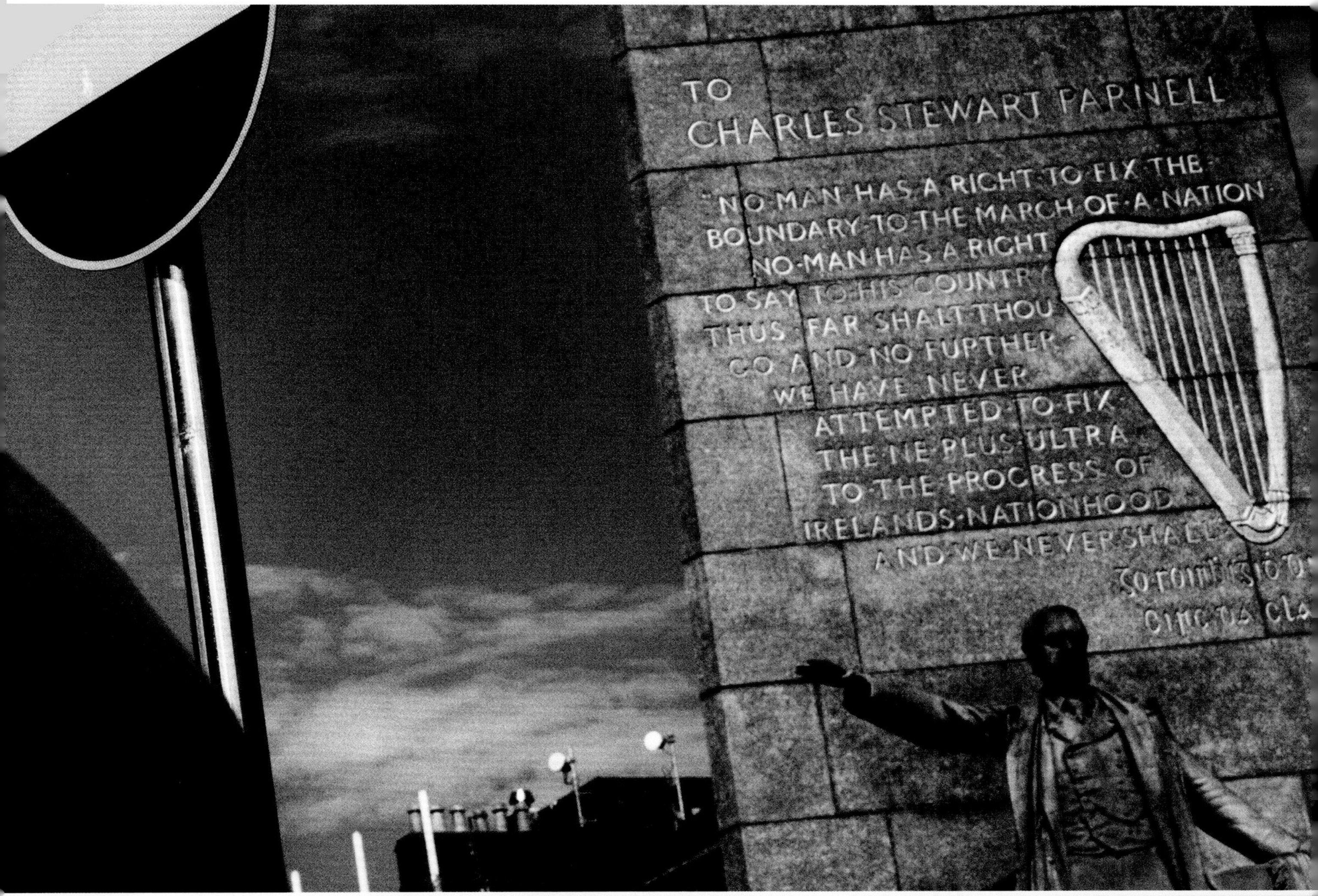

TO
CHARLES STEWART PARNELL
"NO MAN HAS A RIGHT TO FIX THE
BOUNDARY TO THE MARCH OF A NATION
NO MAN HAS A RIGHT
TO SAY TO HIS COUNTRY
THUS FAR SHALT THOU
GO AND NO FURTHER
WE HAVE NEVER
ATTEMPTED TO FIX
THE NE PLUS ULTRA
TO THE PROGRESS OF
IRELANDS NATIONHOOD
AND WE NEVER SHALL

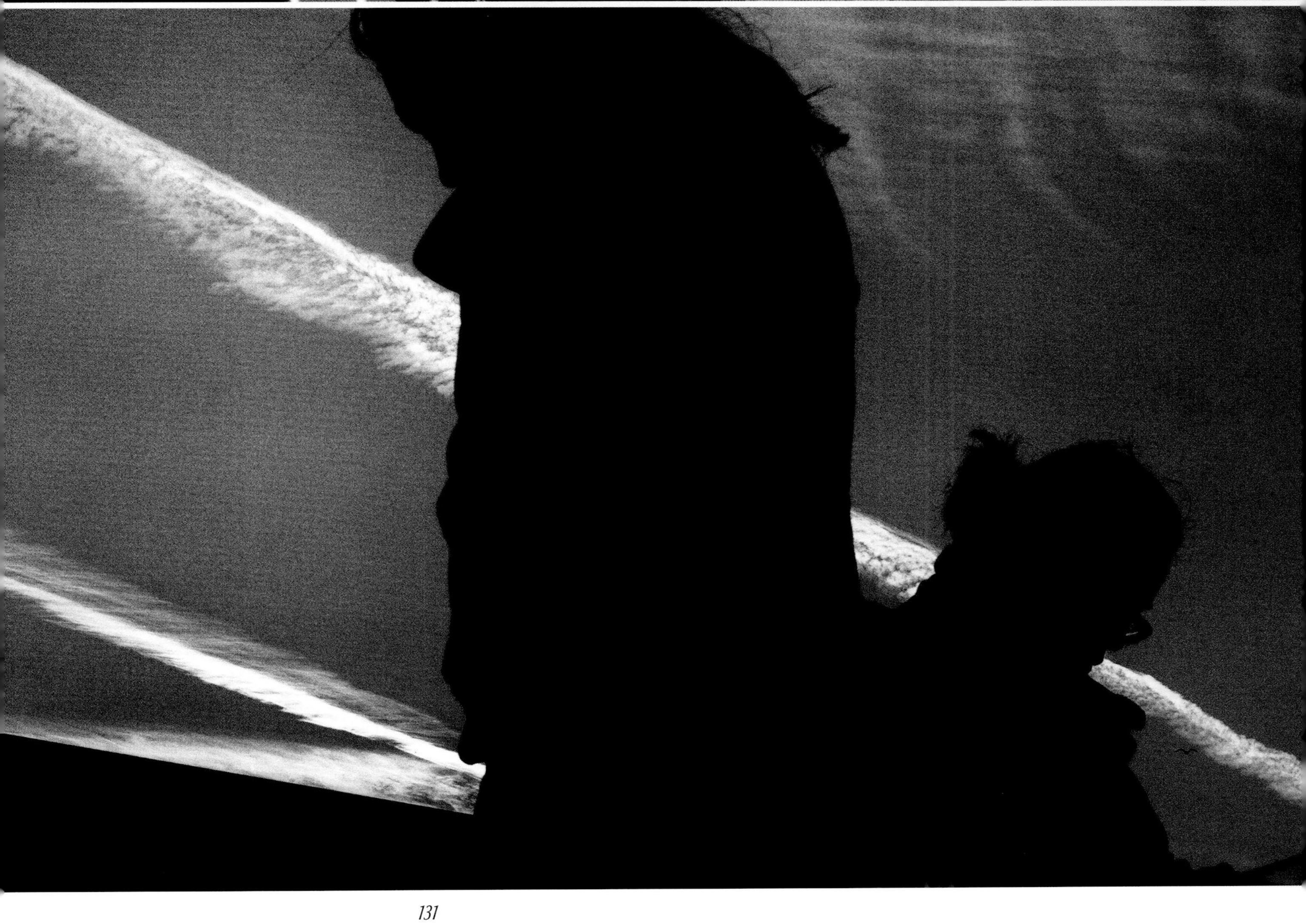

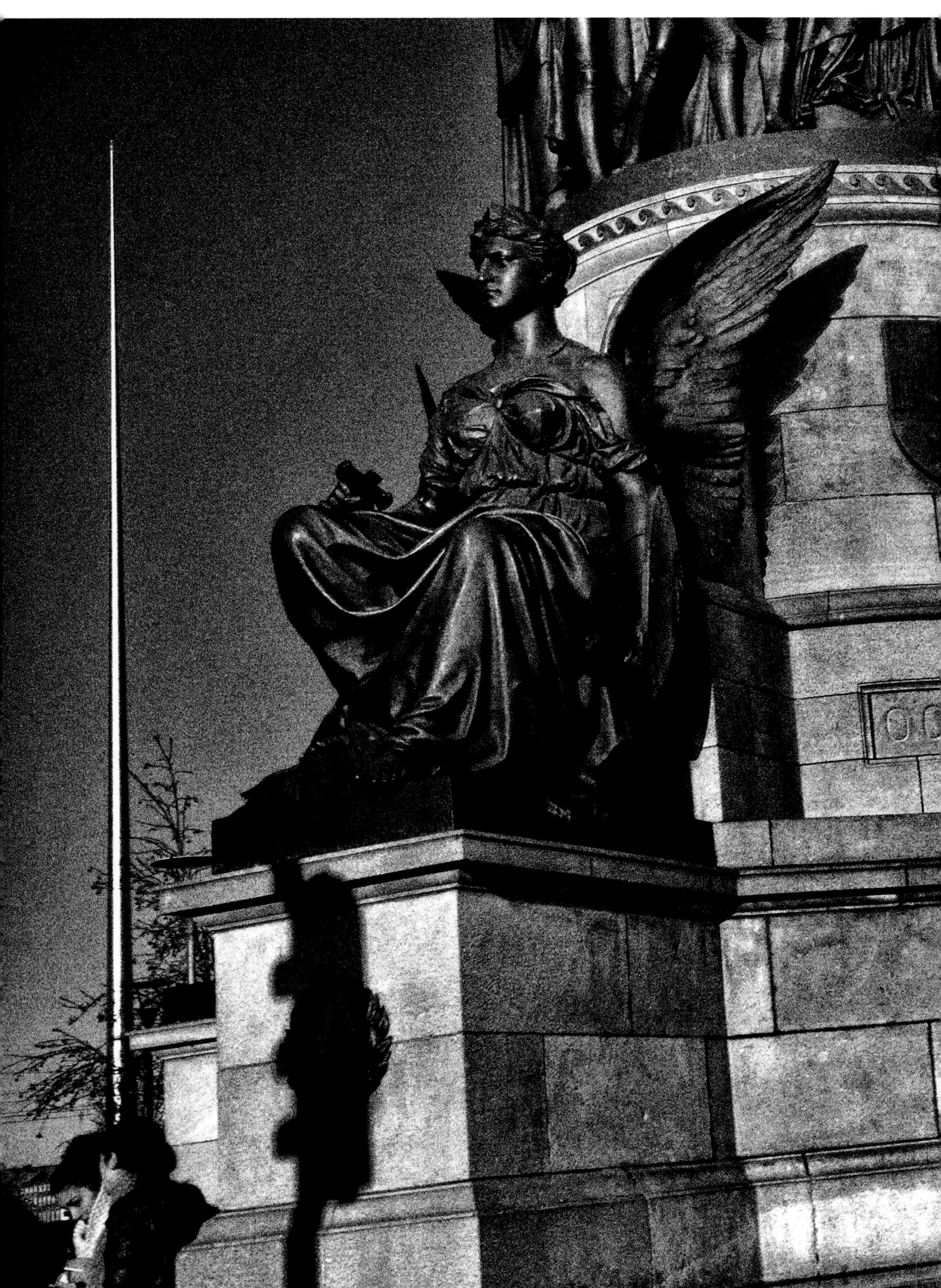

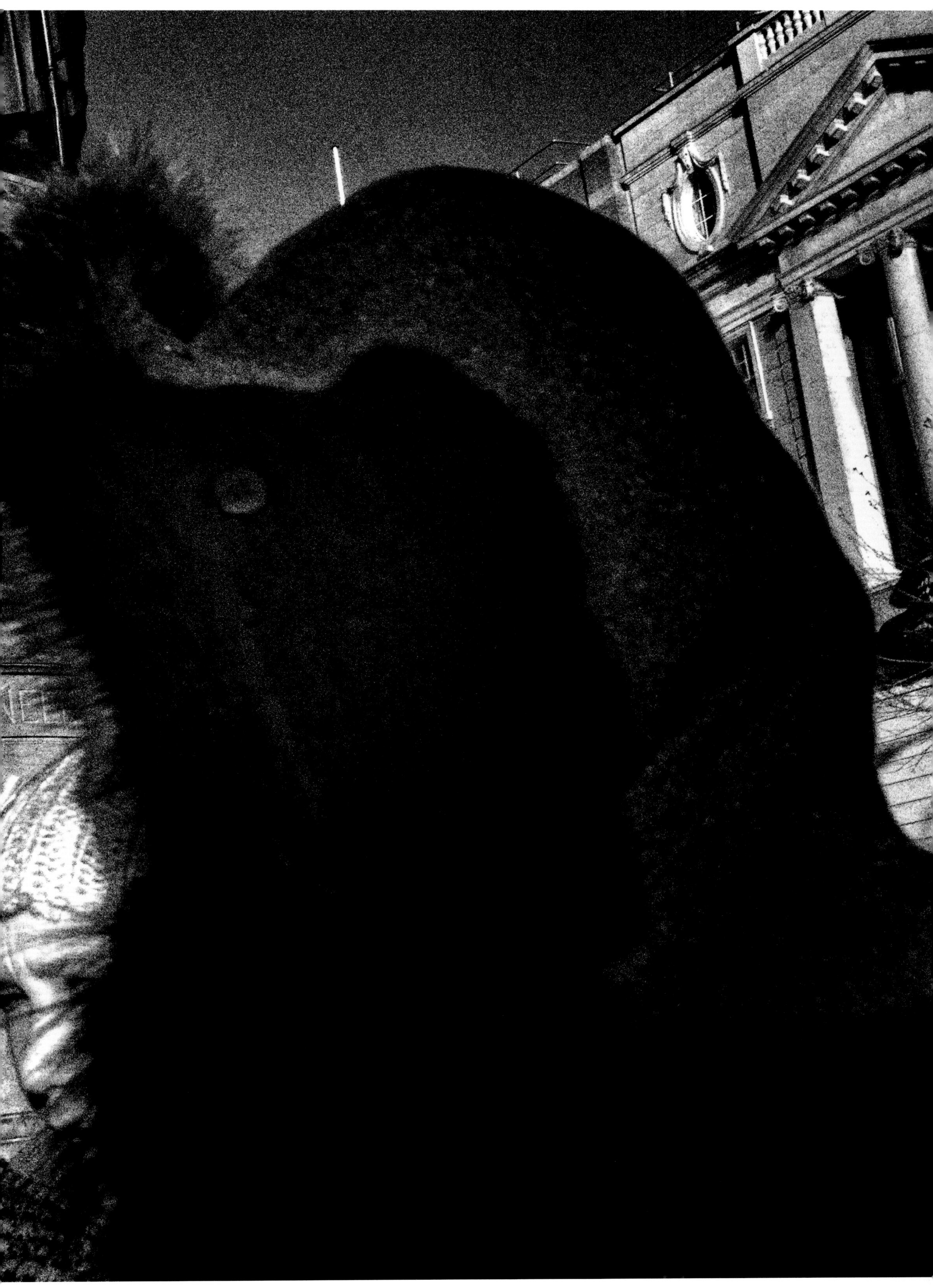

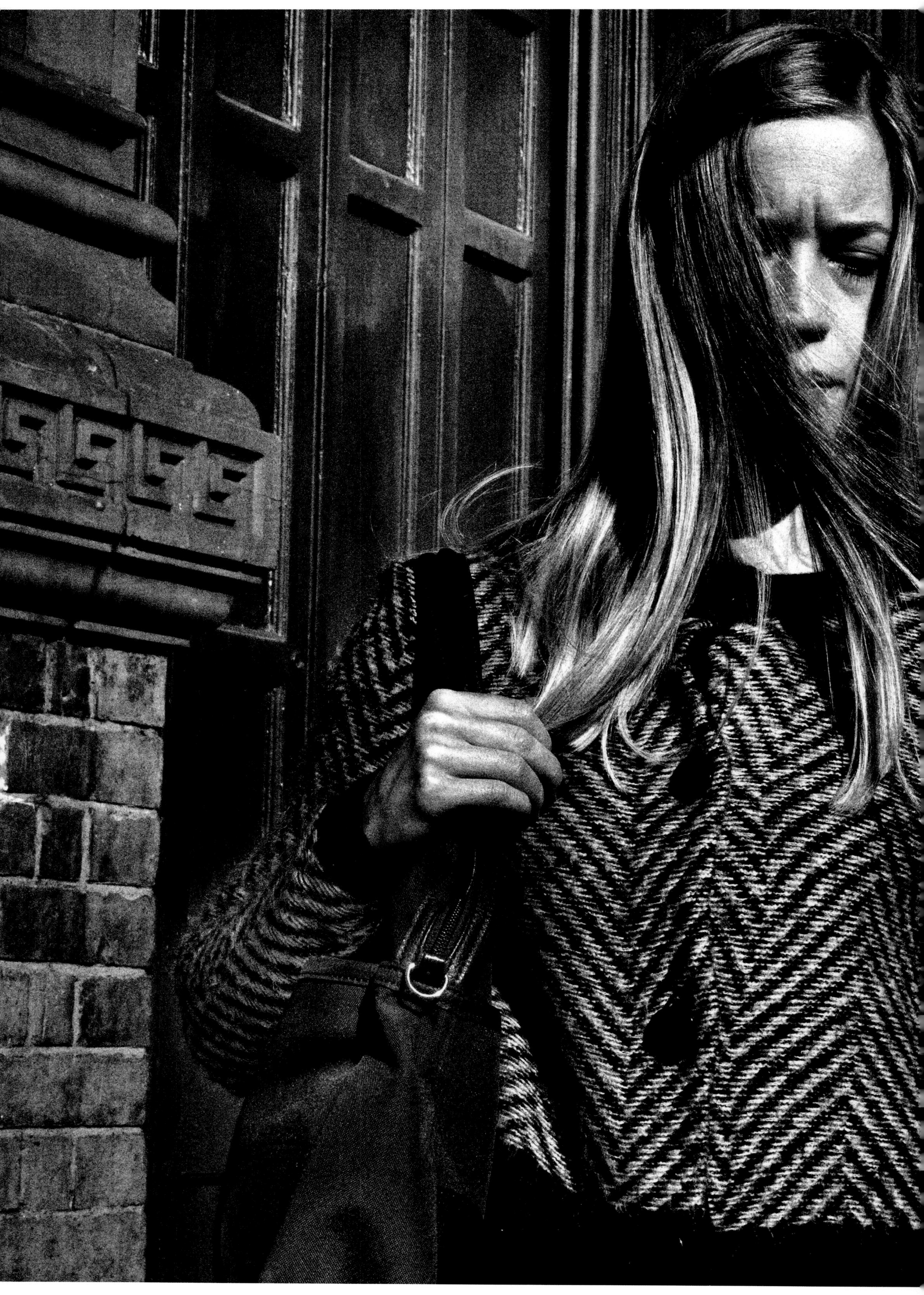

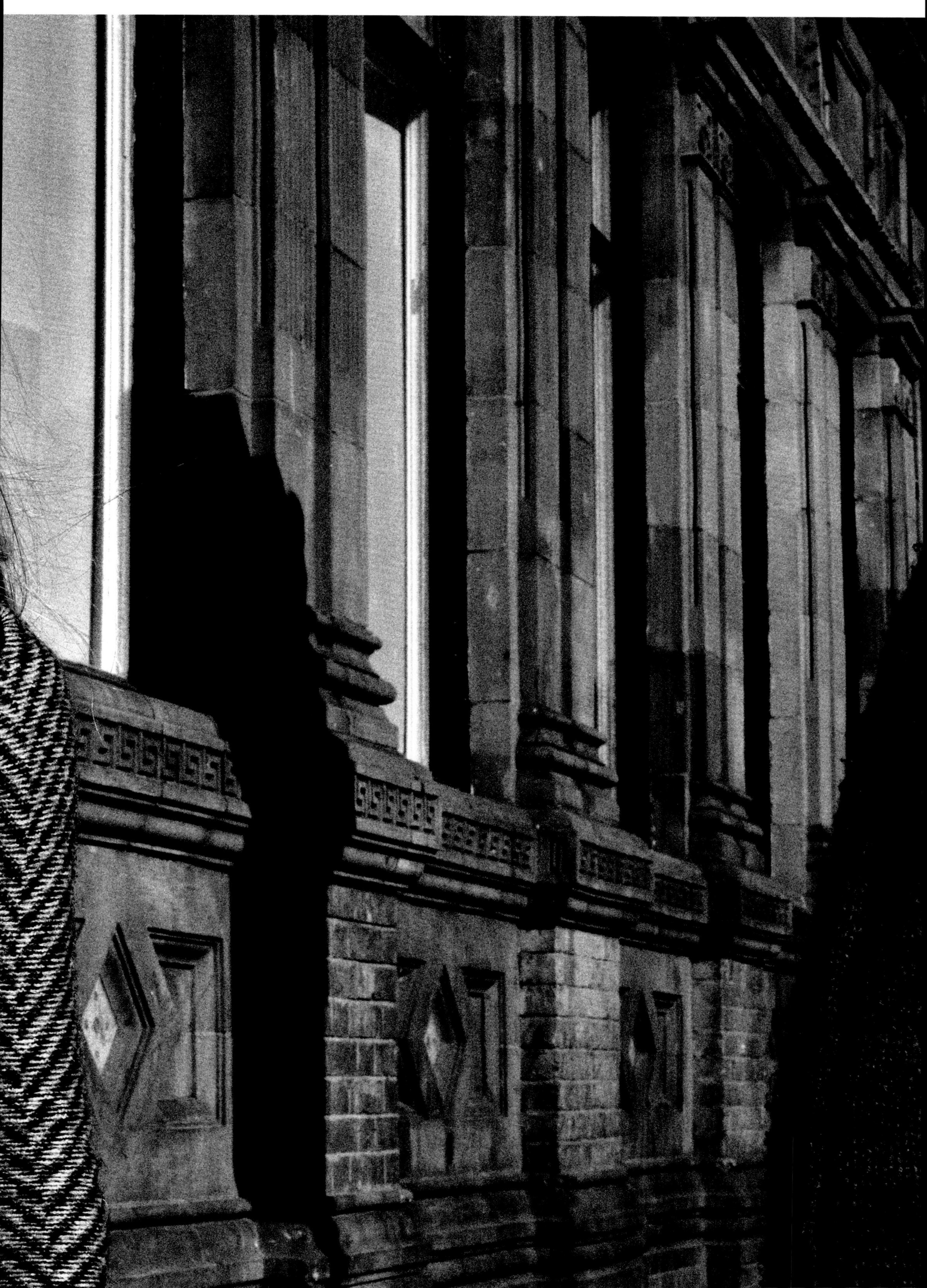

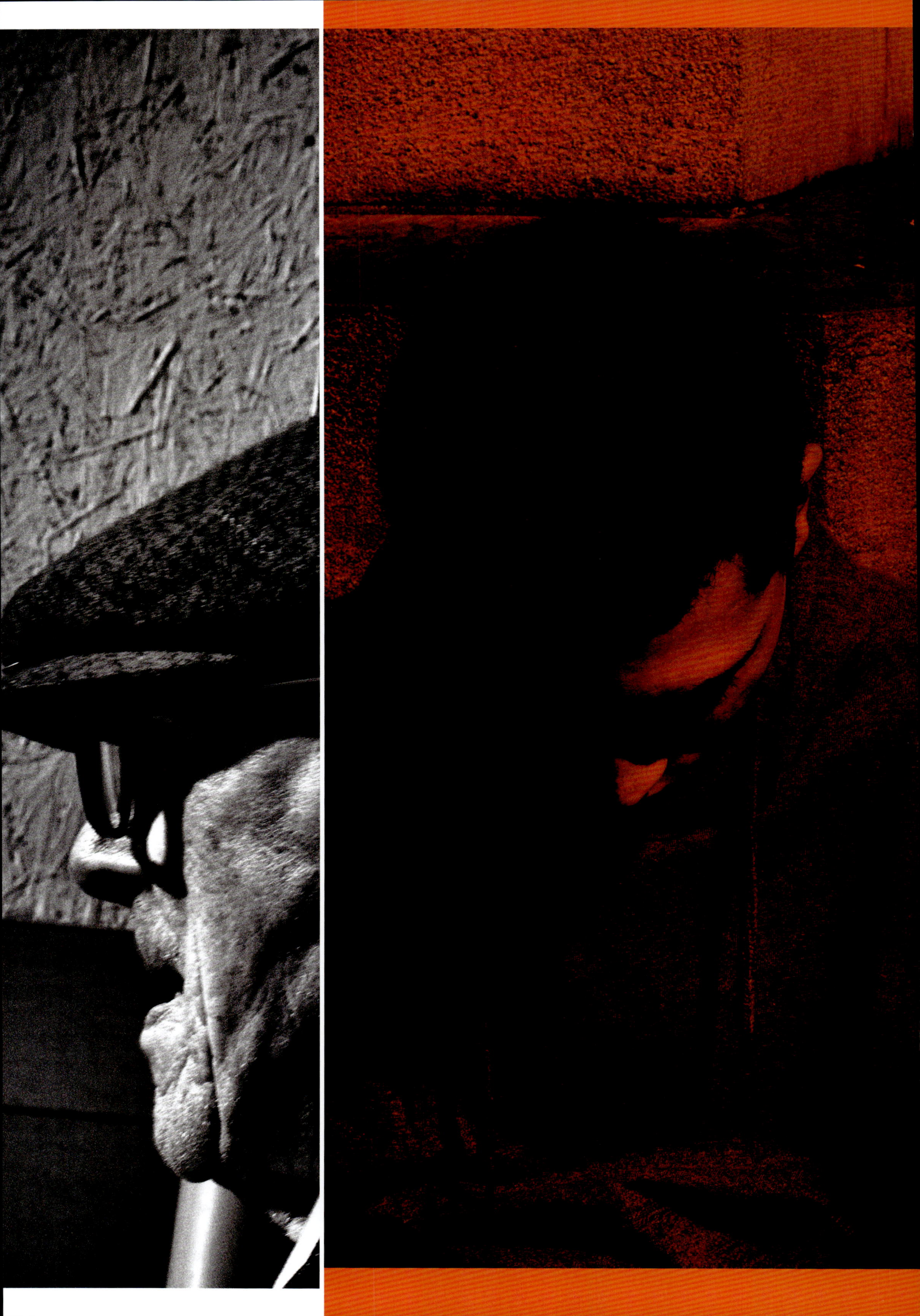

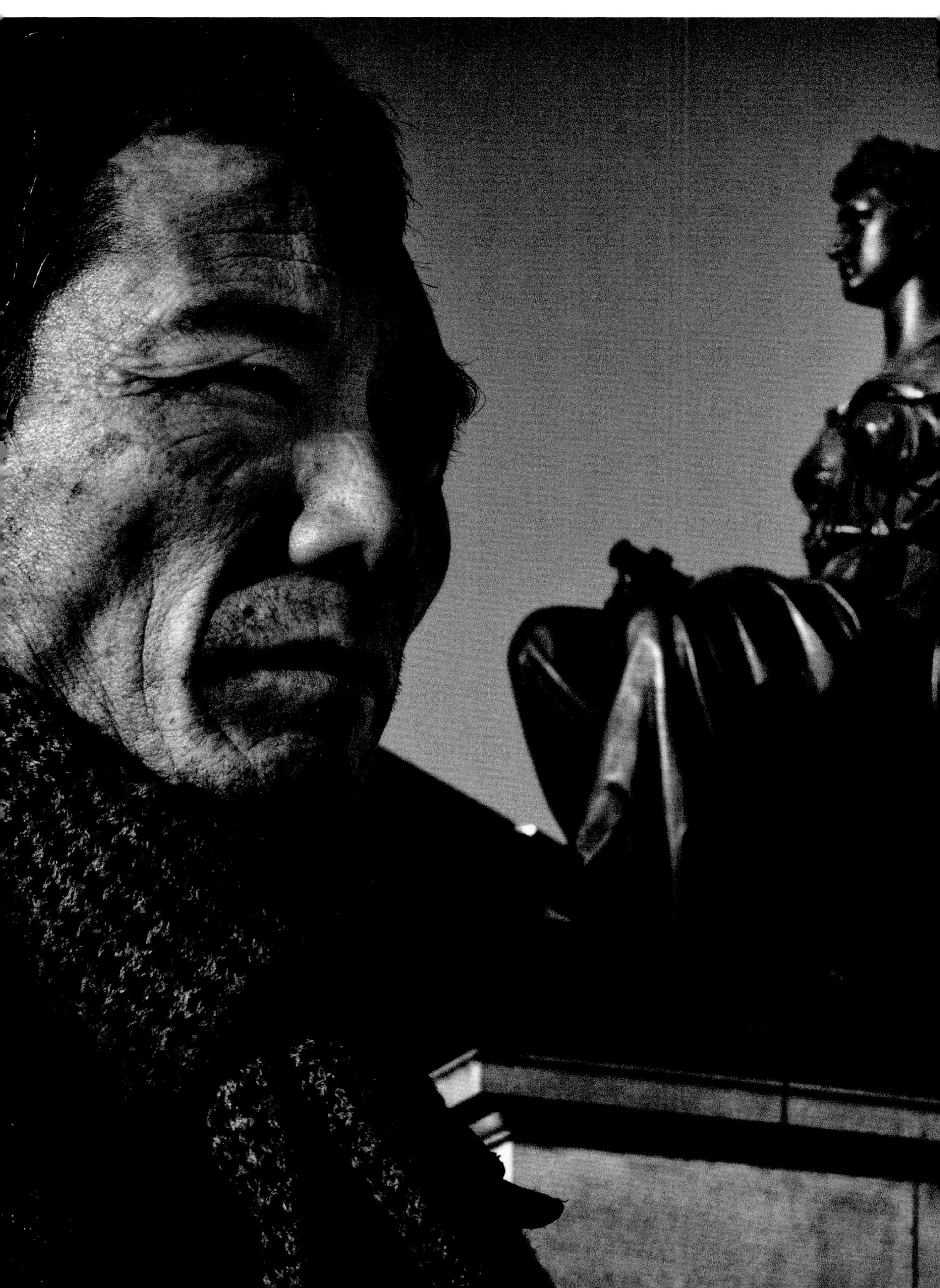

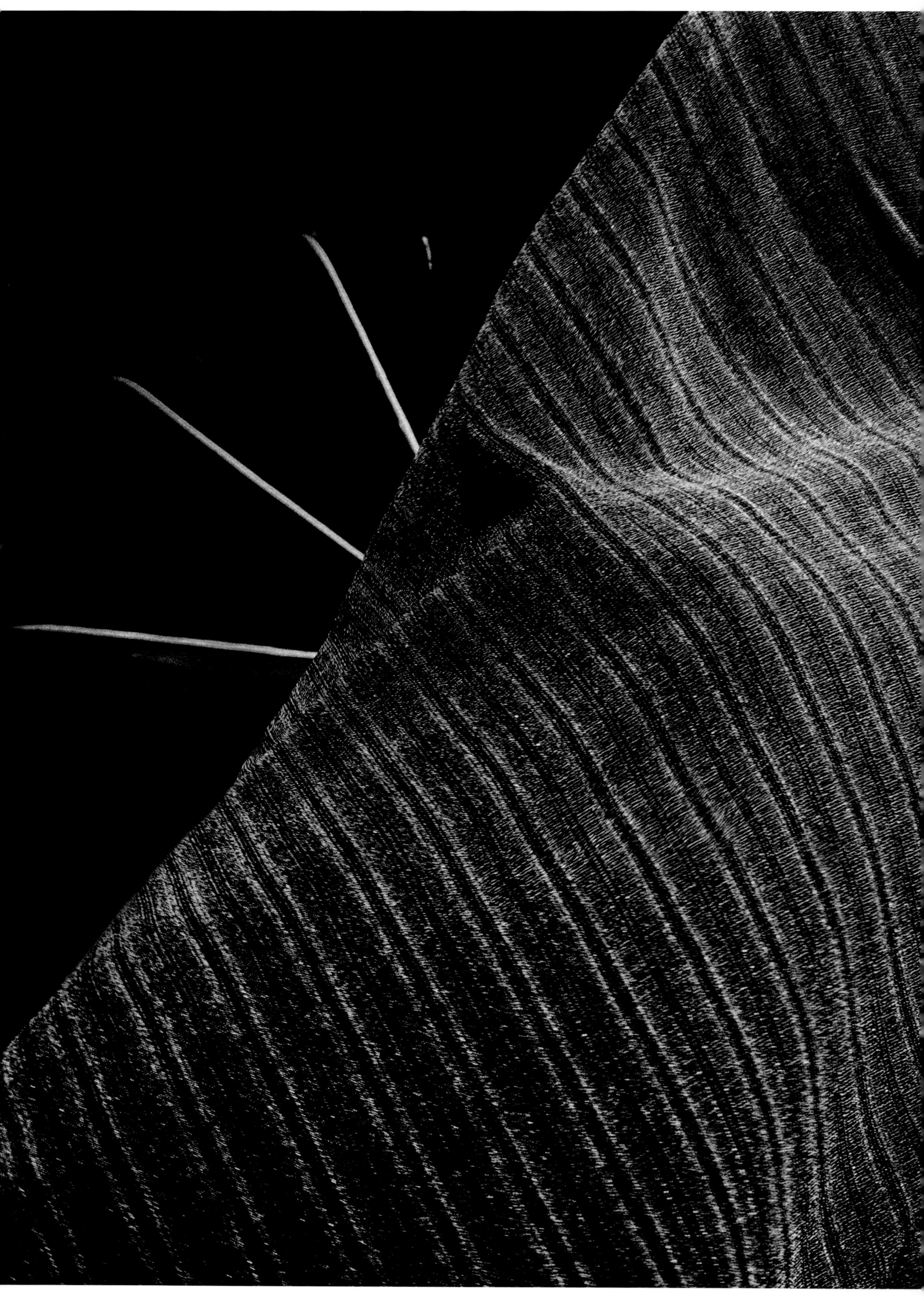

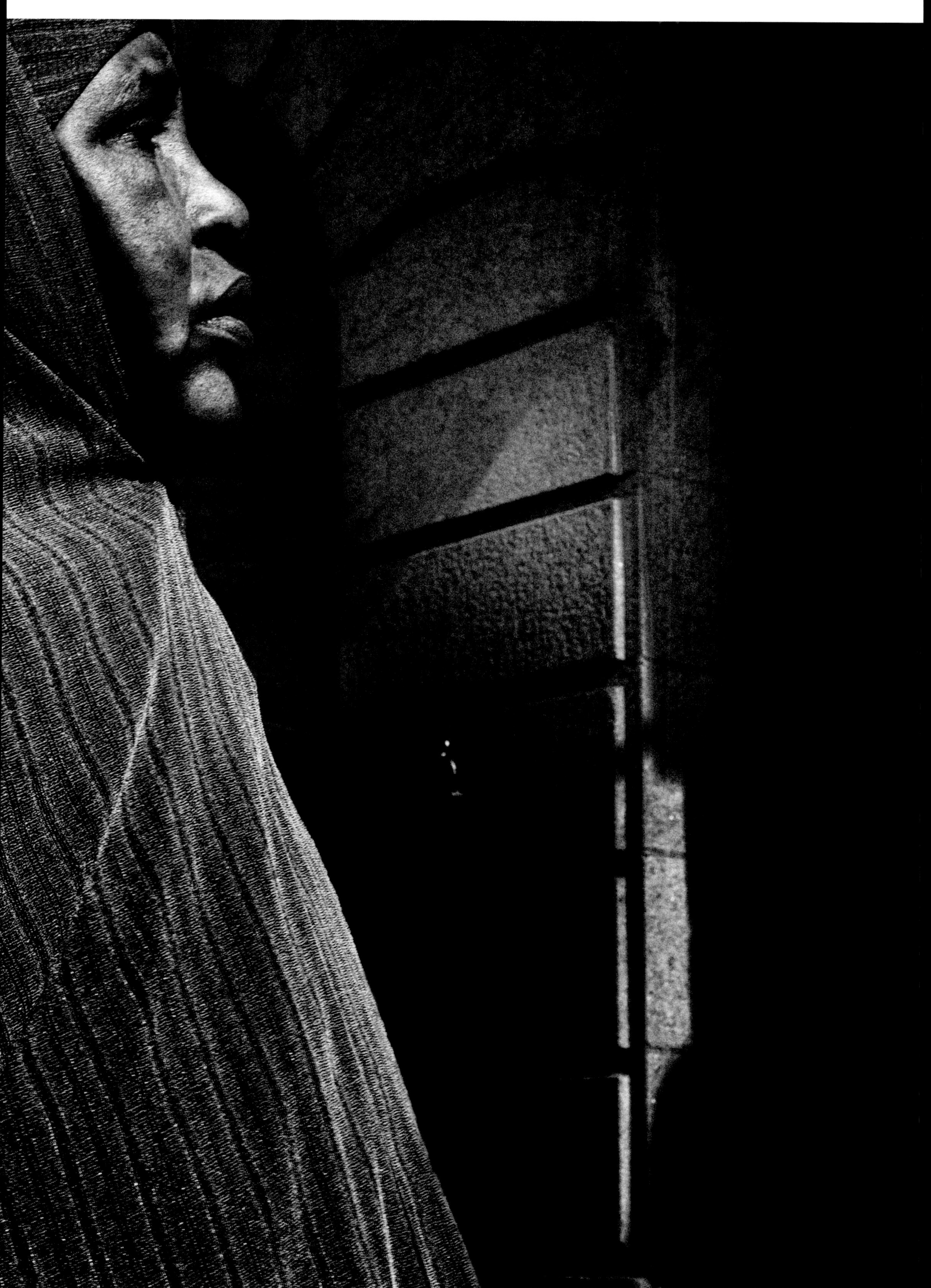

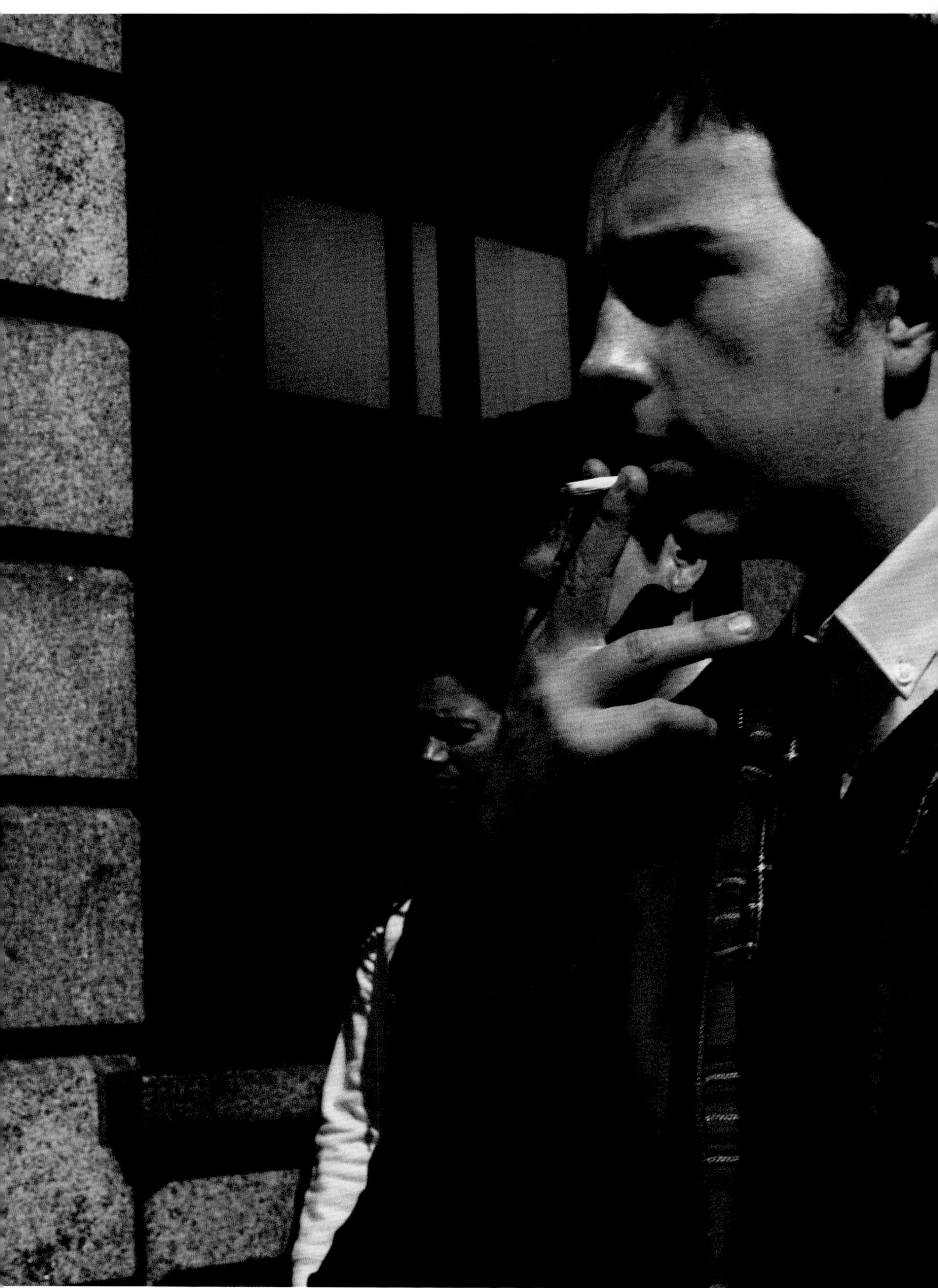

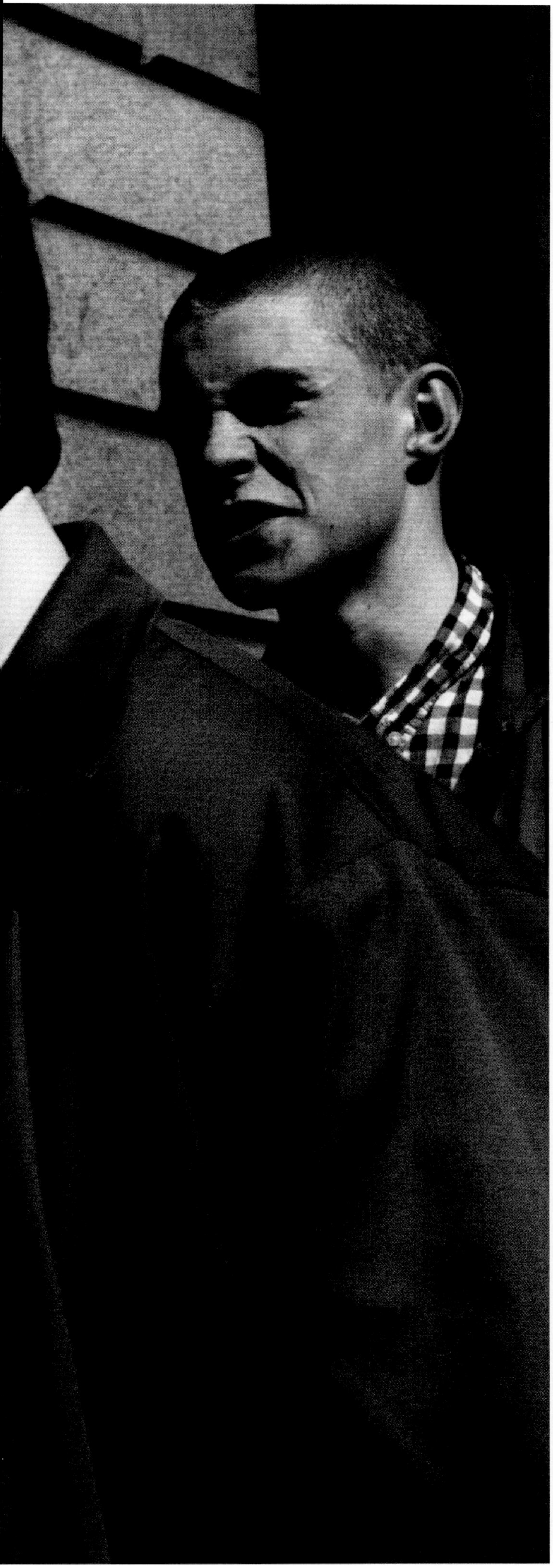

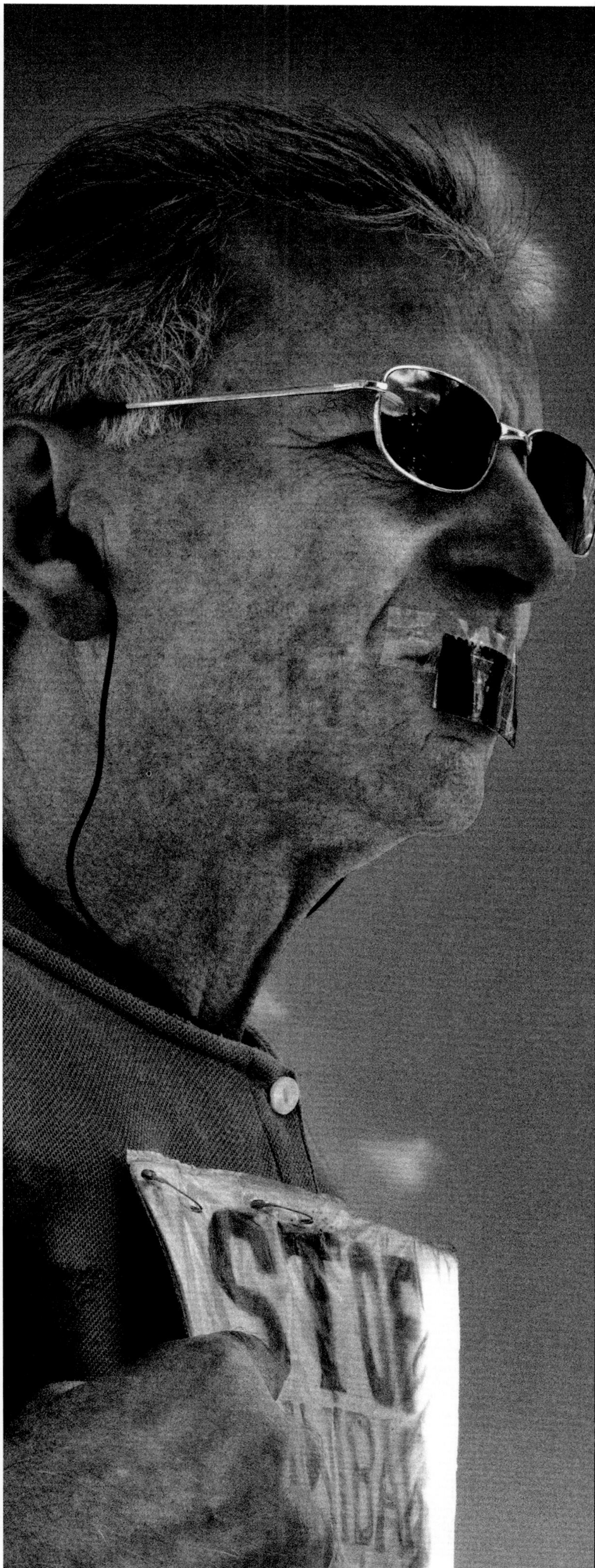

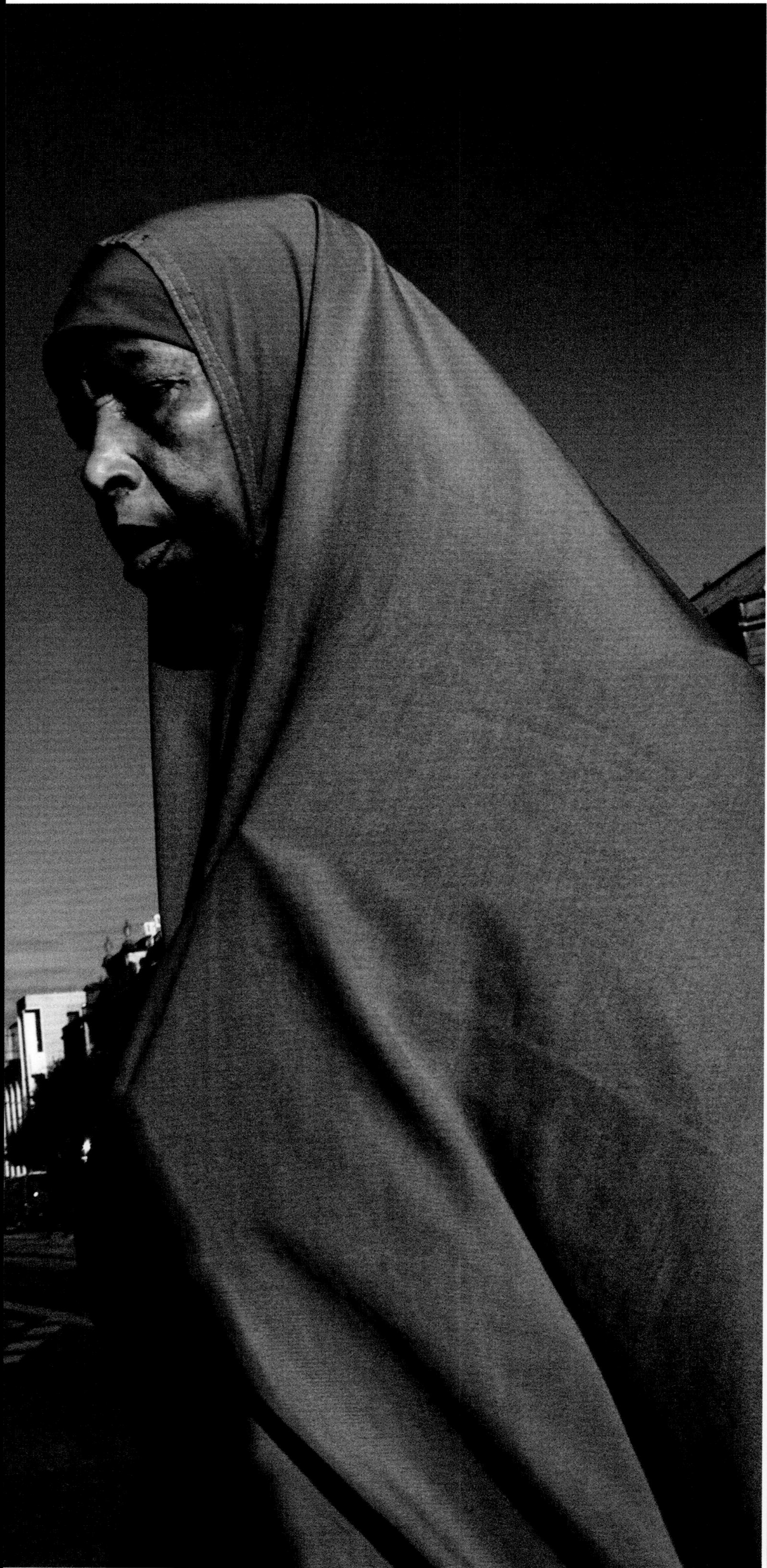

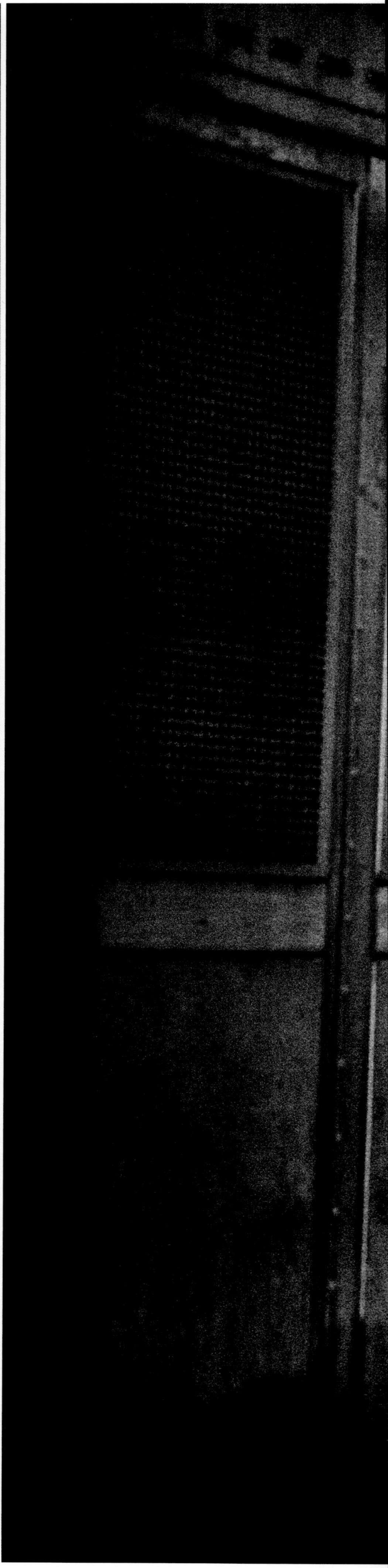

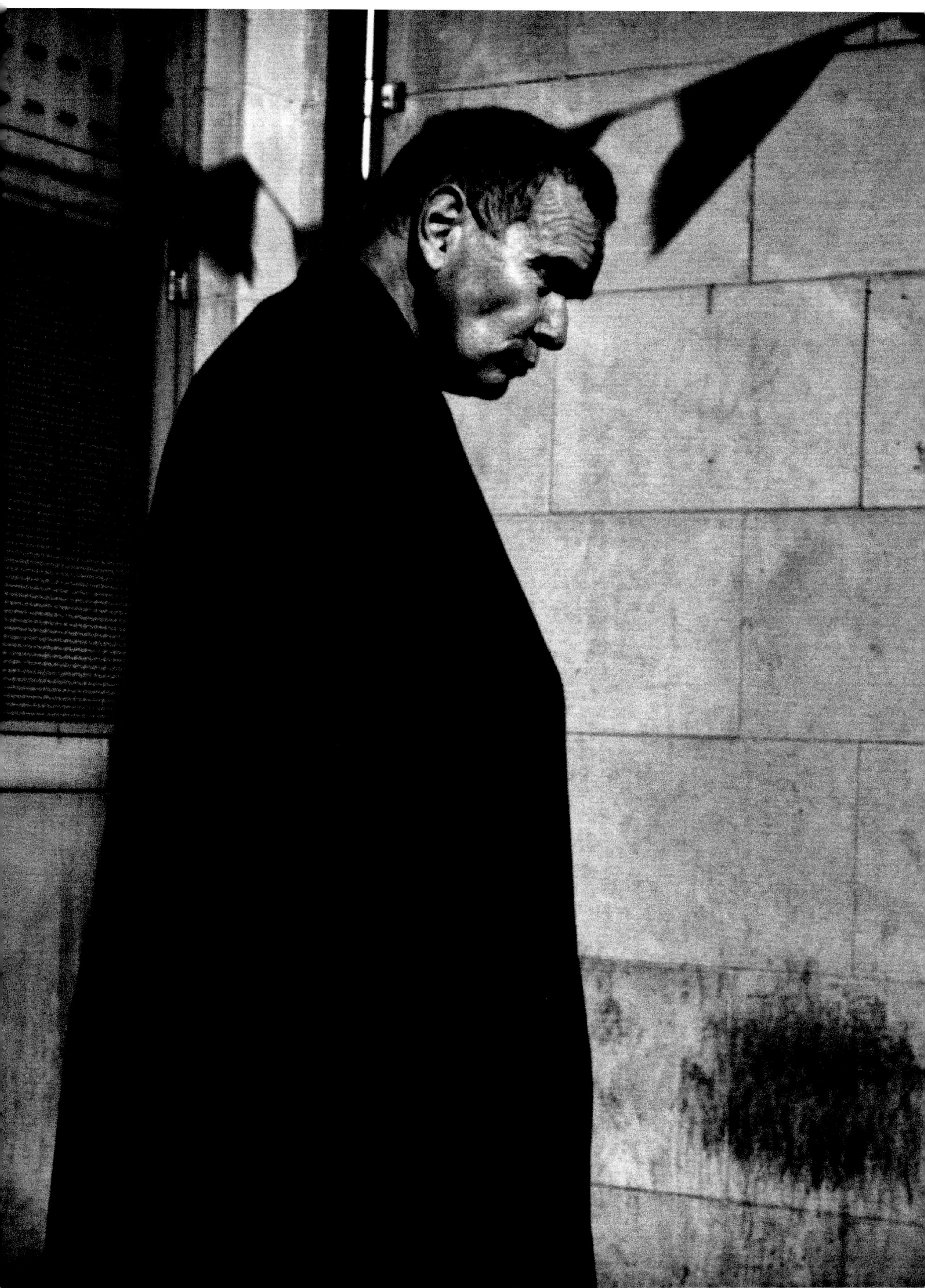

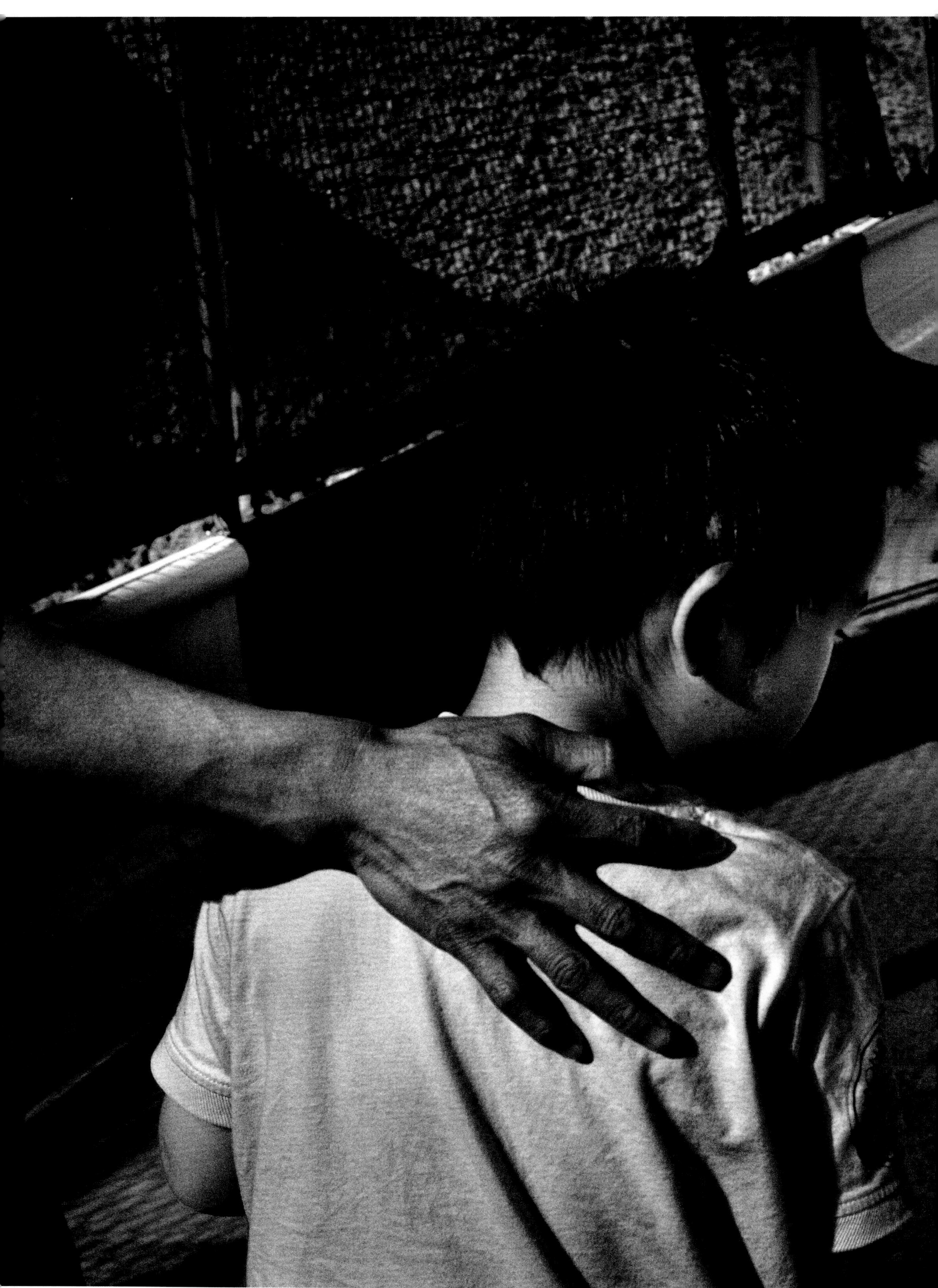

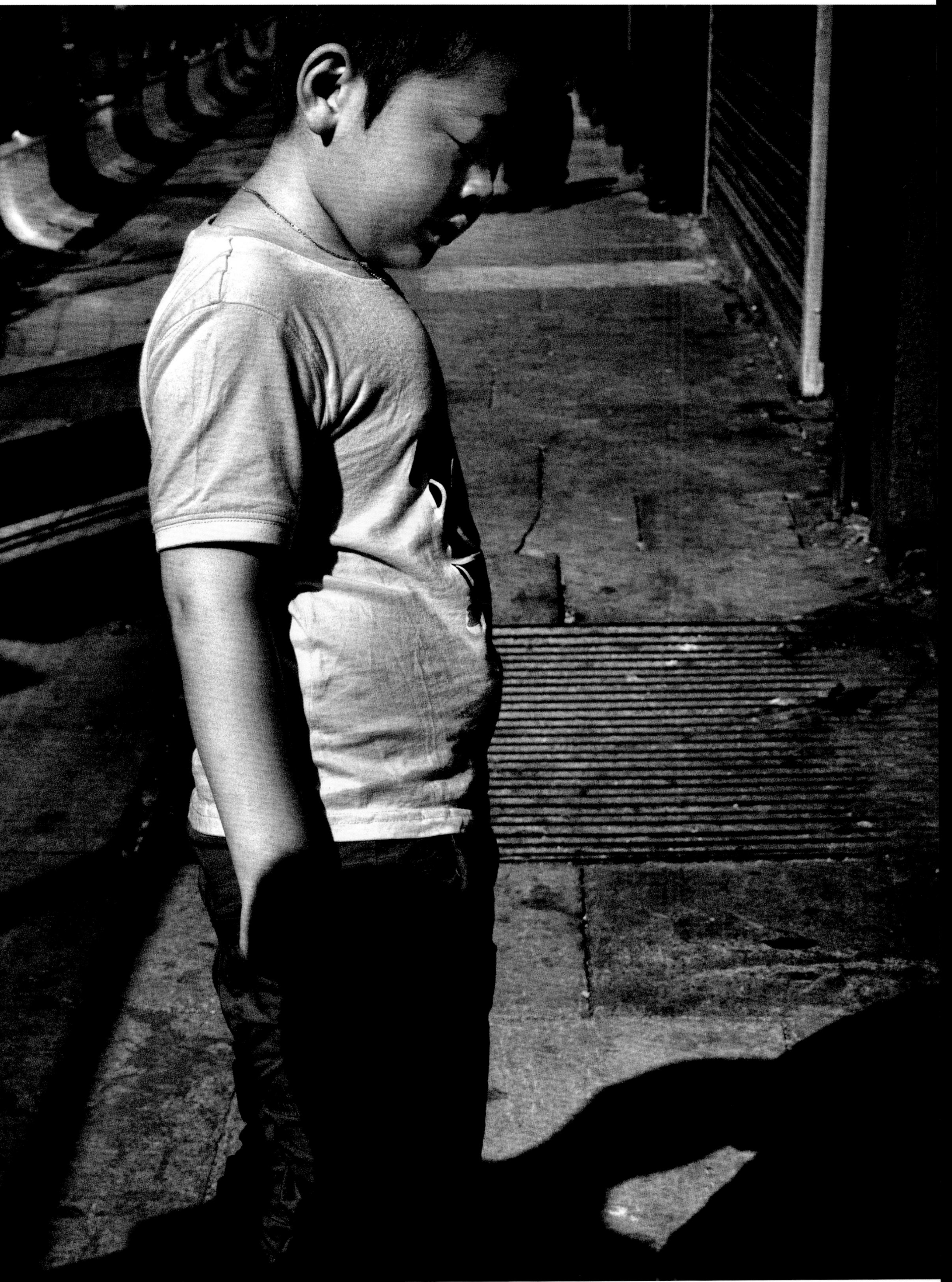

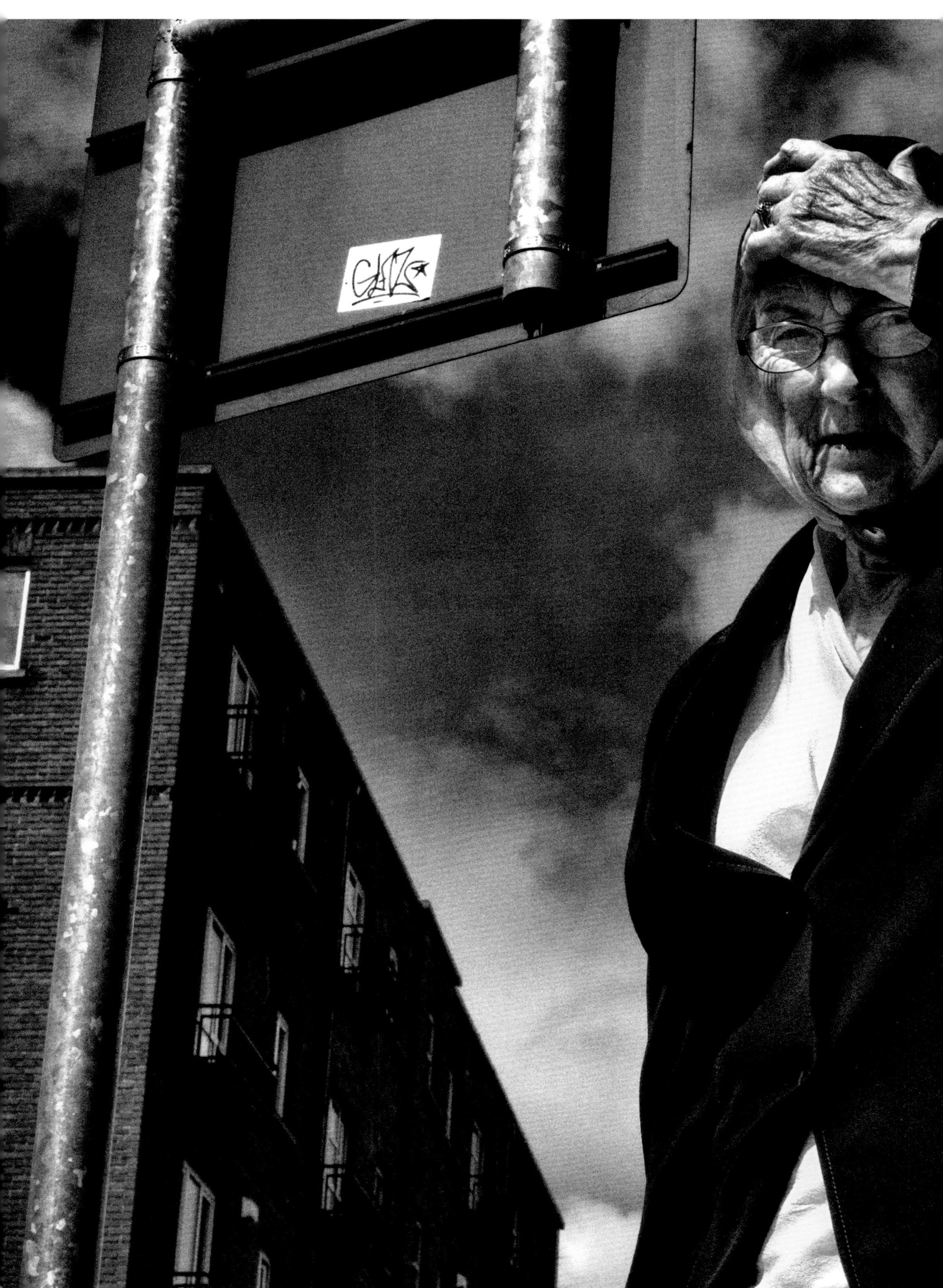

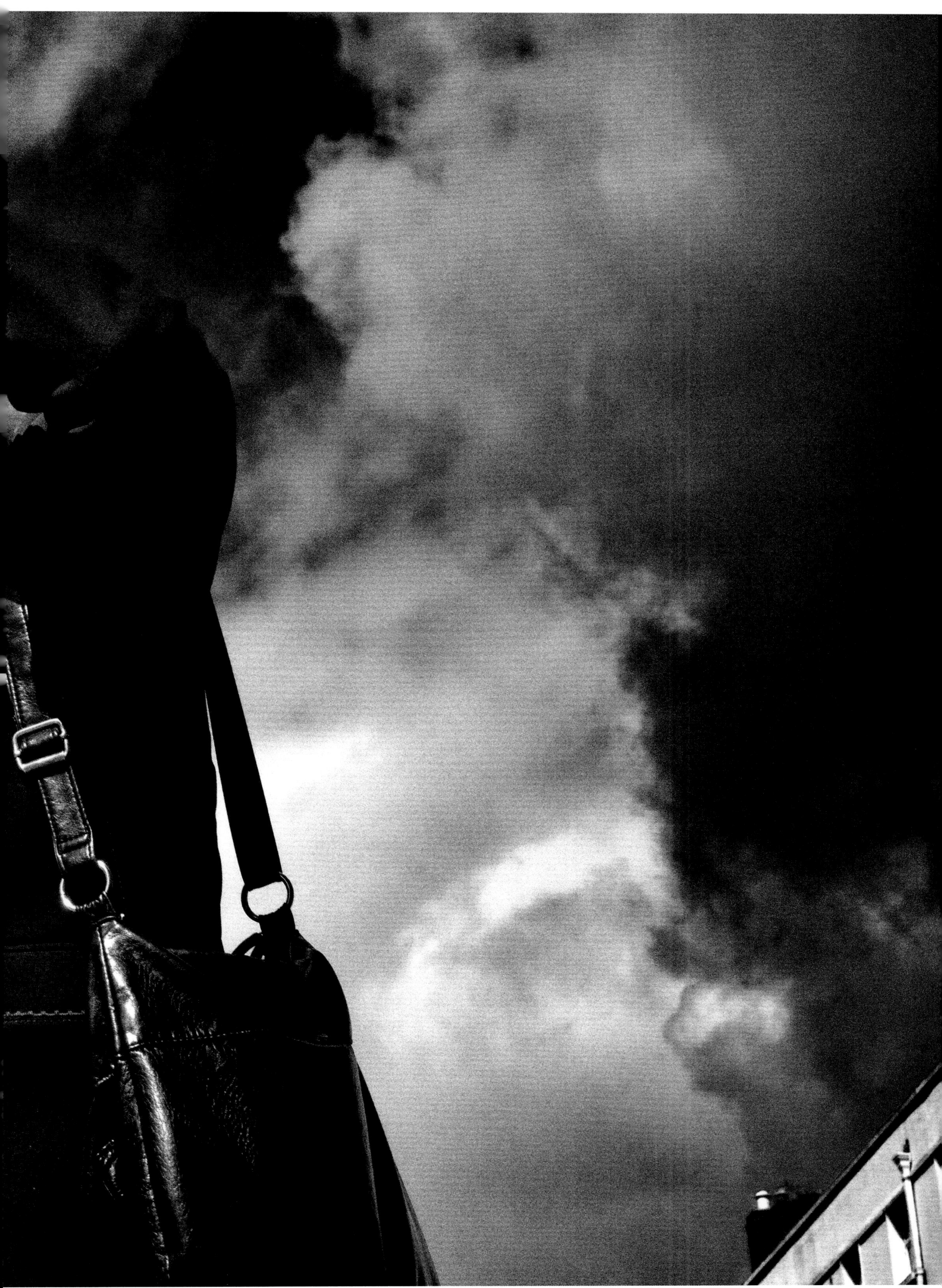

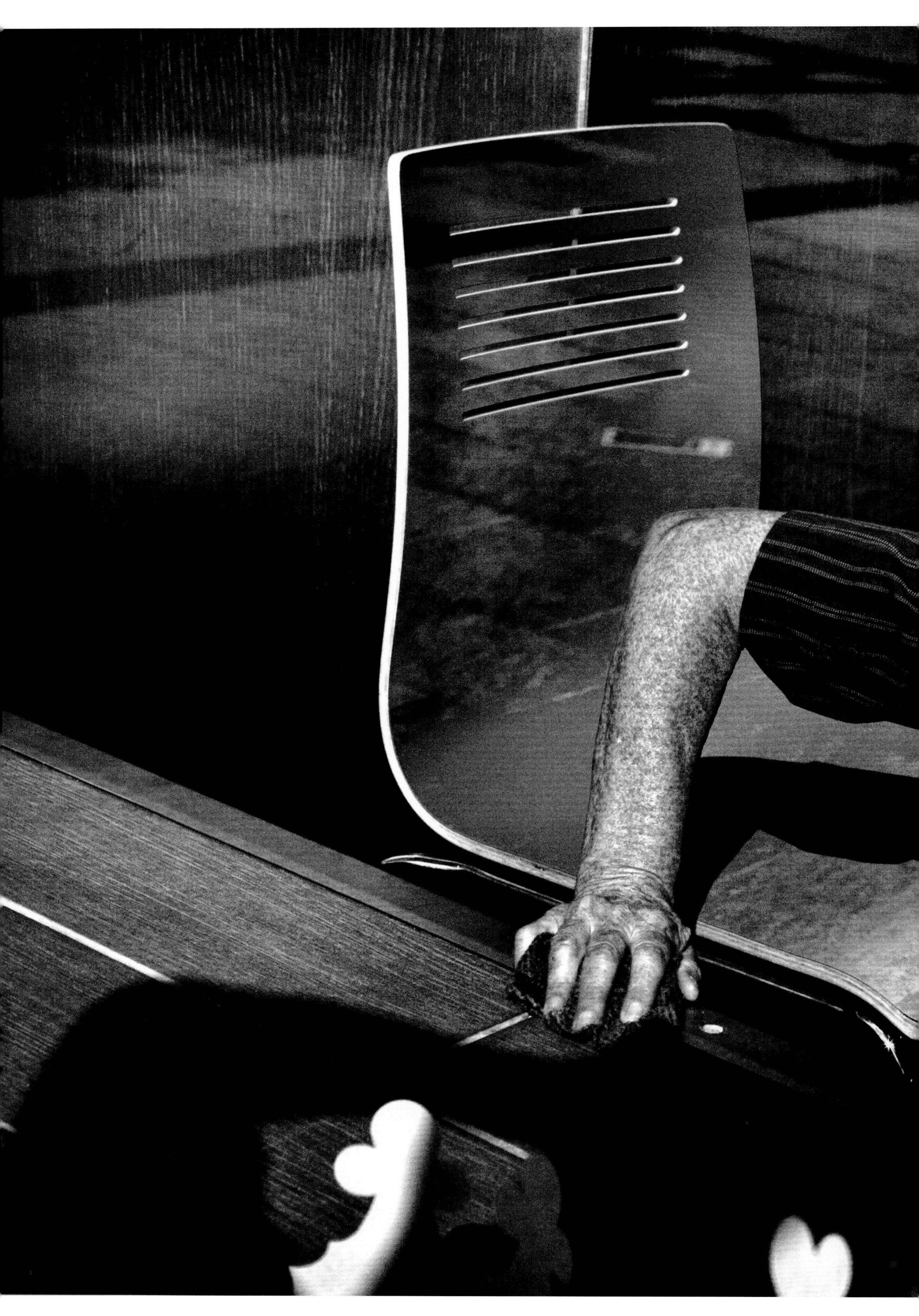

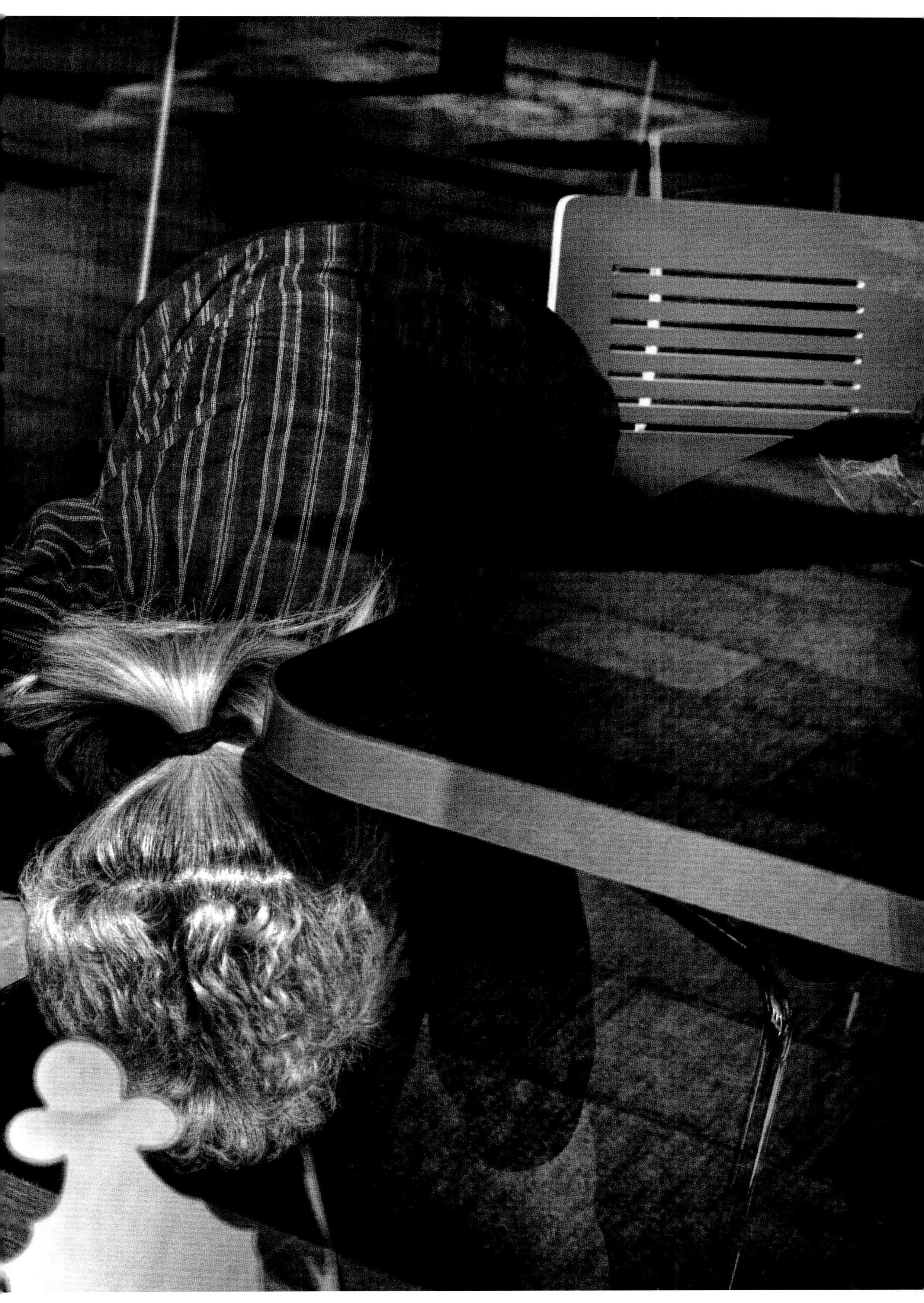

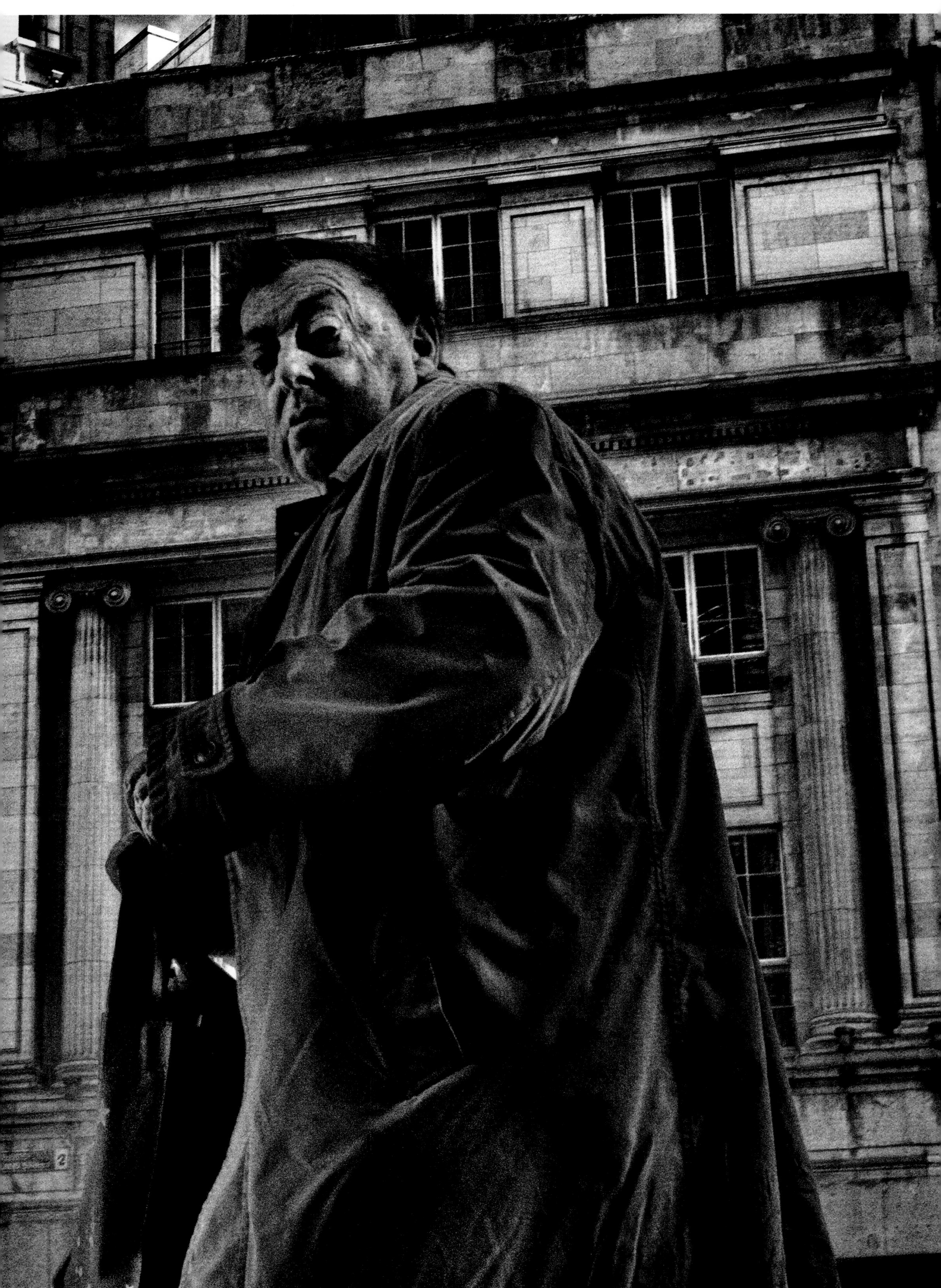

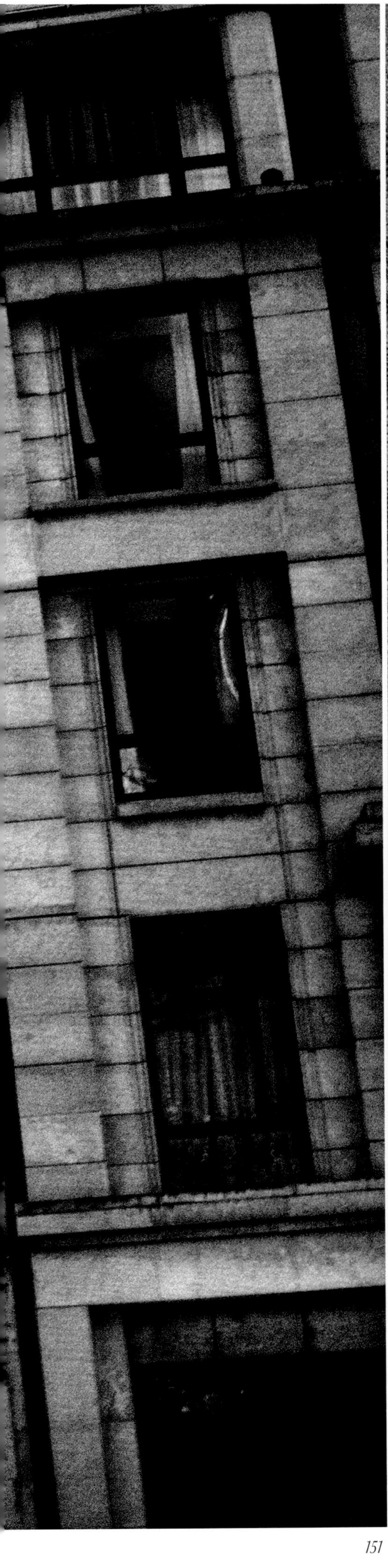

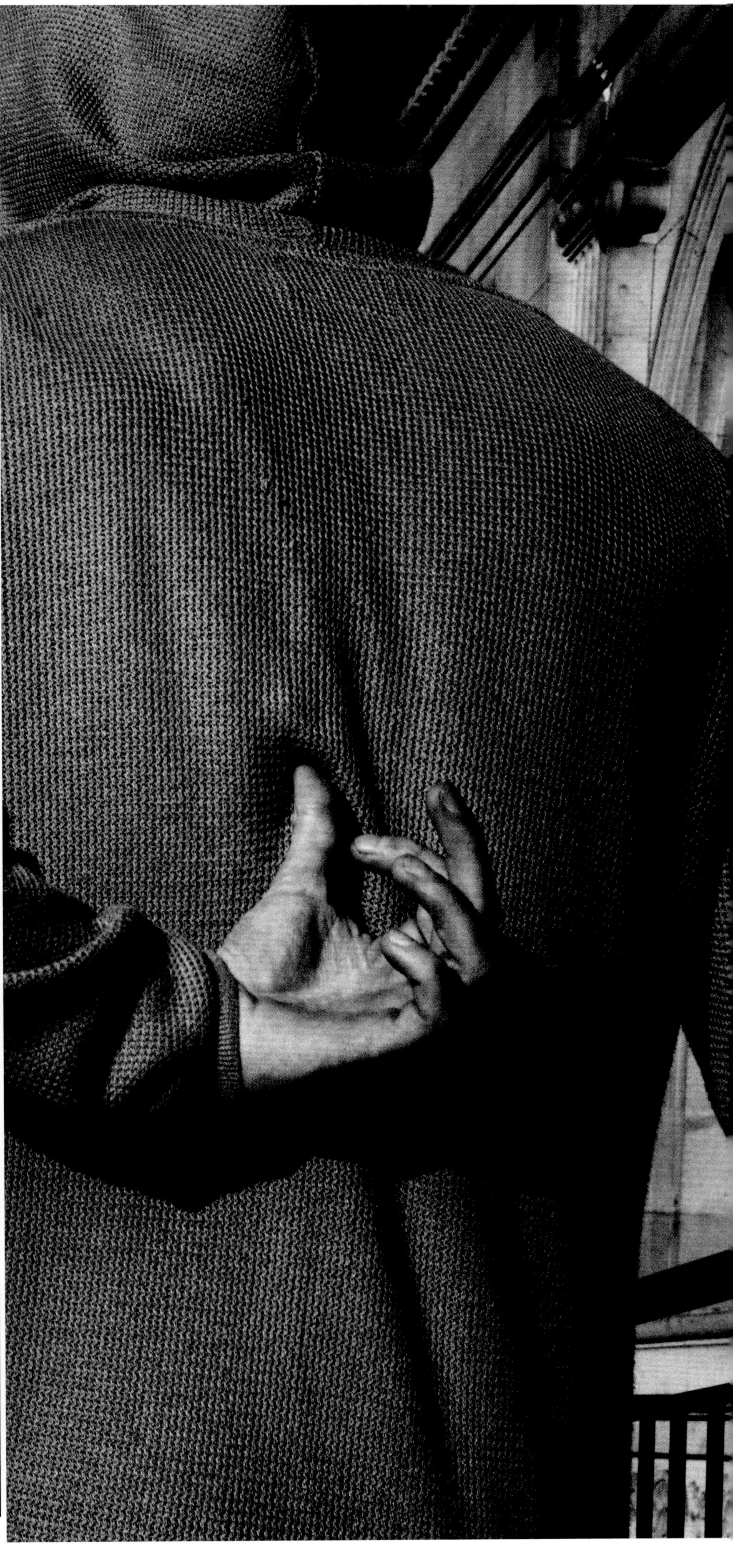

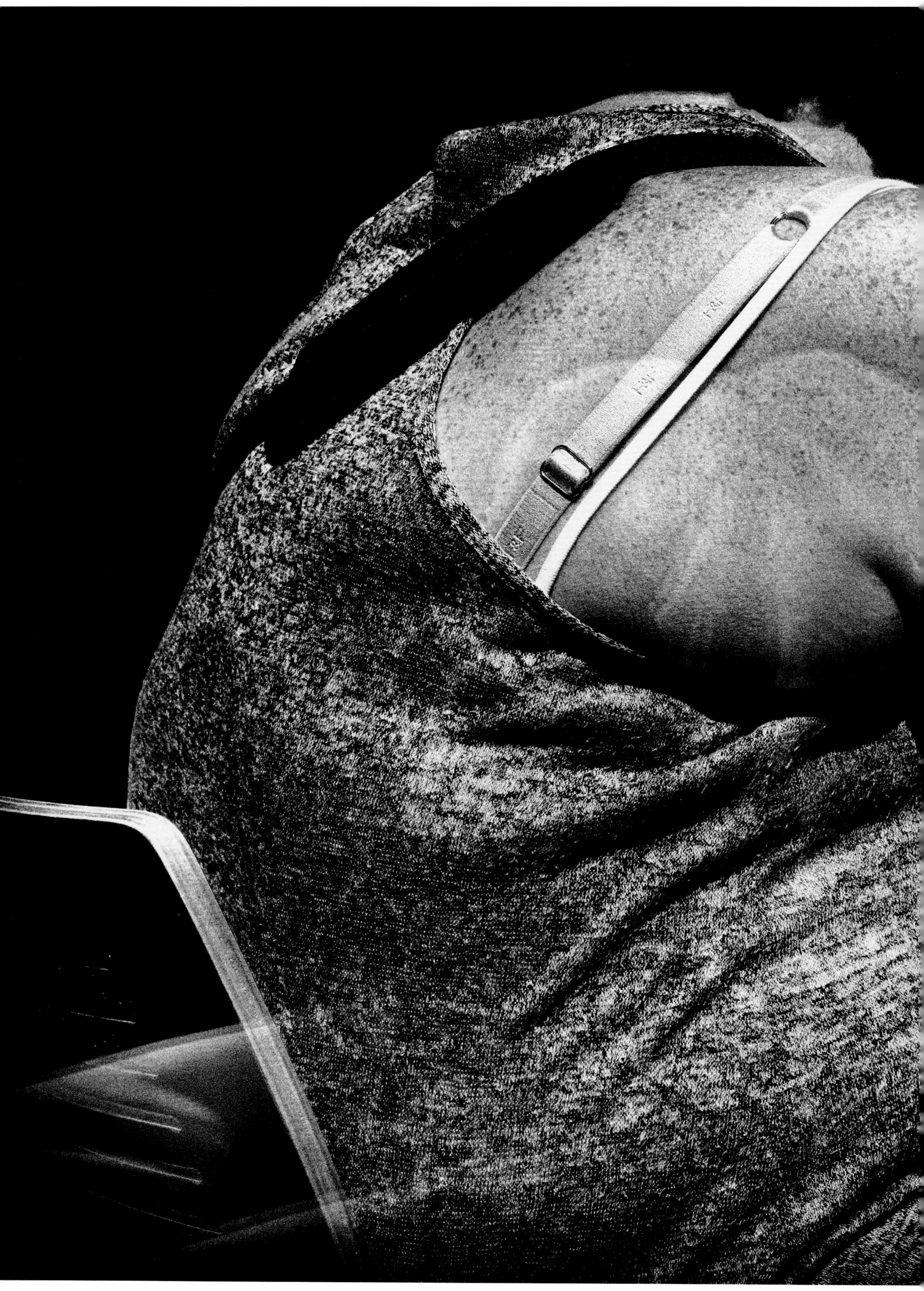

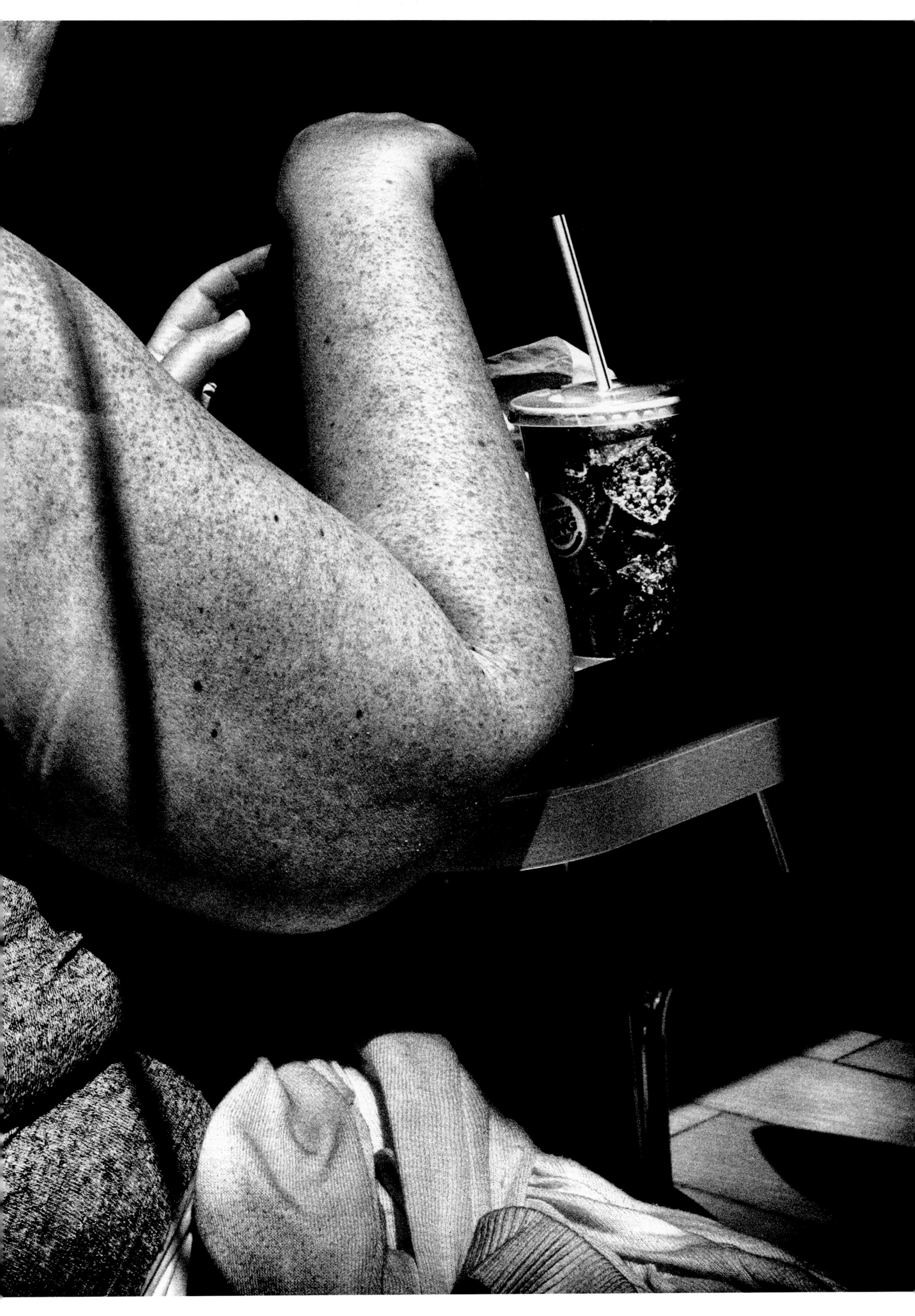

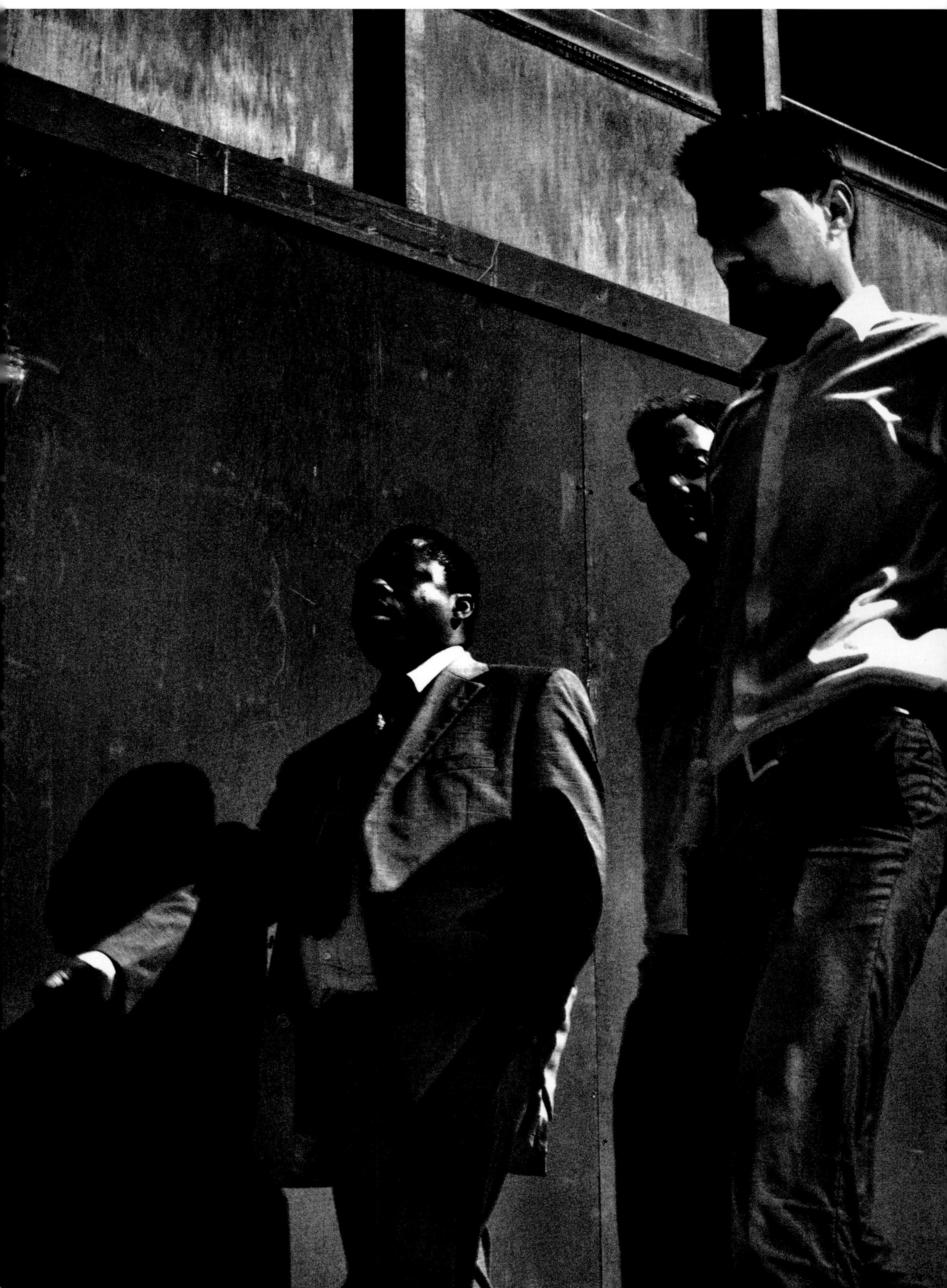

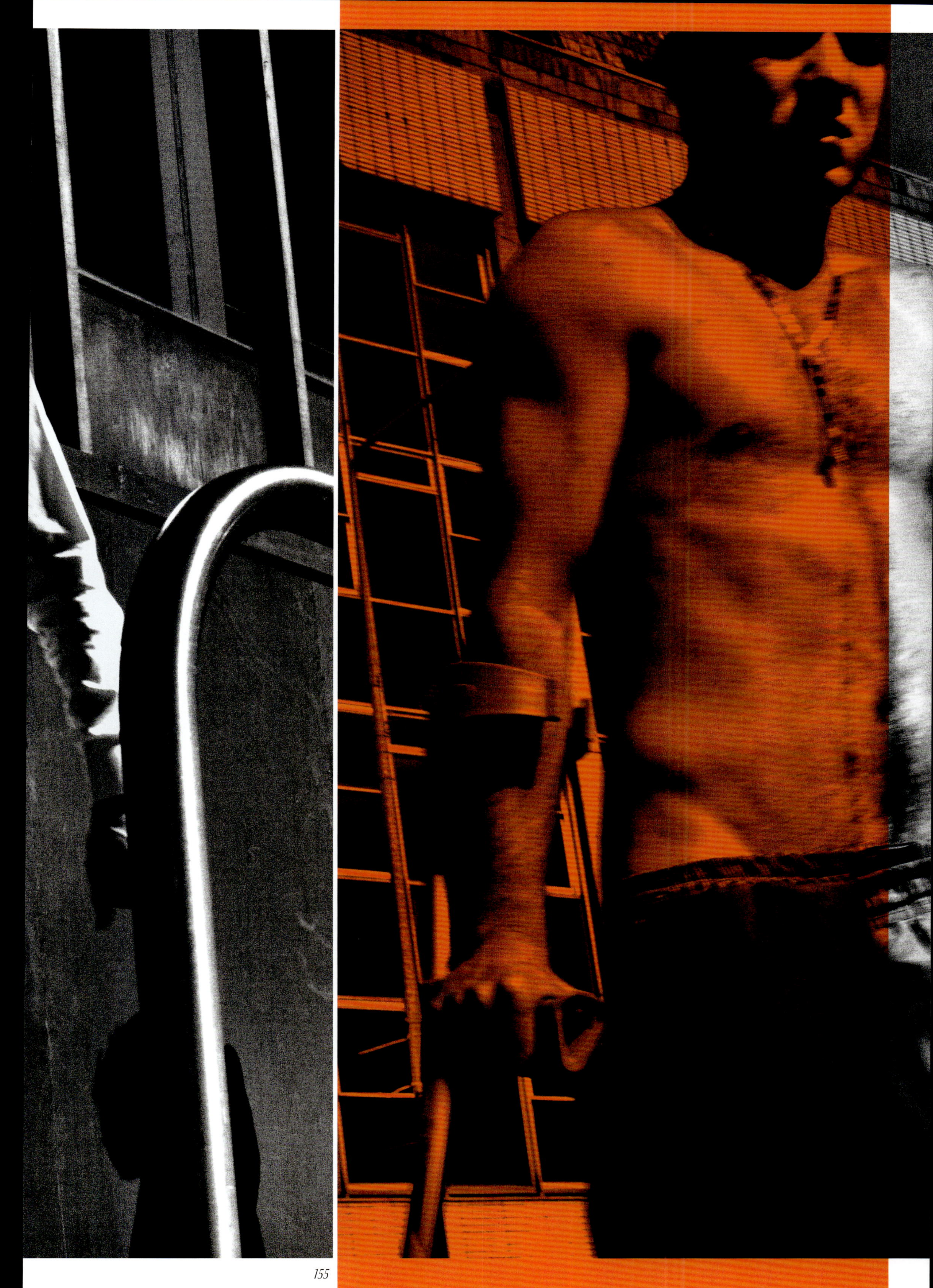

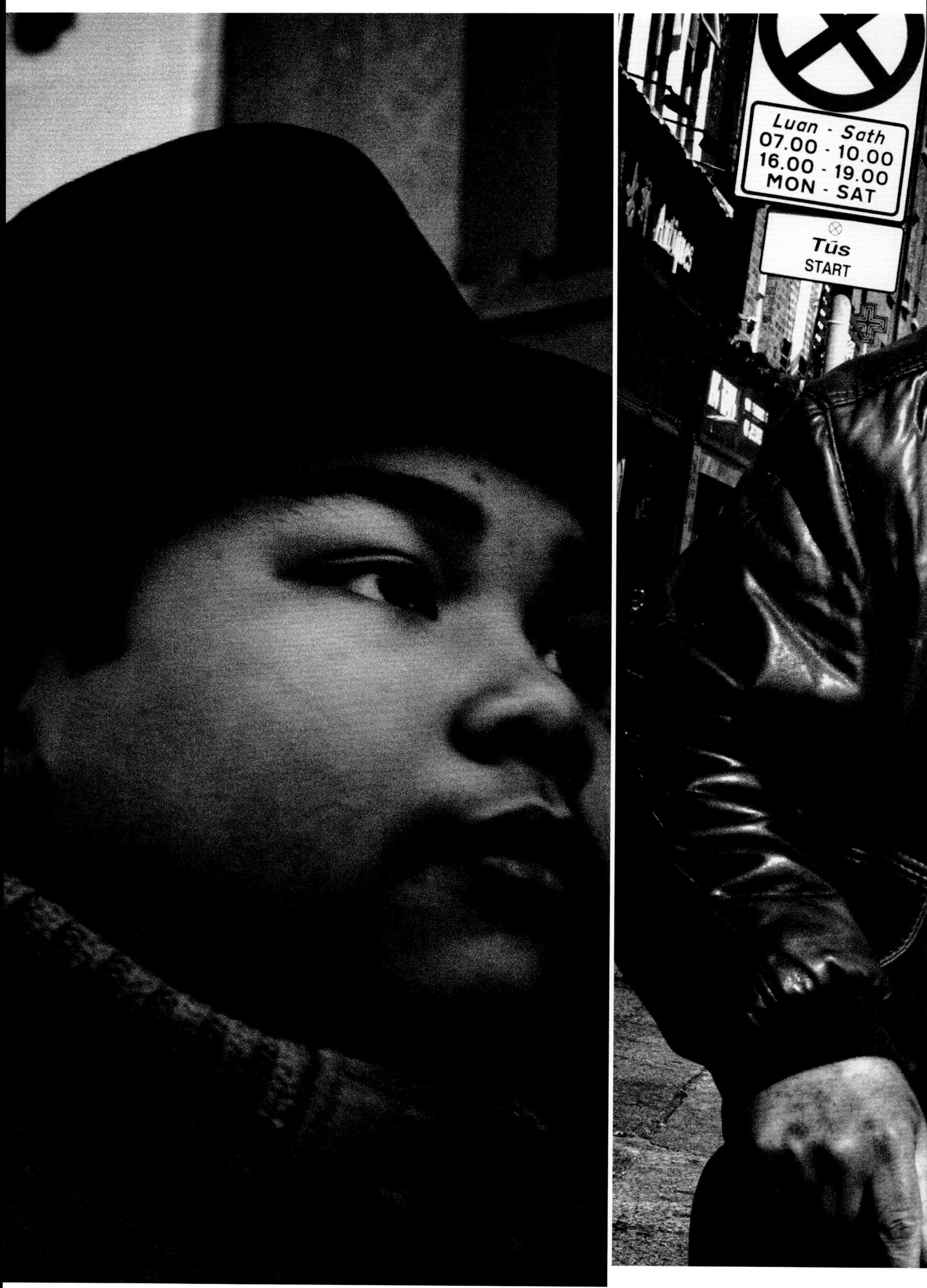
Antiques
Luan - Sath
07.00 - 10.00
16.00 - 19.00
MON - SAT
Tūs
START

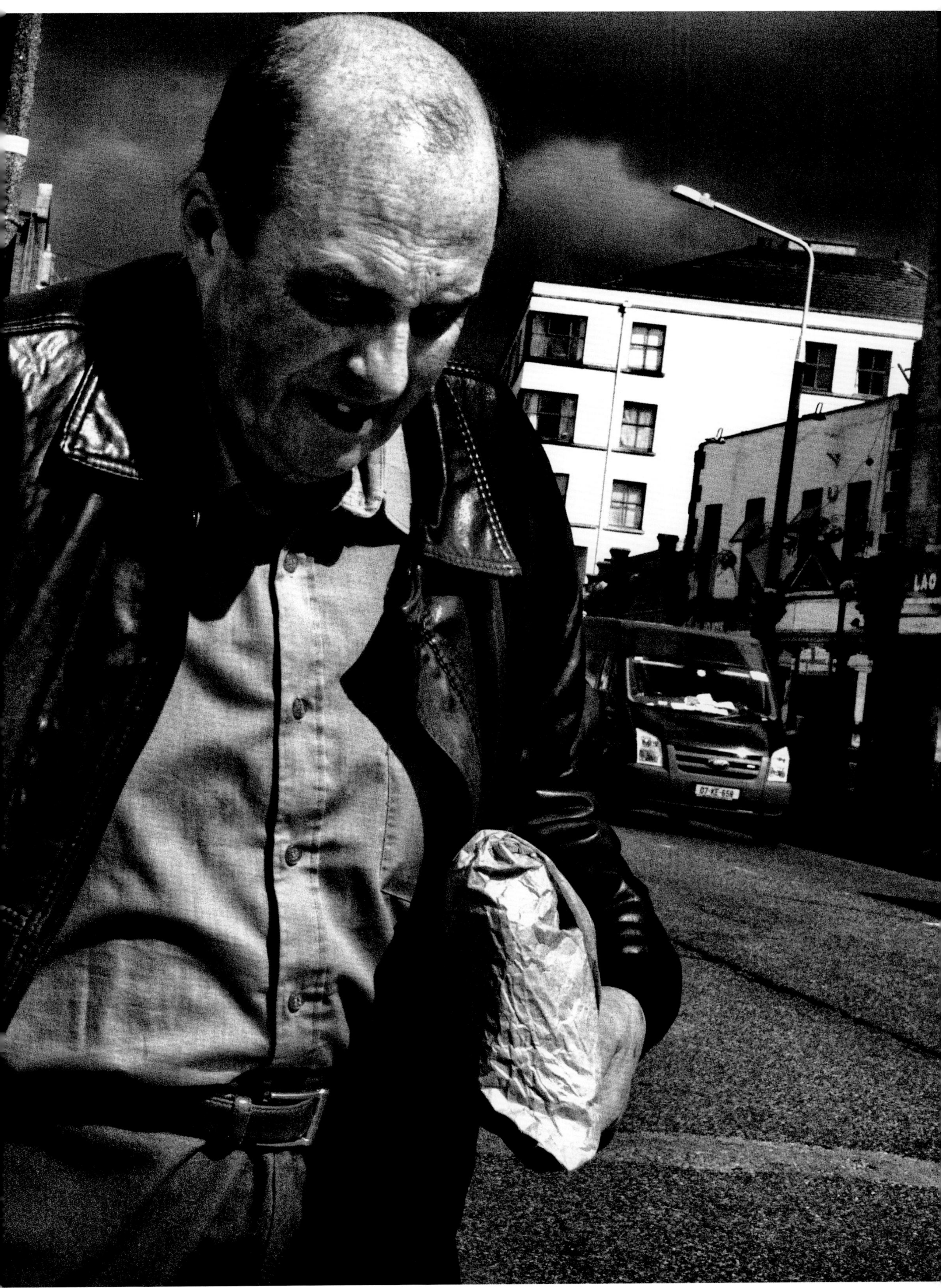

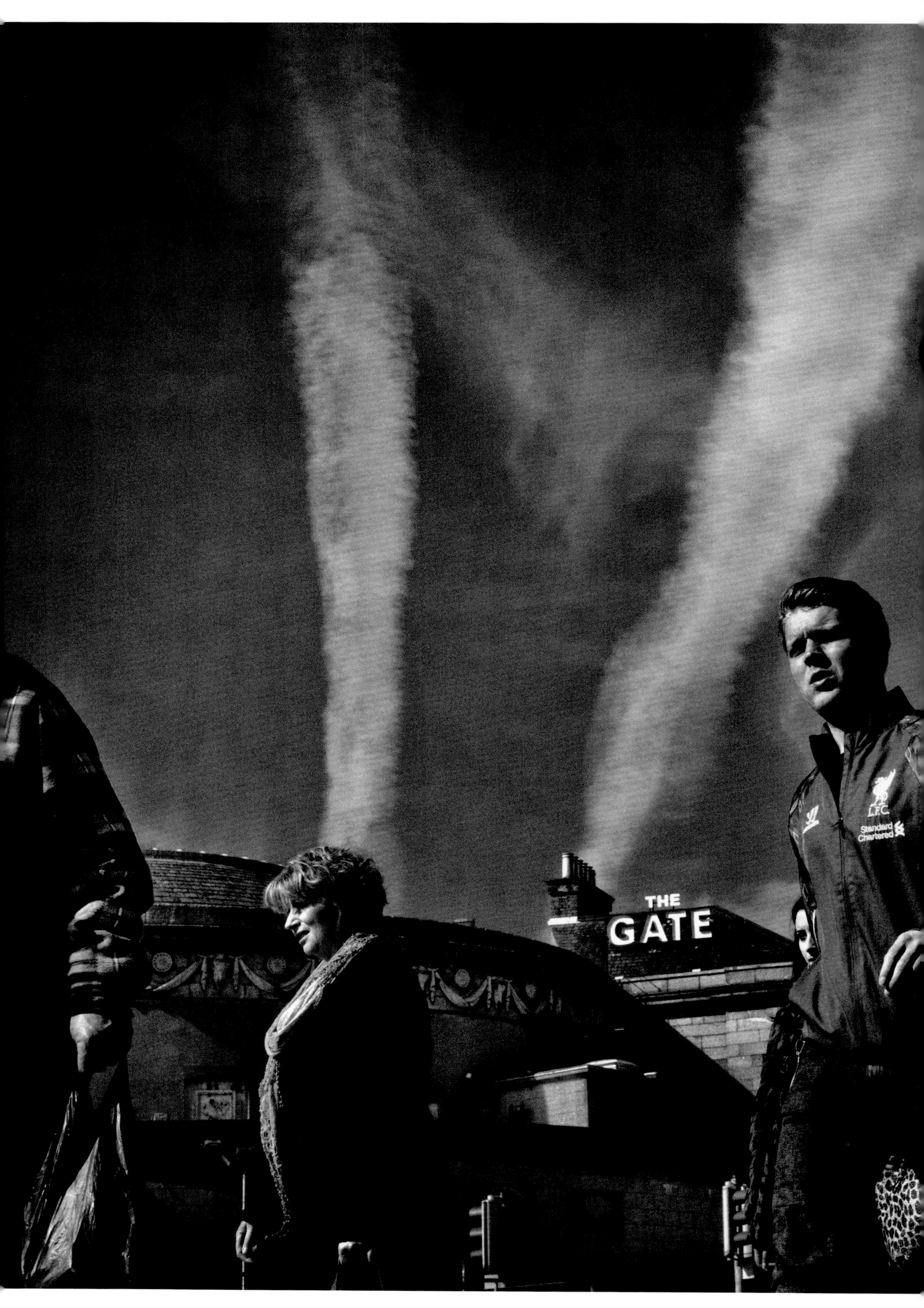
THE
GATE
LFC
Standard Chartered

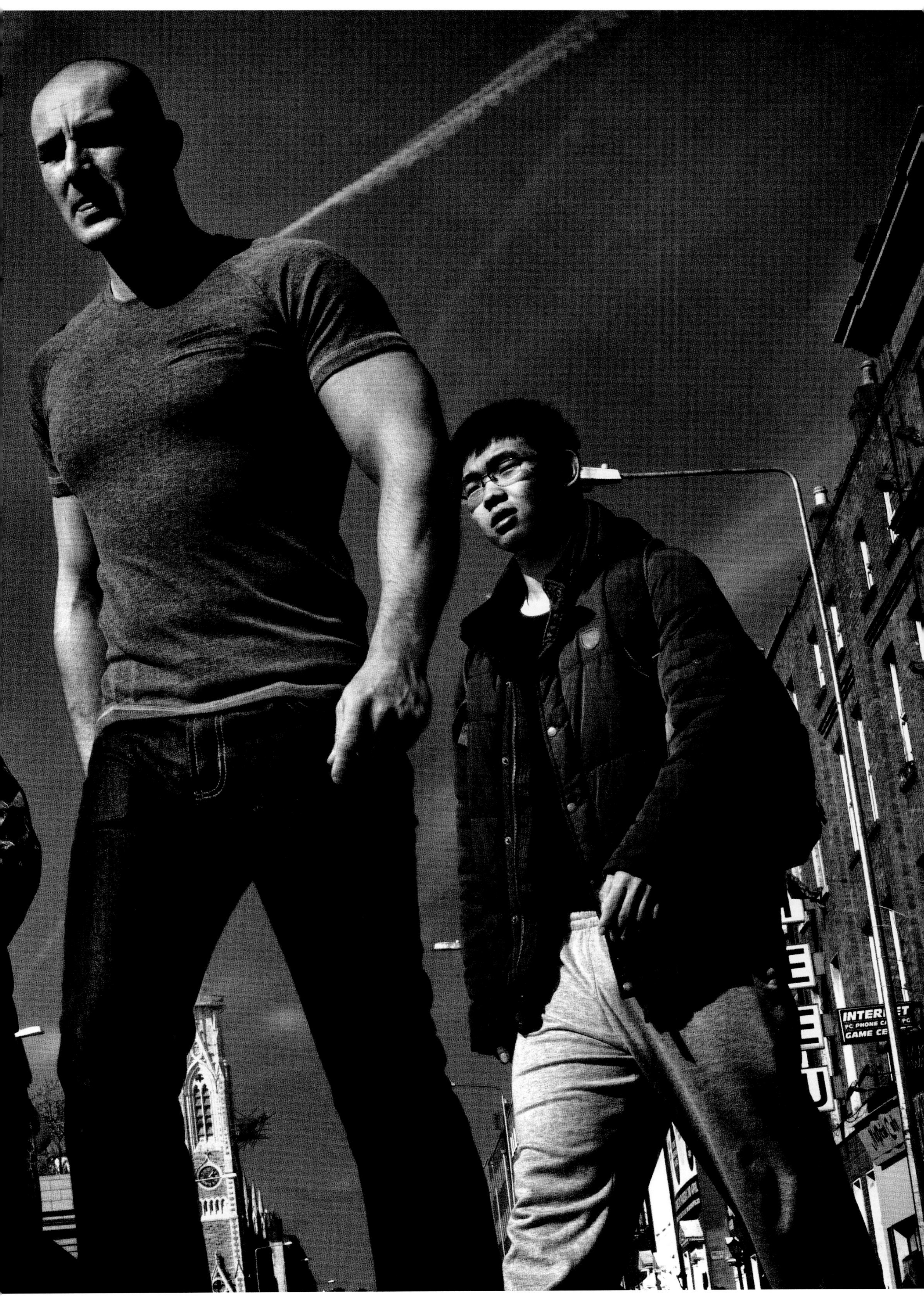

INTERNET
PC PHONE CA   PC
GAME CE

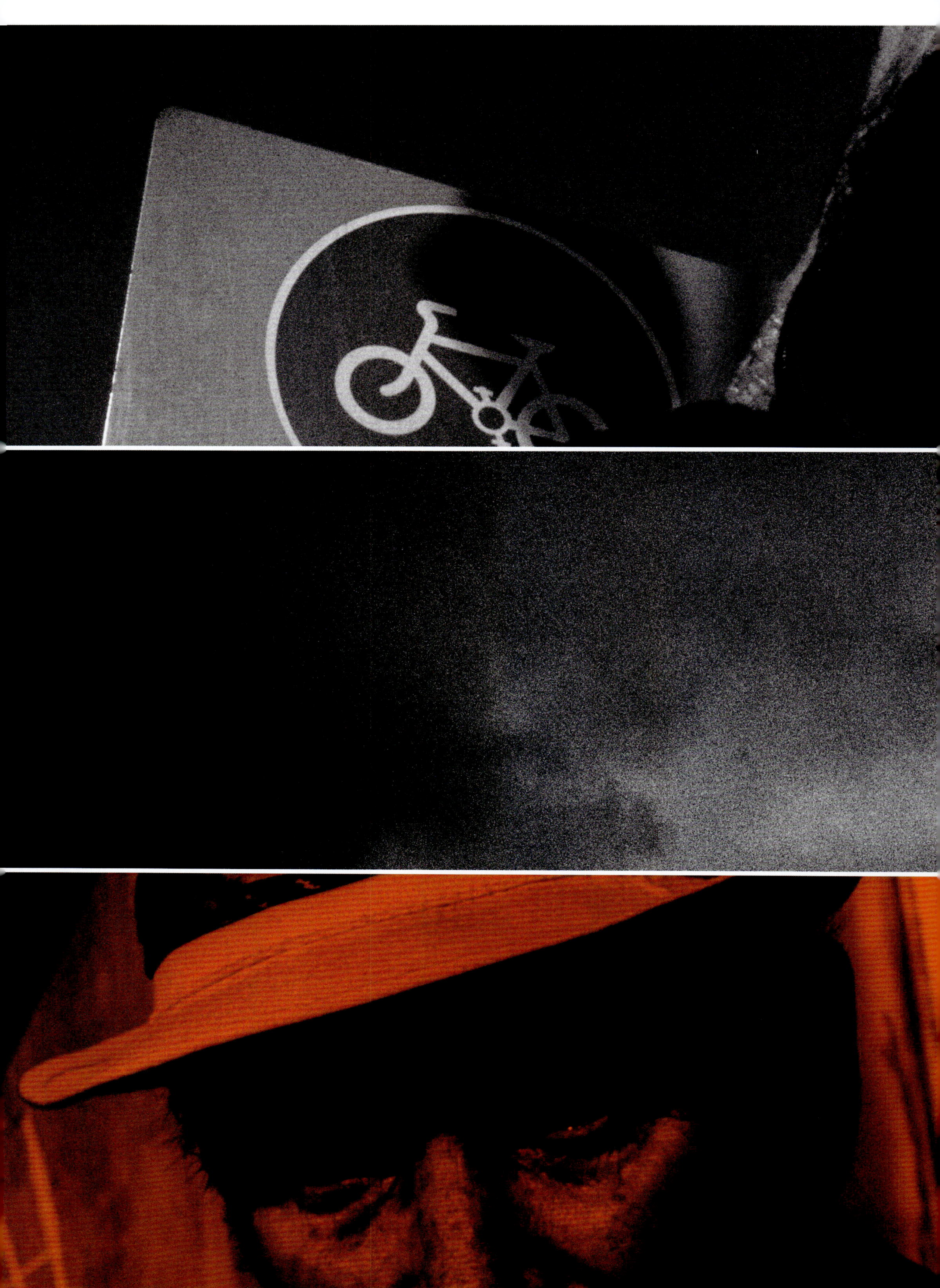

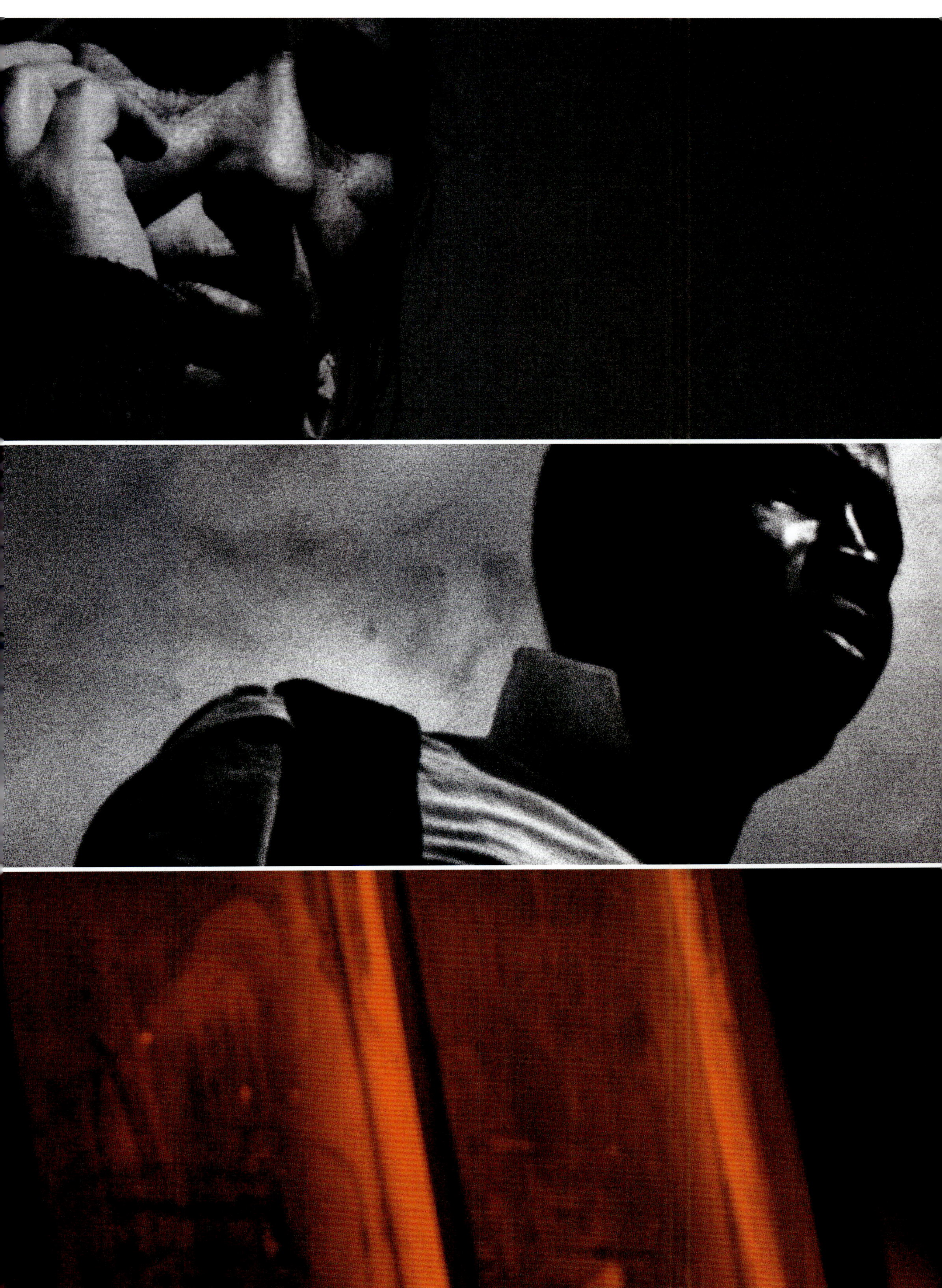

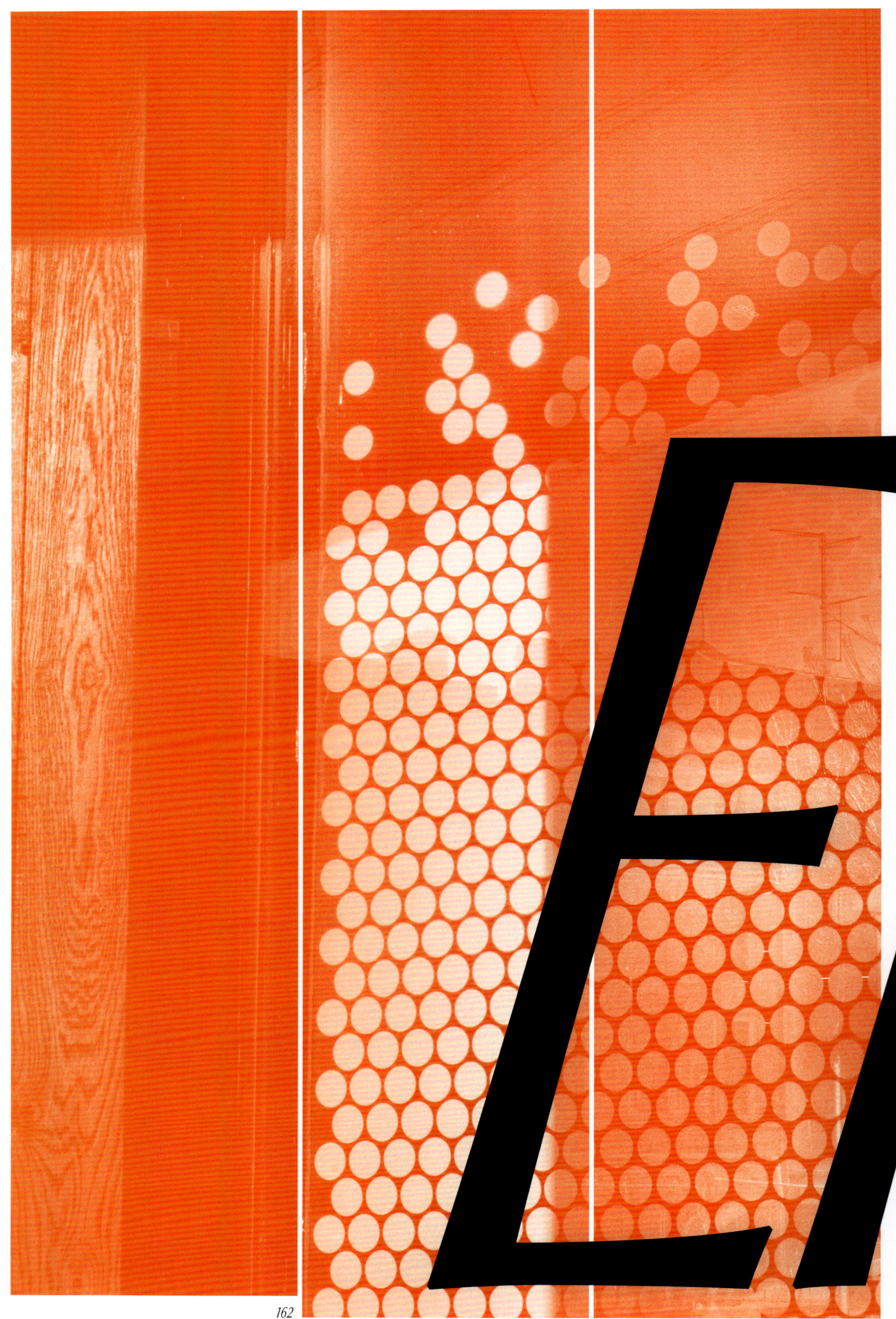

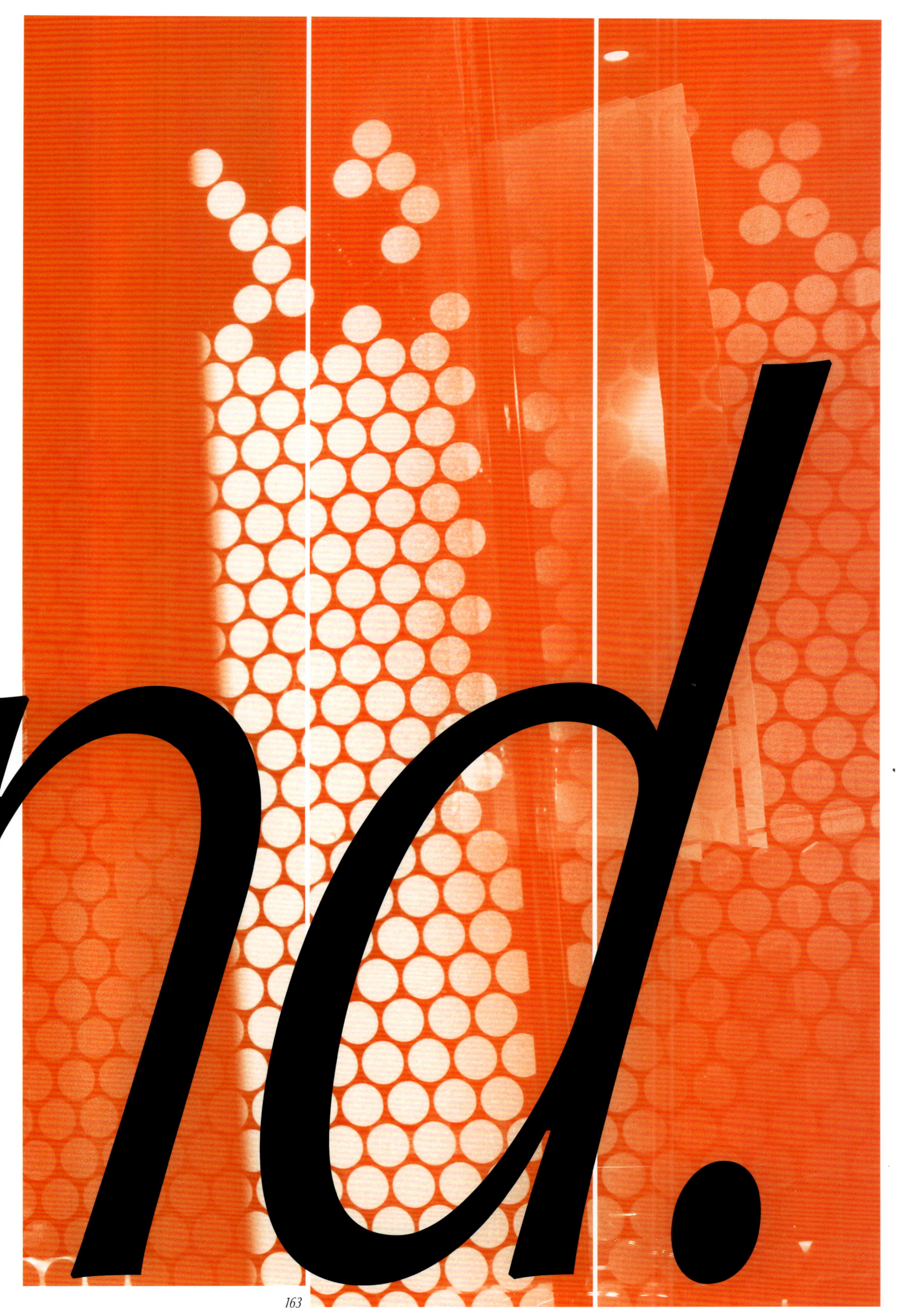

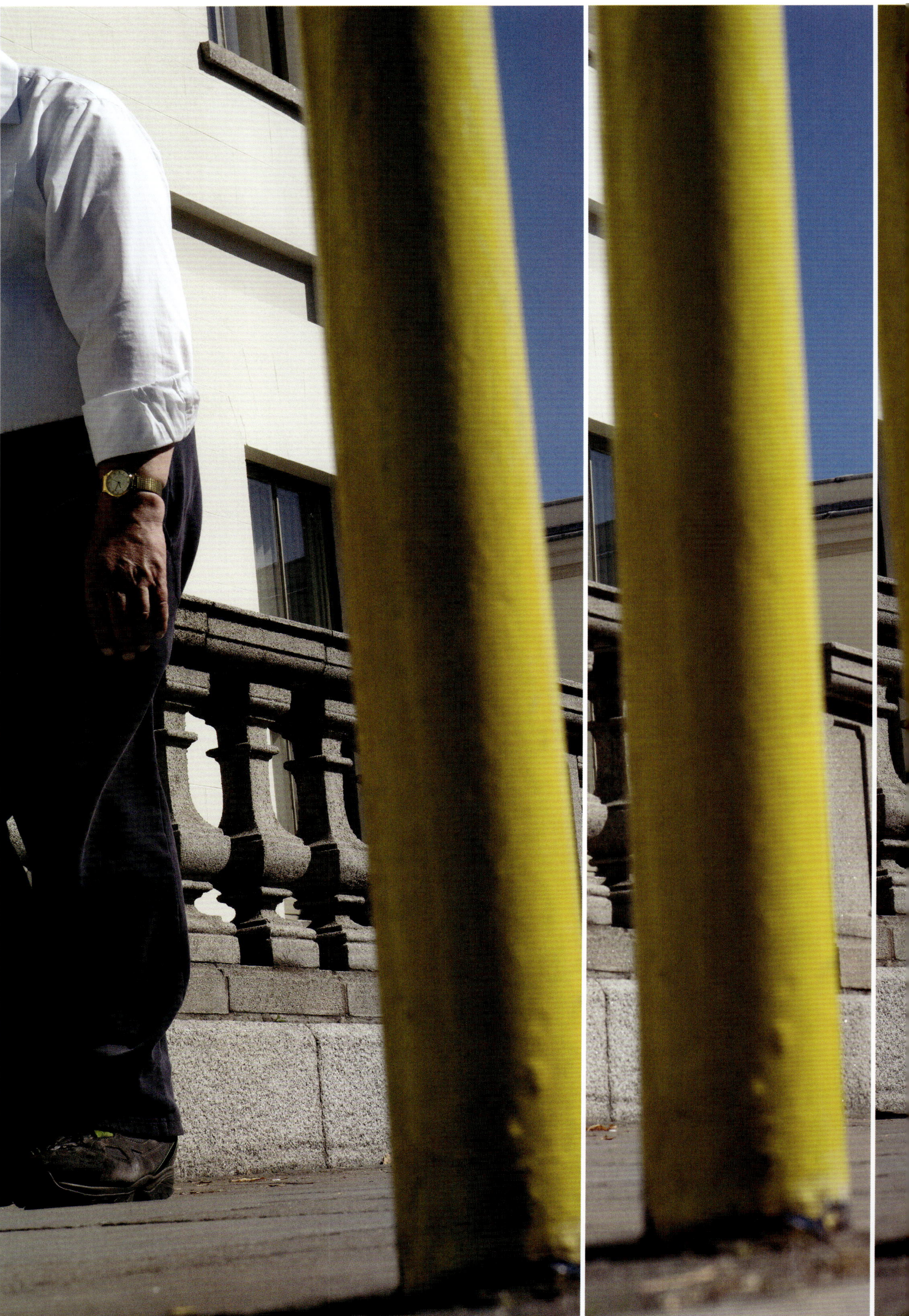

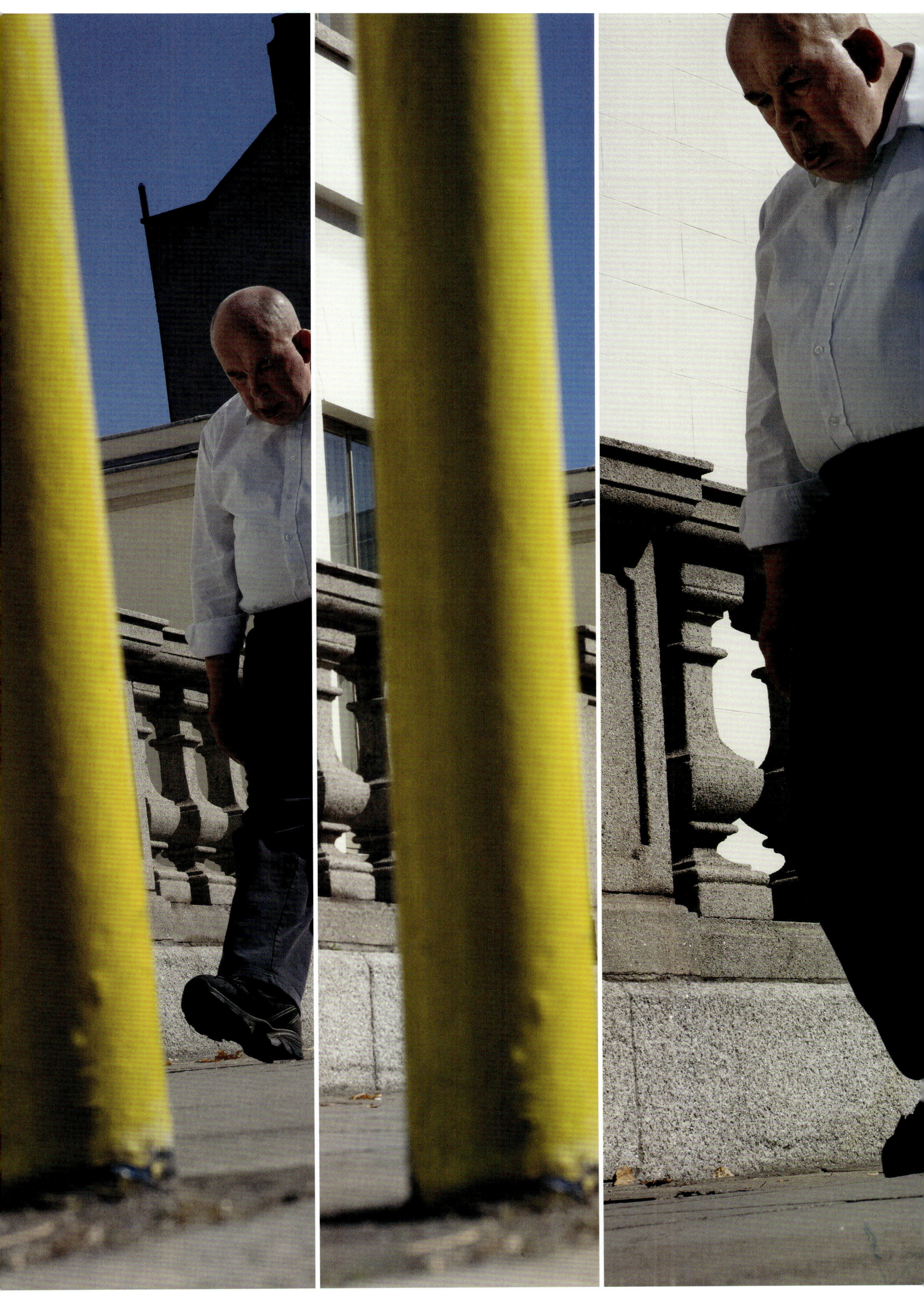

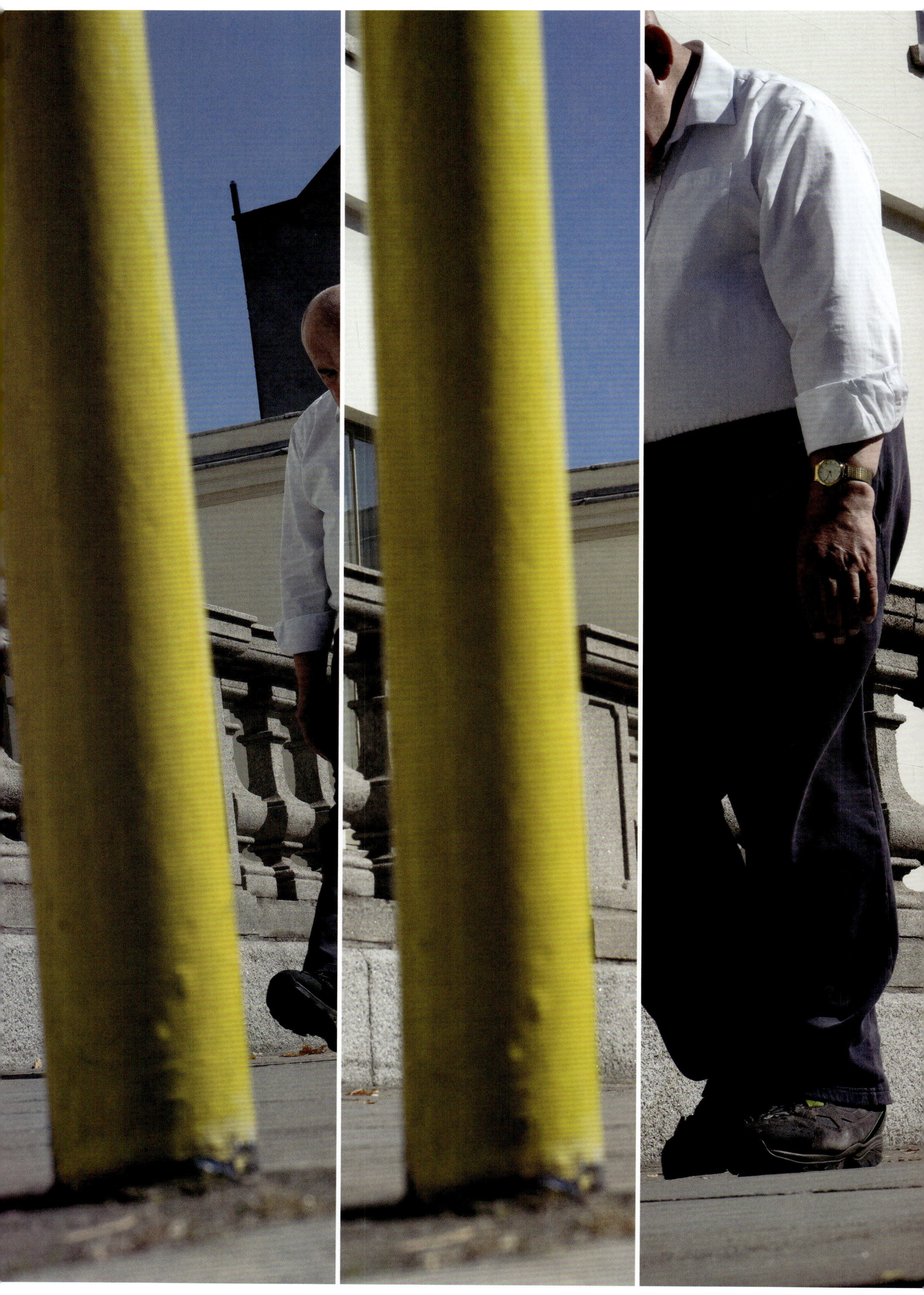

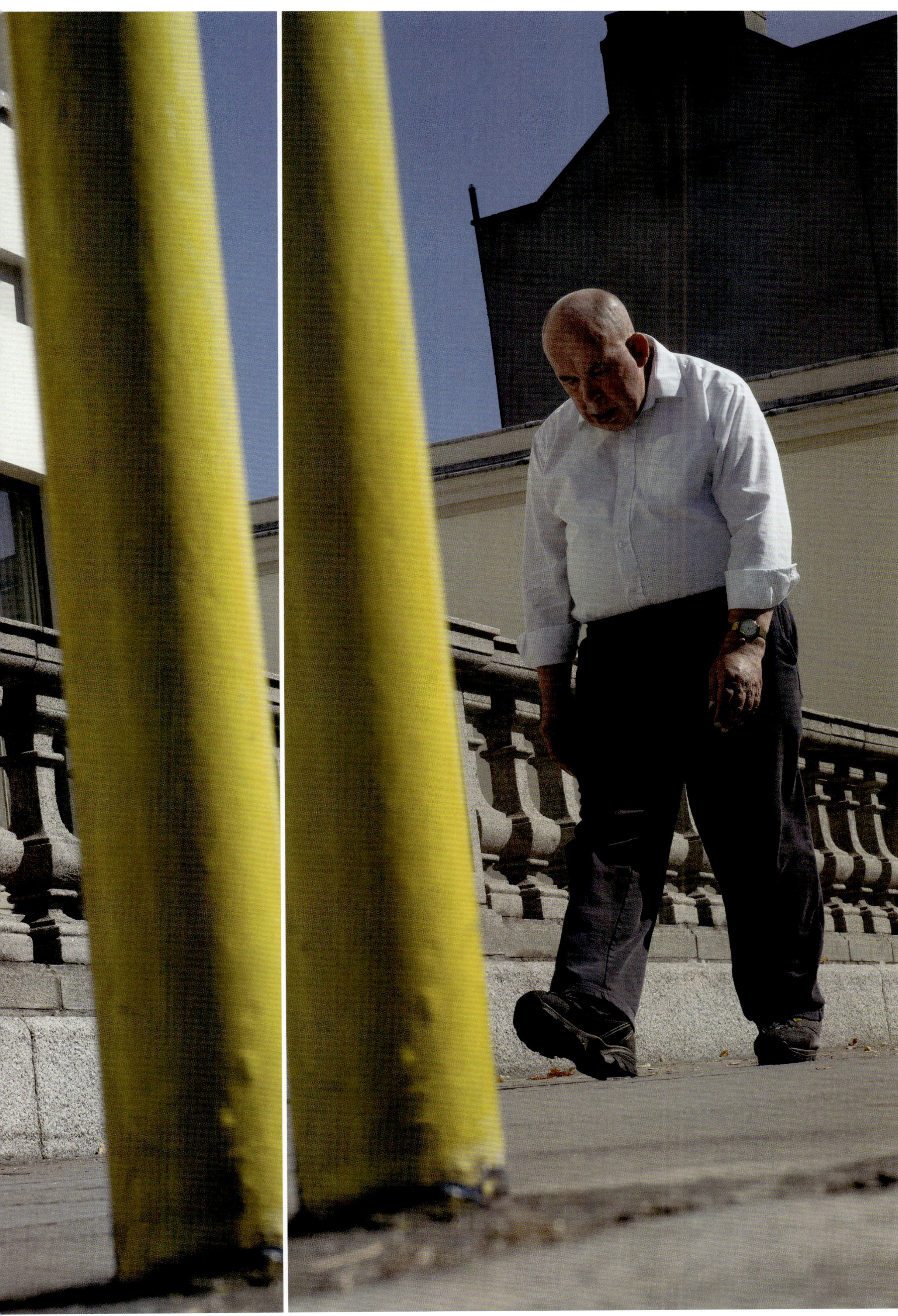

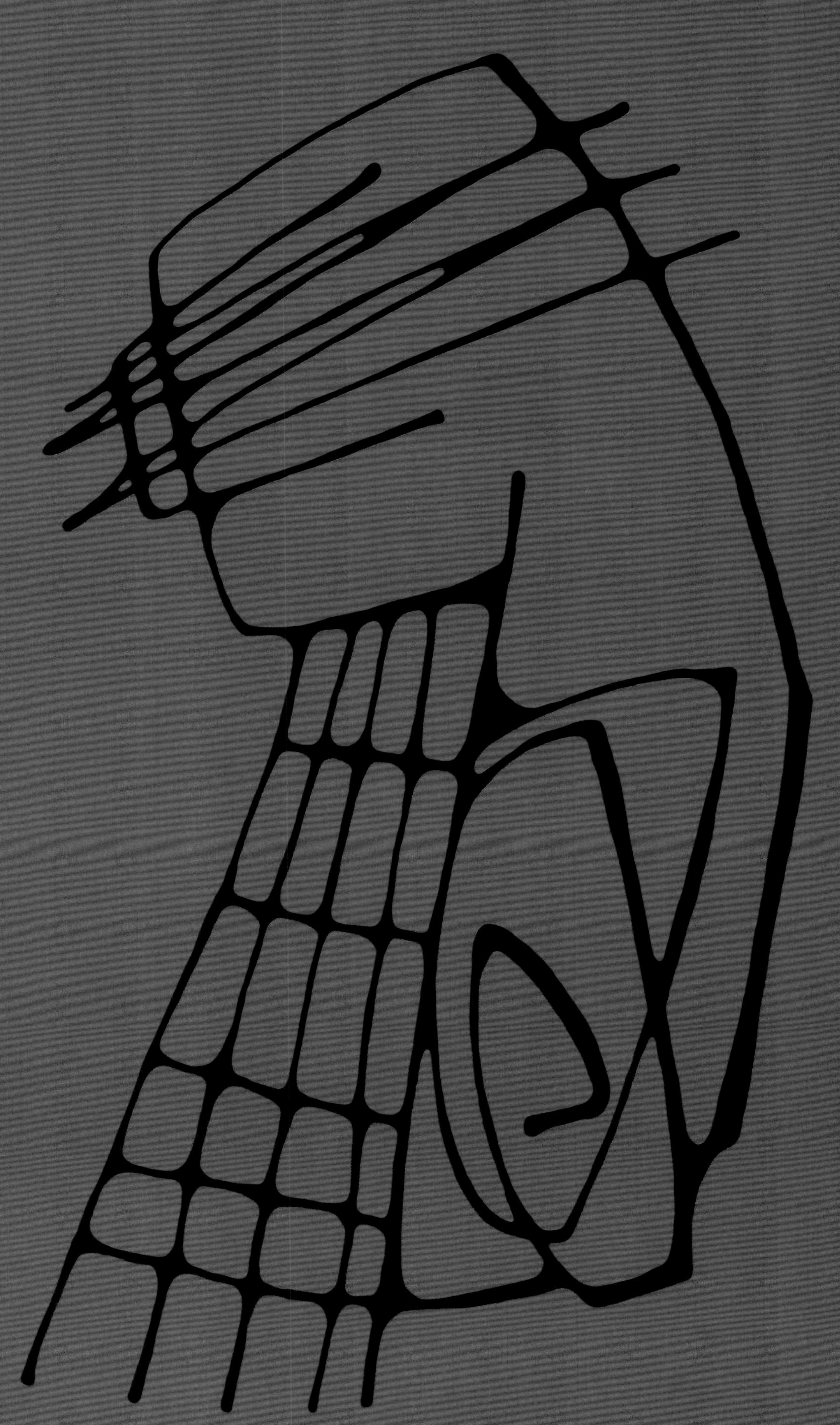

AND THE NEXT THING, I was walking down
from the Five Lamps when something very odd happened
to me. As I came along Summerhill there was a sensation
of floatiness — is all that I could call it — and it was by the moment
getting stronger. By the time I hit Parnell Street I could feel
the surface of the path falling away from beneath me — it was
as if I was rising up. I don't know how to describe it really.
It was like that feeling from years ago when you have a whitener
in a nightclub. That feeling when suddenly the music goes woozy
and your tongue goes thick and you feel as if you've been lifted up
away from yourself. Hoisted! Hoisted is the word I am looking for.

And suddenly in this way I was lifted above the street —
I was way, way above it — and I could see it clearly for the
first time.

I could understand then the way that it makes us move.
The way that it dictates the pattern of our stride. The way that
it makes our forearms beat back the fume-thick air.

And as I looked down I saw the way that time could come
loose. And then the traffic disappeared. And the Chinese writing
faded away. And the horses appeared. And there were gas lamps.
There was a fight outside a public house between men in hats.
There was a brasser in a doorway, calling. There was a child
looking at her face in a puddle and clowning.

It became still an older time down there. I could smell
the countryside nearby. The wailing of beasts. The heavy,
thudding movement of a stockyard. Animal screams.

And then it started to spin forward again on a loop.
The Chinese writing emerged again. The traffic announced
its recovery with coughing and barks. I was suspended above
the future of the street. There was music of a type I could
not identify. It came from a kind of underground cavern.
Faux-leather suits were in and these came in fabulous tones —
there were inky rioja reds, hot pinks, cool forest greens.
There were big silver boots and wedge heels. There was a new
type of streetlight that was dimmer and gave a somewhat
gloomy air, an eeriness even. But the people moved in the
same way still. They beat back the air with forearm smashes.
They did not pause to check their stride.

And then a great silence enveloped the street and it
held for a moment, and then more, and everything stopped,
and was frozen, and it felt something like peace.

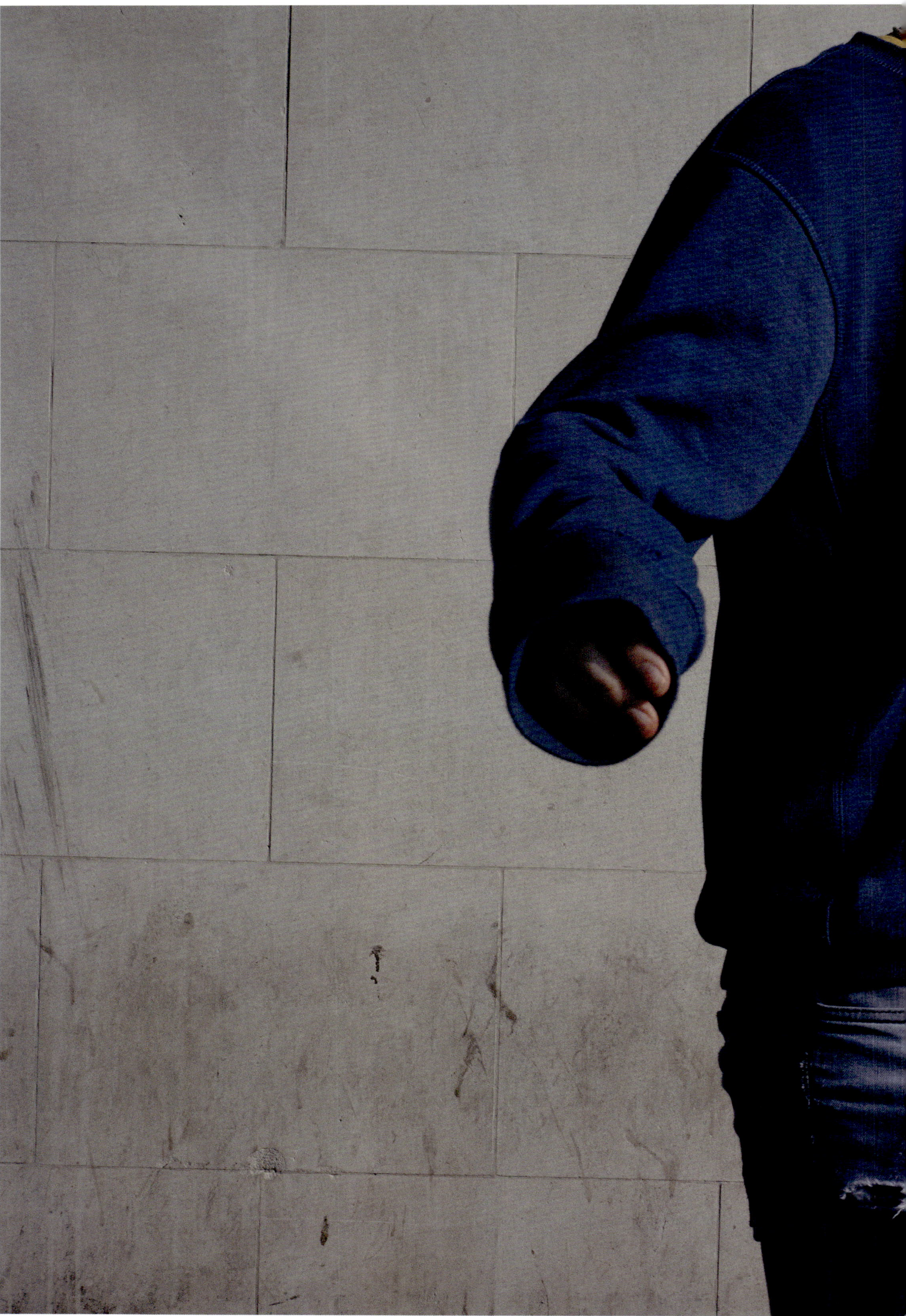

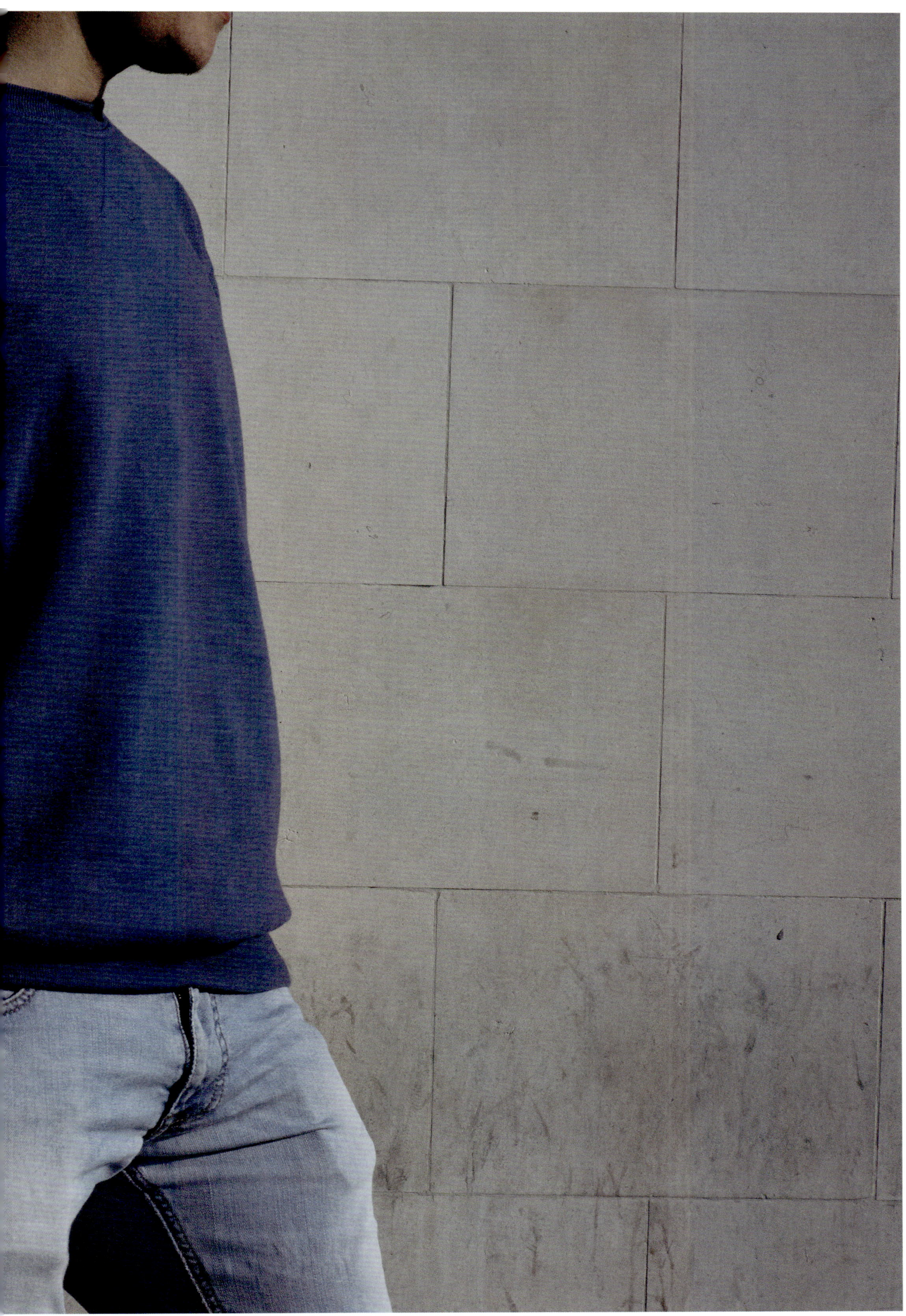

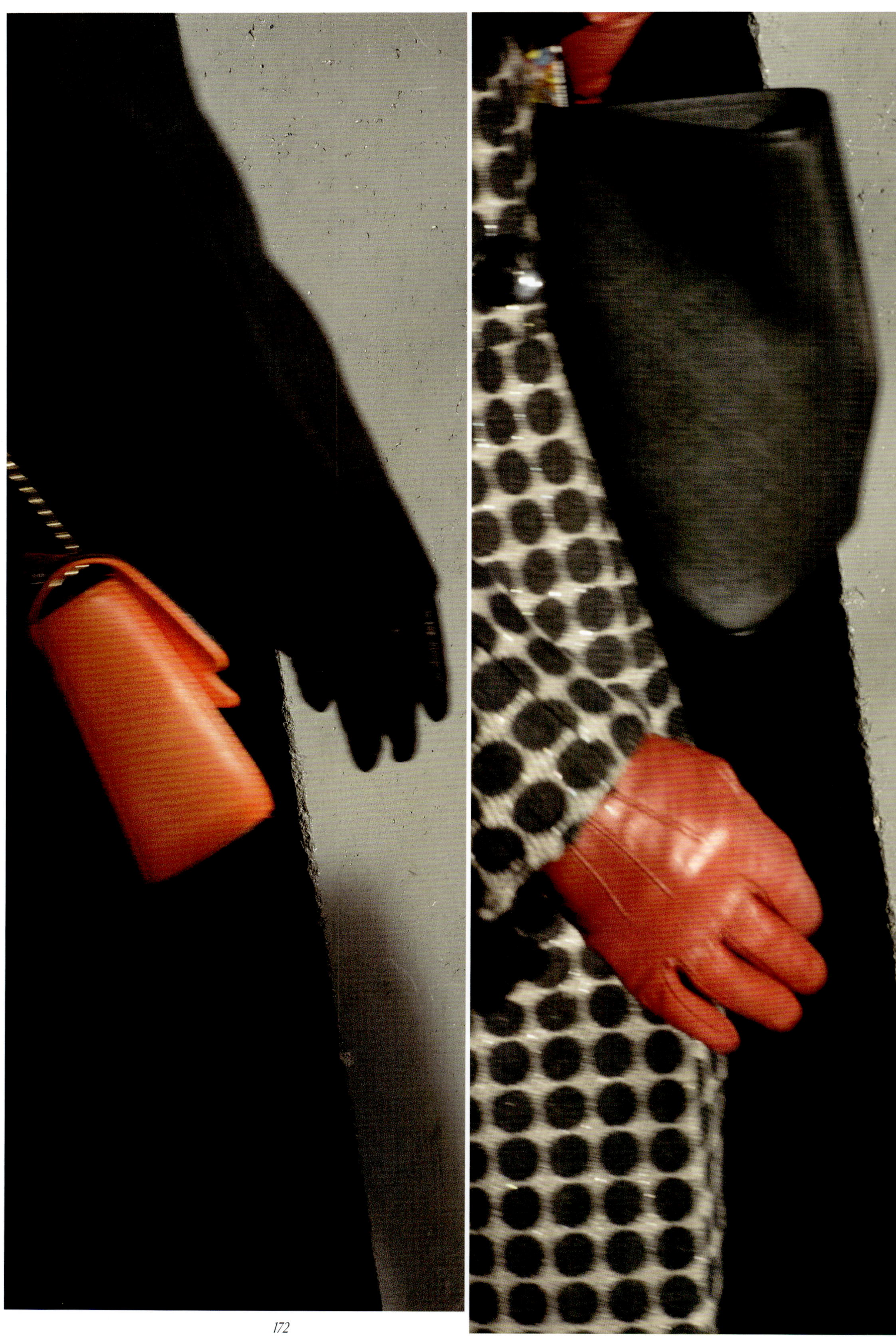

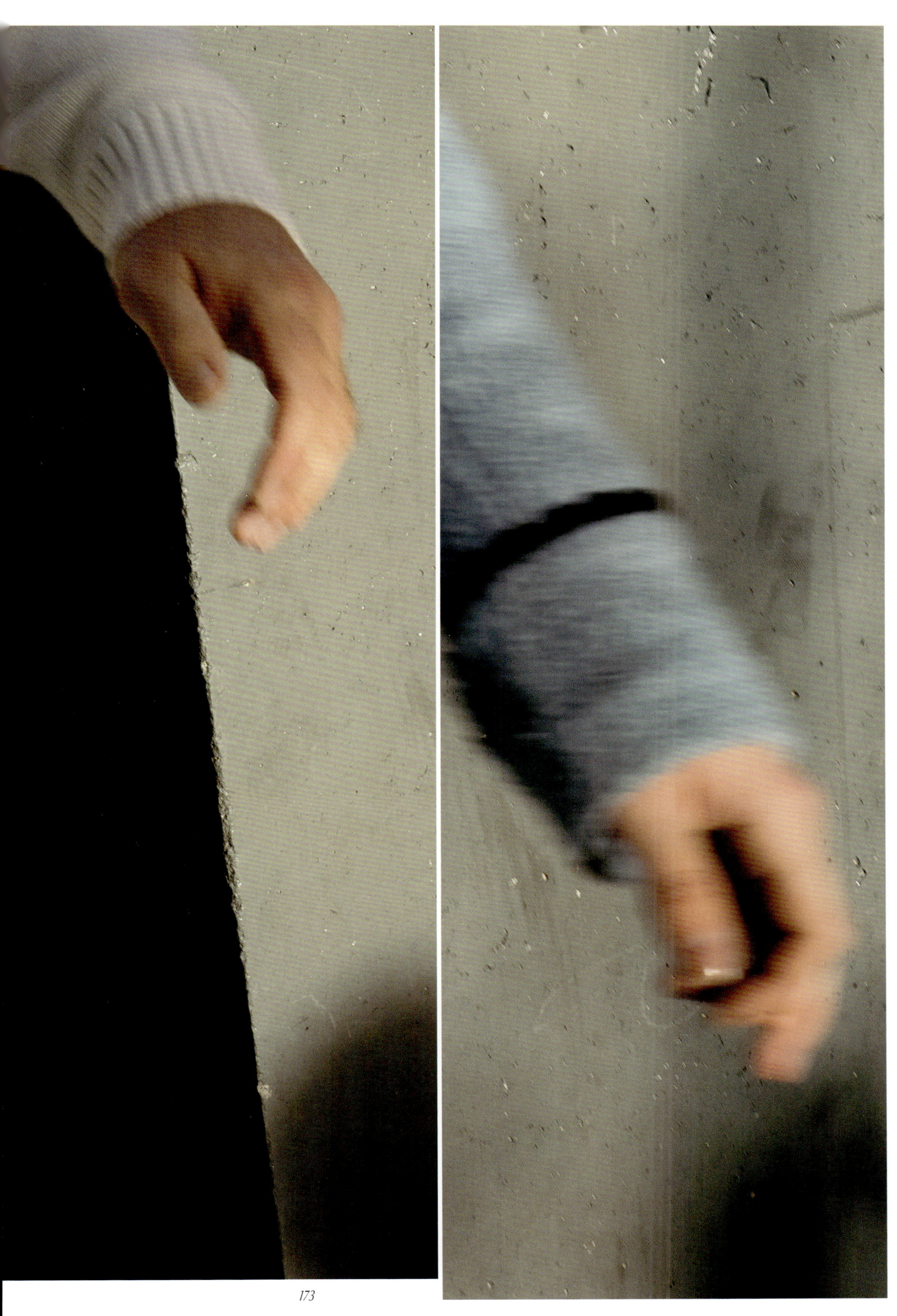

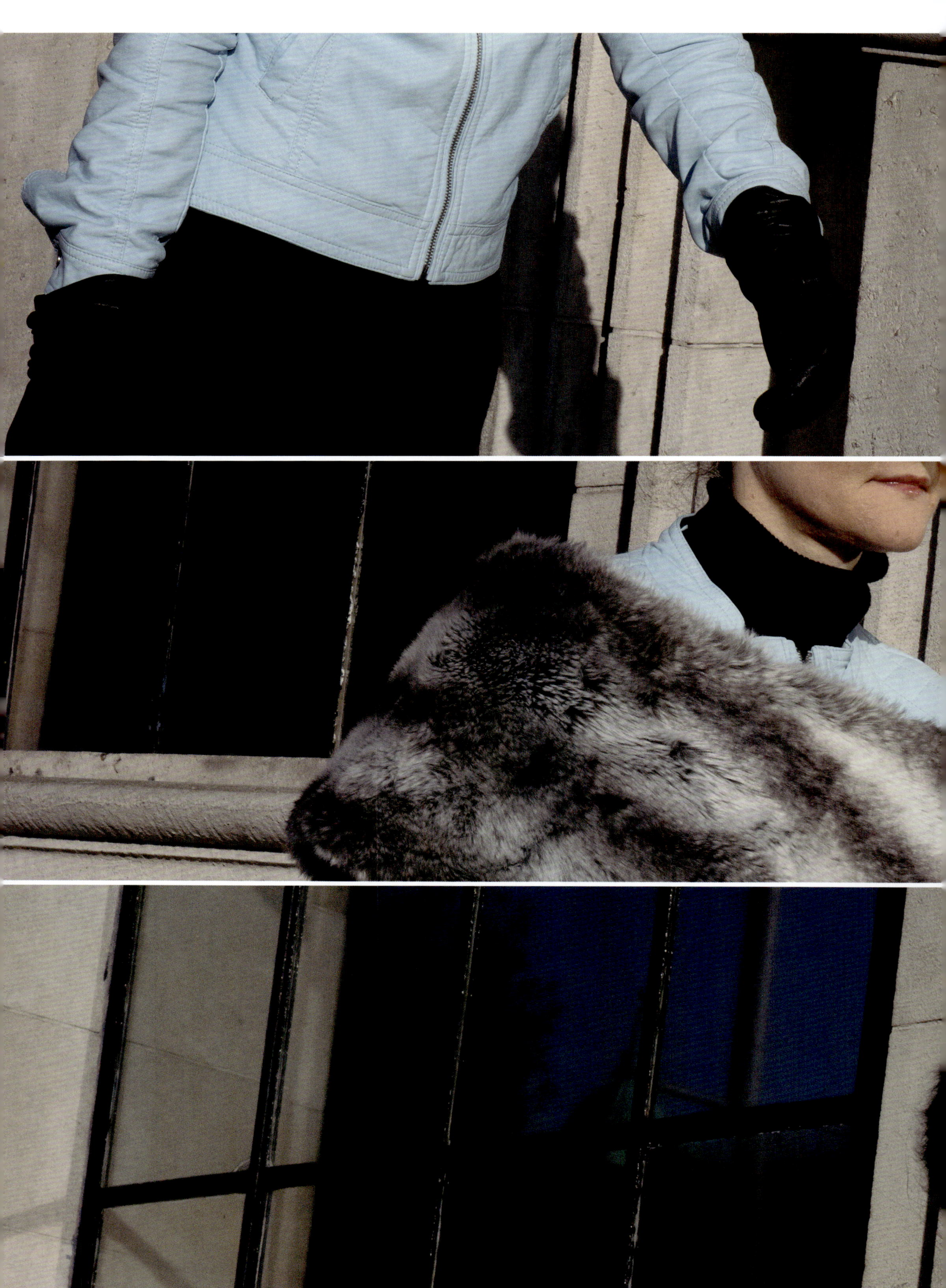

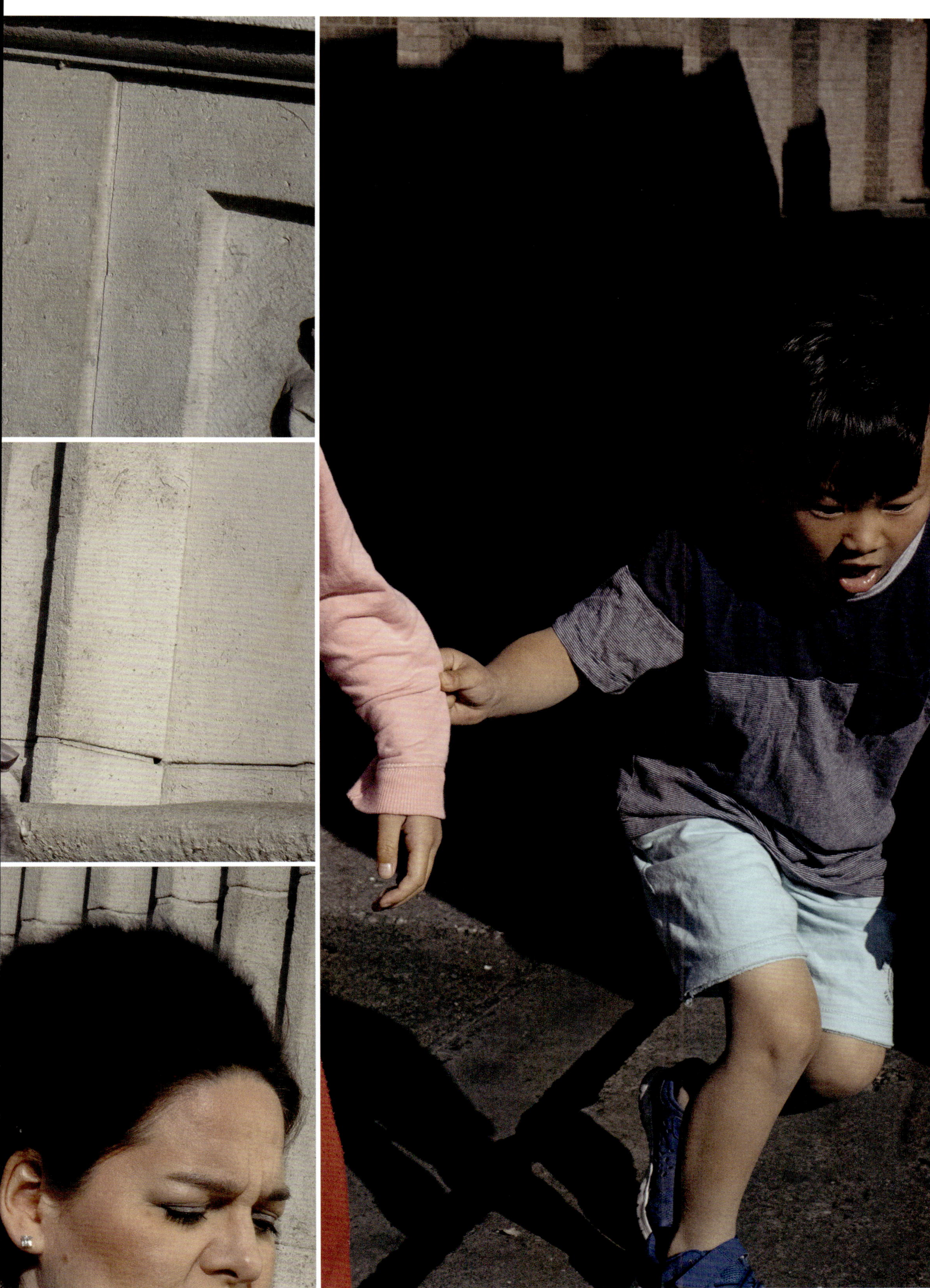

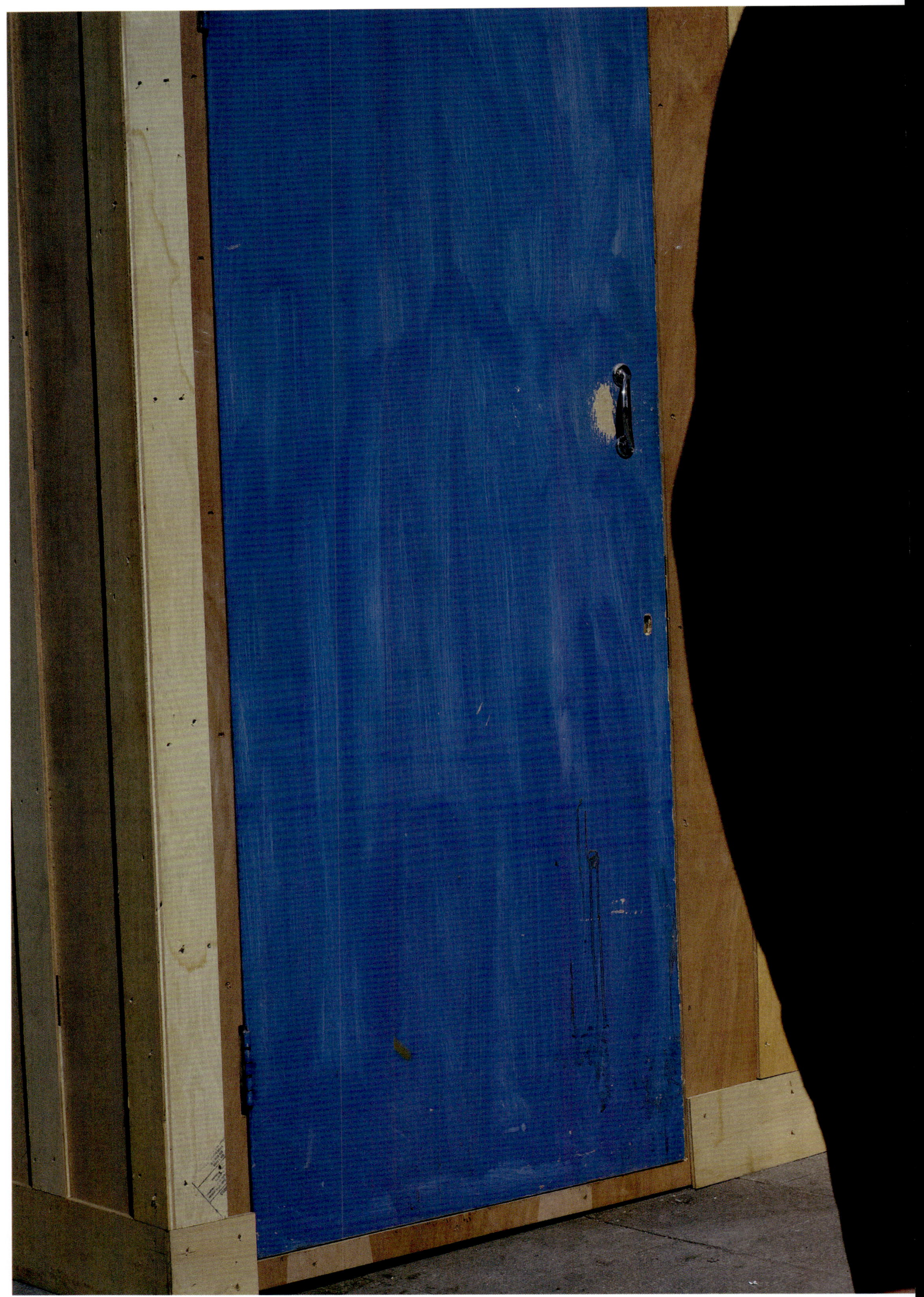

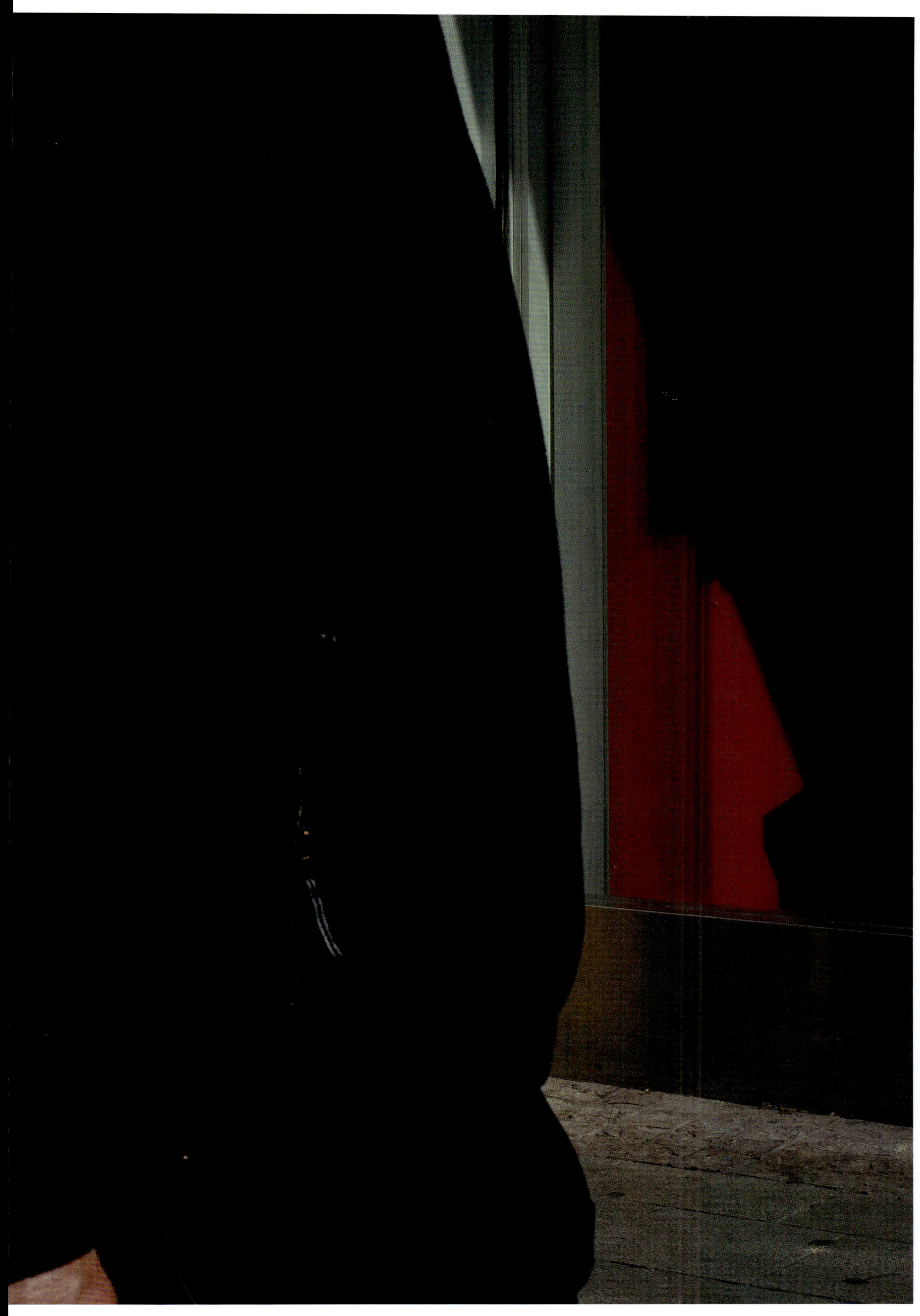

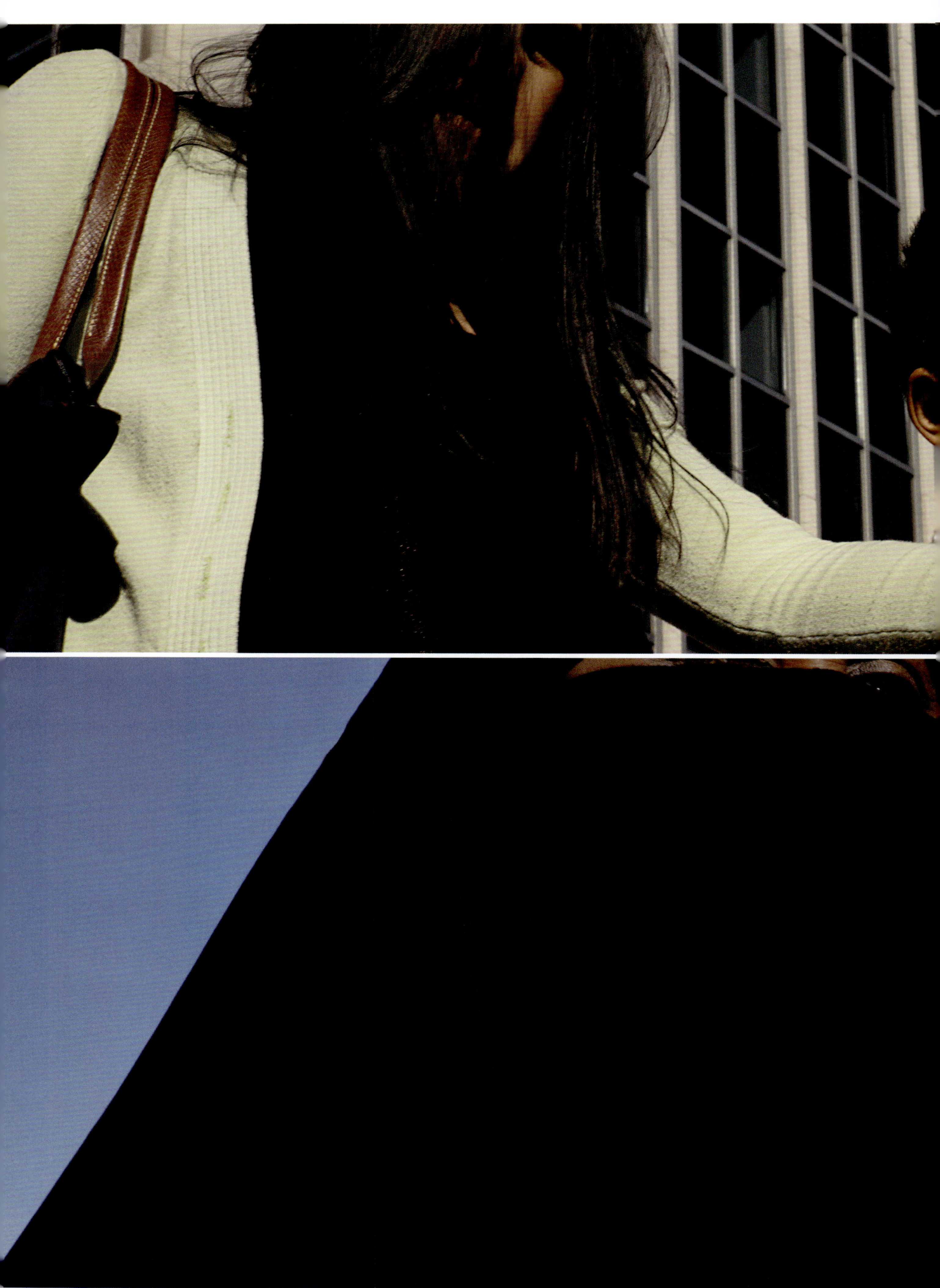

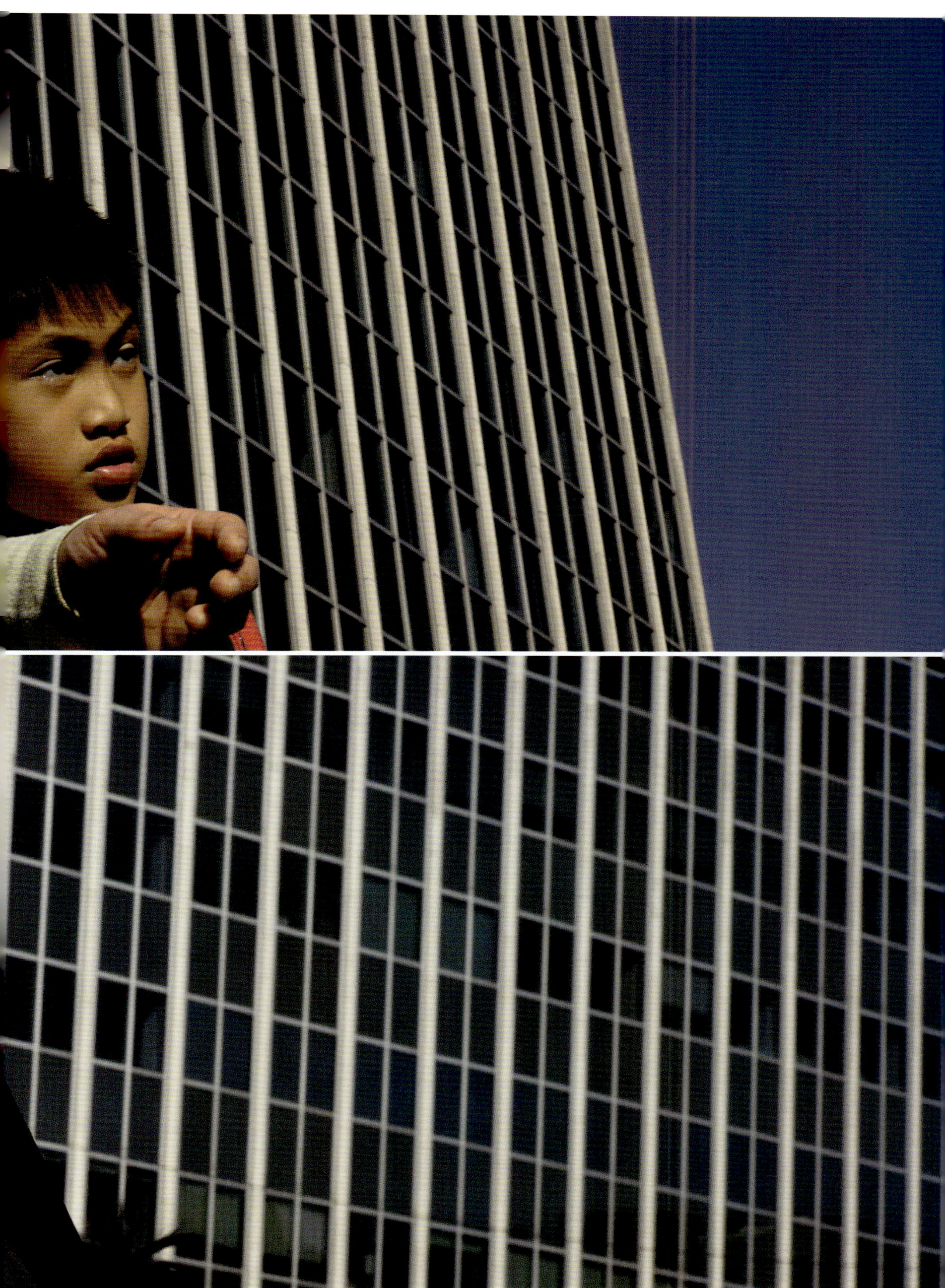

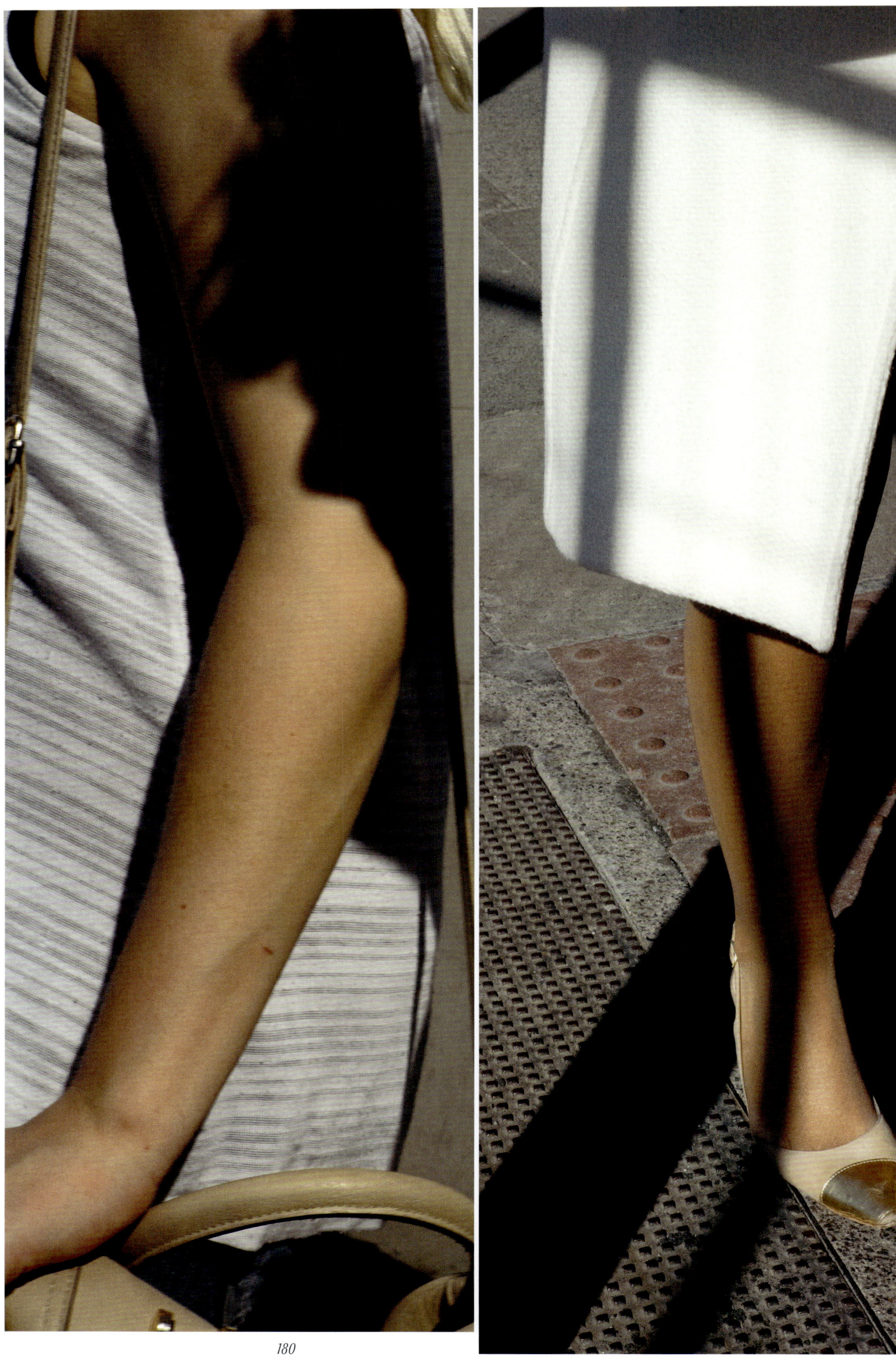

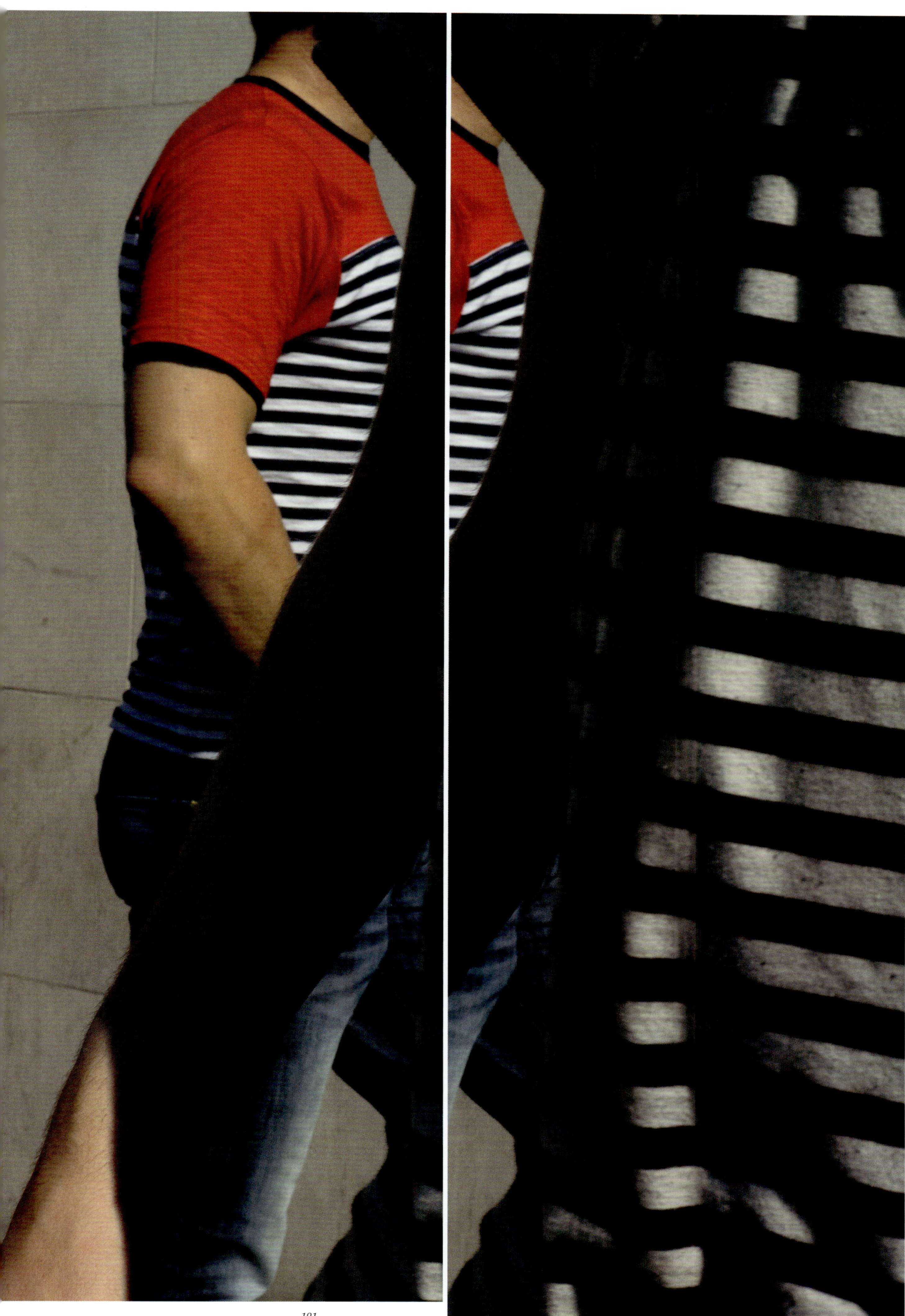

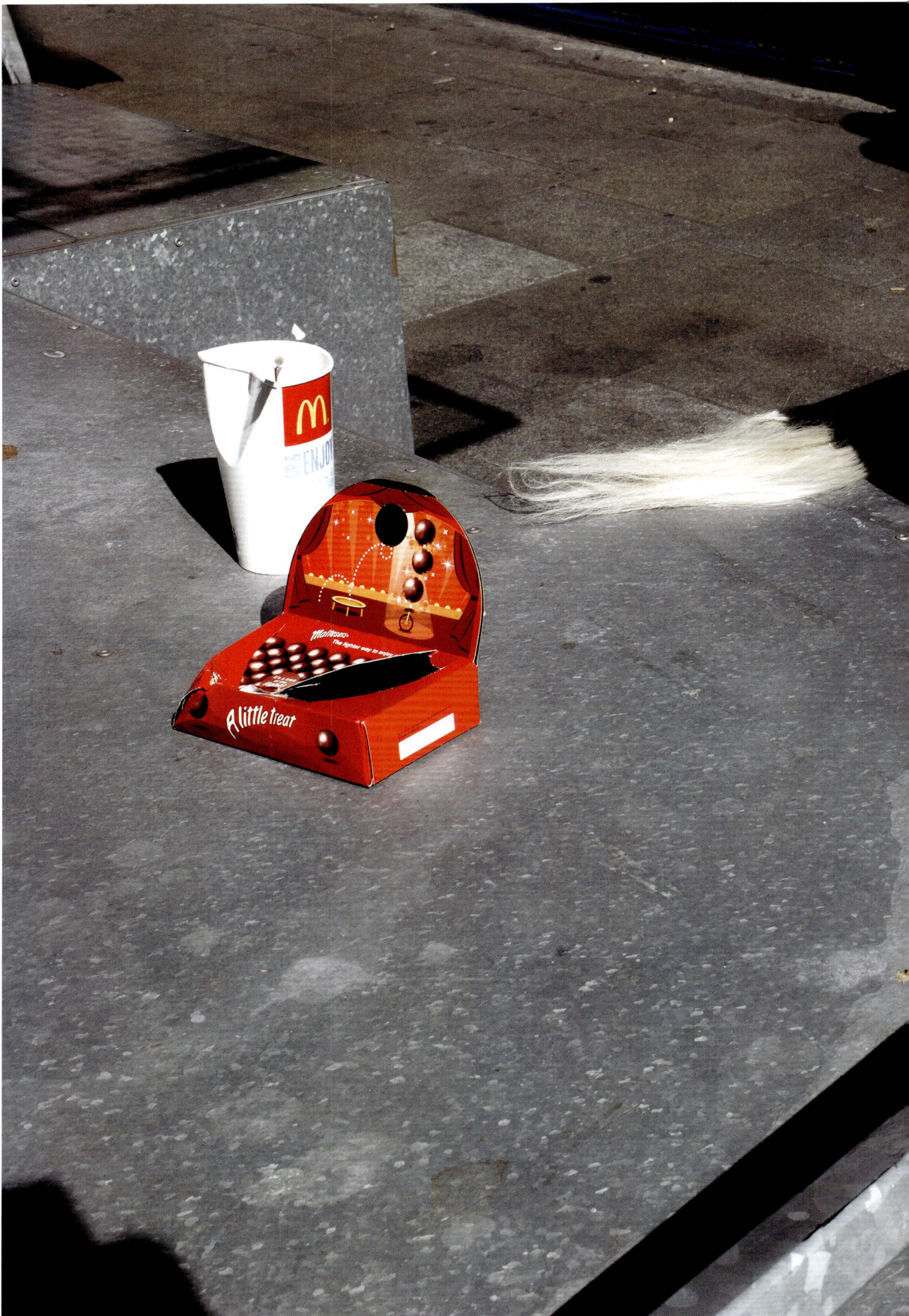

M
ENJOY
Maltesers
The lighter way to enjoy
A little treat

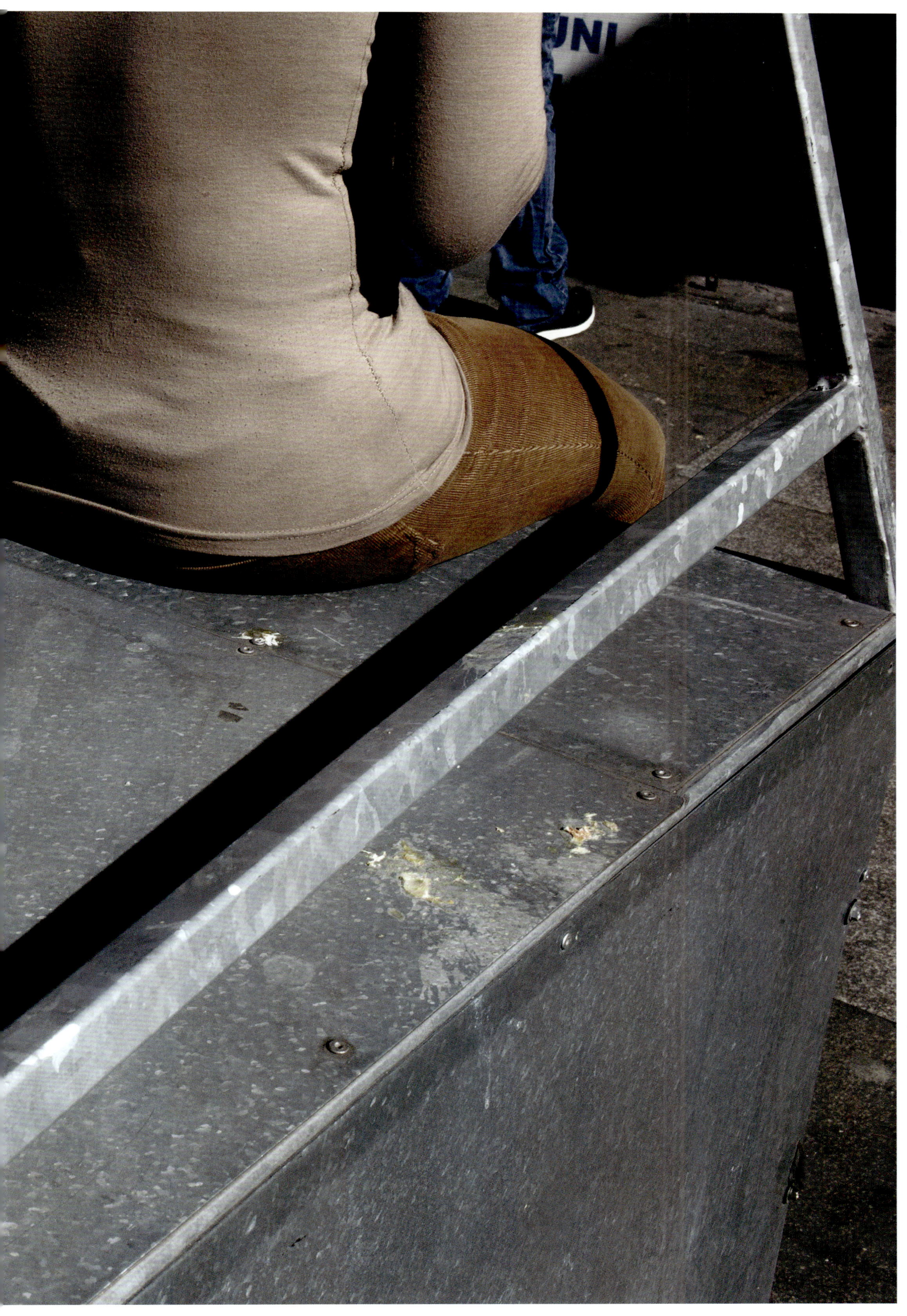

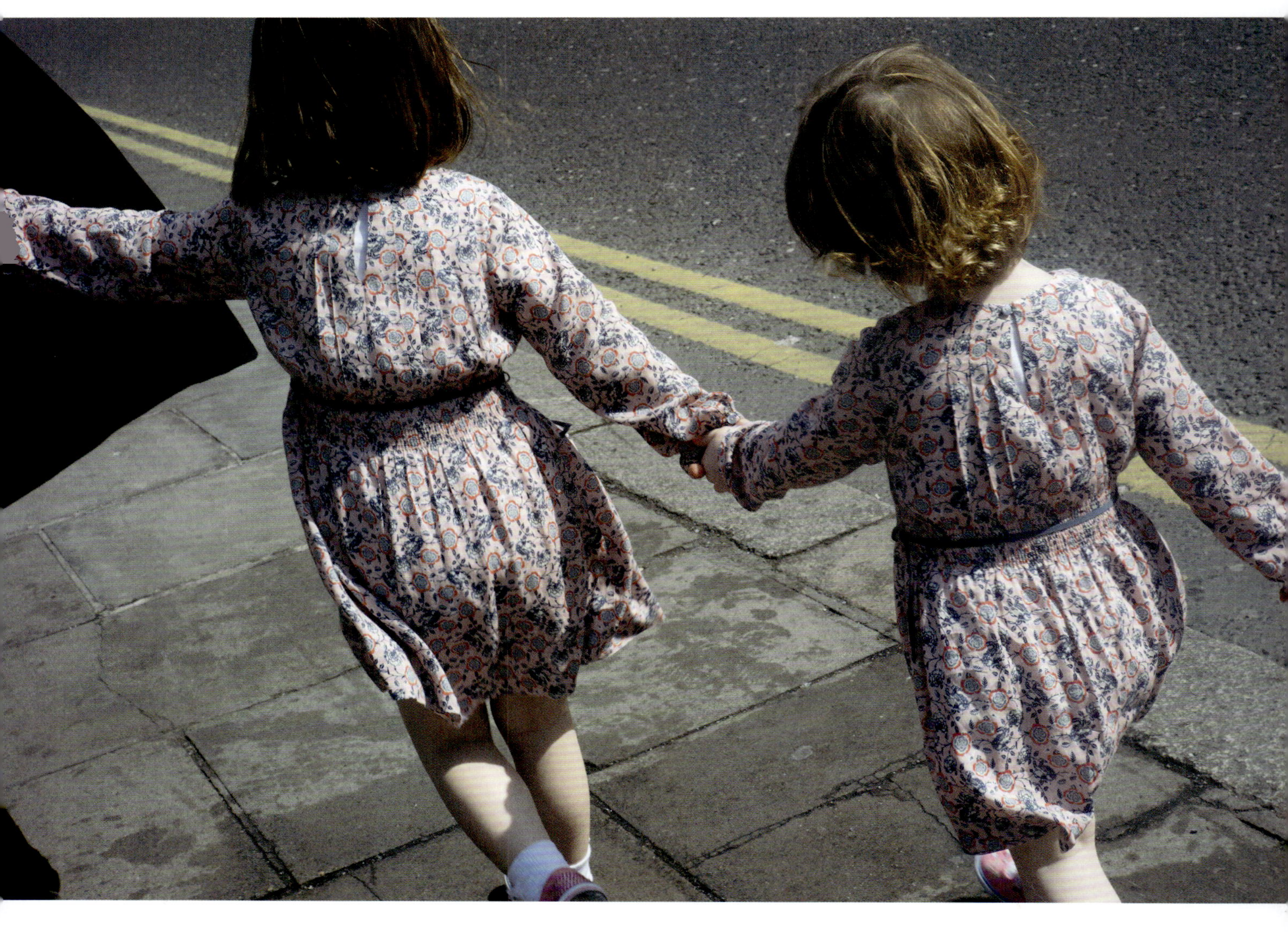

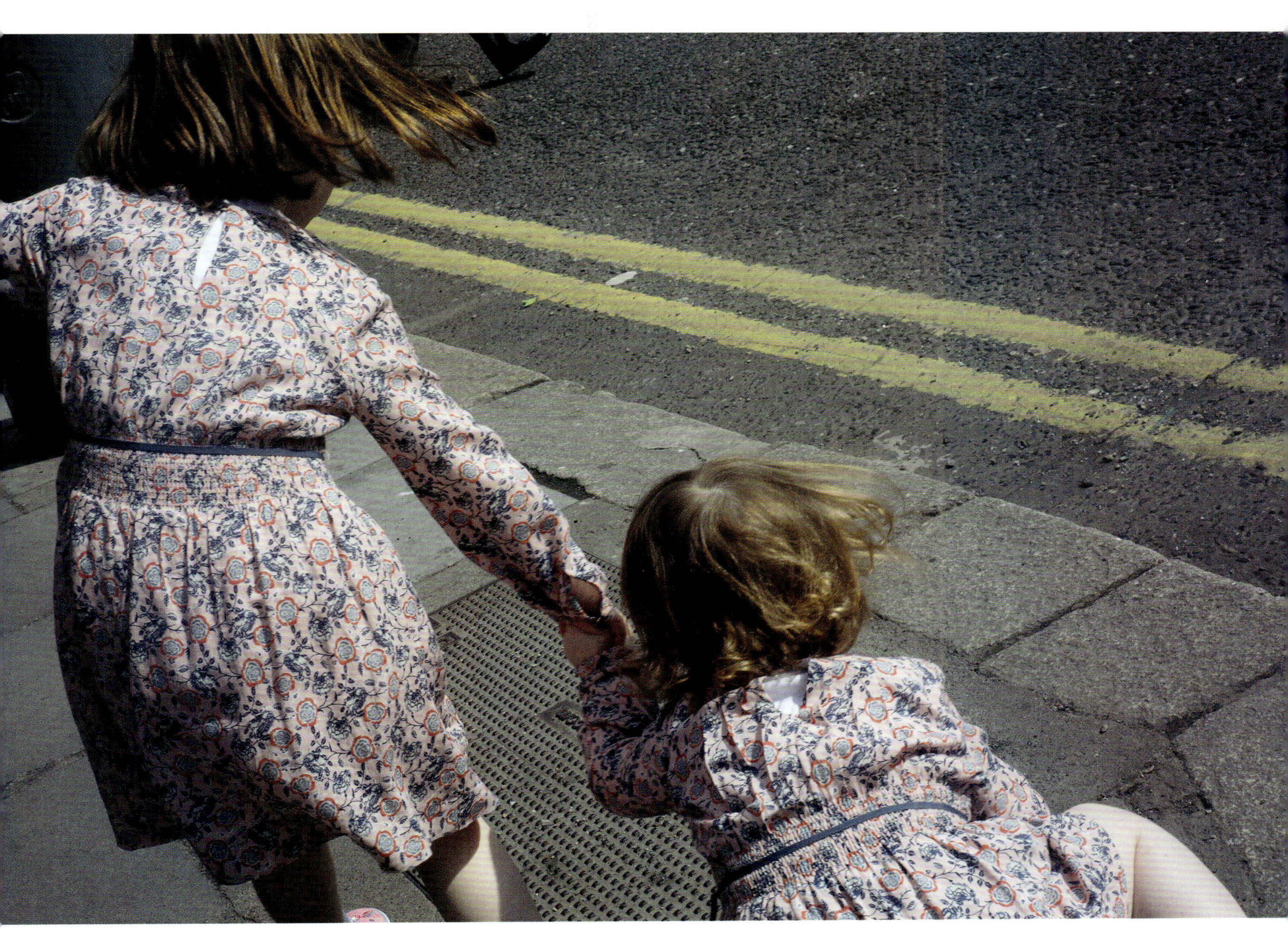

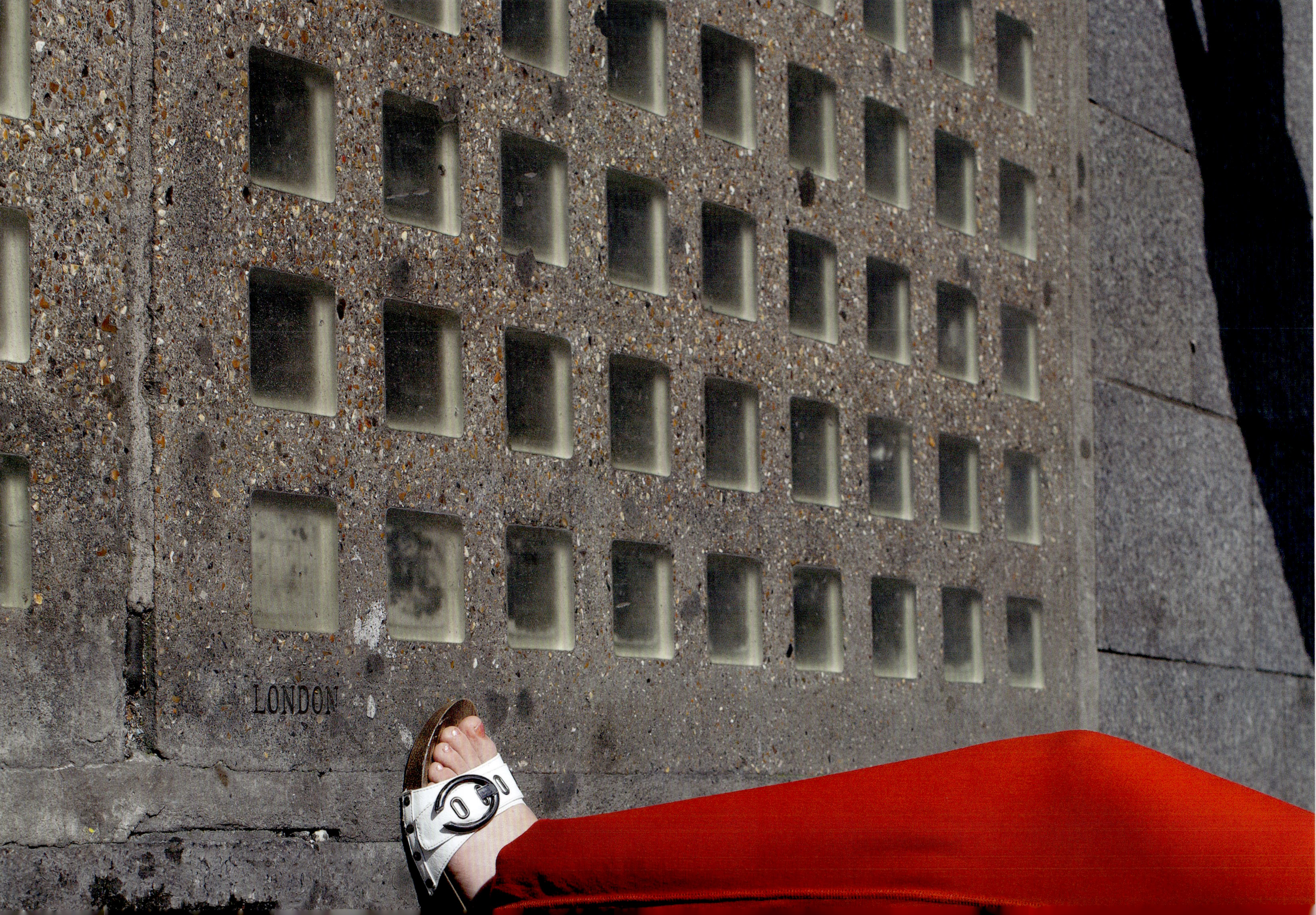

LONDON

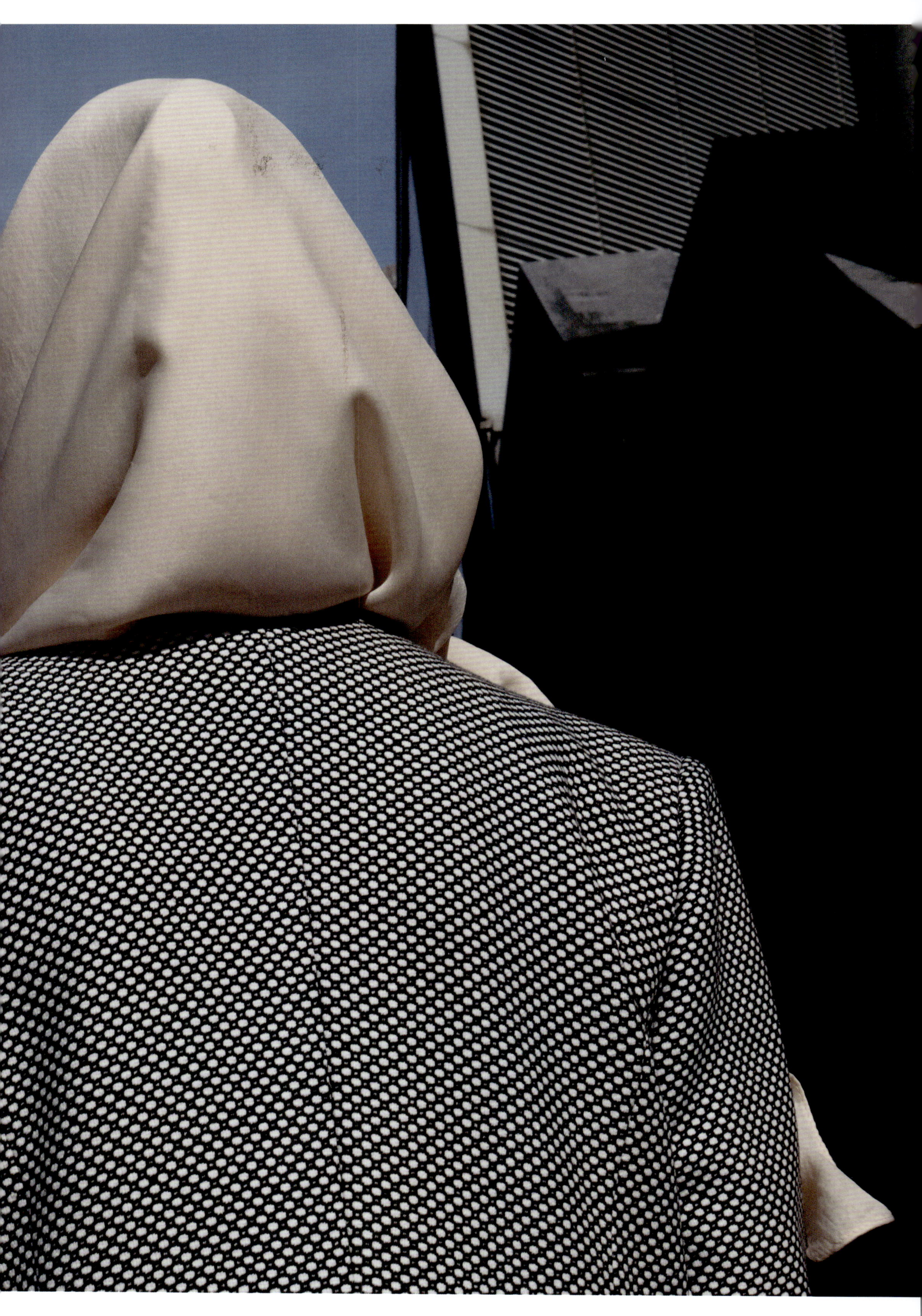

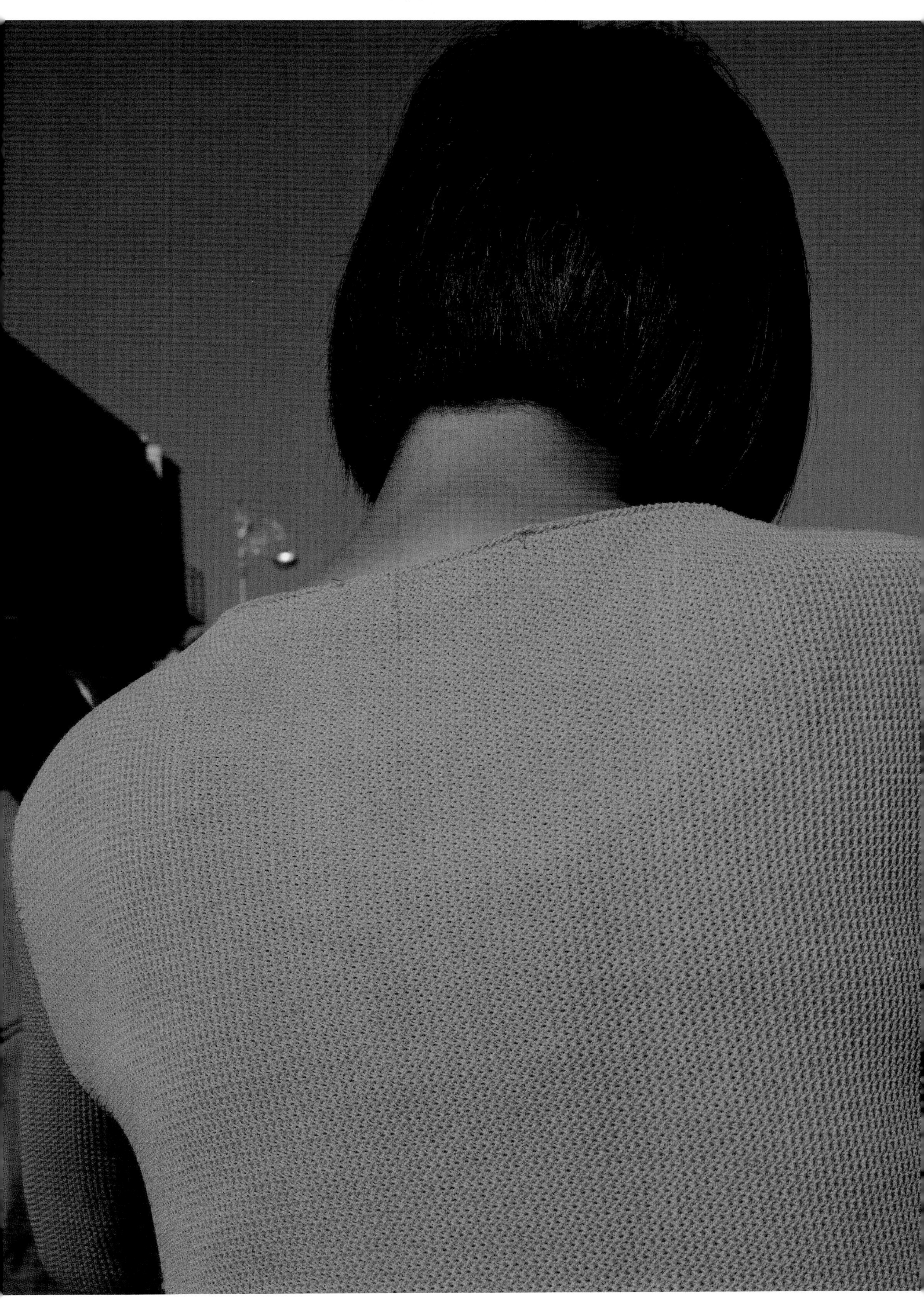

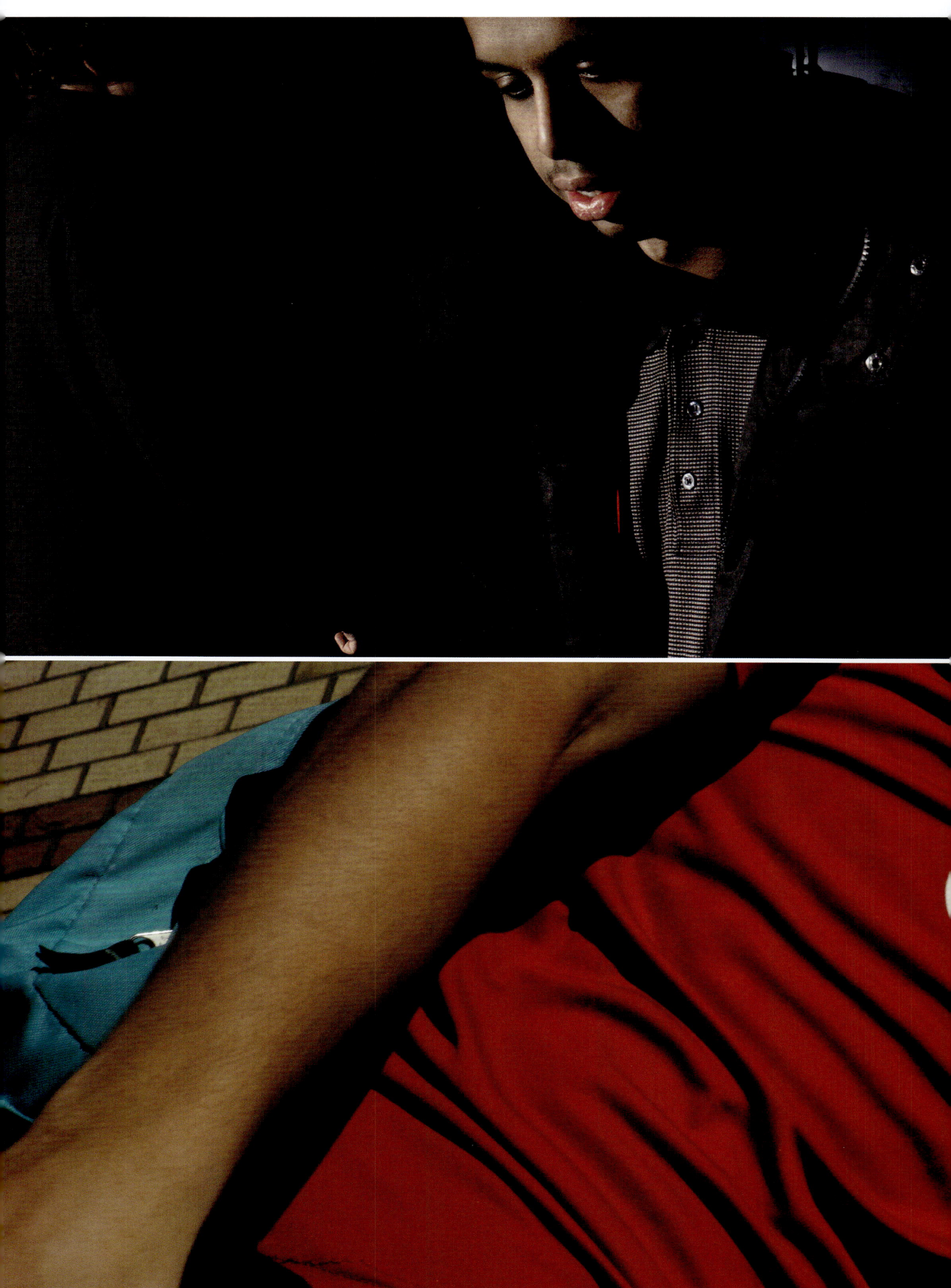

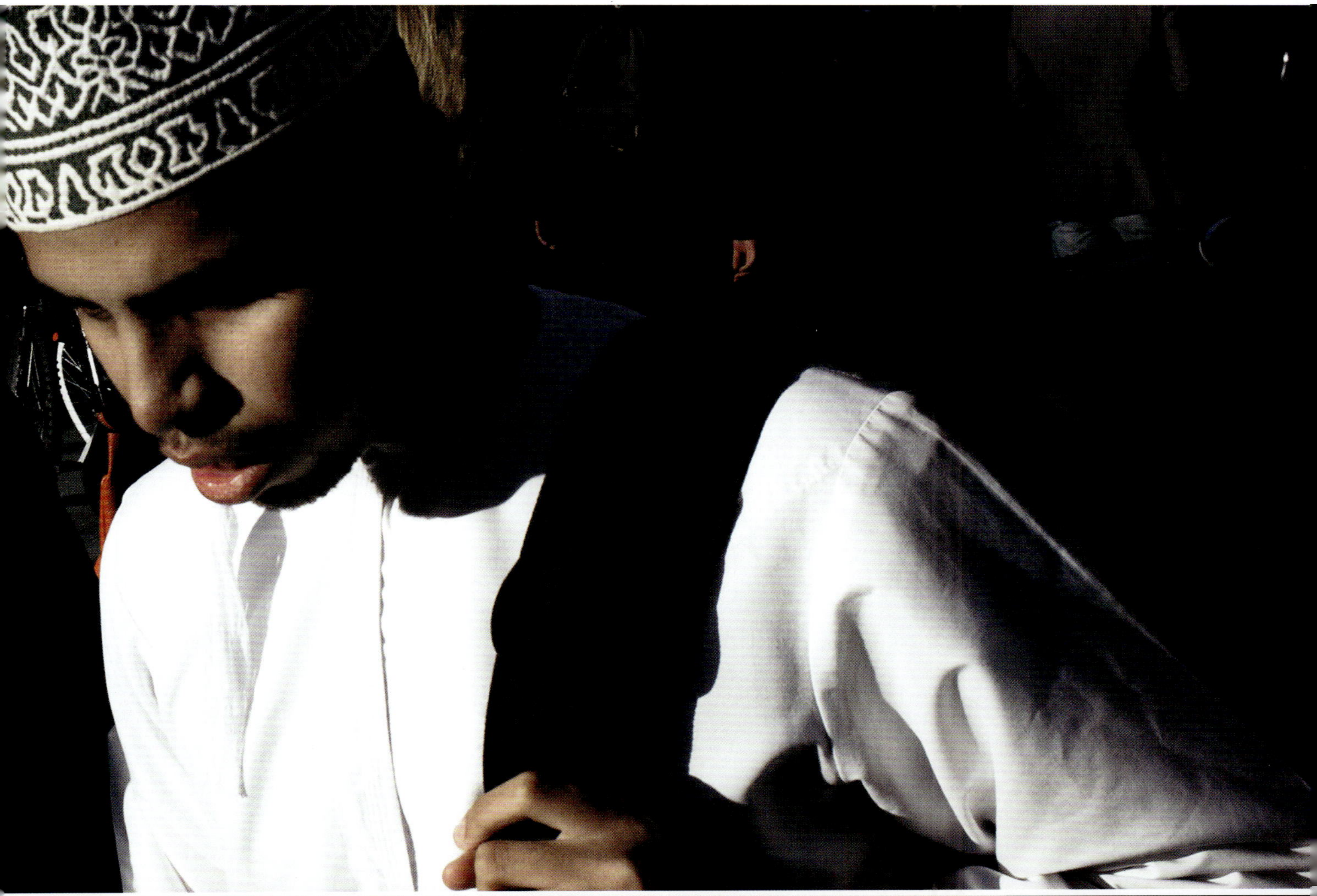

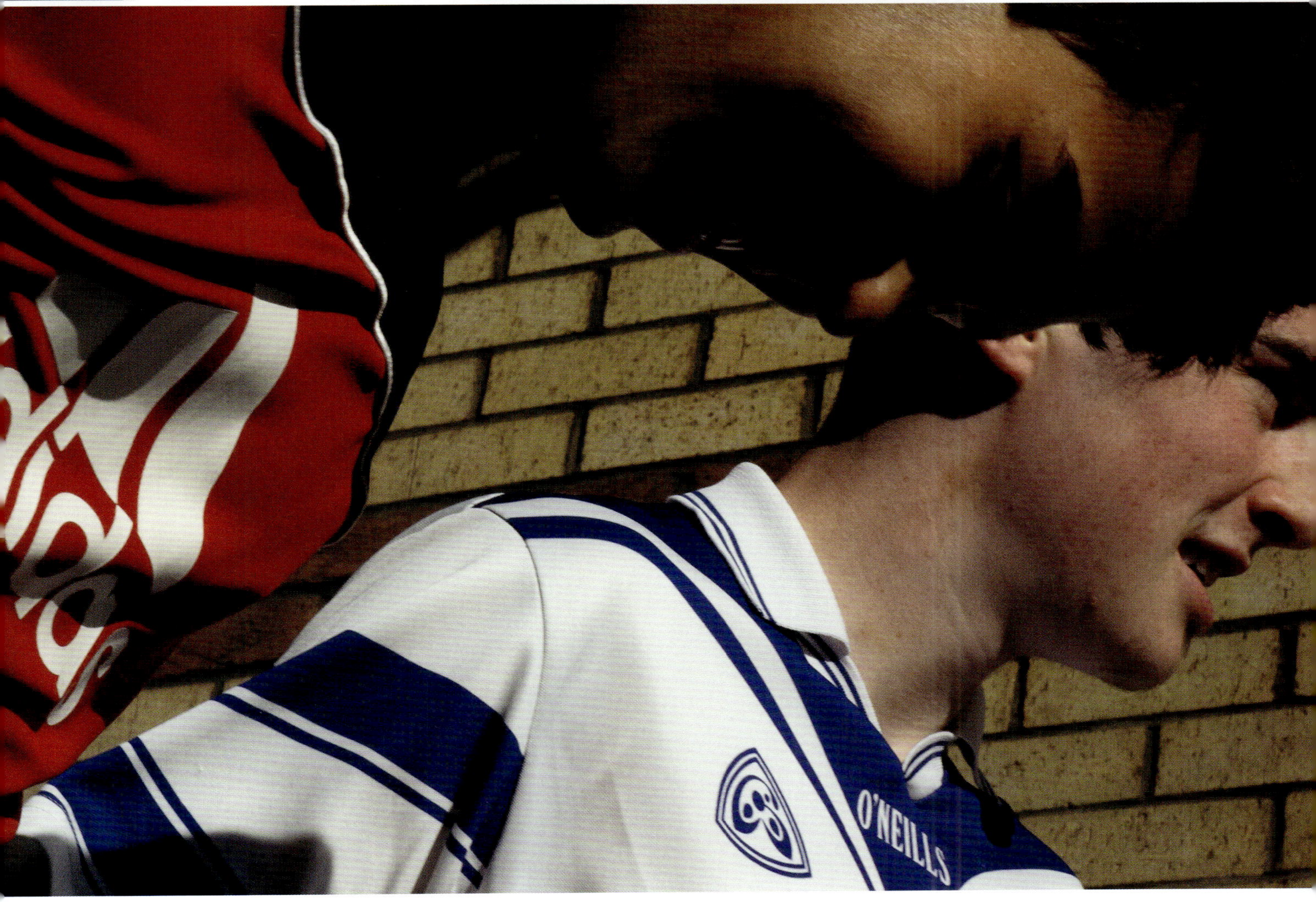

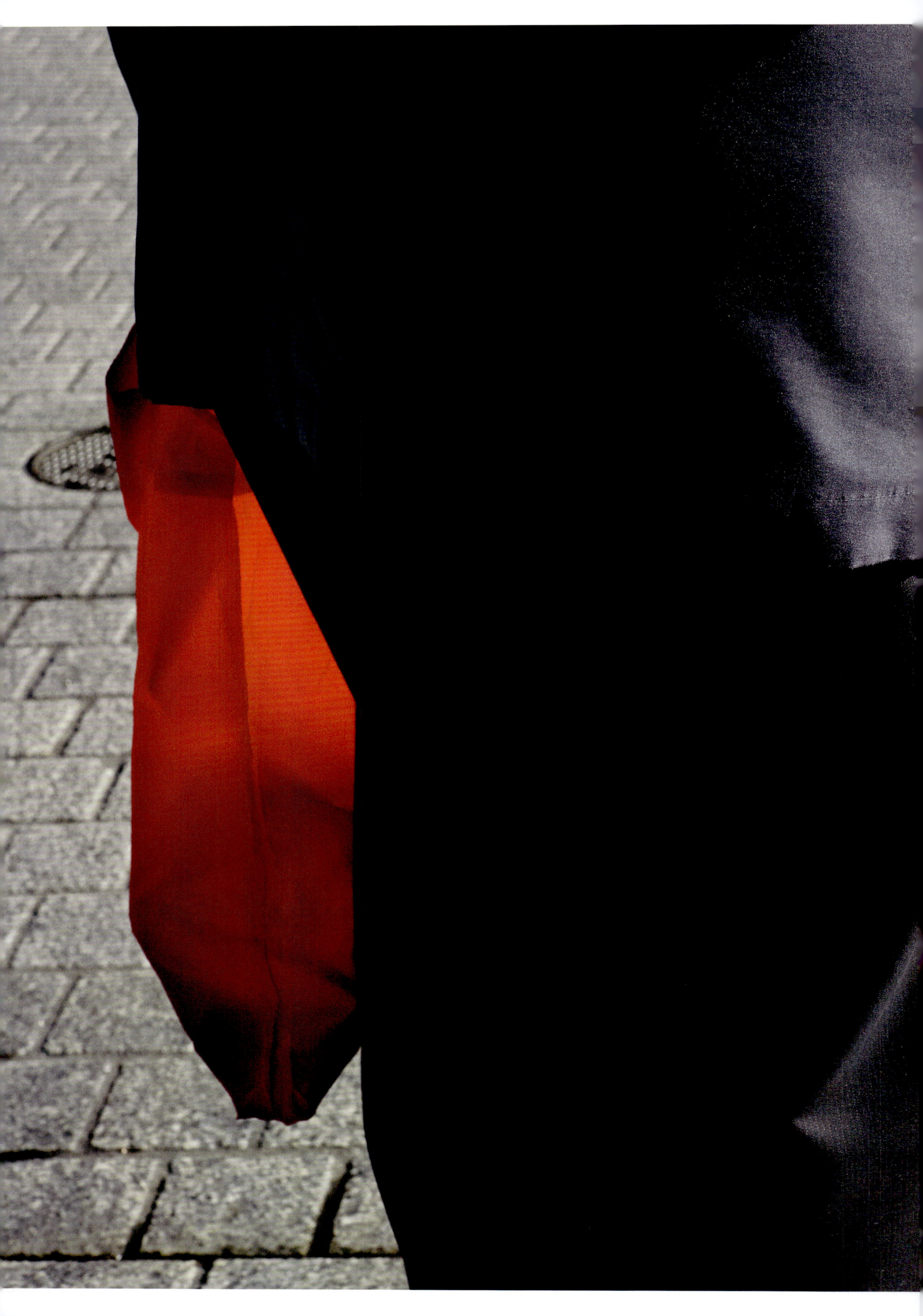

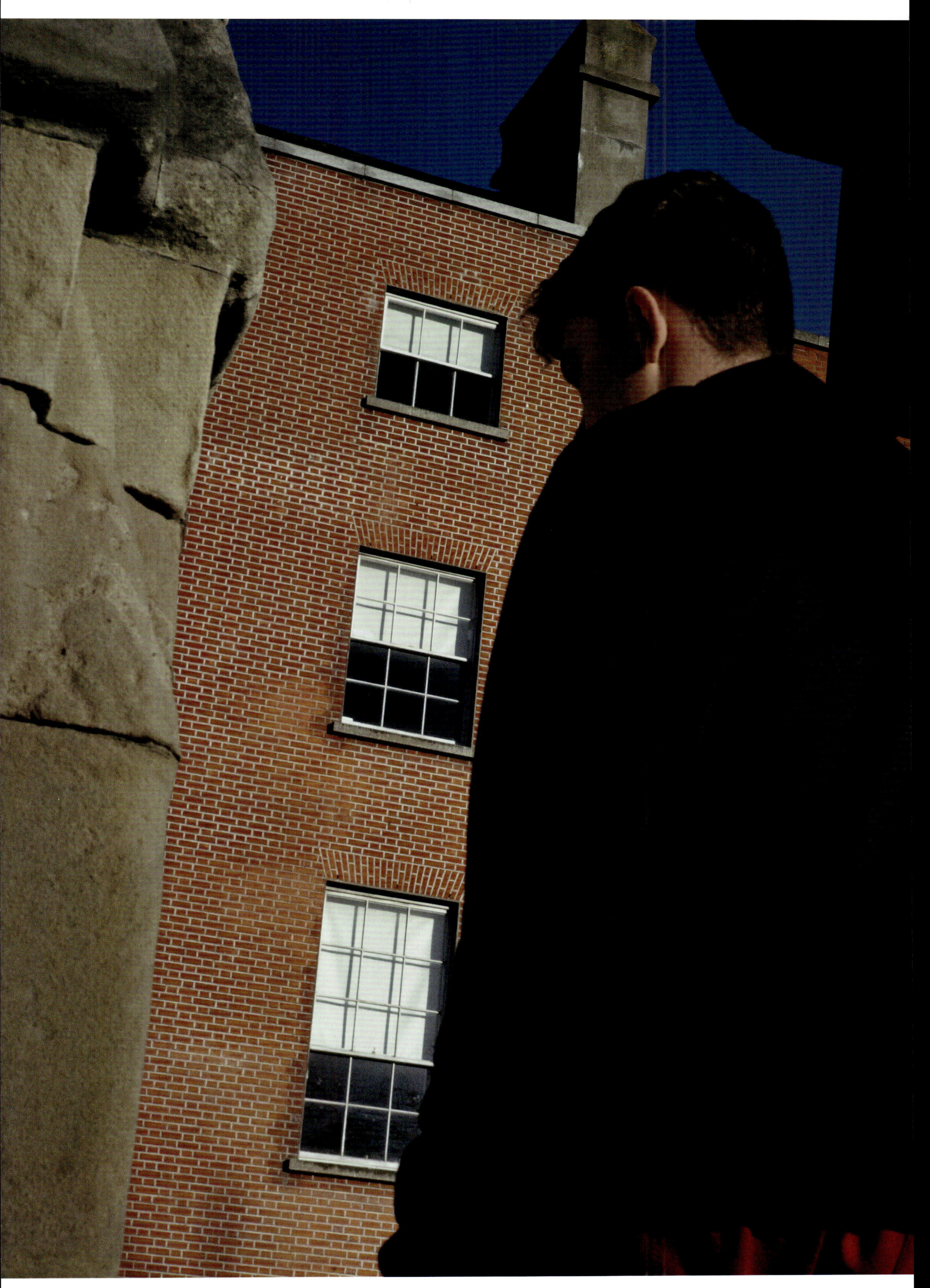

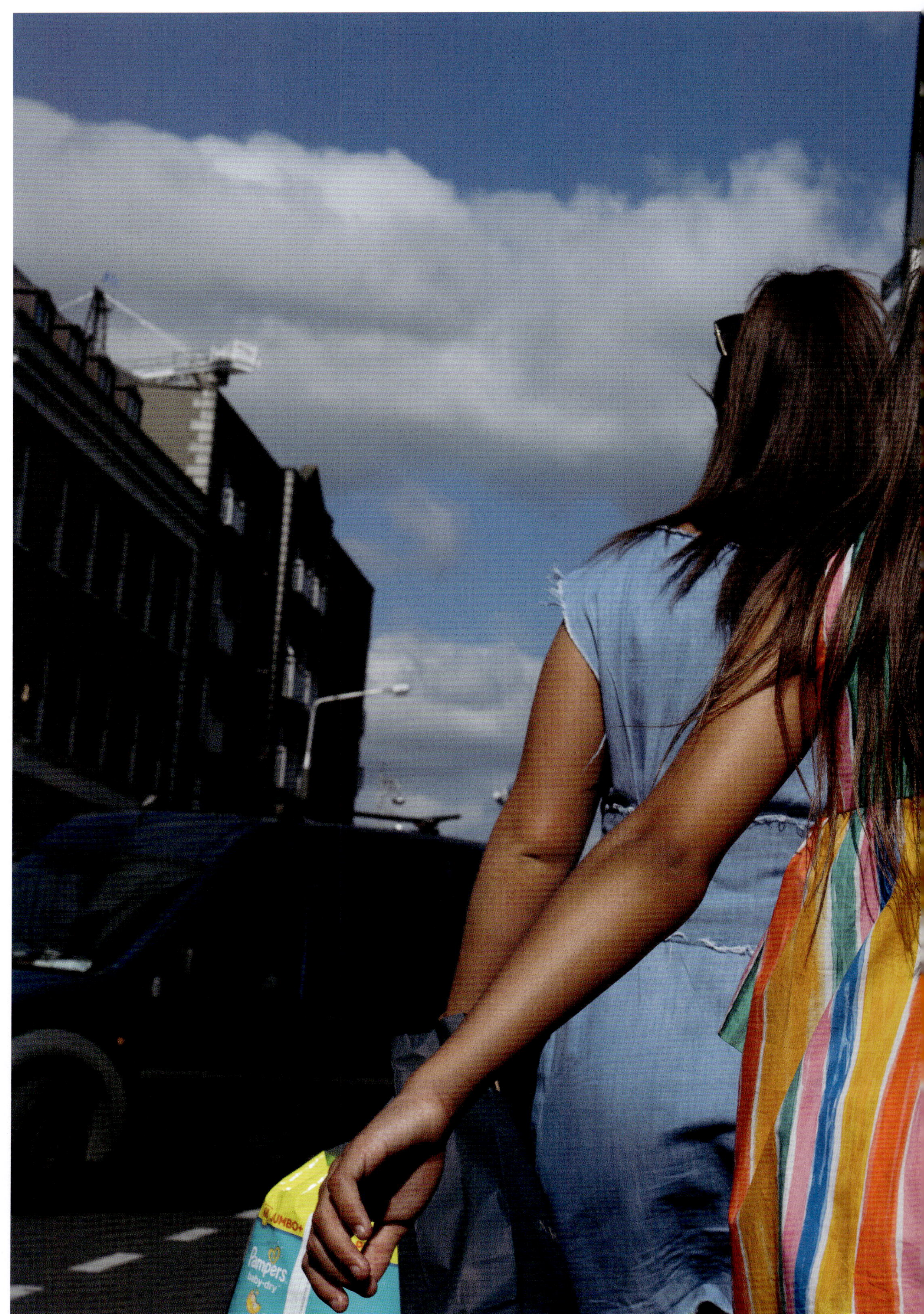

JUMBO+
Pampers
baby-dry

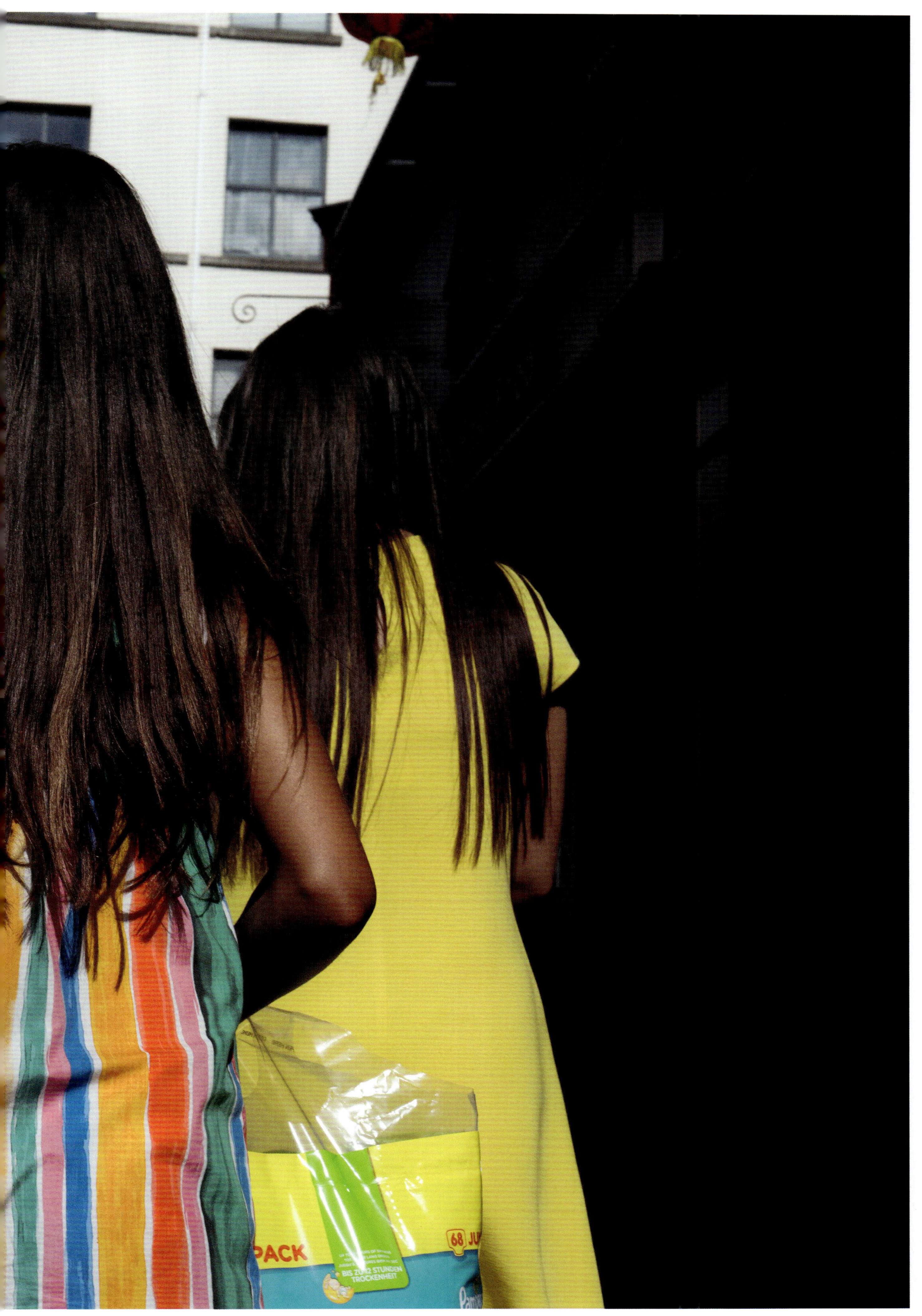

PACK
68 JU
BIS ZU 12 STUNDEN
TROCKENHEIT

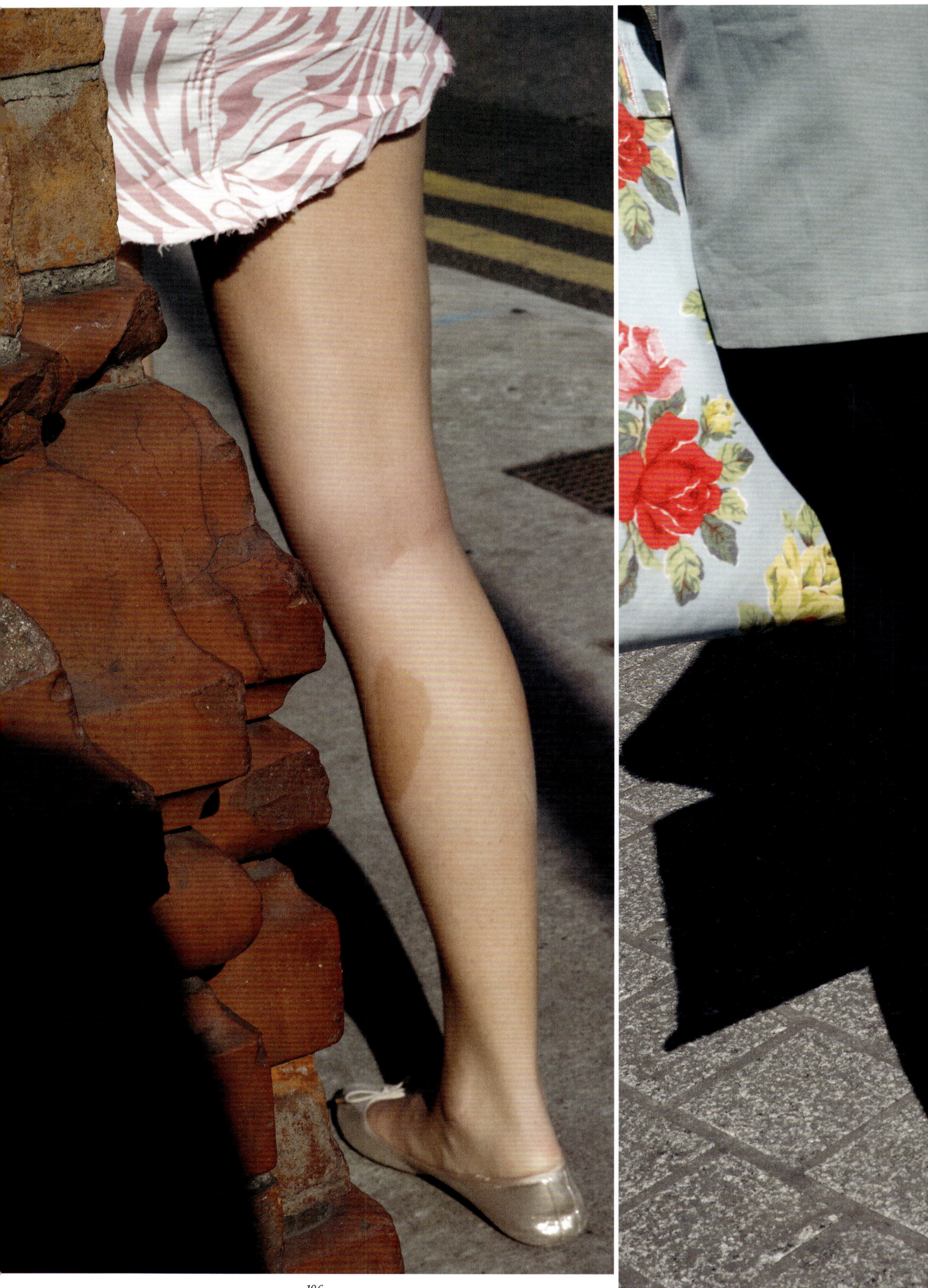

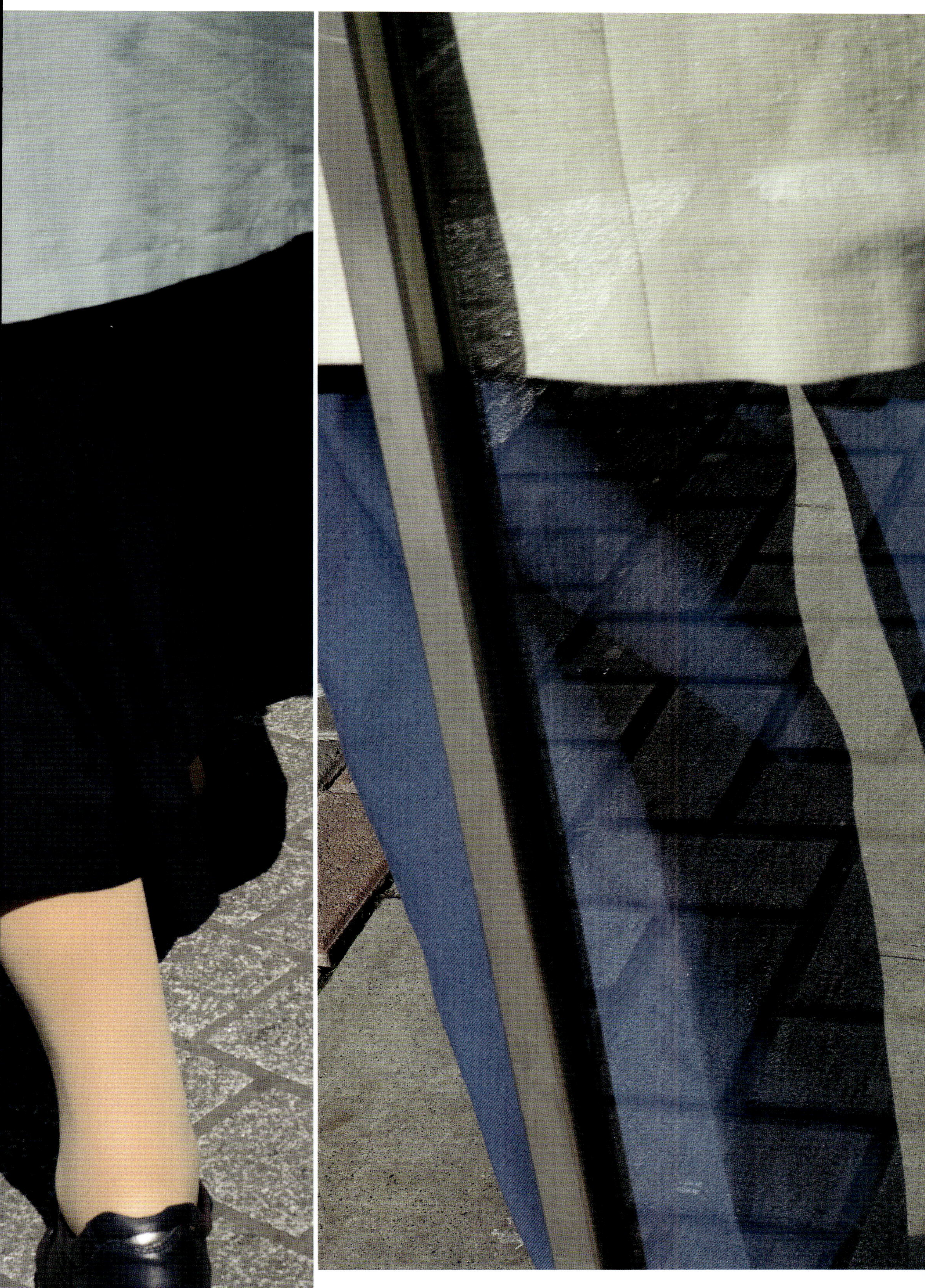

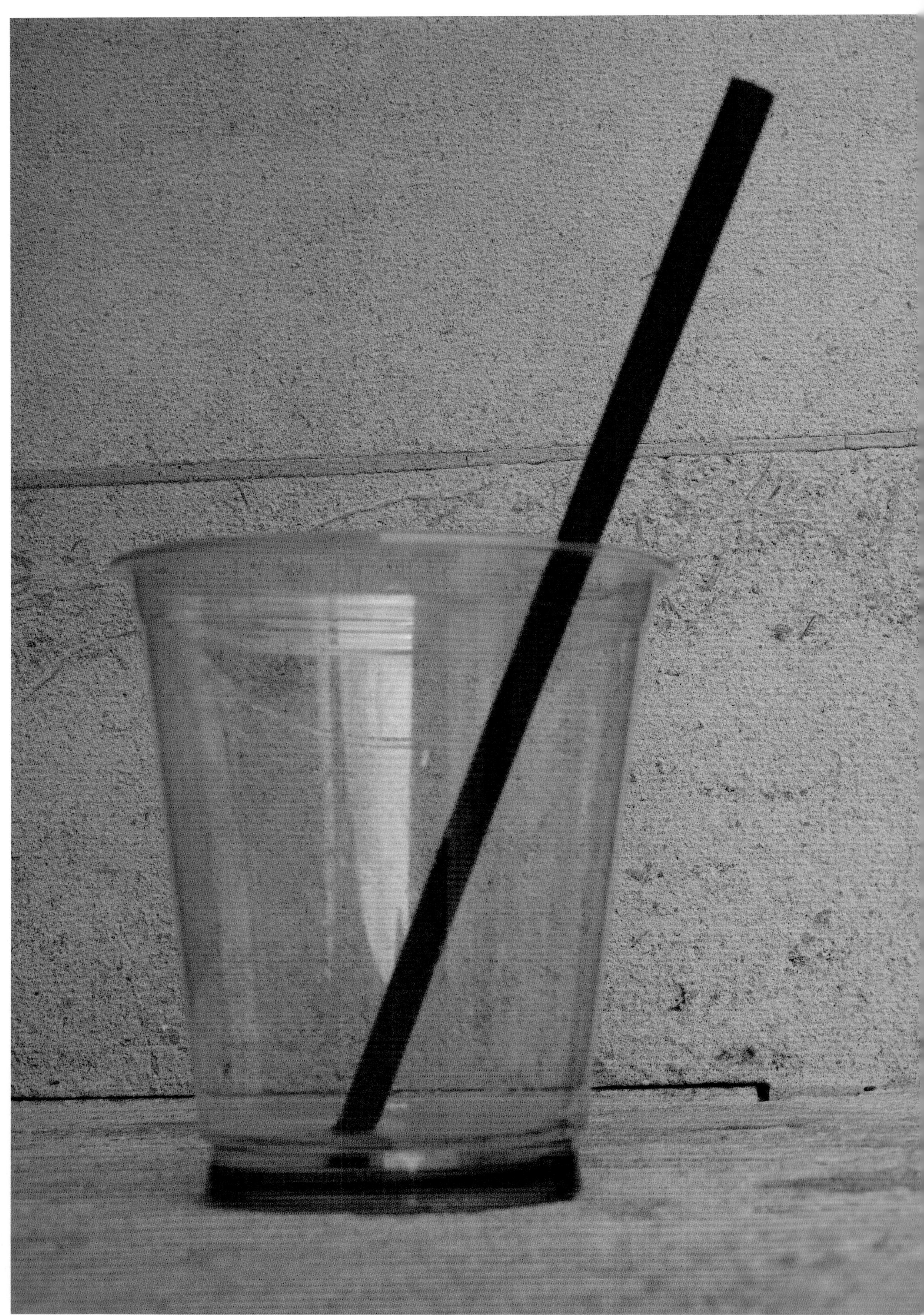

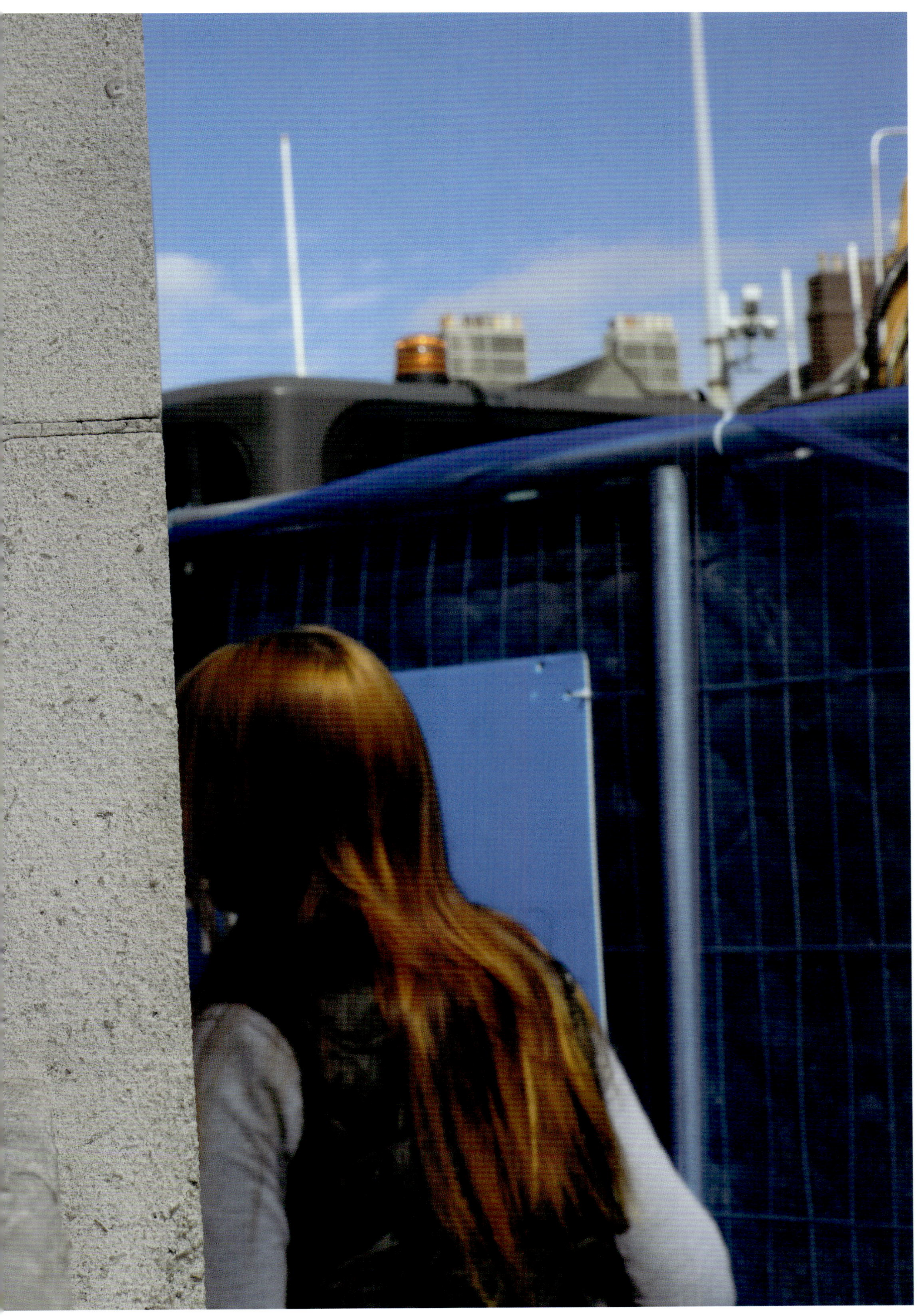

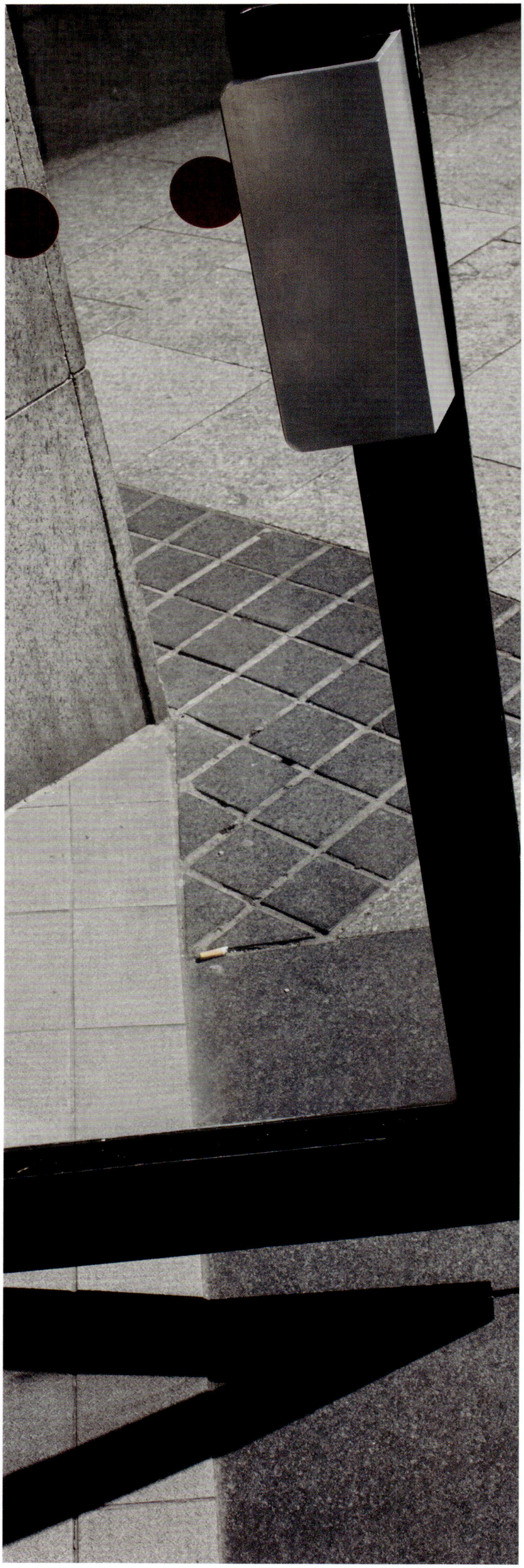

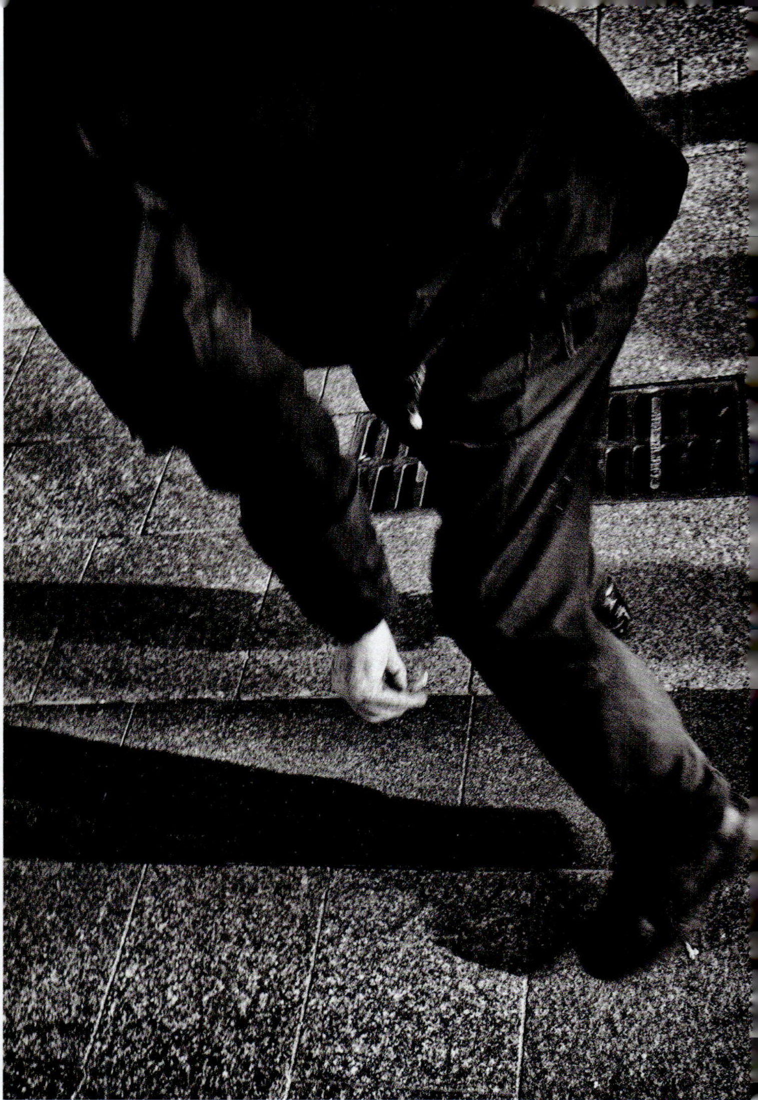

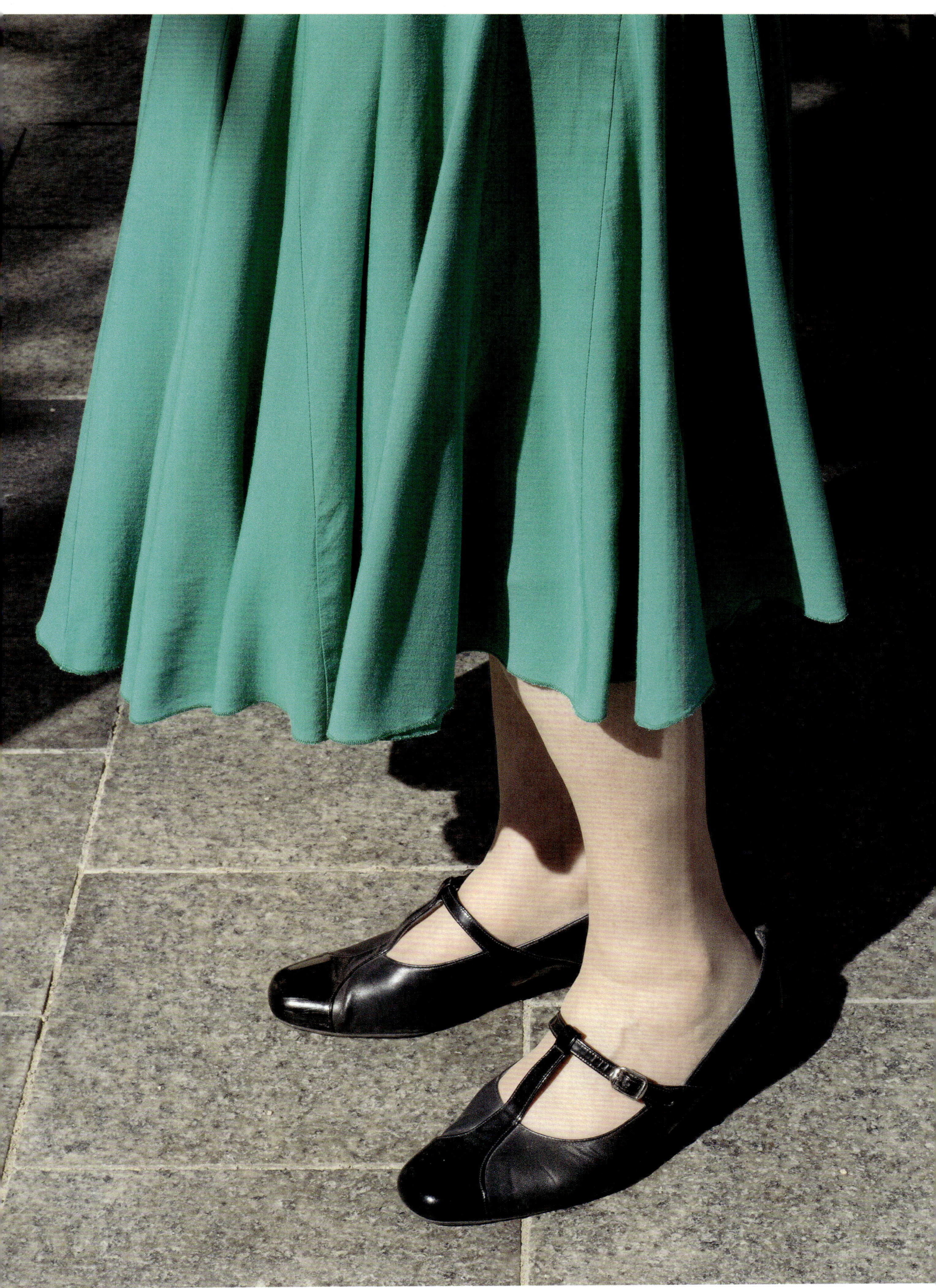

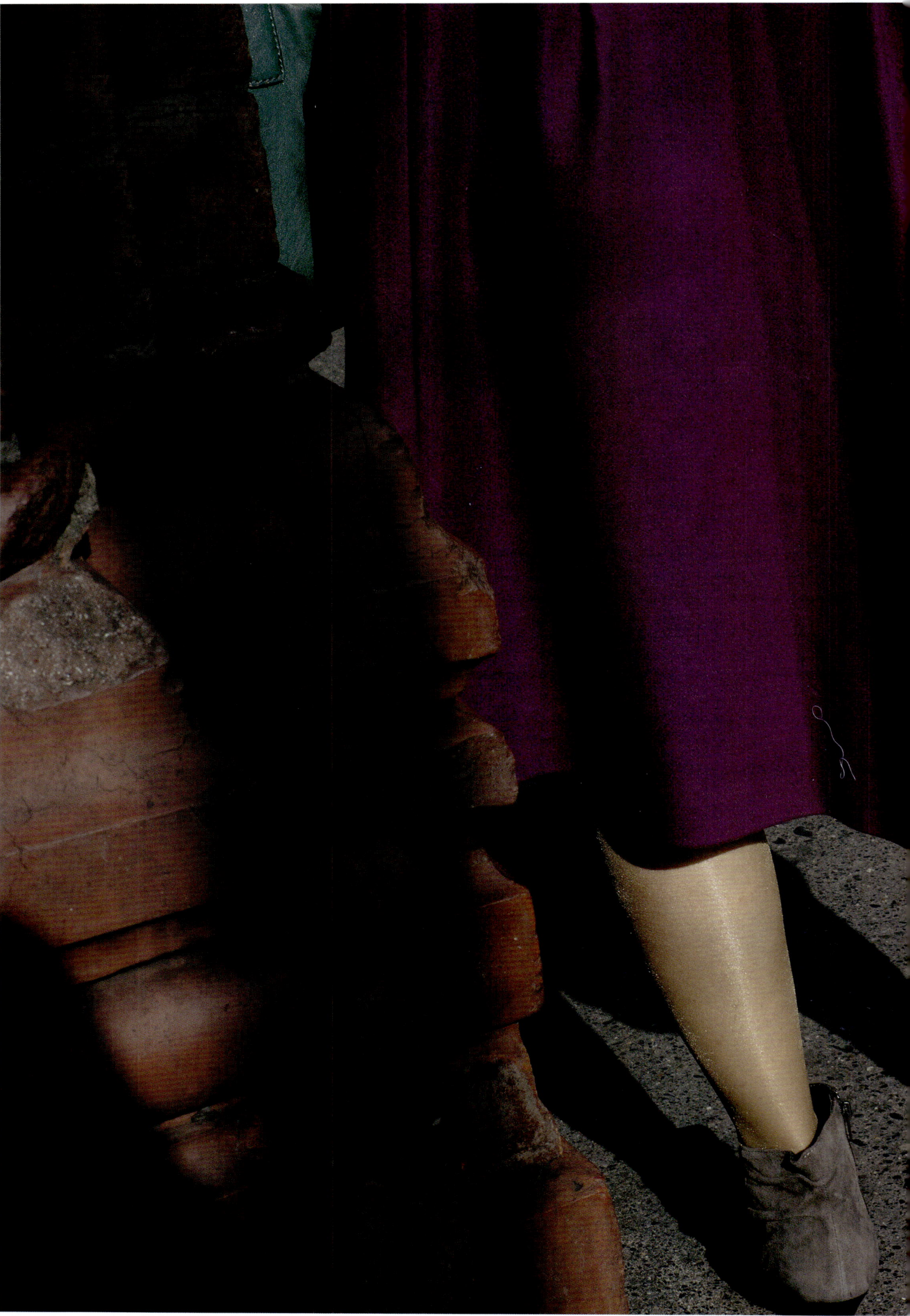

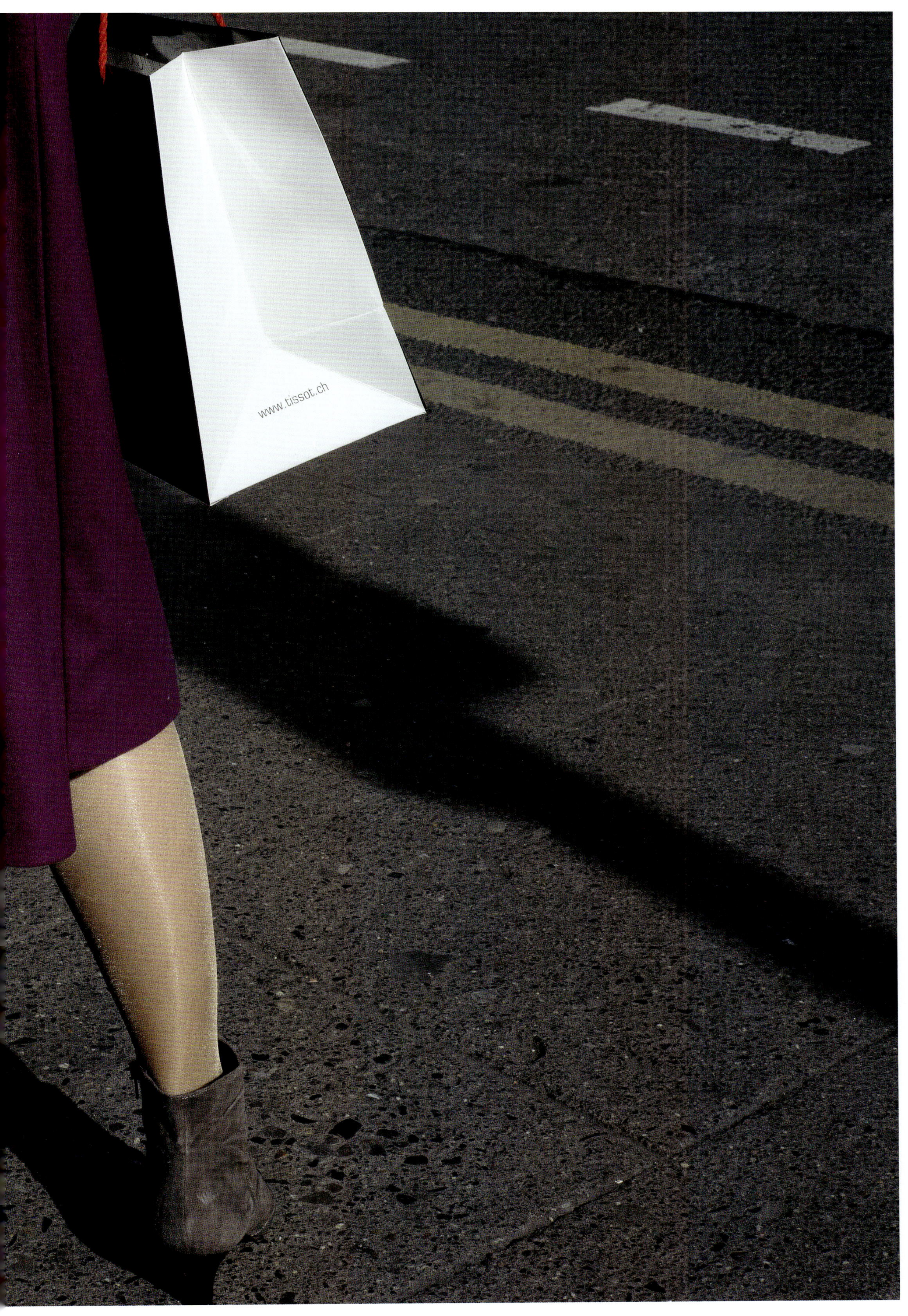
www.tissot.ch

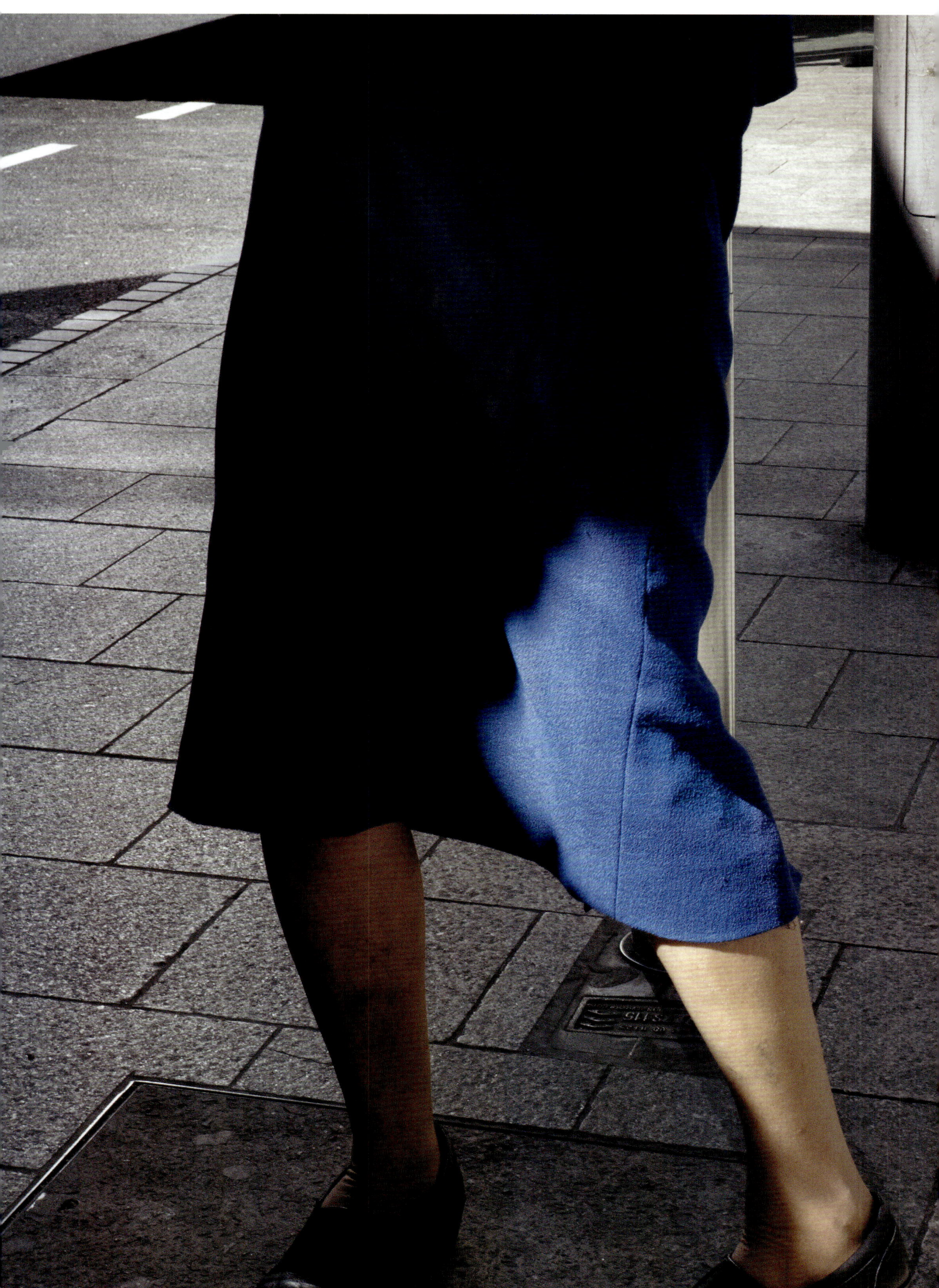

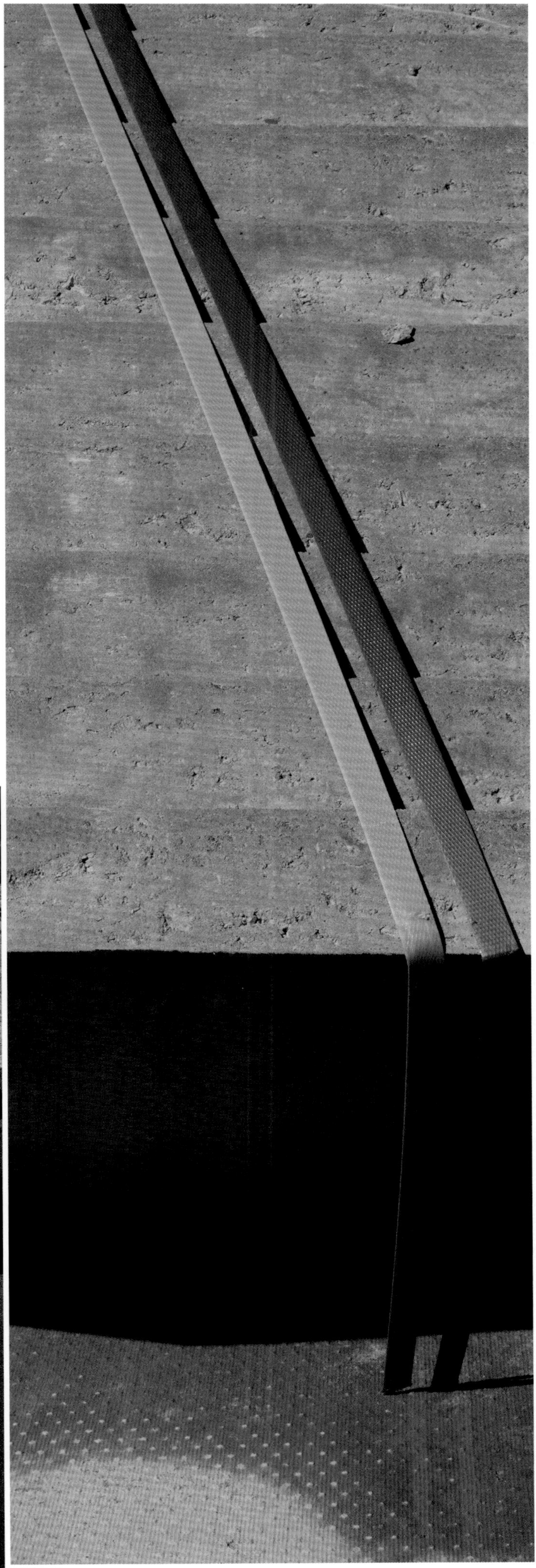

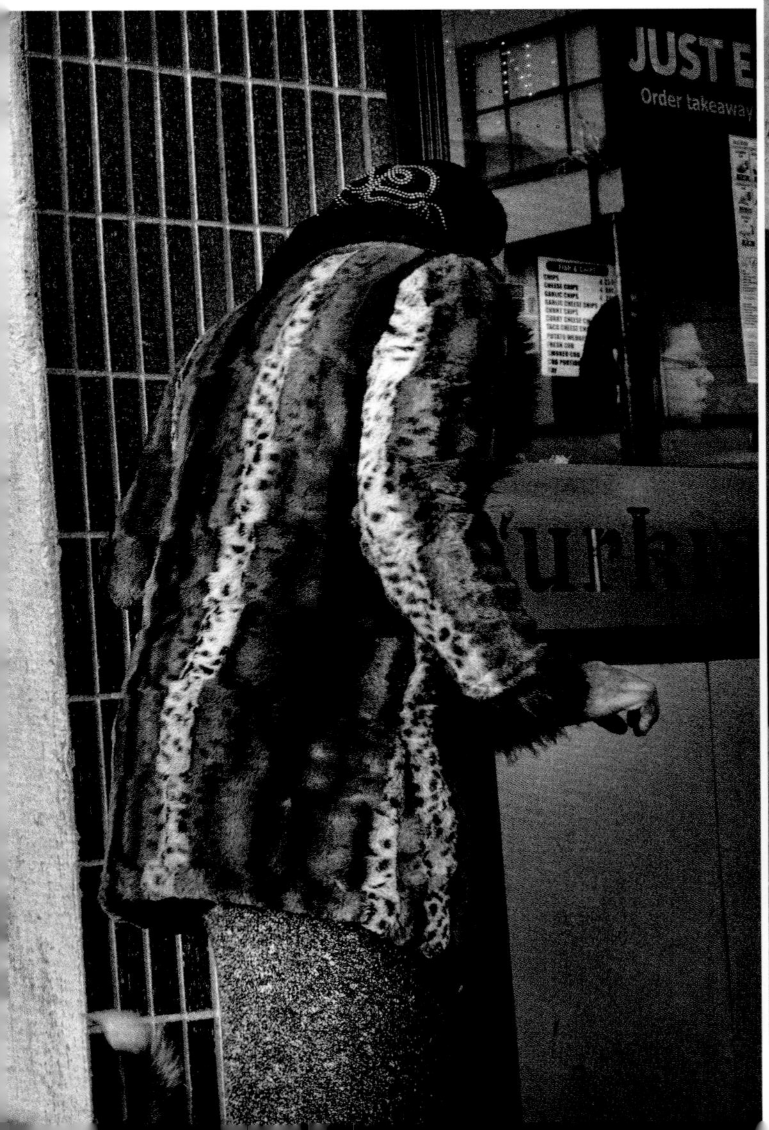

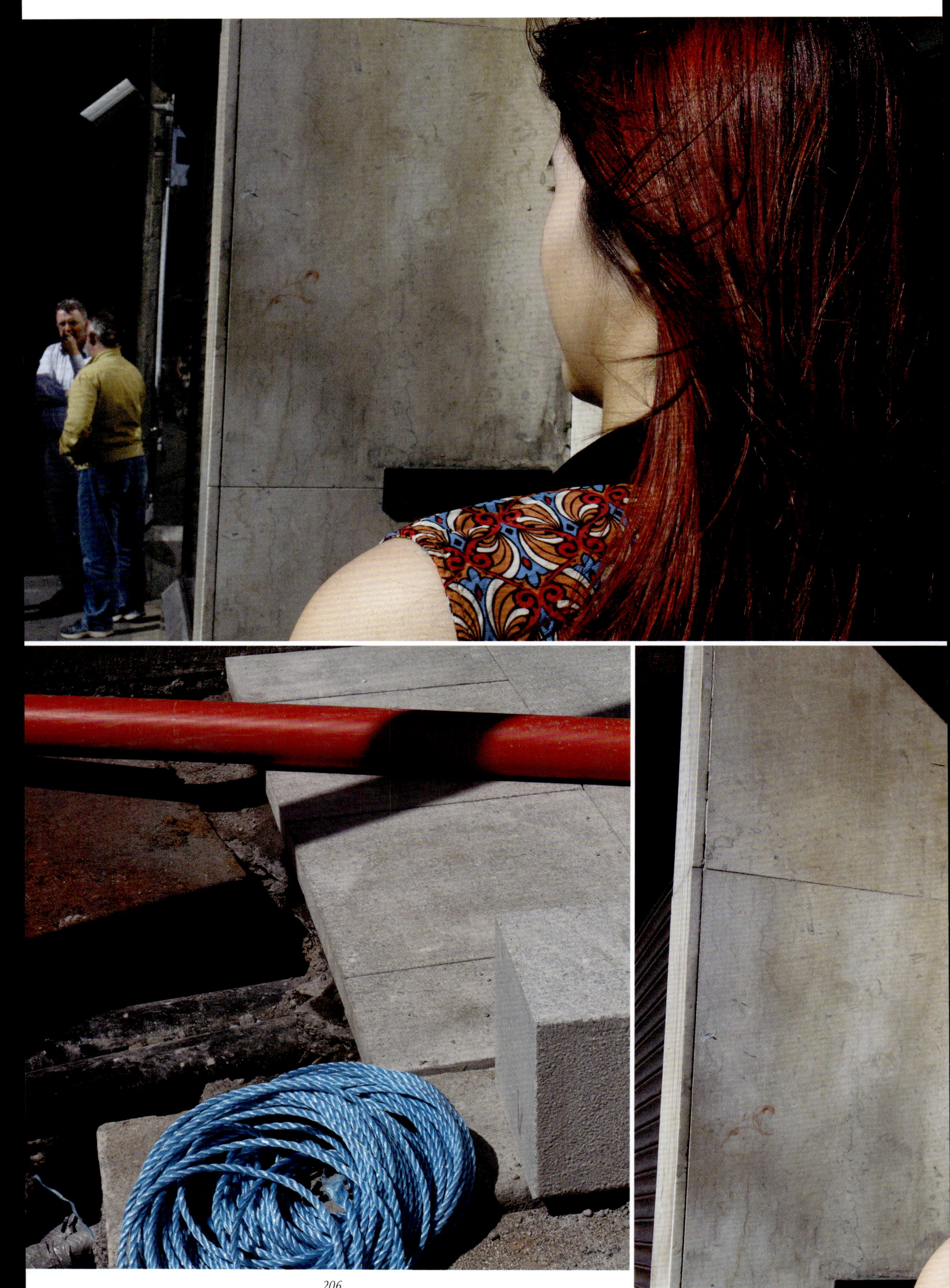

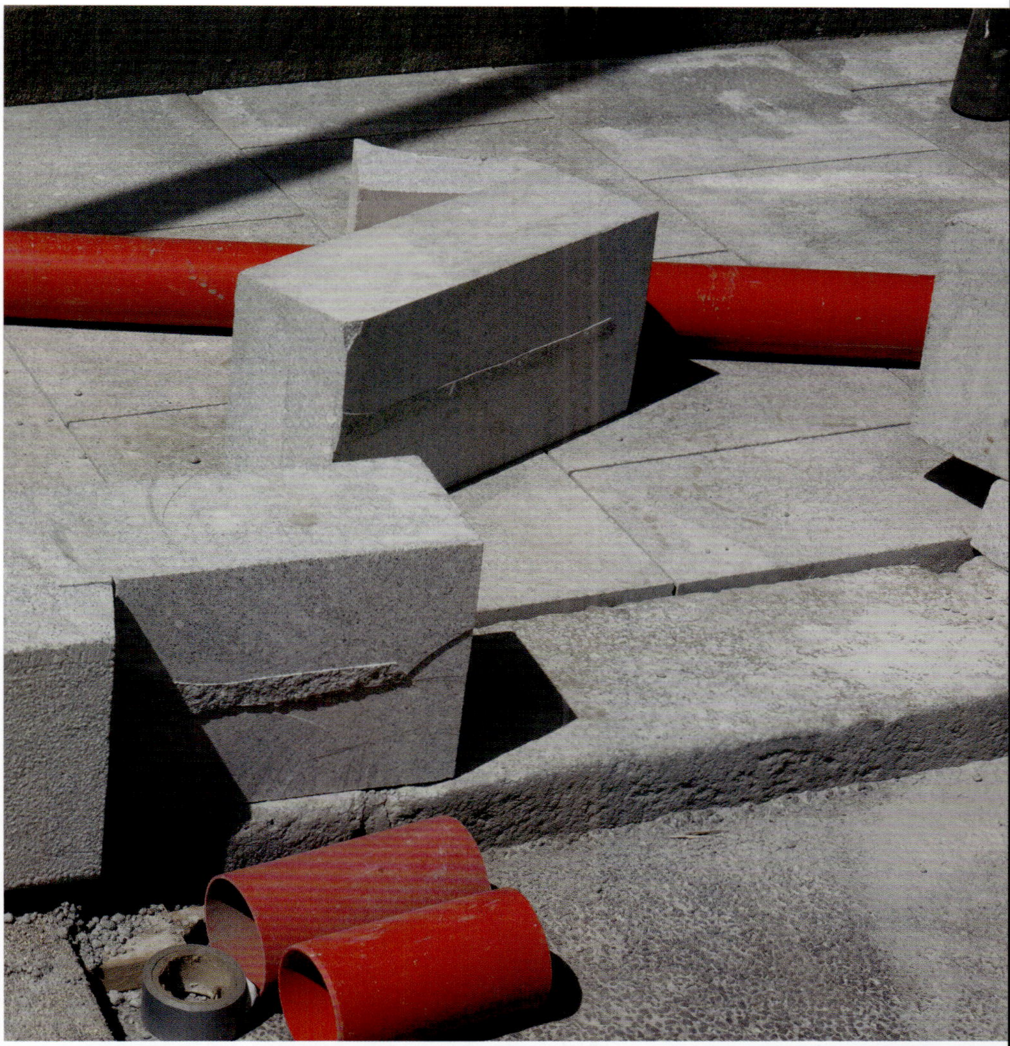

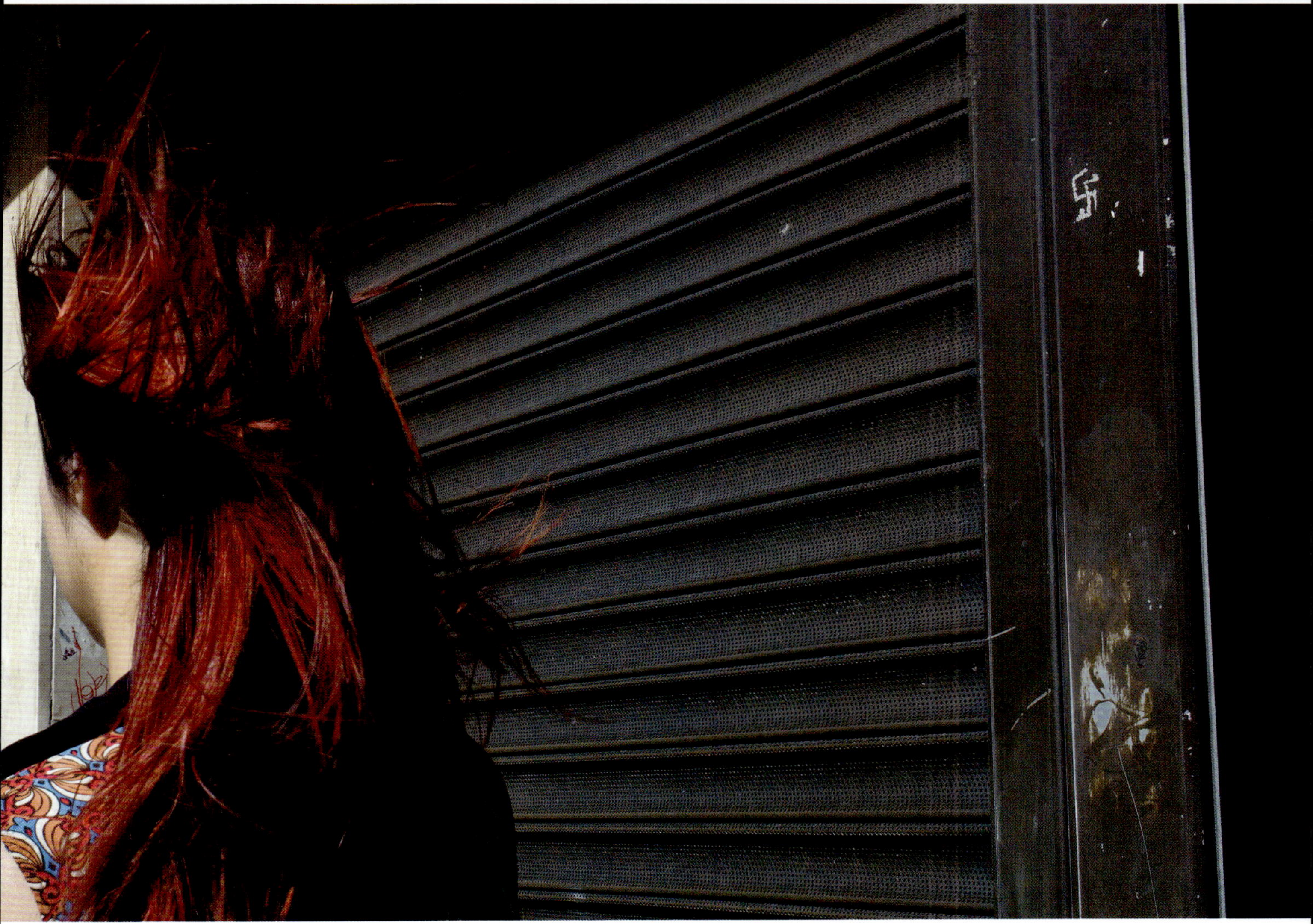

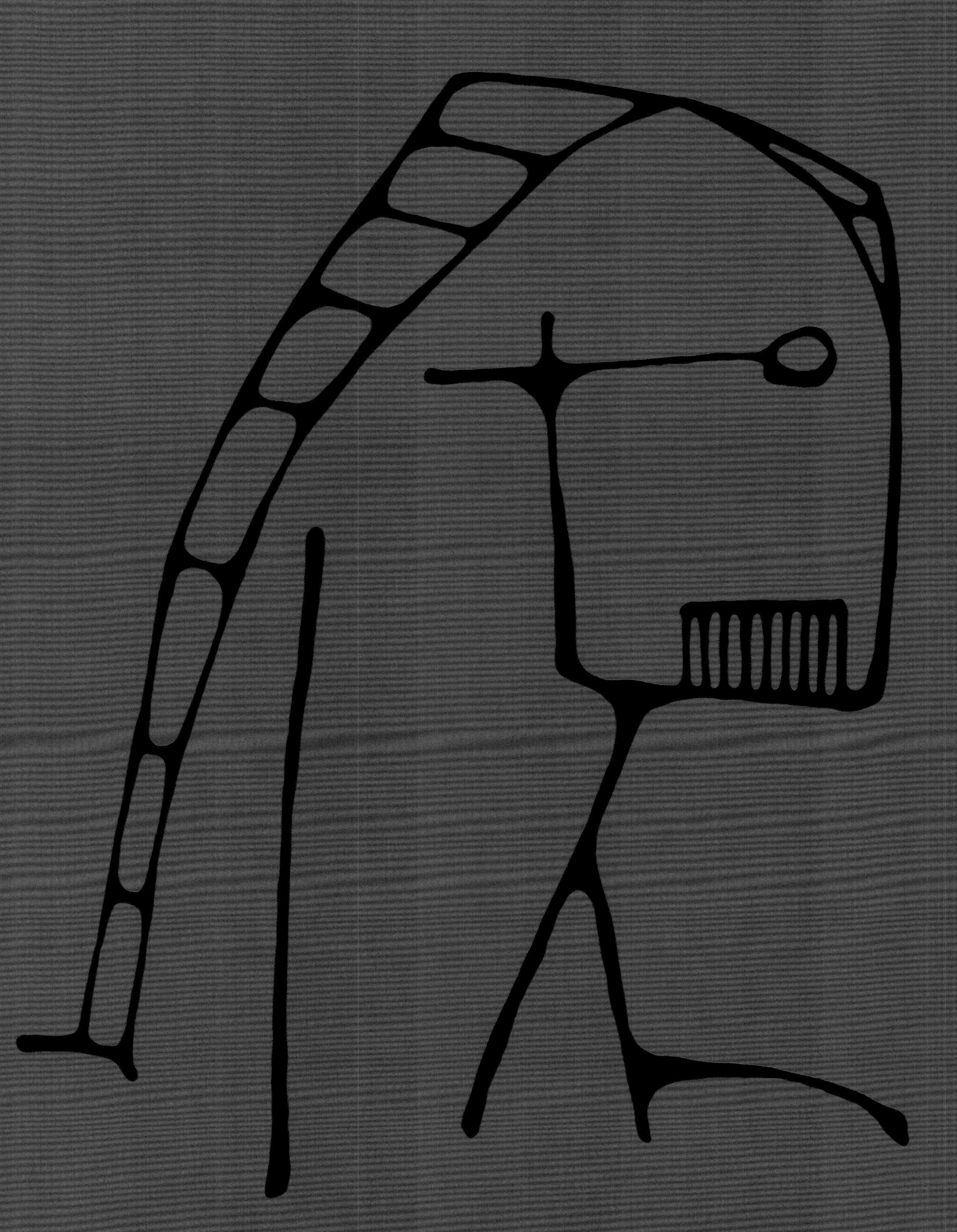

THE EVENING IS SPREAD OUT across
the sky.
A child's bawl flies from a high window.
Guided by voices, a taxi-cab roams.
Sometimes it feels like you're on the next street over
and you can't quite hear yourself.
There is intrigue on the street.
There are assignations.
A moment from 1965 plays out again.
A moment from 1843.
A moment from 2134.
Night falls.
The lights rise up.
There is laughter in the crevices.
The fat man shows a mouth of vandalized teeth.
The sexy young woman walks a ritual path.
Until morning comes ...
... and the beer barrels are sent to bounce and roll
into the basements of the pubs — the sound of this has both
a timeless and a jaunty quality.
A sizzle of fat from the fryers of the Vietnamese.
As we walk we sail into clouds of
hilarity,
rage,
lust.
And beneath the street now there is a threaded pulse.
It tells us once more that

time is passing.

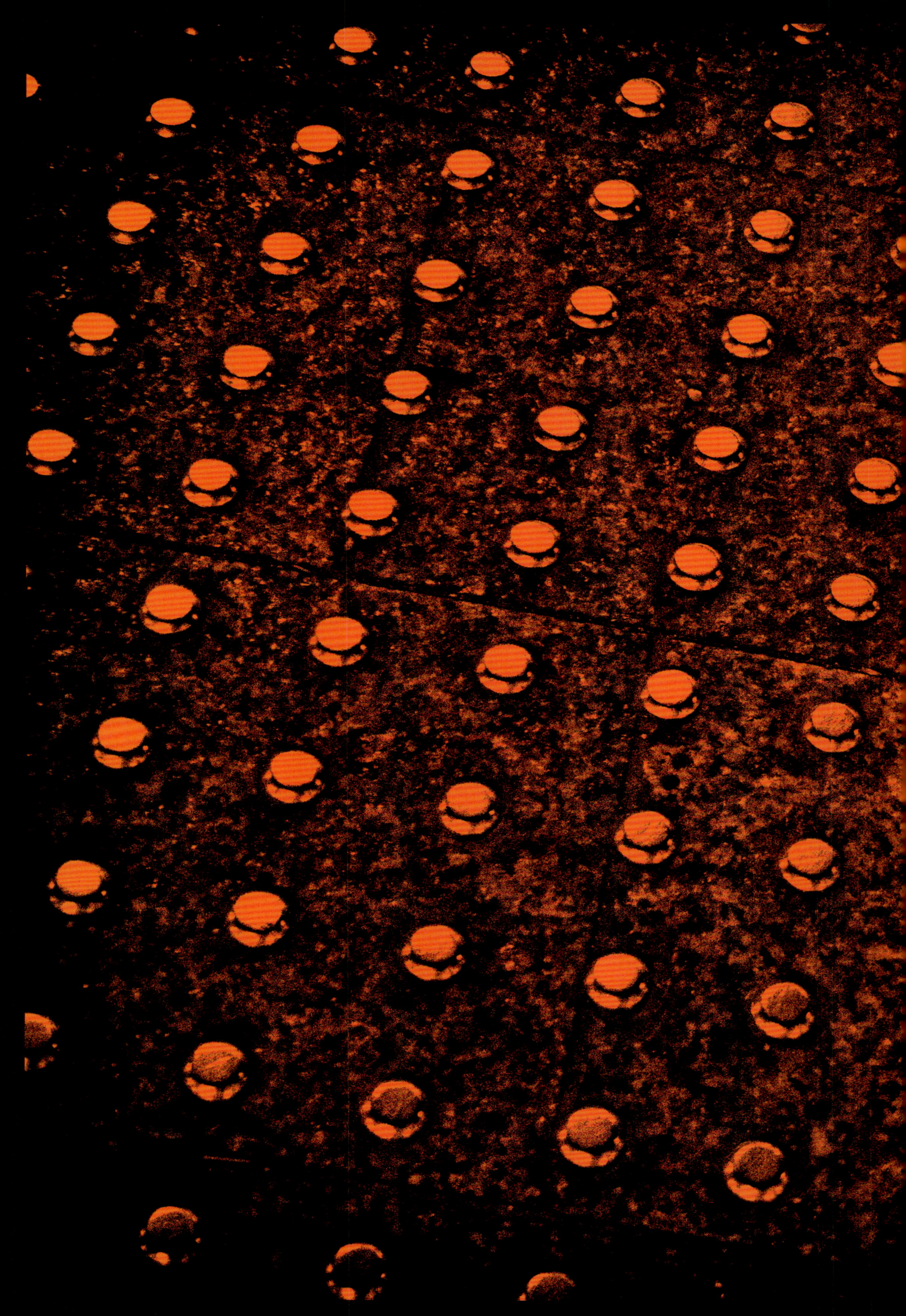

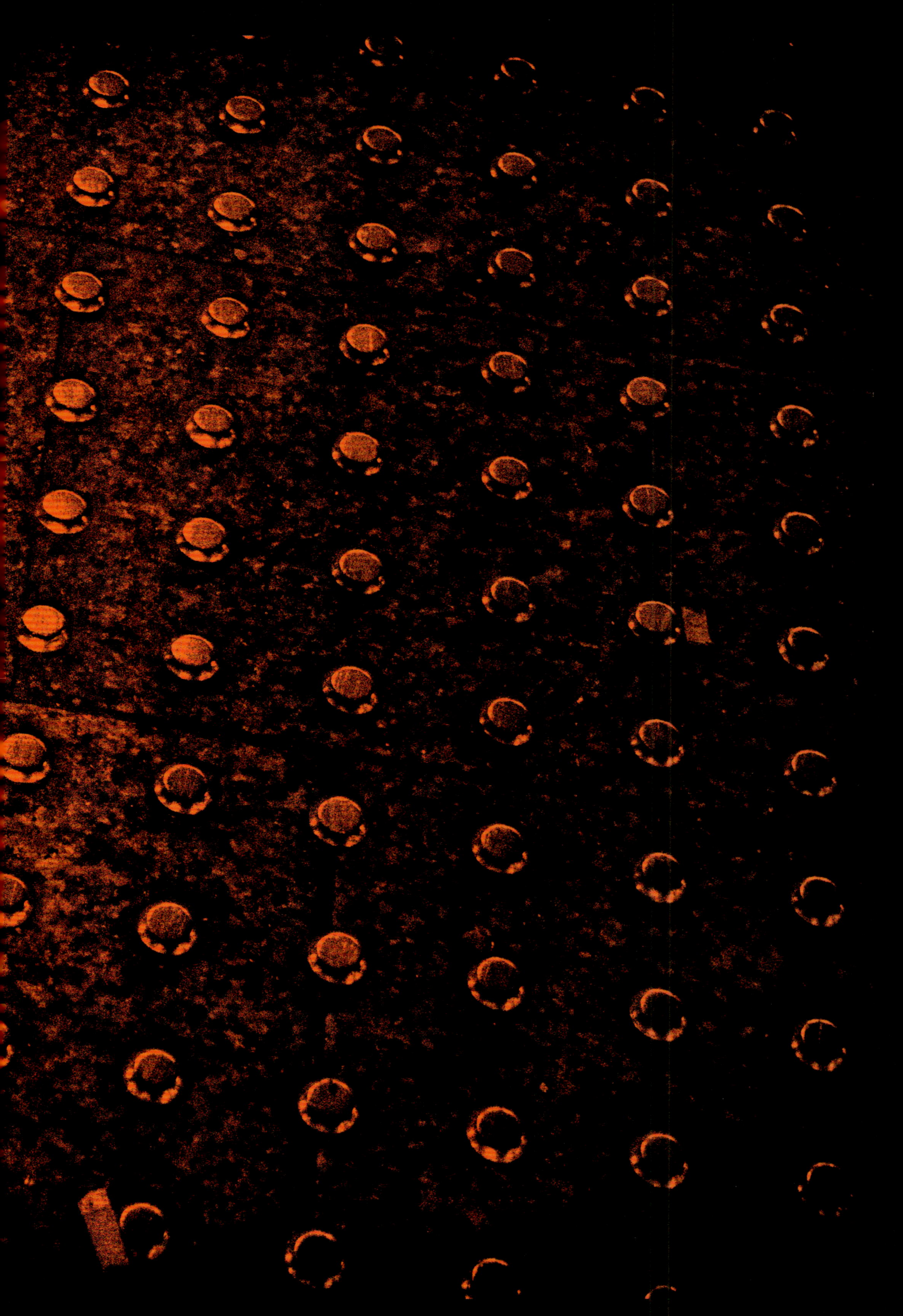

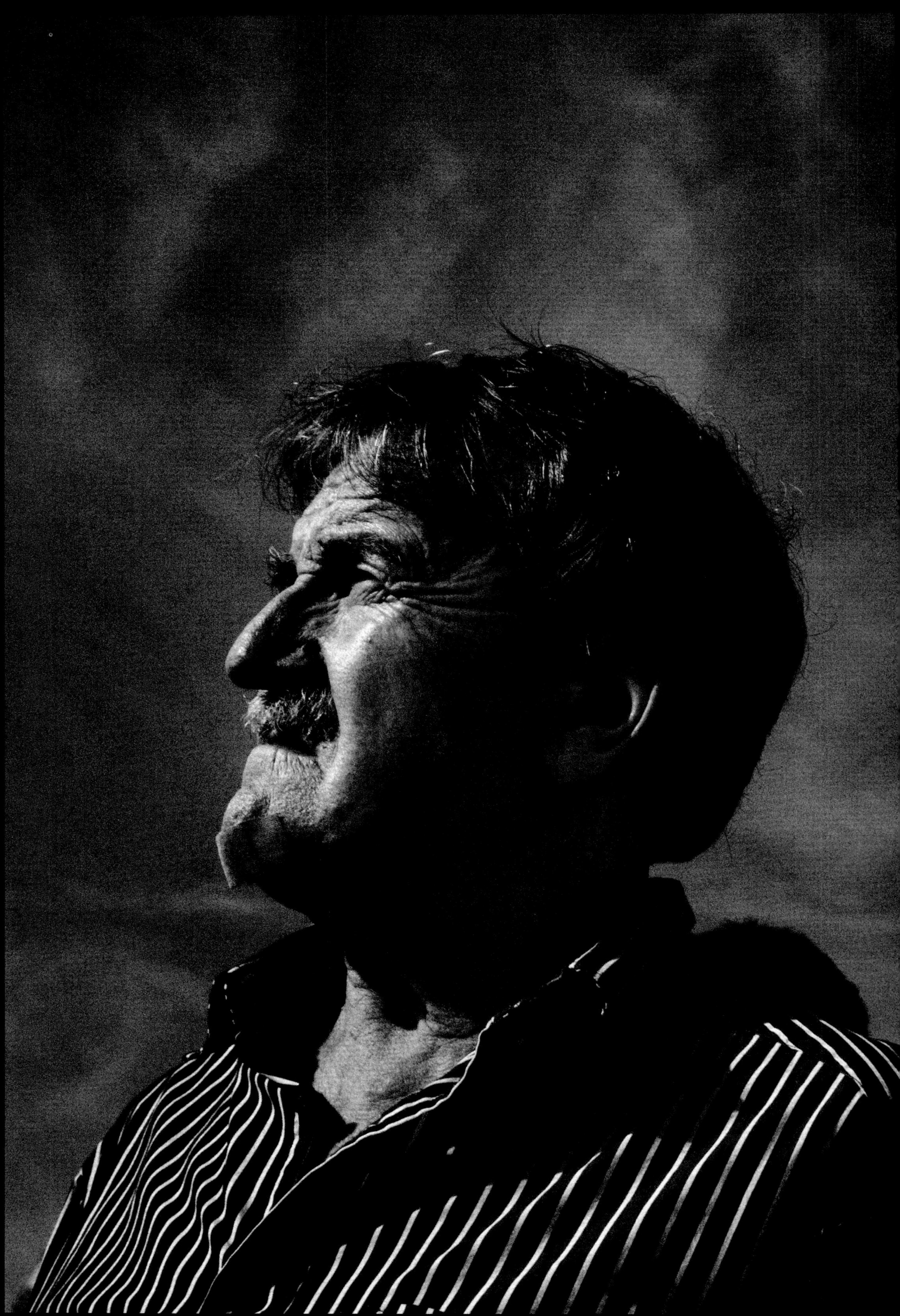

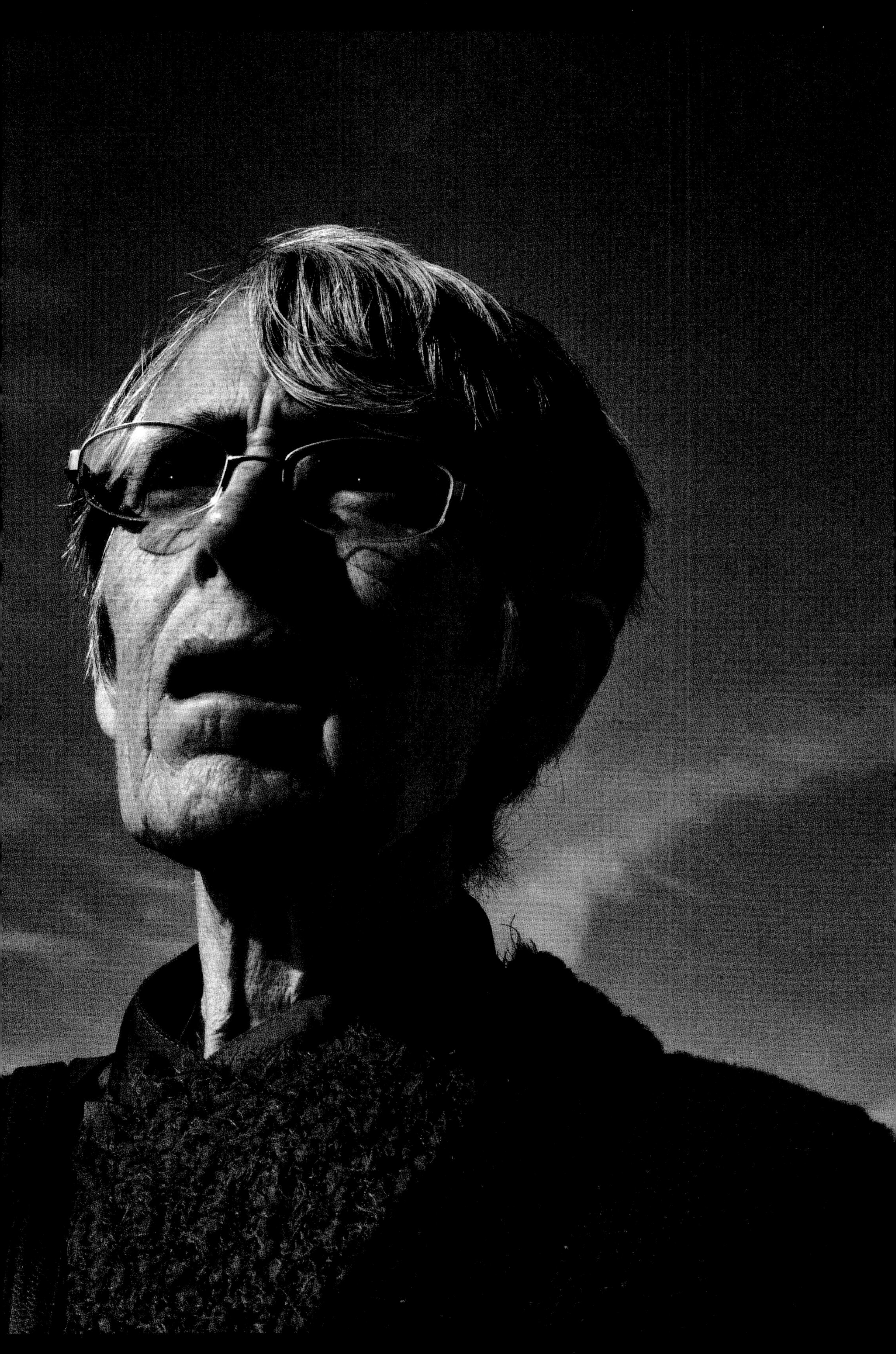

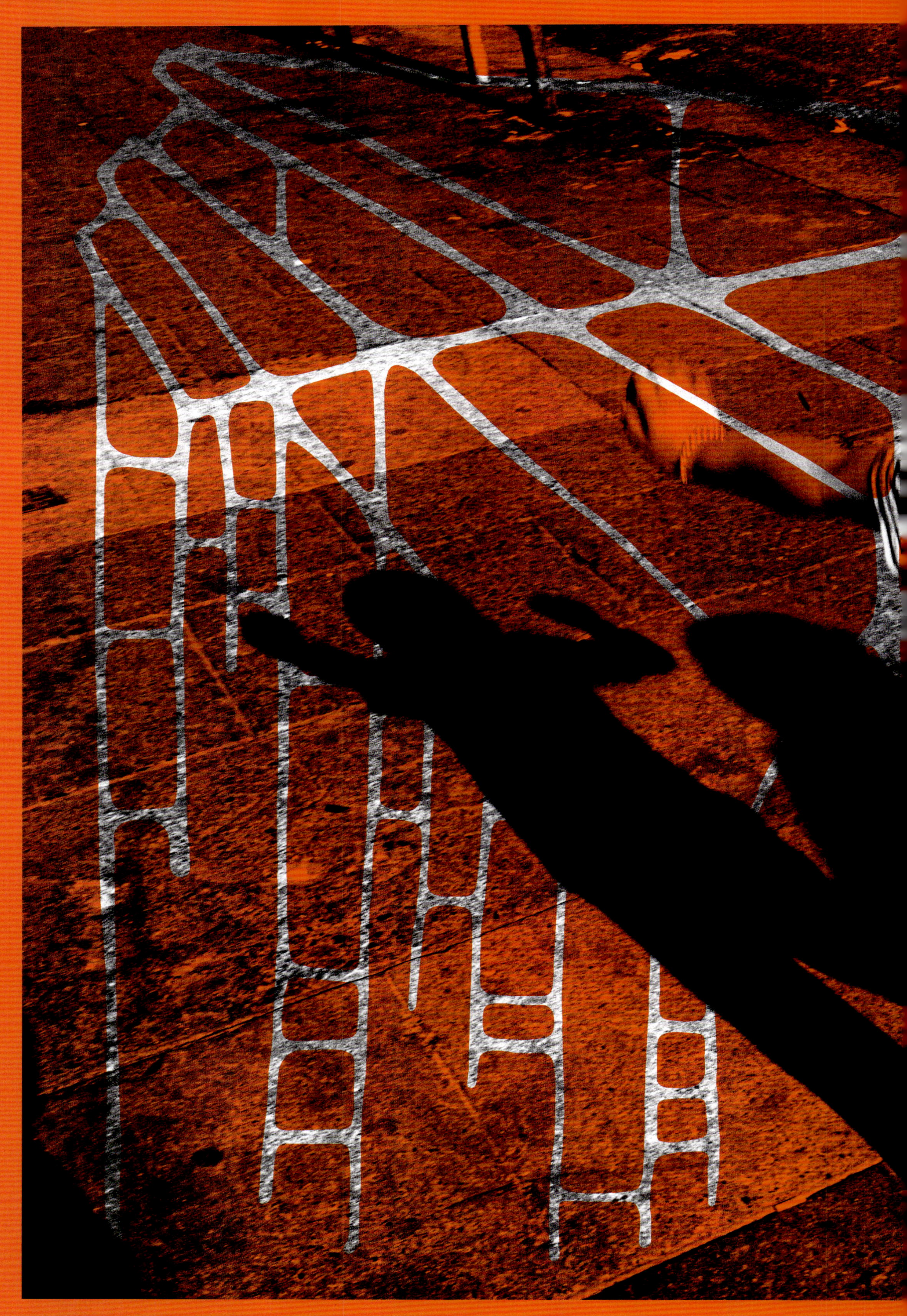

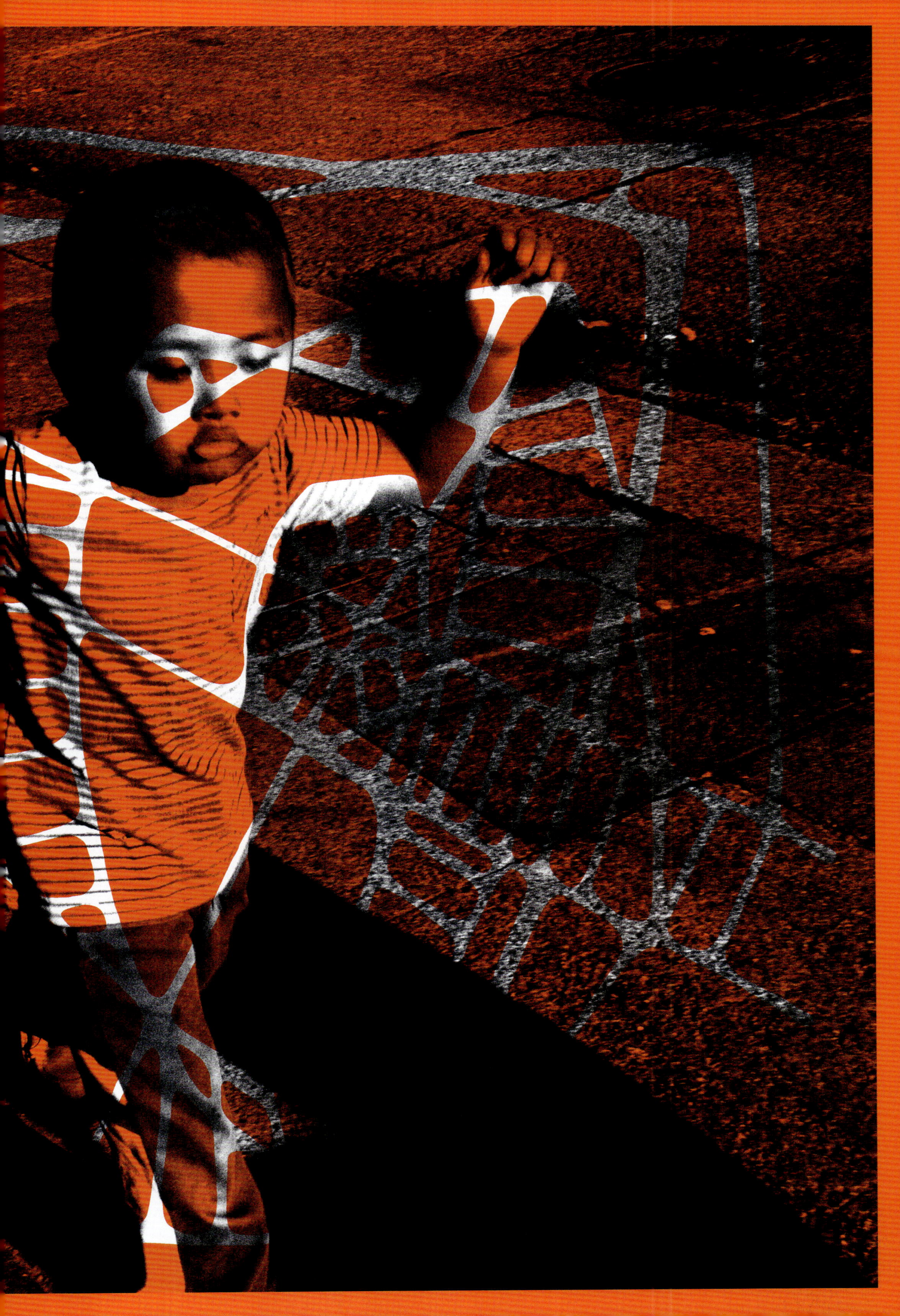

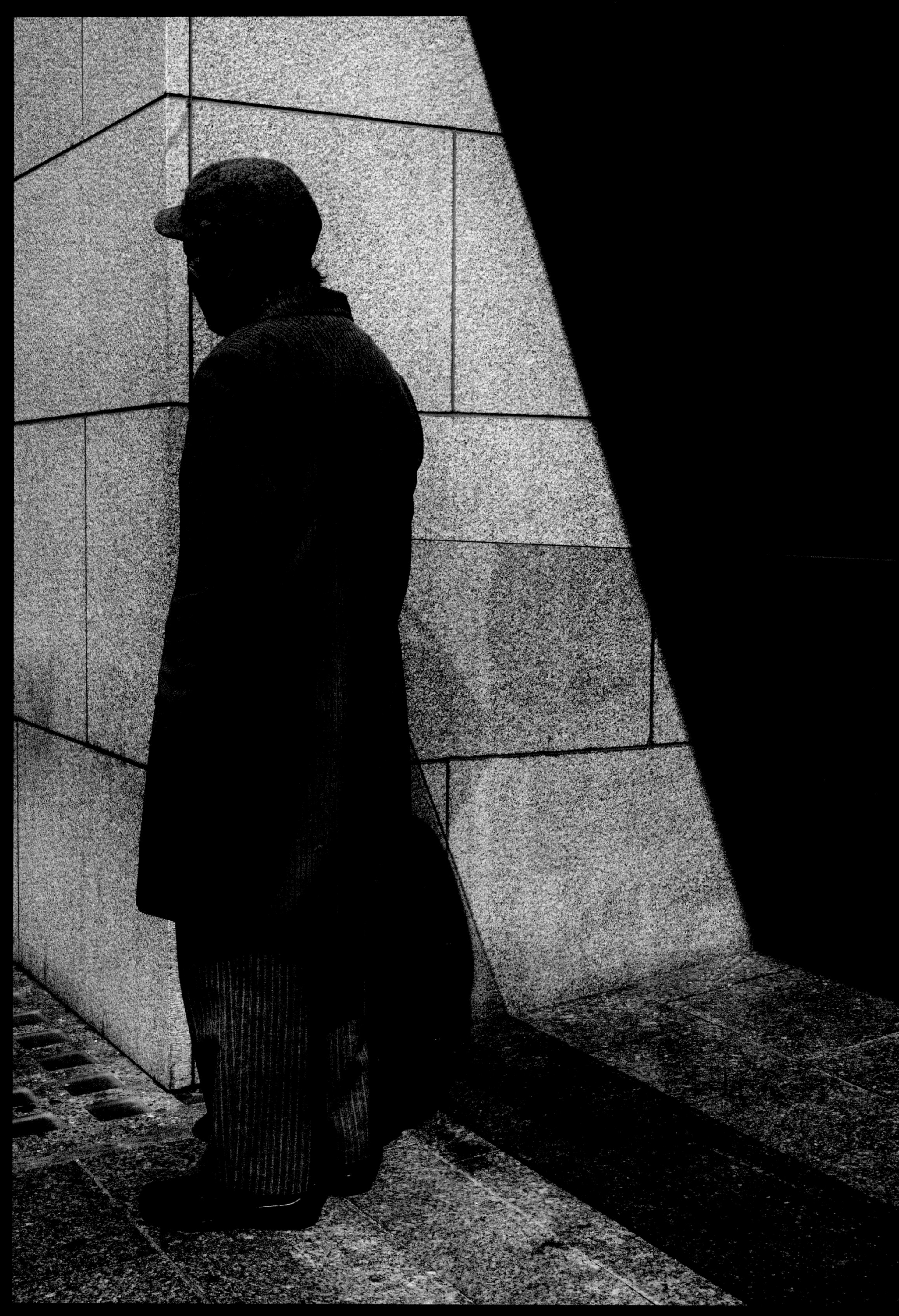

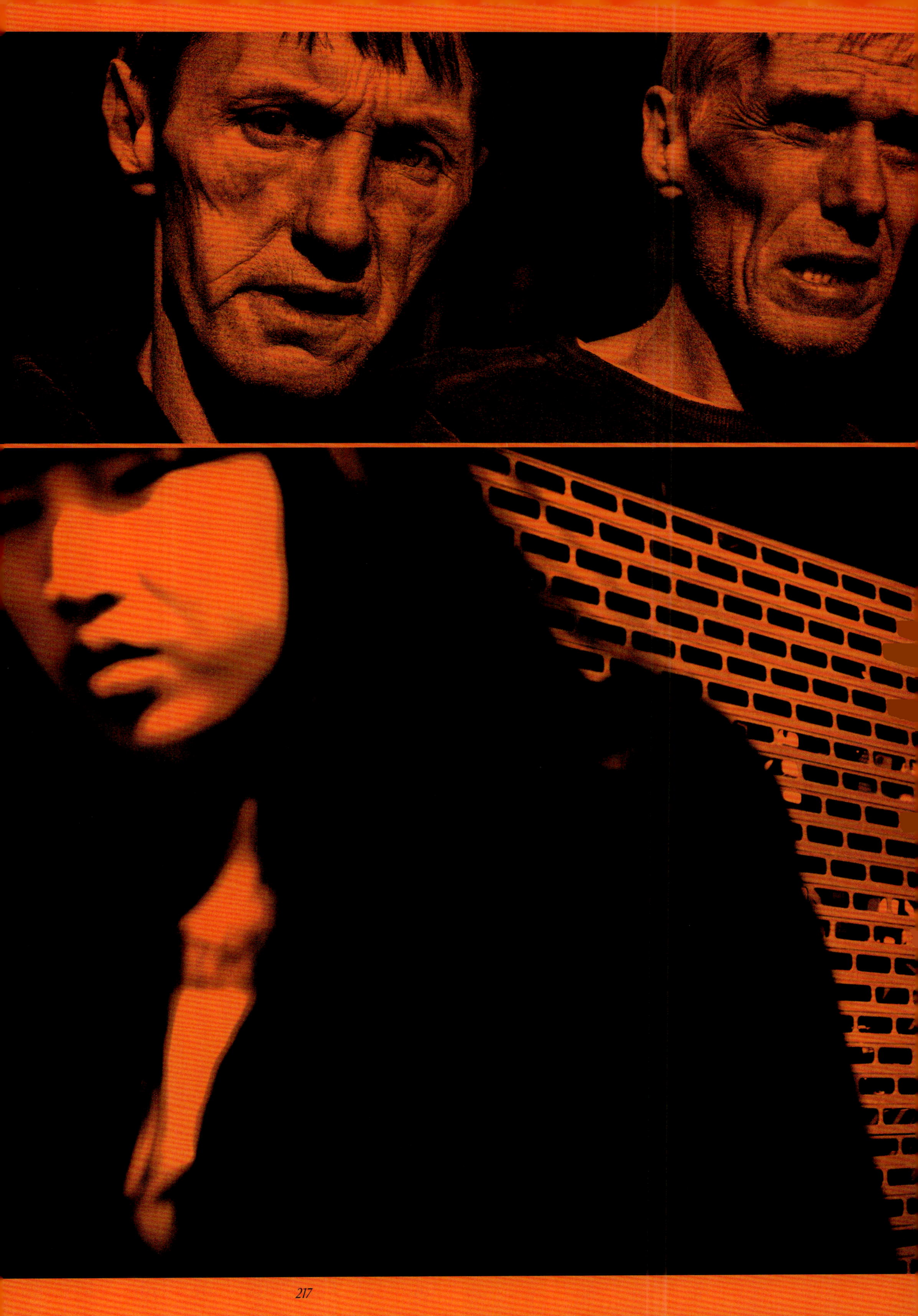

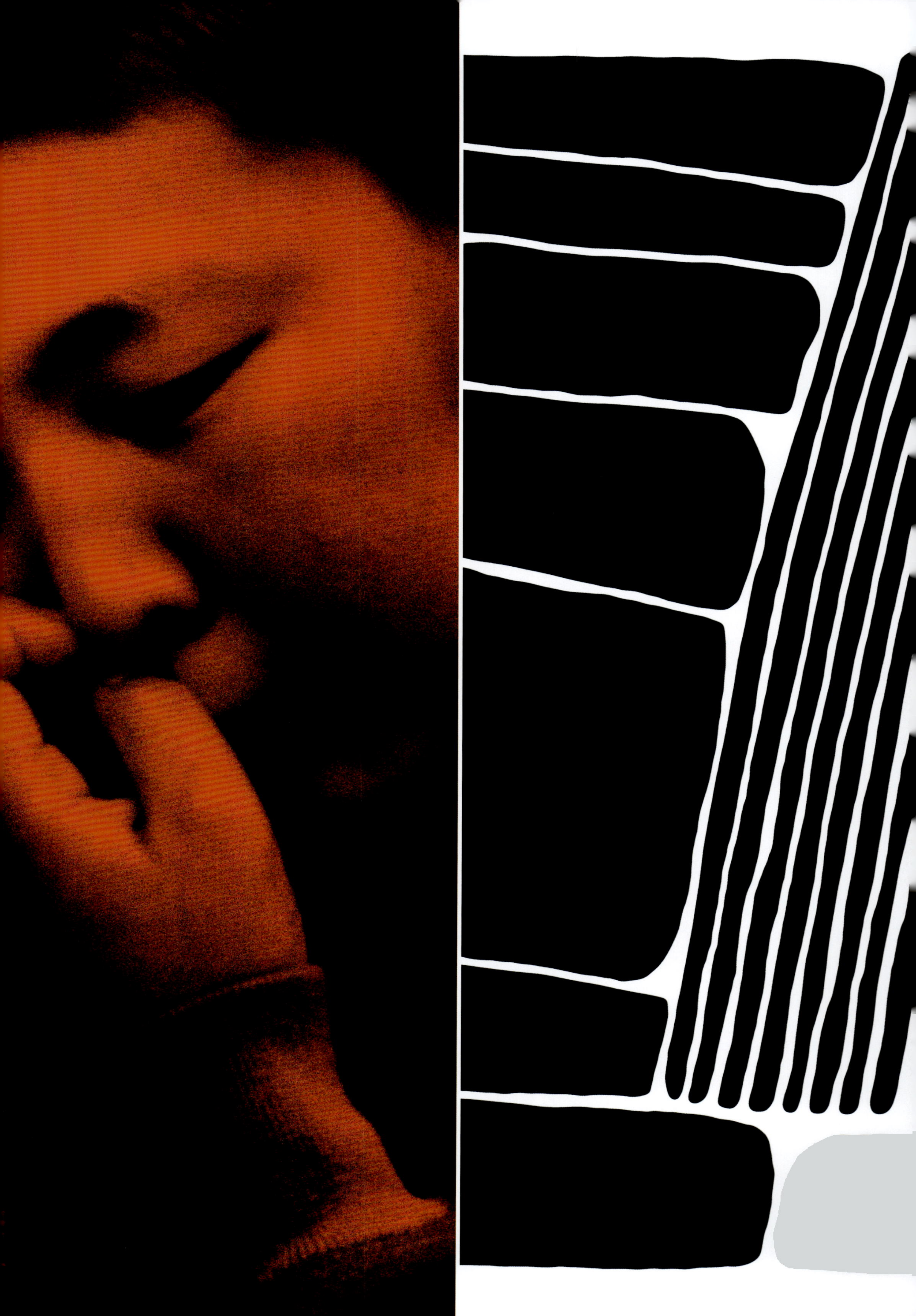

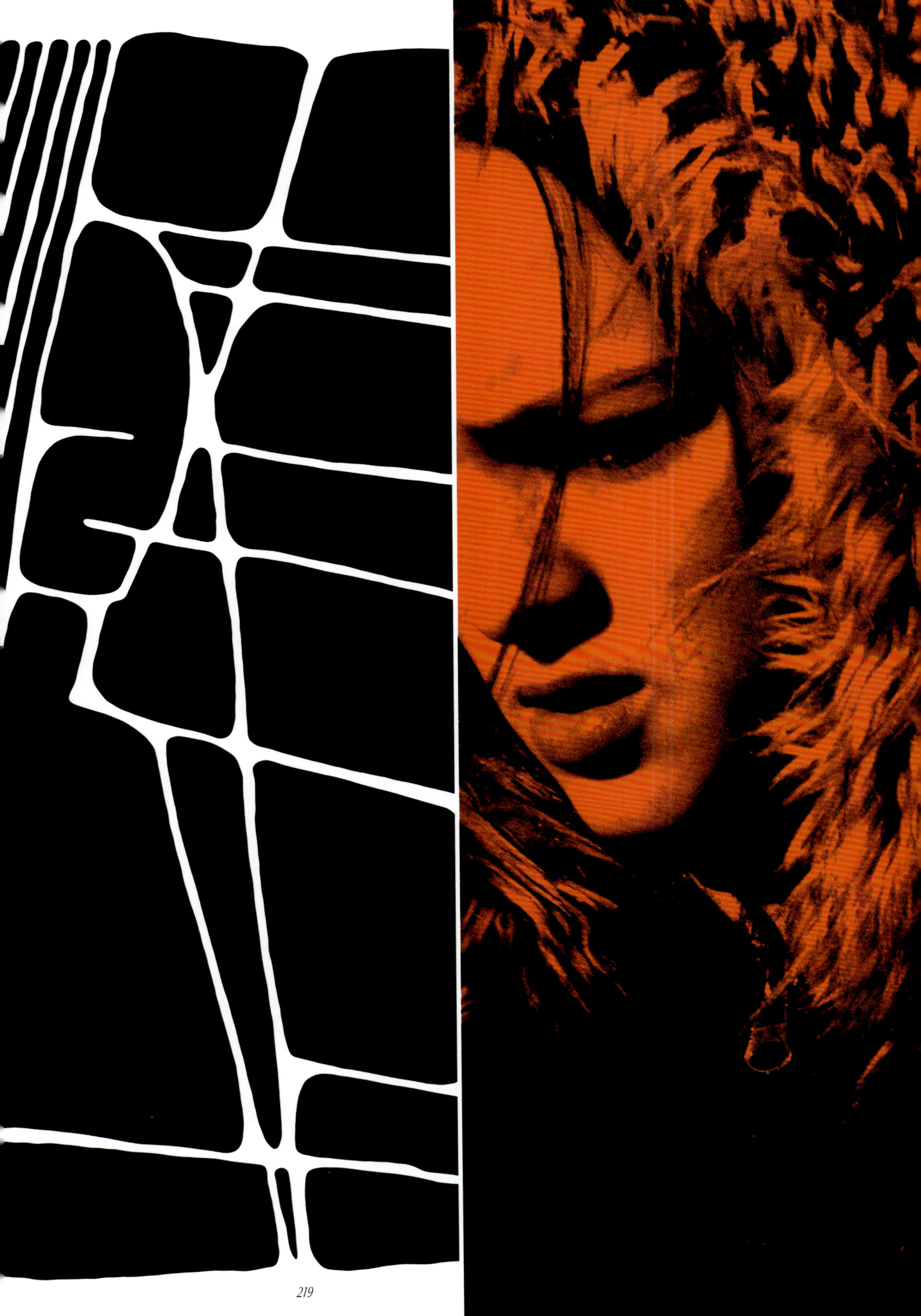

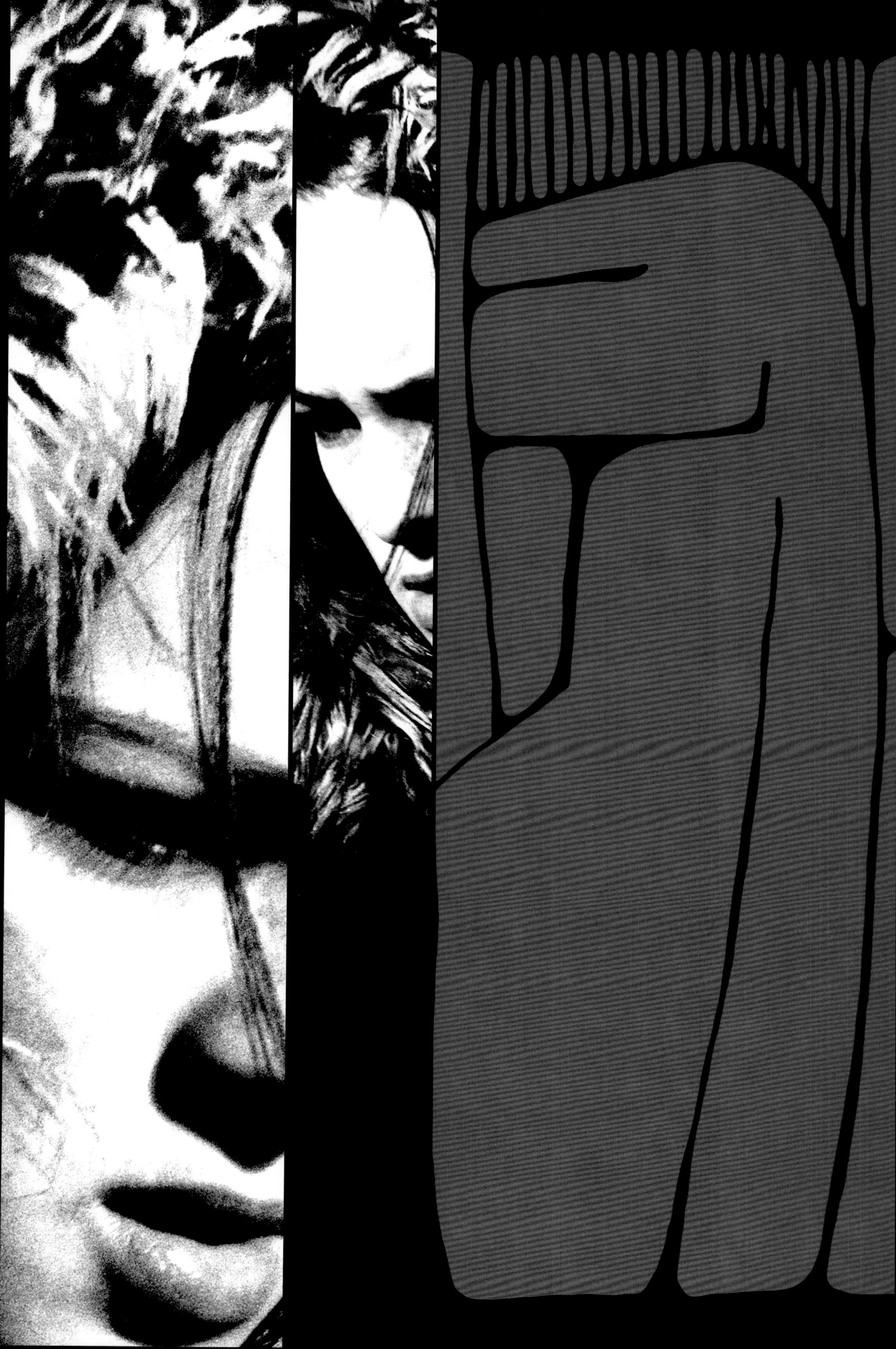

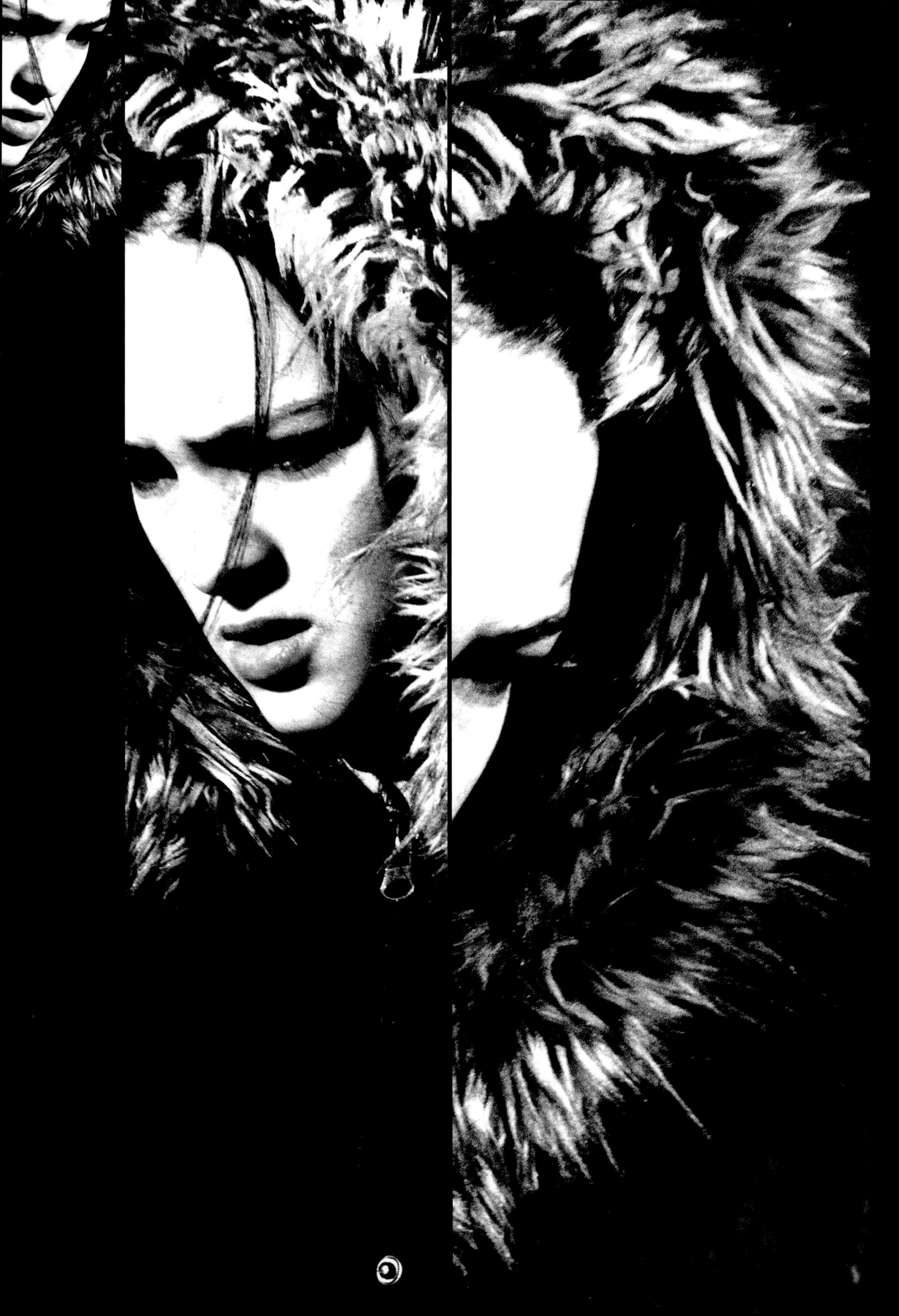

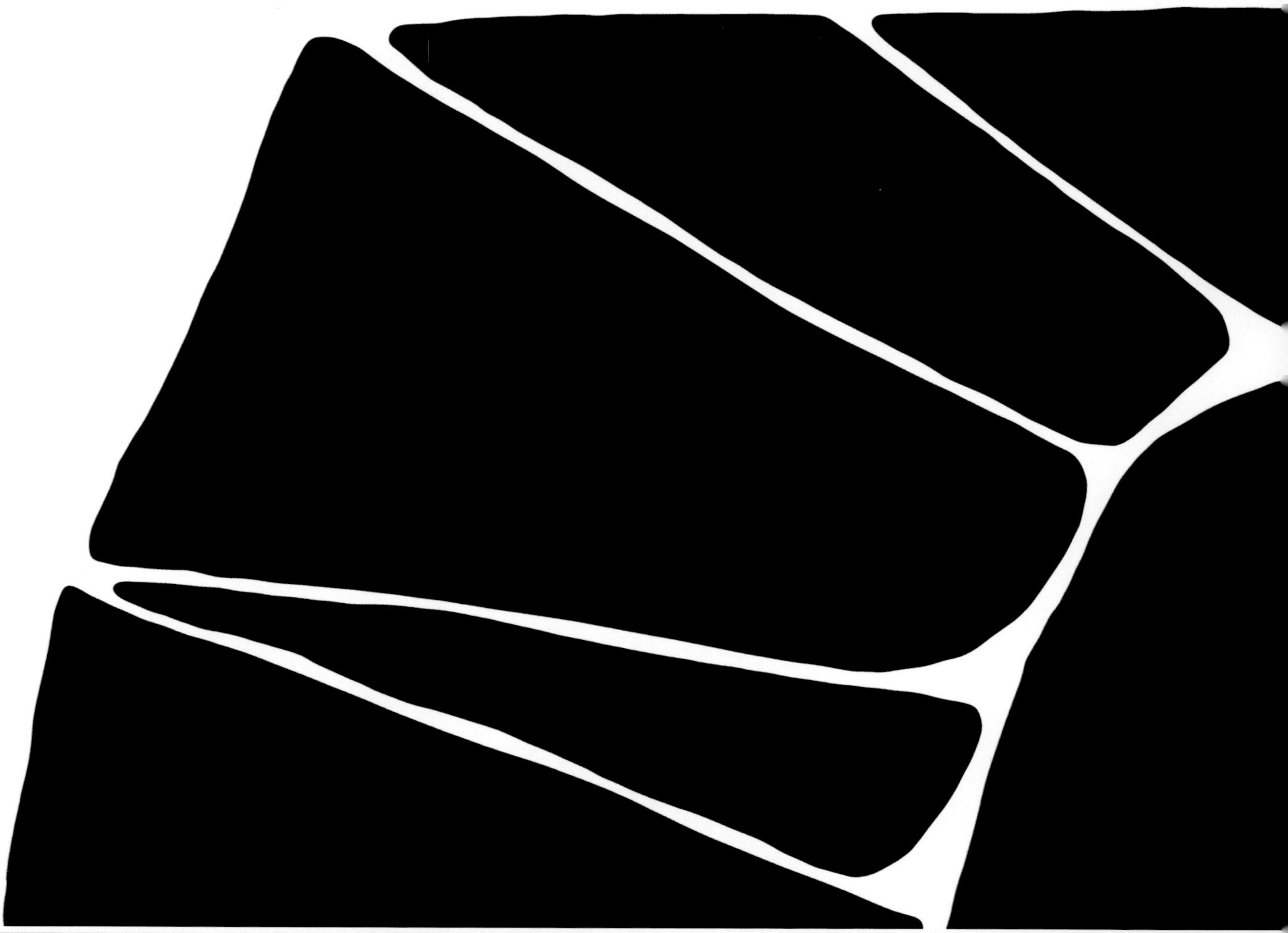

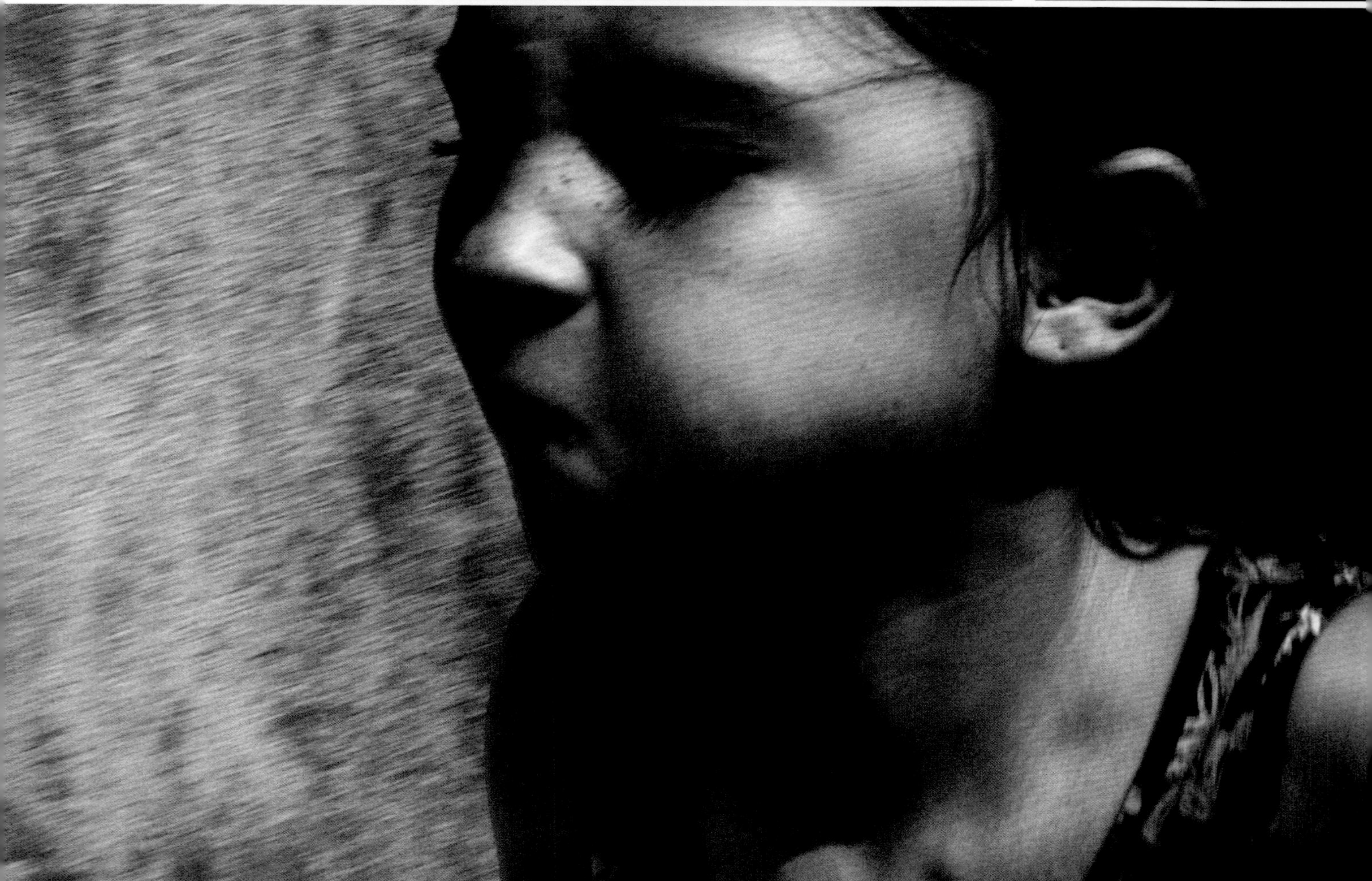

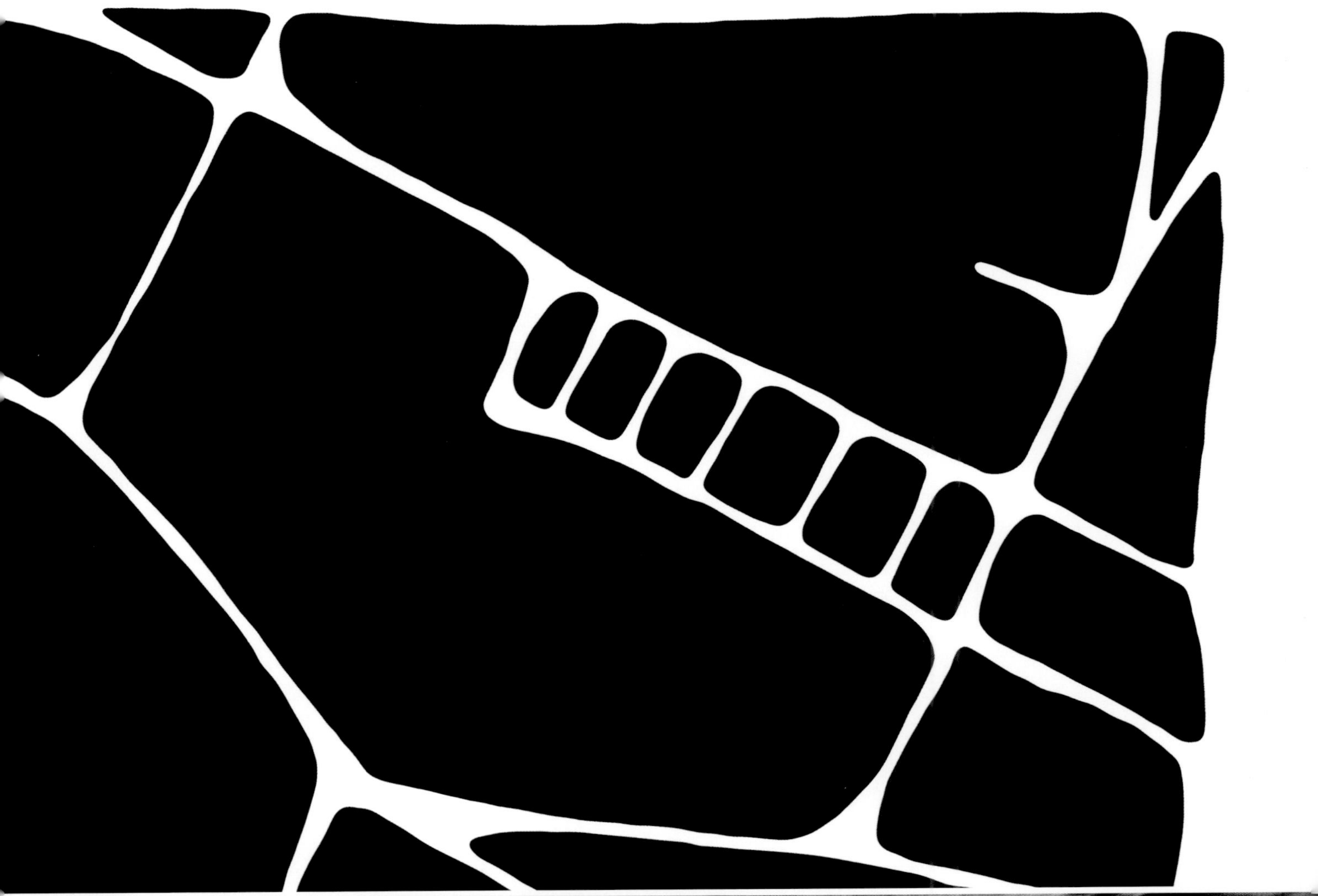

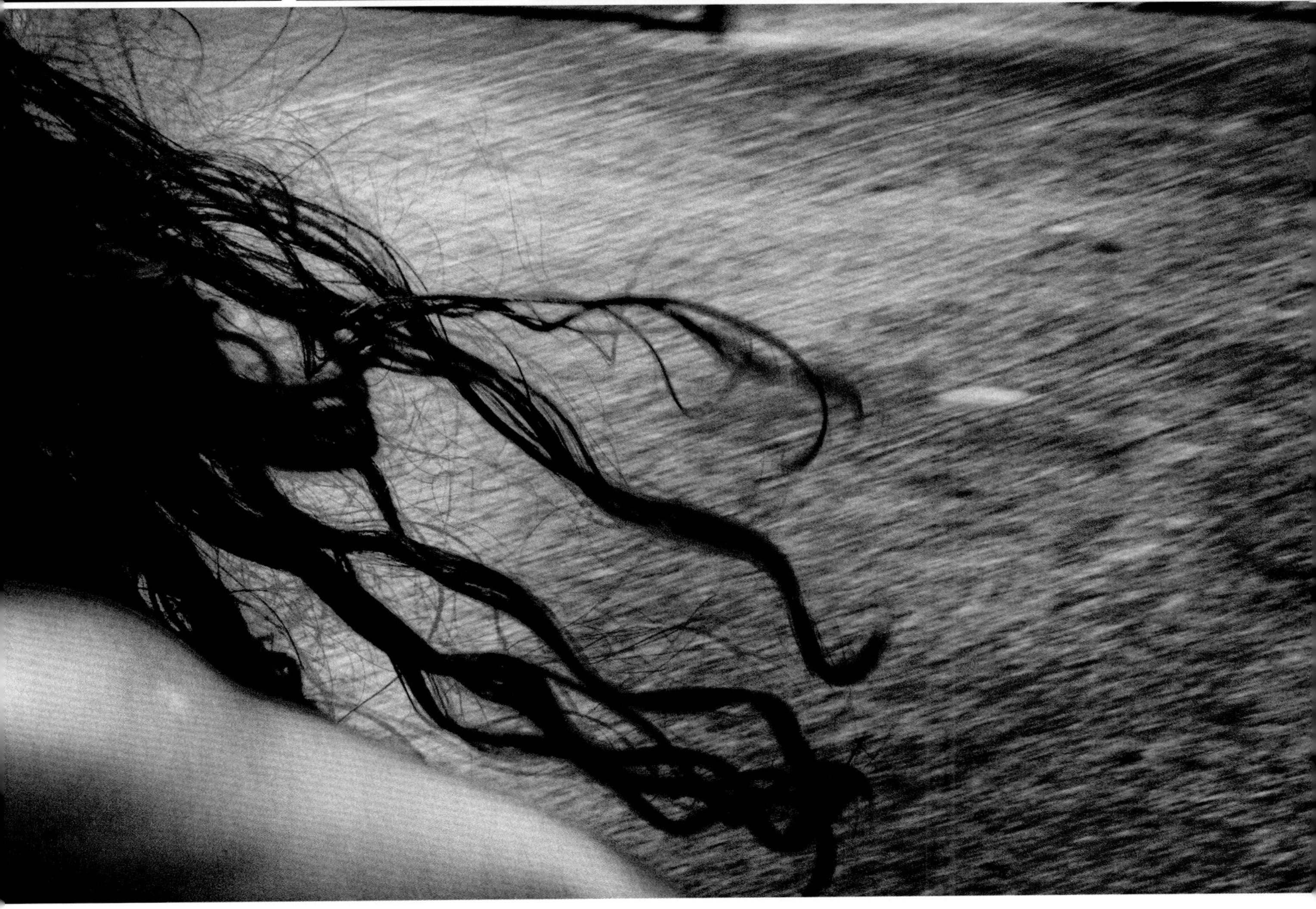

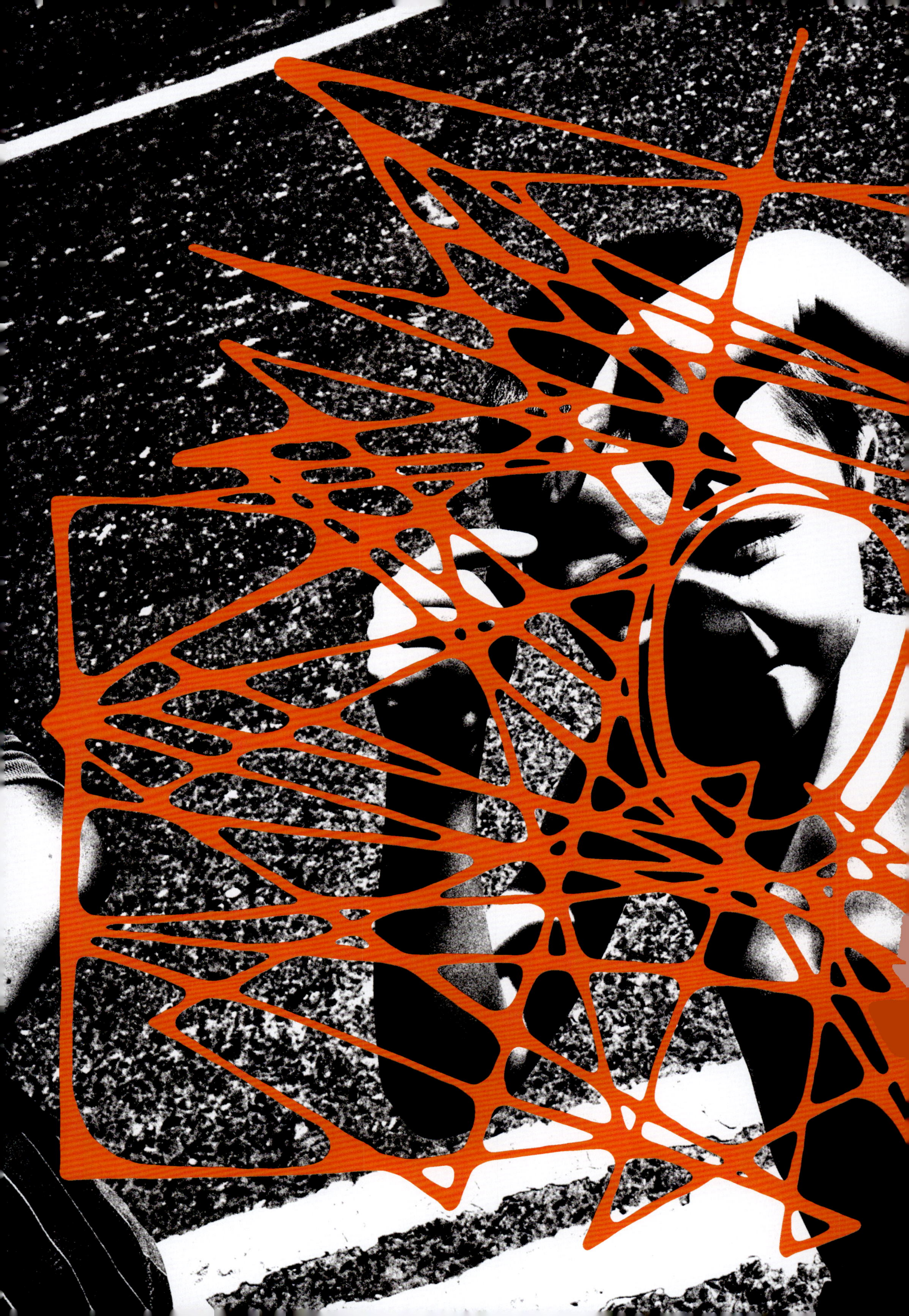

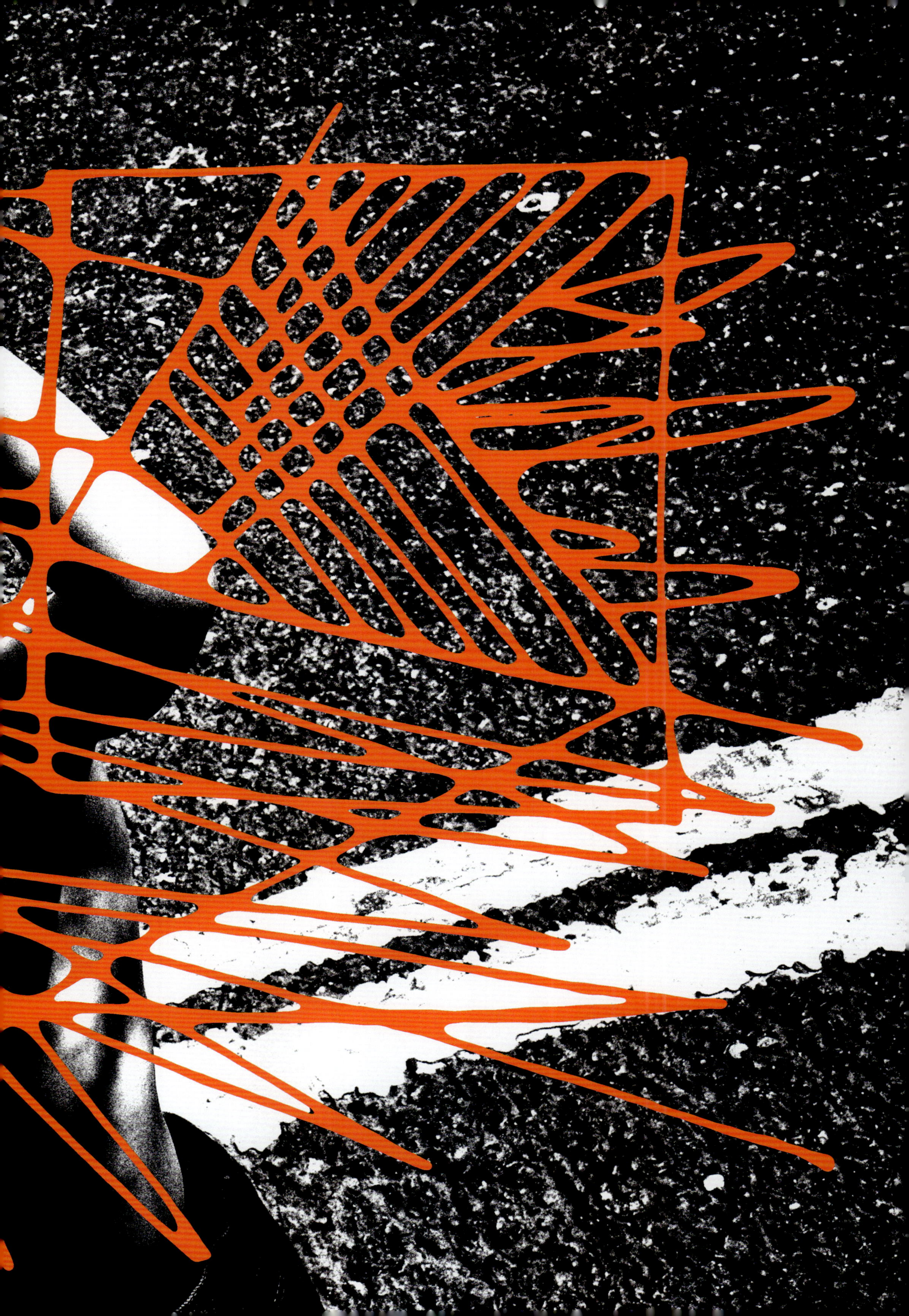

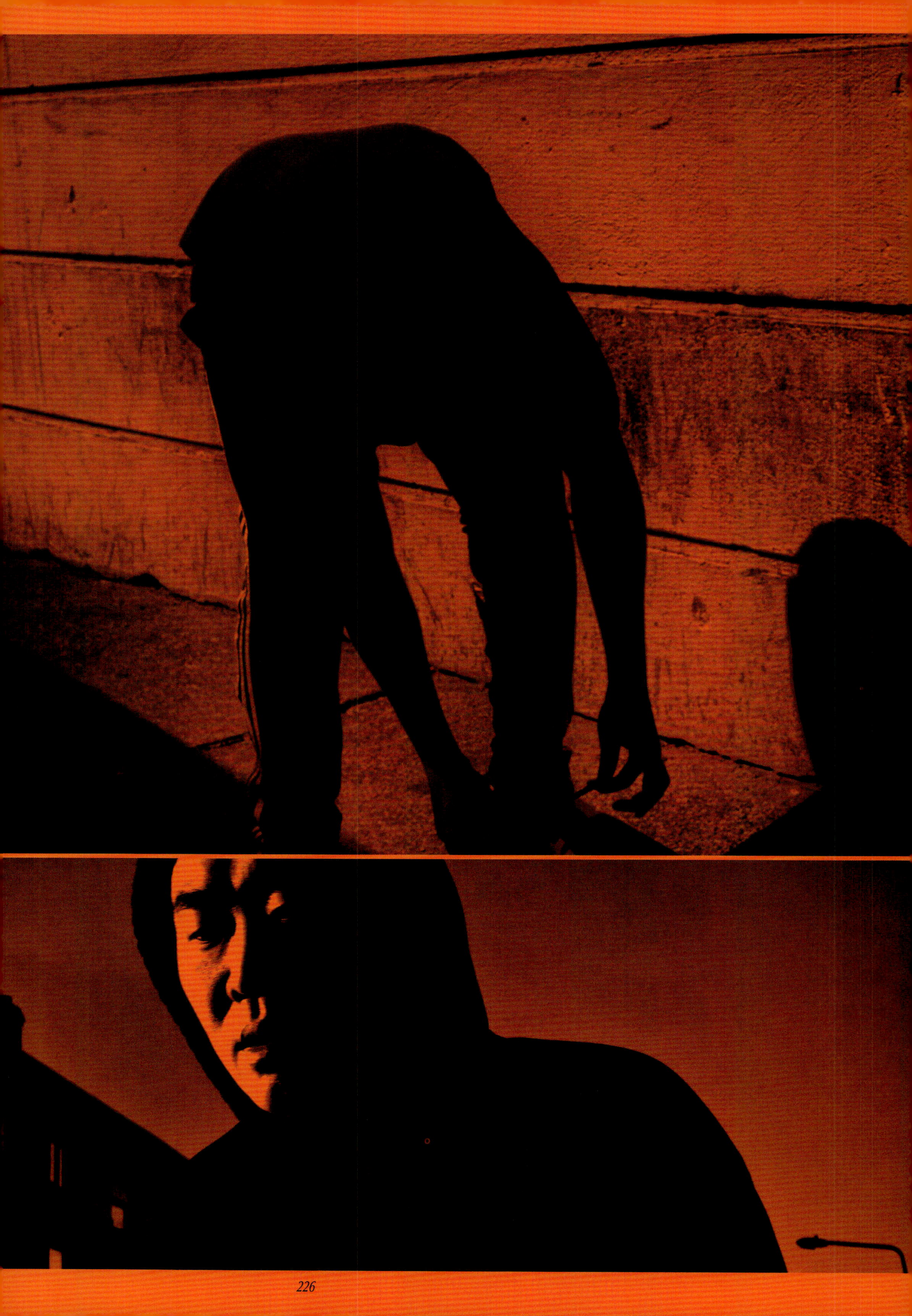

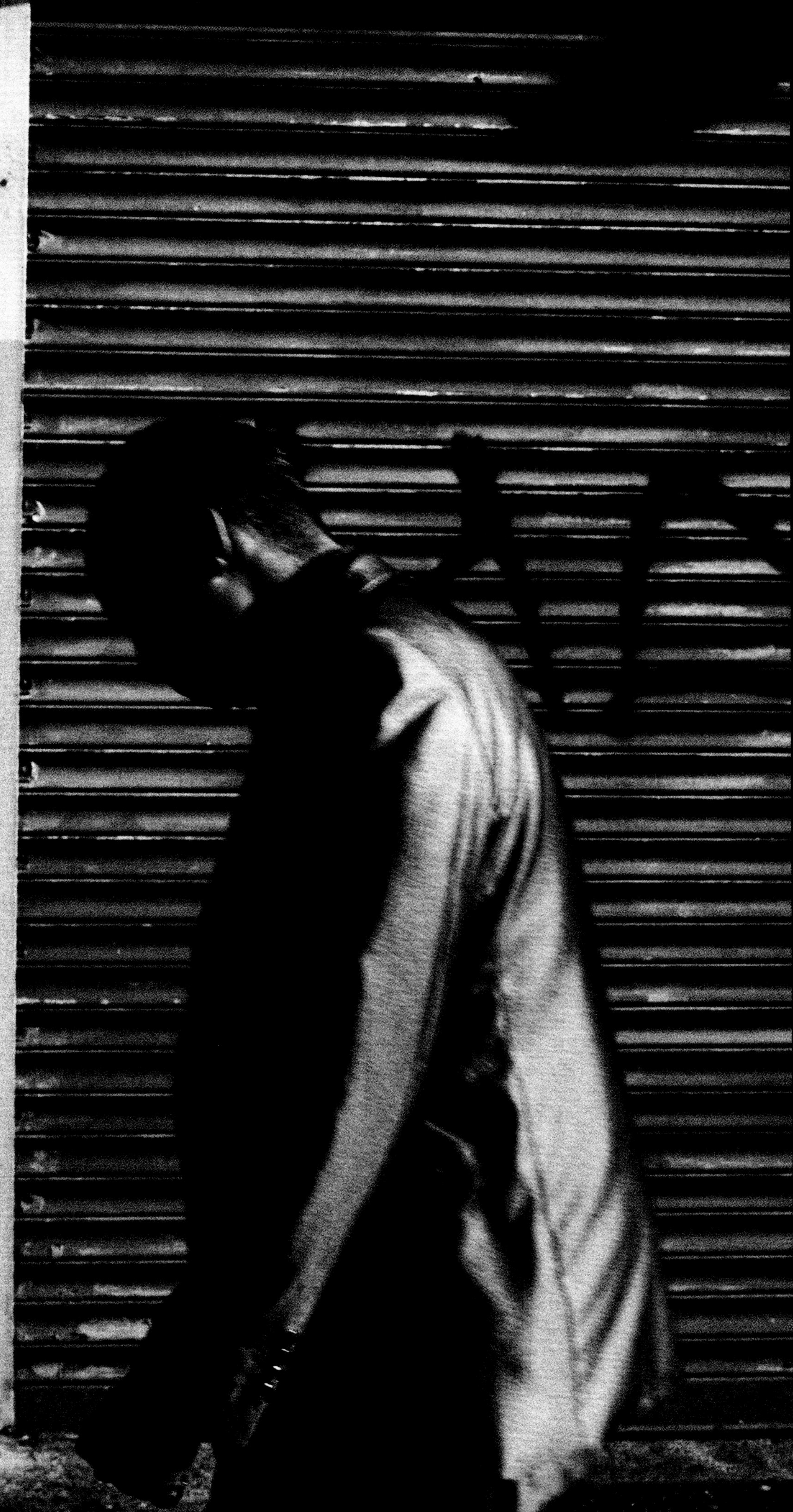
BIKE
LOCK
FRAMES
LIGHT
BULBS
BINS
MOPS
BRUSHES
BASINS
BUCKE
READIN
GLASSE
CUTLER
TRAVEL
ADAPTO
HANGER
CLOT
HOR
KETTL
ALAR
CLOC

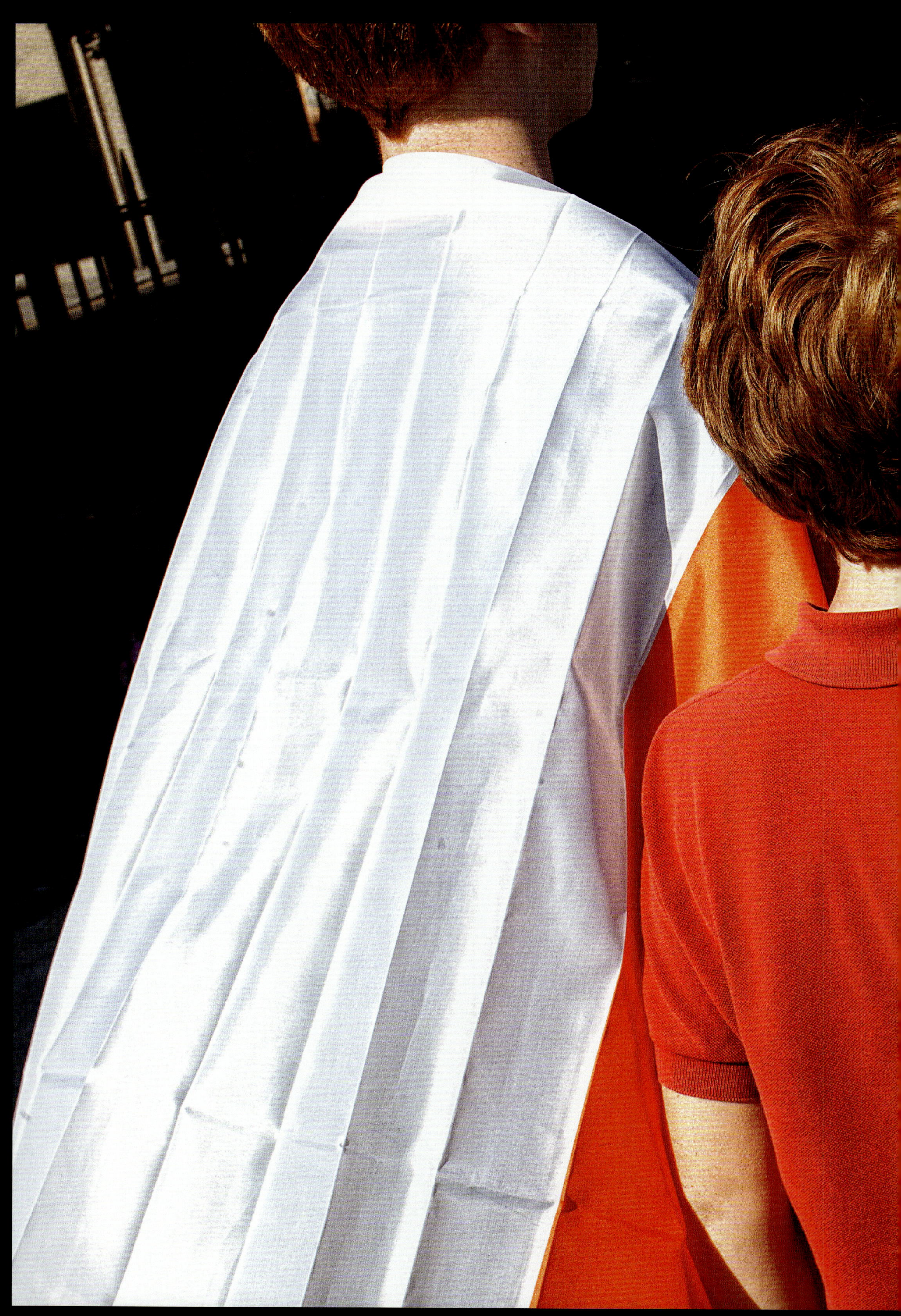

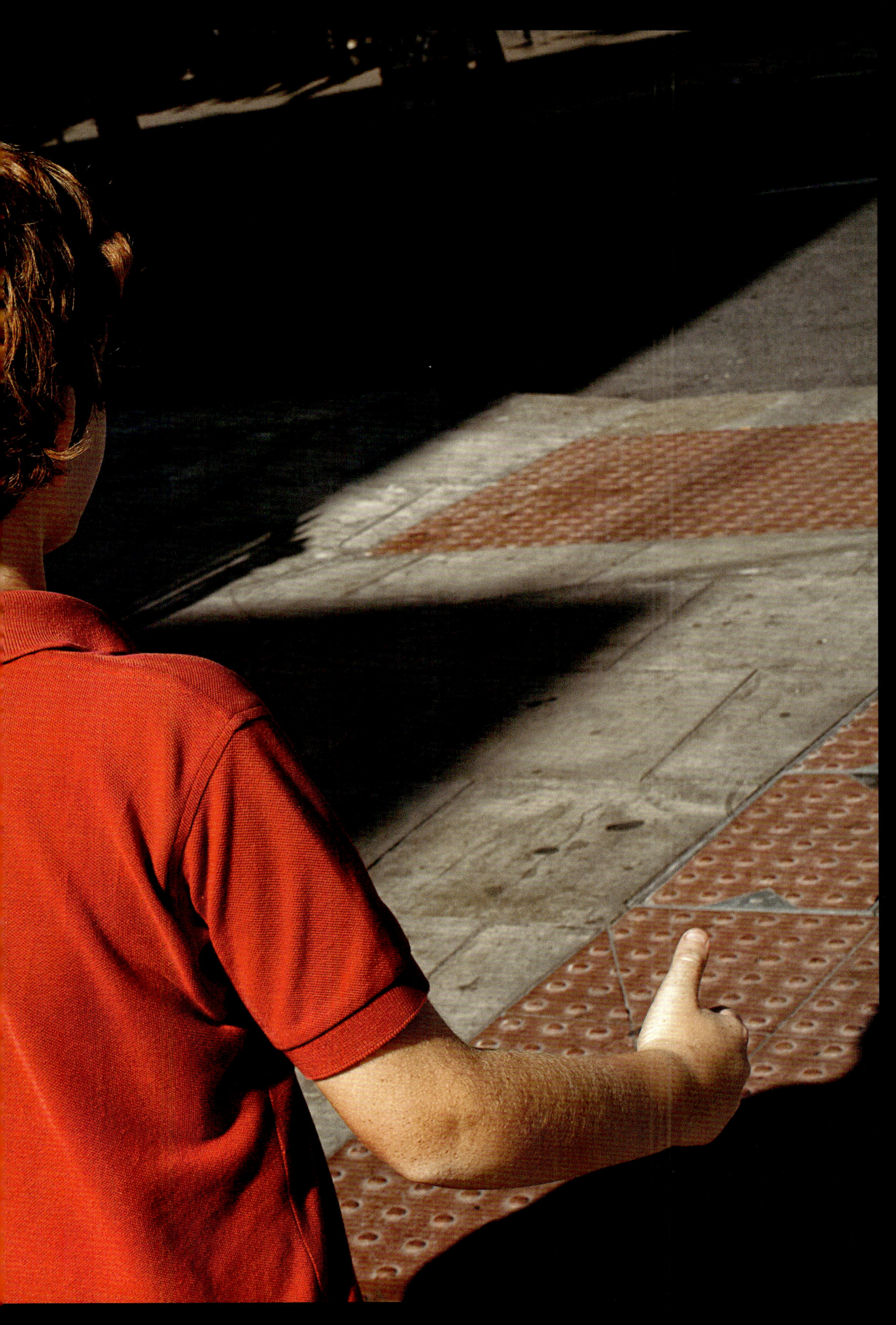

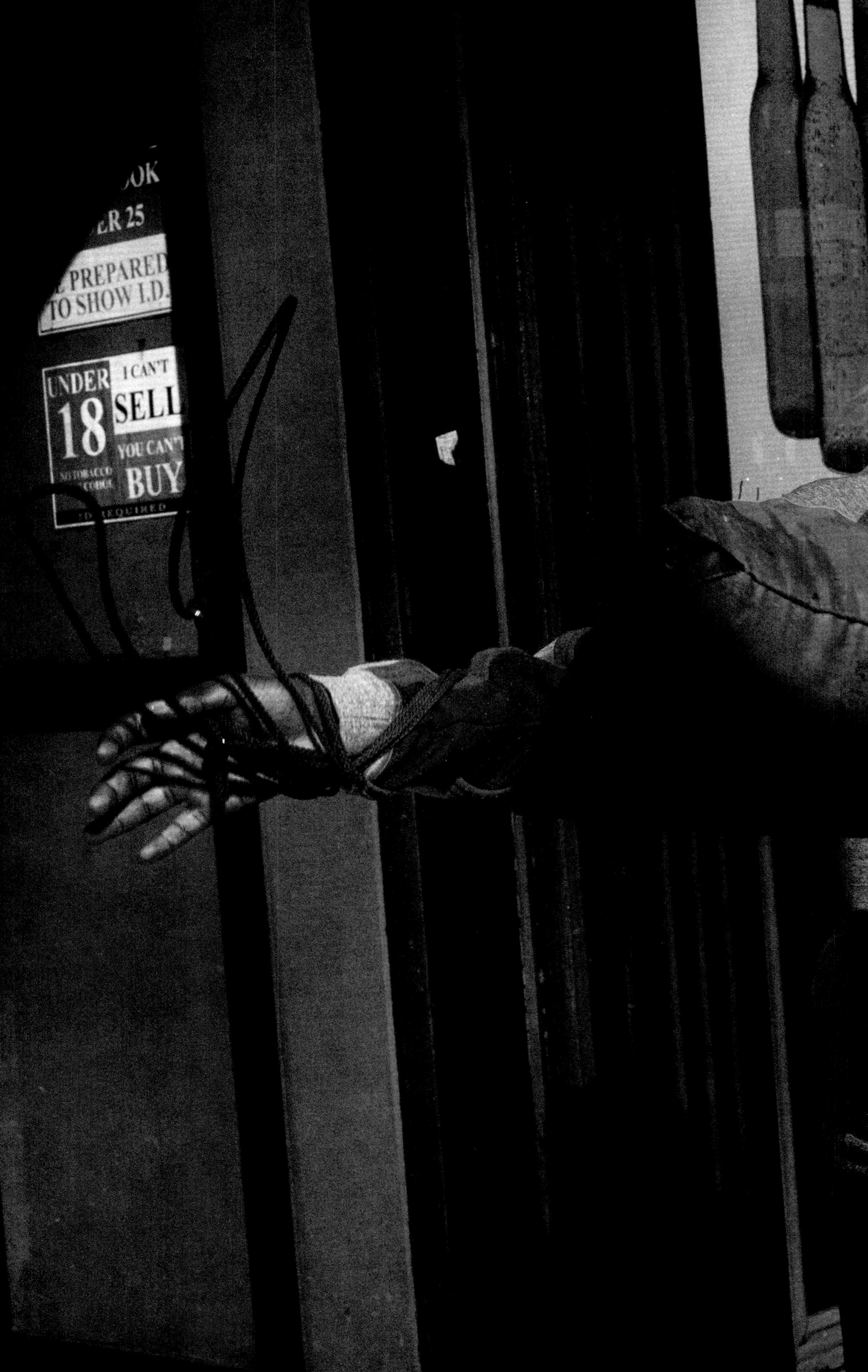
OK
ER 25
PREPARED
TO SHOW I.D.
UNDER
18
NO TOBACCO
ALCOHOL
I CAN'T
SELL
YOU CAN'T
BUY
ID REQUIRED

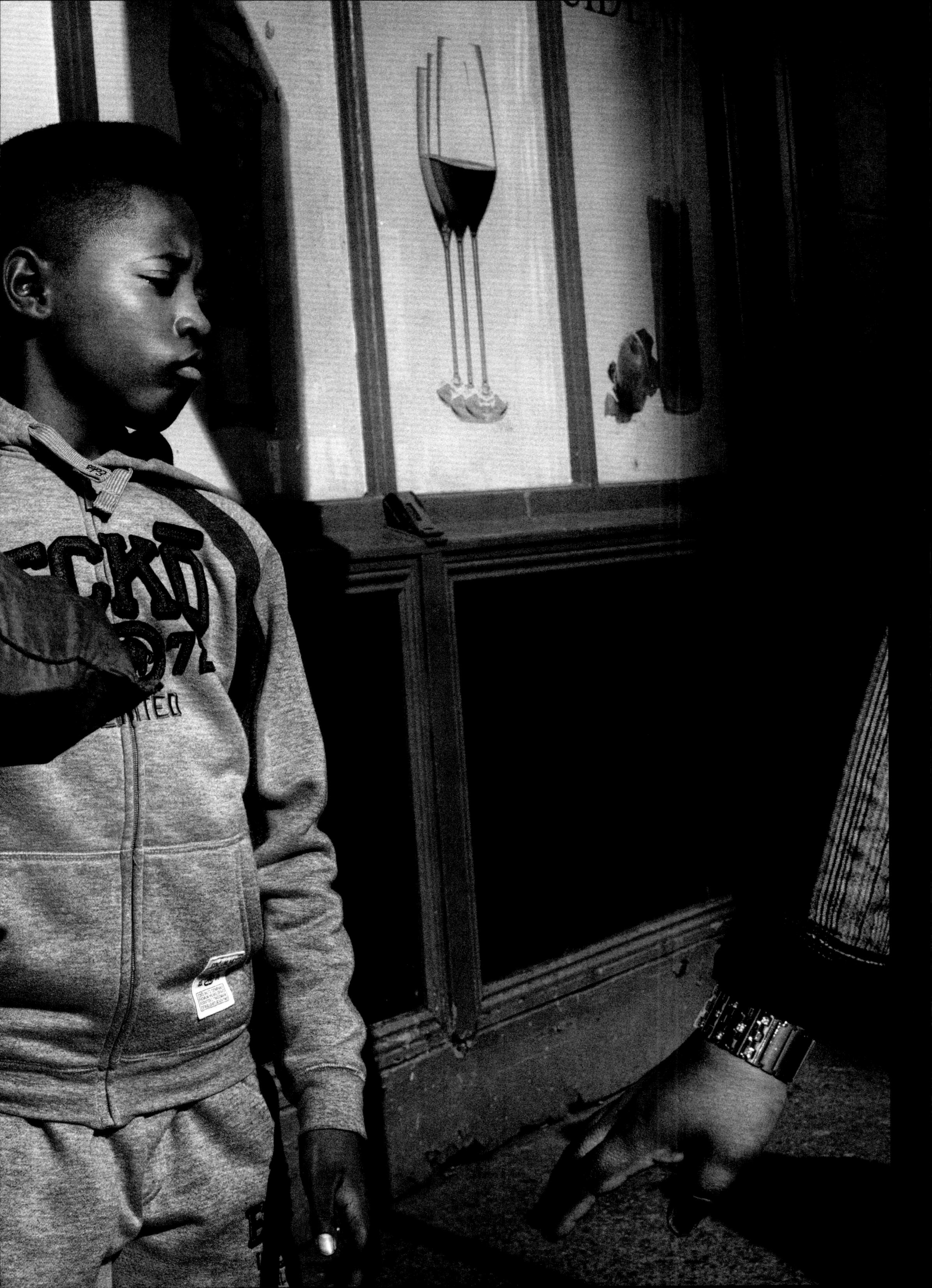

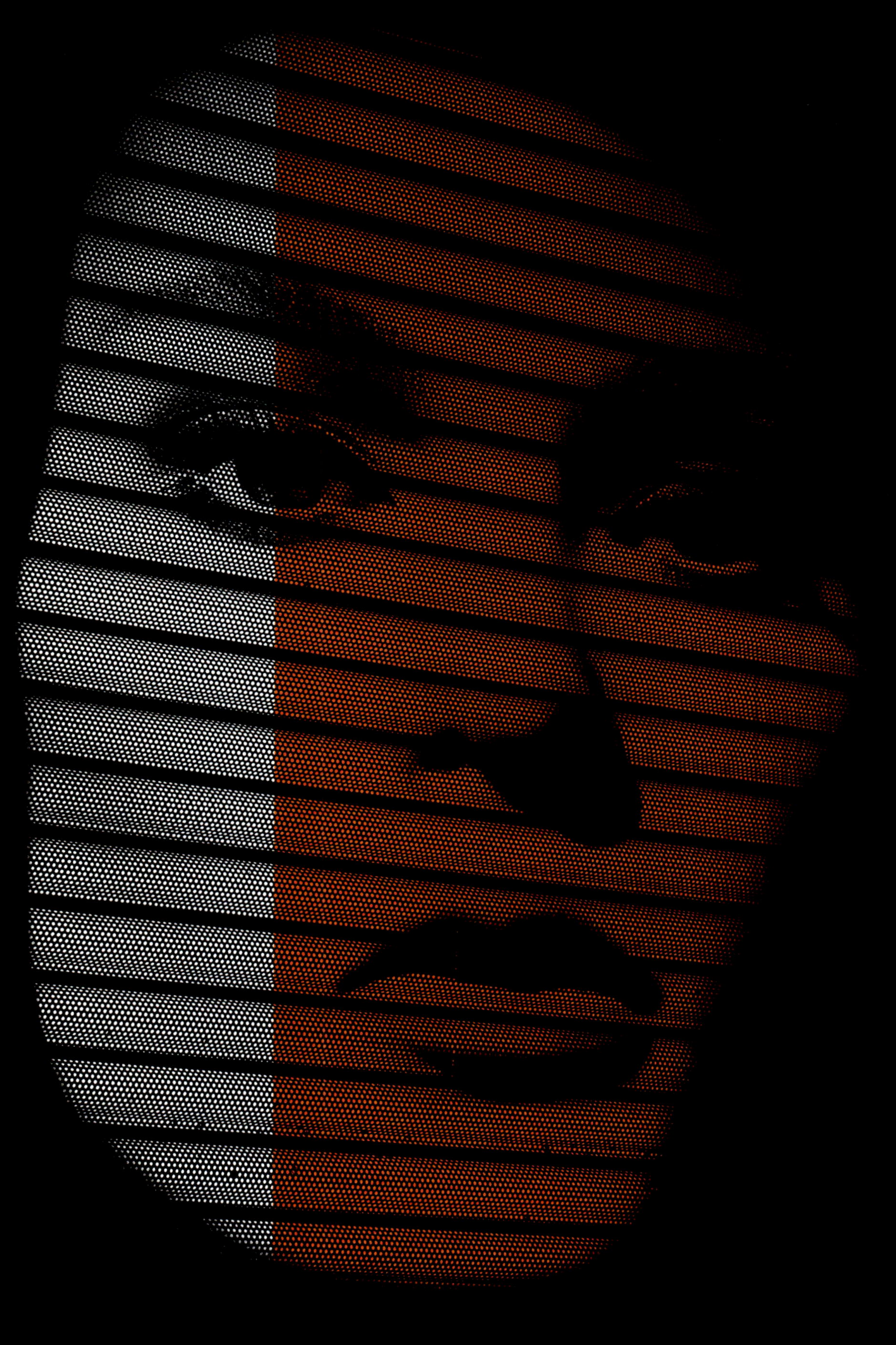

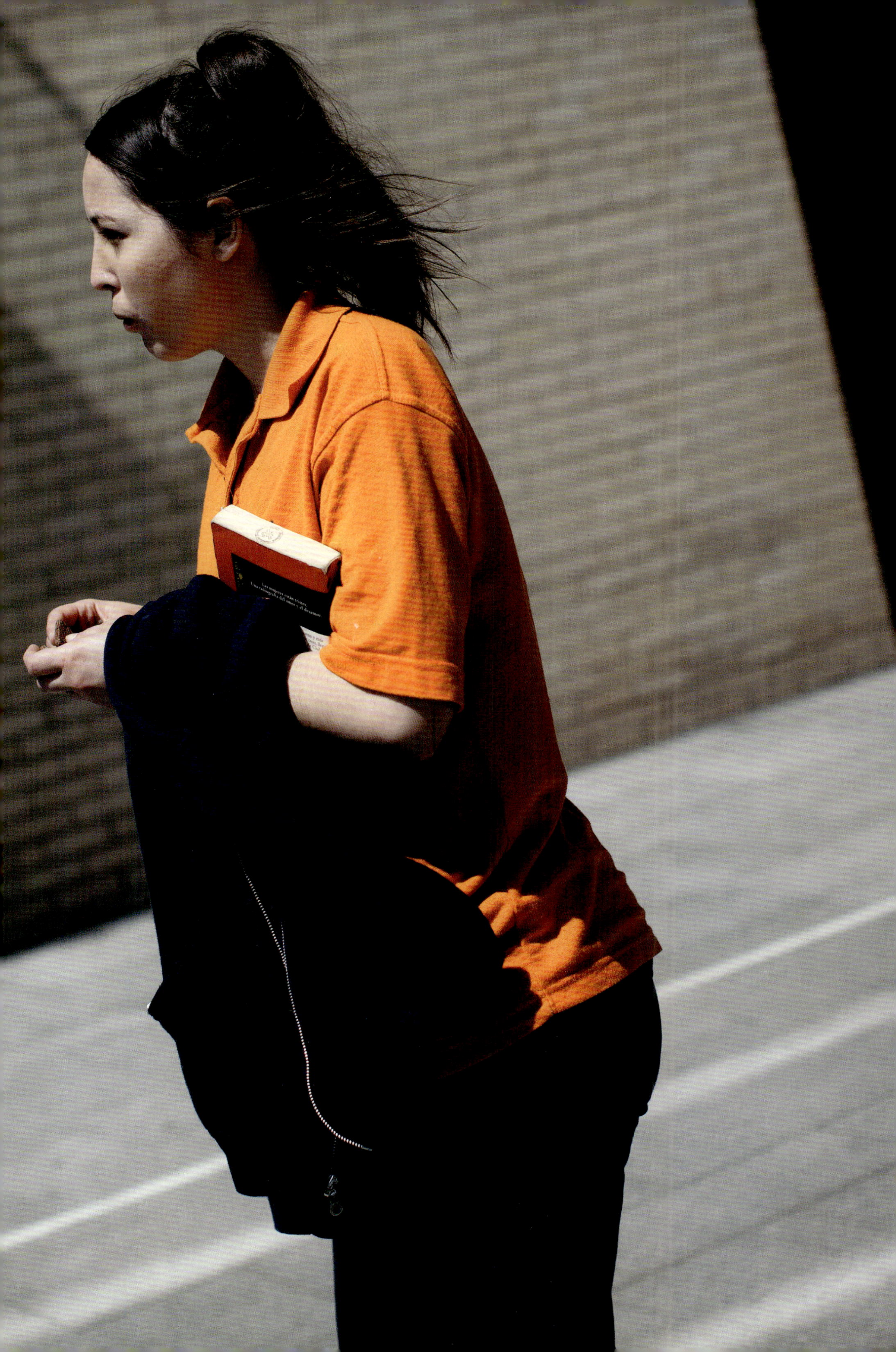
Las mujeres están tristes.
Una radiografía del amor y el desamor.

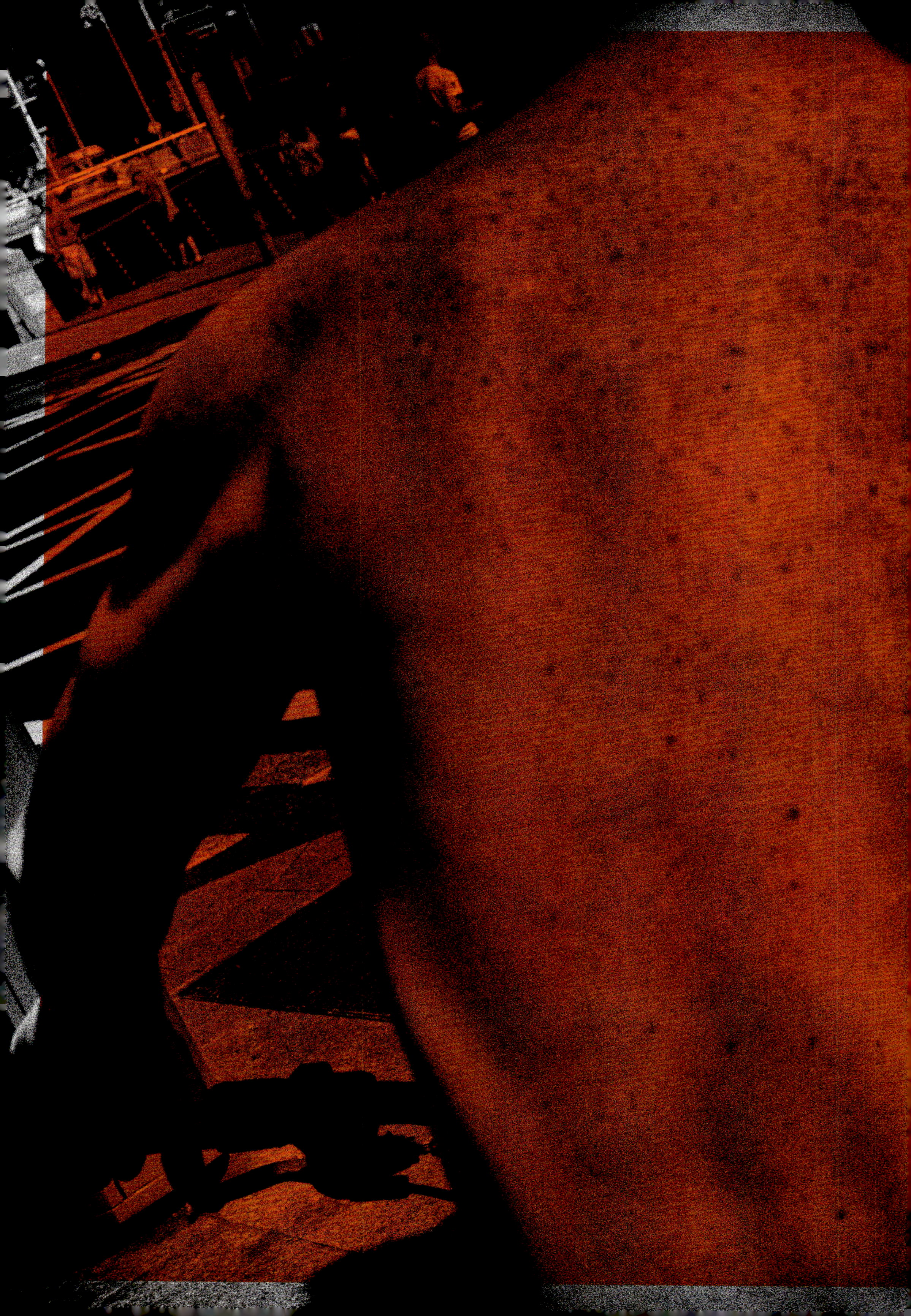

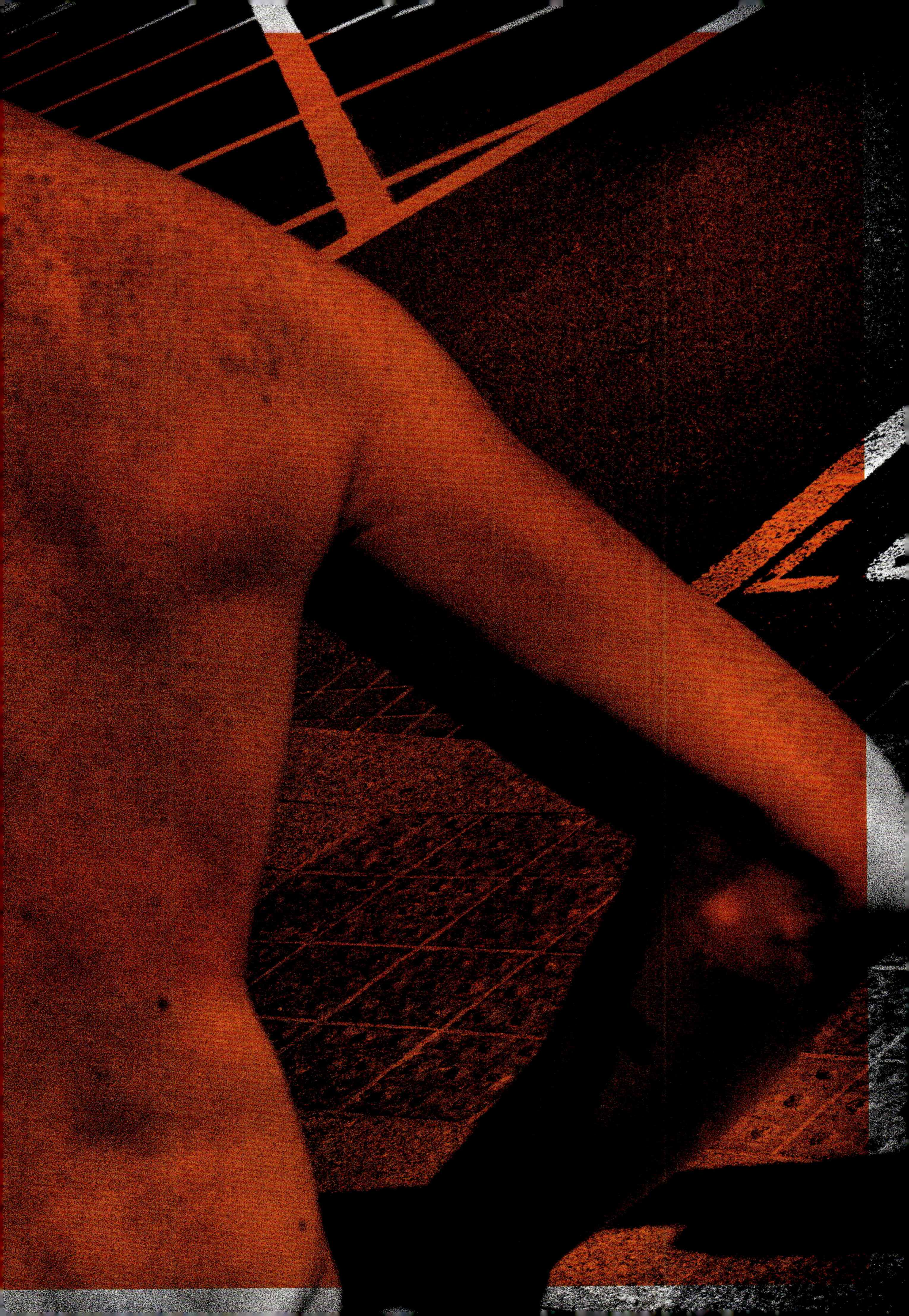

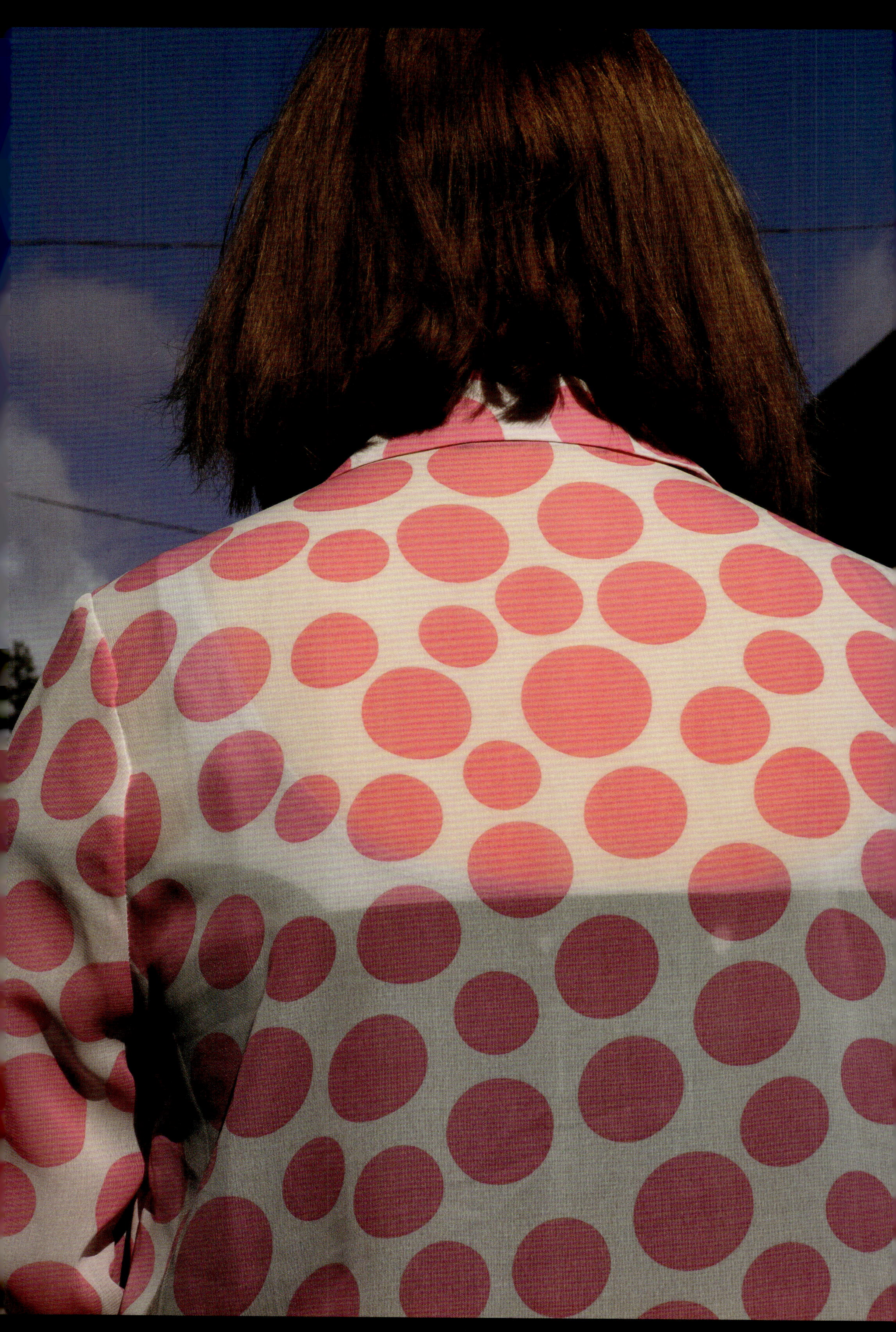

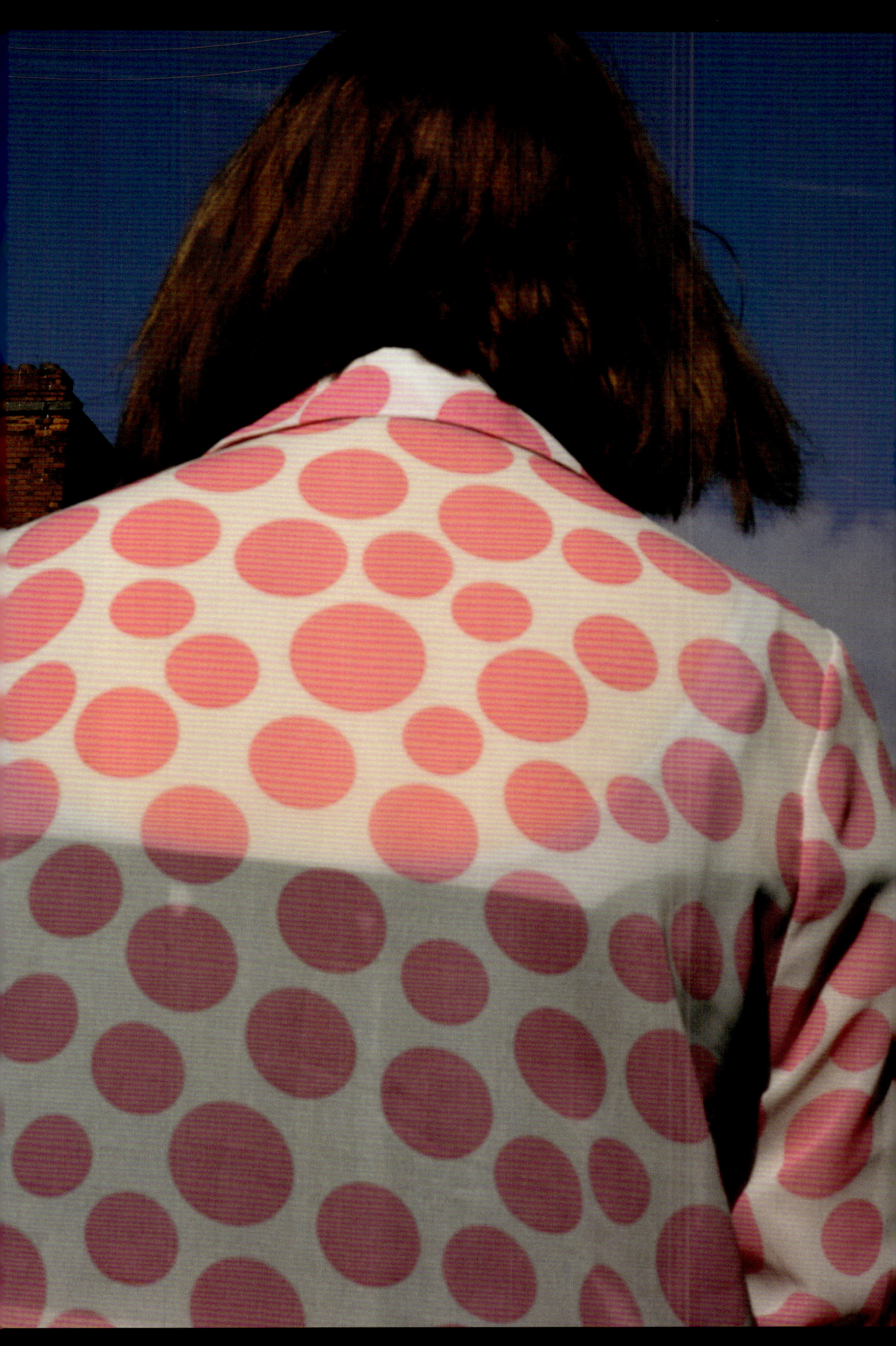

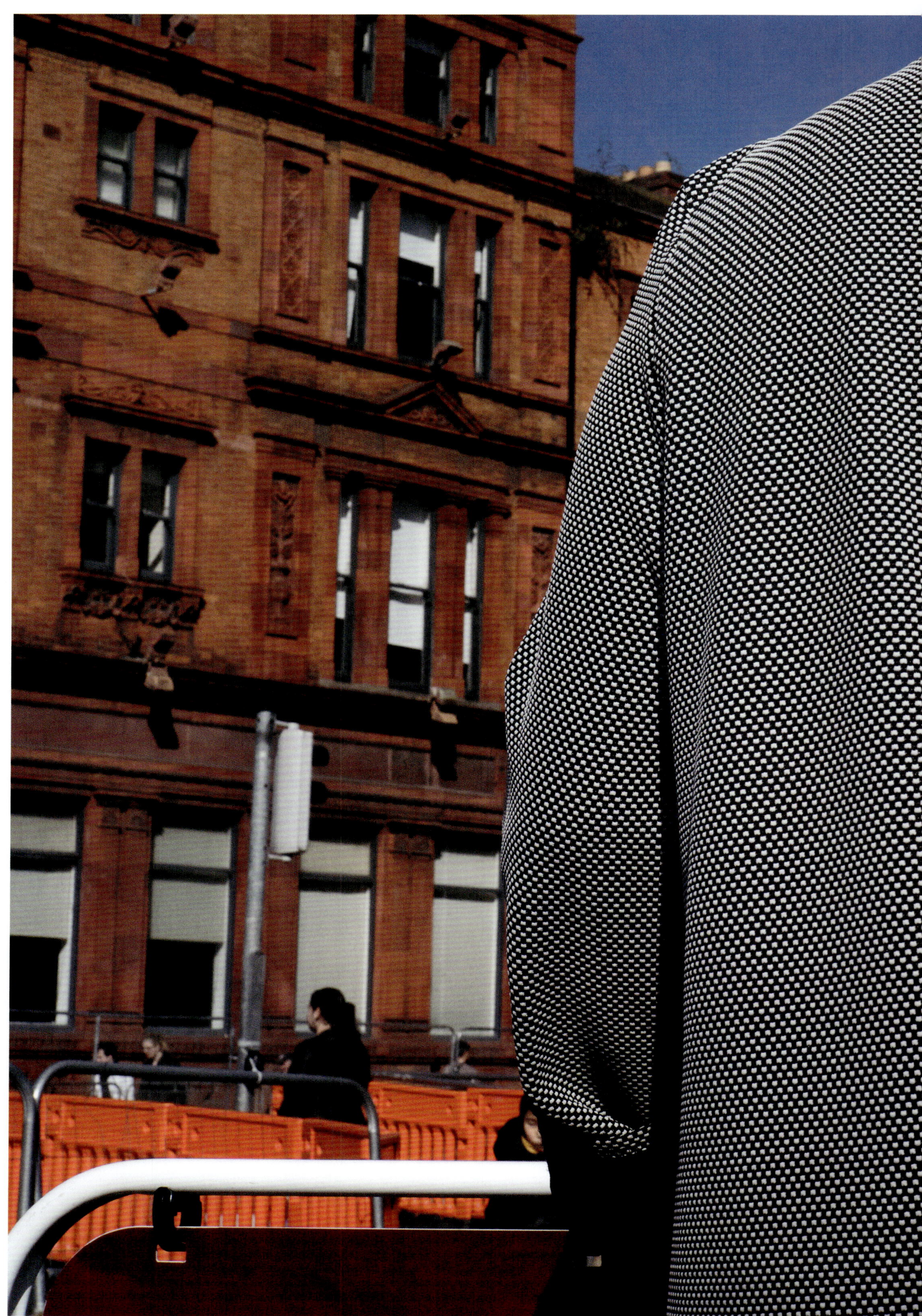

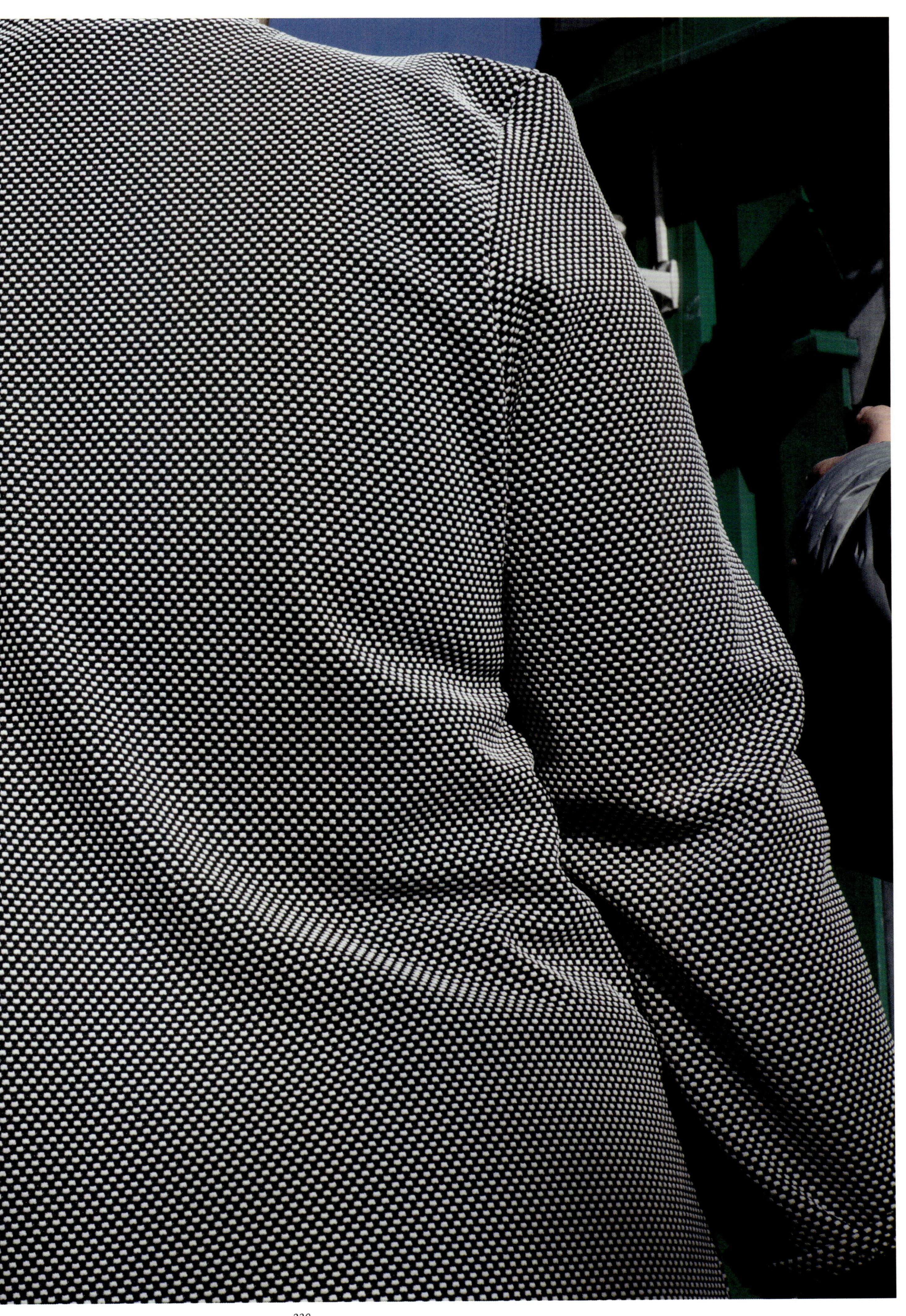

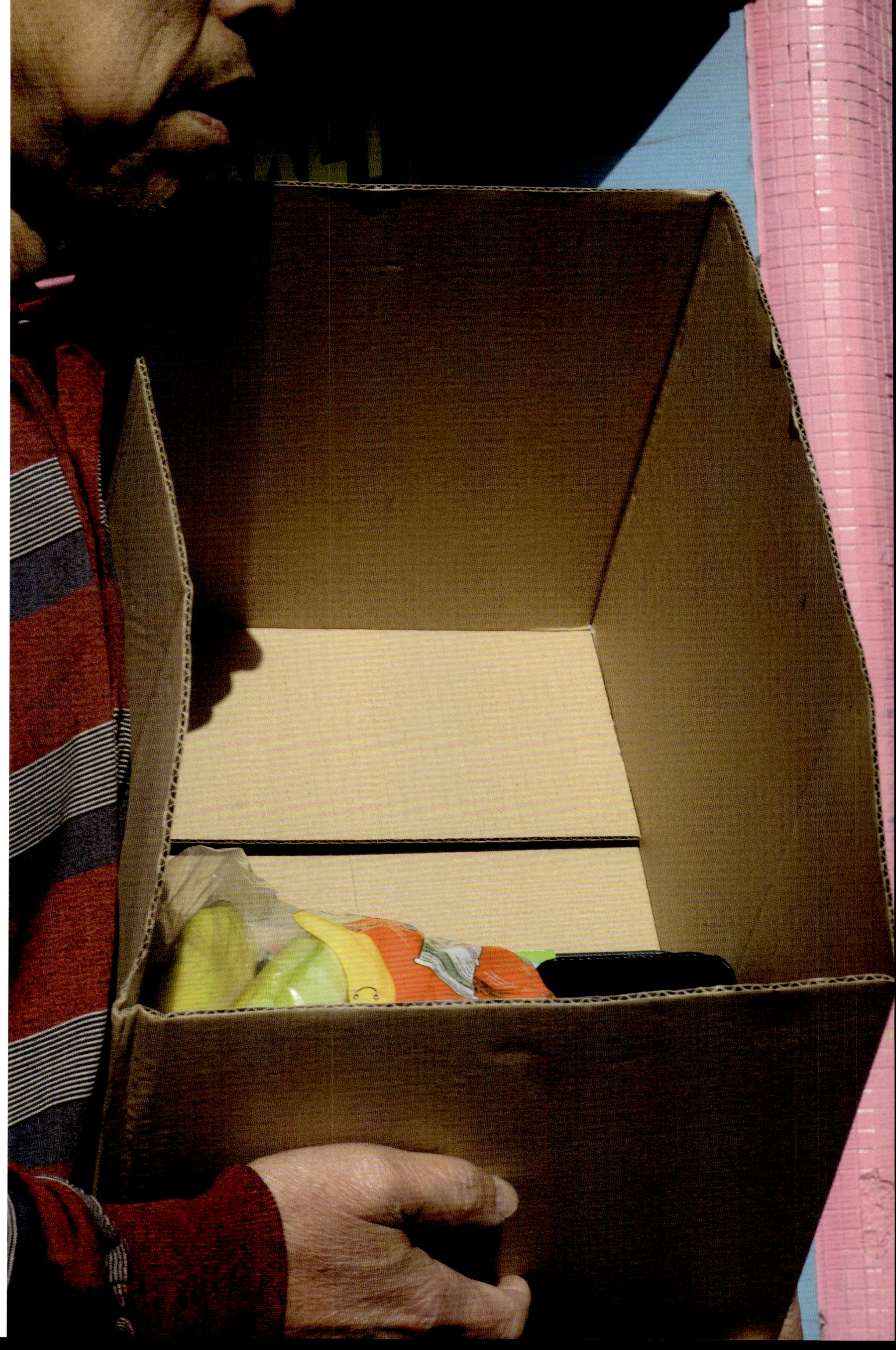

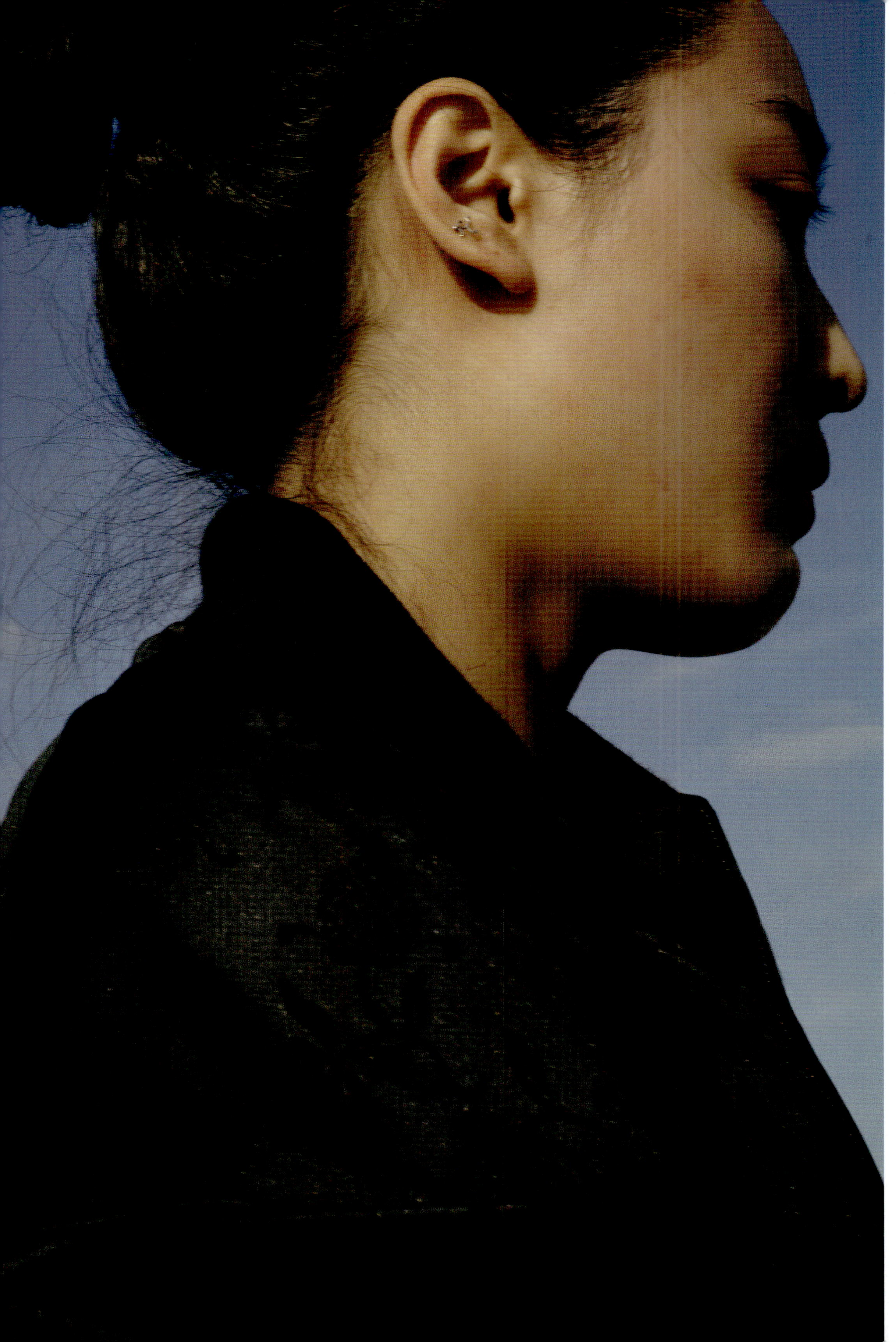

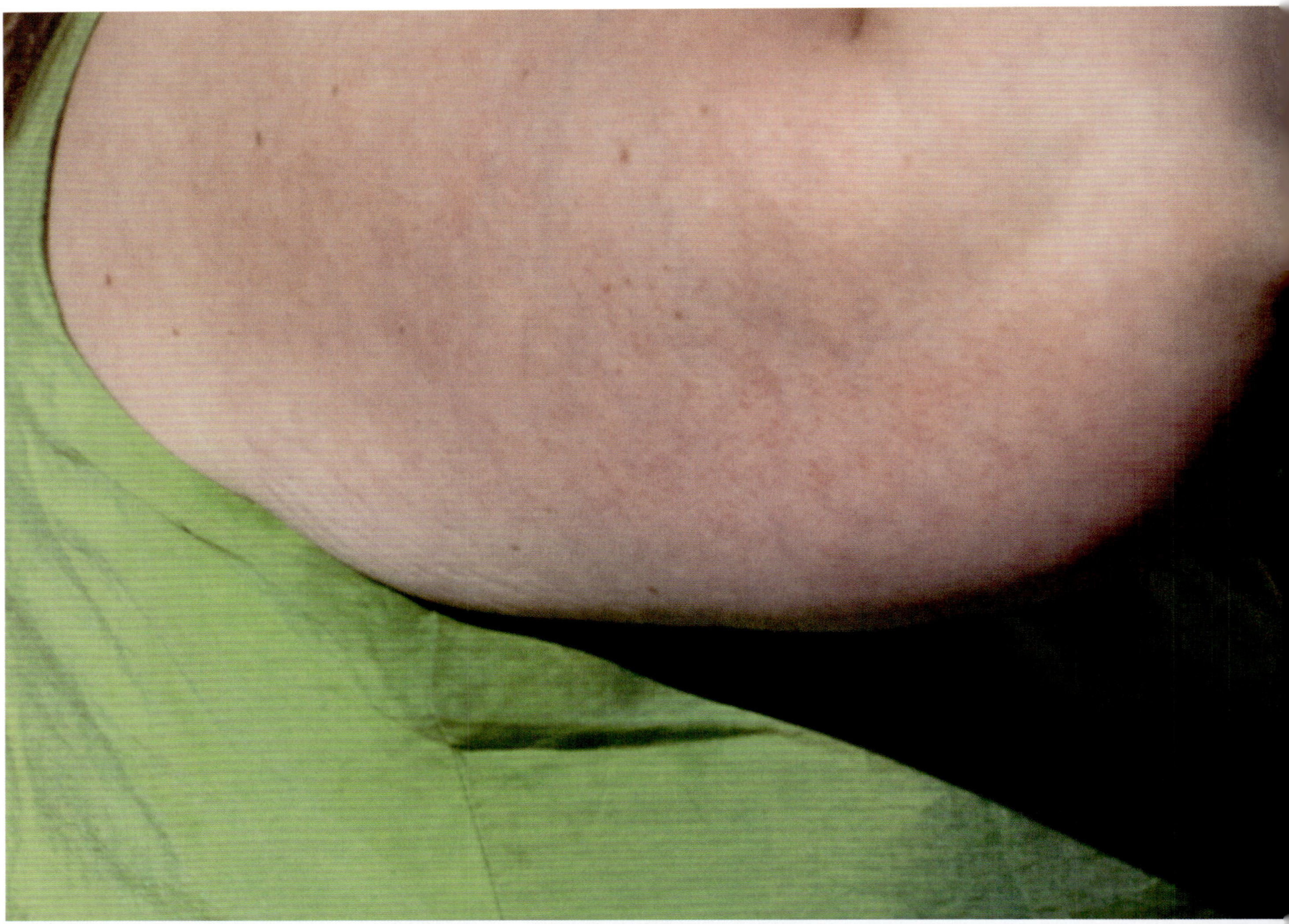

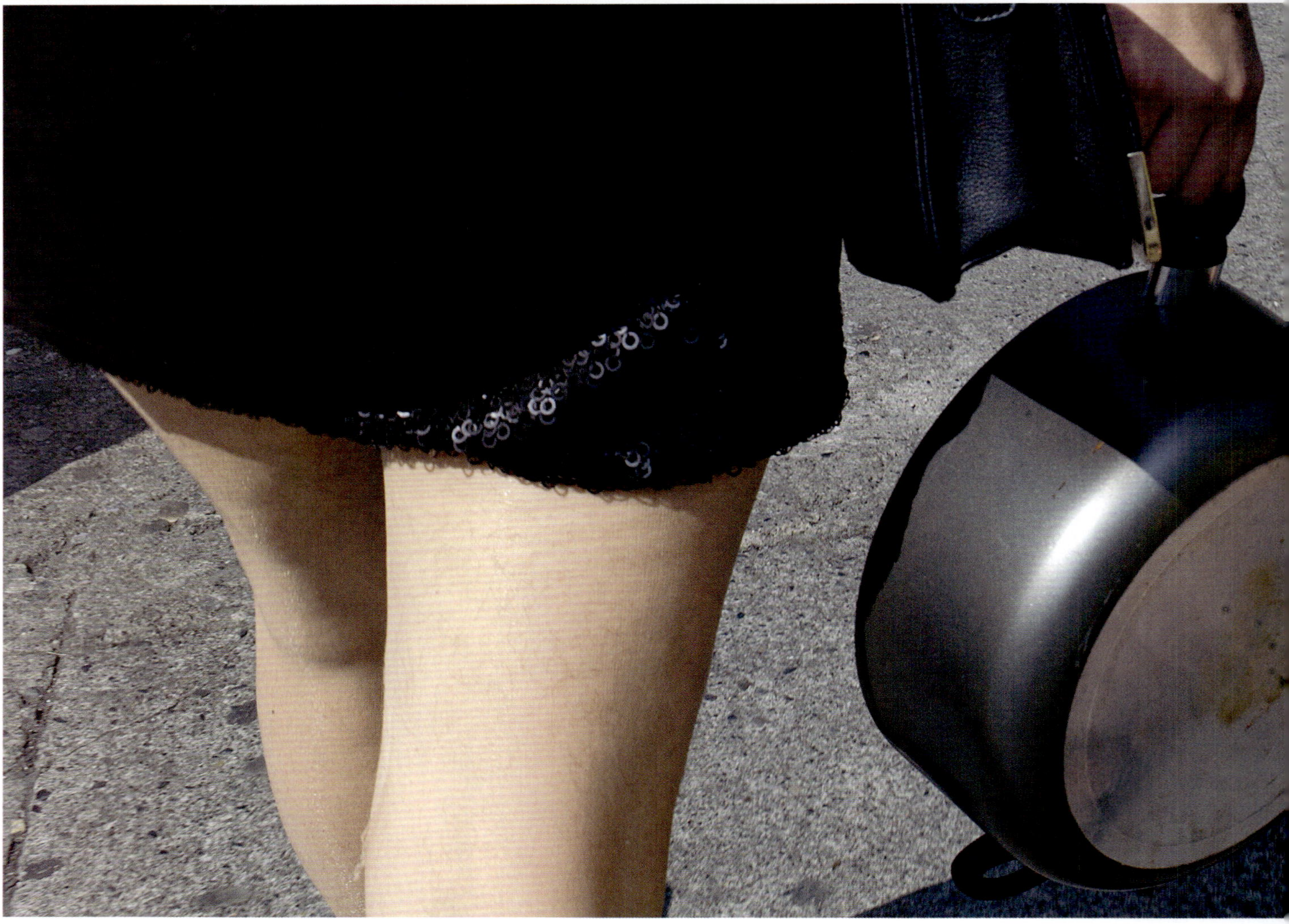

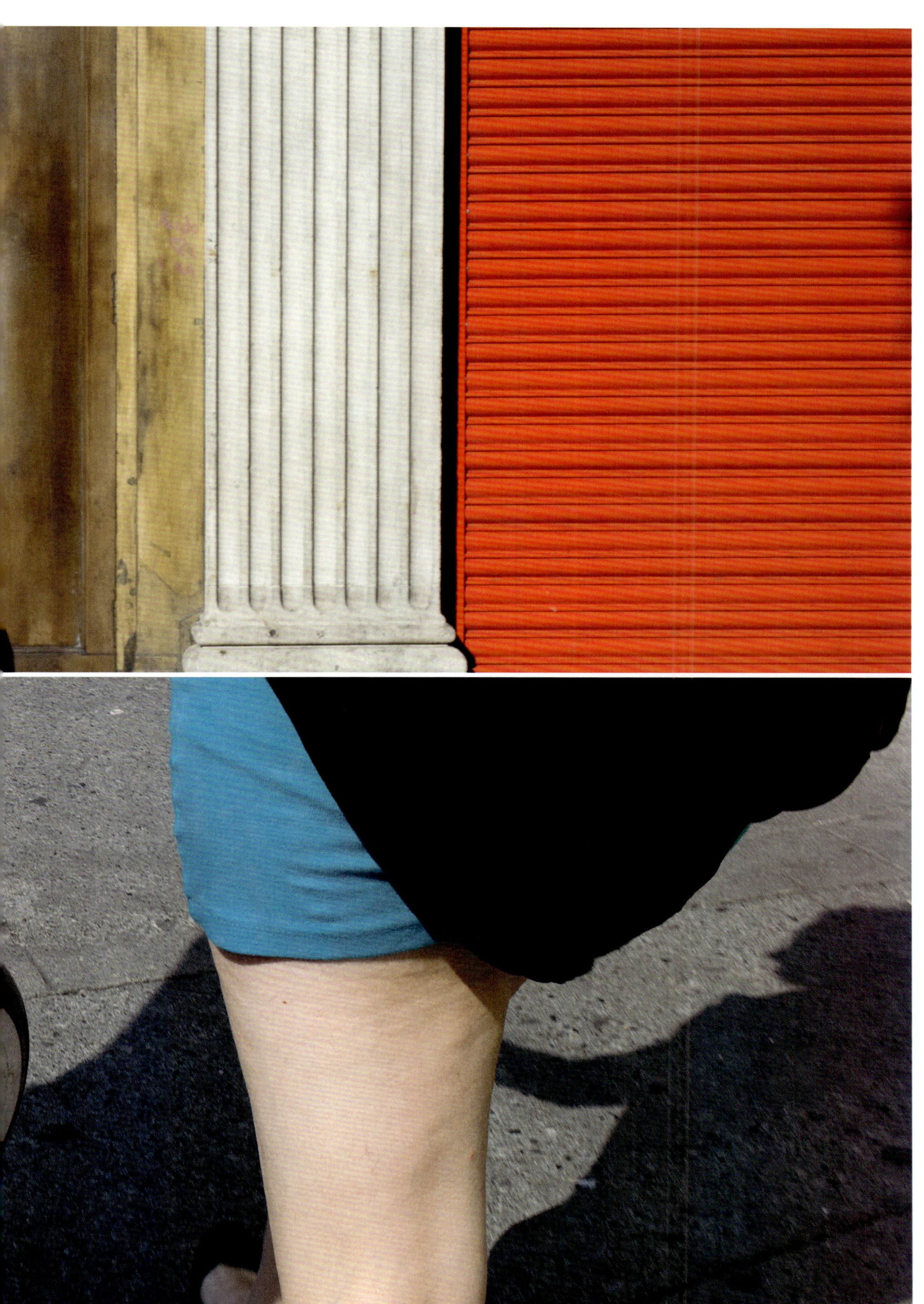

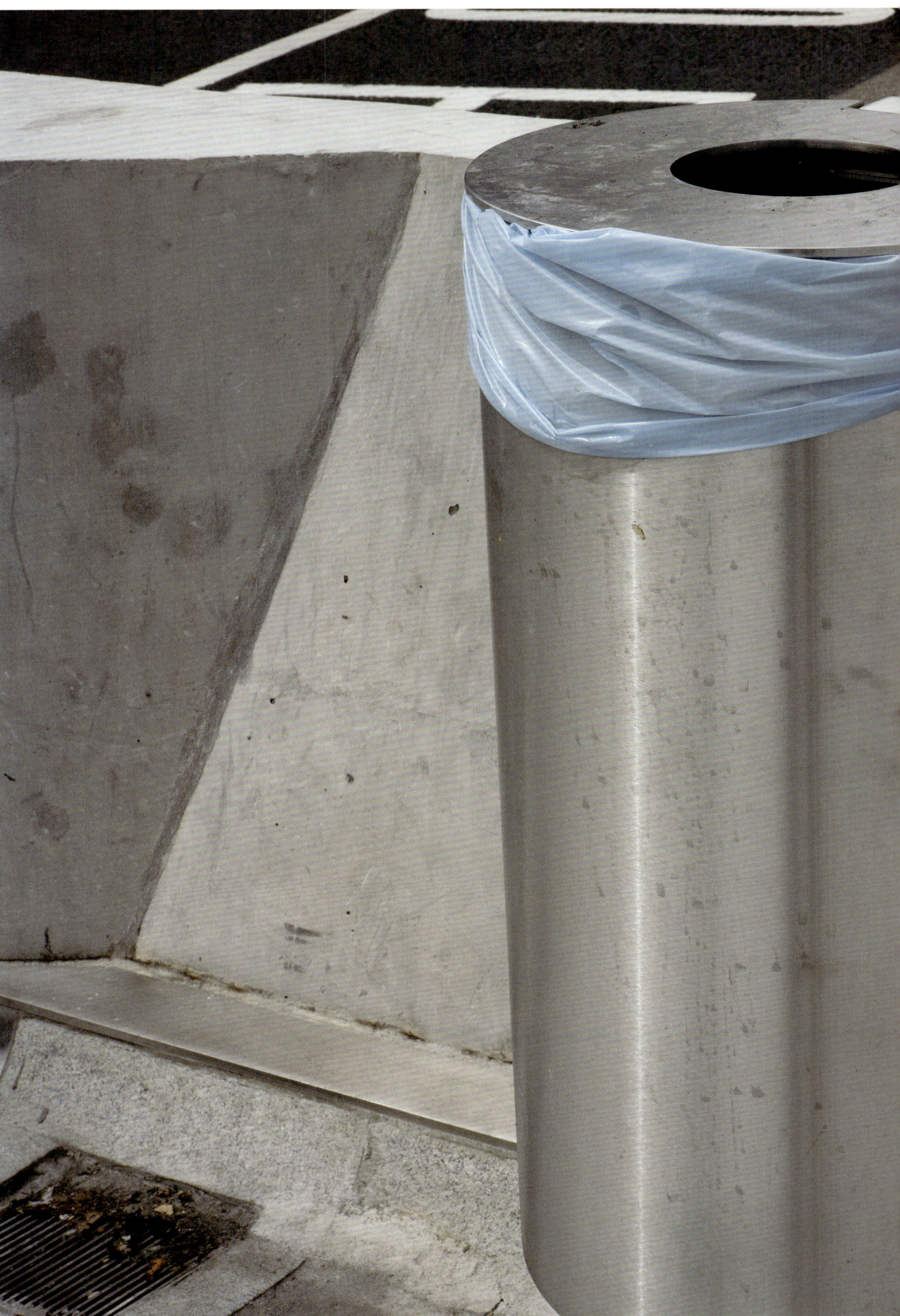

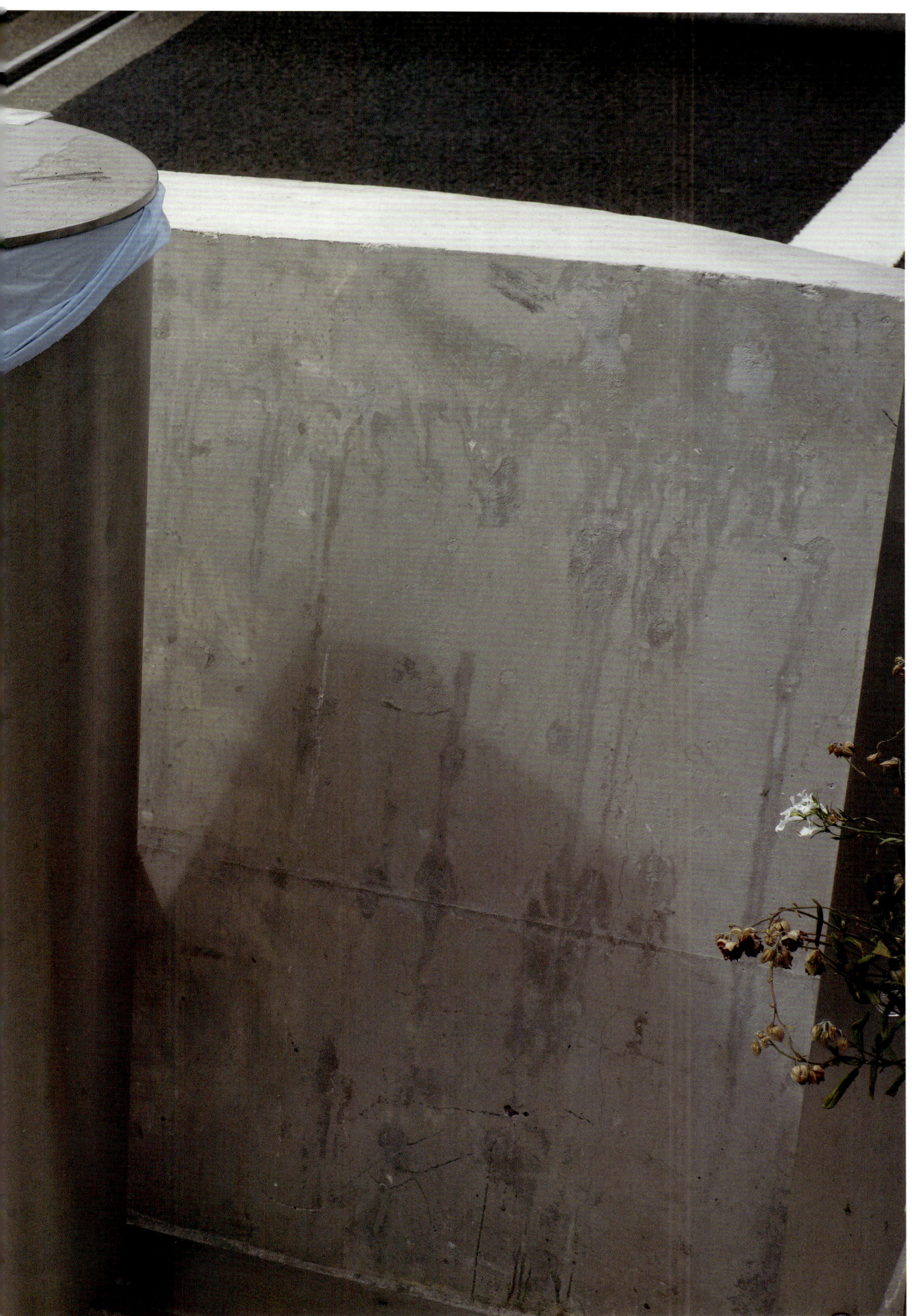

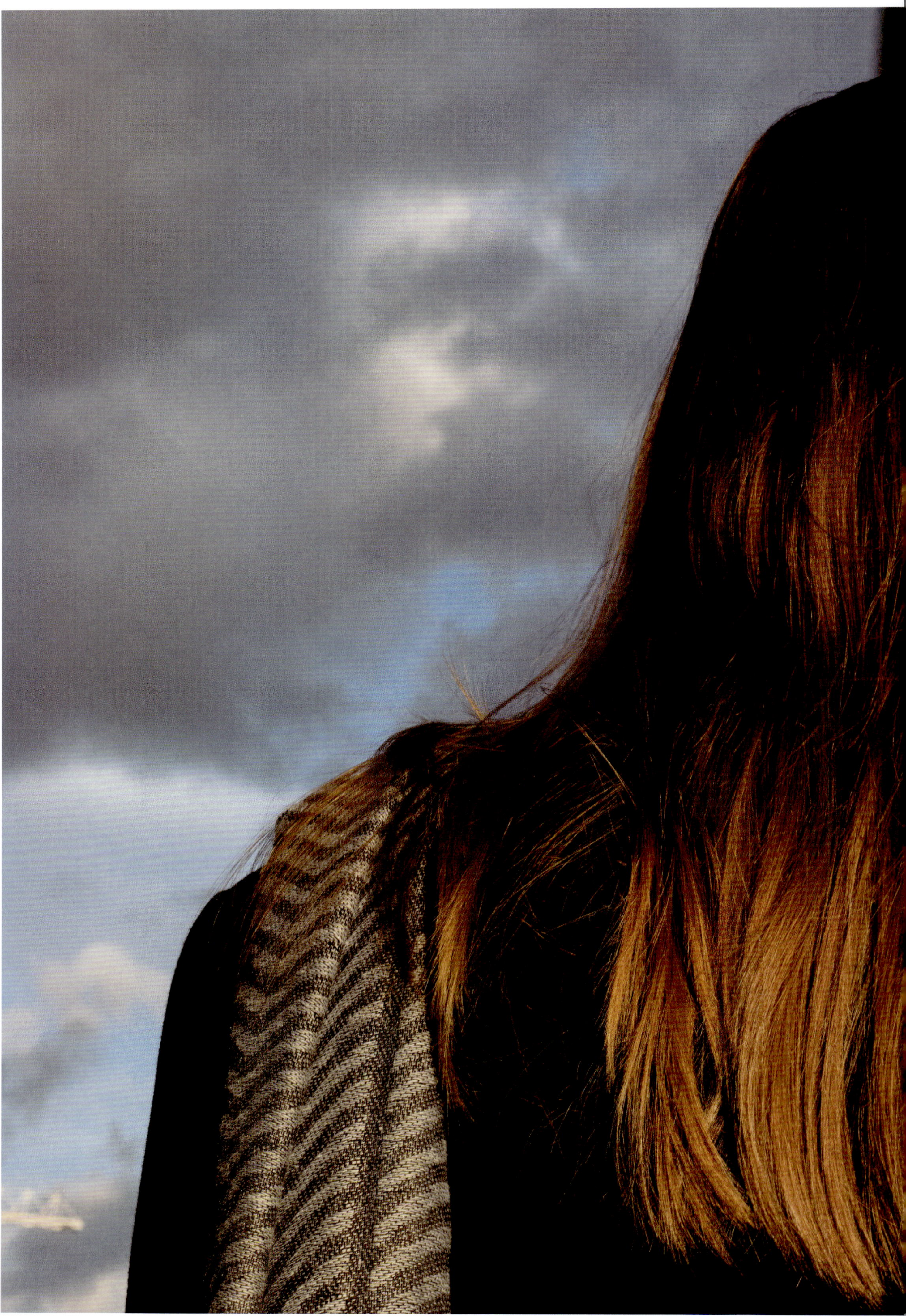

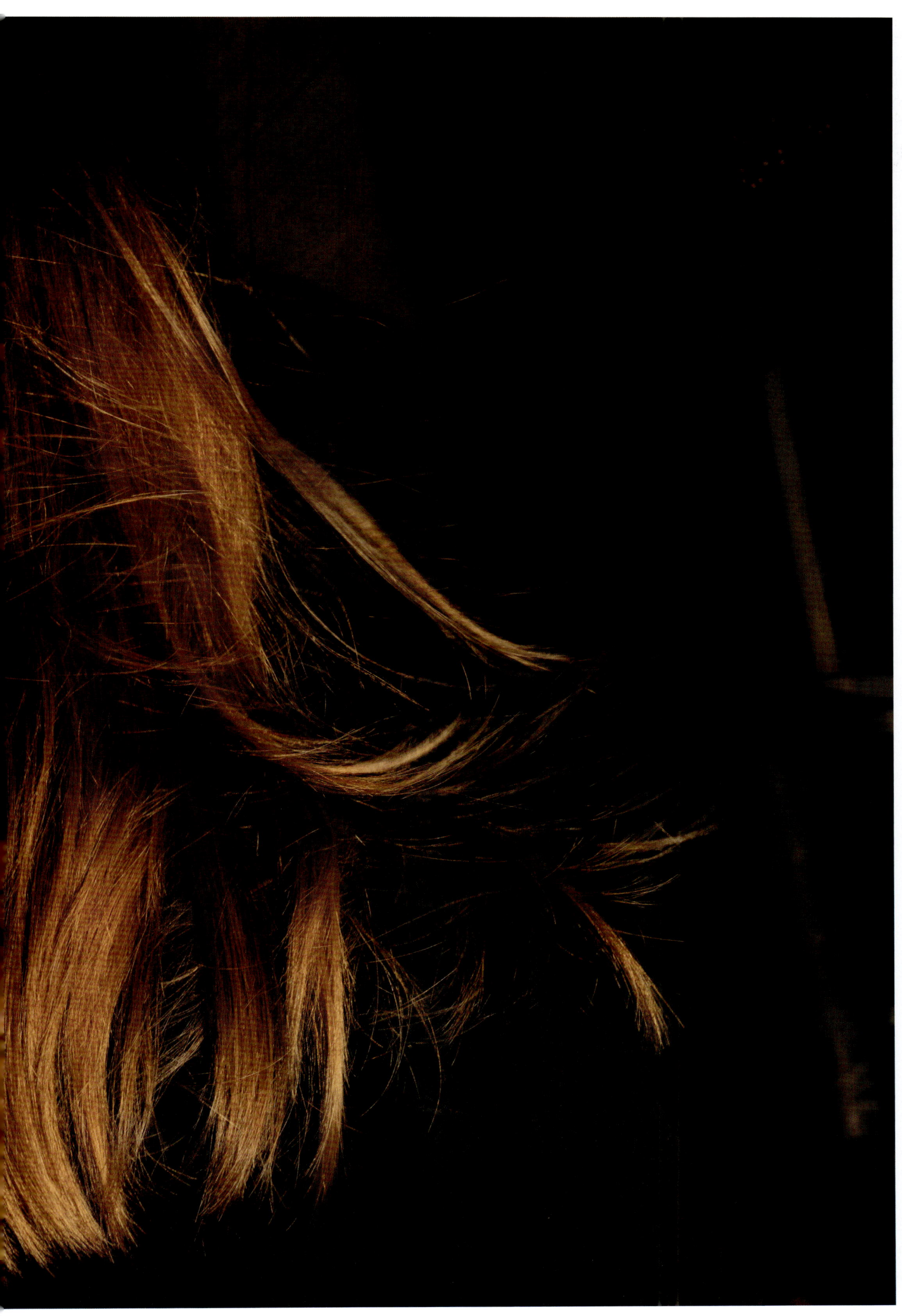

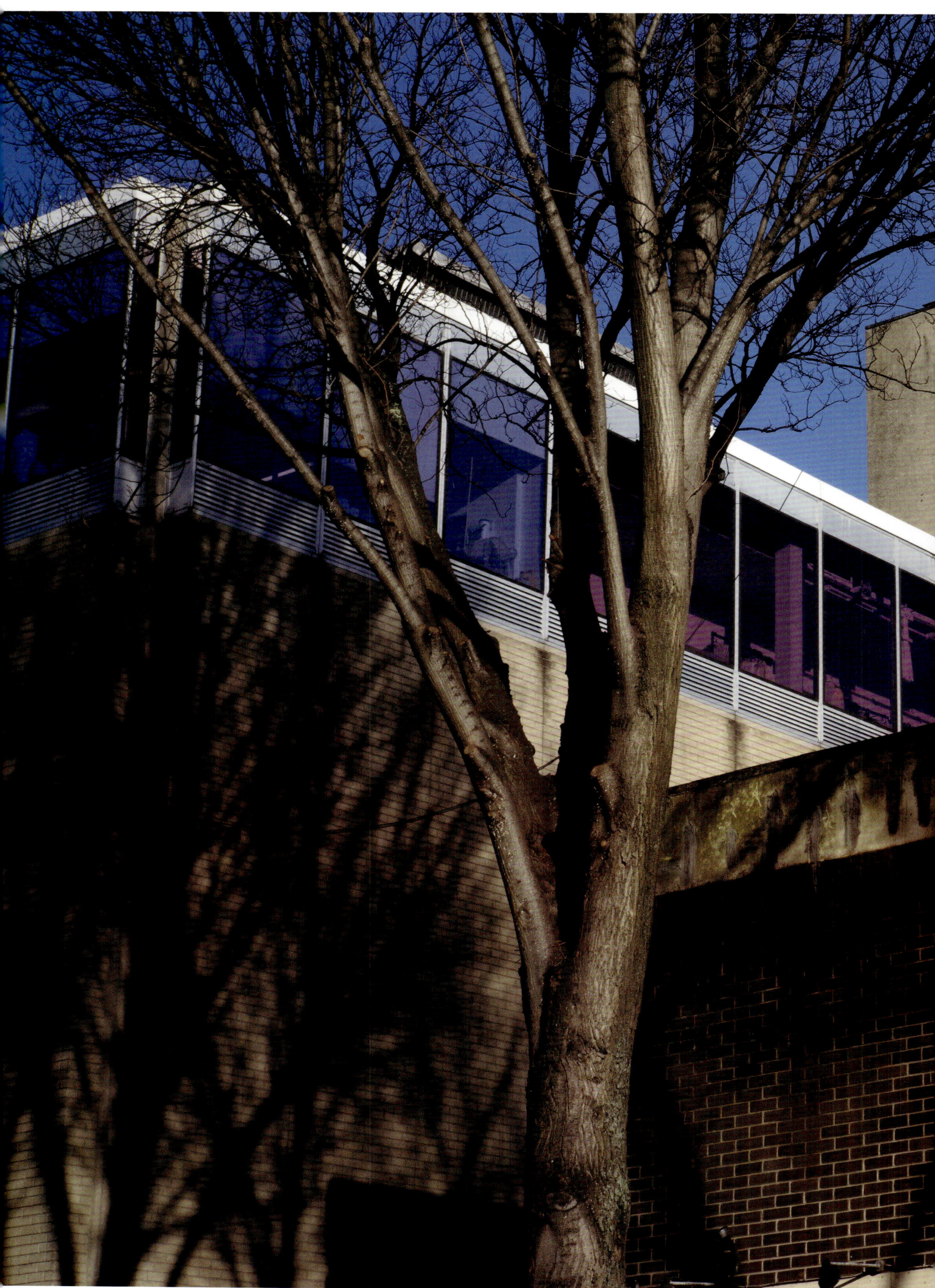

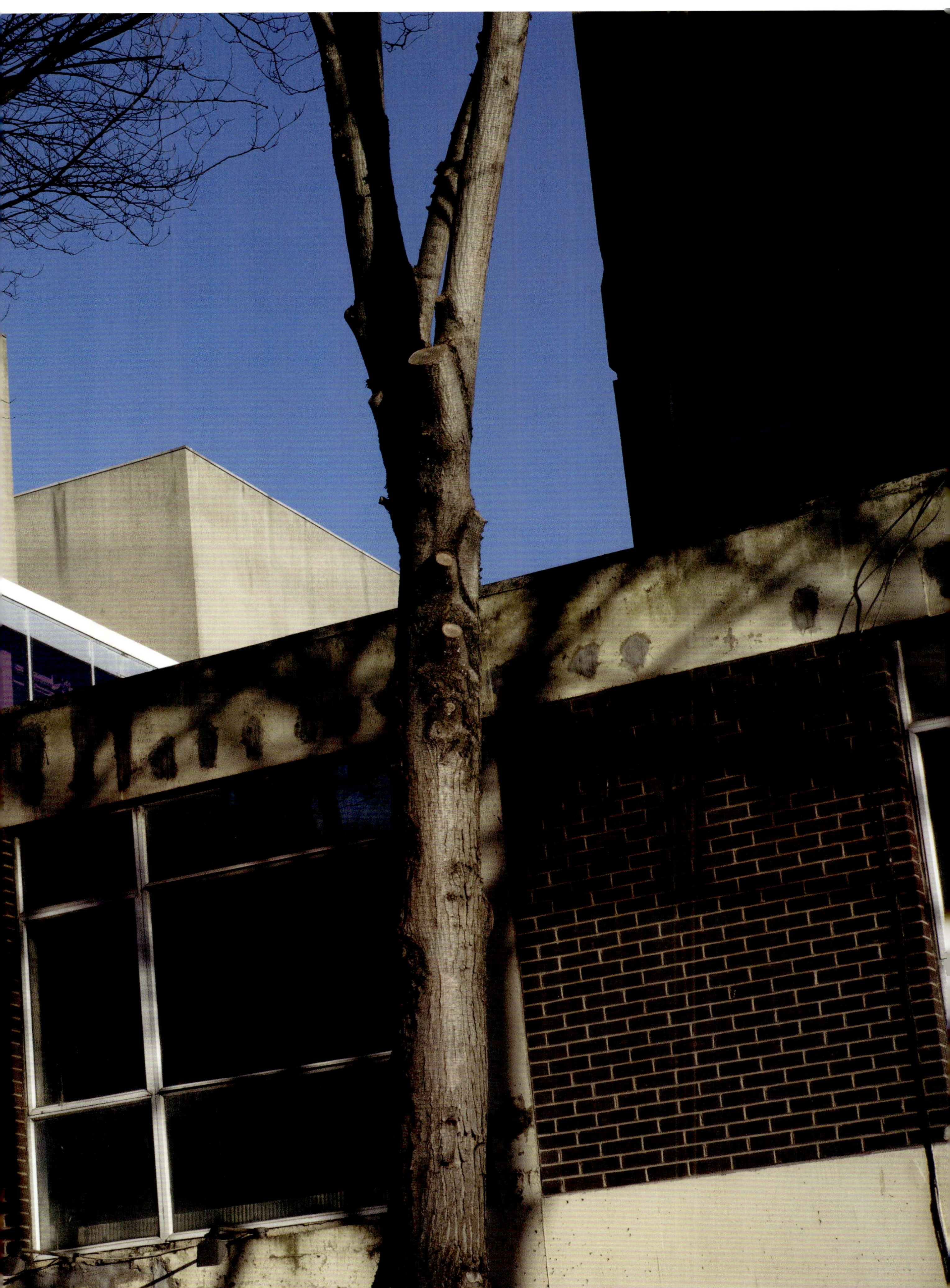

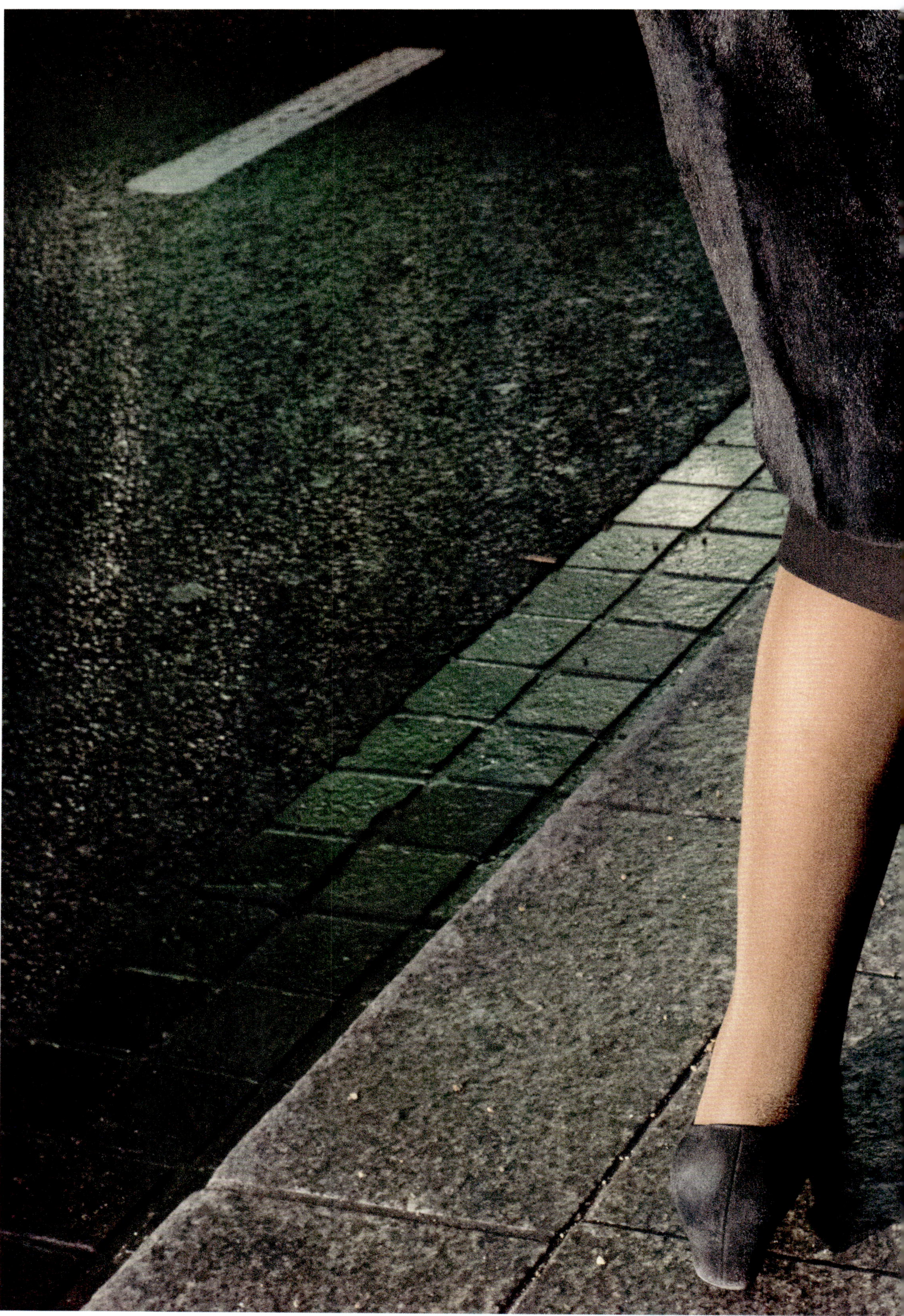

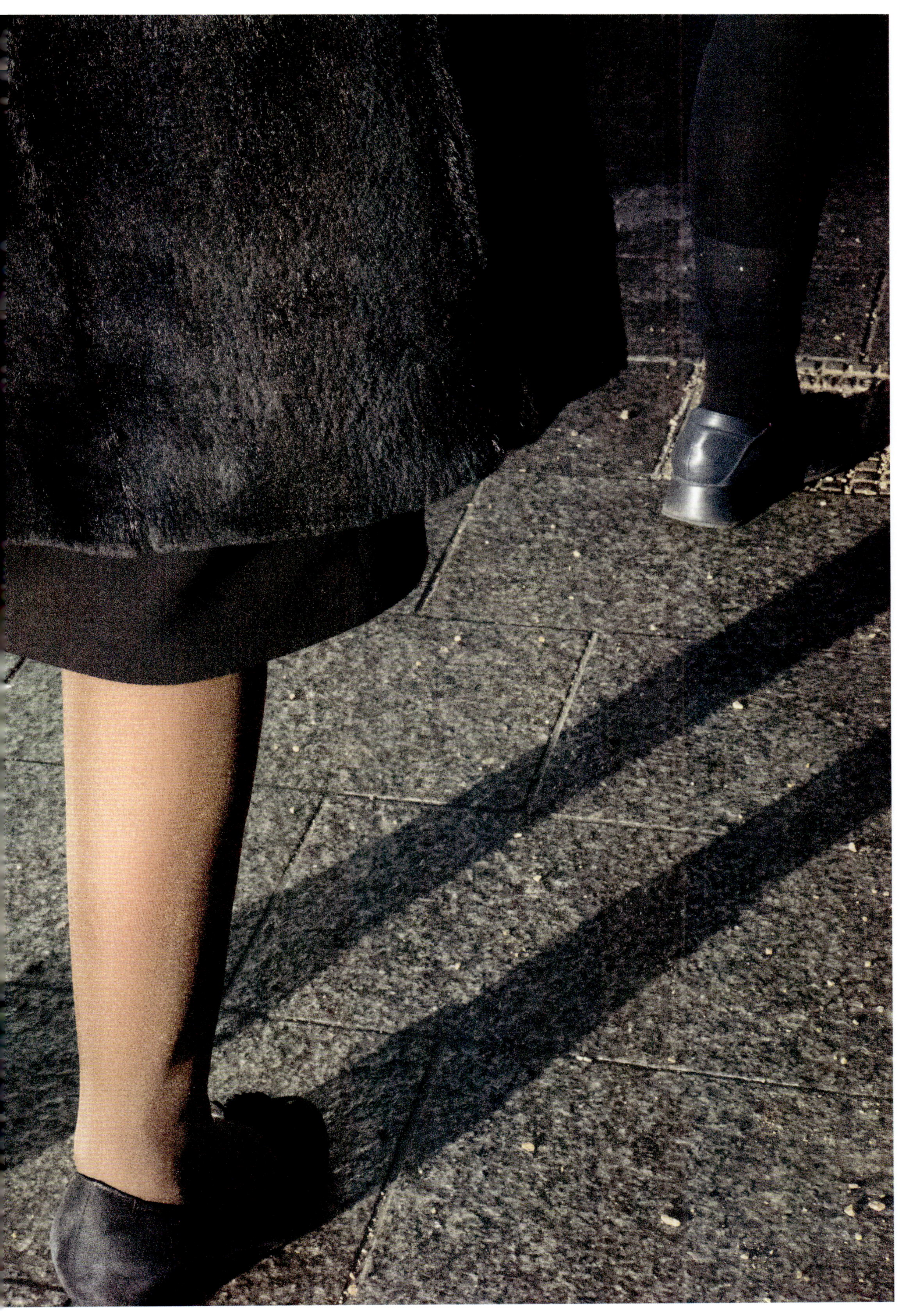

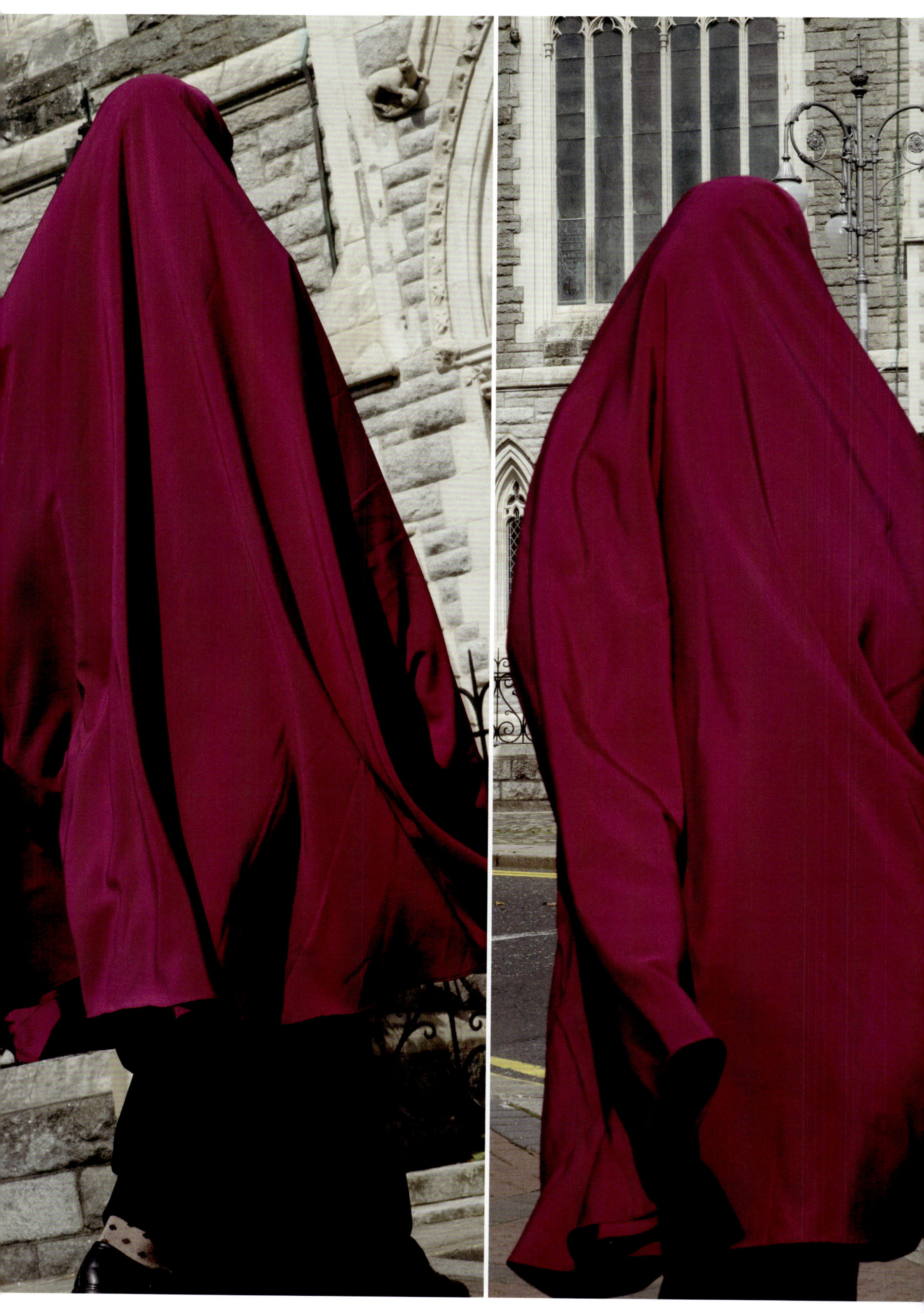

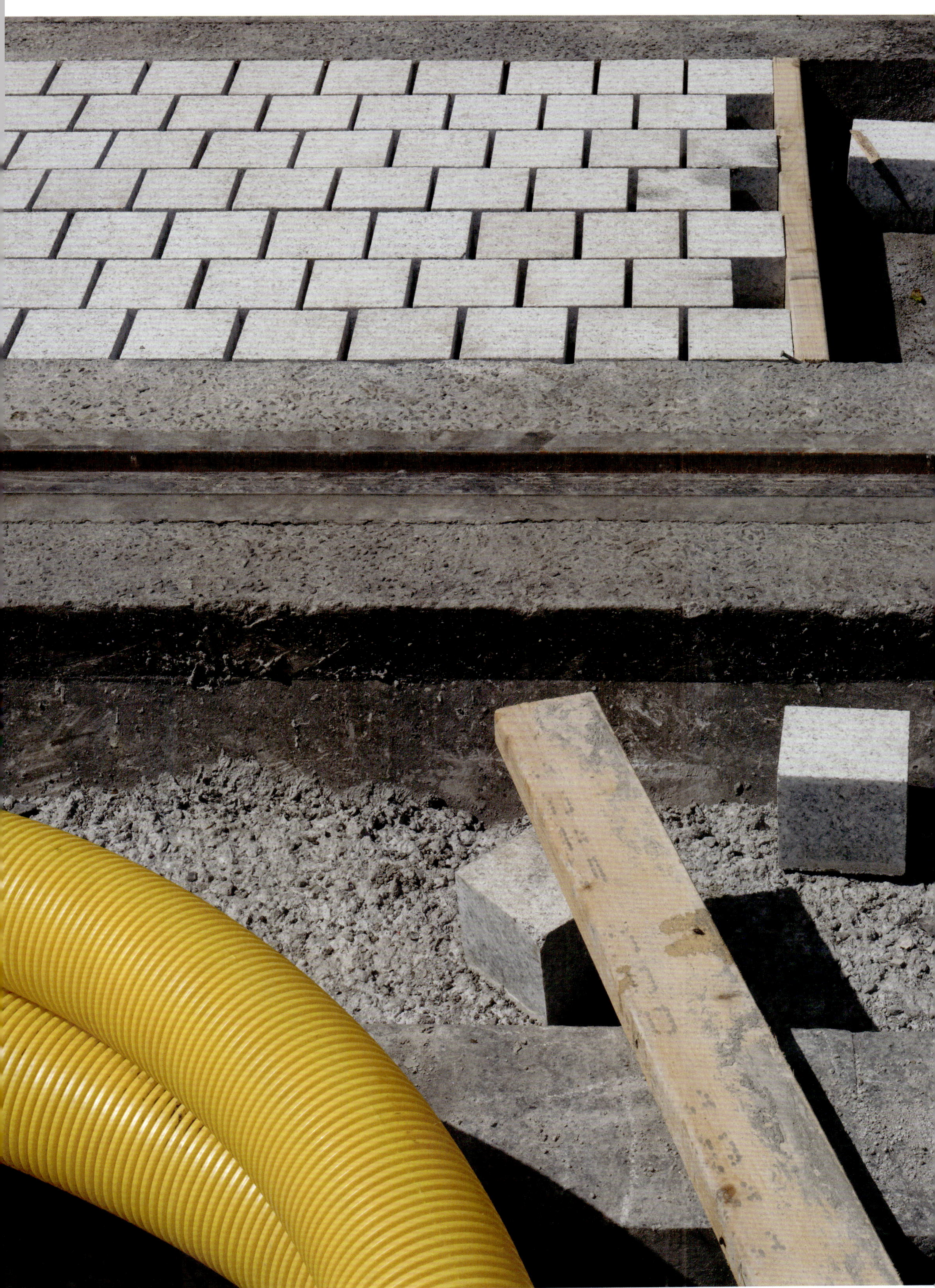

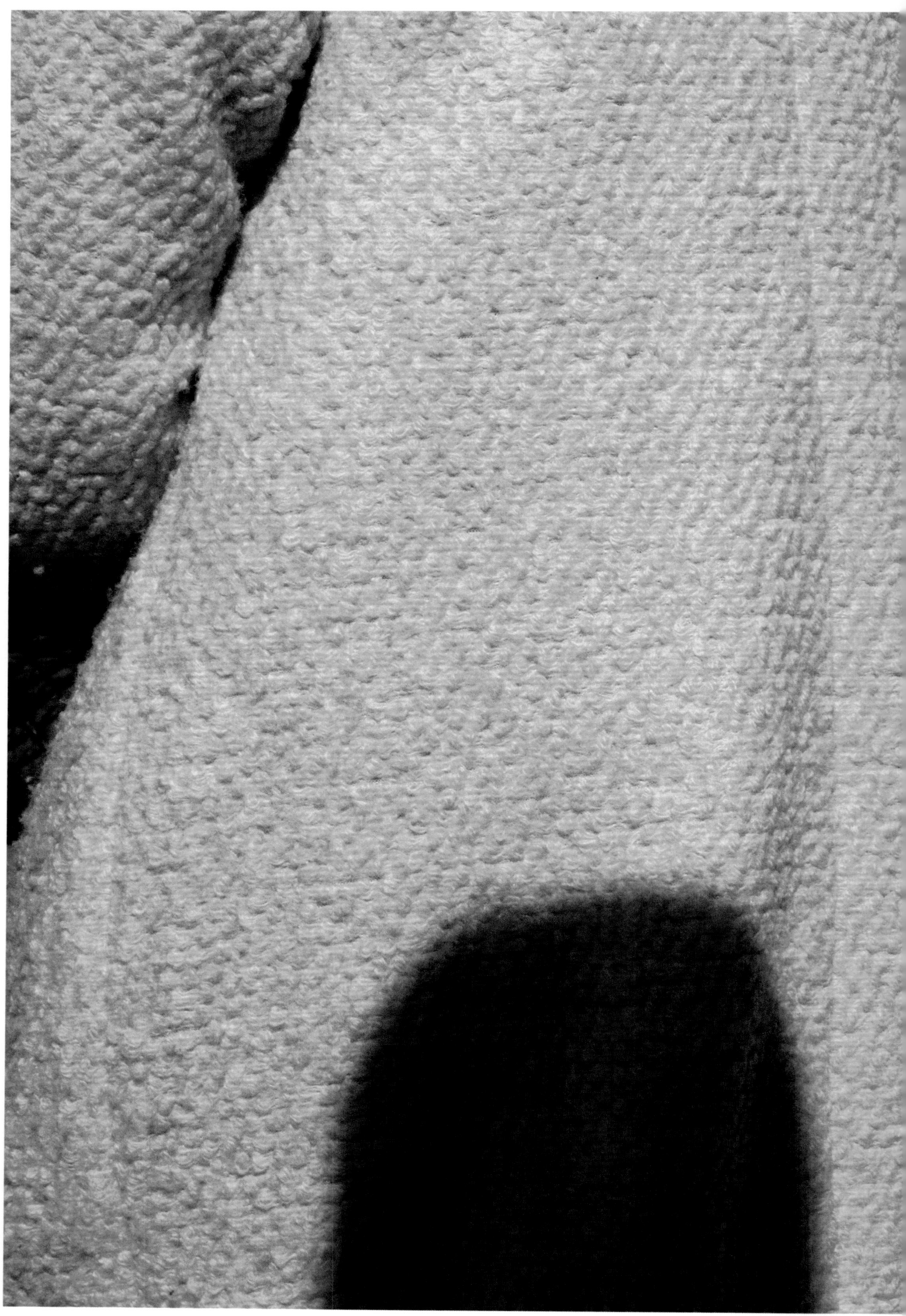

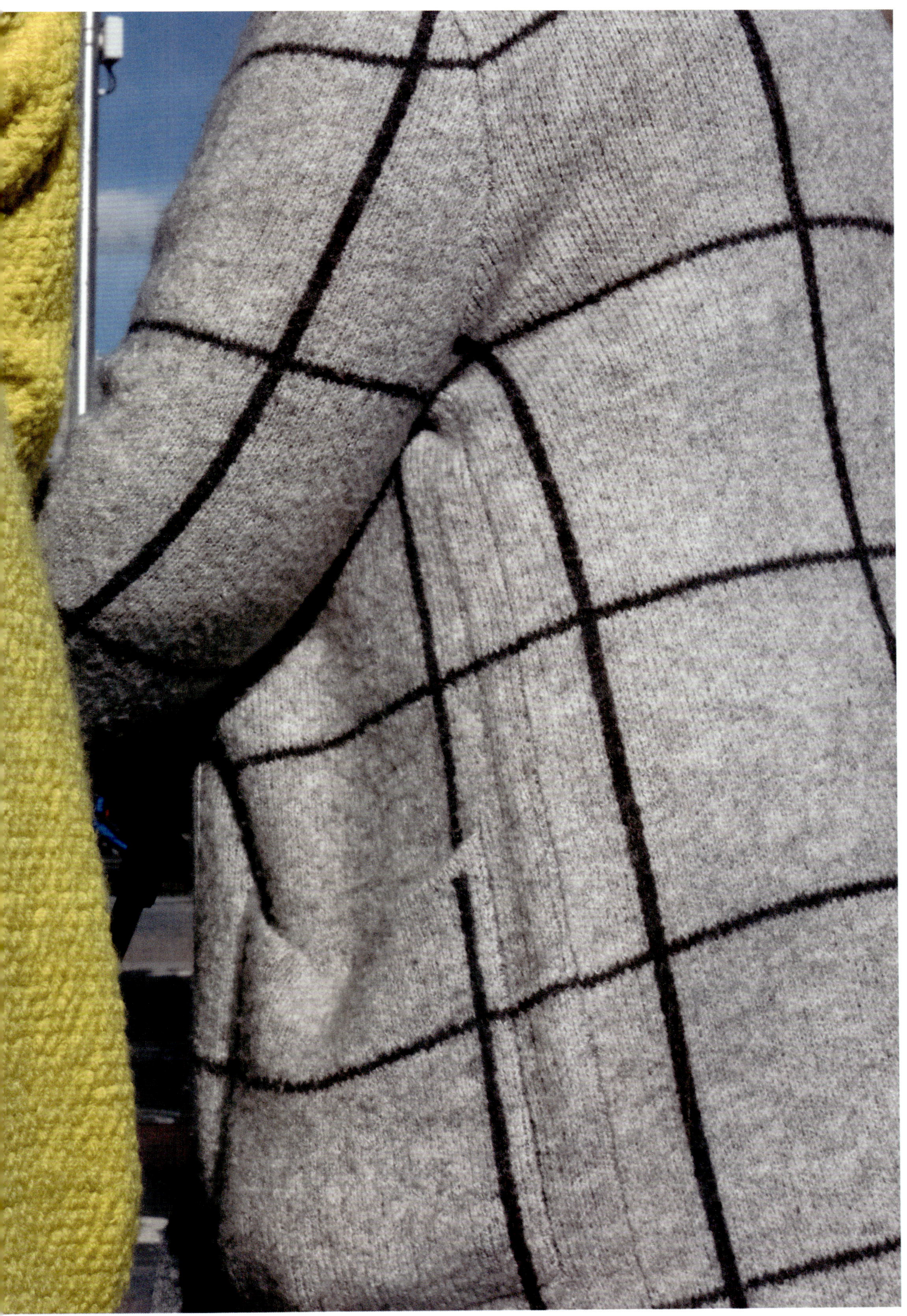

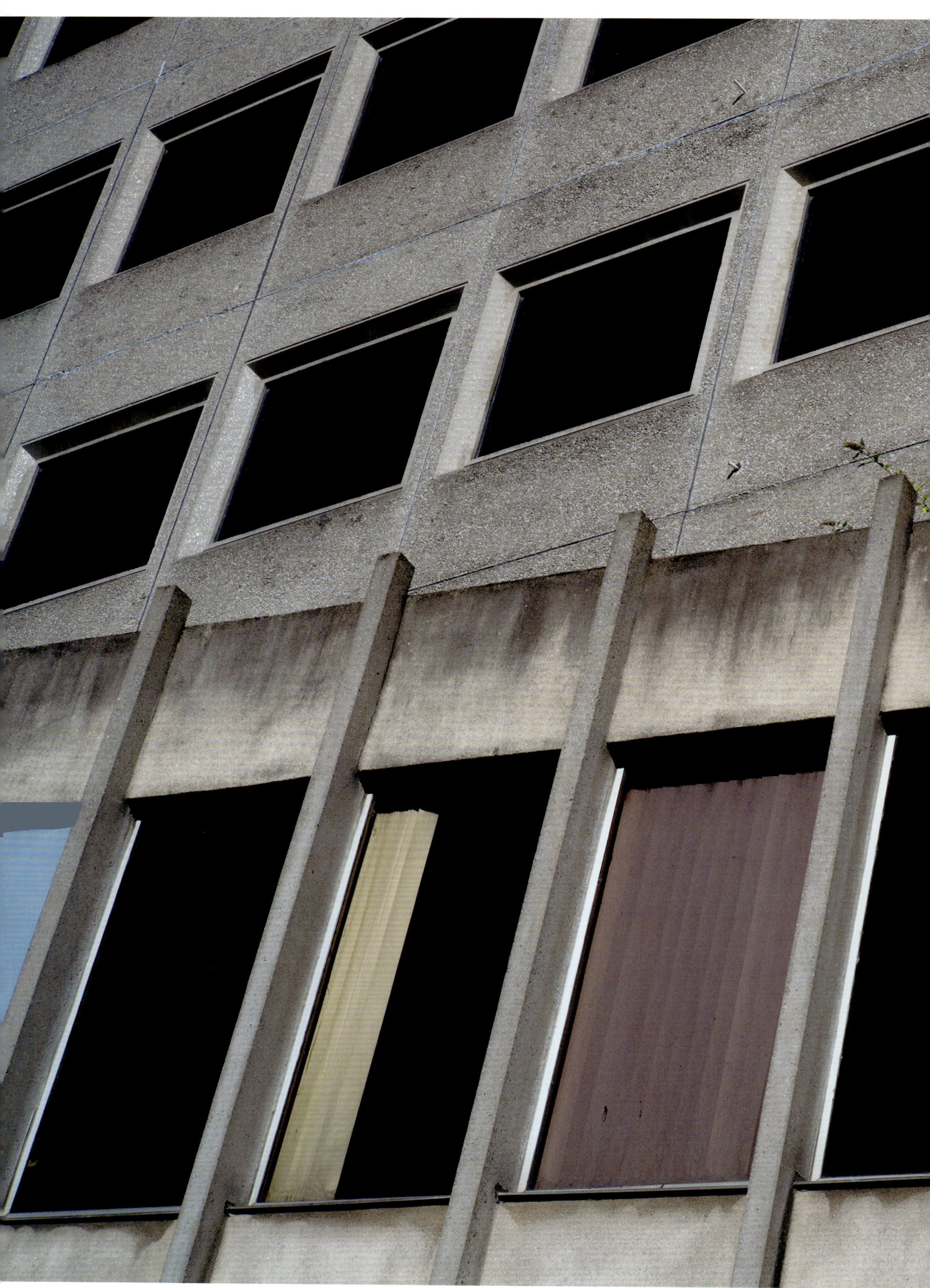

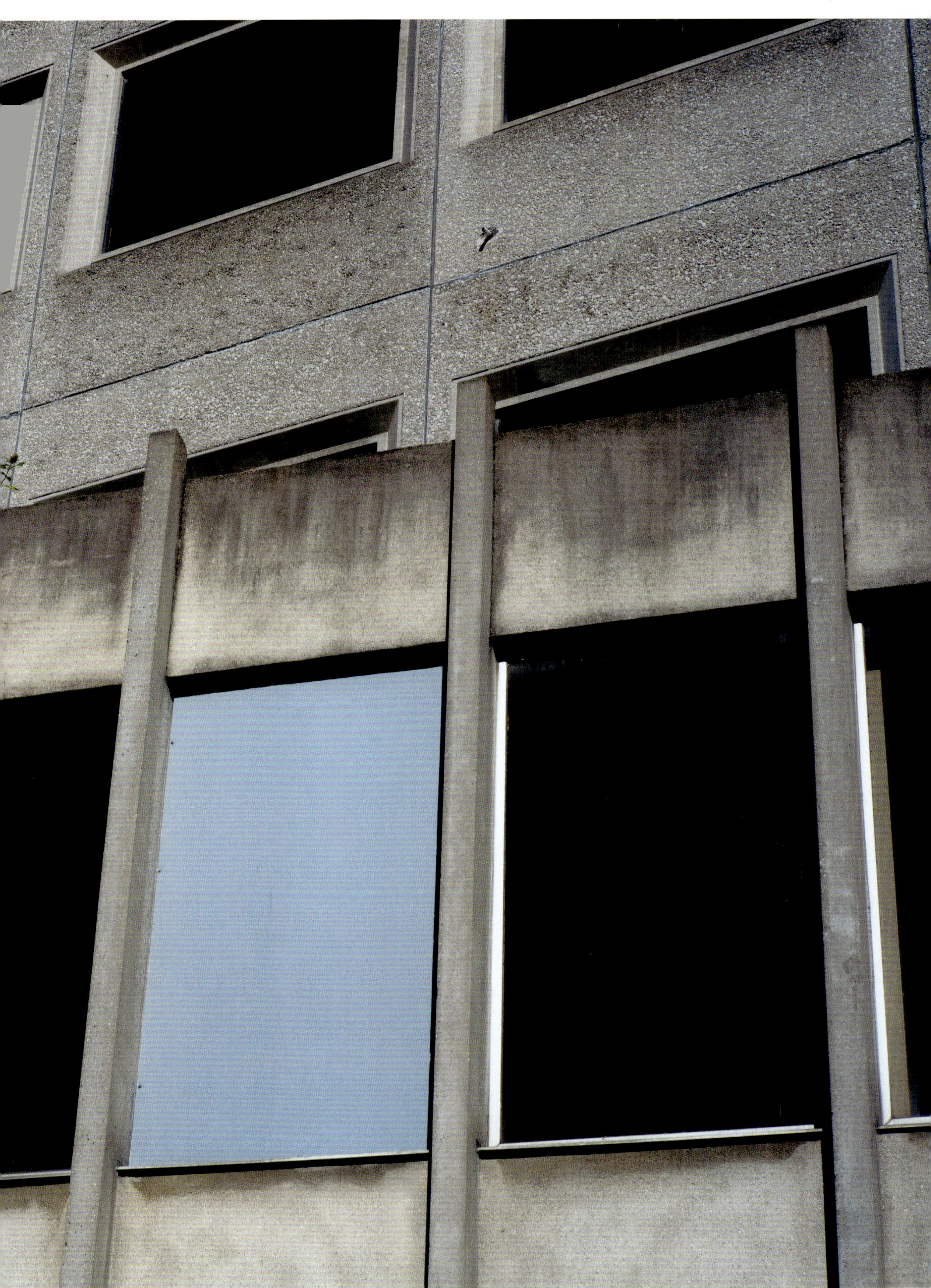

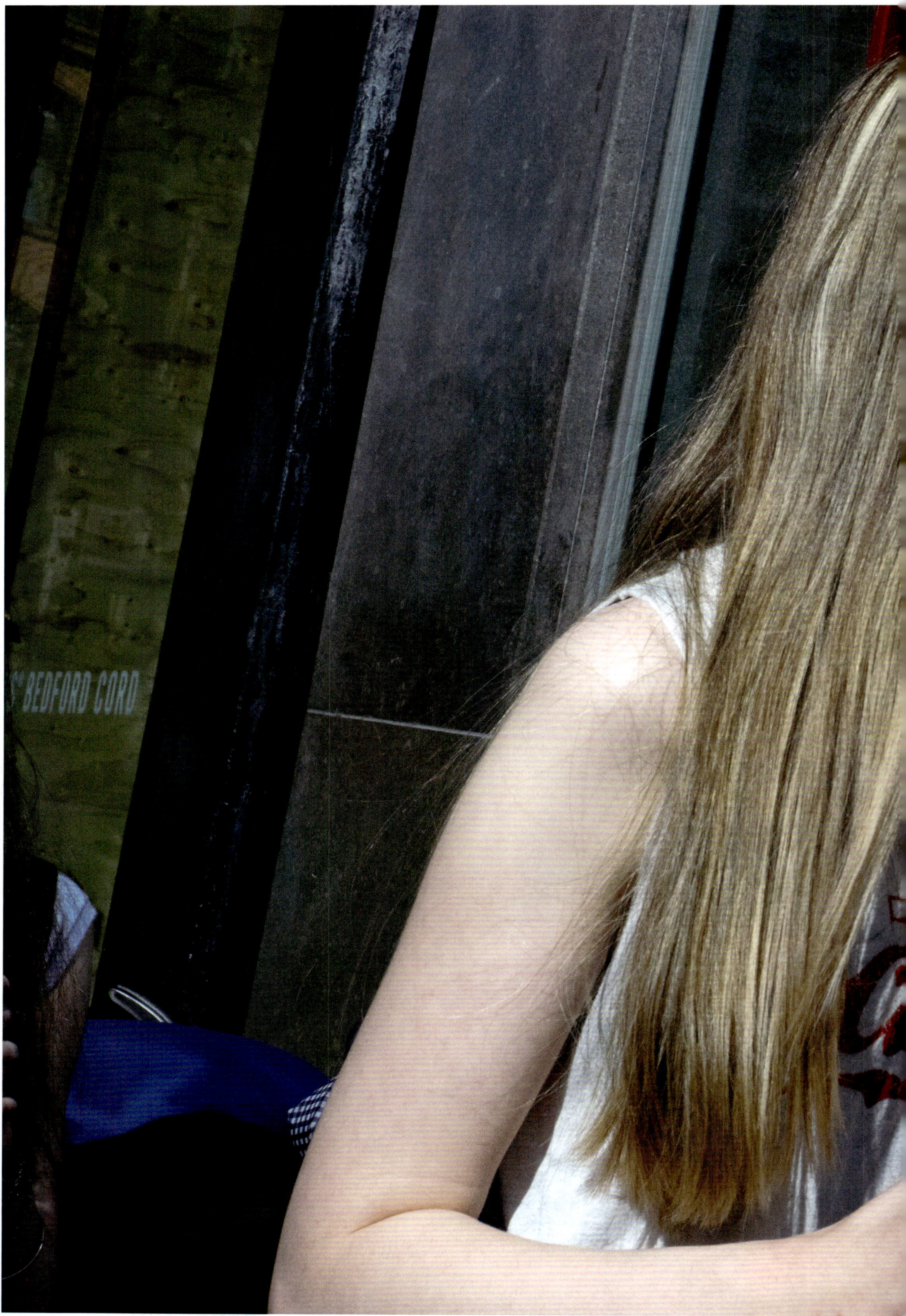
BEDFORD CORD

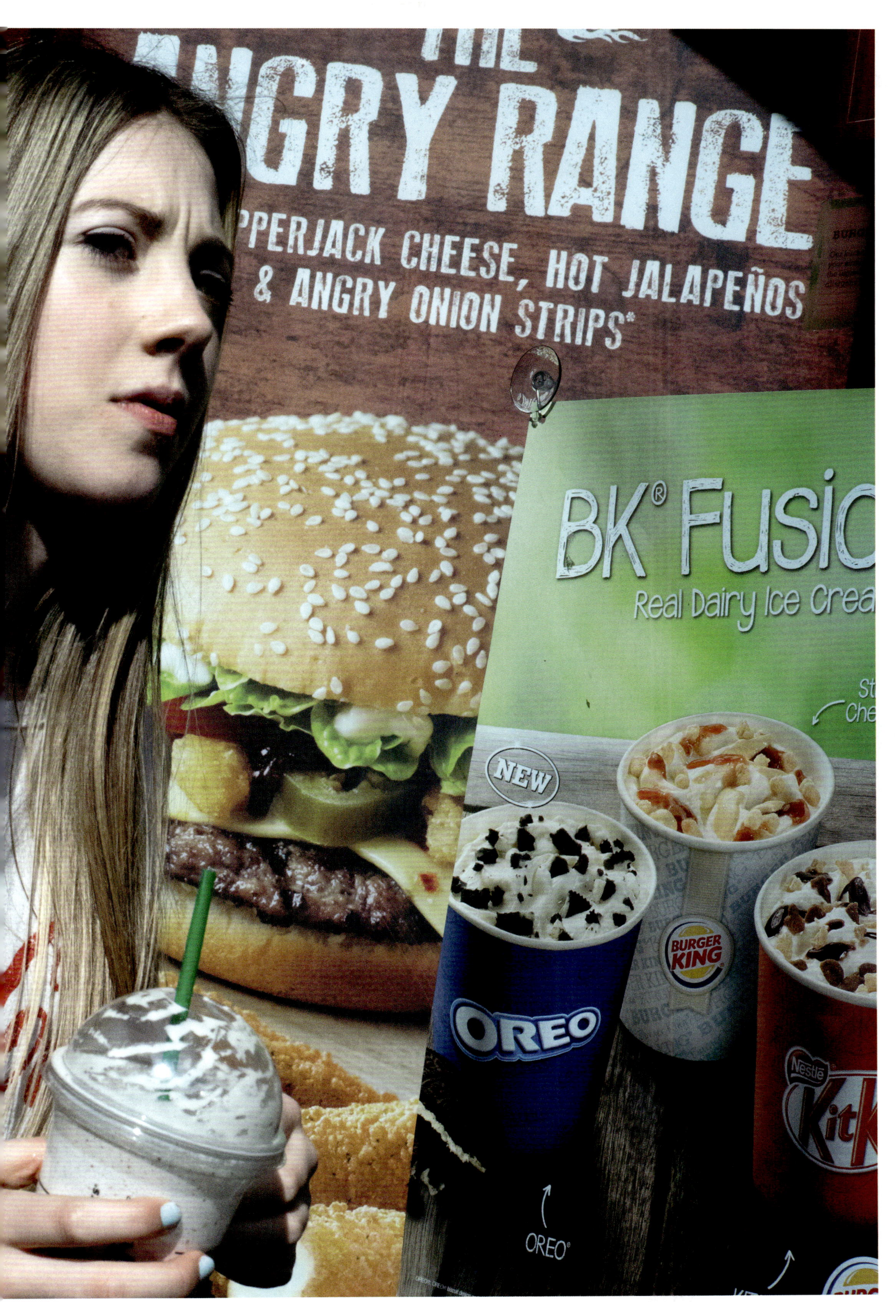
THE
ANGRY RANGE
PPERJACK CHEESE, HOT JALAPEÑOS
& ANGRY ONION STRIPS*
BK® Fusio
Real Dairy Ice Crea
NEW
OREO
BURGER KING
NESTLE
KitK
OREO®

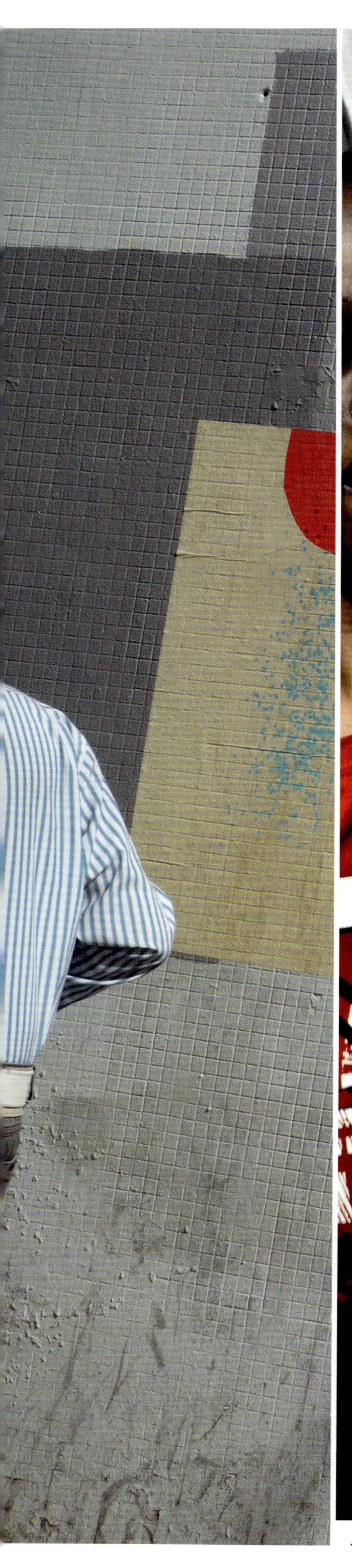
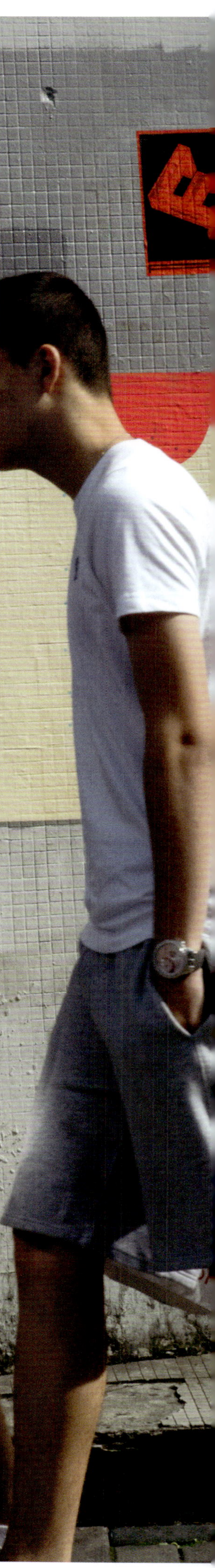

W62
75
STREET
FREE SPIRIT
HORIZED
AREA

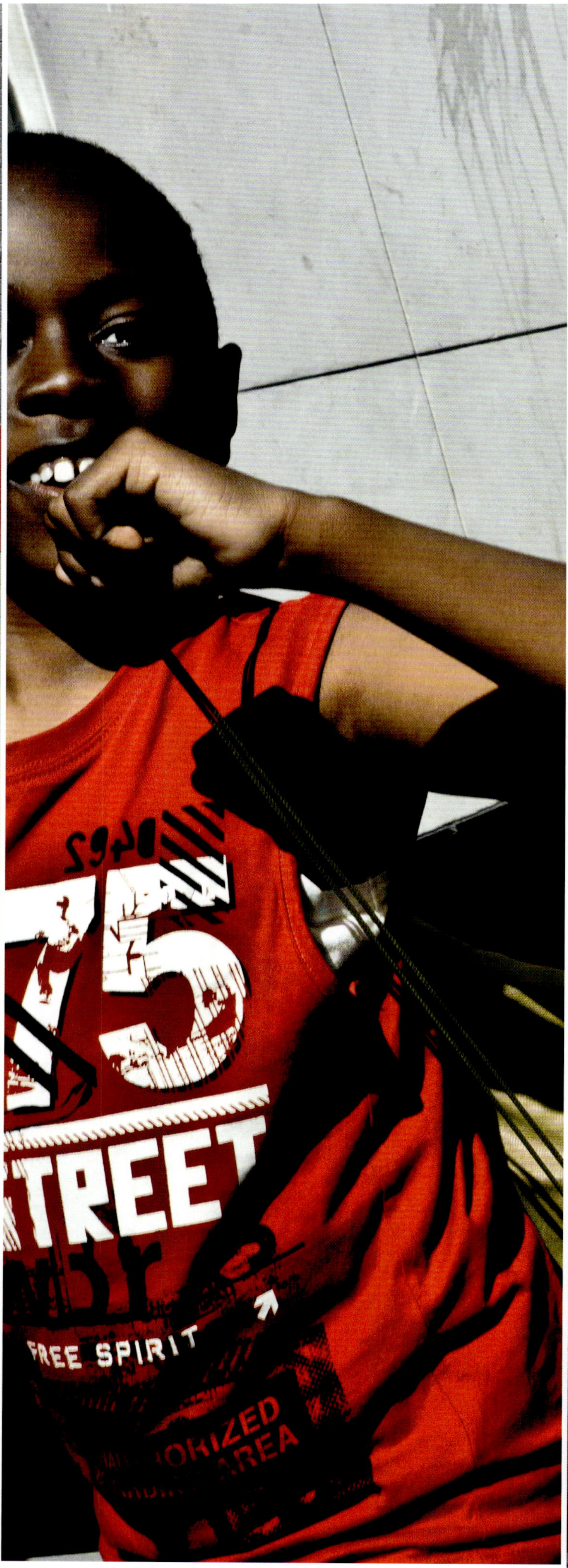

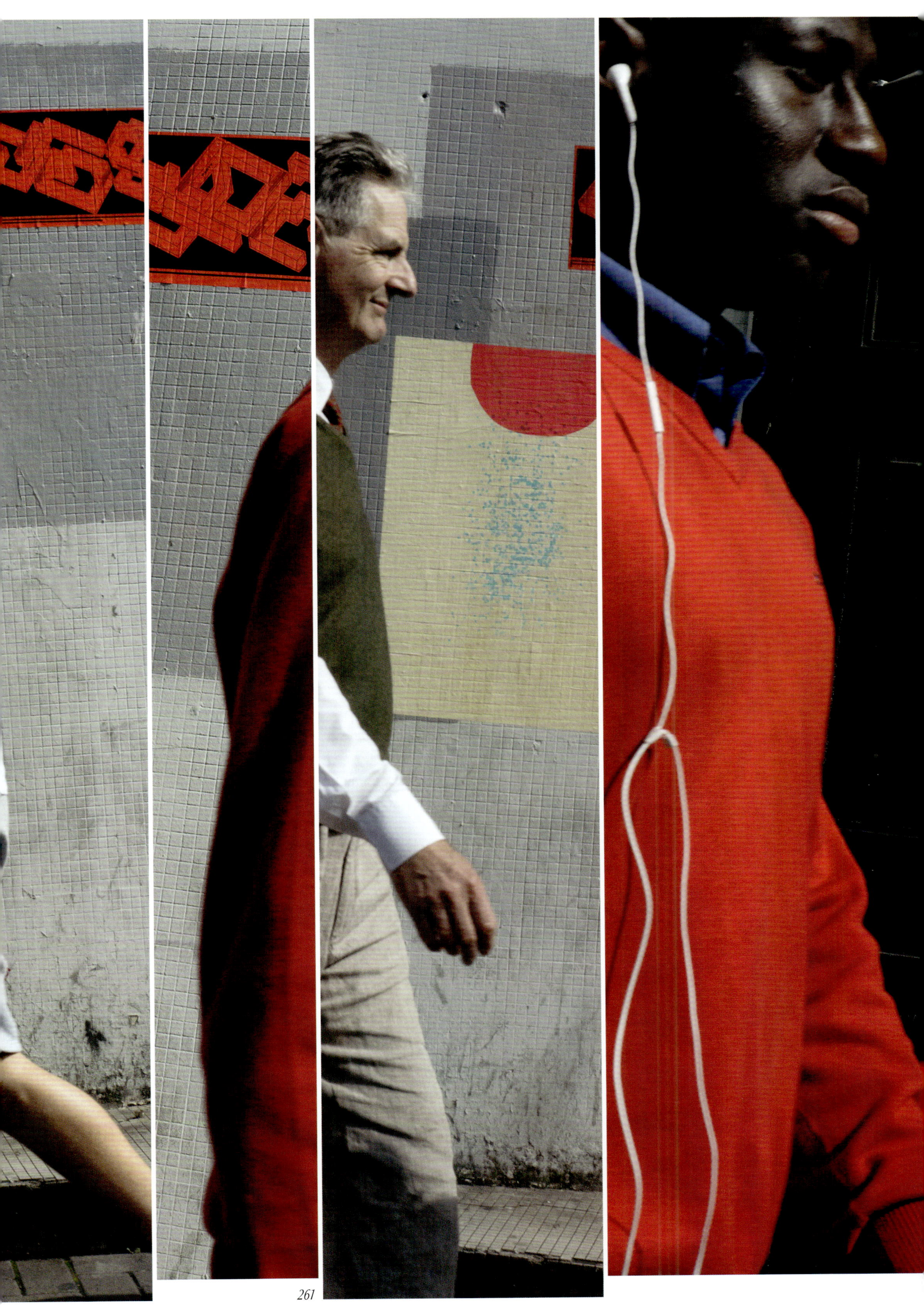

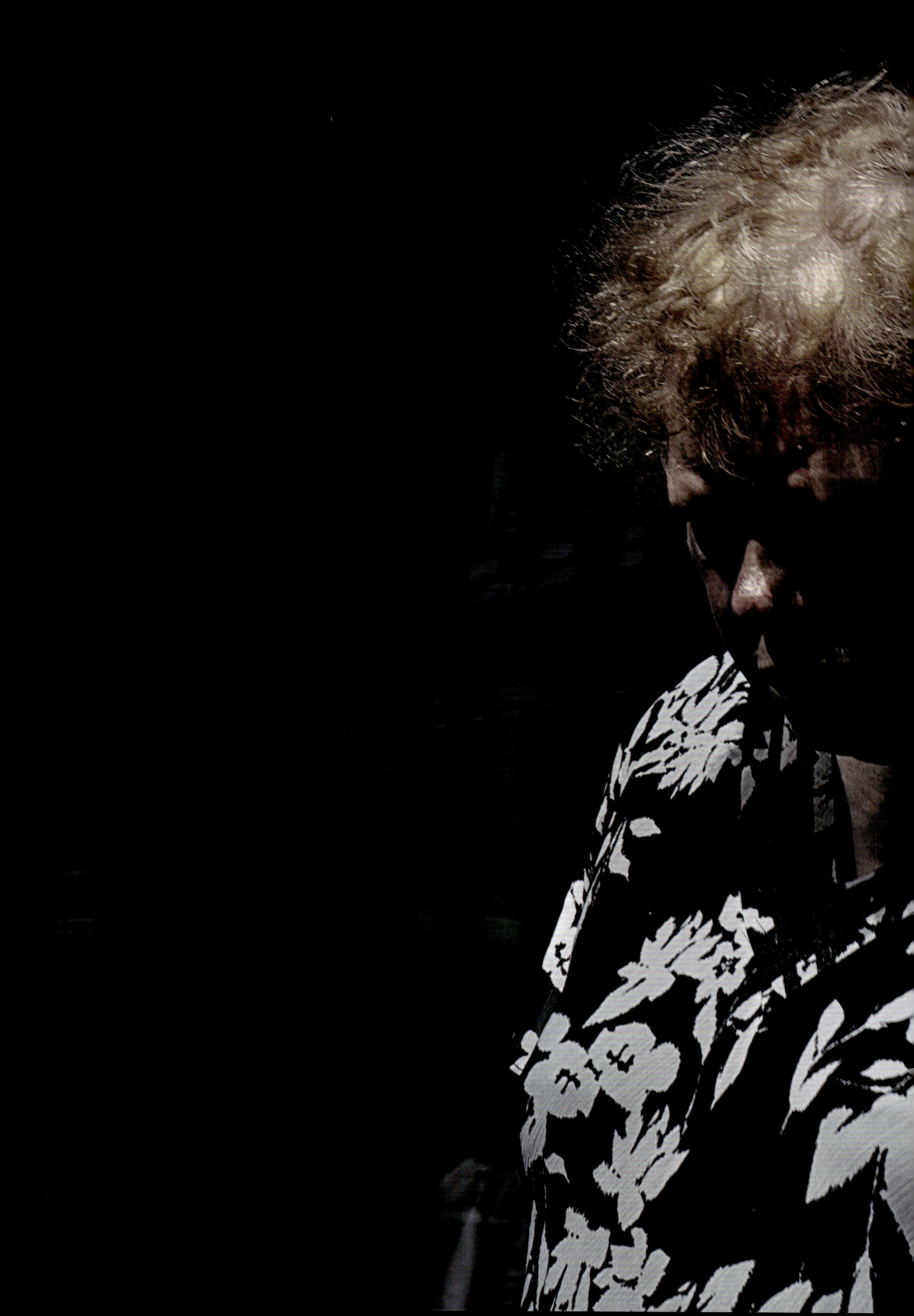

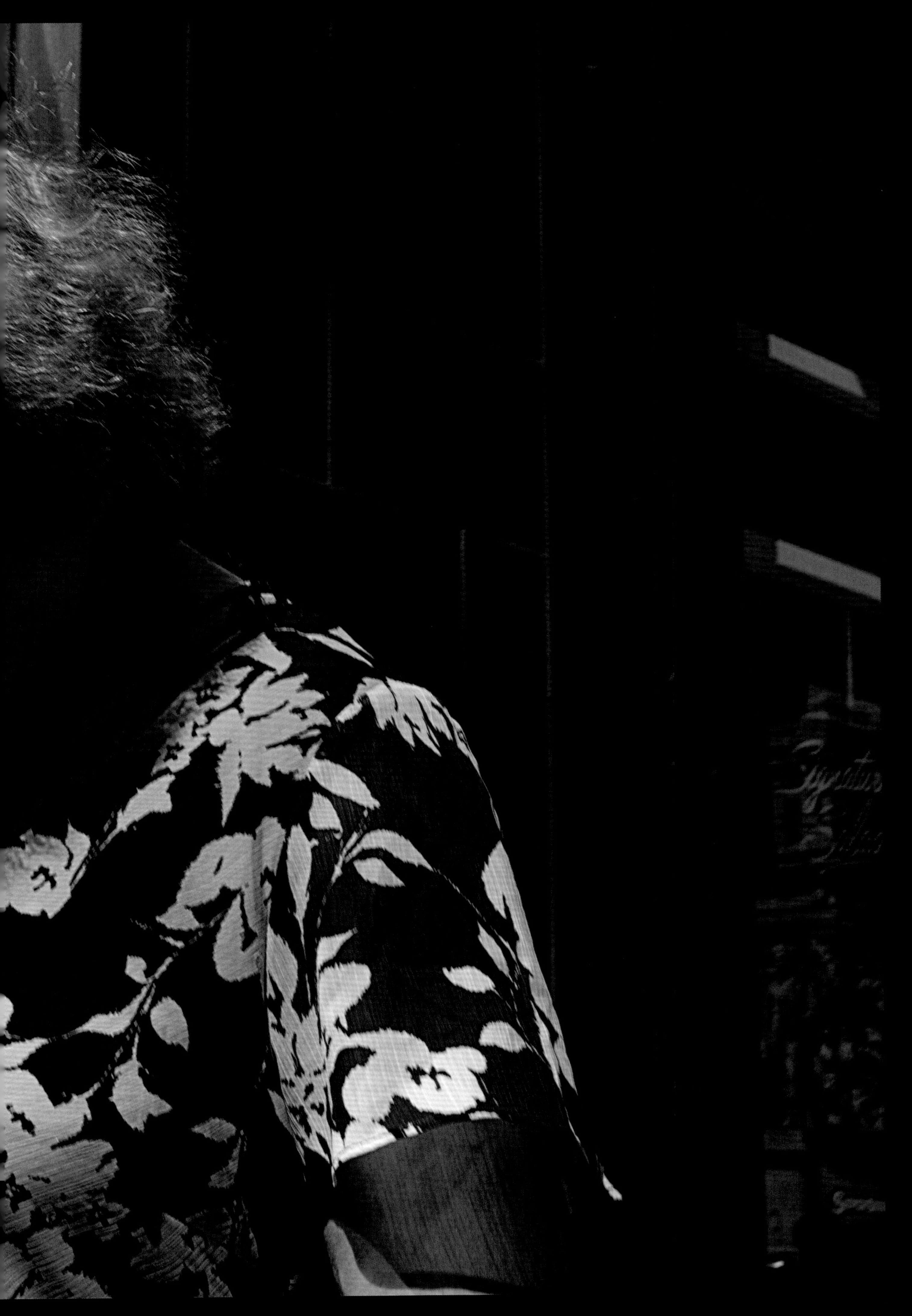

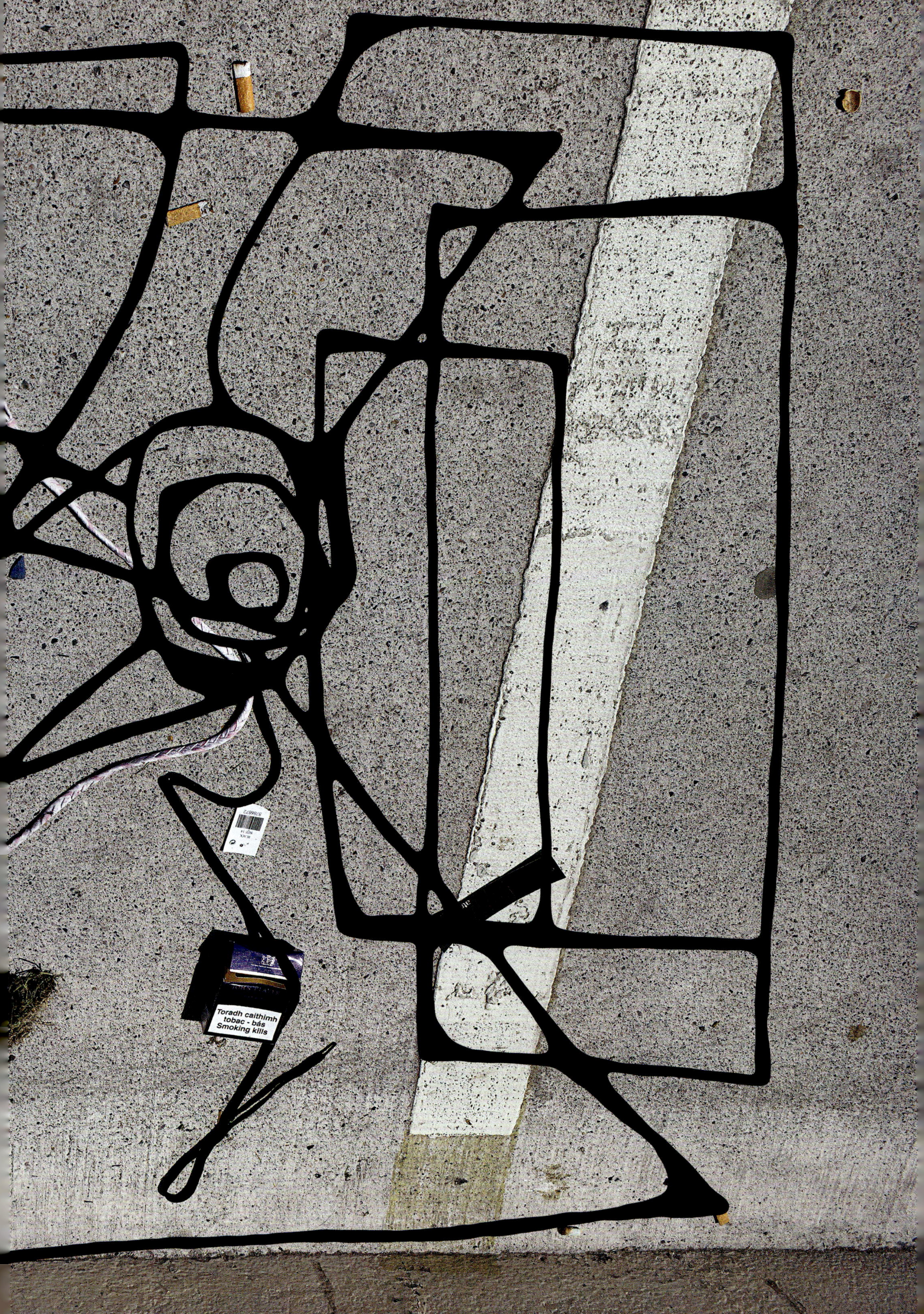
Health Warning
Tobac...
Smoking kills

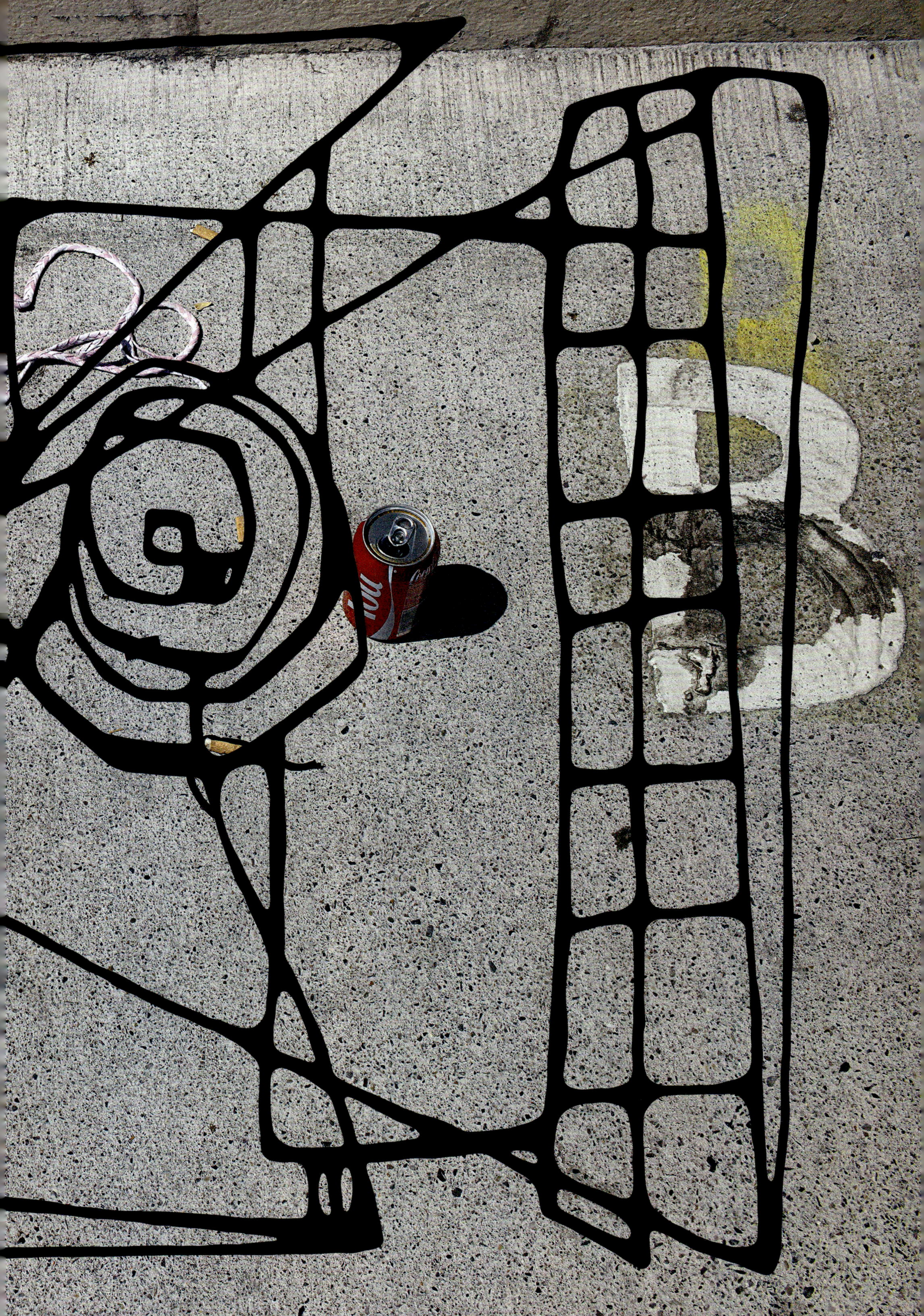

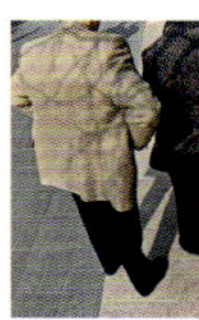

i (series)
untitled 11
2013
p. 65

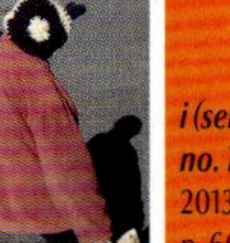

i (series)
no. 12
2013
p. 66

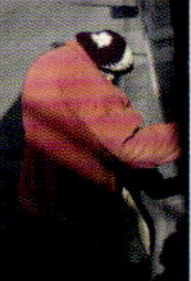

i (series)
no. 13
2013
p. 67

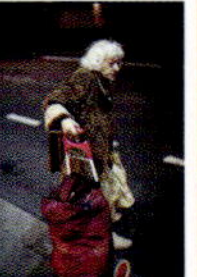

i (series)
no. 9
2013
p. 68

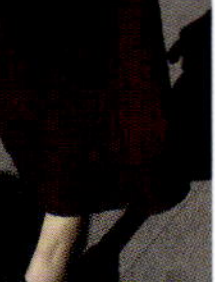

Nassau Street
2017
pp. 68–69

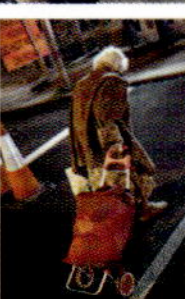

i (series)
no. 8
2013
p. 69

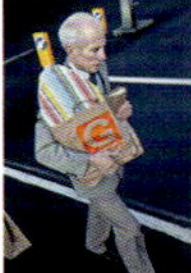

i (series)
no. 4
2013
p. 71

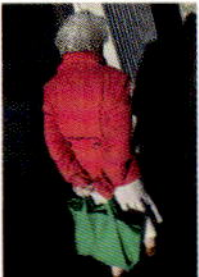

i (series)
untitled 12
2013
p. 72 (detail)

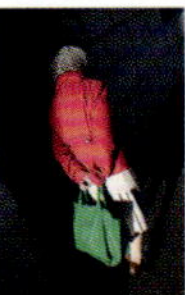

i (series)
untitled 13
2013
p. 73 (detail)

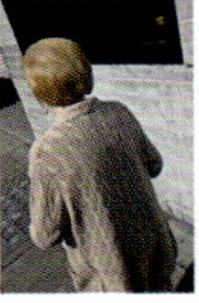

i (series)
no. 30
2013
p. 74 (detail)

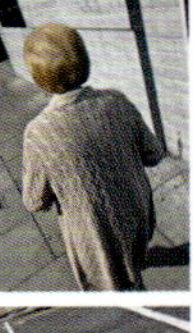

i (series)
no. 29
2013
pp. 74–75

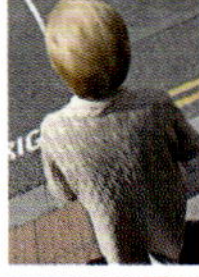

i (series)
no. 31
2013
p. 75 (detail)

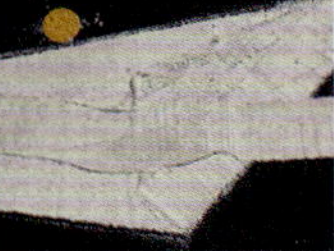

Parnell Street
2018
pp. 76–77 (detail)

ON

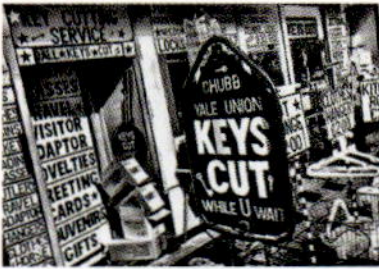

**Frederick Street
North**
2014
pp. 78–79

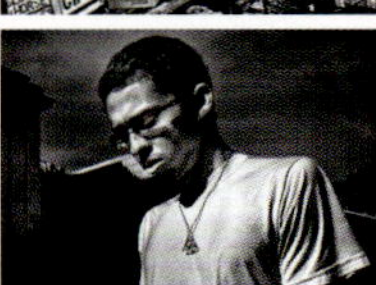

ON (series)
no. 17
2014
p. 80 (detail)

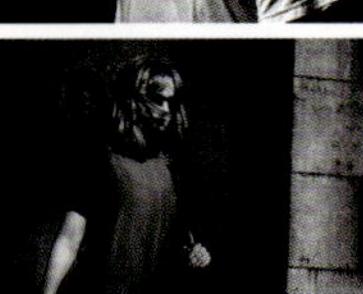

ON (series)
untitled 1
2014
p. 80 (detail)

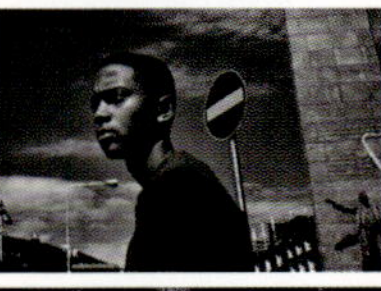

O'Connell Street
2016
p. 81 (detail)

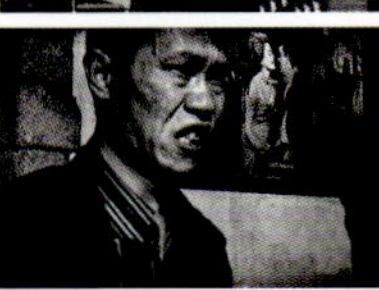

ON (series)
untitled 2
2014
p. 81 (detail)

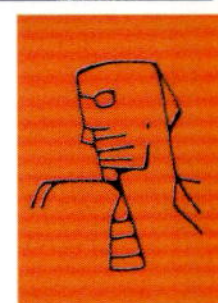

**End.
Head 12**
2016
p. 82

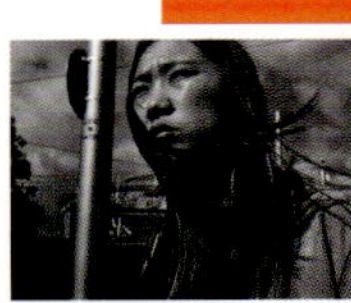

O'Connell Street
2017
pp. 84–85

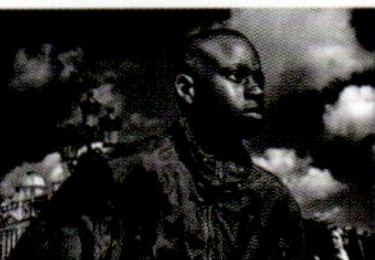

ON (series)
no. 5
2014
pp. 86–87

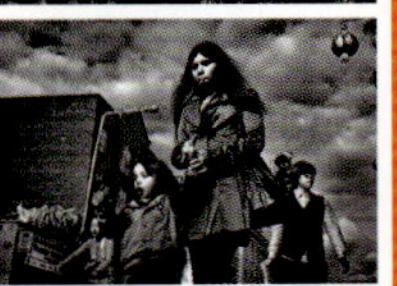

ON (series)
no. 48
2014
pp. 88–89

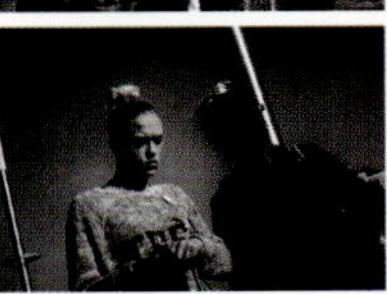

Parnell Street
2016
pp. 90–91 (detail)

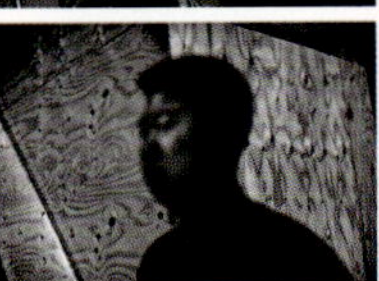

ON (series)
no. 19
2014
pp. 90–91 (detail)

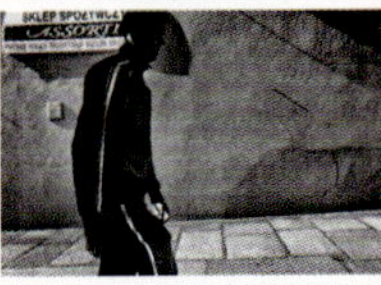

ON (series)
no. 16
2014
p. 92 (detail)

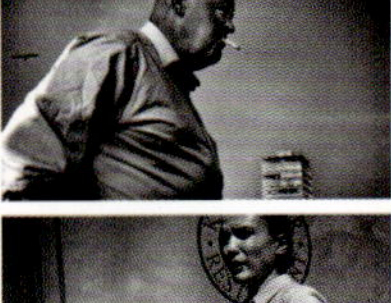

ON (series)
no. 38
2014
pp. 92–93 (detail)

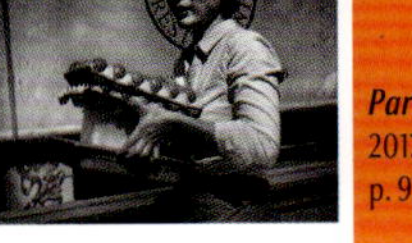

Parnell Street
2017
p. 93 (detail)

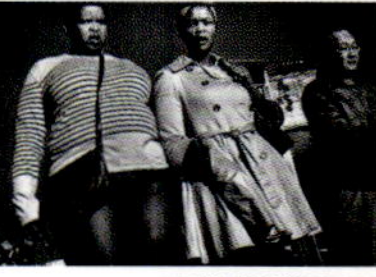

ON (series)
no. 2
2014
pp. 94–95

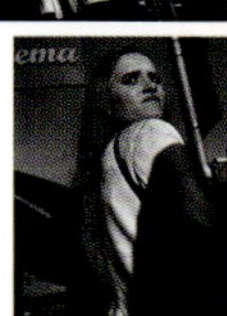

Abbey Street
2017
pp. 96–97 (detail)

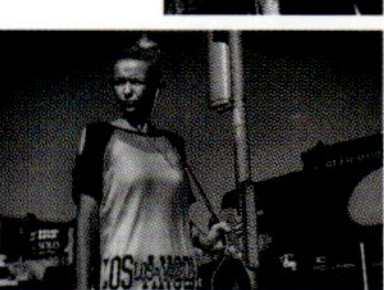

Church Street
2016
pp. 96–97 (detail)

ON (series)
no. 47
2014
pp. 96–97 (detail)

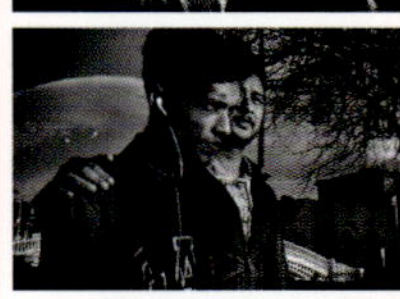

ON (series)
no. 14
2014
pp. 98–99

Burgh Quay
2015
p. 100 (detail)

ON (series)
no. 20
2014
pp. 100–101 (detail)

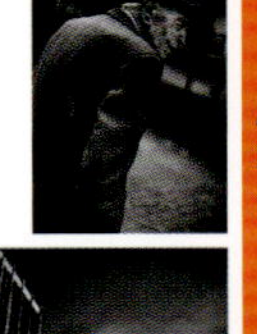

Moore Street
2014
p. 101 (detail)

ON (series)
no. 12
2014
pp. 102–103 (detail)

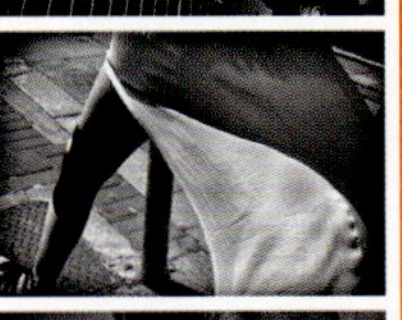

ON (series)
no. 4
2014
pp. 102–103 (detail)

ON (series)
no. 22
2014
pp. 104–105

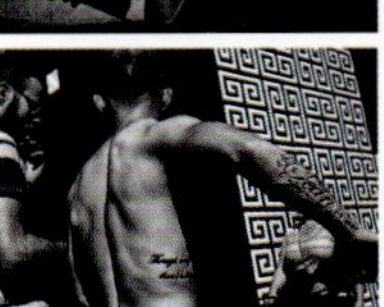

Grafton Street
2017
pp. 106–107

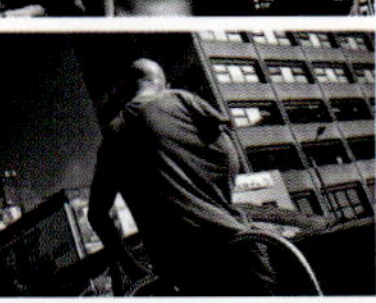

ON (series)
no. 21
2014
pp. 108–109 (detail)

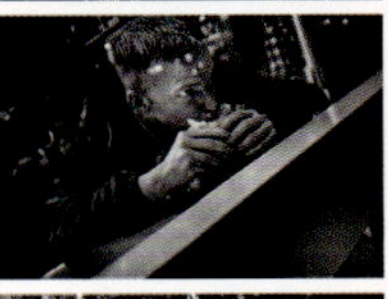

ON (series)
no. 29
2014
p. 109 (detail)

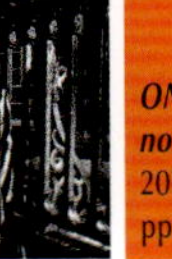

ON (series)
no. 27
2014
pp. 110–111

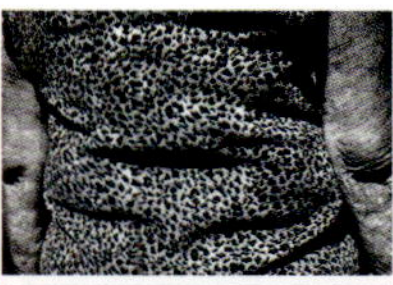

ON (series)
no. 44
2014
pp. 112–113

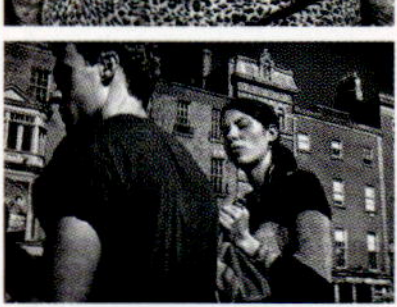

ON (series)
no. 3
2014
p. 114 (detail)

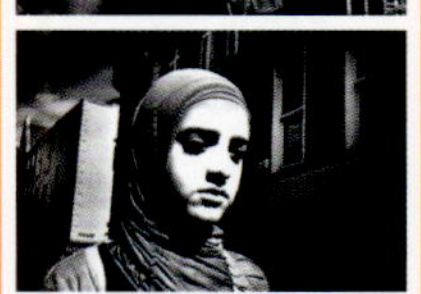

ON (series)
no. 24
2014
p. 114 (detail)

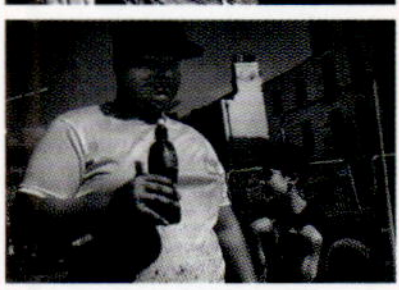

ON (series)
untitled 3
2014
p. 115 (detail)

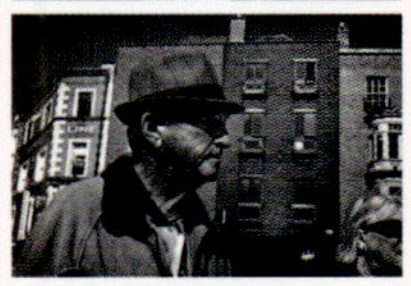

ON (series)
no. 4
2014
p. 115 (detail)

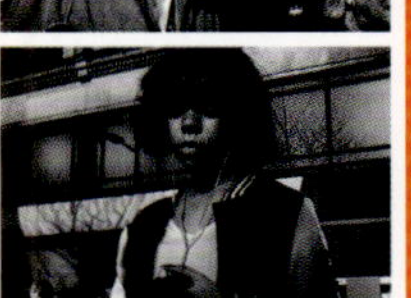

ON (series)
no. 40
2014
pp. 116–117 (detail)

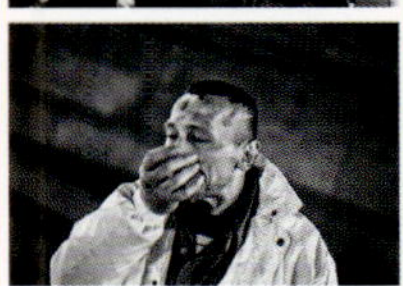

ON (series)
no. 26
2014
pp. 116–117 (detail)

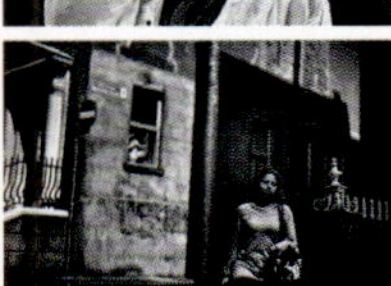

ON (series)
no. 50
2014
pp. 118–119

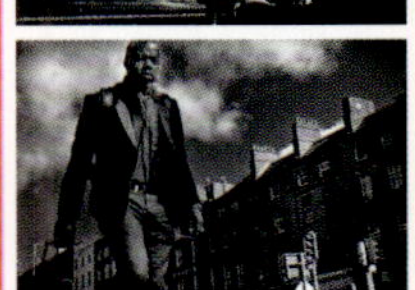

ON (series)
untitled 4
2014
p. 120 (detail)

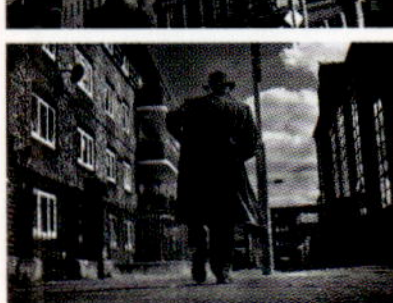

ON (series)
no. 45
2014
pp. 120–121 (detail)

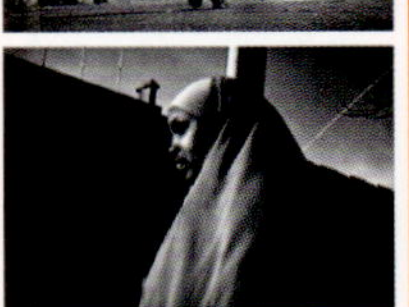

ON (series)
no. 31
2014
pp. 122–123 (detail)

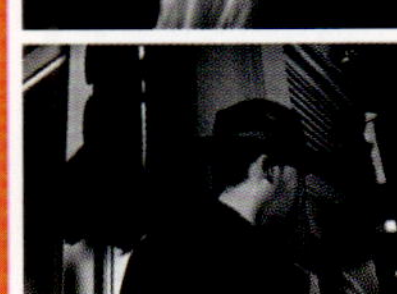

ON (series)
no. 23
2014
pp. 122–123 (detail)

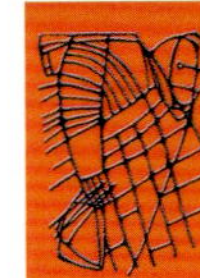

**End.
Head 18**
2016
p. 124

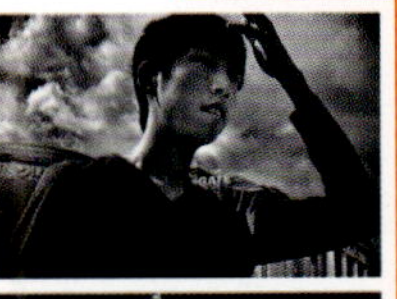

ON (series)
no. 35
2014
pp. 126–127

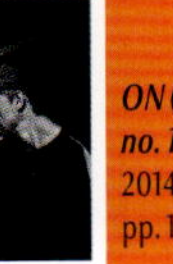

ON (series)
no. 11
2014
pp. 128–129

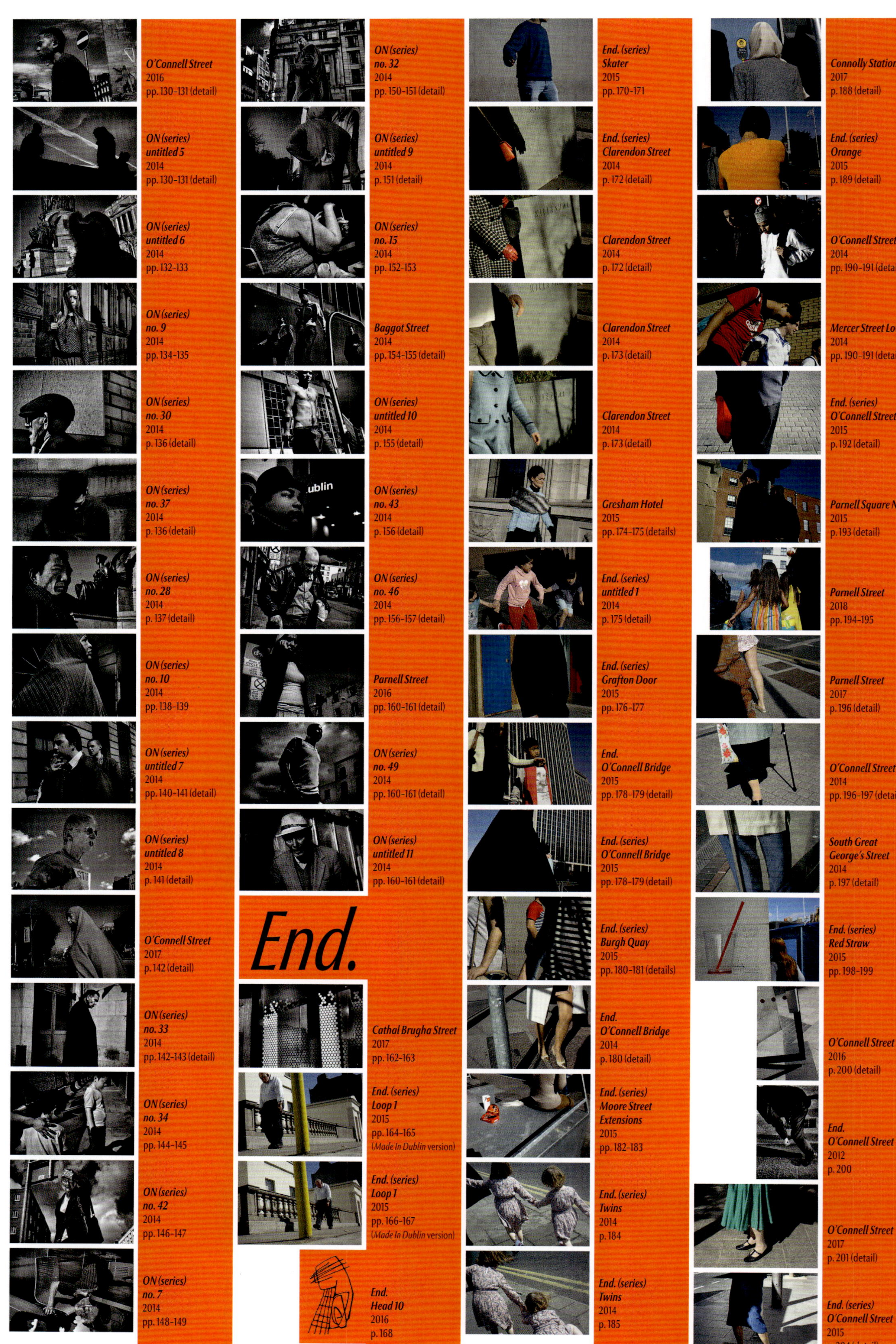

O'Connell Street
2016
pp. 130–131 (detail)

ON (series)
untitled 5
2014
pp. 130–131 (detail)

ON (series)
untitled 6
2014
pp. 132–133

ON (series)
no. 9
2014
pp. 134–135

ON (series)
no. 30
2014
p. 136 (detail)

ON (series)
no. 37
2014
p. 136 (detail)

ON (series)
no. 28
2014
p. 137 (detail)

ON (series)
no. 10
2014
pp. 138–139

ON (series)
untitled 7
2014
pp. 140–141 (detail)

ON (series)
untitled 8
2014
p. 141 (detail)

O'Connell Street
2017
p. 142 (detail)

ON (series)
no. 33
2014
pp. 142–143 (detail)

ON (series)
no. 34
2014
pp. 144–145

ON (series)
no. 42
2014
pp. 146–147

ON (series)
no. 7
2014
pp. 148–149

ON (series)
no. 32
2014
pp. 150–151 (detail)

ON (series)
untitled 9
2014
p. 151 (detail)

ON (series)
no. 15
2014
pp. 152–153

Baggot Street
2014
pp. 154–155 (detail)

ON (series)
untitled 10
2014
p. 155 (detail)

ON (series)
no. 43
2014
p. 156 (detail)

ON (series)
no. 46
2014
pp. 156–157 (detail)

Parnell Street
2016
pp. 160–161 (detail)

ON (series)
no. 49
2014
pp. 160–161 (detail)

ON (series)
untitled 11
2014
pp. 160–161 (detail)

End.

Cathal Brugha Street
2017
pp. 162–163

End. (series)
Loop 1
2015
pp. 164–165
(Made In Dublin version)

End. (series)
Loop 1
2015
pp. 166–167
(Made In Dublin version)

End.
Head 10
2016
p. 168

End. (series)
Skater
2015
pp. 170–171

End. (series)
Clarendon Street
2014
p. 172 (detail)

Clarendon Street
2014
p. 172 (detail)

Clarendon Street
2014
p. 173 (detail)

Clarendon Street
2014
p. 173 (detail)

Gresham Hotel
2015
pp. 174–175 (details)

End. (series)
untitled 1
2014
p. 175 (detail)

End. (series)
Grafton Door
2015
pp. 176–177

End.
O'Connell Bridge
2015
pp. 178–179 (detail)

End. (series)
O'Connell Bridge
2015
pp. 178–179 (detail)

End. (series)
Burgh Quay
2015
pp. 180–181 (details)

End.
O'Connell Bridge
2014
p. 180 (detail)

End. (series)
Moore Street
Extensions
2015
pp. 182–183

End. (series)
Twins
2014
p. 184

End. (series)
Twins
2014
p. 185

Connolly Station
2017
p. 188 (detail)

End. (series)
Orange
2015
p. 189 (detail)

O'Connell Street
2014
pp. 190–191 (detail)

Mercer Street Lower
2014
pp. 190–191 (detail)

End. (series)
O'Connell Street
2015
p. 192 (detail)

Parnell Square North
2015
p. 193 (detail)

Parnell Street
2018
pp. 194–195

Parnell Street
2017
p. 196 (detail)

O'Connell Street
2014
pp. 196–197 (detail)

South Great
George's Street
2014
p. 197 (detail)

End. (series)
Red Straw
2015
pp. 198–199

O'Connell Street
2016
p. 200 (detail)

End.
O'Connell Street
2012
p. 200

O'Connell Street
2017
p. 201 (detail)

End. (series)
O'Connell Street
2015
p. 204 (detail)

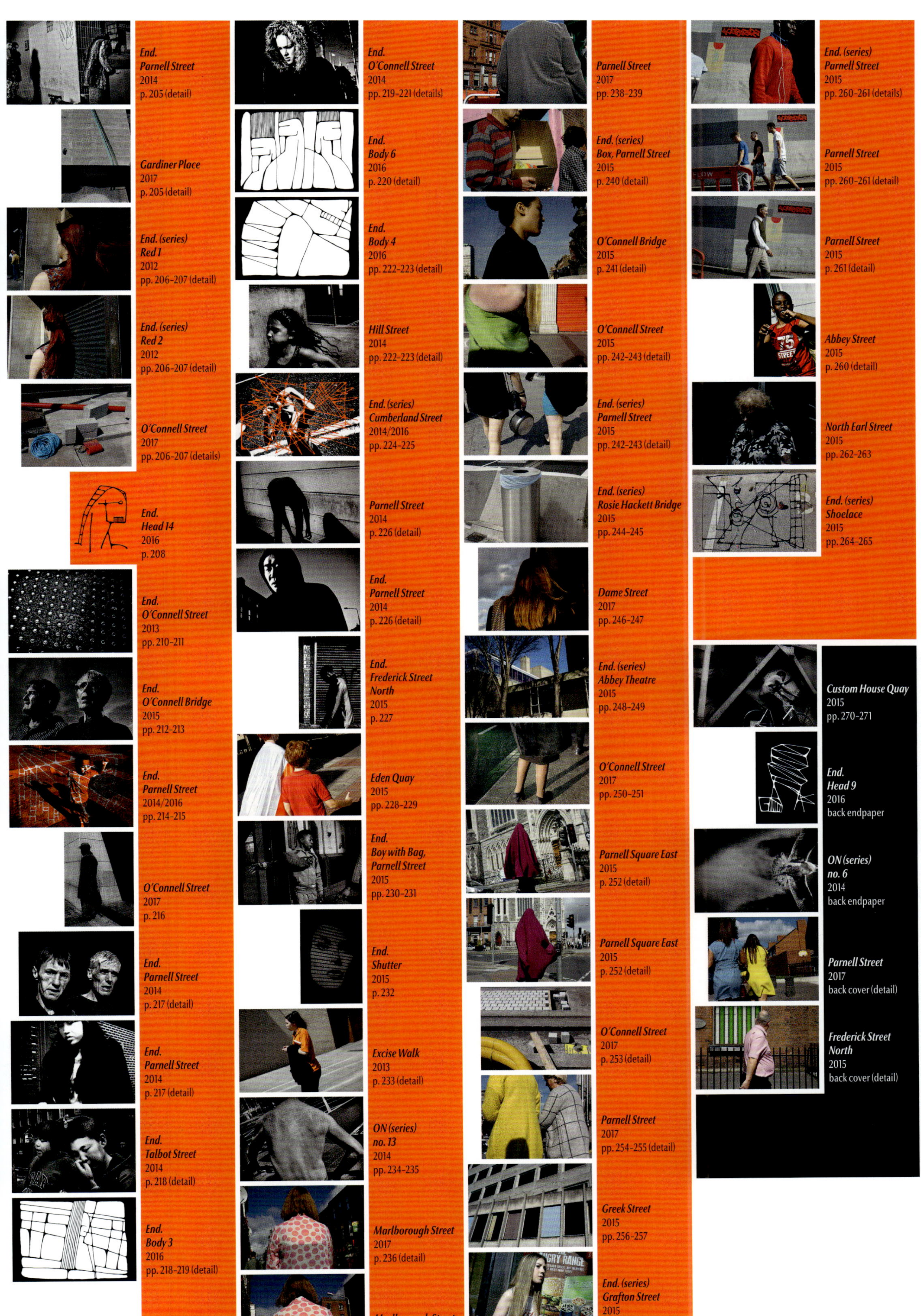

End.
Parnell Street
2014
p. 205 (detail)

Gardiner Place
2017
p. 205 (detail)

End. (series)
Red 1
2012
pp. 206–207 (detail)

End. (series)
Red 2
2012
pp. 206–207 (detail)

O'Connell Street
2017
pp. 206–207 (details)

End.
Head 14
2016
p. 208

End.
O'Connell Street
2013
pp. 210–211

End.
O'Connell Bridge
2015
pp. 212–213

End.
Parnell Street
2014/2016
pp. 214–215

O'Connell Street
2017
p. 216

End.
Parnell Street
2014
p. 217 (detail)

End.
Parnell Street
2014
p. 217 (detail)

End.
Talbot Street
2014
p. 218 (detail)

End.
Body 3
2016
pp. 218–219 (detail)

End.
O'Connell Street
2014
pp. 219–221 (details)

End.
Body 6
2016
p. 220 (detail)

End.
Body 4
2016
pp. 222–223 (detail)

Hill Street
2014
pp. 222–223 (detail)

End. (series)
Cumberland Street
2014/2016
pp. 224–225

Parnell Street
2014
p. 226 (detail)

End.
Parnell Street
2014
p. 226 (detail)

End.
Frederick Street
North
2015
p. 227

Eden Quay
2015
pp. 228–229

End.
Boy with Bag,
Parnell Street
2015
pp. 230–231

End.
Shutter
2015
p. 232

Excise Walk
2013
p. 233 (detail)

ON (series)
no. 13
2014
pp. 234–235

Marlborough Street
2017
p. 236 (detail)

Marlborough Street
2017
p. 237 (detail)

Parnell Street
2017
pp. 238–239

End. (series)
Box, Parnell Street
2015
p. 240 (detail)

O'Connell Bridge
2015
p. 241 (detail)

O'Connell Street
2017
pp. 242–243 (detail)

End. (series)
Parnell Street
2015
pp. 242–243 (detail)

End. (series)
Rosie Hackett Bridge
2015
pp. 244–245

Dame Street
2017
pp. 246–247

End. (series)
Abbey Theatre
2015
pp. 248–249

O'Connell Street
2017
pp. 250–251

Parnell Square East
2015
p. 252 (detail)

Parnell Square East
2015
p. 252 (detail)

O'Connell Street
2017
p. 253 (detail)

Parnell Street
2017
pp. 254–255 (detail)

Greek Street
2015
pp. 256–257

End. (series)
Grafton Street
2015
pp. 258–259

End. (series)
Parnell Street
2015
pp. 260–261 (details)

Parnell Street
2015
pp. 260–261 (detail)

Parnell Street
2015
p. 261 (detail)

Abbey Street
2015
p. 260 (detail)

North Earl Street
2015
pp. 262–263

End. (series)
Shoelace
2015
pp. 264–265

Custom House Quay
2015
pp. 270–271

End.
Head 9
2016
back endpaper

ON (series)
no. 6
2014
back endpaper

Parnell Street
2017
back cover (detail)

Frederick Street
North
2015
back cover (detail)

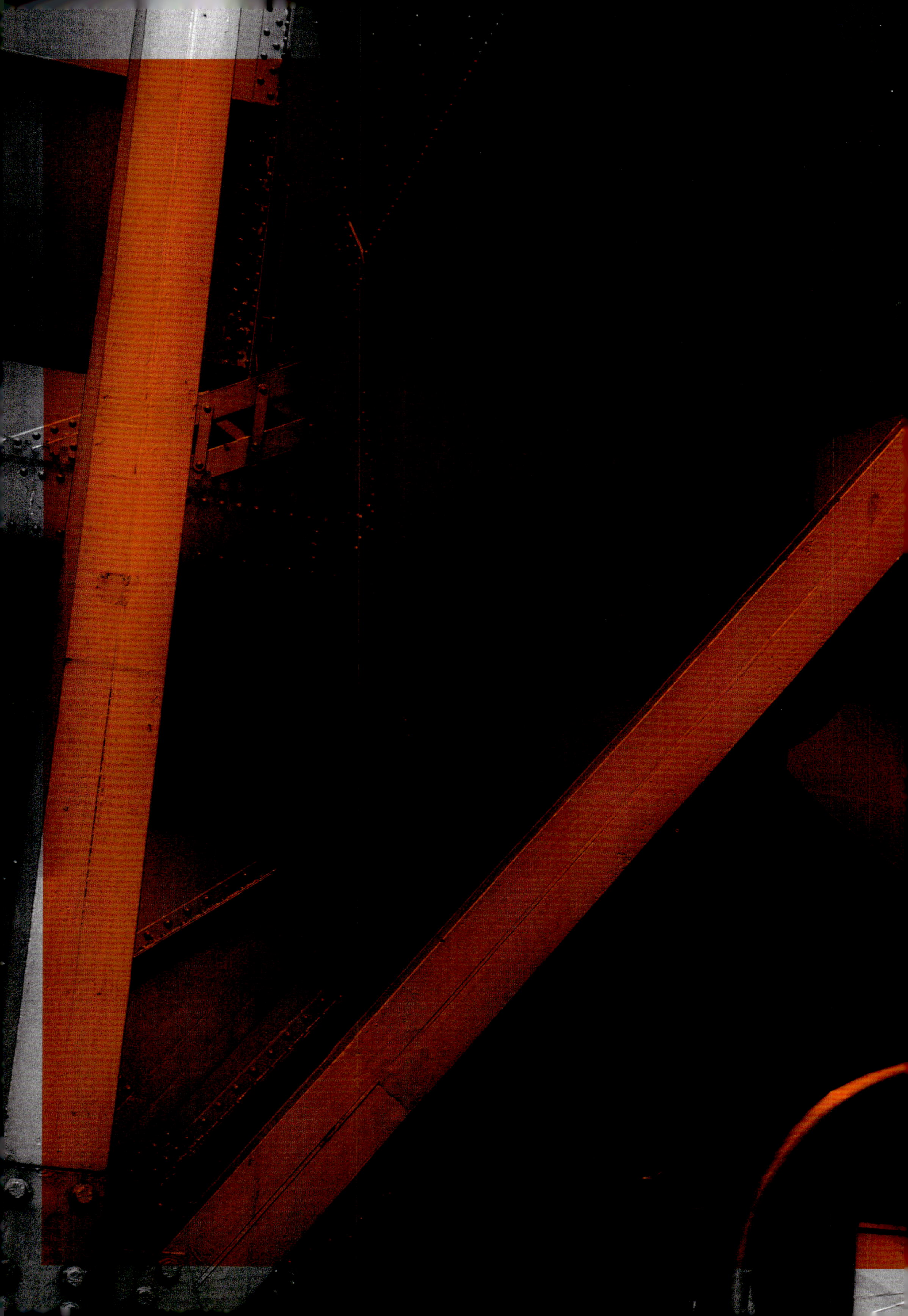

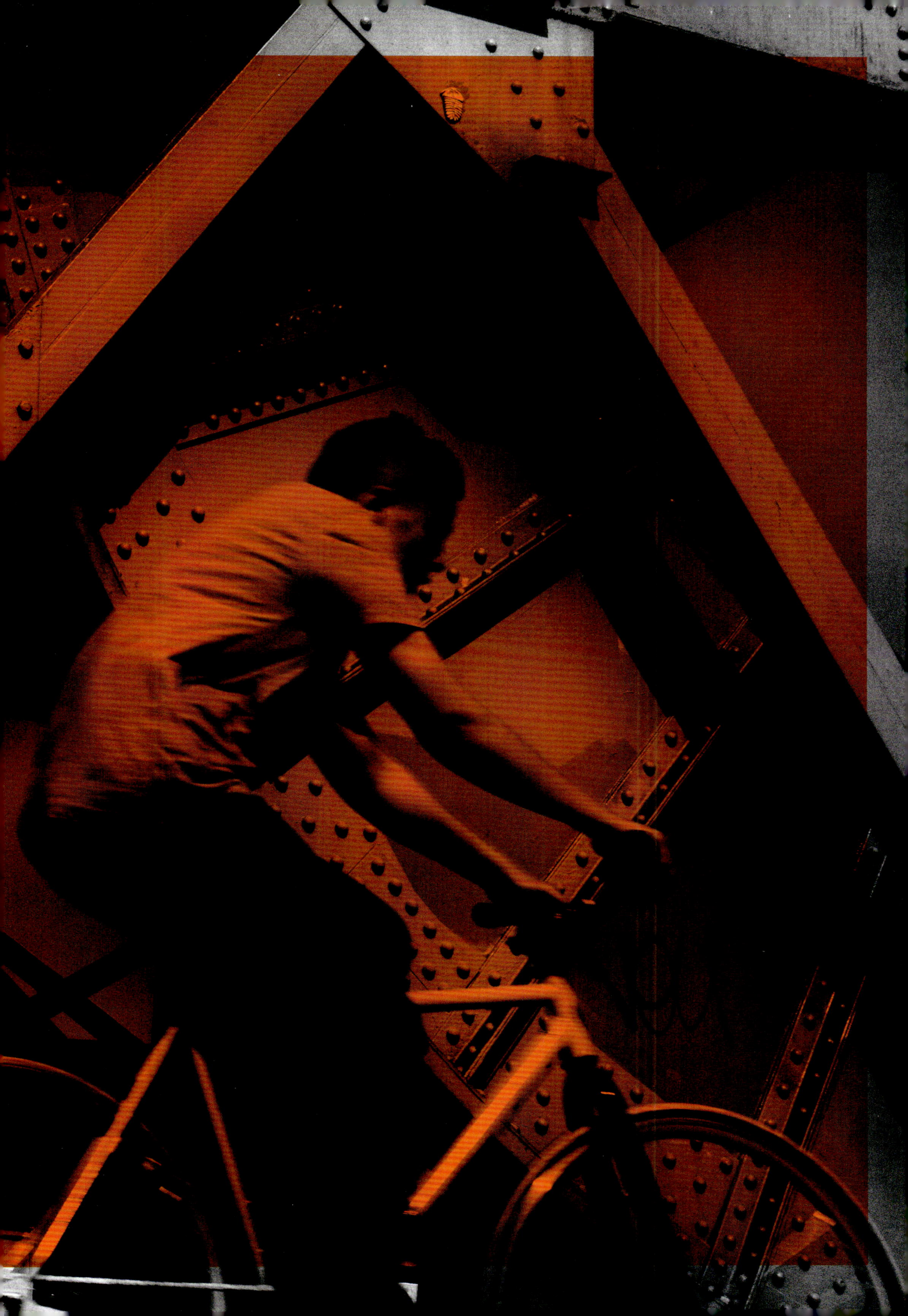

ACKNOWLEDGMENTS

Made In Dublin was the name of Eamonn's first series of D1 Recordings music events that took place in Dublin during the mid-1990s.

Made In Dublin is also the name of a multi-screen surround-sound panoramic installation by Eamonn Doyle, Niall Sweeney and David Donohoe, originally commissioned by ThisIsPopBaby for *Where We Live*, 2018.

Eamonn & Niall would like to thank:

Mum & Dad.

Johanna Neurath and Ginny Liggitt, for vision and nous in realizing this book. Musician and composer David Donohoe, an integral collaborator in the ongoing evolution of Eamonn's work. Kevin Barry, whose visceral words now feel embedded in the Dublin trilogy.

Michael Hoppen, Martin Parr, Jim Butler, Ed Dunne, Nigel Truswell, Karen Walshe, Sean O'Hagan, Marcel Meesters, Karim Rehmani-White.

And you, and those who brought us here, and all the visitors, passing through.

BIOGRAPHIES

EAMONN DOYLE

Born in Dublin in 1969, Eamonn studied photography and painting in the late 1980s. He spent much of the next twenty years producing music and working in the independent music business, founding the Dublin Electronic Arts Festival (DEAF) alongside the record labels D1 Recordings and Dead Elvis. He returned to photography in 2010. His debut photobook *i* was self-published in March 2014 and followed by *ON* and *End.*, also self-published. Regularly exhibited around the world, his photographs now feature in many private collections. Eamonn is represented by the Michael Hoppen Gallery, London.

NIALL SWEENEY

Born in Dublin in 1967, Niall studied art and design in the 1980s, after which he ran a small collective studio working in design, art, technology and nightclubs. He moved to London in 1998 to complete an MA in Typo/Graphic Studies, where he then co-founded the award-winning studio Pony Ltd in 2000 with electronic musician and designer Nigel Truswell. Niall has worked with Eamonn since the 1990s, from the early years of music through to the book collaborations and exhibitions.

KEVIN BARRY

Born in Limerick City in 1969, Kevin Barry is the author of two collections of short stories, *There are Little Kingdoms* and *Town and Country: New Irish Short Stories*, and the novels *City of Bohane*, which won the 2013 International IMPAC Dublin Literary Award, and *Beatlebone*, which won the 2015 Goldsmiths Prize. His contribution to this book is the first time he has written on Dublin.

SEAN O'HAGAN

Irish journalist Sean O'Hagan is the *Guardian*'s photography critic and a feature writer on art and culture for the *Observer*. In 2011 he won the J Dudley Johnston Medal from the Royal Photographic Society 'for major achievement in the field of photographic criticism' for his writing in the *Observer* and the *Guardian*. He curated the exhibition 'The Lost Moment – Civil Rights, Street Protest and Resistance, 1968–69', held at the Gallery of Photography, Dublin, in 2018.

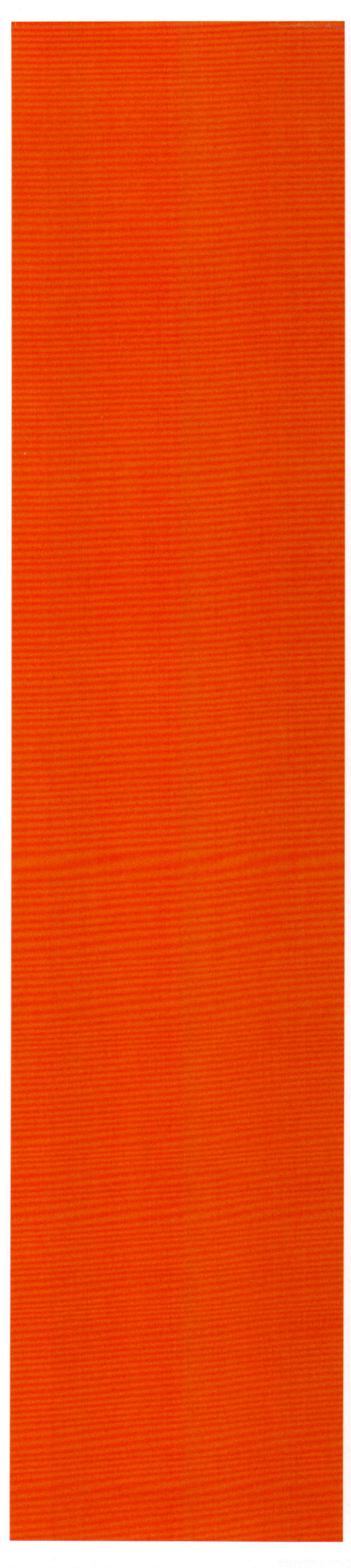

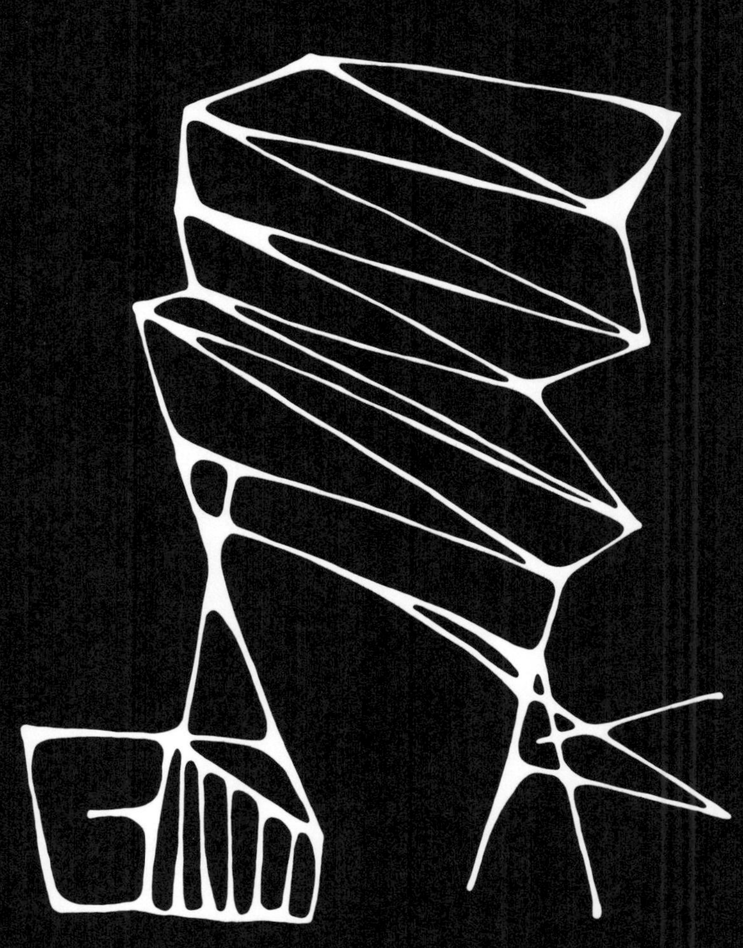

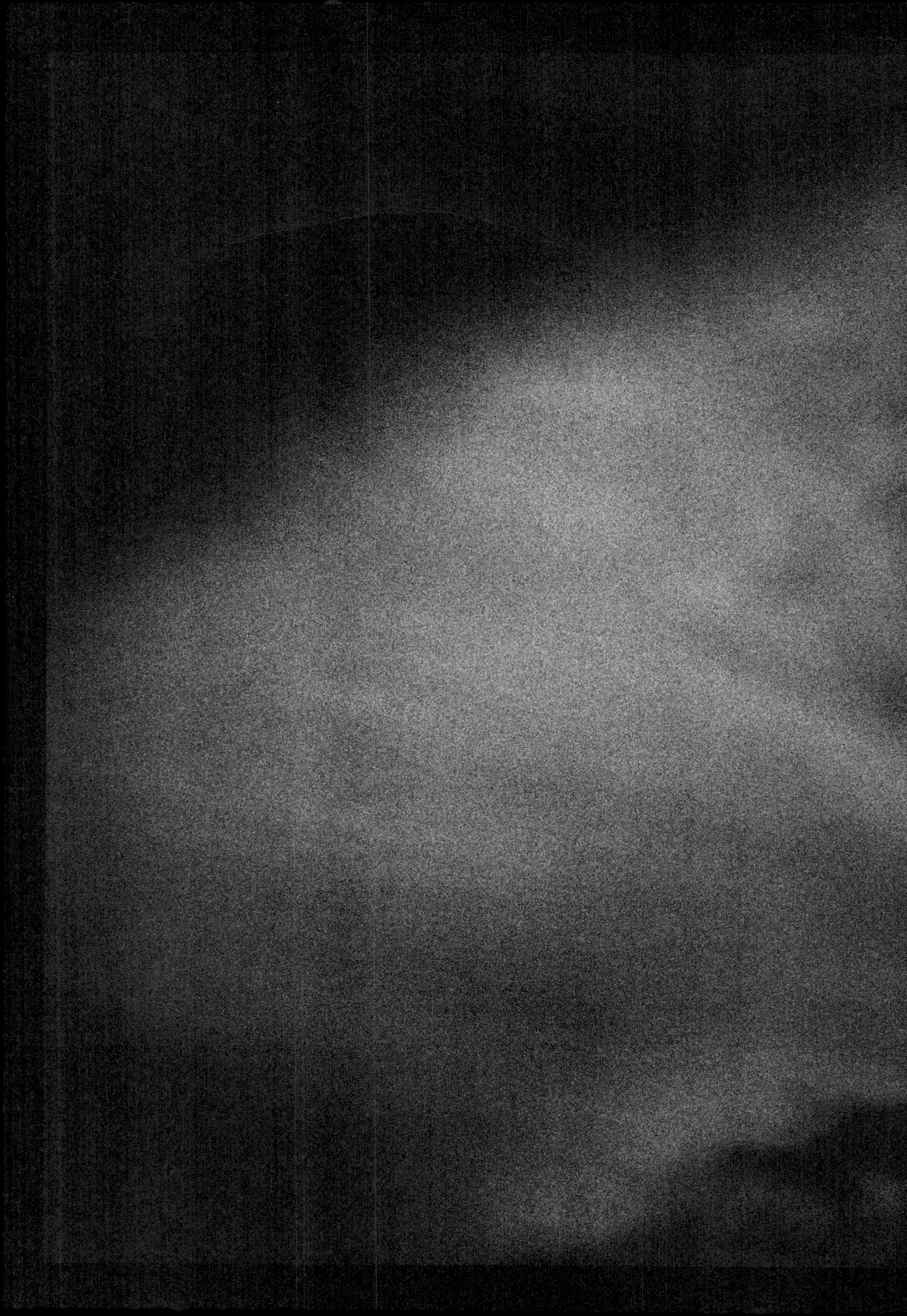